TENNYSON

TENNYSON

MICHAEL THORN

St Martins Press
New York

T 19805

TENNYSON
Copyright © 1992 by Michael Thorn.

ISBN 0–312–10414–6
'A Thomas Dunne Book'

Printed in England by Clays Ltd, St Ives plc

First published in Great Britain by
Little, Brown and Company

First U.S. Edition: December 1993

10 9 8 7 6 5 4 3 2 1

CONTENTS

ACKNOWLEDGEMENTS

My first thanks must go to Richard Beswick who asked me to write this book and then gave advice and support as it was required. It has been a pleasure to work with so responsive and good-humoured an editor.

Martin Seymour-Smith, in the course of conversations mainly about cats and cricket, boxing and publishing, gave me many a clue to follow up. My decision to pilfer one of his literary terms and apply it to Tennyson was, however, made independently.

My long-time friend, Tim Johnstone, read the very early drafts at a time when he was distracted by two young children. His responses, as a reader with a neutral view of Tennyson, proved invaluable.

Brian Hinton, poet, librarian and Tennyson enthusiast, plied me with tea and anecdotes in the tiny Freshwater Library staff-room at the beginning of my researches. Then, while I was preparing the final manuscript, he did the same in a tea-room overlooking Freshwater Bay. If the Isle of Wight does not figure prominently enough in this biography it is not for want of Dr Hinton's spirited advocacy.

Richard Hutchings, co-editor with Brian Hinton of the English edition of Emily Tennyson's Journal, offered me more access to his papers than in the event I was able to take advantage of. Sadly, he died in the summer of 1991, thus depriving the Centenary of a guiding light.

Joy Lester, organizer of several exhibitions on the Isle of Wight, showed me her extensive collection of photographs and illustrations, and copied for me a Lewis Carroll print which I had had trouble locating. Her knowledge of local affairs can only be described as breathtaking.

Christopher Sturman, teacher, archive historian and editor of a Lincolnshire archaeological journal, passed on to me notes on the Tennysons' departure from Somersby (though I believe we have arrived at different conclusions about this event). I have not had room to include much of his detailed research into family history, but his various articles have helped fill out my view of Tennyson's early years.

A chance meeting in Somersby churchyard with descendants of the Baumber family led directly to a fresh interpretation of an important incident. I thank Mr and Mrs Bamber for their help.

The present owner of Park House, Maidstone, kindly spent an hour showing me over the grounds (then under threat from the Channel Tunnel rail link) and the staff at the Farringford Hotel gave me carte blanche to wander the building both on a preliminary visit and later as a paying guest.

Susan Gates and her assistants at the Tennyson Research Centre, administered by Lincolnshire County Council, were tireless carriers back and forth of the well-catalogued correspondence. Miss Gates helped with several specific queries and advised on the availability of illustrations.

The public libraries in East Sussex have been most accommodating. For this I must thank mainly Neil Beck at Eastbourne Library for imaginatively authorizing a change of status from individual to 'institutional' borrower. The assistants at my local branch library in Hailsham have been very tolerant of the anomalies that appear on their VDU screen as a result of this decision.

The library at the University of Sussex has been able to lend me most of the published letters, journals and memoirs that I have required. Several of these books have been on uninterrupted loan to me for a matter of years, an indication perhaps of the low profile which Tennyson has on the syllabus of that university.

At Trinity College Library I must thank particularly Diana Chardin who looked out for Tennyson references while recataloguing part of the Houghton collection. The staff at the Bodleian Library are to be commended for managing to mix rigour with cordiality.

Of previous writers on Tennyson I must acknowledge the work of Robert Bernard Martin, who produced the first full-scale objective biography. His book was published before the bulk of correspondence and related materials became widely available in published form and the quality of his scholarship has been widely acclaimed. My task would have been more difficult without Professor Martin's book, but its view of Tennyson is very different from the one I have arrived at.

The biography by the poet's grandson, Charles Tennyson, is a readable and sympathetic portrait, and even the two-volume *Memoir* by Tennyson's son, Hallam, for all its faults, is plump with anecdote and interest.

Of critical books I am most indebted to Christopher Ricks, Valerie Pitt and Jerome Hamilton Buckley.

The three volumes of Tennyson's letters, edited with such wit and informative energy by Lang and Shannon, have saved me much delving.

Jack Clemo personally authorized the use of an extract from one of his poems, for which I thank him.

My wife has seen the towers of Tennysonia in our bedroom growing ever taller and my children have had to accept holiday routines dictated by my working habits. It has been a great blessing that they have been, (relatively!), uncomplaining.

Needless to say, any faults, errors or instances of zany thinking are entirely my own.

INTRODUCTION

'A morbid and unhappy mystic' HAROLD NICOLSON
'Afraid of death, sex and God' HAROLD NICOLSON
'Of all the great poets undoubtedly the stupidest' W.H. AUDEN
'The brains of a third-rate policeman' G.B. SHAW
'The saddest of all English poets' T.S. ELIOT
'Pre-eminent Victorian' JOANNA RICHARDSON

O f all these characterizations, it is probably the last and
most polite that has done the greatest damage to
Tennyson's reputation. And despite Robert Bernard Martin's
magisterial biography of twelve years ago, Philip Larkin's statement made in the 1970s – 'The general reader's image of Tennyson is pretty much as Harold Nicolson left it in 1923' –
remains true today. It is still the commonly held view that
Tennyson's lyrical ability had as good as deserted him by 1850,
the year in which he married and became Poet Laureate.

The primary aim of this book has been to re-animate for the
general reader the popular image of the poet. To achieve this the
focus is predominantly personal and literary, and I have set out
to tell a single story, that of an artist moving from one collection
of poems to the next. Tennyson, and not the social milieu, is the
indisputable hero of this book and, as Samuel Johnson observed,
'The business of a biographer is often to pass slightly over those
performances and incidents which produce vulgar greatness, to
lead the thoughts into domestic privacies and display the minute
details of daily life, where exterior appendages are cast aside and
men excel each other only by prudence and by virtue.'

Those two qualities are unfashionable criteria for judging an
artist's reputation; so much so that ever since Tennyson's death,
beginning with the inevitable backlash against the general
adulation he had received as Poet Laureate, there has been a
tendency to pick out for emphasis the darker aspects of his life

xi

and character. First we had the revelations of his 'unhappy' childhood. Life in the Rectory at Somersby, we learned, was not all babbling brook and humming bee, but was peppered with scenes of drunkenness, violence and insanity. Then we were told that Tennyson's own mind was dangerously unstable and that like Edward Lear, but to a lesser degree, his life was a struggle with epilepsy.

It is time to put in perspective this way of looking at Tennyson and to bring before the reader a fresh way of seeing the poet, uncoloured either by romantic suppositions of what a poet's life should be like or by general assumptions of what being a 'Victorian' meant. Some readers of poetry will never forgive Tennyson for his popularity or for becoming wealthy enough from his writing to be able to buy not just one, but two mansions with his royalties. Such largess is permissible for novelists but not for poets, and many of the unkind (and ultimately stupid) comments about Tennyson's intellect stem from just this form of inverted snobbery.

Frank Harris, when comparing Tennyson with James Thomson, put the case with self-incriminating simplicity: 'Between these poles you can find England: the one man, supremely endowed with genius for words but the mind of a sentimental schoolboy, was ruined by too great adulation and too many rewards; the other, of far higher mental endowment, bred as a charity orphan, was gradually disheartened by neglect and finally broken by the universal indifference that kept him a pauper.' It is Harris himself who had the mind of a sentimental schoolboy, hung-up on the belief that true poets had to die in the gutter.

Harris was neither the most astute nor the most influential of critics, but Tennyson's reputation has certainly suffered from similar judgements made by more substantial figures. Auden hammered it home most famously, when he described Tennyson as 'the great English poet of the Nursery'. Readers will have to form their own opinion from the evidence given in the following narrative, but this certainly begs the question of the role of the intellect in the composition of poetry. From the straightforward point of view Matthew Arnold was clearly Tennyson's intellectual superior, but was he the greater poet?

Tennyson has also suffered in comparisons with the other member of that triumvirate of Victorian poetry, Browning. There can be no doubt, it is claimed, who has had the greatest influence on twentieth-century poets. Browning, it has to be said, is more likely to be cited by modern poets as an overt influence, but Tennyson's work has more modernist affinities than is often acknowledged. John Heath-Stubbs, reading 'The Eagle' on BBC radio recently, drew attention to the fact that this short poem can be seen as a forerunner of the Imagist school, and the 'medley' organization which Tennyson made use of for many of his longer poems has been widely copied, most notably of course by T.S. Eliot.

The best-received of Tennyson's medleys, *In Memoriam*, and the relationship with Arthur Hallam which occasioned it, have tended to tinge the whole of his career with qualities of elegy and mourning, so that the colour most readily associated with him is black – his 'black' hat, his 'black' cape (one, at least, of his capes was in fact dark purple), his 'black' beard, his 'black' blood. This is probably the first biography of Tennyson to refer to the television soap opera 'Neighbours'. In the notes the reader will find a reference to an episode of the programme in which a gift of a bouquet is accompanied by a quotation from Tennyson. The verse is intended to console the recipient for the death of one of the characters in the soap opera: a prosaic example, perhaps, but still indicative of the view of Tennyson as the poet of mourning.

I want readers of this book to acknowledge that there were other tones both in the life and in the work, and other colours to associate with Tennyson's character. As for his relationship with Arthur Hallam, I hope I have been more willing than previous biographers to speculate about the emotional complications in their friendship and to show that the stimulus for *In Memoriam* was something other than the straightforward expression of grief.

Was Tennyson a Christian poet? Did he, as some have claimed, help to mould for two or three generations what the English meant by marriage? These questions are connected and I do not attempt to answer either of them in isolation. I judge his religious conviction by the standards of his lifelong obsession with the nature of the after-life and, in maintaining the close domestic focus through to the end of Tennyson's life, I have attempted to give the reader a view of his relationship with Emily which does not always accord with the accepted story of their marriage.

There are two aspects of Tennyson's life about which

previous writers have been rather coy or lacking in percipience – sex and drugs. As for the first of these we have been led to believe that Tennyson was incurably cold-blooded. Such a view goes against the grain both of the documentary evidence of his life, and the recurrent issues in his work. All that I need say in these introductory paragraphs about Tennyson and opium is that the popular perception during his own life that he used the drug was more widespread and lingering than the effort to brush it aside has implied. According to Yeats there was a man at the Savile Hotel who told him that 'Tennyson used to come there, to him, calling out for opium, and that his arms were all punctures from the needles.' It is not so much the veracity of such stories which is at issue, simply their existence. On the Isle of Wight, Tennyson's home for the greater part of his married life, you can still hear off-the-record (and off-the-wall) saloon-bar theories about the poet's amatory exploits. They are probably as wide of the mark as the more sedate fabrications enshrined in Tennysonian legend.

Another aspect of this legend is the picture of Tennyson as Tory squire with reactionary, nationalistic views, a misconception rather comically demonstrated at the Farringford Hotel where, adorning the walls of both the bar and the library, are paintings of horse and hounds gathering for the Hunt. Tennyson loathed fox-hunting, he never took part in that aspect of country life, and was a prominent anti-vivisectionist – qualities which ought to endear him to some quarters of his modern audience.

Many of his contemporaries found his fantasies of invasion comical (some, including Jowett, thought he had moved to the Isle of Wight for added personal security) and for much of the time he was a thorn in the side of the government of the day, whether it was Tory or Liberal. Such nationalism as he did adhere to was based on his love of old English patriotic ballads and stoked up by his essentially conservative temperament. He lived through a period of rapid social and political change, and his responses have subsequently gained rather than lost in impact. Where his contemporary readers could ignore the general thrust of poems like 'Locksley Hall' and 'Locksley Hall Sixty Years After' in favour of carping about particular allusions and references, we can read them with a more open mind and, in the manner of all enduring art, allow our own circumstances and attitudes to 'invade' and illuminate the work.

I end this book with a quotation from 'The Passing of Arthur'. The irony is intended to be gentle and affectionate, as those readers who are kind enough not to skip any passages on their route to the final chapter are bound to acknowledge. Tennyson always possessed, to a high degree, a self-observing and heroic conception of himself. In an early sonnet he wrote, 'We live but by *resistance*, and the best/Of Life is but the struggle of the will.'

This is the story of his own resistance and struggle. On completing it I made a final visit to the Isle of Wight and decided that the best place to collect my thoughts for an Introduction would be at Farringford itself. There are many literary shrines that one can visit for an hour or two, pay one's admission price, take the odd photograph, sup of the atmosphere, and depart. But the Farringford Hotel provides a rare opportunity to live as a guest in a poet's house. Despite the inapposite paintings, the management observes a link with the past by maintaining Tennyson's study (not his original one at the top of the house, which is now a guest room, but the one he had built in the 1870s) as a library and miniature museum. The view from the drawing-room is still impressive and, apart from the addition of a large dining room, the outer shell of the building has been little altered. The greatest sense of identification with the past, however, is to be obtained by taking the path out of the green gate at the edge of the grounds, walking the mile down to the cottages near the bay, and standing at the back gate of Dimbola, once the home of Julia Cameron. The neighbouring house, also part of the original Cameron residence, is under threat from developers, and by the time this book goes to print may well be no more than rubble, despite a spirited campaign to preserve it as a museum dedicated to Cameron and her circle.

If the house is demolished and replaced by a block of flats, this act will symbolize the 'cockney' invasion and development which Alfred and Emily tried so hard to resist. On a Saturday night the invasion encroaches the hallways of Farringford itself, when upwards of a hundred resident and non-resident guests fill the dining-room to eat from the table d'hôte menu and dance until midnight to the accompaniment of a versatile duo who, on the night of my own visit, demonstrated a repertoire which ranged from old-time favourites to Motown. It was not, after all, the atmosphere in which to write this introduction.

And on Sunday mornings, Tennyson's cherished lawns, much of which are given over to a nine-hole golf course, swarm with the bright and pastel shades of leisure-wear. It is all, from one point of view, a perfectly healthy manifestation of changing times, but as Tennyson's biographer I can perhaps be excused for wishing that the poet might suddenly manifest himself one weekend and, spreading out his cape and appearing like a fiendish predatory bird (in the guise that so terrified the local children of the island), return the house and the park to its original gentility.

TENNYSON

PART ONE
Phosphorus

1   A Father's Ghost

Dear lips, loved eyes, ye fade, ye fly,
Even in my fear ye die,
And the hollow dark I dread
Closes round my friendless head,

And far away, to left and right,
Whirlwinds waste the dizzy night,
And I lie and toss and mourn,
Hopeless, heartless and forlorn.

('IN DEEP AND SOLEMN DREAMS')

A night at the end of March, 1831. Alfred Tennyson, twenty-one and a half years old, has been called home from Trinity College at the onset of his father's final illness. His student days are over.

The body of the man who has terrorized the Rectory at Somersby during the last few years has been removed. Carried out to the church by six local clergymen, it has been laid in the ground near the church door, beneath a tombstone costing thirty-three pounds, one shilling and a penny-halfpenny.

The bed which held the raving and broken patriarch of the family during his month-long ordeal, and for another ten days in the repose of death, now holds the young poet.

What is Alfred Tennyson doing in his father's bed?

We know that the house was crowded. All of the immediate family was gathered, and although not many distant relatives attended the funeral there *were* extra guests in the house. Present-day squeamishness about using other people's beds, particularly the beds of the recent dead, was undeveloped in the time of the poet's youth. He had probably slept in his father's bed countless times in the past whenever the house became unduly cramped, perhaps sharing it with a brother, or even the irascible and touchy Doctor himself.

But Tennyson, in recollecting this incident, took it more momentously. He wanted to see his father's ghost.[1] Any one of us who has lost a parent prematurely will know that, however

3

awkward the relationship with that living parent has been, death induces a craving for *rapprochement*. Even so, the young Alfred Tennyson's behaviour suggests something a little stronger than the common reaction. He actually wanted to see his father's ghost.

Dr Tennyson had been a hard and erratic taskmaster and a cold but ineffective disciplinarian. As the self-appointed educator of his sons, particularly the three eldest, his efforts to mould them in the image of what he would like to have been himself – a classicist, a scholar, a poet – had weighed heavily on each of them. Though it was their mother who took the most gleeful interest in their writing – standing out with them on the road to Louth, awaiting delivery of their first joint volume – they would have known that, despite his lack of demonstration, their father was secretly proud of their abilities.

It was Alfred, by this time, who had by far the greater claims to that paternal pride. Ten months before his father's death his first individual volume, *Poems, Chiefly Lyrical*, had been published, and noticed in such places as the *Westminster Review*. And long before this his father had pronounced, 'If Alfred should die, England will have lost a great poet.'

What was now to become of the young man's poetic ambition? His grandfather and uncle – gruff and practical men – would try to dragoon the brothers into remunerative occupations.

In later life Tennyson never once spoke disparagingly of his father and repeated many of his stories with affection. The death, and the family history which led up to it impressed him deeply, in the way that such events do affect quiet and outwardly unresponsive individuals.

A deep and instinctive belief in the personality's ability to survive death would have given seriousness as well as mock Gothic-romanticism to this lying awake for his father's ghost. His desire for evidence that his father was enjoying a continuing existence beyond the grave was absolutely in earnest, and thoughts about death and the after-life would become the hallmark of much of Tennyson's poetry. A conception of life as 'the war of Time against the Soul of Man' eventually gave his work both its optimistic and its pessimistic power, and at this moment prompted him to self-dramatize his predicament, so that he felt the first *frisson* of an individuality stripped of its parentage.

If the rededication of his life to the ancient Muse (he would later refer to this as following a 'gleam') occurred anywhere, it occurred here, in his father's bed, in the ghostless dark of the Somersby night.

The summons home had been received at the end of February. The night of departure was mild and, after dining at Trinity, friends gathered in Alfred's rooms at 57 Corpus Buildings. James Spedding was there; Arthur Hallam was not. (Having spent the previous Christmas at Somersby and fallen in love with one of the Tennyson sisters, he had spent much of the new year trying to persuade his father to accept their engagement, and was in London continuing the campaign.)

There must have been much portentous calling of toasts in those Trumpington Street rooms, in the knowledge that Alfred and his brother Charles (Frederick, the eldest, was already at home) were unlikely to return to Cambridge. A few days after they had left, Spedding wrote to his brother 'their father is dead or dying. Alfred will probably not return to Cambridge.'

The coach did not leave town until late. By the time they all arrived in the yard of the Bull Inn they were merry and tipsy enough to dance a quadrille on the flagstones.

It being winter, the two brothers took inside seats. As the coach pulled out through the Cambridge streets, past college walls and shop entrances, and onto the flat and straight Huntingdon road, they both sank into sombre and silent contemplation, while regaining their breath after the exertions of the quadrille.

Riding a stage could be an uncomfortable and arduous affair. 'Eight miles an hour, for twenty or five-and-twenty hours, a tight mail-coach, a hard seat, a gouty tendency, a perpetual change of coachmen grumbling because you did not fee them enough, a fellow-traveller partial to spirits-and-water – who has not borne these evils in the jolly old times?'[2] Before rededicating himself to poetry in his father's bed, Alfred Tennyson spent much of this cold night-ride perched on the hard seat beside his brother in silent recollection of the past.

2 The Days That are no More

Memory! why, oh why,
This fond heart consuming,
Show me years gone by
When those hopes were blooming?

('MEMORY')

T ennyson's grandfather was born in 1750 and, by the time Alfred was living, had retired from legal practice in Market Rasen, to establish a country house at Tealby on the western edge of the Lincolnshire Wolds. Much of his wealth stemmed from earlier family inheritance. On his mother's side the Claytons owned a good deal of property in Grimsby, and a sensible marriage, in 1775, to Mary Turner brought with it extra landed interest in and around Caistor, to the north of the Wolds (which was later to have its significance for Alfred's brother Charles).

George Clayton Tennyson and his wife had four children: Elizabeth, the first-born (later to become 'Aunt Russell'), Mary (later 'Aunt Bourne'), George (the eldest son, father of Alfred and future vicar of Somersby) and, after a six-year gap, the youngest child, Charles (a future Member of Parliament).

Mrs Tennyson wrote to her mother on discovering that she was pregnant with Charles that 'at dead of night I would awake frightened and flutter'd for I scarce knew why till a little recollection brought it to my mind.'

But how unplanned and unwanted was the pregnancy? It seems that even as a younger child George in some way disappointed his father. There was dark talk of a clumsy, ungainly Clayton inheritance. The new child, temperamentally very different from his elder brother, quickly became the paternal favourite. No amount of delving into the archives has managed to show precisely when George Clayton Tennyson decided to ignore the principle of primogeniture and favour the younger son in his will.

Certainly the favouritism was felt and resented long before it was firmly established. It gave rise to family mythology, such as the story that Charles had been sent to Eton. Much of the other evidence of preferment is difficult to prove. Hallam, Alfred Tennyson's son, in the two-volume memoir of his father, quotes a local squire, Heneage of Hainton, warning George, 'If you do this you'll be damned, you will indeed.' But such evidence smacks of family bias.

The strongest signal that young George was not the chosen heir came in 1801 when, following his degree, his father persuaded him to take priest's orders. A year earlier he had sent the boy's tutor, Mr Hutchinson, to Cambridge on a spying mission, but the report, disappointingly, was not incriminating:

Holywell Feb 11th 1800

Dear Sir

I made inquiry and heard nothing blameable in his conduct. I have since called upon him, always found him reading and so lately as this day week he was so deeply engaged to enter the schools for his degree ... that he declined dining from College ... I am sure his conduct is proper ... and his morals pure.

Unfortunately for George, this affidavit was ignored. Forcing him into ordination signified that the living at Benniworth, secured as long ago as 1791 and which would traditionally have been kept for the younger son, was now earmarked for the eldest, who appears to have acquiesced in these designs, except in one regard.

In the autumn of 1801, before entering the life of the church, he set out for Moscow to see the coronation of Tsar Alexander. The colourful stories which he brought back from this extraordinary trip, including a flight on horseback to the port of Odessa (after making dinner-table accusations in which he named the previous Emperor's murderer) were often repeated in future years by Alfred.

That Tennyson's father went to Russia is undoubted. That he did not return to England for another five months is also recorded. He was in bad shape when he turned up in Cambridge in February 1802, and his brother detained him for a week before permitting him to resume his journey home. 'I think, if I may judge from his appearance when he came, that had he gone

7

on immediately, it would have been little less than suicide', he wrote to his father.

The story of romantic adventure and danger survived probably contains some truth. It is also likely to be largely invention – a way of explaining to those who listened that the Vicar of Benniworth was not your average country parson. Indeed he was not, and Alfred Tennyson grew up in no average vicarage household, if any such existed then or now.

In 1806 George became Rector of Somersby and Bag Enderby, by which time he had married Elizabeth Fytche, a niece of the Bishop of Lincoln. (The stories of Russian adventure may have been used to impress Elizabeth. She is reputed to have turned down no less than twenty-five previous proposals of marriage.) Ecclesiastical law allowed him to remain the incumbent at Benniworth, a curate being appointed to manage affairs there. Before moving, he spent two years having the Rectory at Somersby rebuilt.

Commonly misunderstood because of the close connection with the word 'wild', the term Wolds is likely to conjure up the wrong image of the poet's birthplace. Situated in one of the prettiest parts of the Lincolnshire Wolds, halfway between Alford and Horncastle, Somersby[3] is, and was, neither desolate nor wild. The Rectory, in which Tennyson grew up, lies between two ranges of gentle hills. Through the valley runs a small brook. The region is likely to strike today's visitor as a geographical curiosity – a portion of idyllic and quintessential English rural landscape in the southern style transported to more northern regions. The copses and old farmhouses might suggest Sussex, rather than Lincolnshire. Only the squat, square-towered churches would seem out of place.

The Rectory, its garden, the Somersby lanes, the brook, the Holywell Wood, and the long flat road to the sea – these formed the boy's landscape for the entire period of his childhood. It was a comforting and cosy environment for children to be born into, but remote enough for their domestic life to be claustrophobic.

Dr Tennyson (he was known by that title from 1813 onwards, after paying for the degree of Doctor of Civil Law) has been given a bad press. Depicted as either a debauched alcoholic, a deranged epileptic, or a grotesque mixture of both, the impression has been created that the childhood of Alfred and his siblings was one long ordeal. Close reading of the evidence – of which there is plenty, from both the Somersby and Tealby sides of the family – gives a rather different picture, at least for the first dozen years of Alfred's life.

At the outset George Tennyson seems fully in command of his affairs, attentive to the needs of his rapidly-increasing family. In July 1807, before moving into the Somersby Rectory, he wrote to his father:

24 July 1807

You were so good to say that you would contribute £200 towards the building of the house at Somersby. All the materials of the house and stables have been procured and the house partly finished ... The house was in so miserable a state that I have been obliged to take down the ceilings of the whole house, above and below, except of two rooms. This together with the enlarging of the kitchen, which was only ten feet wide, the building a nursery over it and two servants rooms over the nursery ...

Far from his being openly cantankerous about the so-called dis-inheritance, he appears to have accepted it with meekness and mildness. Only in time did it rankle, and become exacerbated by further real or imagined slights. The relationship with his brother Charles which, after such a Biblical act of favouritism, might have been expected to founder on recrimination or even violence, remained extremely cordial. Charles was a frequent visitor to Somersby, and when he married Frances Hutton and began a family the two groups frequently holidayed together.

Elizabeth Tennyson lost her first child in infancy. Frederick was born in 1807, Charles in 1808 and Alfred in 1809, on 6 August, by which time the family was settled in the rebuilt and refurbished rectory. (The timing of Tennyson's birth is highly significant. In later life he claimed to have been born five minutes before midnight, on the 5th August; this ambivalence towards his birth-date has been used by many commentators to account for the prevalence of twinned poems or companion-pieces in his work.)

A further eight children were born during the ensuing ten years, giving Alfred six brothers and four sisters, the youngest, Horatio, being ten years his junior. So rapid was the family's increase that further improvements to the Rectory had to be made and in 1820 a large extension was added in the form of a dining-hall, designed and built by the Rector himself, with the help of his coachman Horlins.

The population in the parishes of Bag Enderby and Somersby has shrunk since Tennyson's day, rather than increased, and the impression of remoteness gained by the modern visitor is probably more acute than it was in the early nineteenth century. Nevertheless, for some years the family did not have its own pony and trap (the Doctor having to walk the mile or so between his two churches – 'What a clip he used to goä', said the Somersby rat-catcher) and the children were thrown upon themselves for company and diversion.

The three eldest boys, rooming together in the attic of the house, formed a self-contained unit. Alfred was closest to Charles. Frederick could be cussed and volatile, but Charles was always kind and caring. They would often be together, especially in later years when they were both writing poetry, and composing out in the open. It was their habit to walk on opposite sides of a hedge, vying with each other for memorable lines, and shouting them across at one another in a kind of poetic ping-pong. Alfred remembered one of his winning volleys to his sixtieth year: 'With slaughterous sons of thunder rolled the flood.'

Intimate and confined though the childhood was in one sense, it also had an open aspect. In 1806 George had begun a library by buying books from the sale of Bennet Langton's collection at Langton Hall, and he added to these rapidly, concentrating on collecting folio editions of classical authors. From an early age the children were encouraged to read books from these shelves, and later he arranged, through his brother Charles, to have a daily paper posted from London.

For a time the eldest children attended the local village school, run by a Mr Cadney in Holywell Wood, but even then Dr Tennyson would add his own personal tuition. He was far more interested in his children's education than he was in parish work, although he was highly sociable and valued as a raconteur at gatherings and functions. Sometimes there were entertainments at the Rectory itself, particularly when Charles was expected to visit en route from London. In the summer of 1818 George complained to Charles about his non-appearance: 'You were a pretty fellow to pass us, after having promised to be with us on Monday. You don't know perhaps that I asked a large party to meet you and sat up half the night awaiting your arrival.' Such disappointments gradually embittered him.

Dr Tennyson was not so popular with the rustics. They treated him suspiciously, and servants at the Rectory spread rumours regarding his temper and strange habits. It was said that he would retire to his study and play his harp, glowering at the walls, which were covered with pictures of naked gods and goddesses.

Financially the family was comfortably off. The parish at Benniworth continued to bring in money over and above the cost of employing a curate. In 1814 both Charles and George were given an annual allowance of £250 by their father. And in 1815 a third living, at Grimsby, was acquired for George, which was expected to bring in an extra £500 a year. All told this added up to a healthy upper middle-class income. George was awarded an additional increase in his annual allowance in 1816. The friendliness between the two brothers at this time is made evident by Charles' reaction to this (he had not been given the increase). Charles is writing to his father:

4 Mar 1816

... With respect, to my not receiving an annual allowance equal to that you pay my brother which you say was the point which you would like me to attend, I trust you will believe me when I say it was not likely to produce any observation from me. George's situation and mine are very different. I cannot be so blind as not to feel that you have fixed my annual allowance at less than George's, I could not possibly have obtained what I have in marriage without your support and the advantage of your covenants. This corresponds with the preferment George has obtained by your means but the advantage is decidedly mine as the property I obtain is permanent and not clogged as livings are by duties and restrictions ... This too is supposing that my brother and myself are equal in *rights* if such a term be not odious in itself.

A letter more easily written by the favoured party, and one which neatly states the relative positions of George and Charles at this time – that the short-term advantage was with George, but the long-term well and truly with Charles, as heir to the Tealby and other estates.

Legends abound as to when Alfred first began composing poetry and few of them are worth repeating. His young brother,

11

Arthur, claimed that Alfred always 'felt that he was a poet, and earnestly trained himself to be worthy of his vocation', but something similar could have been said of Frederick and Charles, as applied to their childhood and youth.

Alfred himself wrote, in old age, that before he could read he would like to spread his arms to stormy days and cry out, 'I hear a voice that's speaking in the wind' and during his first weeks at Cambridge he wrote the homesick poem which begins 'Playfellow winds and stars, my friends of old'. Other homesick poems of that later period — 'The Outcast' and 'Inverlee' — suggest a breezier, more sociable growing-up than many accounts have offered.

As an example of the solemn and over-wrought treatment which the Tennyson childhood has received can be cited the absurd interpretations put upon the trance-like state which the poet experienced 'quite up from boyhood':

This has come upon me through repeating my own name to myself silently till all at once as it were out of the intensity of the consciousness of individuality the individuality itself seemed to dissolve and fade away into boundless being . . .[4]

That explanation was given by a sixty-four year-old, grown articulate in talking about 'consciousness' and 'individuality'. But the practical activity of repeating a name, or any word, over and over until its sense evaporates, is commonly indulged in by young children. To take this confession of Tennyson's as indicating an infirmity of mental health, or even a proclivity towards epilepsy, is too far-fetched.

The real significance of the recollection is that Tennyson admits to using his own name instead of someone else's, or a common noun. Not insanity, but a significant self-absorption is indicated here.

Epilepsy is a diagnosis which has more basis in the cases of Tennyson's father, the Rector, and his uncle Charles. Both men appear to have begun suffering fits and seizures some time between 1810 and 1820. But in neither case is epilepsy the only or even the most likely explanation. We know that Dr Tennyson drank increasingly (claret in the beginning, but ultimately whisky) so that when, for instance, his wife and mother discovered him one day in 1816 with his head in his hand, oblivious to their questions, they may conceivably have over-reacted to a drunken stupor:

he did not answer – we repeated, he made no Effort to speak & was insensible – when he open'd his eyes they rolled without meaning and then he spoke incoherently for a minute, this wandering of the intellect is alarming.

Medical opinion seemed to indicate that, if these states were indeed fits, the condition was cataplexy rather than epilepsy, a view supported by the fact that Dr Tennyson seems never to have collapsed in paroxysm as might be expected in a full epileptic, and the fact that anger is thought to induce cataplectic fits.[5]

This being so, the condition, whatever its cause, would not have been apparent to the children until the onset of the Doctor's first serious physical and mental breakdown in 1822, by which time any organic illness or disease had been compounded by several years of alcoholism. After that date the whole Tennyson household could not help but be intimately familiar with Dr Tennyson's morbid condition.

3   Old Man of the Wolds

I would be a merman bold,
I would sit and sing the whole of the day;

('THE MERMAN')

There was an ordinary, unexceptional side to Tennyson at this time, both in his personal life and in the life of the family at Somersby – an ordinariness manifested, not contradicted, by the way he entered his name in his copy of Virgil: 'Alfred Tennyson, Somersby, in Lincolnshire, in England, in Europe, in the World, in the air, in space' (what young boy or girl has not indulged themselves in this way?) – and it needs early emphasis in order to balance whatever preconceived notions the experienced reader may bring to this book.

Until he was thirteen years old, that is until his father's first significant breakdown, the childhood of Alfred was happy and sociable. There were visitors, gatherings, even parties; the continual arrival of babies into the household; a growing number of younger brothers and sisters. A house filled with children aged between three and fifteen cannot have lacked its moments of uproar, both playful and heated.

There were, as well, such familiar ingredients of family life as holidays at the seaside. The Tennysons began making regular trips to Mablethorpe, a place which, unlike Somersby, is significantly changed – some would say ruined, although all such judgements are purely comparative. Even in 1813 George had been able to write to his brother Charles complaining of the overcrowded nature of the coast and disapproving of the other trippers:

> 19 Aug 1813
> ... At Trusthorpe, a small village near Mablethorpe, where I went yesterday, every miserable shed is occupied by ... greasy and pot-bellied grocers and linendrapers. As for the Inns you cannot at all be decently accommodated in them. They are stinking, filthy places, not fit for a pig, and at Sutton a bed-ridden person has existed in the kitchen amongst the cooking for the last 20 years.

Nevertheless Charles was invited to come and join them:

> Little George can bathe with our children* and I have a covered cart on purpose to take them to the sea and for them to dress in.
> *of whom we have four here ...

Alfred was then four years old. Three years later, at the age of seven, he was sent to Louth Grammar School (already attended by Frederick and Charles), lodging in term-time with his aunt and grandmother Fytche in Harvey's Alley. He stayed at the school until 1820 and disliked the place intensely – so much so that in later life he refused to walk down the same street. Before he went there his father forced him to memorize the four books of the *Odes* of Horace, one book on four successive mornings – a prodigious feat and an indication of the father's standards and expectations.

It was while returning from dropping the boys in Louth one day that Dr Tennyson called in on Rev Rawnsley, a curate at

14

Spilsby. The two men got on well. George stayed the night, and a lasting friendship – one which would bring the Doctor and his family much-needed support in later times – was begun.

Not much is known of Alfred's spell at Louth Grammar School, other than the fact that he hated it. This is a pity because he went there when he was seven, and left when he was eleven, a significant period in any person's childhood. It might well have been the sheer misery of these years – at least, those parts of the year when he was away at school – which gave his mind its cast of morbid self-absorption.

By the time Alfred returned to a settled life at the rectory, in 1820 – the Doctor deciding to turn full-time tutor – he must have noticed the deterioration in his father, whose physical ill-health fuelled and fed upon a developing jealousy of both his brother and his sister.

The sister had married a wealthy, but uneducated, business-man called Matthew Russell. With their wealth they extravagantly renovated the ancestral castle Brancepeth and in 1818 Charles, having long harboured political ambition, was elected to parliament as the MP for Grimsby, helped in his electoral campaign by financial support from the Russells. Increasingly it appeared to the Rector at Somersby that a mysterious vindictiveness had caused his father to reverse every privilege that should have been due to him as oldest son, and that his prospering younger brother and sister were cutting him further and further adrift.

One of those privileges, it seemed to Dr Tennyson, was that he should have been sent to Eton. Certainly his own eldest son would go there. And off he packed Frederick in 1818, at the age of eleven – a decision that he came to regret more than any other.

This meant that Charles and Alfred were thrown closer together, in the hot-house that the Somersby academy became. The father was quite open about his motivation:

> I have known some satisfaction in thinking that my boys will turn out to be clever men. Phoenix-like, I trust (though I don't think myself a Phoenix) they will spring from my ashes, in the consequence of exertions I have bestowed upon them.

Such was the way he saw things in 1824, writing to his brother. The education the boys received was hard and grand, in the

15

classical manner, with a decided emphasis on the literary. Based very much on the Doctor's own library it included ingredients which would not have been part of Frederick's curriculum at Eton – the *Arabian Nights,* Persian poetry, the Koran, and many books on folklore and myth. But Alfred and Charles also spent large tracts of time conventionally translating from Latin and Greek and copying out standard commentaries. As a diversion from his studies Charles was in the habit of doodling in the margins of his text. A two-volume edition of Horace contains some small, rudimentary but evocative portraits of his brother (see plate 2).[6] Their translations were mostly in the style of Pope's *Homer.* One example has survived. 'A Translation of Claudian's "Rape of Proserpine"' was composed when Alfred was roughly twelve years old and consists of 134 lines of heroic couplets. The notion that 'it describes something closely resembling Somersby Rectory at its worst: a Hell dominated by a gloomy tyrant. Pluto, bitterly resentful of his unjustly privileged brother, Jove'[7] is more than a rather clever matching of myth to circumstance. The atmosphere at the Rectory was definitely degenerating and Doctor Tennyson becoming increasingly unstable.

At the same time we have still to guard against the Gothic view of Somersby. 1820 was the year in which the Rectory was extended. (How much this was simply in response to the increased family, and how much an attempt to make the Rectory a more baronial residence is a moot point.) In the same year the family began to keep their own horse and cart and they had, by now, quite a retinue of servants, working and living-in – a coachman, a nursemaid, a cook, housemaids, gardeners, and a new valet, the previous one having been sacked for seducing the housemaids.

Alfred's sister Cecilia cherished a pretty memory from this time and would later talk of how on winter evenings by the firelight 'Alfred would take her on his knee, with Arthur and Matilda leaning against him on either side, the baby Horatio between his legs' and tell them 'legends of knights and heroes among untravelled forests rescuing distressed damsels.'[8] Such memories may be rose-tinted and over-suggestive of Victorian postcard scenes of family groups round the fireside, but the Somersby children must have known at least some times like this.

Elizabeth Tennyson had given birth to her final child in 1819.

As long as his family was increasing, it seems, the Doctor was able to sublimate his most extreme feelings of being outcast. After the birth of his youngest, Horatio, those feelings welled over to be expressed in unrestrained terms. This extract from a letter written in 1820 speaks for itself:

14 Aug 1820

My dearest Father

I find to my great disquietude, that you have thought proper to attribute to my suggestion or instigation, certain expressions which may or may not have been used by Miss Fytche reflecting upon your conduct as a parent. I utterly disdain to exculpate myself from this charge. I did intend to have visited Tealby, but an accusation so unjust, so frequently reiterated and so totally unsubstantiated has so far oppress'd my spirits and irritated my feelings that it is impossible I can do so with any pleasure. With the sentiments you entertain and have entertained for more than twenty years, I cannot wonder you told Mr Bourne you had not a spark of affection for me. The rude and unprecedented manner in which you first addressed me at Hainton, after a long absence, on your return from York (I quote your words, 'Now you great awkward booby are you here') holding me up to utter derision ... You make and have always made a false estimate of me in every respect. You look and have always looked upon me with a jaundiced eye ... Conscious also that I am thrown into a situation unworthy my abilities & unbecoming either your fortune or my just pretensions, & resisted in my every wish to promote my own interests or that of my family by removing to a more eligible situation, unaccountably kept in the dark with respect to their future prospects, with broken health and spirits, I find myself little disposed to encounter those unprovoked and sarcastic remarks, which tho' they may be outwardly borne, are inwardly resented, and prey upon the mind – the injustice, the inhumanity & the impropriety of which everyone can see but yourself, and which in your last visit were levelled against the father of a large family in the very presence of his children, and that father between forty and fifty years of age ... You may forget or pass off as a jest what penetrates and rankles in my heart; you may break what is already bent, but there is a tribunal before which you and I may speedily appear, more speedily perhaps than either of us desire or expect – there it will be seen whether you through life have treated me with that consideration and kindness which a son has a right to expect from a father, and whether (as you have been accustomed to represent me to myself & others) I have been deficient in filial affection & obedience.

I am, My dear Father
Your affectionate Son
G.C. Tennyson

Perhaps the letter does not quite speak for itself. Its style and tone should warn us against taking it too literally, although there are certainly truths contained in it. It is a fact, for instance, that for some time the Doctor had been pressing his father to allow a transfer to the Grimsby living. The idea seems to have been resisted because the Old Man did not want George interfering with Charles' parliamentary reputation. But despite its apparent lucidity the general drift of the letter is unnatural and inebriated. It is a letter written in a state of sodden self-pity. Indignation that others do not take us at our own value can lead to the kind of paranoia exhibited here. The letter does not represent a true state of affairs, and the Old Man, wisely, did not attempt to justify himself. Instead, he made it known that George's younger children would have £20,000 settled on them collectively in his will.

A significant feature of the letter is that some hearsay remarks uttered by a member of Mrs Tennyson's family are cited as the sparks which ignited the incident. Elizabeth Tennyson hardly features in the story so far, but her role becomes significant after her husband's death, and her later antipathy towards the Tealby set gives rise to the suspicion that her husband's sense of being wronged may well have been inflamed by the kind of baiting that can occur between any married couple.

Despite this developing rancour, contacts between the two sides of the family were still close. Only a year previously the Doctor had entertained his parents at the rectory and Frederick had written home from Eton:

11 May 1819

My dear Grandpapa and Grandmama
... I hear you have come to stay a week at Somersby. I am

now learning to play at Cricket and I like to play at it very much indeed.

... Tell Miss Bousfield I will write to her soon ... Tell Mamma I am glad to hear my pony goes on so well and that it does not stumble at all ...

A month after that the entire household had gone down with measles (Matilda becoming dangerously ill) and Elizabeth threatening a miscarriage after her constant travelling up and down stairs.

In September of that year Charles and Fanny lost a child and the Old Man wrote, 'Though I am unnatural enough not to feel much regard for ... the loss of new born babes, yet I feel for you and Fanny and am sorry for her even.' This is a telling note. Not many a father, or father-in-law, would have put it quite like that. But George was his own man. He said what he felt like saying and others took it the way they pleased. He didn't dwell on secondary meanings and others shouldn't either. Emotional reactions made him impatient. Life was a simple and straight-foward business. As he continued to play an important role in the life of the family after his son's death it is important to realize that there are alternatives to the Somersby view of him as the wicked Old Man of the Wolds.

Several years later, when Charles and Fanny wanted to move from London and set up home in Bayons Manor, they found out at first hand how bloody-minded and unpredictable the Old Man (then grown fully old) could be. In other words, the ill-treatment which Tennyson's father enumerated in his letter of August 1820 was as much an aspect of his natural character (bluff, unfeeling etc.) as of any predetermined vindictiveness. It is just about possible to imagine the phrase 'great awkward booby' being spoken in an off-hand, semi-affectionate manner.

4   Ducks to Water

Every portion of the surface of our bodies is
pierced with fountains. These fountains will run
with foul water, so long as there are impurities
within man, and with distilled water from the
moment that these are expelled. Thus the nauseous
effluvium that belongs to impurity is giving us a
warning. The impurities of man come from within,
the cleansing power of man also comes from himself.
Disease is only filth.[9]

In the spring of 1822 both Dr and Mrs Tennyson went to
Cheltenham for a water-cure, just missing brother Charles.
The Old Man wrote to Charles: 'It was lucky you left [Cheltenham] before your unbrotherly brother arrived. I fear he will stir up much strife.'

The English prediliction for water-cures was notorious. As long ago as 1790 Horace Walpole had been able to observe, 'One would think the English were ducks; they are forever waddling to the water.' The cure at Cheltenham had been established in 1738 and became a royal spa fifty years later when George III came to remedy a stomach disorder. The new development which this royal patronage stimulated – 'rows of white tenements with green balconies', according to Cobbett – made it a centre for the leisured classes.

Embarking on a cure became part of the annual round for many people, one season among many, and was approached as if it were a holiday, with more attention paid to the other temporary residents of the town than to whether the water from tap number 2a or 4a was the most likely to elicit a cure for those aches and pains which were the merest excuse for the visit.

However, for every person who was able to use a water-cure in this indulgent and conscience-free way, there was another conditioned into thinking that their body definitely needed the water-treatment, and without it they would sicken, and ultimately perish. The symptoms associated with hypochondria are now considered to be manifestations of an illness affecting the mind. But in the early part of the nineteenth century hypo-chondria was distinguished from melancholy as having 'cor-poreal' rather than 'mental' attributes. In other words the hypochondriac could be cured with proper attention to the physical symptoms.

Since the eighteenth century and the publication of George Cheyne's *The English Malady* (1733), nervous illness had been considered the prerogative of social élites. The possession of highly-strung nerves was a mark of distinction. As for nineteenth-century visitors to spas, many liked to give the impression that their anxieties and exhaustions were the result of intellectual labours rather than general dissipation.

Dr Tennyson could have claimed the need for treatment on both counts. His sister Mrs Russell was also at the water-place and her presence prevented the Tennysons' stay being as restful as intended, for while they were there news came through that Matthew Russell was dangerously ill and not expected to live. A day or two later a communication was passed to George telling him that Mr Russell was dead. At the time George handled things with tact and sensibility. Charles' wife, who had remained in Cheltenham, wrote: 'She bore the tidings extremely well, your brother breaking it to her in the mildest way, for indeed he is all kindness and feeling on this unfortunate business, and I know not what would have been done had he not been there.'

She wrote again, in December of the same year, 'Your brother improves every day and talks of leaving us next week ... [He] flirts away with Miss Taylor, who dined here the other day and fine romping we had I can assure you.'

George had returned to Cheltenham in November and this report shows how variable could be his mood and condition. It is quite possible that Alfred overheard adult chatter at this time concerning marital infidelity, and this may have been in his mind when he came to compose, at the age of fourteen, the strange dramatic poem *The Devil and the Lady*.

The existence of the play was unknown to the general reader of Tennyson until 1930. Although there is no doubt that the greater part of the play is the work of a fourteen year-old – its similes are often based on schoolboy mathematics, with conceits made out of such themes as vulgar fractions and recurring decimals – different manuscript versions suggest that revisions were made to it over a period of years. The most adept passages may have been added in at a later date, but even so the play must represent one of the most impressive pieces of juvenilia left behind by a writer, and certainly shows how immersed in Jacobean drama Tennyson was at this time.

> The summer fly
> That skims the surface of the deep black pool
> Knows not the gulf beneath its slippery path.
> Man sees, but plunges madly into it.
> We follow through a night of crime and care
> The voice of soft Temptation, still it calls,
> And still we follow onwards, till we find
> She is a Phantom – and we follow still.

(THE DEVIL AND THE LADY III, ii)

Back in Somersby the tedium of Dr Tennyson's parish round, and the demands of his schoolmastering at home, quickly undermined whatever restorative benefits the romping and the waters of Cheltenham had induced.

The memory of what he had done for his sister in her time of need, the special attentiveness he had given her, began to nettle him, especially when he heard, in January 1824, that she was behaving, in his eyes, inappropriately:

I hear that Mrs Russell is very gay at Brighton; her gaiety is no business of mine. When I last saw her, I requested she would write to me but I suppose she is so utterly absorbed by amusements and the things of this world and its pomps and vanities that she either does not care or does not deign to take any notice of my wish. I think it is not the way I ought to be treated – I, who gave up the express purpose for which I went to Cheltenham, the recruiting of my health, to administer to her solace and support, might reasonably have a line from her when I requested it. I say that I devoted my health and time and money to her (the time I was with her cost me £30 at Cheltenham) and she little recollects when in bad state of health (as I now am) how she trespassed upon that health by being almost the whole night in my room for a series of nights. This I vow to God in the most solemn manner I have never recovered. My wife knows it as well as myself. I did not think that Mrs Russell had been so ungrateful and callous ...

Her indifference, and I must say ingratitude, has nettled me to the quick. The only reason which she can alledge for this conduct is that when lately she offered to come and see us we had not accommodation.

This I suppose is to cancel all former benefits. *We are three and twenty in family and sleep five or six in a room.* Truly we have great accommodation for Mrs Russell and her suite. We have not the house at Brighton nor the castle at Brancepeth ...

There is something about that 'My wife knows it as well as myself' which suggests again that Elizabeth had been goading him over the matter. 'You are put upon, George – put upon', or something of that sort, would seem to have niggled him into protest.

In the following year, 1825, the Doctor's health deteriorated further and he had to give up the education of at least some of the children. The girls continued with their governess. Dr Bousfield from Horncastle was called in to examine George in March of that year, following the resumption of seizures. Having not observed the fits, Bousfield remained non-committal as to whether they were epileptic or not.

By the beginning of July Dr Tennyson was strong enough to take Frederick to Cambridge, in order to enter him at college. Alfred and Charles went too and this trip, Alfred's first to Cambridge and possibly the longest journey he had yet undertaken, must have made a deep impression. He was fifteen years old and had seen no place like it before, the only other towns he had visited being Dalby, Mablethorpe and Louth. But the whole trip was overshadowed by the regard that had to be given to his father's condition, a regard tinctured with genuine filial affection. When they had returned to Somersby, Alfred was moved to write to his uncle:

My dear Uncle
It is with great sorrow that I inform you that my poor Father is not any better than before. He had another violent attack of the same nature yesterday. Indeed no one but those who are continually with him can conceive what he suffers, as he is never entirely free from this alarming illness. He is reduced to such a degree of weakness from these repeated attacks, that the slightest shock is sufficient to bring them on again ... He has already had two of these since my Grandfather was here

which is not much more than a week ago and some time previous to that had three each night successively. He was not able to attend the Bishop's Visitation on Friday. With kindest Remembrances to my Aunt and Cousins[10]

To Dr Tennyson's fits and general depression was added a chesty complaint for which he began taking laudanum and 'other soporifics'.

By this time Alfred was acting as bearer of news between Somersby and Tealby, sometimes walking the twenty miles between each. The anxiety induced by his father's ill-health eventually took its toll on his own condition and in the summer of 1826 his father insisted he should go away to Skegness for a few days' sea-bathing. Both Frederick and Charles, no doubt somewhat jealous, wrote to their grandfather trying to cadge the means of joining Alfred. Frederick pleaded that he was also unwell. Charles, characteristically open, confessed to a simple 'wish to accompany my brother and a strong relish for the breakers'.

5   Scorpions in the Closet

For bitter thy tears will trickle
'neath misery's heavy load,
When the world has put in its sickle
To the crop which fancy sowed.

When the world has rent the cable
That bound thee to the shore,
And launched thee weak and unable
To bear the billow's roar;

('THE PASSIONS')

At the turn of the year (1827) the Doctor's indignation with his father broke out a second time. In writing to thank the

Old Man for agreeing to pay Frederick's Cambridge expenses, he added a further protest at reported insults:

22 Jan 1827
...I have been credibly informed that you make it your business to speak in the most disrespectful terms of me to everyone and to one person you represented me as 'the greatest lyar that ever spoke,' and this you had said immediately prior to writing me a very affectionate invitation. How you can think so ill of me and yet write so kindly is more than I can comprehend. I regret exceedingly you should continue to speak of me in so injurious and unkind a manner, as it absolutely precludes me from visiting you, when I know you harbour so unjust and unfavourable opinion of me, neither can it be pleasant for you to receive me, a person, according to your description, of so despicable a character.

The Old Man scrawled a rude and brusque reply on the back of this letter, but did not send it. His actual response was to increase George's allowance from £700 to £1000, 'premissing that you will pursue proper plans of education for your children and that I shall be precluded from further applications'.

The Rector had been under a good deal of family pressure to put out the children to proper schools but by this time had become increasingly fanatical about his teaching. This was what he lived for – to make the most of his boys' abilities in the hope that they would indeed rise, Phoenix-like, from the ashes of his own failure.

The wide reading which the Somersby syllabus encouraged, or at least gave room for, is openly on display in Alfred's first published verse. *Poems by Two Brothers*[11] was published by Jacksons of Louth, in April 1827. The Doctor appears not to have been connected with the publication. He had long ago described Jackson as an 'infernal rogue' and took no interest in the book's release. It was their mother who stood out with Alfred and Charles (Frederick being in Cambridge) on the road from Louth, awaiting delivery of the first proofs.

The two accredited poets were paid an advance of £20 (£15 in cash and £5 to be taken in books), a significant part of it being spent on hiring a carriage to drive them to Mablethorpe on publication day, 20 April 1827.

Alfred and Charles were drunk with exhilaration on that

carriage ride, and must have displayed their excitement at first publication with extravagant behaviour, for Charles later wrote: 'I think if anyone had met us they would have thought us out of our minds.' In their Preface to the book the brothers had written, 'We have passed the Rubicon, and we leave the rest to Fate.' Fate received the little book quietly, as is often her way with first works.

Most of Alfred's contributions were written between the ages of fifteen and seventeen. There is a sickly precociousness about them. Frequent quotations are used to establish authority. These, and other literary references, have been traced by scholars directly to books in the Rectory library. The overriding influence is Romantic (how could it not have been in 1827?) with particular debts to Byron and Shelley. When news of Byron's death reached Somersby in 1824 Alfred had rushed out of doors and scratched 'Byron is dead' in sandstone. He had felt that 'everything was over and finished for everyone – that nothing else mattered'.

Rushing out of the house (sometimes into the churchyard to lie amongst the graves) became Alfred's stock response to heightened emotion and was a way of escaping increasingly violent domestic outbursts. The opium and calomel treatment which had been prescribed for the Doctor's 'Cholera Morbus' and continuing drunkenness were inducing turbulent ranges in his mood.

A month after publication of their book Alfred and Charles accompanied their mother to St Albans, where she visited a cousin, Mr Wheeldon. While in the south Alfred went to stay with his Aunt Russell in Berkeley Square. Although it was his first visit to the capital he seemed strangely slothful and un-interested. 'I wish he had something in Life to interest him as well as his beautiful poetry', his aunt informed Tealby. 'Westminster Abbey was the only thing which particularly charmed him, it suited the pensive habit of his soul.'

Between Elizabeth and her cousin there must have been a good deal of talk regarding the state of her marriage and it seems she returned to Somersby resolved to bring matters to a head. A friend of the Fytche family, Rev William Chaplin, was called in to mediate and on 10 October he wrote to the Doctor's brother describing the seriousness of the situation and suggesting that the only solution was for Dr Tennyson to be declared insane and removed from the house.

... You must know that he has long been most singular in conduct. I am sorry to add is now dangerously disposed to his wife and children: I dread the fatal effects towards some of them, which would consign him to perpetual confinement for his life ... The children are alarmed at him and the wife in the greatest fright both in day and night. I may in truth say in daily danger of her life ...

Charles immediately sent Dr Bousfield to the Rectory. The report was sober and mild in tone. Bousfield found the Doctor had 'the same acuteness of mind and playfulness of manner as when I first met with him more than thirteen years ago'. However,

I found that Mrs Tennyson really does labour under the apprehensions at which your letter hinted, from the violent state of nervous irritation which breaks out occasionally in her husband. It is more however on her children's account than her own that her placid disposition appears so greatly unhinged ...

A week later, no doubt having heard that Rev Chaplin's scare-mongering missive had not been fully supported by Dr Bousfield, Elizabeth's sister Mary (with whom Arthur and Horatio were staying) wrote directly to the Doctor in a vein designed to bring the cauldron well-and-truly to the boil:

You have deprived her of all authority in the family, & encouraged the servants to insult her, she is not allowed to have any Money, & if she asks for some for the necessary expenses of the family, she is refused in such language as I should be ashamed to transcribe, these circumstances are so public that your poor Children here are told of them every day by their schoolfellows, & we should consider ourselves as accessories in your violence did we neglect by any means in our power to deliver Eliza from such brutality.

A transcript of the letter was also sent to Old George, who responded by inviting Elizabeth to Tealby, presumably to talk things over with her. But her sister's letter had had predictable effects in the Rectory and she had to write from there on 30 October that she was now forbidden to leave the house:

... George will not allow any of the children to come with me nor will he let me have the Carriage unless I promise to remain from home half a year a condition which of course I cannot comply with as I dare not leave the children with him ... We had a terrible evening on Sunday. I wish very much to have some conversation with you and shall be happy to see you at Somersby as soon as is convenient to yourself.

In an interesting postscript to this letter we learn that Alfred was out of the house and staying with his grandfather, no doubt to protect his own health. How long he had been there, and how much of the violent climax to the marital breakdown he was spared, cannot be known with certainty, but he does seem to have protected himself from its worst aspects. The two boys who *did* witness all of this at first hand, Edward and Septimus (Charles already having left home, Frederick being at Cambridge, and Arthur and Horatio at school in Louth) were the two Tennyson children to suffer, subsequently, the most extreme mental derangement.

Some time early in November the Old Man and Uncle Charles conspired together to propose a trip to the Continent. The Doctor would go to Paris, accompanied by Charles. It was, after all, the rest-cure that the sensible Dr Bousfield had advised.

Before Uncle Charles and George set off for France they both went to Bayons Manor. Alfred flew, not wishing to meet his father. He set off for Cambridge with £100 in his pocket, an amount that had been given to him by his Aunt Russell for the express purpose of employing a mathematics tutor. He was set down at the Blue Boar Inn, Trinity Street, on 9 November and went straight to his brothers' rooms in the recently-erected Rose Crescent.

6 Farewell

Oh! Harp of my fathers!
Thy chords shall decay,
One by one with the strings
Shall thy notes fade away:

('THE EXILE'S HARP')

Life is rarely as grandiloquent as a chapter-break contrives to make it, and Charles and Alfred were home from Cambridge within a month, the beginning of Alfred's university career turning out to be an untidy interlude complicated not only by his father's imposed exile but by Charles' love affair with the Tennyson sisters' governess, Miss Watson. The Cambridge years were to be intricately cross-cut by the chequered progress of the Doctor's illness, as well as other family matters, and that is exactly how they began.

Charles, writing to his grandfather to thank him for overseeing the arrangements for the Doctor's trip to Paris, mentions Miss Watson directly: 'Two of my Sisters are with you I believe; are they not? It will be very pleasant for them and Miss Watson, who, I suppose accompanies them, and she is a lively woman to boot and will amuse you during these drowsy, hazy, onubilated, gloomy, wet, blue-devil-begetting, sunless, hopeless, joyless, days of November: that such are her powers and animation I well know.' On the same day that Charles was thrilling to Miss Watson's charms his grandfather sent a message to his son in London, saying, 'I am sorry to find Charles is attached to Miss Watson, and that she is in debt, however she does not know that I suspect anything . . . This Miss Watson is a bad concern.'

The middle part of this letter makes it clear that the Old Man has taken over temporary custodianship of the Somersby children and plans have been made for their future. Edward is to become a clerk, Arthur should join the Navy, and Septimus should continue at school in Louth, joined by Horatio. Alfred, it appears, had removed himself just in time. The letter also contains the surprising assurance that, 'Eliza speaks most affectionately of her Husband and she and her children, at home, are looking forward with delight at the prospect of his return with amended health.' If this was a true, rather than a polite assertion, it shows a remarkable ability to forgive and forget the violent scenes of three weeks beforehand.

It was Mrs Tennyson herself who had sounded the first alarm regarding Miss Watson. A small indication of the governess's character is given by Dr Tennyson, writing from London a day before setting off for Paris. 'This is a very awkward business and if it really be the case the sooner Miss Watson goes the better. She is far from being an undesirable governess and is a most admirable Music Mistress ... she is a kind hearted and Amiable Woman – though a little inclined as all young Women naturally are to be somewhat fatigued and ennuied with the listlessness of Somersby.'

Charles was carrying on a correspondence with Miss Watson from Cambridge and there was a suspicion that he was arranging some form of elopement, especially when the governess declared on 25 November that she could not go to Bayons as requested but had to leave for home at once to attend a sick parent. This sounded too much like subterfuge.

The Old Man immediately confronted Charles with the consequences:

I find Miss Watson has gained your affection, and that you are carrying on a correspondence with her. I must confess this distresses me and your family most seriously, and may if persisted in, prove the utter ruin of you and her. It would interrupt your studies and prevent your ever providing for yourself and a family of your own. Besides your persisting to a conclusion at present would instantly leave you penniless, for you could not expect any fortune from your *uncle Turner*, from your father, or myself.

He wrote again two days later, warning Charles not to take any 'clandestine steps', and added a note for Frederick, urging him to prevent any skullduggery. Meanwhile Miss Watson, having been arrested at Somersby (presumably by the next-door neighbour and Constable, Mr Baumber) for a debt of £24, had escaped in the middle of the night.

In Cambridge Alfred quickly found rooms of his own. When he wrote to his grandfather on 5 December he described his lodgings as being 'some distance from my college'. As Rose Crescent is practically opposite Trinity he can no longer have been staying there.

Having sorted out his accommodation it was time to go home for the Christmas vacation. Charles and Alfred again travelled together, arriving in Somersby exactly a month after they had left it. Edward and Septimus were still at Bayons. Mrs Tennyson was worried by the former's dizzy turns caused, she thought, by constipation. She also warned the Old Man that Septimus had worms.

Dr Tennyson did not remain on the Continent for long. He returned to England in mid-January but was then detained in London for a few days, hunting for a governess to replace Miss Watson.

Charles and Alfred, fearing his imminent arrival in Somersby, spent the final days of the Christmas vacation in Louth, staying with Grandma Fytche. It was a holiday which stirred conflicting feelings in both of them. With their father temporarily out of the way the Rectory was redolent of happier family times, before his violent rages came to rule the home. On the other hand, the growing age of the children and the fact that some of them were being looked after at Tealby contributed to the feeling that the family unit, for so long a compact and self-contained one, was disintegrating. It was a disintegration which increasingly manifested itself in illness amongst the Tennyson children. Dizziness and worms were only minor and premonitionary symptoms of deeper emotional disturbances. Finally the vacation must have been an embarrassing one for Charles. Teased by his sisters, rebuked by his elders, Alfred's romantic brother had to put the well-advertised powers and animation of Miss Watson out of his mind.

Charles was older than Alfred and therefore more likely to be flirting and falling in love, but in general ways too Alfred was much more withdrawn and centred in upon himself. All of his emotions were fuelled by family relationships and by reading. Like many adolescents who are serious about being called to serve the Muses, his interest in flesh-and-blood females was somewhat retarded.

Of the three brothers published in the Jackson volume Alfred had been by far the most industrious and versatile. The metrical experimentation and hungry trying-out of different forms revealed in the book are significant. They are not so much the usual searching for a single characteristic style – the writer trying to discover his voice; Tennyson remained capable of writing in many different voices – the work of his old age is extremely varied. This aspect of his poetry, which was quickly identified as 'Tennysonian' (the term was in use while he was still at the height of his fame and powers), has more to do with his typical preoccupations than with specific features of his poetic voice. These characteristic preoccupations – memory, parting, death, exile, suicide, the far-away – were already evident in the verse included in *Poems by Two Brothers*, but their presentation was, to use a word attributed to them by one of Tennyson's foremost modern critics, Christopher Ricks, far too 'stiff'.

Less stiff, and really of much more interest, are the poems from this early Somersby period which Tennyson did not publish for fear that they were too unusual. One of the best of these, 'The Exile's Harp', gives a sense of the keen flourish with which Alfred eventually left Lincolnshire, arriving in Cambridge a self-conscious exile, in flight from his childhood and adolescence. The Harp hung up on the willow tree was his own Past, both immediate and inherited. Events of the previous two years, the breakdown of his father, and the break-up of family life in the Rectory, had 'consigned to sorrow'[12] most of the early pleasure he had taken in living at Somersby.

> Oh! Harp of my fathers!
>   No more in the hall,
> The souls of the chieftains
>   Thy strains shall enthral:
> One sweep will I give thee,
>   And wake thy bold swell;
> Then, thou friend of my bosom,
>   For ever farewell!

PART TWO
Meridies I

1   Tall and Melancholy

What shall sever me
From the love of home?
Shall the weary sea,
Leagues of sounding foam?
Shall extreme distress,
Shall unknown disgrace,
Make my love the less
For my sweet birth-place?

('HOME')

At the age of eighteen Alfred Tennyson had grown to more than six feet in height. His appearance was impressive. He had a large head, aquiline nose, and dark skin; long black hair; broad shoulders; a way of walking which was both proud and shy. Friends of his Cambridge days remembered him as a 'sort of Hyperion' and he came to rely on making just this kind of impression.

He was already addicted to tobacco, a habit which he had begun at the age of fourteen, having been introduced to it by the coachman, Horlins. Liking his weed strong, he would smoke it in cheap clay pipes. Extremely short-sighted and too vain to wear an eye-glass yet, he would often appear withdrawn and isolated, but he also lacked any form of social embarrassment, and when in company would frequently cause surprise by a slovenly manner. He did the things which were just not done – put his feet up on chairs and sofas, asked embarrassing questions and spoke the first thing that came into his head.

He was egocentric in the most literal sense – self-conscious not in a bashful way but in a way which assumed that those who made up any particular company were uniformly focussed upon him.

He came to Cambridge a 'poet', and the time he spent there was used mainly for developing his craft and accumulating the verses that would be published in his 1830 and 1832 volumes. He left the university without taking a degree and with little evidence of having followed any serious course of study.

The Spedding drawings give the most vivid impression of

Tennyson at this time. Reading a book close to his face, with hair all over his head, very prominent eyelashes and full lips. It is important, for those who know only the later Laureate face, with its beard and hooded eyes, to look long at these Spedding drawings (see plate 2), and to have this image of Alfred in their minds as they follow him through the next few years.

His build is also important. In those physiologically-minded times, it was one which, despite its outer appearance of strength and vigour, predisposed him to melancholy. In a book not published until 1846, but expressing views which had prevailed for some several years, we are given a description of the 'melancholy man':

> ... persons of this temperament are tall, have long necks, narrow shoulders, flat breasts, long narrow heads laterally flattened, with expanded foreheads, well-proportioned countenances, small acute features, thin lips, and they are slow and sedate in their manner and habits ...
>
> All the universe seems inconvenient to the melancholy man, and whether his gloamy sensibility arise from a morbid body or a mistaken view of Divine Providence, his self-complacency is alike disturbed, and he feels his individuality not as his faith dictates, but as his senses inform him, so that he is oppressed by the weight of his own helplessness, instead of casting himself with all his cares upon the Almighty.[1]

Such physiological interpretations of character persisted throughout the nineteenth century. Leslie Stephen attributed the difference in poetic styles between Shelley and Tennyson to differences in their physical stature. If Shelley had been as tall and broad as Tennyson, Stephen suggested, he would not have been so impetuous and excitable.

Because such a view of personality was widely adhered to, it is necessary to treat it seriously, so that Tennyson's morbidity, often attributed (even by himself) to a mysterious 'black-bloodedness' in the family, and by some to a fear of inherited epilepsy, may have arisen because he fitted the stereotype fairly precisely (despite the full lips).

Tennyson's first associates at Cambridge were quick to realize that he was prone to moods of unutterable misery which he took a long time to shake off. On other occasions he was genial enough, and could be positively sociable, which only served to highlight his propensity to melancholy.

In his first months at Trinity he was more prone to such moods than usual, for he did not take to the place. It was fortunate that Frederick had been there a year already, and Charles, with whom he was so close, had a more approachable manner. Through his two brothers he slowly made acquaintance with the young men who would form his Cambridge set – with Blakesley, Brookfield, Spedding, Trench. But these friendships were made and cemented slowly. The first term was solitary. He bought a snake to keep in his attic room and spent long hours idly watching its sinuosities on the floor.

He did a lot of writing. (That sentence is consciously bland and could be inserted at regular intervals in the text to remind the reader that poems are the result of long and arduous composition. An ironical illusion which biographies of writers give rise to is that, by stressing the active elements in the narrative of a life, they suggest that the creation of those works by which the subject has become well-known somehow took shape with a limited amount of time and effort, as a natural by-product of the experiences undergone.)

Confronted with contemporaries who had all been schooled together, or at least schooled in the same sort of social manners, both Charles and Alfred felt conspicuous outsiders. So pronounced was this feeling that when they first attended dinner in the college hall, the noisy sociability of the place and the mass of faces chattering away to one another was so different from the atmosphere of Somersby that they fled in panic, feeling all eyes upon them.

They were quickly known as Frederick's younger brothers. Frederick had won a university prize for a Greek ode and had arrived at Cambridge from Eton (where he had been captain of the school) with a reputation for brilliance. Some also made the association with their Uncle Charles who was by this time making waves as a Radical MP. Clearly they were no country bumpkins.

What Alfred missed most about Somersby was the female presence. Up until this point in his life there is no evidence that he had indulged in any flirtations with Lincolnshire ladyfolk – his brother Charles was more advanced in this regard – but he missed the close and sympathetic relationship with his mother and sisters. That strange narrative poem *The Lover's Tale* was begun at this time, and is a minefield of psychological significance. Tennyson knew it well enough – he later withdrew the poem at the last moment from his 1832 collection, giving as excuse that it was too 'full of faults'. More to the point, especially in that year, were the personal suggestions which it made. Although loosely based on a tale from Boccaccio, the passages describing the love affair between Julian and his foster sister/cousin Camilla could suggest that an intensity of feeling above the normal might have existed between Alfred and one of his sisters. Away from Somersby, his affection for this sister became the inspiration for the poem.[2]

In January one of the Tennyson daughters (it is not known which) actually tried to run away from the rectory, possibly to join Charles and Alfred in Cambridge. But the attempted escape was too unplanned and came to nothing.

> O blossomed portal of the lonely house,
> Green prelude, April promise, glad new-year
> Of Being, which with earliest violets
> And lavish carol of clear-throated larks
> Filled all the March of life! – I will not speak of thee,
> These have not seen thee, these can never know thee,
> They cannot understand me.

(THE LOVER'S TALE)

The poem is forged out of intense homesickness (as are several others of this period) and longing for a lost childhood, accompanied by his memories of closeness to a sister. Having completed the poem he could see better than most, not its stylish faults, (it does in fact contain some fine Keatsian description and the horror of Moxon and Hallam at its exclusion is quite understandable) but its thematic daring. Only Tennyson knew quite how literal some of his poetry was. When The Lover's Tale was pirated in the 1860s it made him furious.

The Easter vacation should have been relished but was dominated by a grisly incident involving his father. The cook accidentally set fire to herself and the Doctor, in trying to put out the flames and rescue her, had his hand horribly singed. The poor woman did not die at once, but was too badly burned to live. She remained in the house for a few days 'in a dying state' and her agony must have been terrible to witness. The injury to his hand, and the burden of having to make arrangements for the woman's funeral, had calamitous consequences for the

Doctor's health and seemed to undo the limited benefits of his jaunt to Paris. Matters were exacerbated by a malicious rumour in the village to the effect that the cook's death could be attributed to her fear of the Rector's temper. Rather than rush directly to his study for assistance she had run up and down in the yard screaming. This unrealistic interpretation of events was later compounded by the suggestion that a water butt, placed outside the kitchen door, had been positioned there by the Doctor with instructions to the new cook that should she too ignite herself she was to jump into this barrel of rainwater and not disturb the household.

We know that Charles and Alfred were in the house soon after this tragedy for on 3 April they both wrote to their grandfather – Charles mentioned the dying cook and Alfred thanked the Old Man for an advance of £20.

Back in Cambridge by the middle of April, and once again conscious of the contrast between his new life there and his old life at Somersby, Alfred wrote to Aunt Russell who was something of a fairy-godmother to him, giving him a £100 annual allowance (which he continued to receive even after he was married) and many irregular gifts.

I am sitting Owl-like and solitary in my rooms (nothing between me and the stars but a stratum of tiles) the hoof of the steed, the roll of the wheel the shouts of drunken Gown and drunken Town come up from below with a sea-like murmur. I wish to Heaven I had Prince Houssain's fairy carpet to transport me along the deeps of air to your Coterie – nay, I would even take up with his brother Abdoul-something's glass for the mere pleasure of a peep. What a pity it is that the golden days of Faerie are over! What a misery not to be able to consolidate our gossamer dreams into reality! Be it so. I must take my cigar philosophically and evaporate them in smoke, twirl my thumbs rotatorily, cross one leg over the other and sink back in my chair. NO – it won't do. The eternal riot of this place, the wear and tear of mind and body are a very insufficient balm to the wound of recollection. When my dearest Aunt may I hope to see you again? I know not how it is but I feel isolated here in the midst of society. The country is so disgustingly level, the revelry of the place so monotonous, the studies of the University so uninteresting, so much matter of fact . . . [3]

That crossing of the legs, twirling of the thumbs, and pretending to be untouched by strong emotion was an aspect of the masculine company at the university which Tennyson loathed. His poem 'A Character' deals devastatingly with just this self-satisfied easy-mindedness:

> With a half-glance upon the sky
> At night he said, 'The wanderings
> Of this most intricate Universe
> Teach me the nothingness of things.'
> Yet could not all creation pierce
> Beyond the bottom of his eye.

The summer of 1828 was cool, with temperatures rarely rising beyond 65°F, and the long vacation at home in Somersby was disappointingly grey. Dr Tennyson was once again 'excessively ill' and towards the end of September, shortly before the brothers returned to Cambridge, Charles wrote to Tealby, at midnight, saying that his father was having to lie out of bed, on the bare floor, to ease the spasms in his chest.

For the Tennyson girls, and for their mother, the departure of Frederick, Charles and Alfred must have been a despondent occasion. Once again they were to be left to cope with the Doctor's awkward turns, and the memory of the previous winter's violence made that a terrifying prospect.

This next term the Somersby Tennysons were joined at Trinity by their Tealby cousin. George found all three of his relatives friendly and helpful. They assisted him particularly with the finding of lodgings. He did not want to pay as much as either Frederick or Alfred, whose rooms cost them each a guinea per week. But he wanted a better room than the 'miserable and stinking' place Charles lived in for twelve shillings. Eventually he secured a good compromise in a room over a tobacconist in All Saints Passage, for a rent of sixteen shillings a week.

His father prompted him from the Houses of Parliament to distance himself from the Somersby trio and seek wider society. 'One object of going to Cambridge is to cultivate a variety of acquaintance and therefore I wd. not have you confine yourself entirely to them or the circle to which they may introduce you ... Your cousins are I doubt not very respectable young men and very clever – but their *habits* may be confined and their society limited.'

He even suggested a change of name (to Hildeyard) – 'in order to secure a permanent distinction from others of your family.' But George seems, at first, to have been dangerously impressed by his maverick cousins. 'I think the society they keep is by no means *middling*', he wrote back to his father. And then rather daringly described how they disparaged Christopher Wordsworth (the brother of William, and Master at Trinity) as a 'complete humbug' and scarcely ever went to Chapel – despite early-morning attendance being technically required several times each week.

George, though, soon turned conventional dud and within a month or two was echoing back paternal rectitudes: 'I scarcely see anything of Charles or Alfred. They only move in one sphere; their society so far is good, being literary; but I think to be a man of the world one ought to live in different societies.'

This new self-righteousness seemed justified, though, at the end of that autumn term, when Frederick was summoned by the Dean to explain his continued absence from Chapel. Frederick was supercilious and stupid enough to refer to the Master's own son, who had also missed chapel but escaped similar reprimand. The Dean took the matter further and when Frederick remained unapologetic he was rusticated for three terms, a punishment which was to have profound implications for the Tennyson family.

2   The Village Constable

We laugh, we cry, we are born, we die,
Who will riddle me the *how* and the *why*?

('THE HOW AND THE WHY')

That vacation Charles and Alfred received a summons of their own – but only to go to Tealby to be lectured by their grandfather. Although the Doctor, on cross-examining Frederick, was convinced that the punishment he had received was over-severe, he was concerned that the two younger brothers should not risk their careers, and the hopes of his whole existence, in the same way.

The Old Man found that their manners had deteriorated since they had gone to Cambridge. He tried to impress upon them that their bills at the university amounted to nearly half their father's income and that with what was left there were four other boys, four girls, a wife and a household to support. They must not waste their time there, but ensure that money being spent on them prepared them for lucrative professions.

Such talk has rarely gone down well with young under-graduates and the Old Man had to write to the Doctor, saying that although Charles and Alfred had not acted with outright disrespect 'they are so untoward and disorderly and so unlike other people I don't know what will become of them . . .' After they had returned to Cambridge the Doctor asked the Old Man if he would repeat, in writing, the lecture he had given them at Tealby, so little faith did he have in its being taken to heart.

Frederick of course, despite the intercessions of a Dr Maltby, had to remain at home. Far from being contrite, he acted in a high and mighty way and haughtily assumed, with the sym-pathetic support of his mother, a position as head of the family. It was now that the Doctor regretted the day he had sent the boy to Eton. Disinherited by his own father, he was not going to be dislodged by his own son, and he commanded Elizabeth to tell Frederick that he must get out of the house. He could take with him either an allowance of £100 a year or, should be prefer it, steps would be taken to enter him as a barrister.

At the same time, in an action which shows how hemmed-in by the rest of the family he was becoming, the Doctor wrote to the Old Man asking him to take in the Somersby ponies because, 'my family do nothing but ride about the country especially in my absence, running me bills etc. etc'.

The ultimatum given to Frederick sparked the Rectory's worst scene of domestic violence. On Friday 20 February, having been given his options, Frederick stood his ground and refused to leave the house. The ensuing argument between father and son, both verbal and physical, reached such a pitch that the Doctor eventually had to call for the next-door neighbour, Mr Baumber, who was also the village Constable, to come and take Frederick away.

That, at least baldly, is what occurred. It is possible to cast the Doctor in a blacker light and some previous biographers have done so – by not making plain that it was *he* who sent for the Constable and by making its sound as if the man of the law was an anonymous figure who took Frederick away to a distant 'cottage'. Although the Baumber family were held at arm's length by the Tennysons (the four children, contemporary with the Tennyson boys and girls, were not close playmates) and the single tradition that has been handed down concerning their occupancy of the Manor House is the dubious one of the young Alfred reaching out from one of the rectory windows to steal apple pies from the Baumber pantry, the very proximity of their dwelling puts a different cast on Frederick's 'arrest'.[4]

Certainly the Doctor seems to have had no support in the rest of his family for this action. 'His mother as usual has taken his part,' he reported to Tealby.

On Saturday 21 February Elizabeth attempted to go to Louth by pony and chaise, but the Doctor, fearing what calumnies would reach his father through Miss Fytche, refused to let her leave. (It was this which prompted his dispatch of the ponies to Bayons.)

The next day, Sunday, Elizabeth and the two eldest Tennyson daughters, Mary and Emily, begged to be allowed to go to Tealby on foot and speak to the Old Man in person. The Doctor said they could, so long as they stayed away a reasonable time – that being anything from two weeks to two months. There was not the slightest chance that Elizabeth would consent to leaving the younger children alone in the Rectory for so long a time.

On Monday she wrote to the Old Man requesting the return of the family's favourite grey pony. Mr Tennyson could hardly countermand a decision of his son's so openly and sent a diplomatic, but firmly negative, reply: 'It would give me much satisfaction to return the pony but under the circumstances it was sent me I cannot at present do so with propriety. You say you have a friend who will keep it for you. I beg to substitute myself for that friend ...'

On Tuesday Frederick was prevailed upon to leave Somersby. Elizabeth took him to Louth, where she risked staying the night in order to give her mother and sister an account of recent events. When she returned on the Wednesday it was to hear from her husband that she was no longer fit to look after her children and all but Mary and Emily were to be sent from her care.

On Friday, having dwelt for forty-eight hours over the things

43

discussed at Louth, Elizabeth finally resolved that it was time to make the Old Man face the reality of the situation in the Rectory and to inform him of her 'final resolution to separate from [her] husband' in order that she and her children might escape his 'ungovernable violence'. In the course of this letter she defended Frederick's role in the recent disagreement in an account which is not substantially different from the one given by Dr Tennyson:

> I believe that you have been informed that Frederick said he would murder his Father. The words that Frederick made use of were these – 'We may thank God that we do not live in a barbarous Country, or we should have murdered each other before this.' George did everything to irritate Frederick a few days ago and though Frederick said nothing disrespectful ... he sent for the Constable (Mr. Baumber) and turned him out of doors.

Much more disturbing than the petty reverberations of this particular dispute was the more general picture which Elizabeth gave of a prevailing atmosphere of savagery in the house.

> There is another and perhaps a stronger reason than any I have given for our separation, the impression which his conduct may produce upon the minds of his family not to mention the perpetual one of such degrading epithets to myself and children as husband and a Father and above all a person of his sacred profession ought particularly to avoid. A short time since he had a large knife and loaded gun in his room. The latter he took into the kitchen to try before he went to bed. He was going to fire it off through the kitchen Window but was dissuaded. With the knife he said he would kill Frederick by stabbing him in the jugular vein and in the heart.

She quitted the house within the next day or two, taking all the children with her to Louth. The Doctor was left alone for ten days. (It is unclear what the servants were doing. In all likelihood, if Elizabeth's account of the large knife and gun was true, they kept well out of their master's way.) At the end of that time Mr Baumber, fearing for his neighbour's health of mind and body, sent for the Rev Rawnsley, who took the suffering creature back to his parsonage in Spilsby, and wrote to the Doctor's brother in London as follows:

> When I arrived on Monday, I found your brother *feeding upon himself*, and most miserable ... He *must* not return to his family, and the sooner he takes another trip to France, or elsewhere, the better for him and all concerned for him. He leaves this place on his journey to Town for your counsel and advice at noon and will tarry a day on the road, which will afford you an opportunity of receiving this before he knocks at your door.

But after spending forty-eight hours in one of the parsonage beds the Doctor decided that he no longer wanted to go to London and returned to the Rectory on Friday 13 March.

On the same day Frederick and Emily set out on foot from Louth, wishing to talk to their father. They were with Mr Baumber (a further indication of the friendly terms in which the Constable was held by the whole family – not just the Doctor) when their father arrived home. But he refused to meet them and they had to return to Louth.

Meanwhile, Rawnsley travelled to London himself to speak directly to the Doctor's brother and to reaffirm his proposal for a second continental trip. Charles, taking the view that George had been shamefully treated by his wife and children but agreeing with Rawnsley that only if the Doctor left home would it be safe for Elizabeth and the family to return to the rectory, travelled to Tealby to secure the Old Man's permission for instigating such a scheme.

Taking his sick brother with him, Charles went back to London on 20 April. After spending time arranging for the cover of his parishes, and some further prevarication, the Doctor left for Paris in mid-May, on the understanding that Charles would join him there shortly.

He was to be out of the country for over a year.

3   Prize Winner

There was a beating in the atmosphere,
An indefinable pulsation
Inaudible to outward sense, but felt
Through the deep heart of every living thing,
As if the great Soul of the Universe
Heaved with tumultuous throbbings on the vast
Suspense of some grand issue.

('ARMAGEDDON')

C harles and Alfred were not at home during the height of these family traumas. It has been suggested they were, on the basis that none of the letters of the period say they were not. But there are letters from their cousin George at the end of both February and March stating that Charles and Alfred were in Cambridge, that they had heard from home, but were not mentioning anything about the matter. George, of course, in the gossipy way of this family, had been kept up-to-date with all the goings-on.

Some readers may question the necessity of recounting incidents that the poet himself did not witness. In Tennyson's case the details of his family history are important in several regards. They have been narrated often enough before but usually in terms of a Gothic melodrama devoid of circumstantial detail. More crucially, as Tennyson was to be heralded, both in his own lifetime and after, as an emblem of what the English meant by marriage[5], we should know what his own early experience of family life was like. Finally, we can be certain that Mrs Tennyson, along with Mary and Emily, in their letters to the 'boys', gave graphic reports of progress in the disrupted household. Where events of this kind are concerned, absence can have a more powerful influence than direct experience.

Dr Tennyson left the country too soon to hear that Alfred had won the Chancellor's Gold Medal for his poem on the set subject 'Timbuctoo'. This was a pity, for it was he who had encouraged entry.

My prize poem *Timbuctoo* was an altered version of a work I had written at home and called *The Battle of Armageddon*. I fell out with my father, for I had no wish to compete for the prize and he insisted on my writing. To my amazement, the prize was awarded to me. I couldn't face the public recitation in the senate House, feeling very much as Cowper felt; Merivale declaimed my poem for me . . .

As the subject for the poem had been announced in December 1828, and entries had to be in by March, the Doctor must have persuaded Alfred to enter during the Christmas vacation. The prize was announced on 6 June.

Tennyson refrained from reciting the poem in person due to an embarrassed surprise at his success rather than any characteristic reticence. He had entered the competition half-heartedly, by patching up and adapting to the set subject a poem called 'Armageddon', which he had begun when aged only fifteen and redrafted in January 1828.

The decision of the examiners was controversial because the prize had never before been awarded to a poem in blank verse. It was important because it established Tennyson as a poet with serious prospects amongst his growing coterie. It was significant because Arthur Hallam had also entered for the prize.

4   One in the Crowd

the time is well-nigh come
When I must render up this glorious home
To keen *Discovery*

('TIMBUCTOO')

This is not the place to bore the reader with thumbnail sketches of various members of Tennyson's set. Men like Merivale, Frere, Brookfield, Lushington, Spedding, Blakesley, Trench and Monckton Milnes, all of whom Tennyson knew by this time, are best described in the course of events, as and when they have a particular part to play. Precedence is given to the friendship with Arthur Hallam because of the mythology surrounding it – a mythology generated by a work of literature, *In Memoriam*, almost as much as by details of biographical history.

Arthur Henry Hallam, born on 1 February 1811, was Alfred's junior by eighteen months. He was the eldest son of the revered historian Henry Hallam and grew up in an environment quite as charged with books and learning as that at Somersby, but one more organized and academic.

The furthest Tennyson had travelled at this date was London. His childhood had rarely taken him beyond the Lincolnshire border. Hallam's childhood, on the other hand, had been cosmopolitan. He went abroad with his family annually.

After leaving Eton, where he had excelled in the debating society, Hallam lived in Italy for eighteen months, and fell in love with an 'older woman', Anna Wintour. A friend from Eton, James Milnes Gaskell[6] (a cousin of Monckton Milnes) was in Italy too, and also fell in love with Miss Wintour. Both young men wrote poems to their beloved and the literary sparring between them seems to have motivated Hallam in his infatuation as much as Anna herself. He was very unhappy not to be going to Oxford with Gaskell (and his other friends Gladstone and Doyle), but his father regarded close friendships as threatening impediments to his son's intellectual career, and he had been entered for Trinity College, Cambridge.

Hallam was matriculated at Trinity in the autumn of 1828. He missed Gaskell and Gladstone miserably; pined conventionally for Anna Wintour. Although, by the end of this first term, Hallam was beginning to mention in his letters to Oxford some of the men who belonged to Tennyson's circle – Frere, Lushington, and Milnes for example – it was mostly at a distance, having heard them speak at the union, or having met them in fairly formal circumstance.

It was not until the early months of 1829 that there is any evidence of contact between Hallam and Tennyson, and although they hardly fell upon one another (in any sense), there are indications that their mutual regard was instinctive and immediate. Hallam was keen to make a friend whom he could relate to on the same terms as Gladstone and Gaskell. Tennyson needed someone other than his brother Charles with whom he could share his poetic development. We do not know how or when they first met but it was under circumstances which led to a literary collaboration.

Tennyson might not have wanted to enter the competition but he was alert to the opportunity. In addition to pleasing his father, he saw it as a chance to prove to the Old Man that one at least of the Somersby grandsons had taken his strictures to heart and was pursuing his university career with a new sense of purpose.

But the subject – Timbuctoo – did not prompt anything from Alfred's pen, and so he sent home for a copy of a much earlier poem, 'Armageddon', and started to cut it about and rejig it to fit the competition theme. The early poem had been begun at the age of fifteen but the version of the poem which Tennyson based his competition entry on had been worked over less than a year beforehand.

At this point Hallam and Tennyson discussed their separate entries, giving one another advice. Later references suggest it was a fairly formal collaboration, but one which held out sufficient promise for a joint venture to be proposed.

The two new friends collaborated on more than their poetry. A 'flu epidemic was rampant at Trinity during those late winter months and, with self-supporting morbidity, they each dramatized their symptoms. 'For the last quarter of a year I have been much distressed by a determination of blood to the head,' Alfred wrote to his grandfather.[7] And writing with the benefit of hindsight, but using a telling similarity of phrasing, Mr Hallam described his son's symptoms thus: 'In the first year of his residence at Cambridge, symptoms of disordered health, especially in the circulatory system, began to show themselves ... A too rapid determination of blood towards the brain, with its concomitant uneasy sensations, rendered him frequently incapable of mental fatigue.'[8]

Alarmed at these signs, and perhaps worried that his son was again forming too distracting a friendship, (Arthur was also trying to persuade Gaskell to transfer from Oxford to Cambridge), Mr Hallam insisted that he take a long, convalescent summer tour, with the result that Hallam spent upwards of five months in Italy and Scotland.

No direct correspondence from Tennyson to Hallam has survived but we know that Alfred did not send a letter this summer, because Arthur complains as much. It is from Hallam's letters, and from some of the replies which he received from Gaskell and others, that we pick up clues to the early beginnings of this consequential relationship.

Although Tennyson's junior, Hallam was confident enough to be critical. Of 'Timbuctoo' he wrote, 'The bursts of poetry in it are magnificent; but they were not written for Timbuctoo; and as a whole, the present poem is surely very imperfect.'[9] Modern readers will concur with this estimation. Too much is overblown in a cumbersomely Miltonic vein. The fascinating aspect of the poem is its counterfeit title-piece quotation from Chapman. This has been interpreted as some kind of hoax, a jape played on the examiners – the quotation has never been identified – but it is more likely that Tennyson was making a statement about the whole poem. Here is a work parading in pretensions.

Hallam claimed that Tennyson 'borrowed the pervading idea from him', but quite what this meant is impossible to establish. Although he was able at the same time to state, 'I consider Tennyson as promising fair to be the greatest poet of our generation,'[10] there was, in the fact that their friendship began in open competition, a similarly open but also significant jealousy which has too often been passed over. In any relationship negative emotions are always present alongside positive ones. Good friends manage to suppress, but not annihilate, the negative ones. (Mythological friends, perhaps, are not allowed to have negative feelings.)

Of course, it is good to have a competitor. Poetry is not a sport, but creativity thrives on seeking to impress those who are similarly engaged. And so it is not necessarily surprising that Alfred and Arthur were already planning to publish a joint volume and that in this joint venture Alfred was taking an authoritative position. He had accepted Hallam as partner in preference to his brother Charles and rejected Monckton Milnes because he did not want any third parties.

Hallam had already left England when the result of the competition was announced on 6 June. Immediately, a flurry of interest was shown in Tennyson, and for the rest of his time at the university his poetic talent was taken seriously.

Alfred, however, continued to worry about his health. He had been seeing spots and went to London to have his eyes cupped by a renowned oculist who practised at 6 Cork Street.[11] While in town he spent time at Hampstead with his friend Merivale, who had won the medal in 1828. Sitting together one morning Tennyson was seized by a presentiment that one of Merivale's grandmothers was dead or dying. In the end he mentioned that both of his had died some time ago, and asked Merivale if either of his were still living.

A few days later Merivale's grandmother did die, suddenly – a fact referred to without any overdue forboding (he states only that it was 'rather remarkable') when writing to Merivale to ask him if he would read 'Timbuctoo' at the prize-giving, Alfred himself being, in Merivale's astute words, too shy or too proud to exhibit himself on such an occasion.

5   Churlish Curmudgeon

Alone my hopeless melancholy gloometh
Like a lone cypress, through the twilight hoary,
From an old garden where no flower bloometh,
One cypress on an island promontory

(SONNET: 'ME MY OWN FATE TO LASTING SORROW DOOMETH')

B y the time Alfred left London for Somersby, at the end of his treatment from the oculist, the Tennyson family was once again settled at the Rectory. Frederick was not amongst them. He had spent the spring exchanging letters with his grandfather and trying to sort out his future – begging that his name not be removed from the college boards.

In the end he secured a post as a tutor and set off for Paris in mid-June, quite possibly meeting up with Alfred in London on his way. But it seems he missed a face-to-face reconciliation with his father, the Doctor having left Paris for Switzerland in a mighty huff because he had been waiting three weeks for the promised arrival of his brother, Charles. (It has to be said that the attitude of the Doctor's family during his exile, particularly that of his father and brother, is difficult to defend. That Elizabeth Tennyson and her children, after all they had been through, should sever communication is understandable, but that Charles should break his promise, and that the Old Man should fail to reply to any of George's letters, which became increasingly frantic for news of his family, is harder to condone.)

When one of George's letters was read aloud in the Rectory, visitors from Bayons were hypocritically shocked by the 'cold indifference of the Somersby household'. In fact there was nothing cold about Somersby during this summer. A veritable social renaissance took hold of the rectory and there was partying and dancing through the long days of July and August.

Bayons did not approve of this either and it is from this period onwards that the divisions between the two Tennyson lines become more and more pronounced. To assert his authority over the family the Old Man vetoed Mrs Tennyson's choice of tutor and again refused to return the horses. This meant that for the regular balls at Spilsby and Horncastle the Tennysons had to hire a carriage.

At the Somersby gatherings Mary would play the Doctor's harp for guests to dance to under the trees, and there would be recitations of poetry out on the lawn beneath the starlight and the elms. Flirting couples could wander off along one of the paths to Holywell Wood.

Alfred's mood on these occasions was variable. He might be vivacious – dancing with the twelve year-old Sophy Rawnsley and amusing the company with one of his famous acts of mimicry – or he might be quiet and distant. He particularly remembered this summer for the onset of a sudden sense of sadness:

> I remember that sometimes in the midst of the dance, a great and sudden sadness would come over me, and I would leave the dance and wander away beneath the stars, or sit on gloomily and abstractedly below the stairs. I used to wonder then, what strange demon it was, that drove me forth and took all the pleasure from my blood, and made me such a churlish curmudgeon.

Some writers are morbid and melancholy only to the extent that they recoil from, and sometimes actually repel, the intrusive qualities of society and pleasure. Tennyson's sense of individuality was always strong, and perhaps cultivated too assiduously. To be really on his own Alfred would take himself to Mablethorpe or Skegness and wander off to the sea-wilderness of Gibraltar Point. In such a place he could truly be absorbed within himself. Accounts gathered from aged local people about the early days of the famous are notoriously unreliable but in all the memories collected from Lincolnshire locals towards the end of Tennyson's life, there is a consistent theme. The young Tennyson would walk around the lanes, hills or sand-dunes, reading a book, or declaiming some experimental lines, oblivious of the day, hour or situation. One old codger from near Skegness remembered:

> ... as if it wur nobbut yisterdaÿ, my man, as was a fiddler bit of a fellow, was off to Heldred's theer at Skegnest, to play fur quolity at a dance; and he was cooming hoam in the morning early, and, bedashed, who should he light on but Mr Alfred, araävin' and taävin' upon the sand-hills in his shirt-sleeves an' all; and Mr Alfred said, saäys he, 'Good morning,' saäys he; and my man saäys, 'Thou poor fool, thou doesn't knaw morning from night,' for you know, sir, i' them daäys we all thowt he was craäzed.

Many of the poems eventually published the following summer took shape at this time, and reflect his increasing experimentation with metre and rhyme. And there was one, not included in the 1830 volume, which presaged some of Tennyson's later preoccupations. Entitled 'The Idealist', it is an early companion piece for a poem which he would not write for another forty years, 'The Higher Pantheism'.

> A mighty matter I rehearse,
> A mighty matter undescried;
> Come listen all who can,
> I am the spirit of a man,
> I weave the universe,
> And indivisible divide,
> Creating all I hear and see.
> All souls are centres: I am one, I am the earth,
> the stars, the sun,
> I am the clouds, the sea.
> I am the citadels and palaces
> Of all great cities: I am Rome,
> Tadmor, and Cairo: I am Place
> And time, yet is my home
> Eternity: (let no man think it odd,
>   For I am these,
> And every other birth of every other race;)
> I am all things save souls of fellow men and
>   very God!

6   Interpreting the Oracles

If I were loved as I desire to be,
What is there in the great sphere of the earth,
And range of evil between death and birth,
That I should fear, – if I were loved by thee?

(SONNET)

It was during the autumn term at Cambridge in 1829, that Tennyson's friendship with Arthur Hallam deepened, and his association with the Conversazione Society, otherwise known as the Apostles, began.

Much more than an intimate debating society, the Apostles were exclusive, secretive, and masonic. It was assumed that, by definition, the members were the most astounding minds of their generation and that their self-appointed task was to give a sort of judicial hearing to some of life's metaphysical mysteries and then, after a straightforward vote, to issue a supreme court verdict. Merivale, who was also an Apostle, looked back in later life with wry detachment at the pomposities of the group. 'We soon grew, as such youthful coteries generally do, into immense self-conceit. We began to think that we had a mission to enlighten the world upon things intellectual and spiritual ... It was with a vague idea that it should be our function to interpret the oracles of transcendental wisdom to the world of Philistines, or Stumpfs, as we designated them ...'

Tennyson was elected at the end of the summer term, probably just before his success with 'Timbuctoo', but equally probably owing to some clandestine whispering of his imminent triumph. He was elected as a poet, not a thinker, and it is unlikely that he would have been accepted without objective measure of his capabilities.

Arthur Hallam's election occurred early in the autumn term. It was a foregone conclusion. His reputation as a debater at Eton, and his natural prediliction for philosophical discussion in college rooms, marked him out as a quintessential Apostle.

In addition to its loftier aims the society served the usual purpose of a close-knit club – providing mutual support and reciprocal flattery, with a smattering of ritual. Each Apostle meeting would begin with the consumption of anchovies on toast, and thereafter the course of discussion was simplicity itself. One of the members would deliver a paper on a given subject, a discussion would ensue, and finally a vote was taken and the result recorded. There was no more to it than that.

For some reason Tennyson missed the first meeting of term and had to pay a five-shilling fine. The debate was on whether clergy should be allowed to sit in the House of Commons. On 14 November they discussed libel law and whether it allowed both freedom of discussion and protection of the individual. On 21 November they considered whether Shelley's poems had an immoral tendency – Hallam and Tennyson voted 'NO'. On 28 November both Hallam and Tennyson voted 'AYE' to whether there is any rule of moral action other than general expediency. On 5 December they voted 'NO' again, to whether the existence of an intelligent First Cause can be deducted from the phenomena of this Universe. Hallam read the paper at this meeting.

Apart from registering his vote, Tennyson took little active part in discussions. His quietness has been attributed to shyness, but this is to evade an alternative interpretation: perhaps he was simply not up to the witty and ironical repartee which characterized Apostle debate. Despite the theoretical priggishness of the group it displayed, in practice, the usual exuberance of student clubs. On one occasion Douglas Heath[12] had huge quantities of table salt poured over his head for talking nonsense.

A key member of the group at this time was Richard Monckton Milnes. Opinionated and frivolous, extrovert and self-confident, a magpie-minded gossip, he was the antithesis of Tennyson, engaging life at Cambridge head-on, rather than submitting to it. Besides Tennyson it was Milnes of all the Apostles of this vintage who, as Lord Houghton, made the greatest mark in later life. His political career was somewhat muted but he became the champion of unpopular causes and developed a special interest in American affairs. He played a significant role in persuading the English to read Emerson and, at the time of the Civil War between North and South, he supported the Union, against the initial tide of public opinion. A keen bibliophile, he gathered an extensive collection of erotica and was especially proud of such curious treasures as a volume which used the dried skin of a murderer as its bookmark. Short, chubby and double-chinned, Milnes once said, 'the thing I was intended for by nature is a German woman ... I think Goethe would have fallen in love with me and I am not sure that Platen[13] didn't.' It is quite unthinkable that Tennyson would at this time have made such a saucy comment about himself.

Late in November Milnes, Hallam and Sunderland (another Apostle, and the reputed subject of 'A Character') set out through the snow on a sortie to Oxford. Their mission, to defend a motion in the Oxford Union that Shelley was a better poet than Byron. In order to obtain an exeat Milnes boasted that he had fooled the Master, Christopher Wordsworth, into thinking that the competition was between Byron and William Wordsworth.

Sunderland was the best speaker of the three, Hallam being less dramatic and Milnes less incisive. (On Hallam's debating skills Milnes said, in a letter to his brother on 8 November 1829, 'He would be a splendid speaker, if he had more nerve.')

It was all good fun and afforded Hallam a chance of meeting three school-chums, Gladstone, Gaskell and Doyle, from whom he was only now beginning to wean himself. Gladstone, who even at Eton had found Hallam a fickle friend, grew jealous at all the talk of Tennyson and Arthur's obviously deepening regard for him.

Such jealousy was neither unmanly nor untypical of the age – an age which prized male friendship almost as highly as marriage. Monckton Milnes also had reason to be jealous of Tennyson, because he would like to have been Hallam's 'special' Cambridge friend.

It was with Milnes that Hallam had communicated by letter during his long summer abroad, and two passages from these summer letters give a good indication of the melodramatic self-scrutiny to which the eighteen year-old Arthur Hallam was prone:

York. August 15th 1829

... I really am afraid of insanity: for God's sake, send me letters, many letters, amusing letters. Mountains, or metaphysics; jokes, or arguments ... anything to distract me; anything to give me hope, sympathy, comfort! Do you ask what is the matter? I cannot tell you: I am not master of my

56

own mind; my own thoughts are more than a match for me; my brain has been fevering with speculations most fathomless, abysmal, ever since I set foot in Scotland. As soon as I reach Malvern I must fling on paper what I have been thinking of, in order to know what I *do believe, what I can believe*. But though I write at present under the influence of a dark hour, think not I have had no sunshine: my poetical faculty has developed itself marvellously: it burns now in my heart: God grant me, if I am to have a Poet's destiny, at least a Poet's power! I have sat within the voice of cataracts, & looked on the silent faces of hills: & have felt glorified by the strong Imagination within me, till I forgot my cleaving curses, and recked of nothing but love to God & man. . . .

> The Lodge. Great Malvern. Worcester. Sept 1st 1829
> . . . I could not, I think, return to Italy, the land that is indeed my country, without such heart-sorrow, as would embitter my outward enjoyments. They whom I loved would be there no more, the wellknown spots, bitterly dear because their feet had pressed them, would look otherwise upon me: the thought would burn in my brain, and be there, & make me know it was there, whether I turned my mind from it, or not, that I am not what I was, not in happiness, not in goodness, not in intellectual energy. My soul was dawning then, and the sky, all but the little black cloud in the horizon no bigger than a man's hand, was very clear: now the dayclouds have settled down on it, and the time has gone by! My last letter to you (that from York) was a strain of madness: I am calmer now. I past some days with Gaskell, which strengthened me: and visited a Lunatic asylum, which gave me a very awful, and elevated sense of sadness: so I am calm for the present.[14]

We learn a great deal from Hallám's letters. He had imbibed the Romantic frame of mind as deeply as any late adolescent is inclined to imbibe the literature of the period they most admire. Whatever had passed between Tennyson and Hallam in the early months of 1829 had left one of the two far from tranquil. 'If I am to have a Poet's destiny . . .' he says. The use of the conditional is very revealing, for it shows that in his collaboration with Tennyson, both in the Chancellor's Medal entry and in the proposed volume of poems, Hallam was working from a position of initial insecurity. To understand the two young men properly, as their relationship develops, it is vital that this is grasped.

Since the summer Arthur Hallam's mental state had become less tumultuous and the regular Saturday night Apostle meetings were largely responsible for this. He had found his niche. Tennyson was still somewhat a figure standing back in the corner, but the friendship between himself and Hallam would increasingly bring him out of the shadows.

7   Ghosts

A spirit haunts the year's last hours
Dwelling amidst these yellowing bowers,
To himself he talks;

('SONG')

At the end of the autumn term Hallam took both the Tennyson brothers to London for a few days. It was only the second visit that Alfred had made to the city and his friend proved a more inspirational guide than had his Aunt Russell. (On that first, morbid trip to London he could not get it out of his head that 'in a few years all its inhabitants would be lying horizontal, stark and stiff in their coffins'.) Jack Kemble, one of the Apostles, had a sister called Fanny who was already making a name for herself on the stage, and the gang went along to the theatre to catch her in one of her characteristically unhistrionic but magical performances. All were captivated.

The Tennysons were also introduced to some of Hallam's Etonian friends. Doyle[15] found Alfred likeable but strange. Charles he thought nice enough, but clearly not a part of the set. (Charles, no longer Alfred's sole literary collaborator, was quietly going his own way and preparing for publication an individual collection of sonnets. His unswerving dedication to the sonnet form was a graphic illustration of the difference in temperament between him and his more experimental brother.)

The Hallams lived at 67 Wimpole Street. Their town residence, formal and a little starchy, must have struck Charles and

Alfred as a world apart from their Somersby home. The same was true for Hallam when, on the 20 December, his hospitality was returned and he was welcomed at Somersby for the first time. This stay was brief. He was back in London for Christmas, but the powerful Rectory atmosphere – warm, informal, faintly eccentric – enthralled him. The weather was mild. He and Alfred played in the garden with the Tennysons' pet monkey. Charles's sense of isolation, as he looked out of the attic window on this scene, became more potent, while along the 'strong current of his memory'[16] flowed stringent reminiscences of his and Alfred's intimate apprenticeship, shouting fabulous hexameters at one another across the hedgerows and galloping out to Mablethorpe in the first flush of publication fever, with mint-fresh copies of *Poems by Two Brothers* in their hands.

For Mary and Emily and the younger Tennyson children this visit of one of their brothers' young friends from Cambridge was an excuse for celebration and excitement.

A special thrill can attach itself to being introduced to the sisters of one's best friend. They have been spoken about and imagined. They possess intimate knowledge of he who is the cause of the introduction. They are imbued with the novelty of the setting, so that the more different the friend's home-life turns out to be from one's own, the more likely it is that the sisters will be found alluring. And if, in addition, they are beautiful, and of suitable age, it is almost inevitable that the friend, the visitor, will fall in love.

The impact that Somersby made on Hallam was assisted by the continued absence of the Doctor, who was at this time miserably holed-up in a very rainy Naples. However, this first visit was exceedingly fleeting and a letter from Hallam to Milnes, written early in the New Year, before he returned to Cambridge for the Lent term, gives no indication that he harboured instant romantic designs on any one of the Tennyson girls. On the contrary, he seems in these early weeks of the year to have become openly infatuated with Fanny Kemble, in the same affected, literary way that he had doted upon Anna Wintour. The romantic poems of this period are addressed to Miss Kemble and not to a Tennyson sister.

This public infatuation became something of an embarrassment to his friends. Gaskell moochingly complained of Hallam's infidelity to Anna Wintour, the love they had each declared for her being, in his sight, eternal and unimpeachable. Blakesley wrote to Alfred from London telling him that Hallam had made himself unwell and that moreover he was 'submitting himself publically *to the influences of the outer world more than a man of genius ought to do'*. But the italics were added by a later generation. The quotation is taken from manuscript materials collected in preparation for Hallam Tennyson's two-volume memoir of his father. He commonly excised questionable sections of text and replaced them with bland paraphrases. Of course, this sort of practice often suggests worse than the (probably) minor indiscretions it is seeking to cover-up. The biographer is duty-bound to guard against thinking the worst, but integrity has to be balanced by speculation. Blakesley's bowdlerized advertisement of Hallam's dissolute behaviour in London is enough to give the lie to the idealized view of Hallam which later developed, nourished by the following kind of pronouncement which appeared in Mr Hallam's memorial essay on his son: 'His premature abilities were not more conspicuous than an almost faultless disposition sustained by a more calm self-command than has often been witnessed in that season of life.'

Arthur knew himself better than that. 'I am one of strong passions, irresolute purposes, vacillating opinions,'[17] he told Gaskell after having been reprimanded for his inconstancy towards Anna Wintour.

The weather proved just as irresolute and the mildness of December gave way to an exceedingly chill January. 'So intense was the cold on Monday night last that Fahrenheit's thermometer fell to 6 degrees, being 26 below the freezing point,' reported the *Cambridge Chronicle* on 22 January 1830. The icy conditions prevailed into February and one Trinity student, named Longmure, had a thigh broken when a stage on the London route skidded and overturned just outside Ware. Alfred's set kept themselves warm by acting out pantomime versions of Shakespeare. In March they performed *Much Ado About Nothing* with Kemble as Dogberry, Hallam as Verges and Milnes as Beatrice. The latter played it outrageously, breaking a couch with his weight, falling to the floor and kicking his legs in the air to show off his petticoats. It is hard to imagine Alfred taking a role in this informal production but he was often called upon to read or declaim his poems at other evening gatherings.

The Apostle meetings continued but Alfred was forced to tender his resignation in February when he failed to take his turn as 'Moderator' and read an essay on the agreed subject 'Ghosts'. Only the prologue of his paper has survived, prompting the thought that perhaps Tennyson never got any further than the three paragraphs it contains. Once again his friends attributed this failure to shyness. And once again, from this distance, that explanation does not convince.

As these few lines constitute the only prose work which Tennyson left behind (apart from a limited correspondence, odd annotations to manuscripts and notebooks, and his prose drama *The Promise of May*) – a fact which makes him thoroughly untypical of the age – they deserve to be quoted in full:

He who has the power of speaking of the spiritual world, speaks in a simple manner of a high matter. He speaks of life and death, and the things after death. He lifts the veil, but the form behind it is shrouded in deeper obscurity. He raises the cloud, but he darkens the prospect. He unlocks with a golden key the iron-grated gates of the charnel-house, he throws them wide open. And forth issue from the inmost gloom the colossal Presences of the Past, *majores humano*; some as they lived, seemingly pale, and faintly smiling; some as they died, still suddenly frozen by the chill of death; and some as they were buried, with dropped eyelids, in their cerements and their winding sheets.

The listeners creep closer to each other, they are afraid of the drawing of their own breaths, the beating of their own hearts. The voice of *him* who speaks alone like a mountain stream on a still night fills up and occupies the silence. He stands as it were on a vantage ground. He becomes the minister and expounder of human sympathies. His words *find* the heart like the arrows of truth. Those who laughed long before, have long ago become solemn, and those who were solemn before, feel the awful sense of unutterable mystery. The speaker pauses:

'Wherefore,' says one, 'granting the intensity of the feeling, wherefore this fever and fret about a baseless vision?' 'Do not assume,' says another, 'that any vision *is* baseless.'

One can see how it might be impossible to continue after such a prologue. Follow that, as they say. And even supposing that more of the essay existed, Tennyson would have felt nervous about delivering this unconventional beginning. The spirit world, life after death, the question of whether there was matter in heaven, were obsessive concerns for Tennyson (long before they became public ones), but he would have been conscious of his audience, and the type of essay they expected. An inability to produce a cogent argument, and to make it coruscate with flashes of wit or learning, rather than the stagey dramatization on display in this introduction, probably lay behind Tennyson's failure to deliver; not shyness. He was able to hold an audience. He wasn't bashful when it came to his poetry.

The other members were forced to accept his formal resignation but Tennyson continued to attend all the Apostle meetings as an unofficial honorary member, (a position which was formally ratified twenty-five years later, although Tennyson never attended any reunions).

Perhaps he was simply too busy to finish the essay, having to get extra poems completed and revised to fill up some of the space which Hallam's work would otherwise have occupied. (Mr Hallam, having set eyes on some of his son's amatory verses would not allow him to publish them. Arthur himself tried to give the impression that it was his own decision, that he had decided his compositions were too crude besides those of Alfred's. Some of his poems were later printed secretly and quietly circulated amongst his friends.)

Certainly Alfred was too self-absorbed to bother with the clamouring of other Trinity fellows who were carrying on a campaign to have their dinner-hour moved from 3.15 pm to 4 pm.

8   Fugitive Pieces

Two children in two neighbour villages
Playing mad pranks along the healthy leas.

('CIRCUMSTANCE')

The job of copying out was already nearly finished by the time of the spring vacation, and Alfred completed the task in the Rectory.

Hallam visited again, this time for a longer stay, and in the seasonal weather was treated to a more sustained dose of Somersby social life. 'I have floated along a delicious dream of music and poetry and riding and dancing and greenwood-dinners and ladies' conversation till I have been simply exhaled into Paradise,' he wrote to Blakesley from the Rectory.

It was at this time that Arthur Hallam began to look at Emily Tennyson in a romantic light. Tradition has it that their first yearning glances were exchanged in Holywell Wood and that a day or two later Alfred came upon Emily Sellwood in exactly the same spot. The Sellwood sisters, Emily and Anne, were regular guests at the Somersby soirées and very friendly with the Tennyson girls. They frequently drove over from Horncastle and often met the Tennysons at the Horncastle balls.

What does a brother feel when his best friend falls in love with a favourite sister? (Mary had always been closest to Charles, and Emily to Alfred.) At the very least, such feelings are not likely to be uncomplicated. But Alfred had too much on his mind at this time to consciously register any conflicting emotions, for soon after completing a fair copy of a new book of poems he lost the manuscript while walking from Spilsby to Somersby late at night. It was not recovered and the copying had to be done again. In some cases whole poems had to be re-written from memory.

Charles had already had his collection *Sonnets and Fugitive Pieces* published in March, by a friend at Cambridge. Alfred, however, had chosen to be published by a London bookseller, Effingham Wilson. The agreement, which had probably been negotiated and signed by Hallam when it still seemed likely he would be co-author, was for half-shares on both risks and profits.

Six hundred copies were issued at a price of five shillings each. The publication date (mid-June) was not propitious, as King George IV died on 26 June. Parliamentary elections were in preparation and the agitation for reform which was to break out later in the year was already simmering. Revolution was affecting France and Belgium. With such goings-on at home and abroad there was little chance that Tennyson's first solo performance would attract immediate notice, although it was advertised in the *Athenaeum* on 19 June, and in the *Literary Gazette* on 26 June.

Tennyson was not impressed by his new publisher. On the 18 June he wrote:

I hear complaints from various quarters that persons are not able to procure my book of the booksellers: I am likewise informed that you told Ridgeway that I desired the publication not to take place till the conclusion of the present week. There must be some mistake in this report, though I am at a loss to account for the origin of it. At any rate the book has been delayed much too long and I must request you to disseminate it immediately, as everybody is leaving town.

Alfred was about to leave town as well.

Dr Tennyson arrived back in England at the beginning of July. He went directly to his brother Charles in London, and several days later Charles reported to Tealby: 'My brother is still here and seems very uncertain what to do. He seems quite unwilling to join his family.'

This indecision was both pitiful and predictable. His letters home had become increasingly distraught, complaining over and over of the 'dreadful state of anxiety' induced by the lack of news regarding his family. The feeling does not escape the student of these affairs, and cannot have escaped the Doctor himself, that his family would have preferred it if he had stayed away forever. The bizarre stories which he eventually began to tell of narrowly-escaped death – how he was nearly buried alive by an avalanche, nearly fell over the edge of a precipice, was hurtled headlong to the rim of a ravine in a runaway coach – were obvious invitations to the family to declare their real feelings.

Uncle Charles' own family life was far from tranquil at this time, the following letter from his wife Fanny suggesting that the Old Man's favourite son was just as volatile and irascible as his older brother:

You cannot suppose, after what passed when you were last here, that I can be very comfortable. The too frequent repetitions of such scenes have long ago destroyed my peace ... It is enough for the head of a family to speak, without its being resented by their offspring, but if you are determined to place them above me, I cannot blame them altogether ... If I am a despicable person, why leave others of the family with me – take them, and let me remain in solitude and be at peace.

She finishes by complaining about the 'great impropriety of conduct between men and maids' in the household, an impropriety in which, it is implied, Charles was himself involved.

Elizabeth Tennyson wrote to her brother-in-law confessing to the 'greatest dread' at hearing the news that her husband was back in the country. 'May God protect my family.' Frederick, mercifully, was still away from Somersby. Alfred immediately left home, travelling to London on a matter of 'life and death', his mother supposing that his purpose was to consult a Physician, although the dramatic phrase may have had less personal connotations.

When the Doctor finally bucked up the courage to travel to Lincolnshire, he went not to Somersby, but to Tealby. He had been there more than a week before his presence was known at the Rectory. On hearing the news Charles and Emily immediately fled to Mablethorpe, leaving their mother and Mary in the front line with the younger boys. Mrs Tennyson wrote a neutral letter to her husband which was hardly a loving welcome home but was sufficient to encourage the Doctor back to the house.

He was not at all well. In August he exchanged letters with his father in which, amidst concerns for the future of the younger boys, particularly Edward and Arthur (who were now seventeen and sixteen respectively) the two men vied declarations of illness with one another. The Doctor complained of diarrhoea and vomiting. The Old Man wrote back that he was 'passing blood in urine'. The atmosphere at the Rectory had been changed at a stroke and it is not surprising that Hallam spent no time there that summer.

9　Brothers in Arms

There lies a vale in Ida, lovelier
Than all the valleys of Ionian hills.

('ŒNONE')

Alfred and Hallam had other plans. Looking back on this summer's adventure, Hallam wrote to Trench later in the year, in rather throwaway style, 'Alfred went, as you know, with me to the south of France, and a wild, bustling time we had of it. I played my part as a conspirator in a small way, and made friends with two or three gallant men.' There was rather more to it than that.

Since 1823 a group of Spanish exiles had been in London, having fled their homeland when the monarchy was restored. The ensuing ten years, up to the death of King Ferdinand, and the start of the Seven Years (Civil) War between the Queen and Ferdinand's brother, Don Carlos, are known as the 'ominous decade'. The expatriate group, led by Jose Torrijos, would gather in Euston Square, wrapped up in long black cloaks, and importune passers-by for support, much as Iranian or Kuwaiti exiles have done more recently. One afternoon Sterling was amongst the crowd at Euston. He was picked out by Torrijos himself and, impressed by the Spaniard's cause, invited him to Cambridge to meet the other Apostles.

The result was that the society colluded in a plot to reinstate the liberal constitutionalists. Sterling's cousin, Robert Boyd, invested the whole of his inheritance in buying and fitting out a warship for the exiles. But just as they were about to embark, the river police, acting on a tip-off from the Home Secretary, prevented sailing and attempted to arrest the Spanish crew. Most were able to jump overboard and escape and they continued their efforts by taking passage to Gibraltar where Kemble and Trench were already in communication with rebels on the southern mainland.

The timing for an attack was delayed further and further. Sterling eventually left for the West Indies. Trench was the second, and Kemble the third to lose their initial revolutionary zeal. Only Sterling's cousin, Boyd, stayed on to see the rebellion through to its lethal conclusion.

Alfred's and Arthur's role in all this was to convey money and secret instructions to the men in the north of Spain. Their mission was therefore to travel through France into the Pyrenees, and there is no reason to believe that they were any less enthusiastic about the cause, at this stage, than the other Apostles.

When Mrs Tennyson wrote her letter mentioning Alfred's 'life and death' visit to a doctor, and his need to remain in London for a fortnight, the two friends had already left for France. It seems clear enough that a mother was being deceived, either wilfully to conceal the mission from her and spare her consequent worry, or by an ironic remark not properly understood.

After stopping in Paris for a short while, and possibly meeting up with Frederick, they continued on their way south. It was a tiring and dusty journey and Alfred, who suffered from hayfever all his life, became too unwell to continue. The two of them held up their journey at Montpelier for a few days and then continued westwards towards the Pyrenees.

The landscape between Narbonne and Perpignan inspired 'Mariana in the South', which Tennyson began to write rattling along in a diligence across the dry terrain.

Behind the barren hill upsprung
   With pointed rocks against the light,
The crag sharpshadowed overhung
   Each glaring creek and inlet bright.
Far, far, one lightblue ridge was seen,
   Looming like baseless fairyland;
   Eastward a slip of burning sand,
Dark-rimmed with sea, and bare of green.

('MARIANA IN THE SOUTH', 1832)

At a border village between the rivers Gaube and Marcadou the two undercover agents handed over their smuggled money and messages to Ojeda, the rebel leader. He knew no English, and they no Spanish, so they conversed in French. Ojeda, thanking them for everything, said that the funds and instructions would help them 'couper la gorge à tous les curés'.[18]

They had hoped to meet Frederick at Bagnères but instead found only a curt note inviting them to follow him back to Paris. This they were both too tired to contemplate and instead they remained at Cauteretz, recouping their strength.

Their mission accomplished, the two friends could now relax and enjoy the scenery, with Tennyson acquiring a new poetic territory quite different from Somersby and the Lincolnshire Wolds. It was one in which 'Œnone', 'The Eagle', 'The Lotos-Eaters' and 'In the Valley of Cauteretz' came to life. Climbing the pine-sided crags with Hallam, looking over precipitous drops, running hands in the deep cold waters of glacier lakes, then descending again into the hot mountain valleys – these were heady days for Alfred and Arthur. Their fatigue soon left them but they were content to spend several days in the region.

Some unsubtle suggestions have been made as to what went on in the valley of Cauteritz to give it such a lasting significance in Tennyson's work and thinking. It is probably sufficient for all of us to find, in our own past, a period of cameraderie with a single or select few friends, in a foreign or strange landscape, to understand that it is the absence of sexuality in such experiences which gives them their poignancy. Typically they occur at the end of youth.

Alfred and Arthur were not attracted to one another sexually, but on the horizon, certainly for Arthur (who would by now have confided in Alfred his love for Emily) and inevitably for Alfred, rolled the divisive undertow of sexual attraction between a man and a woman.

The term 'homoeroticism' is often used by those wanting to stop short of suggesting a homosexual relationship. But even this is not an accurate way of describing Arthur and Alfred's relationship. A better one might be 'platonic possessiveness', and Robert Bernard Martin is right, but too hesitant, in his biography *The Unquiet Heart*, to see such possessiveness and inherent jealousy as the thematic subtext to 'Œnone', which tells the story of Paris's desertion of his first love for the temptress Helen. Spoken by the abandoned one, the poem seems to give voice to Tennyson's acknowledgement, in the midst of this interlude of happy companionship, that erotic love will soon come between himself and Hallam and 'all the colour of my afterlife/Will be the shadow of today.'

> I wish that somewhere in the ruined folds,
> Among the fragments tumbled from the glens,
> Or the dry thickets, I could meet with her
> The Abominable, that uninvited came
> Into the fair Peleian banquet-hall,
> And cast the golden fruit upon the board,
> And bred this change ...

These themes of possessiveness and jealousy became more articulated and conscious as time went by, so that Tennyson later looked back at the days in the valley as representative of the intense ideality of his friendship with Hallam, a friendship which he could, without feeling abashed, describe as love, knowing that this did not imply sexual attraction, but did imply concomitant feelings of fidelity, jealousy, and other emotions, both negative and positive, which attach to a loving relationship.

Eventually the two of them decided it was time to return home. They went to Bordeaux and on 8 September boarded a steamer bound for Dublin. Travelling on the boat were Mr and Mrs Harden of Cumberland and their three daughters, to whom, on the first day, Alfred read aloud his newly composed 'Œnone', and on the second day, Arthur, recovered from initial sea-sickness, read from a new single-volume edition of Scott's novels.

The two sketches which Mr Harden drew of the scene on deck are amusingly evocative of what Hallam referred to, in a letter to Charles Tennyson, as, 'that more relaxed and more pleasant freedom of society, which is usual in seavoyages. In the presence of that awful element human beings forget the colder maxims of convention, which may be suitable enough between the four walls of drawing-rooms.' Relaxed enough for the men perhaps – they are shown lounging on the sunny deck amongst books and bolsters, Tennyson wearing a long cape possibly given to him by the Spanish insurrectionists – but the three young women sit alongside one another on a hard bench, each one wearing an identical coal-skuttle hat (see plate 3).

10   Desire

Wantoning in orange groves
Naked, and dark-limbed, and gay,

('ANACAONA')

The timing of their crossing from Dublin to Liverpool was auspicious, for it enabled them to be amongst the passengers on the first train to run between Liverpool and Manchester. A mistaken impression that the train ran along grooves (like a tram), rather than raised rails, later gave rise to the famous line 'Let the great world spin forever down the ringing grooves of change' ('Locksley Hall').

Alfred would not permit Arthur (in his letter to Charles) to warn Somersby of his imminent return. He wanted to produce a 'poetical effect by appearing improviso'. (Hallam adds that his own maxims of conduct were extremely different: 'I confess to an avaricious appetite for the sight of sympathies excited, necks stretched out, and butlers looking round the corner, not to mention a well-aired bed, and a providently augmented dinner.')[19]

Alfred, arriving home in much better bodily health than when he had left, was always likely to deny he felt well, and by the beginning of October he was suffering under an imagined indisposition sufficient to delay his return to Cambridge for the new term. Like many hypochondriacs Tennyson lived to an old age but rarely felt himself to be in the peak of health. At this time of his life he was troubled mainly by headaches and grey spots in his vision. Susan Baur, in her book on hypochondria,[20] makes ample reference to Tennyson (as well as Darwin) to illustrate nineteenth-century attitudes towards the illness. She is over-dismissive of the grey spots, suggesting that they are an archetypal symptom of all hypochondriacs. Those of us who, like Tennyson, are short-sighted, will know that excessive reading or lack of sleep can easily bring on a parade of these disconcerting 'musculantae'. Tennyson's exaggerated sensitivity to them, and his fear that they indicated incipient blindness, need to be put in the context of the belief, inculcated in all adolescents and young men of that time, that failing vision was one of the consequences of masturbation.

The popular image of the compulsive masturbator was uncomfortably close to a description of the young Tennyson. William Acton wrote, 'he becomes careless in dress and uncleanly in person. His intellect has become sluggish and enfeebled ... He may end in becoming a drivelling idiot or a peevish valetudinarian.' The last characterization was to be tellingly echoed a few years later by Edward FitzGerald. Apart from insanity, masturbation was thought to be capable of causing impotence, consumption, apathy, loss of memory, lack of concentration and a loss of physical energy.[21]

Once Alfred had summoned up sufficient energy, he returned alone to Cambridge on 2 November. Charles had already decided not to resume his studies. Possibly he felt obliged to remain behind with his mother and protect her from the unpredictable behaviour of his father. Possibly he was infatuated with the new governess. Possibly he had already begun to make too frequent use of opium, a habit which was to debilitate his life; and possibly he simply felt concerned that he was not yet ready to sit his exams.

A new poem of Alfred's quickly became a favourite with the Apostles. 'Anacaona', written in Somersby, but full of the sensuality which was the inheritance of his Spanish trip, entranced his friends with its sunny eroticism. They copied it out for one another. They urged Tennyson to publish it. And this was odd because we are supposed to believe that it was these loftily-minded friends who were trying to steer Tennyson towards verse with a more serious purpose. 'Anacaona' tells, in a sonorous swoon, the story of the Queen of Xaraquay, killed by Spanish conquistadores. There is little narrative in its eighty-four lines, and the poem does not contain a description of Anacaona's death. Tennyson's friends responded to it for its unabashed delight in naked innocence:

> A dark Indian maiden
>   Warbling in the bloomed liana,
> Stepping lightly flower-laden,
>   By the crimson-eyed anana,
> Wantoning in orange groves
>   Naked and dark-limbed, and gay,
> Bathing in the slumbrous coves,
> In the cocoa-shadowed coves,
>   Of sunbright Xaraguay,
> Who was so happy as Anacaona,
>   The beauty of Espagnola,
>   The golden flower of Hayti?

One of the Trinity crowd who enjoyed this poem (and kept his own manuscript book of as many Tennyson poems as he could get copied) was the unlikely John Allen[22], who, at school, had been forced to toast bread at the fire with his naked hands for refusing to look at a set of rude engravings, and, as an undergraduate, made a daily catalogue of the vices to which he was prey. These, it has to be said, are rather uncolourful – Indolence, Pride, Folly, Gluttony, and Whispering in Chapel. For a young man passionate about not wasting his time and who, to this end, was continually making resolutions (to play cards no more, to give up dancing, etc.) reading poems about naked Spanish maidens was apparently a morally safe and worthy pastime. No one would want to suggest otherwise, but it is interesting to speculate what it was about 'Anacaona' that Allen and others found so entrancing.

While still at home Alfred had exchanged letters with Hallam, who was staying in a country house near Leyton, in Essex. On 4 October Hallam wrote to Somersby a letter which, ostensibly, gives no indication that the days in Cauteritz had given rise to any intensification of his regard for Alfred. He talks of the Spanish trip exclusively in terms of its politics ('Spanish affairs, you will have seen in the papers, go on slowly') and quizzes Alfred about his reactions to unrest in Europe, particularly in Belgium and Saxony. The letter survives only in Hallam Tennyson's transcript. It is, therefore, possible that other passages have been excised, but the nature of the letter suggests it is complete. Indeed, all the evidence tends to indicate that the ardency of feeling generated by the days in the Spanish valley were one-sided.

The Apostles' revolutionary zeal was put to the test during the following few weeks, when the rick-burning and general unrest which accompanied Parliamentary debate of the Reform Bill swept the Cambridgeshire countryside. There were riots in Huntingdon and in December the *Cambridge Chronicle* reported: 'Some apprehension having been entertained that in consequence of the excited state of the labouring classes in many villages, riotous proceedings might occur on Market day, the Mayor and magistrate of the town, as a precautionary measure, swore in, as special constables, about 500 of the inhabitants.' A rumour that the university library would be attacked spurred many of the undergraduates to augment the special constabulary with the formation of vigilante units, armed with pointed ash sticks. As Spedding put it, 'Visions of broken heads & arms, scythes & pitchforks, disturbed the purity of our unselfish contemplations, & the idealism of our poetical imaginings.'

In the event, there was only one incident. Merivale was in Hallam's room at 6.30 pm when they both heard a hubbub in the court below. Grabbing their sticks they rushed down to the main gate to see a red glare hanging over the Master's lodge. But the actual fire was some distance away, on the road to Coton. Twenty-three ricks were alight. Farmworkers were standing casually watching them blaze, and some sabotaged the students' attempts at fire-fighting by cutting the water-pipes.

Tennyson helped to man one of the engines, allegedly muttering that it was time a stop was put to such goings-on, but in general the Apostles affected an aloof and circumspect attitude towards the local panic. Merivale reported, disdainfully, that some undergraduates were too terrified to go to bed at night without checking underneath the mattress for firebombs. And Hallam felt that most of the alarm had been the result of 'hoax and humbug'. The vigilante groups were disbanded before the end of term.

It is a little too facile to argue that Tennyson's set had been panicked into showing their true colours; that the libertarian mission of the summer was revealed as humbug. Romantic insurrectionists abroad, they were hard-headed protectors of order at home. The same could be said of many a revolutionary when put to the test.

Like Wordsworth, Tennyson was temperamentally conservative. A strong belief in justice was balanced by just as strong a desire to see as little change as possible. It is futile, no doubt, to guess at what kind of poetry Tennyson would have written had he been born a century earlier, but it would surely have been less varied, and more of a piece. As it was, he had to cope with a period of momentous changes in social, industrial and political life. Because of his nature, they were changes which he tried, with considerable success, to isolate himself from, but in the end they could not be ignored and he was forced to acknowledge them. Wordsworth's retirement and isolation in the Lakes is ultimately less compelling partly because he only lived to see the beginnings of a change in the world order.

On 19 September Spedding, whose father had gone to school with Wordsworth, invited the poet to his rooms for evening coffee to meet several of the Apostles and friends. Wordsworth sounded off at some length in an alarmist way about revolutions and reigns of terror. He defended 'passive obedience' (not passive disobedience), quoting scripture in his support, and carried on until 1 am, saying nothing profound or original.

Hallam and Tennyson were not there. They had already caught the coach for Louth, on their way to Somersby. Arthur stayed at the Rectory for only a few days, the three weeks he had spent there in the spring seemingly a very long time ago, the Spanish adventure having intervened, and the Doctor having returned to the house in the meantime. Hallam had not met Alfred's father before, and there is no record of his first impressions, but whatever they were like they were not so bad as to prevent him reconvincing himself of his love for Emily before going home to Wimpole Street to spend Christmas with his family.

11　Upon What Love is

He saw through life and death, through good and ill.
He saw through his own soul.

('THE POET')

At the turn of the year reviews of *Poems, Chiefly Lyrical* began to appear. One of the quaintnesses of this literary period is that months, frequently a whole year or more, could elapse between a book's publication and the appearance of a review in one of the major quarterlies. (This contrasts with the breakneck speed of today, when a book is quite likely to be reviewed before its official publication date and to receive all the notices that it will get during a single week.) It is important to appreciate the much more leisurely speed of the nineteenth century because it allowed for subtle (and not-so-subtle) campaigns of influence to be waged by the friends and supporters of an author.

In May 1830, more than a month before the book was due out, Tennant had written to William Bodham Donne, an Apostle who had left Cambridge shortly before Tennyson's time, saying that Tennyson would 'want some helping hand in the reviews & other authorised guides of the public taste; if you have any snug corner in any of the said poetometers I recommend you to write a notice if not a full & critical review.'

But by mid-January 1831 Hallam, also writing to Donne, and referring to the possibility of himself writing a review, said, 'I bide my time. I have no direct influence with any reviewer at present, nor, as criticisms of some kind are already bringing the book into general notice, is there any need for hurry: I shall however very probably stir myself in this way next summer.'

Amongst the notices that had already appeared was a piece in the *Westminster Review*. The reviewer, W.J. Fox, liked the collection, finding the poems graceful, animated, and impassioned. He singled out the amatory poems particularly, which dealt with a topic of 'incalculable importance to society'. Writers pay special attention to their first full-length review, especially if it is largely congratulatory, and the following paragraph was to have significant influence on Tennyson:

Upon what love is, depends what woman is, and upon what woman is, depends what the world is, both in the present and the future. There is not a greater moral necessity in England than that of a reformation of female education. The boy is a son; the youth is a lover; and the man who thinks lightly of the elevation of character and the extension of happiness which woman's influence is capable of producing, and ought to be directed to the production of, in society, is neither the wisest of philosophers nor the best of patriots. How long will it be before we shall have read to better purpose the eloquent lessons, and the yet more eloquent history, of that gifted and glorious being, Mary Wollstonecraft?[23]

The amatory poems which Fox was here responding to have not been universally liked and they are still pounced on by detractors of Tennyson keen to ridicule him.

'Claribel', 'Lilian', 'Madeline', and 'Adeline' are superficial poems beside 'Mariana', but collectively gave the book its air of originality. There had been few straightforward poetic portraits of women before Tennyson picked on these ladies, evolved, he said, 'like the camel from my consciousness'. They also contrast well with the stranger, more philosophical poems: 'The How and the Why', 'Supposed Confessions of a Second-Rate Sensitive Mind (not in Unity with Itself)'[24], 'Nothing Will Die', 'All Things Will Die' (like 'The Mermaid' and 'The Merman', an early example of Tennyson's intriguing propensity for paired poems), 'Circumstance' (a short meditation on the number two, compelling in its simplicity), 'All Thoughts All Creeds', and 'Dualisms'.

Tennyson's own later estimate of this collection was severe. Not many of the poems were ever reprinted and those that were were labelled 'juvenilia'. But 'Mariana' and 'Ode To Memory', the two most outstanding poems in the book, though written early, are hardly the creation of a juvenile mind or talent.

The first of these is the story of a young life languishing in vain expectation of a lover who will never come:

> With blackest moss the flower-plots
>   Were thickly crusted, one and all:
> The rusted nails fell from the knots
>   That held the pear to the gable-wall.
> The broken sheds looked sad and strange:

Unlifted was the clinking latch;
Weeded and worn the ancient thatch
Upon the lonely moated grange.
    She only said, 'My life is dreary,
      He cometh not,' she said;
    She said, 'I am aweary, aweary,
    I would that I were dead!'

Passivity and frustration became the hallmark of much of his early verse about feminine figures. The tight verse structure is maintained throughout the seven stanzas of the poem (another attribute of Tennyson's early work) with just slight and subtle variations in the wording of the refrain. The form of the poem increases the sense of constriction and claustrophobia built up by the homely imagery (nails, sheds, latch, and – in the rest of the poem – curtain, doors, hinges, clock). Feminist commentary has been right to see in 'Mariana' and 'The Lady of Shalott' pictures of a panting, nubile sexuality waiting to be assuaged, but wrong to assume, in the language of sexual politics, that they are also miniature masques of masculine oppression. It is one of the special features of Tennyson's poetry that he could imagine himself so effectively in the female role and in doing so produce poetry which has a universal application. What 'Mariana' ultimately says is that all of us, not just yearning girls, will find life full of disappointed desires.

In 'Ode To Memory' Tennyson speaks as himself, but the mood is identical. He waits – thirsting – for the return of his lover, Memory. The poem has been called 'decorous'. I think it a good deal more powerful than this word implies, but it approaches its subject conventionally, in a style not entirely Tennysonian – more of a mixture of Keats and Shelley. This highlights the importance of even the very lightweight female figures, because in them he developed his own characteristic way of speaking about the human condition. We can hear the voice of Mariana in the opening lines of the Ode:

Thou who stealest fire,
From the fountains of the past,
To glorify the present; oh, haste,
    Visit my low desire!
Strengthen me, enlighten me!
I faint in this obscurity.
Thou dewy dawn of memory.

Panting eroticism, although a feature not to be overlooked, was always a figure of a deeper hunger for inspiration and enlightenment.

12   In an Old World

Hark! death is calling
While I speak to ye,
The jaw is falling,
The red cheek paling,
The strong limbs failing,
Ice with the warm blood mixing,
The eyeballs fixing.

('ALL THINGS WILL DIE')

The Lent term was to be Tennyson's last at the university, although he did not know it at the time of his return in January. It was Hallam who came back from London with the greater sense of foreboding, his father having reacted badly to the idea of his nineteen-year-old son marrying. What news reached him of the Tennyson family did not help him to view the prospect of an engagement to Emily sympathetically. He wrote to Dr Tennyson pointing out that it would be quite impossible for him to provide Hallam with an allowance sufficient for the support of both himself and a wife and that, therefore, until Arthur gained his majority, it was best that he should not visit Somersby again. Dr Tennyson agreed and a separation of the two lovers was enforced. (Subsequently it became clear that in Mr Hallam's eyes the separation, as agreed with Emily's father, included a ban on correspondence.)

Arthur could not have been fully aware of this edict at the beginning of term, although his father's opposition to the love affair had been abundantly clear during the Christmas holiday, and knowledge of the bullying way in which past friendships had been impeded could not promote optimism. To counter this he threw himself into what a friend described as an 'exuberant loving-kindness towards others', one result of which was that, on 18 January, he wrote to Leigh Hunt, then editor of the *Tatler*, enclosing both Charles' and Alfred's recent volumes of poetry. Apart from Hallam's rather shady dealings with Effingham Wilson, this was his first action as Alfred's unofficial agent.

He continued to be anxious about Kemble and Trench, for news reached London making it clear that there was no hope for the Spanish rebellion. In February he heard that they would soon be back in England – leaving just Boyd, of the original band, behind in Gibraltar.

February brought bad news as well as good. His father, no doubt having looked into his son's financial affairs to help illustrate his view that an engagement was impossible, wrote to Arthur complaining of the debts he was running up. He complained particularly of the expense of his 'ill-advised and unauthorised expedition' to Spain, the costs of which he had been forced to defray.

At the end of the month Charles and Alfred received first news of their father's worsening condition, and then their summons home. For Charles it had been a busy term, and he had been working hard to prepare himself for the degree which he hoped to pass in the summer. Alfred, though, gave academic work scant attention. Early in the term he completed 'Mariana in the South', the 'pendant poem' (Hallam's term) to the first 'Mariana'. He was paying so little heed to his studies that his friend Merivale reported 'Alfred is trying to make his eyes bad enough for an aegrotat degree', awarded to those who have a sickness certificate.

By now Tennyson was thoroughly at ease within the Church at Cambridge, as the Apostles were known. Excused from the need to compete in discussion, he simply joined in the social gatherings, reading a new poem when he had one ready, reciting an old one, or one of the traditional ballads he knew by heart, when he did not. As for the ban on Hallam's meeting his sister, he had mixed feelings about it. It would mean an extension of the period of male comradeship, but it would also mean that he would be unable to invite Hallam to Somersby until February 1831, when Arthur would be twenty-one.

Their relationship was changing anyway. Hallam was now the ascendant partner. This was a consequence of several things. The trip to Spain had occurred at Hallam's instigation and was paid for by him (or rather, by his father). As the more widely travelled party Hallam naturally took the initiative. More and more Hallam was to promote Alfred's cause in literary circles, and in the summer an unsigned review by him was to appear in the *Englishman's Magazine* and provoke a notable response. (Although Hallam was still writing verse himself he had withdrawn as a literary competitor and collaborator.) The very fact that he was in love with the poet's favourite sister, and she seemingly in love with him, also put him into a superior and mildly adversary position. The fact that Mr Hallam was a man of high reputation, and that the Wimpole Street home was so much more conventionally middle-class than Somersby, compounded Tennyson's sense of social and personal inferiority. He may also have become conscious of the same fickleness which Gladstone had complained of in Hallam. A few months later, when it was known beyond all doubt that Alfred would not be returning to Cambridge, Hallam wrote to Emily, while waiting for Charles to arrive on the stage, 'Would that Alfred were with him! but that will not be & perhaps ought not to be, "the days are awa" that we have seen.'

Here Hallam recognized a truth which Tennyson would take a long time to accept. Much art is not the celebration of truth, but the fight to deny it, (where 'truth' is understood as the actual way of the world). Two parallel poems published in the 1830 volume are at first sight contradictory. 'Nothing Will Die' says the 'world will change, but it will not fade'. 'All Things Will Die' says 'the old earth must die'. But underlying both poems there is a sombre sense that we are indeed living in an old world and the power of rejuvenation is growing faint. 'The old earth/ Had a birth,/As all men know,/Long ago' ('All Things Will Die'). ''Tis the world's winter;/Autumn and summer/Are gone long ago' ('Nothing Will Die'). So, like Mariana in her rusted, weeded and worn surroundings, we have to seize on the rare Indian-summer brightnesses of life and cherish them. Taking life as it comes might have been appropriate in the spring-time of the world, but not any more. Arthur Hallam was like some sunny Greek in comparison to Tennyson's mossy blackness.[25]

Alfred could have done with Hallam's company during the weeks that followed his father's death and funeral; could have done with someone to speak up for his vocation as a poet. He was not, whatever happened, and whatever vague assurances he might give to his uncle and grandfather, going to follow in his father's footsteps and enter the church to become a reluctant and wholly unsuitable parson.

Relationships between Somersby and Tealby had already worsened again due to ill-feeling surrounding the funeral and burial. Uncle Charles did not manage to make the trip from London to attend the ceremony, a lapse for which he had a good alibi (depending on the view one takes), but a lapse which was bound to be read as an insult. Charles's excuse was that on the night of 23 March (thirty-six hours before the funeral) he had to attend a late sitting in the House for a reading of the first Reform Bill, and he sent his father a result of the vote, lest it be thought his presence there had been unnecessary:

For the Bill	302
Against	301
Maj.	1

If I had not gone, the Speaker's casting vote wd. have cast out the Bill. I thought I was something better of my sciatica but leaving the House much heated at 4 this morning and encountering a fierce East wind, I am today suffering from rheumatism, sore throat and face ache ...

To this it must be added that the Old Man did not want him to attend the funeral anyway, and young George was given the job of passing on his father's apologies. After the funeral George surprised and alarmed his father and grandfather by returning to Cambridge in the company of Frederick.

Mrs Tennyson had wanted her husband buried at Tealby rather than Somersby. There was probably another reason for this, apart from the fact that Tealby was the family seat and not to bury George there would cast the last die on his disinheritance. If the family was to stay at the Rectory as hoped, the further away Dr Tennyson could be buried, and the less they were reminded of the torment he had recently caused, the better. But it was not to be. Eventually, Elizabeth's brother John convinced her that the 'great expense it would occasion' was unwarranted.

Charles was allowed to keep to his resolve of returning to university and arrived back just a few days late for the start of the new term, to live in rooms arranged for him by Hallam.

This left Alfred the oldest male in the household, and some have suggested that he remained at home with the noble purpose of overseeing the family's affairs, but it is more likely that it was the hopelessness of his academic prospects which kept him in Somersby. Although this is not to deny that he gave his mother valuable moral and emotional support in the ensuing weeks and months, the Doctor's financial affairs were brought into order, as these things tend to be, by representatives of the older generations – by Uncle Charles, Rawnsley, and the Old Man.

Rawnsley began to meddle in the Tennysons' affairs with well-meaning, Christian solicitude. He had taken Frederick aside on the day of the funeral, at which he officiated, and received assurances from the chastened young man that he would pursue his profession. On 4 April Charles and Alfred were called to the Rectory at Spilsby to receive the same pep-talk and urged to 'put their great talents into exercise'. (To this they might have replied that they were so doing, and shown Rawnsley Leigh Hunt's review in the *Tatler*, a copy of which had just arrived at Somersby along with a letter from Hallam to Emily. It was a glowing review, allowing equal space to both poets, but preferring, on balance, the less conventional Alfred.)

Hallam had gone to London at the start of the vacation 'girded up for warfare', ready to fight 'like a true knight' for the rescinding of his father's edict. He failed, and in his first letter to Emily after the death of her father, wrote: 'I would to God I could be with you now, Emily, following all the currents of your sorrow ... Oh Emily, will it not be sad to leave Somersby?'[26]

The patron of the livings of Somersby and Bag Enderby was William Burton, but Burton's son[27] was not yet old enough to take orders and so another incumbent, a bachelor named Robinson, had been selected to fill the interregnum. The Tennyson family hoped that the Rectory would be too large for the needs of a single young man and that they would be allowed to stay there for the time being.

Rawnsley took up their cause, encouraging the Old Man at Tealby to 'accede to Mrs Tennyson's earnest wish to remain at Somersby'. (Here she was revealed as very much more her own woman than she is often given credit for, since to press this case she had to counter the views of her brother John who thought it would be best for the family to get away from Somersby.)

The next three months were untidy ones dominated by the efforts to sort out the Doctor's financial affairs. In May, Uncle Charles, his sciatica presumably better, ventured up from London to visit Somersby. Together with Elizabeth and Rawnsley he went through the Doctor's bills and bank account, in which there was only £30 remaining. Of more concern than the Doctor's own debts, however, were the debts run up at Cambridge by the three eldest boys.

The future of all the Tennyson children was tacitly taken to be in Tealby hands, as is shown by this long extract from a letter Charles wrote to his father immediately following the consultations in the Rectory:

Alfred is at home, but wishes to return to Cambridge to take a degree. I told him it was a useless expense unless he meant to go into the Church. He said he would. I did not think he seemed much to like it. I then suggested Physic or some other Profession. He seemed to think the Church the best and has I think finally made up his mind to it. The Tealby Living was mentioned and understood to be intended for him. Frederick it was said intends to go into the Church and is anxious for a pupil at Eton. This is a *choice of his own* and a calling he seems *very desirous of filling*. Charles requires no consideration. Edward is understood to be unfit for *any thrift*, and I fear must remain at home, but Alfred says he really fears that his mind will at length so prey upon itself, that he cannot answer for consequences. It is difficult to devise anything for him as an employment with a *real* object. Alfred says he should if possible, for the sake of his mind, go from home and be amused. He has often fancied he should like to be a farmer, but as farming requires as much wit as any calling, I do not think we can look at the matter seriously. If Eliza should finally move to Buckden which *Mr Fytche seems to think advisable*, then he might get into some variety of life which might relieve his mind ... Arthur is a nice looking sprightly fellow. He is quick enough, but not, they think, qualified for any profession requiring considerable talent. He has a turn for drawing and has been at Mr Espin's at Louth for some time ... I will look out immediately on my return to Town for a Post for him within my own department at the ordnance or elsewhere in a good office. He is 16. ...

As to Septimus, he is a clever sharp fellow, and all seem to think he should be a Solicitor. He is now 15 and perhaps (if you approve) the sooner he is articled the better. ...

Horatio is at Louth School – the only one there. I saw him. He seems a nice little fellow – 11 years old – and being yet young enough for the Sea, I proposed to his Mother that on my return to Town I would endeavour to get him into the Navy. She consented with a grace that did her credit, considering her maternal fears.

These maternal fears were not to be so easily steam-rollered. On 2 July, after Charles had spoken to his friend Captain Duncan of the Ordnance, she wrote to the Old Man, 'I fear [Charles] is going to get [Horatio] into the Navy, which will make me completely miserable for the remainder of my life and to which I can never give my consent.'

The Old Man became increasingly frustrated with this Tennyson intransigency. The girls were equally trying. Emily wrote to her grandfather in July, begging for money to help her make a visit to Cheltenham:

> ... I am very ill, and have been so a long time, and feel assured, if you know how I suffer, you would immediately furnish me with the means of going to Cheltenham. Dr Bousfield says it is the only place for me, the pain in my side evidently increases, and my life is so wretched, that sooner than pass another year as the last, I would be content to follow my poor Father to the grave....

13   The Inaudible Invisible Thought

One very dark and chilly night
Pride came beneath and held a light.

('LOVE, PRIDE AND FORGETFULNESS')

Hallam, naturally enough, had mixed feelings about Emily's continuing ill-health. His letter to her on 7 May 1831 gives an insight into her depressed condition and his half-suppressed impatience with it.

I have heard from others that you are better: why will you not let me hear it from yourself? ... I am conscious indeed that we may be deceived, as others have been; that distress may continue with each of us until the end: there are moments, I know, in which you think so, when you lie on the sofa, and weep ...

Three weeks, and several letters, later he continued:

My dearest Emily, it is a hard thing for me to say that I do not believe you, yet I cannot but feel you make the best of your sufferings to me ... You may suffer more in imagination perhaps, than in what is called reality; but that does not make the case better.

Emily was not the only one to give him concern. Merivale had misjudged Alfred's eyesight problems. Although he would have been quite willing to play the infirmity for all it was worth to gain a doctor's certificate, it was not entirely concocted. With the typical thoroughness of a hypochondriac he was so well-read in medical lore that when he finally went to consult Sir Benjamin Brodie in London, the physician joked that he never saw medical students without charging an extra fee. As a result of this examination Alfred was advised to go on a milk diet.

Hallam must have felt at times like the Old Man of the Wolds, exasperated by the Somersby indolence and impracticality. Replying to Frederick just before going to Hastings for several weeks, in a letter which gives sober advice to Frederick over his plans to propose to one Miss Bellingham, he says:

Poor Alfred has written to me a very melancholy letter, What can be done for him? Do you think he is really ill *in body*? ... Alfred's account of Emily is worse than yours; but it is clear as daylight that change of place and society would do her good. It is horrid that I should not be allowed to be at Somersby now; if nothing else, I should break the uniformity of her life.[28]

The Hallam family's summer residence in Hastings was at 6 Brede's Place. He found the resort dull, and knew no one, (indeed so desperate for company was he that he asked Alfred to tell him if Aunt Russell was in the town). He turned his energies to continuing his campaign as Alfred's agent and posted off a sonnet ('Check Every Outflash') to Edward Moxon, publisher of the *Englishman's Magazine*, having been tipped off by Milnes that Moxon wanted to publish a piece by Tennyson.

On the same day he contacted Alfred, urging him to send Moxon a copy of 'Rosalind' or something similar. 'If you choose I have no doubt that you can become a permanent contributor on terms; and why should you disdain a mode of publication which Schiller and Goethe chose for their best compositions. It will not interfere with your collecting the pieces hereafter into a volume.'

It was now that Hallam began to think seriously of contributing a critical essay on Alfred's 1830 volume to the Moxon periodical. 'I am not sure that a clever attack by a friend might not do Alfred good', he told Milnes. The article took less than seven days to write, and was published in the August issue, along with Tennyson's sonnet.

Typically, Alfred himself had done nothing about sending material to Moxon, and Hallam had to confess:

You perhaps will be angry when I tell you that I sent your sonnet about the 'Sombre Valley' to Moxon, who is charmed with it, and has printed it off. I confess this is a breach of trust on my part, but I hope for your forgiveness.

It had indeed been a tremendous liberty, but Alfred appears not to have taken undue offence, mollified perhaps by Hallam's fulsome review which was, in due course, to rebound upon Tennyson in a particularly nasty way.

Hallam followed up his and Alfred's joint appearance in the magazine by persuading Merivale to call upon Moxon and to ask how much he would be willing to pay Alfred as a monthly contributor, and whether he would be interested in bringing out the poet's next volume. 'You might dexterously throw in that I have a promise that any article I might write should be admitted either into Edinburgh or Quarterly.' This admirable forthrightness was motivated by the desire to demonstrate that Alfred could put his poetry to profit, and therefore better withstand the pressure to push him into the church.

The Old Man gave Emily the money to go to Cheltenham, but only sufficient for herself. It took a further letter from Mrs Tennyson, pointing out that Emily would need an escort –

someone used to travelling – before he agreed to the extra expense.

Alfred was the chosen consort. His first visit to Cheltenham, in the company of his favourite sister, must have been highly charged. They were both unwell – Alfred still worried that he was going blind, Emily suffering with a pain in her side – with their mutual dependence on Arthur Hallam locking them into a magnetic triangle of emotion. When Alfred exaggerated his sister's frailty and attempted to delay her union with Hallam, whom was he trying to preserve for himself – Arthur or Emily? We shall never know with certainty, and in all probability Tennyson was himself only faintly conscious of his motives. It is well known that when two young people fall in love, a sister or a brother has a tendency to become a rival for the beloved. In nine cases out of ten the rivalry is muted or playful – reflex behaviour without significance. But there are cases where the rivalry is serious – deadly serious, and spiteful. This is the stuff of pulp fiction and it was a theme that the popular novelists of the nineteenth century delighted in. Tennyson himself made use of it in 'The Sisters' and 'The Ring' (as did other distinctive writers, like Henry James in his story of the supernatural *The Romance of Certain Old Clothes*) but those two poems were written much later in his life and the poem which is the key to this strange *ménage à trois* in Cheltenham is *The Lover's Tale*, already in early draft form. In that poem the rivalry corresponds much more closely to the real-life situation where, instead of two brothers or two sisters vying against one another, we have a brother and a sister in competition. There have been many interesting readings (and re-readings) of this poem, but it will never tell us exactly what we want to know about Alfred's regard for Emily. In the poem, the question of incestuous passion is put at one remove by making Julian and Camilla (the name is suggestively close to Emily) cousins, although brought up in the same household.

Psychologically, it has been suggested, the romantic lover remains at heart self-interested, auto-erotic and, by implication, bi-sexual. If this is so, then Alfred's position as both antagonist and intermediary between Emily and Hallam begins to make more sense. Certainly there are passages in *The Lover's Tale* which it is impossible to resist applying to the situation in Cheltenham. Perhaps Emily confided:

all the secret of her inmost heart,
And all the maiden empire of her mind,
Lay like a map before me, and I saw
There, where I hoped myself to reign as king,
There, where that day I crowned myself as king,
There in my realm and even on my throne.
Another!

Hallam managed to sneak a visit to them in September, on a rather roundabout route up to Yorkshire. He stayed a week and found both of them in a precarious state of health, particularly Alfred. They were boarding with a Miss Corgan at Priory House and the week Hallam spent with them there was shot through with a clandestine atmosphere. Hallam knew he ought not to be seeing Emily. 'I made up my mind rightly I still think, though I confess things may be said on the other side', he wrote to Frederick.

And they were. In *The Lover's Tale* the suitor comes, 'like a careless and greedy heir/That scarce can wait the reading of the will/Before he takes possession.' In one of the visionary sequences of the poem Julian dreams that Camilla has died. He comes upon her funeral procession in autumn woods. Flinging himself upon one of the pall-bearers he discovers that he has accosted none other than Lionel.

Always the inaudible invisible thought,
Artificer and subject, lord and slave,
Shaped by the audible and visible,
Moulded the audible and visible ...

'The Lady of Shalott', written at this time, suggests that Alfred really did have nightmares that Hallam's love for Emily would be the death of his sister – as, metaphorically, of course it would, for the enclosed, protected life of her youth would be over and she would lay herself open to all kinds of mortal passions. Tennyson's own commentary on the poem is explicit: 'The new-born love for something, for some one in the wide world from which she has been so long secluded, takes her out of the region of shadows into that of realities.'[29] How many realities are we talking about? Hallam Tennyson, memorably describing the poem as a 'tale of magic symbolism', implies not many. The four lines which he claimed held the key to the poem are not at first reading the most striking:

Or when the moon was overhead,
Came two young lovers lately wed;
'I am half sick of shadows,' said
  The Lady of Shalott.

If this is to tell us something of 'deep human significance'
it can only mean that Hallam Tennyson (with his father's
commentary?) read the poem as the story of a virgin grown sick
with frustration to the point of throwing herself upon the first
gladiator who rode into view between the barley-sheaves.
Alfred found the quickness with which Emily had succumbed to
Arthur Hallam slightly disgusting. It spoke of too keen a lust for
sexual knowledge. Tennyson was always on the side of waiting,
of prolonging the 'suspenseful moment'.

Interestingly, Hallam's friends were not unaware of Emily's
identification with her brother's poetic heroines. Trench, writing
at the time of Hallam's first visit to Somersby after his majority,
informs his correspondent, 'Hallam past through here last
Sunday on his way to visit his Lady Love in Lincolnshire – I
hope she is the Lady of the Mere/Sole-sitting on the shores of
old Romance.'

Throughout this year (1831) Arthur Hallam gave the impression of a young man genuinely in love. Forbidden to meet
his beloved, he sublimated his longing in the busy promotion of
his best friend's poetic career and in frequent letter-writing to
Emily and his Cambridge friends. Emily makes a less positive
impression. We hear of her dissolving into tears upon the sofa.
We hear that she writes too infrequently to Arthur, that her
letters are too short and too miserable. Arthur urges her to join
Alfred in learning Italian but she cannot put her mind to it.

As the year progressed the prospect of Mr Hallam's ban
coming to an end ought to have raised her spirits and improved
her health. But it didn't. What was she afraid of? Was she frightened of dying young? (Being a common fear in those days it is
hard to see how this alone could have rendered her so disabled.)
Or was she conscious, to an exaggerated degree, of the fear
which everyone must experience before betrothing themselves
to one person for life? It should be remembered that she and
Hallam had only met two or three times, and the longest they
had been together was for three weeks. Three weeks can be a
long and delicious time for young lovers, and though absence
may make the heart grow fonder, it does other things too. Fears

and indeterminacies enter the mind where once there were only courage and certainty. The ardency of Hallam and the supreme confidence of his letters seemed to allow her little freedom of manoeuvre. And she had a brother who was demonstrably cool about her prospects.

She and Alfred stayed in Cheltenham until the end of October. Back in Somersby, Alfred, still on his milk diet, found that the Old Man had been continuing to rail against his impracticability. Charles and Frederick had gone to Cambridge, both now determined to obtain their degrees, and resigned to entering the church. (It was only by giving such an undertaking that their grandfather could countenance the expense which completion of their studies would entail.) There was still no way that Alfred could agree to such a future for himself.

In early December he went to Cambridge. He was in the rooms of Francis Garden, a Scot, with Hallam and Tennant on the 7 December but seems not to have stayed at the university long enough to hear Hallam recite his prize-winning essay on the 'Influence of Italian Writing of Imagination on the Same Class of Composition in England'. This recitation took place in Trinity chapel on the 16 December and in a letter posted to Emily on the 15th Hallam makes it clear that Alfred has already left Cambridge. 'My love to Alfred, and recommend his sending back my book.' The rogue had obviously walked off with one of Hallam's books, (possibly a volume of his own writings, for a little later Hallam had to berate Emily for looking into his *Theodicea Novissima* – theological writing should only be read by men, he thought).

14 Crusty, Rusty, Musty & Fusty

The wind sounds like a silver wire

('FATIMA')

T he next eighteen months were to be the fullest and happiest, though not the most intense, period of Alfred and Arthur's friendship. Hallam took his degree at the end of January ('at last my odious labours are finished'), amused that he should be getting his ahead of Frederick Tennyson, who had matriculated two years before him.

Alfred had spent a grievous Christmas. His short visit to Cambridge in December had apparently made him pine for lost companionship. The Old Man remained adamant that return to the university was impossible in Alfred's case. Hallam wrote to Frederick:

I do not suppose [Alfred] has any real ailment beyond that of extreme nervous irritation; but there is none more productive of incessant misery, & unfortunately none which leaves the sufferer so helpless. I trust my coming will be beneficial to him: but meantime nothing should be left undone that may wean him from over-anxious thought. It is most melancholy that he should so completely have cut himself off from those light mental pleasures, which may seem insignificant in themselves, but in their general operation serve to make a man less unhappy, by making him more sociable ... I hope you will do all you can to assist me in endeavouring to restore Alfred to better hopes & more steady purposes. It will be sweet to labour together for so holy an end.[30]

This passage is indicative of their new mode of relationship. Hallam is the nurse, the medicant; Alfred the patient, the sufferer.

As his majority approached, Hallam displays an ever greater

hale-and-heartiness. Moving to Tunbridge Wells, he wrote to his old friend Donne, 'The life I have always desired is the very one you seem to be leading. A wife & a library – what more can man, being rational, require, unless it be a cigar?' This was men's-club thinking and Hallam was public-minded enough to add, 'I am not however without my fears that the season for such luxuries is gone or going by: in the tempests of the days that are coming, it may be smoking, & wiving, & reading will be affairs of anxiety & apprehension.'

Diplomatically, Hallam stayed in Tunbridge Wells for three more weeks after his twenty-first birthday at the beginning of February, and then went to spend the whole of March at Somersby. In one of his first letters from Somersby Hallam says something highly significant. 'Emily is not apparently in a state of health that need much disquiet me, and her spirits are, as I had hoped, more animated by confidence & hope. Every shadow of – not doubt, but uneasiness, or what else may be a truer name for the feeling – that Alfred's language has sometimes cast over my hope is destroyed . . .'[31]

What this plainly indicates is that, at various times during the year's separation, Alfred had gently prepared his friend for disappointment. Whether this means that Emily definitely suffered moods of uncertainty, or whether it was a way for Alfred to express his equivocal attitude towards the love affair, is difficult to determine.

Some of the magic of Somersby, as experienced by Hallam in the spring of 1830, was gone. Emily and Mary did not sing so often, and when they did their voices were not what they had been. Mary was not as beautiful. There were no horses to ride. The dining-room had had curtains hung in it and had become a large lounge. Alfred, though, seemed better and brighter, and had gathered together sufficient poems to make up a volume similar in length to the first. Hallam persuaded him that he should publish without delay.

But in the May issue of *Blackwood's Magazine* the editor, Professor John Wilson, writing as 'Christopher North', published a cutting attack on *Poems, Chiefly Lyrical*. The essay poured scorn on Hallam's piece in the *Englishman's Magazine*, heaping ridicule on it point by point, and taking him to task for spoiling a promising talent with over-lavish praise. In the February issue Wilson had already, in passing, spoken out against Tennyson's band of admirers. 'I have good hopes of

Alfred Tennyson. But the Cockneys are doing what they may to spoil him.'

It is ironic, in view of what Tennyson would say of 'Cockneys' in later life, that Wilson should repeat the charge near the beginning of his long May essay. 'One of the saddest misfortunes that can befall a young poet, is to be the Pet of a Coterie; and the very saddest of all, if in Cockneydom.'

The essay was full of severe phrases: 'infantile vanity', 'puerile partiality', 'idiotic', 'silly', 'clumsy and unwieldy failure', 'painful and impotent straining after originality', matched to close readings of individual poems. That Tennyson had been unduly cosseted from criticism was probably true, and it was a pity that Hallam's essay, once written, did not deliver the friendly criticism which had been intended at its conception. As far as his literary career was concerned the time was right for Tennyson to face up to some cold-faced derision of this kind. But such times rarely coincide with smooth periods in a writer's personal life, and this issue of *Blackwood's*, sent to Somersby by Hallam, arrived when the poet was in the midst of one of his hypochondriac depressions.

With Frederick at home the Rectory was dominated by his aggressive personality and Alfred found himself increasingly unable to cope with the essential incompatibility between them. More than once during this month he had to escape to Mablethorpe or Sutton and be alone. His health remained poor and his eyes continued to worry him. At the end of the month Charles was invited to be examined for ordination. Alfred felt ever more isolated and desperate, and Christopher North's savagery deflated all the enthusiasm that Hallam had built up for a second volume.

In fact, the review had not been without commendation. It spoke of the 'fine music' in 'Ode to Memory', and of the 'profound pathos' in 'Mariana', but praise mixed with criticism always has a bitter, patronizing taste, and Tennyson vented his feelings by scribbling the following attack:

> You did late review my lays,
>   Crusty Christopher;
> You did mingle blame and praise,
>   Rusty Christopher.
> When I learnt from whom it came,

I forgave you all the blame,
   Musty Christopher;
I could *not* forgive the praise,
   Fusty Christopher.

These lines were not written until October and are marred by the sense of an aggrieved man pulling his punches. Perhaps an earlier version, in which the refrain was 'Tipsy Kit', had been harder-hitting. One of the Tennyson sisters, however, found that version 'too sharp', and so he emended it to 'Christopher'.

By the beginning of June he was feeling too hemmed in at the Rectory and left for London, by way of Cambridge. Before he departed, news had reached Lincolnshire of the passing of the Reform Bill and to mark the event Alfred took his sisters across to the church and into the tower where they rang a short discordant peal on the bells. The new Rector, hurrying from his lodgings to find out what was going on, was set upon by the Tennyson dog, a small creature that did the man no harm.

The ringing of the bells and the yapping of the dog marked a parallel moment of a decisive kind – for the nation, the transition from an old, literary and static era to a new, scientific and mobile one, and for the poet, from the pampered and private beginnings of his craft towards the more public career. Many historians see the passage of the Reform Bill – an Act of Parliament which broadened the franchise, which had been more than a year in charting its troubled course through the two Houses, had seen the resignation of Grey and his ministers, their speedy reinstatement, and the continual threat of unrest on the streets – as the effectual beginning of the Victorian era. If it is true that no writer becomes properly professional until they have had their work abused, then Tennyson's mauling by John Wilson did set in motion his public reputation. He had written much poetry already, but in something of a vacuum, for a tiny coterie of family and friends. From now onwards he would be thinking more consciously of his readers.

15   Up the Rhine

We have had enough of motion
Weariness and wild alarm,
Tossing on the tossing ocean ...

('THE LOTOS-EATERS', 1832)

A lfred's main purpose in going to London was to be near
Hallam, but there were other friends there too. Hallam's
own announcement of Alfred's imminent arrival, in a note to
Kemble, is an intriguing mixture of excitement and exasperation.
In his letters to Emily he had repeatedly complained about her
brother's inability to communicate by letter.

Dear John
I have news for you, great news – Alfred the great will be in
town, perhaps today! ... He talks of going abroad instantly,
from which I shall endeavour to dissuade him ... Alfred's
coming seems to be mainly attributable to your letter three
months ago – at least his answer to questions, why he comes
to London, is said to be 'I have never answered John Kemble!'
One would have thought taking pen in hand was less trouble
than coming 50 miles; but different persons have different
estimates of difficulty.[32]

While Tennyson was still in Cambridge, Hallam spoke to
Moxon and secured his (informal) agreement to publish
Tennyson's second volume, as soon as the poems were ready.
Not having Alfred at hand, he wrote to Emily, 'A 2nd book just
now would set Alfred high in public notice, and afford him the
means of putting money in his pocket.'
Edward Moxon, described by Leigh Hunt as 'a bookseller
among poets, and a poet among booksellers' was just eight
years older than Tennyson. A Yorkshireman, he had come to
London as a sixteen year-old and worked as a clerk at Longman.
By submitting some of his youthful poems to Charles Lamb for
criticism, he and the Lambs had become lifelong friends. He left
Longman for Hurst, Chance & Co. and became an independent

publisher in 1830. By 1832 he had made a promising but not inspirational start in the business. His business tactics were conservative and undemonstrative – therefore likely to appeal to the publicity-shy Tennyson. A typical agreement with his authors was based on a half-share of the profits, calculated after the publisher had deducted production costs.

But Alfred did not bring his poems with him to London on this visit. Nor did he stay with the Hallam family at Wimpole Street – the reason being the sensitivity of the relationship with Emily. He stayed instead at Southampton Row, in lodgings previously used by Frederick, and was at once much better, meeting Cambridge cronies, and going with them to see Fanny Kemble perform in *The Hunchback*. The group often gathered at the Kembles and Fanny, who was much taken with Alfred, would sing for the collected company, and Alfred would perform his mimicry. (One of his favourite party-pieces was to enact the coming up and going-down of the sun by means of facial expression, but he was adept at voices too, as his later dialect poems testify.)

Though such society was good for Tennyson, he could not sustain it for any length of time and on the 22 June he left for Richmond, where he began 'The Innkeeper's Daughter' in the Star and Garter Hotel.

By the end of the month Hallam had some 'strange news' to break to Emily. For the entire winter Tennyson had been pining for a foreign trip. So insistent had been the longing for more southern climates that Hallam could not suppress some derisive amusement when he heard of Alfred's excursions to the Lincolnshire coast: 'What can Alfred be doing at Sutton! All his fine talk about "Alps and Appennines, the Pyrennees and the river Po" dwindled to a shabby sojourn at Sutton!'[33]

In Tennyson's longing for travel, and his talk of foreign climes, it is perfectly plain that what he really desired was a renewal of the intense comradeship he had experienced two years beforehand in Cauteritz. Hallam's letter to Emily on 30 June, written only a day or two before their departure, makes it clear that he has succumbed to a sustained campaign:

I have strange news for you, news which will make your dear eyes open wide and full, like – (I am in a hurry, & can't think of any object in nature for a simile). In short I am going tomorrow with Alfred up the Rhine for three weeks! He complained so of his hard lot in being forced to travel alone, that I took compassion on him, & in spite of law & relatives &c. I am going.[34]

They sailed for Rotterdam, aiming to proceed up the Rhine to Cologne and beyond, but they had to spend the first five days cooped up on board the steamer, which lay in quarantine banked on mud-flats. It was an inauspicious start to the three-week adventure. Alfred complained of being 'bugridden, flybitten, fleabitten, gnatbitten & hungerbitten'.

When they were at last allowed to disembark and see a bit of the town of Rotterdam it was as if they had escaped from prison and were breathing the air of freedom once more. But the Dutch countryside was flat and dull, and Alfred found it too much like Lincolnshire to be invigorating.

Reboarding the steamer they began their slow progress up the Rhine, through more flat ugly country. But Cologne, which they reached on 15 July, they found 'a paradise in painted glass' and Alfred at last became reasonably animated. From Cologne they went to Bonn and from then onwards the countryside became much hillier and more interesting. They climbed the Drachenfels and ate cherries under an old castle wall. Things were finally just a little like they had been in the Pyrenees, but very much diluted.

They stayed a night on the river island of Nonnenwerth, and slept in what had once been a Benedictine convent before being converted into a hotel. Then they continued upriver as far as Bingen, where they did more climbing, but the landscape was still too tame ('no more South than England', Alfred proclaimed it) and the sense of cameraderie still too dilute.

Returning by way of Aix-la-Chapelle and Brussels, Alfred became openly miserable. Hallam tried to put a brave face on things but was obviously fretted that an excursion which had not been his idea, and which he had had to have his arm twisted to go on, had been so lacking in value to his friend. 'We have drunk infinite Rhenish, smoked illimitable Porto Rico, & eaten of German dinners enough to kill twenty men of robust constitution, much more one who suffers paralysis of the brain like Alfred. He has written not a jot of poetry.'

This disapproval of Hallam's is interesting. Tennyson's egotistical indolence is being reprimanded. In the ending of 'The Lotos-Eaters'

Surely, surely slumber is more sweet than toil,
  the shore
Than labour in the deep mid-ocean, wind and wave
  and oar;
Oh rest ye, brother mariners, we will not wander
  more.

Critics have been too quick to read an authorial disapproval of the sailors' surrender to their bliss. A letter Tennyson wrote to his friend Brookfield, urging him to quit his opium habit, is often paraded as evidence of the poet's staunch distaste for drugged stupefaction. Actually, the letter only shows us that opium-taking was common amongst the Trinity set. Brookfield was an ordinary enough chap; if he took it, others must have done likewise. No doubt Tennyson was so brusque with his friend, telling him that 'confusion, horror and death' lay in store for him if he did not give up the drug, because he felt such a strong attraction to a numbed life of blissful ease himself. The Arthur Hallam who wanted to marry Emily was the responsible, energetic man-of-the-world, keen to labour in mid-ocean. The Arthur Hallam of two years ago, in the Pyrennees, was more of a Lotos-Eater than he was now. Tennyson, drinking his Rhenish, and smoking his Porto Rico was pitted against him. When Hallam shouted, 'Courage!' and 'To the grind-stone', Tennyson lay back and puffed on his pipe.

Having been careful in his letters home to swear his friends to secrecy regarding his and Alfred's impending return, Hallam accompanied Tennyson back to Somersby. During this visit the 'engagement' between Arthur and Emily became so public that Rev Rawnsley, who had been made a guardian of the younger children in Dr Tennyson's will, felt compelled to write to Hallam's father to ascertain his feelings about the affair.

Hallam's letters make it clear that, as things then stood, although marriage was feasible, it would have to be with his father's very grudging consent, and could not in any case take place for a further two years. Recognition of these impediments had caused Arthur extreme anxiety and depression earlier in the year, and this visit to Somersby reminded him of the painful choice that confronted him. It was one which he confided to Brookfield in a letter from the Rectory in mid-August:

... I have been very miserable since I saw you: my hopes

grow fainter & fewer, yet I hope on, & will, until the last ray is gone, & then – . Emily, thank heaven, is better than she has been, & I think rather more cheerful. Somersby looks glorious in full pride of leafy summer. I would I could fully enjoy it: but ghosts of the Past & wraiths of the future are perpetually troubling me. I am a very unfortunate being; yet, when I look into Emily's eyes, I sometimes think there is happiness reserved for me ... One thing I fear must be – even if I succeed to the utmost of my hopes, I think the affection of my own family, the faces of my home, the faces of my infancy, will be lost to me. Already I see it clearly diminishing ...[35]

Rawnsley had written to Hallam's father in the belief that the affair with Emily was still clandestine. However, Mr Hallam assured him that the news was 'by no means new to me, but has been the cause of great perplexity & solicitude for a considerable time'.

What was news though, was the revelation that Arthur and Emily had been corresponding with one another for the entire duration of what Mr Hallam had considered a wide-ranging ban on all form of contact.

... If this was done with Mrs. Tennyson's approbation, I must say that, making every allowance for a mother's feelings, under distressing circumstances, she had done all in her power to frustrate not only my intentions, but those of her husband, as signified to me. My son considered himself too far engaged in honour by this correspondence, & by the sort of renewal of their mutual promises which had taken place, to marry any other woman – in which it was impossible for me not to concur. But this of course left the objections to their union grounded on *want* of adequate income just as before. Of my son's *present* visit to Somersby I had no knowledge or suspicion, till he informed me of it by a letter from the continent, to which he had gone for a short time with Mr. Alfred Tennyson.[36]

Mr Hallam's view was therefore that Arthur was honour-bound to marry Emily, but that the Tennyson family bore a high degree of responsibility for tricking him more and more deeply into the match, rather than doing the honourable thing and releasing him from a promise made, originally, at the age of nineteen. The remainder of his letter to Rev Rawnsley stated that the most he could allow his son was £600 per year. To make a marriage possible this sum would have to be supplemented by the Old Man.

There then followed several weeks of grisly and unbecoming financial negotiation. Many characteristics of early nineteenth-century life are supremely appealing to the modern mind, but this jockeying for position before a marriage is not one of them.

On 4 September Arthur wrote personally to his uncle Charles. The sum offered by the Old Man had been insultingly small and Mr Hallam felt it was so nugatory as to render marriage impracticable. The difficulty was with the rather vague £300 share likely, but not certain, to come to Emily on the Old Man's death. Hallam's father wanted the Old Man to bequeathe a definite and unalterable £4000. The marriage could then proceed.

That approach was made at his father's direction (although Mr Hallam would later claim that he intended his son to speak to the MP and not write to him). A few days later Arthur wrote to Frederick Tennyson, off his own bat. After bringing him up-to-date with the state of negotiations, he threw a surprisingly foxy proposal:

> It must be a matter of indifference to my father, from what quarter the additional thousand comes, provided it is secure. So if anyone else were to settle 40 or 50£ per ann. on Emily, to come into use at the old man's death, it would be the same as if he settled it ... When your Grandfather departs you, as his representative, become the head of the family. Except in the unfortunate event of further quarrels, you will, there is no reason to doubt, possess a tolerable porportion of what he has to leave ... Is there no possibility therefore of your charging your own future estate with the sum before mentioned? ...
> Am I an impudent fellow to make so cool a proposal?

Hallam had been forced into making this proposal out of desperation, not impudence. But he was certainly guilty of humbug in the ensuing justification:

> ... it is for you to consider whether what is given for Emily's interest is not given for the welfare of the whole family, &

yourself in the number, nearly as much as if you retained it in your own disposal. The hearthstone which you would thus contribute to raise would be a sure & lasting asylum, not perhaps useless or [devoid] of comfort to you all, when the foot of an alien shall be on the soil of Somersby.[37]

The response of the Old Man, communicated by Charles, was as expected. 'He cannot break into the arrangements made for a large family.' And he directed that any future approaches be made via Rev Rawnsley. Thus rapped on the knuckles, Hallam confided in George Tennyson, 'The step I took proved a complete failure, & has made matters worse instead of better.'

All this time Alfred declined to give his friend any advice, and did not intercede on his behalf. Instead, he concentrated on collecting the remaining poems due to be published by Moxon. Hallam received a further batch of them on 24 September, in a packet which included some sonnets, 'My Life is Full of Weary Days', 'Mariana in the South', and new stanzas for 'The Palace of Art'.

Tennyson did well to concentrate on his work during this time. The disintegration of the household, presaged some time ago, was now becoming a reality. Charles had passed his ordination and preached his first sermon – 'in the hubble-bubble way of that family', according to the Old Man. He had been given the curacy at Tealby, and a room for lodgings at Grove House on the estate.

In July Frederick had had a violent contretemps with the Old Man, who wrote to tell his son: 'Frederick has been here a day or two and threatened and left me in the most brutal manner – He is a savage ... On his leaving me I said he would kill me by his conduct, his answer was, You will live *long enough*.' It was for this reason that Charles was allowed only one room at Grove House – 'so that he cannot entertain the Brute'. Partly as a consequence of this latest quarrel, and partly, perhaps, to escape the further embarrassment of a second approach from Hallam, Frederick left Somersby before the autumn, much to Alfred's relief.

But Edward, the young brother for whom Alfred had been long concerned, and on whose behalf he had several times spoken out with uncharacteristic intervention, now gave grave cause for concern. By the end of October a Dr Probart was recommending removal to the Lincoln Asylum. In a rare display of unanimity, both sides of the Tennyson family objected to this proposal on the grounds that Lincoln would be too near for comfort – 'injurious to the poor boy himself and to his Brothers and Sisters', as Uncle Charles put it. They decided, instead, to send him to York, uncertified, and on the understanding that he went as a pupil apprenticed to the medical profession.

Edward went away in mid-November. He remained in the asylum at York for the rest of his life. Of the other boys, Septimus had left home and was working in a solicitor's office; Arthur was at home but very unwell.

16   Then the Event

My sister, and my cousin, and my love,
Leapt lightly clad in bridal white – her hair
Studded with one rich Provence rose

(THE LOVER'S TALE)

At the same time that decisions were being made for Edward's future, Alfred was putting a final packet of poems together for Hallam. This included 'The Old Year', 'Lines to James Spedding', 'O Darling Room', and 'To Christopher North' – the last two Hallam tried, gently, to persuade Alfred to leave out. 'If you have doubts, refrain', he wrote in Greek.

By now Hallam had entered conveyancing and was working in the middle of London. In his long letters to Emily at this time there are signs that his frustration with her continuing poor health was beginning to sow doubts in his mind about their relationship. In several of them he recounts, with gusto, vivacious weekends spent as a guest in country homes and describes, gloatingly, the lively young women and the entertainments indulged in with them.

Following a weekend of charades and amateur theatricals at the home of Charlotte and Catherine Sotheby, Arthur wrote a high-spirited review of his dramatic triumphs:

My most decided success was in the character of Pygmalion.

Charlotte Sotheby was my Statue: she looked it to perfection: when the curtain drew up, & showed her standing motionless on the pedestal, draped in white, & a white veil concealing all her head except the beautiful features not unlike in truth the work of Grecian art – when I, dressed as a sculptor, poured forth a speech (in verse) of my own composition in praise of my supposed statue, ending with a prayer to Venus that she might live, & at the word slowly & gracefully the form began to move, to bend forward, to descend, to meet my embrace – the room rang with acclamations, & I – I thought of several things, but none so much, as of the pleasure I should have in describing this to you, & perhaps on some occasion acting it with you.[38]

What Hallam meant by this was not that he wanted to 'act' such a scene with Emily, but live it. He wanted to breathe life into her, make her more like these agreeable Sotheby sisters, 'full of lively, somewhat satirical conversation, yet not without tokens of deep & strong feeling, ready to come when called for'. Like all people he would have fantasized the impossible. Should marriage with Emily ever become, for practical and monetary reasons, totally out of the question, then he might exchange her for just such a Venus-figure as Charlotte Sotheby. Hallam's subsequent letter, written in another mood, is insufficiently convincing to quash such a suggestion:

Do you know, Nem[39], what is the predominant feeling always in my mind, when I see beauty & talent, & when I address to them the common homages of politeness? I mentally sacrifice them to you with feelings of pride, & almost disdain: I pass among them, as one above them: they seem utterly remote from my own sphere of life: I look at them as a living man might look at empty ghosts. I am enthroned in the love of Emily, & regard all other things as below the concern of my royalty.[40]

Meanwhile, Alfred, who had already slowed up production of his book by insisting that he correct the proofs twice over, let drop the surprise decision to remove *The Lover's Tale* from the volume. On 20 November he wrote to Moxon, saying 'it spoils the completeness of the book and is better away'. Several of the

102

poems lately delivered to Hallam had been finished quickly, to fill up the hole thus left.

Arthur could not believe it. 'Heath is mad to hear of your intention. I am madder. You must be pointblank mad.' But Tennyson was not mad. He had a point about the wholeness of the volume. *The Lover's Tale* would have been out of place.

Much of the poem had been begun when Tennyson was only nineteen, (he was now twenty-three), but he had continued to work at it, and Part III exists in separate notebooks, suggesting its composition was more recent than earlier parts. It is this section of the poem which gives the clearest indication that the initial literary impulse had gathered psychological implications. All writers reveal more of themselves in their work than they are conscious of at the time of composition. Recognition of what has actually motivated a poem or story can be gradual or sudden, but however it develops it is often unsettling. Tennyson's last-minute withdrawal of the poem suggests that just such a realization had occurred to him during the process of proof-reading.

Parts I and II, the only sections of the poem that Tennyson had ever intended to print in 1832, tell the story, in retrospect, through the eyes of the main character, Julian, of his love for a cousin, Camilla, brought up in his household as a foster-sister. Part I recounts the growth of his love for her, through infancy (they had been born 'On the same morning, almost the same hour') and childhood, through to the dreaded 'event' which occurs when they are both eighteen. The event is brought about by the confession of Camilla that she loves Julian's friend and neighbour, Lionel. Julian has had to accommodate himself to the fact that he cannot hope to love Camilla in worldly terms, but the realization that she, so suddenly, has promised herself to another is devastating: 'All my wealth/Flashed from me in a moment and I fell/Beggared forever.' In Part II Camilla has married and moved away. Julian is tormented by disturbing visions. He seems to see her funeral and has nightmares in which, drowning in a storm at sea, he clasps her weight in his arms to try and save her, but phantom-like she disappears.

Part III, printed in full below, is one sustained vision of fifty-nine lines. Sharing both the turbulent, quick-shifting imagery of the pop video, and the magical enchantment of the wedding sequence in Alain-Fournier's *Le Grand Meaulnes* (which it surely inspired), it is one of the most intense and powerful passages in Tennyson's work.

I came one day and sat among the stones
Strewn in the entry of the moaning cave;
A morning air, sweet after rain, ran over
The rippling levels of the lake, and blew
Coolness and moisture and all smells of bud
And foliage from the dark and dripping woods
Upon my fevered brows that shook and throbbed
From temple unto temple. To what height
The day had grown I know not. Then came on me
The hollow tolling of the bell, and all
The vision of the bier. As heretofore
I walked behind with one who veiled his brow.
Methought by slow degrees the sullen bell
Tolled quicker, and the breakers on the shore
Sloped into louder surf: those that went with me,
And those that held the bier before my face,
Moved with one spirit round about the bay,
Trod swifter steps; and while I walked with these
In marvel at that gradual change, I thought
Four bells instead of one began to ring,
Four merry bells, four merry marriage-bells,
In clanging cadence jangling peal on peal –
A long loud clash of rapid marriage-bells.
Then those who led the van, and those in rear,
Rushed into dance, and like wild Bacchanals
Fled onward to the steeple in the woods:
I, too, was borne along and felt the blast
Beat on my heated eyelids: all at once
The front rank made a sudden halt; the bells
Lapsed into frightful stillness; the surge fell
From thunder into whispers; those six maids
With shrieks and ringing laughter on the sand
Threw down the bier; the woods upon the hill
Waved with a sudden gust that sweeping down
Took the edges of the pall, and blew it far
Until it hung, a little silver cloud
Over the sounding seas: I turned: my heart
Shrank in me, like a snowflake in the hand,
Waiting to see the settled countenance
Of her I loved, adorned with fading flowers.
But she from out her death-like chrysalis,
She from her bier, as into fresher life,
My sister, and my cousin, and my love,
Leapt lightly clad in bridal white – her hair
Studded with one rich Provence rose – a light

Of smiling welcome round her lips – her eyes
And cheeks as bright as when she climbed the hill.
One hand she reached to those that came behind,
And while I mused nor yet endured to take
So rich a prize, the man who stood with me
Stept gaily forward, throwing down his robes,
And claspt her hand in his: again the bells
Jangled and clanged: again the stormy surf
Crashed in the shingle: and the whirling rout
Led by those two rushed into dance, and fled
Wind-footed to the steeple in the woods,
Till they were swallowed by the leafy bowers,
And I stood sole beside the vacant bier.

There, there, my latest vision – then the event!

17 Metaphysical Flankers

O Fullness of the worlds!
O termless field,
Relation, difference,
Not all concealed,
Fair feast of every sense
In part revealed.

('EARLY SPRING', 1833)

Hallam, taking his first holiday from conveyancing, spent Christmas in Somersby. He had been looking forward to it for a long time. The industrious letter-writing of the young couple ought to have prepared for an intensification of their relationship, but in practice it had an inhibiting effect. Emily, no doubt intimidated by Hallam's exhilarating portraits of Richmond goddesses, was an invalid for the entire duration of his stay, remaining the greater part of each day in her room, so that the engaged pair were forced, even though under the same roof, to continue their epistolary contact, by writing notes to one another in Italian.

Emily, it seems, had been so frightened of meeting Hallam

again that, in mid-December she had concocted an imminent visit to Aunt Bourne in Dalby. Whether she was serious in this intention, or merely trying to prompt Arthur to postpone his holiday in Somersby, is unclear. But there seems to be no accompanying evidence to support the view of other biographers that the whole family was anticipating a move from Somersby at this time.

Hallam's influence on Tennyson's *Poems* of 1832 had been very considerable. He had chosen the publisher, negotiated the terms, delivered the manuscripts, given editorial advice, and assisted in proof-reading. Even before publication, he was preparing a review of the poems, but it was unsolicited and remained unaccepted – if it was ever finished.

Four hundred and fifty copies of the book were printed in December, each one selling at six shillings. There was an immediate attack on the volume in the *Literary Gazette*, which singled out one of the best poems, 'The Lady of Shalott', for special mockery. There were enough poorer pieces in the book. Some awkward sonnets (Alfred, with few exceptions, did not have his brother's talent for this form), more girly poems, and the two great mistakes, 'O Darling Room' and 'To Christopher North'. These were more than compensated for by 'The May Queen', 'The Miller's Daugher', 'Œnone', 'The Hesperides', 'The Lotos-Eaters', 'The Palace of Art', 'Mariana in the South' and 'To J— S—'.

But in the April edition of the *Quarterly Review* John Croker lashed the new book with the same caustic fault-finding that had helped finish Keats off fifteen years earlier. The review was laced with sarcasm, Coker's main critical technique being to present close readings of the poems, interpolating regular cutting comment and italicized quotations for emphasized ridicule. The weakest poems in the volume were all too vulnerable to such abuse, and Croker had a field day with the opening sonnet and with 'To —'. His mockery of 'The Lady of Shalott' was just rude silliness, but he hit home again with a more justified and sustained attack on the evasive descriptive richnesses of the mythological poems. ('Œnone' *is* overbrimming with swimming vapours, dewy-dark lawns and ingoing grottos.) After quoting a passage from 'The Lotos-Eaters', 'a kind of classical opium-eaters', Croker said simply, 'Our readers will, we think, agree that this is admirably characteristic; and that the singers of this song must have made pretty free with the intoxicating fruit. How they got home you must read in Homer: – Mr Tennyson – himself, we presume, a dreamy lotos-eater, a delicious lotus-eater – leaves them in full song.' But the most sardonic sideswipe of all was directed at 'O Darling Room', Croker, having quoted the last lines of the poem, concluding: 'We have ourselves visited all these celebrated spots, and can testify, in corroboration of Mr Tennyson, that we did not see in any of them anything like *this little room so exquisite*.'

The poem, it has to be said, rather invited such ridicule:

O darling room, my heart's delight,
Dear room, the apple of my sight,
With thy two couches soft and white,
There is no room so exquisite,
No little room so warm and bright,
Wherein to read, wherein to write.

For I the Nonnenwerth have seen,
And Oberwinter's vineyards green,
Musical Lurlei; and between
The hills to Bingen have I been,
Bingen in Darnstadt, where the Rhene
Curves toward Mentz, a woody scene.

Yet never did there meet my sight,
In any town, to left or right,
A little room so exquisite,
With two ouch couches, soft and white;
Not any room so warm and bright,
Wherein to read, wherein to write.

This is so bad – apart from its maudlin sentiment, the middle stanza is about as cack-handed a piece of verse-making as any poet has thought fit to print – it is tempting to think it was included in the collection as a joke (it is impossible to read the poem aloud in anything but a humorously theatrical tone), but there is unfortunately no evidence that it was.

As well as the vilification of the 'hang-draw-and *Quarterly*' there had been an earlier notice by Edward Bulwer[41] in the *New Monthly*. Of 'To Christopher North' Bulwer had said 'an infant of two years old could not be more biting', and he pronounced the whole volume to be redolent of 'effeminacies', shot through with 'an eunuch strain'. Coming from Bulwer this was a bit rich, given his reputation as a 'finished dandy', which involved wearing lipstick and face-paints.

These were crushing reviews and though the Apostles of course praised the volume (and bought it in quantity – seventy-five copies being sold in Cambridge immediately after publication) even they were not convinced. There were hints that some had preferred the earlier collection, and there were rumblings that others disapproved of revisions to such favourites as 'The Palace of Art'.

But Alfred does not present a crushed figure at this time. Indeed he seems to have been in a particularly positive mood during the spring of 1833, as two long jocular letters – one to James Spedding, the other to Aunt Russell – testify. The letter to Spedding is the epitome of late-night, drunken banter between old college friends, but the light frothiness of it all is darkened now and then by perplexing adumbrations bubbling beneath the surface.

> You should not have written to me without telling me somewhat that was interesting to myself (always the first consideration) or that bore some reference to you and yours (always the second) or lastly without giving me some news of the great world; for know you not that I live so far apart from the bustle of life that news (even gossip) becomes interesting to me? Ironical sidehits at a person under the same roof with myself and filling more than a first half of the sheet – (i.e. not the person – but the sidehits – it looks as though I meant that the person in question slept with me and I assure you that we have a spare bed and that the bed is not so spare either, but a bed both plump and pulpy and fit for your domeship, whenever you can come and see us ...) ... ironical sidehits, I say, at my friend and guest, in a letter addressed to me, – moral kicks and punches through the medium of my epistle, and consequently to be delivered by me in a mellowed accent to the unhappy kickee (O fatal necessity and such as ought never to have been imposed!) – metaphysical flankers and crossbuttocks and wherein I was made the unhappy instrument of giving pain to my dearest friend ...

Even when read in context this remains a most peculiar conceit. Unravelled, all that has happened is that Spedding has addressed a letter to Tennyson which is a little too free with moral advice for Hallam. As the recipient of the letter, Tennyson has to pass on the advice. He would have liked the letter to have been of more personal interest. It is almost as if Tennyson volunteers the play on the word 'sheet' in order to put across the suggestion, quickly denied, that Hallam has 'slept with me' (a phrase, it must be said, with none of the connotations that it carries today). Although this is pure fancy – Hallam has used the comfortable spare bed – it leaks over into the ensuing part of the letter and gives rise to the image of Tennyson flagellating his friend with 'metaphysical flankers and crossbuttocks'. Is the conceit too strange to be an innocent whimsicality? The answer is, probably, no.

Tennyson went to Mablethorpe at the end of February and when he returned to Somersby there was a letter waiting for him from his favourite Aunt (Russell). His reply, more soberly written, and more communicative, suggests a mind growing increasingly confident and content with his position in the world.

> ... Willis wrote to me, a week ago, from the Royal Music Repositary stating, that Mrs. Hughes ... had set 'Oriana' to music, and asking my permission to publish it. Of course I gave it ...
>
> Emily, whom you enquire after, is here; she is not yet cured of the liver complaint, which sent her to Cheltenham – most probably it will cling to her all her life – at least I have never heard of anyone, who was cured of a serious derangement in that organ.... For myself I drag on somewhat heavily through the ruts of life, sometimes moping to myself like an owl in an ivy bush ... and sometimes smoking a pipe with a neighbouring parson ...

Then, after giving details of his Rhine visit, Alfred sends his compliments to his young cousin Gustavus Russell, hoping 'for his own peace of mind, that he will have as little of the Tennyson about him as possible'. Finally, in a postscript he tells his aunt not to bother buying his book – he can let her have as many copies as she wants.

On 25 March Alfred took Mary to London. Why not Emily? Was she still afraid of meeting Arthur Hallam? Was she suffering too much from her liver complaint? Or had Alfred's insight into *The Lover's Tale* lessened the intensity of his brotherly feelings for that favourite sister?

Mary was described (by Blakesley) as 'a fine-looking person, although of a wild sort of countenance, something like what Alfred would be if he were a woman, and washed'. The two of them stayed at Wimpole Street, with the Hallams. It being Mary's first visit to London as an adult they occupied themselves with sight-seeing. On 4 April Arthur took them both to the zoo. The next day they went to see the images projected by Carey's Oxy-Hydrogen Microscope. And on 6 April they took a boat to the Tower, with the young Heath family. On Sunday 7 they went to a service in Westminster Abbey and the next day Mary went off with Mrs Hallam and Arthur's sister, Ellen, to 'a great new Bazaar in Belgravia Square, called the Pantechnicon'. The next day they returned to the Gallery of Practical Science and saw some electro-magnets. That night, their last in London, Alfred went to Moxon's for supper and was out till three in the morning, and on Wednesday the 10th Hallam accompanied them to the Times coach-office and saw them onto a stage bound for Cambridge, where they intended stopping before continuing on to Somersby.

It was the last time that Arthur and Alfred would see one another – this rather formal, pleasure-tripping week in London being an exquisitely inappropriate way for their friendship to end. Except, of course, that it did not end there. The close examination of the narrative record of their friendship gives a disappointingly thin substance for so legendary a relationship, but we must remind ourselves that a significant, if not the most significant, part of the legend is dependent upon a poem which, at the date of their parting, was neither written nor conceived.

18   Premonitions

> ... Where the path we walked began
> To slant the fifth autumnal slope,
> As we descended following Hope,
> There sat the Shadow feared of man;
>
> (*IN MEMORIAM* XXII)

In Alfred's recent letter to Aunt Russell he had confessed to not having seen his grandfather for nearly three years. However, his brother Charles, now living at close quarters, brought regular news.

The Old Man was grouchy with gout and their uncle Charles, now with a safe Parliamentary seat in Lambeth, wanted to take up residence at Bayons, to rebuild the house, and adopt the name 'd'Eyncourt', which the family romantically associated with a Lord d'Eyncourt who had once owned the valley in which Bayons Manor was built.

To begin with his father disliked the idea. 'It would hurt my feelings to lay aside the name of Tennyson for this Frenchified name.' But a few days later he gave way. Then, regretting his compliance, and beginning to see the problems, he wrote, 'The name of Tennyson to be retained by my late son Dr Tennyson's family, but would not this be thought partial in me and animadverted to your discredit ... This is a matter for much consideration.'

Charles had his way with the name, as he did also with the move. But not without rancour. To begin with the idea was that the Old Man would stay in the Manor and Charles would move into Grove House. Julia, his daughter, and the Old Man's favourite grandchild, had to mediate in negotiations with the elderly Mr Tennyson, so deep were his feelings against Charles's wife.

'[Grandpapa] declares that he will not live either with or *near* Mamma and seems therefore quite averse to your having the house below', she reported in July. And in August, 'Grandpapa is cranky and crooked and sure to find fault with everything you do.' As the Old Man was well over eighty by now, and on his last legs, this was hardly surprising. Julia was telling her parents

111

to accept the fact that the 'Old Man' had become merely an old man.

Alfred was on the move during much of the summer but was in Somersby sufficiently frequently for there to be the beginnings of a long and significant infatuation with Rosa Baring to distract him. She was the step-daughter of Admiral Eden who was at that time leasing Harrington Hall, which lies on a bend on the Somersby–Bag Enderby road, just a one-mile walk from the Rectory.

'The Gardener's Daughter' was begun at this time, in between a second visit to Mablethorpe, a call on Cambridge, a lightning trip to London, and a longer stay in Scotland. Tennyson's feelings for Rosa did not intensify until the following summer, but the descriptive details of the poem (despite the disguise of placing it on the margins of a city) are obviously modelled on Harrington.

The early summer was exceedingly hot and Tennyson had an idea to go to Jersey. There seems to have been no Cambridge or family connection with Jersey at this time, and Hallam was perplexed by the news. 'Alfred's notion of going to Jersey seems an odd one. What should he do at Jersey? Besides there is a bit of a revolution going on there.'[42] Perhaps it was a notion thrown into the air to entice Hallam away on another jaunt. But this is unlikely. Hallam was already committed to accompanying his father to Austria. And all the indications of these summer weeks suggest that Alfred's attitude towards the relationship had radically shifted. Resigned, now, to Hallam's engagement to his sister, he felt once again the more powerful partner. One cannot help but agree with Charles Tennyson who, in his biography, stated his belief that 'despite the brutal shock of Croker's article and the clouds hanging over Somersby, those spring and summer months of 1833 were the happiest and fullest that Alfred had yet known.' His reasons for so saying – 'ripened friendship with Arthur, Arthur's love for Emily, so understanding and selfless'[43] – are, however, a little ingenuous.

Alfred's 'odd notion' of going to Jersey came to nothing. He went instead of Mablethorpe. In most biographies, Tennyson's visits to Mablethorpe are connected with bleak sandhills, the wind, and roaring surf. But, as we have seen, his early contact with the resort was in the context of family summer holidays, and it has been a Romantic distortion to depict him as being interested in the place only for its wildness and solitude. In hot midsummer it was neither a wild nor solitary place, and its sandhills far from bleak. That Tennyson enjoyed the sun is attested in several instances and in the first week of June Hallam, having heard that Alfred was at the coast, wrote to him there: 'How horribly hot those Mablethorpe sandbanks must be under a sun like this. Anyhow you are baked to your heart's content.'

On 5 July Alfred returned to Cambridge and took with him the early version of 'Thoughts of a Suicide' (later to become 'The Two Voices'). This early version contained a horrible premonition:

When thy best friend draws sobbing breath,
Plight thou a compact ere his death
And comprehend the words he saith.

Urge him to swear, distinct and plain,
That out of bliss or out of pain
He will draw nigh thee once again.

Is that his footstep on the floor?
Is this his whisper at the door?
Surely he comes. He comes no more.[44]

A week later, on 12 July, with Frederick, Monteith, Morton and Rice – friends he was not particularly close to – he paid a quick visit to London, where the group carried on 'a regular Cambridge debauchery style'[45] and where Alfred decided to go to Scotland with Monteith.

Meanwhile Hallam had gone to Somersby to visit Emily. Alfred's avoidance of the Rectory at this time is extremely significant. There was nothing to have prevented his being in Somersby with Hallam and certainly Arthur felt his absence:

I feel tonight what I own has been too uncommon with me of late, a strong desire to write to you. I do own I feel the want of you at some times more than at others; a sort of yearning for dear old Alfred comes upon me and that without any particularly apparent reason. I missed you much at Somersby, not for want of additional excitement; I was very happy. I had never been at Somersby before without you.[46]

This letter is dated 31 July. He asked Alfred to write to him in Vienna 'whither I am going on Saturday with tolerable speed'.

Saturday fell on 3 August. It is highly unlikely that Hallam's letter reached Alfred in Scotland much before the 3rd and even if it did he would have needed a post-chaise drawn by the Furies to reach London in time for a farewell. The 'final parting' as depicted in the *Memoir*, and as followed by both Charles Tennyson and Robert Bernard Martin, is a touching tableau, but it is a fanciful one based entirely on an undated letter from Tennant to Septimus Tennyson.[47]

When Hallam left England on the 3 August he had not seen Tennyson since the 10 May. He had been unwell for several months prior to departure, suffering from a feverish ague. His letters to Emily from the Continent are curiously unromantic – very different from the ardent, tempestuous missives of the winter. The only affectionate parts of them are the greetings and valedictions. In between are long tracts of travelogue, all recorded in a rather dutifully monotonous style. Something must have been played out in the Rectory during July. That something might well have been Hallam's love for Emily. Feckless in his schoolboy friendships, he had already shown (with Anna Wintour) that he could be feckless in his love for a woman. Was his infatuation with Emily on the wane? And if so, how did he view the approaching marriage? He had stepped in too far to pull back now.

The flat, descriptive letters which he posted to his fiancée are oddly reminiscent of the ones sent to Bayons by Dr Tennyson during his year of exile. ('I wish instead of his elaborate description of Mt Vesuvius he had given some of his state of health', the Old Man had then remarked, and a similar thought probably went through Emily's mind when reading Hallam's letters.)

The trip was planned in the late spring by Mr Hallam, who had insisted from the first that Arthur should be his companion. He may very well have been determined to prevent another escapade with Alfred Tennyson, much as he had earlier acted to block Arthur's friendships with Doyle and Gladstone. Arthur was so dependent on his father financially, and for the goodwill that might eventually make marriage to Emily possible (a prospect which he still convinced himself was right), that he had no option but to comply with his father's wishes.

Their departure date, 3 August, was also Arthur's sister's seventeenth birthday, and he sent her birthday wishes. The note affected Ellen 'more than the occasion seemed to warrant' and she burst into tears. Something in her brother's wording possibly gave her foreboding that the trip would end tragically.

They steamed to Calais. It was a rough crossing. The boat was a poor one and most of the passengers, including Arthur were sick. He spent three hours on deck, his head wrapped in his cloak, thinking of Somersby. It was a night crossing and the moon shone beautifully on the tormented sea.

They took the road from Calais to Lille and passed through the countryside of Flanders, observing the harvesting. Sleeping at Cassel, Arthur was reminded of his 1830 trip with Alfred when the Hipocrac (a spiced wine) had been so good, 'and the waiter so perfect'. Then they proceeded to Mons, Tournay, and Namun, travelling very fast, and barely giving Arthur time to write.

Soon they were amongst the Alps. Arthur wrote his second letter from Salzburg, and a third, after much sight-seeing, from Gmunden. This one he wrote while sitting beside a lake surrounded by purple hills. It was, he said, 'My last Alpine view, for tomorrow I leave the reign of mountains, and strike off into plain country toward Vienna.'

His fifth letter, dated 6 September, described the squares and streets of that city, and the contents of the Imperial Gallery. The sixth letter told of an excursion into Hungary and visits to the towns of Presburg, Raab, Gran and Pesth. At last there were some personal touches for Emily (and Alfred) to seize hold of:

... Besides, is there anything more pleasant than to hear the rush & gurgle of the water against the boats, while smoking the best Hungarian tobacco out of a true Meerschaum just beginning to colour, & looking at the lights from both banks twinkling magically through the exhalations which in the evening are sent up from this mighty stream [the Danube]? ... Today is, if I mistake not, Mary's birthday: I shall not fail to drink her health in a glass of *Tokay*, & to wish her all happiness, both in prosperity of circumstances, & peace of mind. *Tokay*, I think, deserves its fame, as the best of the rich, sweet wines; but one cannot drink much of it.[48]

It was Hallam's final letter. Arriving back in Vienna he became unwell, with a return of the ague. Despite the time of year he felt cold and asked for the fire to be lit. Lying on a sofa beside this foreign hearth for a whole day, he told his father he felt better and that he thought the ague was passing off. Mr Hallam, who had sat with his son since morning, said that in that case he would take a walk.

On his return Arthur was still on the sofa, and apparently asleep. Eventually, disturbed by the awkward position of his son's head, Mr Hallam spoke to Arthur but received no reply. He immediately sent for a doctor who, when he arrived, opened a vein in young Hallam's wrist and another in his hand, and when no blood flowed declared him dead.

This was on the 15 September. The death certificate listed a stroke as cause, and an autopsy, performed by Klaus von Rokitansk, one of the leading pathologists of the time, seemed to confirm this.

The different accounts of Arthur Hallam's death (the details here are taken from Doyle's letter to Gladstone, of 11 October 1833[49]), all reported by people who were not in Vienna at the time, seem almost too pat, varying a little, but repeating the same details consistently, almost with the ring of a prepared alibi.

At first reading, the cutting of Arthur's veins by the physician seems a most peculiar way of establishing death. Making the cut in the wrist and the hand at once prompts the speculating mind to wonder whether the cuts were already there, self-inflicted, and this part of the story concocted to disguise the real cause of death – suicide. However, the autopsy has to be trusted, and perhaps Mr Hallam's assessment of the first doctor's action, or later interpretations of it, was mistaken. Maybe the veins were cut, not to establish death, but in an effort to treat a patient who was believed still living. (Blood-letting was a common enough response to feverish illnesses such as the 'ague'.) Finally, if any of Hallam's friends had the slightest suspicion of Mr Hallam's version of the death, they did not show it. And there was plenty in Arthur's previous temperament and physical demeanour to make death by cerebral haemorrhage extremely plausible – in particular the acute headaches and intensely flushed face from which he had suffered ever since adolescence.

Once the autopsy had been completed the body was sealed in a shipment cask and taken to Trieste, from where its passage home was a protracted affair. Delayed by winter storms it did not arrive in England until late December.

Arthur was buried on 3 January 1834, in the church at Clevedon, beside the river Severn, amongst his maternal relatives, the Eltons. News of his death reached Clevedon, where the rest of the Hallam family were staying, on 28 September. Three days later Mr Hallam arrived home and instructed his brother-in-law, Henry Elton, to write to Somersby informing Alfred of the terrible news.

Matilda, having been to a dancing lesson, returned from Spilsby a few evenings later with the day's post. Amongst the letters was one for Alfred, sent from Clevedon. The other Tennysons were all at table, finishing dinner. Matilda handed out the mail then went upstairs to take off her bonnet. As she did so she recalled a strange experience of a few days earlier. Walking with her older sister Mary, they had seen a tall figure dressed in white and as they followed it down the lane it disappeared through a dense part of the hedge. They each believed it to have been a ghost, and later, when they were able to calculate the time of Hallam's death, they both believed, quite sincerely, that it had been Arthur's spirit walking ahead of them.

Downstairs Alfred had opened his letter:

Clifton. 1 Octbr. 1833

My dear Sir,

At the desire of a most afflicted family, I write to you, because they are unequal, from the Abyss of grief into which they have fallen, to do it themselves.

Your friend Sir, and my much loved Nephew, Arthur Hallam, is no more – it has pleased God, to remove him from this his first scene of Existence, to that better World, for which he was Created.

He died at Vienna on his return from Buda, by Apoplexy, and I believe his Remains come by Sea from Trieste.

Mr. Hallam arrived this Morning in 3 Princes Buildings.

May that Great Being, in whose hands are the Destinies of Man – and who has promised to comfort all that Mourn pour the Balm of Consolation on all the families who are bowed down by this unexpected dispensation!

I have just seen Mr. Hallam, who begs I will tell you, that he will write himself as soon as his Heart will let him. Poor Arthur had a slight attack of Ague – which he had often had – Order'd his fire to be lighted – and talked with as much cheerfulness as usual – He suddenly became insensible and his Spirit departed without Pain – The Physician endeavor'd to get any Blood from him – and on Examination it was the

117

General Opinion, that he could not have lived long – This
was also Dr. Holland's opinion – The account I have
endeavor'd to give you, is merely what I have been able to
gather, but the family of course are in too great distress, to
enter into details –

> I am dear Sir –
> your very Obt. Sevt:
> Henry Elton[50]

Alfred left the dining-room and was alone for some minutes,
collecting himself. Then he sent for Emily.

PART THREE
Meridies II

1   Striving, Seeking

> I will go forward, sayest thou,
> I shall not fail to find her now.
>
> ('THE TWO VOICES')

I n 1827 (the year *Poems by Two Brothers* was published) Blake died; a year after Arthur Hallam's death both Coleridge and Charles Lamb were gone; Keats had died a dozen years before, and Byron ten; Wordsworth was still publishing, but as a voice from a departed era – the stage seemed to be clearing for a new generation of poets.

The 1830s, however, were destined to be the decade of the prose writer. Dickens followed up *Sketches of Boz* (1836) with *The Pickwick Papers* in 1837, *Oliver Twist* in 1838 and *Nicholas Nickleby* in 1839. Carlyle's *Sartor Resartus*, *The French Revolution* and *Chartism* came out during the same years. On the Continent Victor Hugo and Balzac were in their prime. Stendhal and Pushkin were also publishing.

But, since the period of Byron, Coleridge, Shelley and Keats, poetry seemed to have hit a flat interregnum, and those poets who filled it are now read chiefly in anthologies, rather than in their own right. People like Southey, Landor, Thomas Hood, Leigh Hunt and Thomas Moore filled the gap between the Romantics and the triumvirate of Tennyson, Browning and Arnold. Of course, each still has his special apologist somewhere, who will be duly and rightly rankled by such judgement; and, as usual, there is the wayward exception – John Clare.

Equally, such a long-distance viewpoint rather obscures the fact that at the time those same poets who now fill only the lower or middle ranks, were puffed up and spoken of in the same terms as the truly great. Nevertheless, there is in Tennyson's behaviour following the death of Hallam the sense of a young man carefully grooming himself to take on the, as yet, unclaimed mantle of greatness. And this sense is rather stronger than that of a person rendered incapable by grief.

The singlemindedness with which Tennyson avoided any kind of paid employment is remarkable. Many a young poet's ambition has foundered at the first fence – the temptation (or the necessity) of a regular paypacket. But even those who fight shy of a settled career usually do a bit of this and that, to make ends meet. For modern poets, modelling themselves on Wallace Stevens (insurance) or Philip Larkin (librarianship), retreating into the obscurity of a humdrum profession has its compensating, monastic and dedicatory aspects.

To be sure, Tennyson's options were limited, but not non-existent. Having turned his back on the church he might have apprenticed himself to an apothecary, as one or two of his younger brothers did (though fruitlessly), or, like Frederick, gone abroad, where the £100 which his Aunt Russell gave him every year might have proved enough for basic subsistence. But he chose to stay at home, earning nothing, and using Hallam's death in several interesting ways.

The word 'using' strikes a sharp note, and requires explanation. All of us are prone to considering the most dreadful scenarios – the death of a parent, a loved one – and the role (usually vigorous, heroic) which we shall play in life's sequel to that loss. At the end of such daydreams, or perhaps day-mares, we are filled with a sense of unspeakable shame, especially when young, believing that no one so despicable as ourselves could possibly contemplate such grisly circumstances, and frightened that our imagining them might actually make them occur.

It is almost certain that Tennyson had already 'used' Hallam's death imaginatively, as a way of keeping his sister for himself. (This seems to be acknowledged by the premonition in the early draft of 'The Two Voices' already quoted). And for that reason his reaction to news of his friend's death became complicated, as most such reactions are, but especially in this case, by feelings of guilt and release.

He was able to use the more conventional and expected aspects of grief to forestall any suggestion that he should find himself an occupation. Aged twenty-four, and having mooched around for two and a half years since his enforced departure from Cambridge, it would otherwise have been at just this moment that family pressure to gain paid employment might have become overbearing.

Suspiciously deconstructive readings of *In Memoriam* have suggested that Tennyson 'used' the death of his friend in a calculating, almost mercenary way. 'Engagement with matters of faith and doubt seemed a responsible move for a poet.'[1] Such readings depend on a perverse and cynical way of interpreting human behaviour; and even the author of the comment has to add, 'It was also temperamentally attractive to Tennyson.' But how very damning is that 'also'.

On the other hand, the traditional view that Tennyson immediately began pouring out his grief in the consoling verses of *In Memoriam* is too simple and inaccurate, as the editorial work of Christopher Ricks and others has, by now, conclusively illustrated. This traditional view was accompanied by a picture of Tennyson in the years immediately following 1833 as withdrawn and nervously unstable, clinging to his mother's apron-strings at Somersby, and using poetry as a form of therapy. The fact that he did not publish again until 1842 was pointed to in support of this view, but the delay had more to do with his determination to make that appearance one which would confirm him as a major poet.

He had no other estimate of himself. He was that or nothing. And the real death of Hallam put a finish to all romantic dalliance with oblivion. Opting for life, he temporarily took charge of his hypochondria.

> Whatever crazy sorrow saith,
> No life that breathes with human breath
> Has ever truly longed for death.

> 'Tis life, whereof our nerves are scant,
> Oh life, not death, for which we pant,
> More life, and fuller, that I want.

> ('THE TWO VOICES')

One thing Tennyson did not do was use poetry as a prop. There are those who see his busy writing during the ensuing months as reliance on a drug which masks the meaninglessness of existence. It is very difficult to read 'Ulysses' and 'Tiresias' in such a way. Hallam's death had reconfirmed the meaning of existence, not shattered it.

'He seemed less overcome than one would have expected'[2] is a typical comment on the poet's demeanour when he arrived in London later in the month. Clearly there were reverberations to Hallam's death which Tennyson did not share with his friends. (The wonderful short poem 'Hark, the dogs howl!' is a case in point. Tennyson never published this fragment, and his son, when quoting the poem in the *Memoir*, was careful to omit a line referring to Alfred's habit of kissing Arthur Hallam's 'brows'. The fragment ends darkly, with a vision of Arthur's spirit looking 'reproachfully' at the poet.) But it is merely a sentimental form of apology, a way of covering up his apparent coldness or callousness, to suggest that Tennyson was actually a broken young man, and that poetry papered over the cracks. It is either that, or a failure to grasp that more guilt than grief was activated by the letter from Clevedon. And this is why the first poems written in the aftermath of that news were fired through with self-loathing ('St Simeon Stylites') and self-regard ('Ulysses'), and only later did a broader view open the way for the composition of *In Memoriam*.

Of 'Ulysses', written on 20 October 1833, less than three weeks after receiving the painful news, Tennyson himself acknowledged, 'There is more about myself in "Ulysses" ... It was more written with the feeling of his loss upon me than many poems in *In Memoriam*.'[3]

> How dull it is to pause, to make an end,
> To rust unburnished, not to shine in use!
> As though to breathe were life. Life piled on life
> Were all too little, and of one to me
> Little remains: but every hour is saved
> From that eternal silence, something more,
> A bringer of new things; and vile it were
> For some three suns to store and hoard myself,
> And this gray spirit yearning in desire
> To follow knowledge like a sinking star,
> Beyond the utmost bound of human thought.

('ULYSSES')

Vile it were to do anything but, in the words of the poem's final line, 'To strive, to seek, to find, and not to yield.' This ending, with its atmosphere of gold lettering on a school shield, invokes the wrong response in the modern reader, but is an accurate measure of the mood in which Tennyson left Somersby at the end of the month, and went out into the world.

From this moment on he was his own man; with a mission and a vision. If the night spent in his dead father's bed was the likely moment of a private dedication to his Muse, Hallam's death was the spur to a more public ambition.

2   The Second Voice

'Come' and I come, and all comes back
Which in that early voice was sweet,
Yet am I dizzy in the track,
A light wind wafts me from my feet.

('YOUTH')

S uch heroic mood was intermittent, as attested by the verses
of 'Youth':

So lived I without aim or choice,
    Still humming snatches of old song,
Till suddenly a sharper voice
    Cried in the future 'Come along'.

When to this sound my face I turned,
    Intent to follow on the track,
Again the low sweet voices mourned
    In distant fields, 'Come back, come back'.

Confused, and ceasing from my quest,
    I loitered in the middle way,
So pausing 'twixt the East and West,
    I found the present where I stay:

Now idly in my natal bowers,
    Unvext by doubts I cannot solve,
I sit among the scentless flowers
    And see and hear the world revolve:

Yet well I know that nothing stays,
    And I must traverse yonder plain:
Sooner or later from the haze
    The second voice will peal again.

('YOUTH')

Two Voices. Come back. Come hither. Passivity and action.
Morbidity and vigour. Hypochondria and health. Doubt and
faith. Death and life. Dualities which were 'temperamentally

attractive to Tennyson' were to become the refrains of what we now call the high Victorian period. More than enough has been said by other writers about Tennyson and 'his age', or about Tennyson the 'pre-eminent Victorian'. Individually such commentaries have been useful, but collectively they have erected a heavy barrier between Tennyson and ourselves. To reclaim his poetry for our own time, a century or more after his death, it is necessary to try and peer past the Victorian gauze.

In October 1833 the high Victorian period of the 1860s and 1870s was still some thirty or forty years away. The public, Tennysonian persona dates only from 1850 (from the time of his marriage and acceptance of the Laureateship), so for the next seventeen years the biographical focus must remain closely personal.

Several of the poems which Tennyson produced in these weeks were worked on in London. Edward FitzGerald, with whom Alfred was not yet on very close terms, wrote to his friend Donne: 'Tennyson has been in town for some time: he has been making fresh poems, which are finer, they say, than any he has done. But I believe he is chiefly meditating on the purging and subliming of what he has already done: and repents that he has published at all yet.'[4] This shows that even a fairly distant acquaintance can be a more reliable source of information than an older brother, for Frederick, a few weeks later, told cousin George that Alfred would 'most probably publish again in the Spring'.[5] Tennyson's next volume in fact came out in the early summer – of 1842.

Clearly Tennyson was not writing quickly to get out a new collection. But nor was he simply responding to nerves and impulses sharpened by loss. A bereavement, or any pronounced emotional experience, will frequently give rise to a creative outpouring, and in part at least Tennyson was simply going with the flow of this imaginative energy. In addition, there does seem to have been a new professionalism about his working approach. During November, when he was once more back in Somersby, he wrote jokily chastizing letters to Cambridge friends regarding the loan of books from the Trinity library. These included Malory's three-volume edition of *Morte D'Arthur* and Thomas Keightley's two-volume *Fairy Mythology*, and are evidence that he was already thinking in terms of a medieval backdrop for some future work. The new professionalism should not be over-stressed – Tennyson's complaints regarded books which *he* had forgotten and left behind when passing through Cambridge on his way back from London, and those who posted them on to him, notably Stephen Spring Rice, did so in little hope of the return date being kept.

Tennyson's trip to London had been at the request of Mr Hallam, who asked Alfred to meet him at Wimpole Street at 1 pm on Thursday 17 October, so that they could share together things which 'we cannot express in letters'. It was probably at this meeting that Henry Hallam informed Alfred of his intention to settle an allowance of £300 a year on Emily. Mr Hallam's personal response to his son's death remained consistent – that nothing could have been done to prevent Arthur's collapse; that had he not died when he did he would certainly have died young, 'at no distant period'; and that, all things considered, it was probably best that he should have died before marrying Emily, 'when the bereavement might have been further aggravated'.[6]

All this time the body of Arthur was still awaiting final transportation. Initially Alfred planned to attend the funeral. Mr Hallam wrote to him on the 9 December, 'I have been informed that you have expressed a wish to attend our dear Arthur's funeral. If that is the case, I have a place for you in my carriage; it is to be at Clevedon in Somersetshire.' He added that as far as he knew the ship had not yet sailed from Trieste and that he had no reason to expect the coffin before the second week in January.[7]

However, things moved more quickly than that. Mr Hallam wrote again on 30 December informing Alfred that the body had been landed at Dover. Some time between the 9th and the 30th Alfred must have communicated his change of mind about attending the funeral, for Mr Hallam was no longer expecting Alfred to share his carriage. Indeed, 'My first thought was not to write to you till all was over.' The tone of Mr Hallam's further comments in this letter suggests that Alfred had given extreme grief as his reason for not going to Clevedon. 'Use your own discretion about telling your sister,' he adds. 'Do your utmost, my dear young friend, to support her and yourself. Give as little way to grief as you may ... I fear the solitary life you both lead in the country is sadly unpropitious.'[8]

Arthur's sealed coffin was taken from the Kent coast to Somerset by a cortège of hearse and three coaches, drawn by sixteen black horses. At Clevedon it was lowered into the family vault in the church of St Andrew. The ceremony was simple and there were no flowers.

Since Alfred's avoidance of Arthur's burial spot persisted for many years, his failure to travel to Somerset in the early days of 1834 must have involved more than funeral-shyness. His behaviour immediately after his father's funeral does not suggest a temperament that would have found simple proximity to a friend's dead body unsettling. And in public he had been well in control of his grief. Tennyson refused to attend the funeral because he wanted to preserve his private reaction to Hallam's death, already knowing perhaps that it would bear creative fruit.

Accounts of the Christmas at Somersby do not make it sound overly melancholy. On Boxing Day all the Tennysons went to visit their friend John Rashdall, curate of Orby, and feasted on oysters. The very day Henry Hallam wrote from London, fearing for the solitary country life the Tennysons were leading, Alfred and Mary were guests at a dinner-dance held at the Rawnsleys'. Alfred stayed the night and spent the whole of the next day talking and smoking with Rashdall and Rawnsley.

When the letter arrived at the Rectory Alfred's friend Tennant was in the middle of a three-day stay, filled, according to the guest, with 'merry Christmas sports, and ... New Year Revels'.[9] And on 3 January, the day of the funeral, Rashdall joined Tennant and Tennyson at Somersby and sat up till three o'clock in the morning.

However, it seems the gaiety was briefly seasonal, for early in January Alfred took it upon himself to write to his uncle in the following manner:

My dear Uncle

I think it my duty to inform you of Septimus's state of mind. My Grandfather talks of letting him stop at home two or three months longer – if this be acted upon I have very little doubt but that his mind will prove as deranged as Edward's, although I trust that his intellect may yet be preserved by getting him out into some bustling line of life *remote from the scene of his early connexions*. I have studied the minds of my own family – I know how delicately they are organised – and how much might be done in this instance by suddenly removing Septimus from all those objects and subjects with which he has been familiar and upon which he has been accustomed to brood ... At present his symptoms are not unlike those with which poor Edward's unhappy derangement began – he is subject to fits of the most gloomy despondency accompanied with tears – or rather, he spends whole days in this manner ... I repeat it, he should be removed as far as possible from home and into some place where new objects and the example of others might rouse him to energy.[10]

Immediately after posting this letter Alfred went to Orby and stayed for three days with John Rashdall. The two of them had become good, pipe-sharing friends and Rashdall recognized a 'mind yearning for fellowship; for the joys of friendship and love. Hallam seems to have left his heart a widowed one.'[11] The final sentence could be quoted alone, to make it appear that Tennyson was pining for his departed companion. The previous sentence, and the actual experience of Tennyson's company, make it clear that the yearning Rashdall detected was not closed and grieving, but open and alive for new feeling. Here was a widow or widower who had already thrown off the weeds.

Tennyson's intervention on behalf of his younger brother was successful (and instructive – that 'I have studied the minds of my family' speaks of a character trying to transcend his own despondency and take on an observational and custodial role), but Septimus had proved incapable of the work expected at a solicitor's office, so he was now apprenticed to the doctor at Horncastle. It is always satisfying when one's good offices bear fruit and this positive outcome set a suitable tone for the New Year.

The deep winter months were to be filled with the sort of study he had shirked at Cambridge. There was a self-imposed schedule to his reading:

Monday	History, German
Tuesday	Chemistry, German
Wednesday	Botany, German
Thursday	Electricity, German
Friday	Animal Psychology, German
Saturday	Mechanics
Sunday	Theology

The German would be replaced with Italian and Greek in

successive weeks. Like the long place-in-space address written inside the cover of one of his early books, how many readers have not made similar optimistic schedules for themselves? There is nothing of interest in the proposed regime, except that it was drawn up at this time, and adds further weight to the view that Hallam's death had nudged Tennyson towards a more forthright use of his talents.

Mr Hallam was in touch again early in February, informing Alfred of his intention to print, privately, a selection of Arthur's poems and essays, to be prefixed by a short memoir. Alfred was asked to communicate, by letter, anything relating to Arthur's habit of mind and favourite pursuits, but in the end he did not contribute in any way to the resulting volume. It was left to other friends, such as Spedding, to help Mr Hallam in the enterprise.

Just a few days after receiving Mr Hallam's request Alfred replied, saying, 'I attempted to draw up a memoir of his life and character, but I failed to do him justice. I failed even to please myself. I could scarcely have pleased you.' This was a rather prompt resignation and would be difficult to accept at face value were it not for Tennyson's chronic inability to express himself in prose. 'I hope to be able at a future period to concentrate whatever powers I may possess on the construction of some tribute ...' This negative response to Mr Hallam probably weighed heavily on the young man, exacerbating his sense of guilt, and acting as a goad for the composition of *In Memoriam* – as is all but acknowledged in the chosen title of the poem.

Frederick was in Somersby during February giving us a second point of view. Alfred's industry – he was now busy composing his 'Morte d'Arthur' – convinced his older brother that he was still aiming for publication in the spring, and this misapprehension indicates that the two kept out of one another's way. Frederick's observations on Alfred's state of health are more reliable: 'His health is very indifferent and his spirits very variable. He too if he does not mind will be obliged when he has lost the plumage of his Imagination to fledge it with Tobacco leaves, if he does not take to some stronger and more fatal stimulant.' This prognosis follows a reference to Charles who was all but killing himself with opium in the village of Tealby. (By now their grandfather had left Tealby and gone to live 'on a sandy moor' – Usselby – where his favourite granddaughter, Julia, moved in with him to act as housekeeper.)

Alfred occasionally visited his favourite brother, according to Mrs Charles Tennyson, who was in effect the landlady. As usual she kept her son George well-informed of the picturesque goings-on: 'Your cousin Charles is living in the house below that the Woodhouses occupied. He is very solitary, alone, tho' occasionally relieved by the visits of his brother and sometimes a sister.' The sister was Mary, whose impending attachment to John Heath provoked a possessive reaction in Charles similar to the one felt by Alfred with regard to Emily and Arthur Hallam. By April Charles had asked to take on Grove House and have Mary live with him. This, of course, was not on.

Mrs Charles Tennyson again: 'It would be very disagreeable in many respects to have a tribe of Somersby people so near us, as of course Mary would expect to go everywhere we did.'

Love was in the air for Alfred too.

At the time of writing 'The Gardener's Daughter' in the summer of 1833, Tennyson was acquainted with Rosa Baring of Harrington Hall, but admired her from a distance. Some time during 1834 their relationship was put on a surer footing, and many poems over the next two years were either directly dedicated to Rosa, or written with her in mind.

Most modern biographies of Tennyson follow R.W. Rader's assessment of Rosa Baring's importance in Tennyson's life, whilst at the same time underplaying the erotic attachment between them. It is as if they are reluctant, on Tennyson's behalf, to admit of any infidelity to Arthur Hallam. Because his love poems are not 'carnal or fleshly' it is suggested, with false reasoning, that he was a man with very low sexual drive. That he was still sexually inexperienced at the time of his marriage in 1850 is usually taken for granted, but there is no simple relationship between the possession of sexual drive and its translation into direct experience.

Part of the pleasure to be had from re-reading 'The Gardener's Daughter' is the innocence with which it evokes the intensity of first love. It is a poem richly and romantically expansive in its decorative descriptions which are imbued with the wistfulness fast becoming the Tennysonian trademark. Essentially a hymn to love-at-first-sight, the sense of rapture contained in the poem is nevertheless recollected. The subtitle is 'The Pictures' and the description is applied with painterly detachment.

Rose, the inhabitant of this Eden (i.e. Rosa Baring, stepdaughter of Sir Arthur Eden) is observed from a distance, every detail of her demeanour erotically savoured. The narrator and his artist-friend, Eustace, spy her from the shadows of the garden.

> the full day dwelt on her brows, and sunn'd
> Her violet eyes, and all her Hebe bloom,
> And doubled his own warmth against her lips,
> And on the bounteous wave of such a breast
> As never pencil drew. Half light, half shade,
> She stood, a sight to make an old man young.

At the end of the poem we discover that the painting of Rose about to be unveiled is the work of an old man, the last tribute to the memory of the love of his life. We are told that she became his wife and that theirs was a happy marriage, but it was only the first throes of romantic attraction that interested Tennyson as yet. Typically, even these he had to deal with at one remove, within a fictional frame which placed the emotion of love not in the present, not in the future, but in the past.

3   Break, Break, Break

> Where is the voice that I loved? ah where
> Is that dear hand that I would press?
> Lo! the bold heavens cold and bare,
> The stars that know not my distress!

(QUOTED IN MEMOIR I 107)

On 3 November 1834 a party was held at Somersby to say goodbye to the Baring girls, who were leaving Lincolnshire to spend the winter in London. Alfred had already (in September) presented Rosa with a birthday poem, so we know that the distant and theoretical admiration which had inspired parts of 'The Gardener's Daughter' was becoming more direct and actual. It is still unlikely that any outright romance had been declared, for Rashdall felt free to remark in his diary that Rosa was 'the prettiest most elegant girl I ever was intimate with. I have parted from her probably for ever!' He spoke with such finality because he was about to take up a new incumbency in the south of England and would not be in Somersby when the Barings returned in the spring.

The following summer Tennyson's infatuation with Rosa would reach its most ardent peak, and would leave as indelible a mark on his life and his poetry as the friendship with Hallam. But in the summer of 1834 the spirits of his own family, and in particular those of his sister, were paramount in his mind.

Emily Tennyson, though still distraught, began to come out into society, stirred by the love affair between her sister Mary and John Heath. It was whilst both John and his brother Douglas were staying in Somersby that she made her first re-appearance in front of company, entering the drawing-room, still dressed in black, but with a white rose in her hair. This dramatic entrance is startling because it seems to confirm the identification of Emily with Camilla in *The Lover's Tale*, stepping out of her death-like chrysalis, 'her hair/Studded with one rich Provence rose'.

Following this visit of the Heaths it was proposed that Alfred, Mary and Emily should spend a week or two in the south – Alfred and Emily accompanying Mary to the Heaths at Dorking, before responding to an invitation from the Hallams to visit them at Molesey Park. But when the time came – July – Emily's lassitude returned and she decided she could not leave home. Mary stayed behind with her, and Alfred ventured forth alone.

He began by passing through London, to bid farewell to Frederick, who was travelling to Corfu to stay with cousin George, then on the staff of Lord Nugent. George's side of the family, when they heard about it, were outraged but powerless to intervene. Frederick's own mother and sisters were surprised to hear about the departure.

Whilst Alfred was in Dorking he received a letter from Emily in which she promised that she still anticipated leaving for Molesey, in about three weeks, when it was proposed that Charles would accompany her on the journey.

I certainly intend to go to Moulsey. Would to God I could begin the journey immediately but it is not in my power. You will be sorry to hear that I have been considerably worse in health since your departure ... You know, Alfred, the great desire I have to become acquainted with the Hallam family, particularly with Ellen; she will perhaps be the friend to remove in some degree the horrible feeling of desolation which is ever at my heart. I can no longer continue in this deepening grave of tears ... depend upon it I will do all in my power to go to Moulsey. What is life to me! if I die (which the Tennysons never do) the effort shall be made ... Take care of thyself that thou mayest return with new health and spirits ...[12]

Alone in Dorking, Alfred did much solitary walking amongst the pines of Leith Hill, composing *en plein air* 'The Sleeping Beauty' and giving such poems as 'Sir Galahad' and 'The Blackbird' their rough beginnings. Heath took his guest to Worthing and proposed a visit to Brighton, but Alfred, who was not in travelling mood, preferred to return to Kitlands, to await news from Emily.

He was anxious, also, to hear of another matter. When he had left Somersby it was in the midst of a scare regarding the Holywell and Enderby woods. The landlord had threatened to cut them down and there was even talk that he was considering turning the Tennysons out of the Rectory. This fear was more or less confirmed to Tennyson in a letter from Tennant, received in Dorking: '[Horatio] tells me they are cutting down all the trees in Enderby Lane and Fairy Wood; I hope the Fairies will haunt them.'[13]

Tennant had fallen in love with the sixteen-year-old Cecilia Tennyson at Christmas. The attachment was not welcomed – whether by Cecilia herself or the family as a whole is unclear. At any rate, Alfred was given the task of informing his friend that his feelings were not reciprocated. It is hinted that something had hatched between Cecilia and Douglas Heath (brother of John), but this might have been a pretext for fending off a man whom Cecilia found unattractive. The whole affair was conducted in a way oddly reminiscent of the restrictions put upon Arthur Hallam when he was courting Emily, with Tennant finally having to beg release from a ban on visiting Somersby.

He was allowed to come in early August, on conditions which he had set out himself: 'that my behaviour to Cecilia should be as heretofore that of a stranger with the affections of a brother.'[14] The awkwardness festered on into the winter, by which time Tennant had taken Horatio Tennyson under his wing, was privately tutoring him, and proposed taking him to Blackheath school, where he had been appointed Deputy Headmaster. But for this, Mrs Tennyson's handling of the matter might have been more forthright, and Alfred's behaviour less considerate.

On his return from the Heaths and the Hallams, Alfred's health became very poor, as it often did in high summer. 'At present I am so unwell as to be almost a prisoner in my own house', he wrote to his grandfather towards the end of August.[15] Such a reaction to the high-octane output of the previous months, and the artificially-heightened level of being from which the poems of the past winter (1833/34) had emanated, was unsurprising.

He spent the autumn corresponding with Tennant and Spedding, sending the latter transcripts of the latest poems – 'Love Thou Thy Land', 'The Blackbird', 'Of Old Sat Freedom on the Height'. What a contrast such poems – espousing love of homeland, cosy hostelry, etc. – are to the heroic spithead stance of 'Ulysses' and 'Tiresias'. As he approached the anniversary of Hallam's death, the rallying call which he had composed for himself in those earlier poems seemed to ring less clearly.

It was not just this impending date which was pressing the memory of his lost friend on Tennyson. In mid-July there arrived at the Rectory a package containing several copies of the *Remains in Verse and Prose*, edited by Mr Hallam, and including the rather austere memoir written by Arthur's father. One of the copies was inscribed especially for Emily and it was again proposed that she should visit East Molesey. This time she was up to the trip. Alfred accompanied her to town in mid-October and stayed with her for nearly a fortnight. A birthday dinner was given in Emily's honour (she was twenty-three) and it was at this function, ironically, that she was first introduced to her future husband, Richard Jesse. Their romance did not openly develop for several years, but Jesse was enchanted enough at this early meeting to ensure that he was invited back to the Hallams' Wimpole Street house a month later, this time to be rewarded with a song from Emily after dinner.

Alfred left his sister with the Hallams and Emily stayed on for Christmas and for the early part of the New Year, growing ever closer to Ellen, Arthur's sister, who taught her to waltz and generally coaxed her out of her melancholy. (When she returned to Somersby she persuaded the family to hold a number of dinner dances. During a warm April evening Alfred danced several waltzes with Sophy Rawnsley, now a nubile sixteen. In later life

Sophy described Tennyson as being 'so interesting because he was so unlike other young men, and his unconventionality of manner and dress had a charm which made him more acceptable than the dapper young gentleman of the ordinary type ... He was a splendid dancer, for he loved music, and kept such time, but, you know, we liked to talk better than to dance together.' She added that most girls were frightened of him.)

How many of the Hallams' social functions Alfred himself attended we do not know. Probably not many. His movements for the corresponding period of time are difficult to trace, which suggests that he moved about in London, meeting his cronies. An early letter of 1835 (to Spedding) mentions promises made between cigars at the Bell and Crown Tavern, Holborn, and in Giddon's Cigar Tavern, Covent Garden. Such places were his likely haunts during November and early December.

He returned to Somersby for Christmas and another visit from John Heath. Several sections of *In Memoriam* were now written, or in the process of composition. Heath took away from his visit copies of 'The Christmas' and 'The Fair Ship' sections.

Tennyson kept up his flirtations with Rosa Baring and Sophy Rawnsley, writing light verse to them both. And he had already spent private moments with Emily Sellwood. Sometimes referred to as 'The Silent Years', this period of time between one published edition and another is often taken as evidence that Tennyson's mauling by the critics had made him reluctant to publish ever again. But it is much more the case that he was determined to make his next appearance one that a mature poet would be able to stand by. Writing to John Wilson back in April he had said, of his old poems, 'I could wish that some of the Poems there broken on your critical wheel were deeper than ever plummet sounded. Written as they were before I had attained my nineteenth year they could not but contain as many faults as words. I never wish to see or hear of them again ...'[16] Here he was speaking of those early poems which he would never re-publish. But as well as having written a sizeable collection of new poems since Hallam's death, he had also been busily revising earlier poems that he did consider fit for re-publication, and this was a process that consumed about as much of his energies as the writing of new verse.

In the New Year he grew restless, and sold his Chancellor's medal (for £15) in return for the freedom to travel. Those promises exchanged over cigars between Spedding and himself had related to a possible visit north, and at midnight on 15 February 1835 Alfred wrote to his friend complaining that his side of the promise had not been kept. 'Despite thy transgression I have an inclination to come and see thee and if possible to bring thee back with me here.'

Spedding lived in the Lakes, and was on friendly terms with Wordsworth and Hartley Coleridge. The trip was to be a substantial one and the selling of the medal may have been specifically aimed at financing this expedition. However, Spedding's written invitation did not arrive until early March, by which time Alfred had arranged to accompany Matilda and Cecilia for a fortnight in Mablethorpe.

Although Alfred loved Mablethorpe at this time of the year, he was growing increasingly bored with Lincolnshire society, and resented having to postpone his visit to the Lakes. Hearing a report of the Hallams entertaining both Wordsworth and Samuel Rogers, he 'growled ... and said he was cut off from all society worth living for – he finished by venting his spleen most mercilessly upon harmless, stout, foxhunting Lincolnshire squires'. This was according to his sister Emily, who was by now keeping up a regular correspondence with Ellen Hallam. A fortnight later she wrote, of the Mablethorpe trip: 'The tides, which thou knowest at this time of year are excessively high and fine, tempted my kinsfolk, and so irresistibly, that they resolved no longer to delay their anticipated gratification, – viz, a sight of the darling breakers.'[17]

Break, break, break,
   On thy cold gray stones, O Sea!
And I would that my tongue could utter
   The thoughts that arise in me.

O well for the fisherman's boy,
   That he shouts for his sister at play!
O well for the sailor lad,
   That he sings in his boat on the bay!

And the stately ships go on
   To their haven under the hill;
But O for the touch of a vanished hand,
   And the sound of a voice that is still!

Break, break, break,
    At the foot of thy crags, O Sea!
But the tender grace of a day that is dead
    Will never come back to me.

('BREAK, BREAK, BREAK')

This poem, so often anthologized, is a perfect example of how biography can be used to reinvigorate a work grown dull with repetition and familiarity. Almost certainly written during this visit to Mablethorpe, (but transposed to a rocky rather than a sandy beach) knowledge of the biographical background creates a cinematically clear image of the cloaked poet looking resentfully at the cheerful fisherman's child, the equally jovial sailor, and the ships at sea. It is one of the great short lyrics, to be set beside Byron's 'So We'll Go No More a Roving', Burns's 'The Rigs o' Barley' and Tennyson's own 'Crossing the Bar'. Christopher Ricks has called it a 'masterpiece of puzzling plainness', in the sense that most good, simple poems, express more than is stated by their straightforward vocabulary.

Once again it is interesting to compare Tennyson's standpoint in this poem, with the poems composed immediately after Hallam's death. Then he was brave and staunch, ready to ride out on the open seas, to continue their voyage alone. Here he is stranded on the shore, cut off both from those who are engaged in life's mature endeavours (the stately ships) and from the idle pleasures of the young and immature (probably the Misses Bourne).

Just as Emily seemed to be getting over Hallam's death, the finality of it was evoking a deep and tragic nostalgia in Alfred.

4   Mismanaged Imagination

Drug thy memories, lest thou learn it, lest thy heart be put to proof,
In the dead unhappy night, and when the rain is on the roof.

('LOCKSLEY HALL')

B efore he left the Rectory with his sisters, news had come
through that their great-uncle Samuel Turner had died,
leaving a big house and the living at Caistor for Charles, who
took the name Turner and immediately removed himself from
Tealby, much to the delight of the d'Eyncourt Tennysons.

His presence there had never been appreciated. The d'Eyncourt
boys referred to him as a 'dogs' meat man', dressed as he
habitually was in a white rabbit-skin hat. And his departure was
greeted with a sense of good riddance. 'There is one good thing
arising from Charles going to live at Caistor, for you will not
then have the swarms of Goths and Vandals down upon you
every week,' one of the boys wrote to his father.[18]

With Frederick away on the Continent, leading the life of a
free-and-easy vagabond, and Charles having come into an
inheritance, Alfred could be forgiven if he felt for the moment as
if his own life had become directionless and had lost
momentum. In addition to the recurrent melancholy and
nostalgia as represented by 'Break, Break, Break' he had to put
up with the company of the two Misses Bourne, Margaret and
Alice, from Alford. According to William Rawnsley, these two
girls were the subject of 'Margaret' and 'Adeline', both
published in 1832. One was a brunette, the other was fair.

Emily joined the others in Mablethorpe towards the end of
April and described Margaret in a letter to Ellen Hallam as 'an
excessively nice girl, who enters much into my way of thinking;
she has not a remarkably sunny mind'. In other words, not
much fun, and a pale substitute for the vivacities of Rosa Baring
and Sophy Rawnsley.

After his stay by the sea Alfred spent the end of April and
part of May in the Lakes. Spedding was still in the family home

at Mirehouse, and living about as inactive a life as Tennyson. He already had another guest — Edward FitzGerald — with whom Alfred was as yet no more than acquainted; but the next month was to seal a lifelong, if awkward, friendship.

FitzGerald had been born Edward Purcell on 31 March 1809, making him just a few months older than Tennyson. His mother was dauntingly beautiful (in a heavy-shouldered and big-bosomed way) and exceptionally wealthy, and when her father died, leaving her a considerable fortune, the family assumed the name FitzGerald. This was when Edward was nine years old. He was immediately sent away, with his two brothers, to attend Bury St Edmunds grammar school, which is where he first met Spedding, and matriculated at Trinity College a year ahead of Tennyson, in 1826. (It was in this year that his father became Member of Parliament for Seaford, Sussex.) Never one of the Apostles or part of Tennyson's set, in spite of his schoolboy associations with Spedding, his most abiding friendship in Cambridge was with Thackeray. After graduation the two of them were together briefly in Paris, where FitzGerald had spent eighteen months of his childhood. It had been there that he developed an interest in bloodshed and criminality, for the family occupied a house in the rue d'Angouleme said to have been used by Robespierre.

Now remembered above all for his translation of the *Rubaiyat of Omar Khayyam* and for his relaxed but cultured correspondence[19], his personality was a good deal more complex than he liked to suggest.

At the time of his Mirehouse visit FitzGerald was living in Boulge Cottage at Woodbridge, Suffolk, close to his family. Like Tennyson and Spedding he had taken no paid employment since leaving Cambridge, but had settled down to become, in his own words, 'a great bear'. Behind apparent similarities there lurked a significant difference between FitzGerald and Spedding, whose nickname — the Pope — reflected a much more serious, puritanical temperament. Spedding was a scholar, and already intended to devote his life to the study of Francis Bacon. FitzGerald talked freely of his Blue Devils, or moods of despondency, and so was immediately in tune with Tennyson and the 'black blood' which occasionally paralysed the poet's willpower. Spedding would have disapproved of the fatalistic surrender to such paralysis by his two companions.

Tennyson spent the duration of his stay, inside and out,

wrapped in his dark insurrectionist's cloak. Spedding remarked that 'it must be a very capable and effective sun that shall make his soul rejoice and say "Ha! Ha! I am warm"'.

On the rare occasions that the weather was fair the three young men would spend the day rowing on Brassenthwaite Water, and Tennyson would read from his red notebook the poems written earlier in the year and recently polished at Mablethorpe. In the evenings, after large rustic teas containing different breads, cakes and jams, there would be political discussion with the older Speddings. FitzGerald, who had no taste for political or moral debate, would sit apart playing solitary games of chess. Occasionally Mrs Spedding would volunteer to be his opponent.

Late in the night it was time once again for poetry and pipes, and for FitzGerald to rejoin the other two. He and Alfred were becoming aware of a growing affinity, bedded in their common literary enthusiasms, and the earlier parts of the evening must have been highly charged for Tennyson, so that as the days went by he grew to resent the Spedding appetite for ironical, speculative banter.

In the middle of the month the three friends went to Ambleside and booked in for a week at the Salutation Inn, but Spedding was soon called back to Mirehouse. FitzGerald and Tennyson were not sorry to be left alone. Alfred was beginning to see in 'Fitz', as he was always affectionately known, a friend who had sufficient sensibility and intellect to begin to play something of a role that Arthur Hallam had filled. Not that there was much in common between Hallam and FitzGerald – apart from the fact that both were more comfortably off than Tennyson.

FitzGerald did not care for Wordsworth, and referred to him disparagingly as 'the Daddy', but bought a copy of *Yarrow Revisited* for Alfred before leaving Ambleside. Although Tennyson's name appears in the Rydal Mount visiting book for May 1835 it is unlikely that he did visit Wordsworth then. Spedding was keen for him to go, but Tennyson kept changing his mind. 'He would and would not (sulky one).'[20] It is most probable that Dorothy Wordsworth copied up the visiting book from some form of appointments diary; that Spedding had made arrangements for both to visit; but in the end went alone. There is no credible reason for Tennyson (or Wordsworth) to have kept the meeting a secret, and both were to give the impression that a later encounter was their first.[21]

After he had left the Lakes FitzGerald wrote to his friend John Allen:

> Alfred Tennyson stayed with me at Ambleside: Spedding was forced to go home, till the last two days of my stay there. I will say no more of Tennyson than that the more I have seen of him, the more cause I have to think him great. His little humours and grumpinesses were so droll, that I was always laughing ... I must however say, further, that I felt what Charles Lamb describes, a sense of depression at times from the overshadowing of a so much more lofty intellect than my own ...

And ten days later the meeting still reverberated, and produced some characteristically astute comment on the comparative styles and subject matter of Tennyson and Wordsworth:

> What you [Allen] say of Tennyson and Wordsworth is not, I think, wholly just. I don't think that a man can turn himself so directly to the service of morality, unless naturally inclined: I think Wordsworth's is a natural bias that way ... Wordsworth is first in the craft: but Tennyson does no little by raising and filling the brain with noble images and thoughts, which, if they do not direct us to our duty, purify and cleanse us from mean and vicious objects, and so prepare and fit us for the reception of the higher philosophy.[21]

It was just this point of view which would make FitzGerald frown at some of Tennyson's later work and inject an uncertainty into their friendship. At this stage the friendship was positive on both sides. But the next eighteen months were bleak ones for Tennyson – so much so, that in January 1837 he would describe himself to Milnes as 'a nervous, morbidly-irritable man, down in the world, stark-spoiled with the staggers of a mismanaged imagination and quite opprest by fortune and the reviews'.

A new chum was not the salvation he was looking for. Had he been anxious to find a Hallam-substitute he would have more earnestly pursued FitzGerald's time and company. The truth of the matter, and the main source of awkwardness between FitzGerald and himself, was that Tennyson had yearnings for *amour*, whereas Fitz did not. And despite what he said to

Milnes, it was to be girl-trouble, as much as a mismanaged imagination, that would make the next year and a half so emotionally unsettled.

5   Home and Country

Love thou thy land, with love far-brought
From out the storied Past, and used
Within the Present, but transfused
Through future time by power of thought

('LOVE THOU THY LAND')

FitzGerald was quick to follow up the meeting with Tennyson. He wrote, on the 2 July, with what proved consummate timing: 'Dear Tennyson, though I am no Rothschild, my wants are fewer than my monies: and I have usually some ten or twelve pounds sitting very loosely in my breeches pocket ...' He would not dare offer money to a small man, 'but you are not a small man assuredly ... It is very difficult to persuade people in this world that one can part with a Bank note without a pang – It is one of the most simple things I have done to talk thus to you ...'[23] These 'ten or twelve pounds' became, in the mouth of Carlyle, '£300 per annum', but most authorities are more inclined to believe the smaller sum.

FitzGerald's letter arrived on the day of the Old Man's death. He had been hanging on, in the miserable isolation of Usselby, for some time, but the end finally came on 4 July. Despite knowing in advance what the probable instructions of the Old Man's will were (he had declared them on several occasions) it appears that the Somersby Tennysons, and Alfred in particular, had been living in hope of a last-minute recognition of their seniority. But the Old Man divided his fortune as originally intended. All that had been inherited he shared equally between Somersby and Bayons. All that he had earned went straight to his son Charles.

It was Mrs Tennyson, Alfred's mother, who came off worst. She had hoped to inherit the tenancy of Usselby Manor but was left nothing in her own name. Instead, Frederick was instructed to allow her £200 per year from his own share. It was probably on his mother's behalf that Alfred felt most angry about the disposition.

Charles had already been provided for at the death of his Uncle Turner so the bulk of the Somersby inheritance went to Frederick and Alfred. Frederick received a life interest in the Clayton estate at Grimsby; Alfred the manor and estate at Grasby. The other seven children benefitted equally from the sale of an estate at Scartho, providing them with £3000 each.

In comparison with the richness of Bayons these were conservative amounts, but with sensible management they ought to have been enough to support the family in reasonable comfort. However, what rankled above all else was the insistence that bonds entered into by Mrs Tennyson and her three eldest sons, at the time of George Tennyson's death, should be deducted from the estate. 'They want the treacherous bond money paying ... and as quickly as possible', Charles complained.

The Old Man's funeral took place at Tealby, after an impressive procession through the town of Market Rasen. At Bayons two thousand mourners followed the coffin from the Manor to the parish church. No Somersby Tennyson was amongst them.

Forgetting their own behaviour at the death of George Tennyson, one of the younger d'Eyncourts (as they now became officially – the royal licence being issued on 31 July) wrote spitefully: 'I hear the family at Somersby are one and all much disappointed at their *handsome* increase of Property – but they expected more, and the girls very handsome futures besides. Some people are never satisfied!!'[24]

Alfred went to Margate, to visit his Aunt Bourne, who had also stayed away from the funeral. Edwin reported, on 1 August, 'Mrs. Russell and Mrs. Hamilton are both here. They are both friends with us again.' Quite what prompted the split in the aunts' ranks is unknown, but whatever it was Alfred got on no better with his Aunt Bourne than usual. 'Alfred I find has been so violent ... that Mr and Mrs Bourne have sent him away from Margate where he was with them', wrote his admittedly biased uncle Charles.

Tennyson went across from the Kent coast to Boulogne for two days, in an effort to clear his head of family matters. Returning to England he wrote to FitzGerald:

Some one says that nothing strikes one more on returning from the Continent than the look of our English country towns. Houses not so big, nor such rows of them as abroad; but each house, little or big, distinct from one another, each man's castle, built according to his own means and fancy, and so indicating the Englishman's individual humour.

I have been two days abroad – no further than Boulogne this time, but I am struck as always on returning from France with the look of good sense in the London people.

English good sense and moderation were the qualities he would ceaselessly set against what he saw as European extremism. Across the Channel reforms could only be forced upon those in power by angry mobs. In England a calculated spirit of compromise in government kept the lid on extremist agitation, by giving just enough at just the right moment. In later life he was fond of quoting Francis Bacon: 'It were good if men in their innovations would follow the example of Time itself, which indeed innovateth greatly, but quietly, and by degrees scarce to be perceived.' And in his recently composed poem 'Love Thou Thy Land', he had written:

Meet is it changes should control
    Our being, lest we rust in ease.
    We all are changed by still degrees,
All but the basis of the soul.

So let the change which comes be free
    To ingroove itself with that which flies,
    And work, a joint of state, that plies
Its office, moved with sympathy.

And yet, he realized that this could not always be the case. Even for the English temperament it was:

A saying, hard to shape in act;
    For all the past of Time reveals
    A bridal-dawn of thunder-peals,
Wherever Thought hath wedded Fact.

Families were just as prone to creating bridal-dawns of thunder-peals as governments. No sooner had the Old Man been laid in his tomb than his son Charles set about reconstructing Bayons

Manor. He issued his instructions from Westminster, sending rough architectural drawings and written guidance for builders. A craftsman was put permanently on site and ordered to carve as many coats of arms and badges on the façade as possible, all depicting the d'Eyncourt descent.

The estate was cleared, with some buildings being demolished. Deer and sheep were set to graze in the park. Portraits and sculptures were commissioned for the interior of the Manor. The drive, which had once run in a straight line from the gates to the front door, was now made to encompass the whole building before turning back over a drawbridge, under several archways, through as many gateways, and coming round again to the front. The effect of this was to add an unnecessary half-mile to the approach to the house.

The Tennysons watched it all with bemused derision. Even Charles's own sons began to worry that their father was piling up debts which in due course they might have to cover. And the obsession with Bayons did nothing for Charles's parliamentary career, which had once been full of promise. From this time on his hopes of advancement diminished, although he still spent the greater part of his time out of Lincolnshire.

6   Cold Coquette

Cursed be the social wants that sin against the strength of youth!
Cursed be the social lies that warp us from the living truth!

('LOCKSLEY HALL')

It was during the next few months that Alfred's involvement with Rosa Baring developed into a passion. The poems to Rosa form the bulk of a limited output between 1835 and 1836 and tell us practically all we know, but all we need to know, of their affair.

Thy rosy lips are soft and sweet,
Thy fairy form is so complete,
Thy motions are so airy free,

146

Love lays his arrows at thy feet
And yields his bow to thee;
Take any dart from out his quiver
And pierce what heart thou wilt forever.

('THY ROSY LIPS ARE SOFT AND SWEET')

This is the first of Tennyson's poems to the beautiful rich girl who had moved into Harrington Hall some time in the autumn of 1832. It was written nearly two years later, on her birthday, 23 September 1834. Her grandfather had been chairman of the East India Company and had left an estate of more than two million pounds on his death. This fortune was sufficient to establish Rosa's father, William Baring, albeit fourth-born son, in comfortable independence. He and his family leased Lulworth Castle in Dorset and it was while rowing nearby that his boat became upturned and he was drowned, with his wife and friends watching helplessly on the shore. Four years after this accident, Rosa's mother remarried, this time into yet another wealthy family. Her second husband was Arthur Eden, who was to become Assistant Comptroller of the Exchequer.

The Baring girls moved to Somersby with their step-father. Harrington Hall was owned by the Cracrofts, a family related to the Sellwoods of Horncastle, so it is tempting to imagine Emily Sellwood being given the task of introducing the Barings to the Tennyson sisters, and thus bringing to Alfred's attention the flighty Charlotte-Rose (Rosa).

At first, and perhaps for the duration of their acquaintance, Alfred was treated as something of a curiosity. In old age Rosa would tell Rawnsley how 'she and one of her girl friends would ride over to Somersby, just to have the pleasure of pleasing him or teasing him as the case might be'. Quoting her directly, Rawnsley continues: 'Alfred, as we all called him, was so quaint and so chivalrous, such a real knight among men, at least I always fancied so; and though we joked one another about his quaint, taciturn ways, which were mingled strangely with boisterous fits of fun, we were proud as peacocks to have been worthy notice by him, and treasured any message he might send or any word of admiration he let fall.'

Alfred, being made the subject of such innocent flirtation, was encouraged into seeing the prospect of romance by the engagement of both his brother Charles (to Louisa Sellwood) and his sister Mary (to John Heath). There is little evidence that

147

the fervent infatuation which developed on Alfred's part was ever seriously reciprocated:

> Rose of roses, bliss of blisses,
> Were not thine the kiss of kisses?
>   Ah! for such a kiss as that!
> Ah! for such a kiss as this is!

('EARLY VERSES OF COMPLIMENT TO MISS ROAE BARING')

On the other hand a superficial and frothy temperament, as all the evidence points to Rosa possessing, is able to give forth a type of personal electricity which can easily be confused with affection. In writing about bliss and kisses Tennyson must have felt that his chances of attaining them were as good as the next man's. It was the gradual realization that this was not the case – both because Rosa was too frivolous to respond to any but the lightest of his verses, and because she was from the moneyed aristocracy – that the affair ended in frustration and anger.

If Rosa and her friends were frequent public visitors to the Rectory, Alfred made equally frequent visits to the Hall. But all mention of his connection with the Hall has a clandestine atmosphere. He waits in the garden for a sight of his beloved. Suddenly she is there:

> The air with sudden odour reeled,
> The southern stars a music pealed,
> Warm beams across the meadow stole;
> For Love through glowing robes revealed,
> Said, 'Open, Rosebud, open, yield
> Thy fragrant soul.'

('THE ROSEBUD')

This fragment, not published until 1885, and quoted here in its Trinity variant, is disturbingly erotic. Disturbing – because it invites the suggestion that at the peak of his rapture Tennyson became something of a Peeping Tom, lurking in the darkness to catch a sight of his beloved. And when it came, the pleasure granted was of a kind which does not marry with the view of Tennyson as an asexual creature. Rader calls the eroticism in this poem 'idealized' but it is only the rather limp final line which can be said to make this so – the penultimate line expresses a clearly carnal yearning.

In the meantime Alfred spent as much of the winter as he could afford away from Somersby, for it was never possible to relax in the Rectory when Frederick was around, and the Barings always spent the winter in London. Where he went and whom he saw has not been recorded except for the odd interlude, although it is likely that when in London he stayed in Spedding's rooms at 60 Lincoln's Inn Fields. Spedding was now working for the Colonial Office. The Cock Tavern was a favourite haunt, and the group enjoying their chops, stout and cigars would often include FitzGerald and Thackeray. Frederick, who had returned from Corfu to take up his inheritance, began to form a fancy for Julia d'Eyncourt Tennyson, but did not declare himself until the following spring. Charles was not so reserved. He had proposed to Louisa Sellwood, the youngest daughter of a solicitor from Horncastle. The Sellwoods had long been associated with the Tennysons and the wedding took place on 24 May 1836.

Charles, who had recently managed to kick the opium habit, resorted to its use yet again in order to calm his nerves before the ceremony, confident that he could exert his will over the drug. The sales of laudanum in Lincolnshire were amongst the highest in the land – due perhaps to the isolated, sombre, flat-countried life led by much of the rural population. Nearly every family carried a supply for dulling the pain of toothache or generally calming a rattled constitution and, by the nature of the drug, a large number of people continued its use beyond the true medical requirement. Going to the altar in a blithely opiated state, Charles was not to know what struggles and strains lay in store as penalties for his enhanced composure.

Emily Sellwood acted as bridesmaid, and Alfred as best man. The close pairing, and the ceremonial situation, prompted Alfred to consider Emily in a new light. He was particularly touched by her display of open emotion. Her eyes began to water in the church, and her sister had to urge her to hold back her tears. 'No tears for me. A happy bridesmaid makes a happy bride.' Alfred, warmly affected by Emily's inability to stifle a tear, pressed her hand. Emily returned the pressure, and the flame of love was lit.

> And all at once a pleasant truth I learned,
> For while the tender service made thee weep,
> I loved thee for the tear thou couldst not hide,
> And prest thy hand, and knew the press returned,
> And thought, 'My life is sick of single sleep:
> O happy bridesmaid, make a happy bride!'

('THE BRIDESMAID')

That the flame was slow-burning gives no reason to doubt the sincerity of this sonnet. Tennyson was still romantically confused and a long way from the day when he would yearn for domestic stability. A previous biographer, taking the view that Tennyson was not of very ardent temperament, finds the poem bloodless and unconvincing. He thinks the line 'My life is sick of single sleep' makes Emily seem an alternative to a hot-water bottle, which is about as cruel a comment as can be found in the reviews of Bulwer and others, and rests on too crude and contemporary an assumption that love, from its inception, must be powered by lust.[25] There are, it has to be added, more warm-blooded ways of reading this line. The poem is only about the first impulse to love – to married love – and to the idea, dawning on Alfred for the first time at the age of twenty-seven, that the time is drawing near for him to find a wife. Neither Rosa Baring nor Sophy Rawnsley had prompted this kind of consideration, though its having arisen did not mean that the idea of marriage was exclusively directed towards Emily. For a while, it seems, Tennyson made serious, albeit covert, overtures for Rosa's hand and her rejection of him is recorded in one or two of the later poems to her, written in the course of the summer of 1836.

After a lovers' tiff involving both Rosa and Sophy Rawnsley Alfred had to make amends in separate poems. The one, 'To Rosa', begging forgiveness for having blamed her for an ill-defined transgression, and the other 'To thee with whom my best affections dwell', apologizing for a momentary harshness.

Whatever the occasion for the quarrel it was the beginning of the end. The following sonnet expresses the emotions of a suitor who has grown thoroughly disenchanted with the object of his quest:

> I lingered yet awhile to bend my way
> > To that far South, for which my spirits ache,
> For under rainy hills a jewel lay
> > And this dark land was precious for its sake,
> > A rosy-coloured jewel, fit to make
> An emperor's signet-ring, to save or slay
> > Whole peoples, such as some great King might take
> To clasp his mantle on a festal day:
> But yet a jewel only made to shine,
> > And icy-cold although 'tis rosy clear –
> > > Why did I linger? I myself condemn,

For ah! 'tis far too costly to be mine,
   And Nature never dropt a human tear
      In those chill dews whereof she froze the gem.
                    (SONNET — 'I LINGERED YET AWHILE TO BEND MY WAY')

Emily Sellwood's free display of emotion had shown Rosa up as being icy-cold. It was but a short step to the inevitable agonies of disintoxication. Rosa's every gesture, her every nuance, became a pain to be rid of. 'A speech conventional, so void of weight/That after it has buzzed about one's ear,/'Twere rich refreshment for a week to hear/The dentist babble or the barber prate.' It would be some time before he would again be able to contemplate Rosa as an object for affection capable of inspiring more generous lines.

A week before his brother Charles' wedding, Frederick wrote to his cousin Julia, finally admitting his feelings:

> Julia, it comes to this. I must know my fate. Dearest, sweetest girl, I have loved you since I was a boy. Since I saw you for the first time, now some twenty years ago, your image has never been absent from my mind.... I am aware that circumstances seemingly inconsistent with this declaration will quickly suggest themselves to you ...

The effort to persuade Julia of his passion was futile. In fact, she never married. After her father became friendly with Bulwer Lytton, who parted from his wife in 1836, it seems she did fall in love but, unable to indulge her affection for a married man, she left home to become a Roman Catholic nun.

Soon after this rejection Frederick returned to Italy, where he settled for the next twenty years, married an Italian, and enjoyed a lazy existence, developing a passion for music and, in due course, the friendship of the Brownings.

With Frederick gone, and Charles settling down to married life, Alfred was once more accepted by everyone at Somersby as head of the household. Earlier, Arthur Hallam had compared the atmosphere in the Rectory with Charlotte Smith's *The Old Manor House*, a novel about clandestine passion. Now, with half the family gone, all the vibrancy seemed to be leaking out of the atmosphere, but Tennyson found his childhood home a comfortable place to be. Reverend Rawnsley wished that Alfred was more interested in 'fame or profit', but added, 'a harmless and quiet life ... is what the ancient poets and philosophers say is after all the highest state of permanent enjoyment.'

Mary, Emily and Cecilia were taking poetry almost as seriously as Alfred, and had formed themselves, together with friends and correspondents, into a society known as the Husks. Like all clubs it had its own husk-speak: favourite pastimes were to 'shuckle' (to meet together to discuss poetry) or to 'sloth' (to sit in the shade at twilight reading a poem), and Alfred was permitted to trespass on much of their slothful shuckling that summer.

It was during the late summer and early autumn of 1836 that Tennyson's passion for Rosa Baring was finally played out and his affections were transferred exclusively to Emily Sellwood. Although no formal announcement was made, by early 1837 it was accepted by friends and family that they were engaged.

Alfred's summer wanderlust went unsatisfied this year, ostensibly because he could not find a walking companion, but probably equally as much because of his romantic troubles. He told Brookfield in the middle of June that he did not expect to get away from Somersby before the autumn and 'perhaps not then'. But he was in good health and apparently enjoying social functions. He ended this short letter with the words, 'I am in a great hurry just going to dine out.'

This was almost certainly on the occasion of a dinner at Horncastle. The special guests were Emily Sellwood's uncle, Sir John Franklin, a famous explorer, and his niece Catherine. So buoyant was Afred's mood this summer, it appears that three objects for flirtation were insufficient for him. Catherine's report of the dinner party makes it quite clear that she became, momentarily, the focus of adoration.

Sitting opposite her at the table Alfred put in his eye-glass and silently ogled her. In due course he returned to his neighbour and mumbled, 'Is she Hindoo?' After the meal, and on retiring to the drawing-room, Tennyson, having in his usual casual manner reclined himself across the seats of three chairs, immediately got up when Catherine began to play the piano. He perched himself extremely close in order to examine, he said, the sparkling jewels she was wearing. Looking intently at her face and her bosom he pronounced her an Eastern princess and named her Zobeide.

This interlude is a good example of how shy and quiet people can be capable of forward and formidable behaviour, and Tennyson was forever shocking people by his lack of observation of the normal social graces.

The dinner at Horncastle was notable for one more reason, since it produced a poem which is typical of the poet's output at this time. Another of the guests was a tall, slender, giraffe-like lady known as Mimosa by the Husks. Her real name was Mrs Neville, and she was one of the Massingberd clan.[26] She had married a young army officer and with two tiny children had gone with him to Australia. But soon after arriving he was arrested for forgery, and deported. She had followed on behind, and arrangements were now in hand for the family to emigrate to America. Alfred was struck by Mimosa Neville's air of nobility in the midst of all her troubles and wrote her the lines 'Woman of noble form and noble mind'.

> Woman of noble form and noble mind!
> Withersoever through the wilderness
> Thou bearest from the threshold of thy friends
> The sacred sorrows of as pure a heart
> As e'er beat time to Nature, take with thee
> Our warmest wishes, silent Guardians
> But true till Death . . .

This is quiet and tame verse – innocuous enough, and hardly Tennyson writing at the height of his powers. In addition to his wide range of style and subject-matter, Tennyson's poetry is characterized by two distinct gears. His ability to compose verse at low throttle was to become a valuable asset.

7   Wishful Thinking

> She is lovely by my side
> In the silence of my life –
> 'Tis a phantom of the mind,

('OH! THAT 'TWERE POSSIBLE')

W inter came early in the autumn of 1836 and Somersby was already deep in snow by the end of October. It was beginning to dawn on the Tennyson family that they were unlikely to spend a further winter in the Rectory. Young Mr Burton was to be married in the New Year and they would be expected to give up the house for him and his bride.

Alfred wrote to Milnes that 'it is not possible for me to come to you at present – family matters prevent me'. It seems he was contemplating following Frederick onto the Continent, for he holds out the hope of a visit to Milnes 'in December, *if I am still in the country*'. If this intention was ever taken seriously, it was dependent on Charles being able to exchange his living for one in the south of England, where Mrs Tennyson and her daughters intended moving. Such, anyway, were the family matters which kept Alfred in snowy Lincolnshire, or, as he put it, *'verrinum in patria'* – in the land of the boars.

Curiously, in the summer, Tennyson had broken his printed silence by offering, via Brookfield, the three year-old 'St Agnes' for publication. This was passed to Lady Emmeline Stuart-Wortley, who published it in the annual *Keepsake*, which came out in November.

Tennyson must have had a special motive for breaking his silence, and for doing so with this poem. Part of the explanation may lie with a retrospective review of his two earlier collections, written by J.S. Mill, and printed in the *London Review* the previous summer. This important essay attempted to qualify the attacks made on Tennyson firstly by 'Christopher North' in *Blackwoods* and then by J.W. Croker in the *Quarterly*. The result was exactly the kind of review which Tennyson had hoped his 1832 volume would attract – a response which treated him as a poet of the very highest quality, whose faults were not to be ridiculed but treated as the inevitable blemishes upon a developing talent.

Mill did not hold back on criticizing where criticism was due, but his censure of Tennyson's failures – amongst which he included 'The Mermaid' and 'The Merman', 'English Warsong' and 'National Song' – was mainly confined to footnotes. The core of the review contained flattering commentaries on 'Mariana' and 'The Lady of Shalott'. In quoting the second of these poems Mill missed out only the final verse, calling it a 'lame and impotent conclusion' and since Tennyson later removed this stanza it seems clear that he read Mill's review and took much of it to heart. It contained some extremely influential general advice:

... every great poet, every poet who has extensively or permanently influenced mankind, has been a great thinker; – has had a philosophie, though perhaps he did not call it by that name; – ... Where the poetic temperament exists in the greatest degree, while the systematic culture of the intellect has been neglected, we may expect to find, what we do find in the best poems of Shelley – vivid representations of states of passive and dreamy emotion, fitted to give extreme pleasure to persons of similar organisation to the poet, but not likely to be sympathiased in, because not understood, by any other persons; and scarcely conducing at all to the noblest end of poetry as an intellectual pursuit, that of acting upon the desires and characters of mankind through their emotions, to raise them towards the perfection of their nature.[27]

'St Agnes Eve' was hardly a direct response to this hefty homily, but its publication seemed well-timed to capitalize upon the fresh interest in his work that Mill's essay might be expected to provoke.

The appearance of the *Keepsake* coupled with Tennyson's November letter (which he had made jolly with recondite geological and meteorological references and other plays upon words, including Freezetown for Fryston – the name of Milnes' home) encouraged Milnes to ask Alfred for a contribution to another annual, this time the *Tribute*, edited by the Marquis of Northampton.

The response was a little delayed (in other words, typically Tennysonian) but forthright:

That you had promised the Marquis I would write for him something exceeding the average length of annual compositions – that you had promised him I would write at all – I took this for one of those elegant fictions with which you amuse your Aunts of evenings, before you get into the small hours, when dreams are true. Three summers back, provokt by the incivility of Editors, I swore an oath, that I would never again have to do with their vapid books – and I broke it in the sweet face of Heaven when I wrote for Lady (what's her name?) Wortley ...

To write for people with prefixes to their names is to milk he-goats: there is neither honour nor profit: up to this moment I have not even seen the Keepsake: not that I care to see it, but the want of civility decided me not to break mine oath again for man or woman. And how should such a modest man, as I, see my small name in collocation with the great ones of Southey, Wordsworth, R.M.M. etc. and not feel myself a barndoor fowl among peacocks?[28]

Milnes, having 'half-promised' Lord Northampton something by Tennyson replied in the panicky tones of a man desperate to avoid looking the fool.

Tennyson was taken aback by Milnes' uncharacteristic pomposity: 'I am the ass in Homer. I am blown. What has so jaundiced your good-natured eyes as to make them mistake harmless banter for *insulting irony*.' Milnes' latest letter made 'me lay down my pipe and stare at the fire for ten minutes till the stranger fluttered up the chimney'. He ended not only by promising Milnes a poem of his own, but one from Charles and Frederick too. At the time of writing (early January 1837) the end of Rectory life was in sight. 'I and all my people are going to leave this place very shortly.'

The 'very shortly', as was so often the case with the Tennysons, became subject to delays and postponements. The move from Somersby, usually given as the spring or early summer 1837, actually took place much later in the year.

But in the meantime Tennyson had his mollifying promise to Milnes to fulfil. In the *Keepsake* he had appeared alongside others of smaller talent and reputation. The *Tribute* was due to contain original work from Wordsworth and Southey, so Tennyson wanted his contribution to be able to stand beside these 'peacocks'.

He chose to extend a set of verses beginning 'Oh that 'twere possible', begun soon after Hallam's death, and eventually published in the *Tribute* as 'Stanzas'.

The poem became, in due course, the germ of *Maud*, but standing on its own it is a curious amalgam of pining for a lost friend and moping for a thwarted love. The 1837 revisions include a clear reference to Rosa Baring:

Alas for her that met me,
    That heard me softly call –
Came glimmering through the laurels
    At the quiet even-fall,

In the garden by the turrets
Of the old Manorial Hall.

But despite the use of the female pronoun throughout the earlier verses, and this reference to a recent romantic attachment, the main source for this painful poem was clearly the loss of Arthur Hallam. Much more vividly than in *In Memoriam* the poem describes the way in which Tennyson felt himself haunted by the memory of his friend. Wherever he goes he is pursued by Hallam's shadow: 'Through all that crowd, confused and loud,/ The shadow still the same;/And on my heavy eyelids/My anguish hangs like shame.' As Christopher Ricks memorably says, there are lines in Tennyson's verse 'which come so shapedly into mind on utterly non-literary occasions, occasions when one is thinking, not about shame and loss in literature, but about shame and loss'. Lines such as:

Then the broad light glares and beats,
  And the sunk eye flits and fleets,
And will not let me be.
  I loathe the squares and streets,
And the faces that one meets,
  Hearts with no love for me;
Always I long to creep
To some still cavern deep,
And to weep, and weep and weep
  My whole soul out to thee.

The revisions (mainly the addition of three or four new stanzas) took Tennyson until March. He posted it off to Milnes with a terse and testy note. 'I vow to Heaven I never will have to do with these books again. So never ask me.'

157

8   On the Move

Ah, clasp me in your arms, sister, ah, fold me to your breast!
Ah, let me weep my fill once more, and cry myself to rest!
To rest? to rest and wake no more were better rest for me,
Than to waken every morning to that face I loathe to see:

('THE FLIGHT')

Soon after sending off the poem he took Septimus to London and during his stay there spent a fruitless few hours waiting for FitzGerald in his rooms. He was anxious to meet Fitz again. So much so, that having left a note at the end of the second hour, he added a postscript after the third and fourth, before giving him up. It was already two years since their stay together at Mirehouse and they had seen far less of each other than was needed for a profound friendship.

The two Tennyson brothers returned to Lincolnshire realizing that it was likely to be the last time they would be making the northward journey home. It had been agreed that they would vacate the Rectory some time in the summer, to make way for the eldest son of the patron, W.B. Burton. Up until this time the Somersby and Enderby livings had been looked after by a Rev Robinson who, as a single man, had had no need of the Rectory.

A date was fixed for a sale of house contents.[29] But the actual move south could not have been made before September. At the end of June Alfred visited his brother Charles at Caistor. Charles's life had settled into the quiet, domestic rhythms reflected in his sonnets. Something of the flavour of the Caistor household is captured in a letter Charles wrote to his goddaughter, Susan Haddelsey, just a month or so before Alfred's visit. 'We have no carnivals at Caistor, but the dear old football was kicked at my window on Shrove Tuesday and made a great mark but did not come through it or I should have kept it and refused to return it.'[30]

Alfred, having decided to accompany his mother and older sisters on their move, gave Charles some of his land at Grasby on which to build, so that he could live much closer to his parish church. The walk from Caistor to Grasby was a particular strain on Louisa.

In July Mary Tennyson went to stay with the Fytches. Her engagement to John Heath had been broken off, in part, it was reported, because of Mary's growing seriousness, and her developing interest in spiritualism and mesmerism – interests which had been influenced by the recent contact with Frederick.

In addition to this emotional hurt she had recently been savaged by a large hound. Nevertheless, Mrs Tennyson d'Eyncourt, seeing her at the Fytches', found Mary 'looking very pretty'. She wrote to her son George on 29 July, 'We invited Mary here but she declined on account of the shortness of the remainder of her time in this country.... Charles is now going to build at Grasby and Septimus and Horatio are going to Demerara to make their fortune (they say) ...' The parenthesis proved as prophetic as it was bitchy. The younger Tennyson brothers did not make their fortune, in Demerara or anywhere else.

These reports show that during June and July the important members of the Tennyson family were still in Lincolnshire. There is further evidence that the family was still in the Wolds yet later in the year.

Aunt Bourne wrote to George d'Eyncourt in December: 'The Somersby people are all gone to live in Essex. Mary, Cecilia and Alfred, driven in Charles Turner's phaeton and accompanied by himself, called to take leave of us at Dalby, they came at ten o'clock at night, wanted supper etc. etc. and were proceeding that night to Rawnsley.'

Clearly the farewell tour was protracted. There is no mention of Mary during Alfred's June visit to Charles. Mary herself, as we have seen, was busy in July. The night-time call at Dalby – less than hospitably received   could not have taken place before August, and, writing of the event in December, Aunt Bourne gives the impression that it had occurred even more recently than that.

Amongst the final poems written in Somersby were 'The Voyage', 'The Flight' and 'A Farewell'. The first of these is lightweight, but of considerable interest. It presages the return of that heroic attitude which gave rise to 'Ulysses', and treats Life as 'the search after the ideal'. Though the crew of the vessel 'know the merry world is round/And we may sail for evermore' they follow on, whether they are blind or lame or sick.

> For one fair Vision ever fled
>   Down the vast waters day and night,

And still we followed where she led,
  In hope to gain upon her flight.
Her face was evermore unseen,
  And fixt upon the far sea-line;
But each man murmured, 'O my Queen,
  I follow till I make thee mine.'

And now we lost her, now she gleamed
  Like Fancy made of golden air,
Now nearer to the prow she seemed
  Like virtue firm, like Knowledge fair,
Now high on waves that idly burst
  Like Heavenly Hope she crowned the sea,
And now, the bloodless point reversed,
  She bore the blade of Liberty.

This states the archetypal Romantic quest which Tennyson has been insufficiently identified with. In 'The Flight', a powerful poem about a daughter deciding to escape rather than agree to an arranged marriage (evidently written in high chagrin at Rosa Baring's eventual marriage, but still suffused with the emotional remembrance of Arthur Hallam – Tennyson speaks through a female character so that he can express his own longing) we are told that 'Love is fire, and burns the feet would trample it to dust'. Somewhere out there will be a safe refuge where she can be re-united with her true love.

        and we shall light upon some lonely shore,
Some lodge within the waste sea-dunes, and hear the waters roar,
And see the ships out the West go dipping through the foam,
And sunshine on that sail at last which brings our Edwin home.

But despite the vigour and poetic ease of these statements they carry less personal commitment than the earlier poems. In his valedictory poem to the brook at Somersby – 'A Farewell' – he acknowledges that more is changing than the simple move of house to house. 'A thousand suns will stream on thee,/A thousand moons will quiver;/But not by thee my steps shall be,/For ever and for ever.' The time has come to move on to another landscape, but it is in a mood of timeless, world-weary resignation, rather than in any fighting, adventurous spirit.

Queen Victoria's accession to the throne occurred in June of

160

this year and Tennyson was moved to write her some hearty good wishes in the form of 'newspaper verse' which he sent off to Spedding with instructions that the poem, entitled 'The Queen of the Isles' should be 'put into the Times or some paper with a circulation'.

> So fill up your glasses and hold them on high,
> Were the health fathoms-deep I would drink it or die,
> And send out your voices and join in the cry
>> To the health of the Queen of the Isles.

Was Tennyson, the 'pre-eminent Victorian', waiting for just this moment? Can his career have been simply a gathering of resources in preparation for the accession of the Queen? Of course it would be absurd to claim that Tennyson suddenly turned from being tortured Romantic to assured Victorian.[*]

The writing of 'The Queen of the Isles' did, however, mark a new direction for Tennyson. It beckoned in a determined (though rather laboured) optimism and a willingness to be seen in print once again.

[*]The term 'Victorian' has been immensely misleading with reference to Tennyson. Prime Ministers can make their mark very much more quickly than sovereigns. It will be perfectly legitimate for future biographers to talk about the influence of Thatcherism on modern writers, despite the fact that it spanned a mere decade. The very length of the Victorian period and its gradual accretion of identifying characteristics make it impossible to be precisely descriptive – to say that such and such a writer was or was not typically Victorian because of this or that attribute. Thatcherism, no less than the Victorian era, was the expression of a collective consciousness which found leadership and direction in a single personality. So closely was it identified with that personality that it died as soon as Mrs Thatcher ceased to be Prime Minister. Queen Victoria, on the other hand, partly because she was a Queen and not a minister of state, did not have her finger so closely on the pulse. The collective consciousness found its expression in a number of very different personalities. And so diffuse became the identification that it is impossible to match the end of the Victorian era with the Queen's death. Many people with imprecise historical perspectives have a conception of the Victorian period which, on close analysis, is coloured by images and descriptions which stem from the Edwardian years. This is hardly surprising. There was much about those Edwardian years which was far more typically 'Victorian' than any milieu Tennyson found himself in before the age of seventy.

161

9   Boozy Bonhomie

Let there be thistles, there are grapes,
If old things, there are new,
Ten thousand broken lights and shapes,
Yet glimpses of the true.

('WILL WATERPROOF'S LYRICAL MONOLOGUE')

By the time the family arrived at their new home in Epping, all the soft fruit had been picked and eaten, but they were in time for the grapes. A long letter written by Cecilia, giving details of the move, is dated Saturday 21 or 27 (the hand is ambiguous) 1838 – but amended in another hand to 1837, and 'Feb' added. In June and July 1837 Saturdays fell on 24th, 31st, 22nd and 29th. Not until October does a Saturday fall on one of the two possible dates – 21st. An autumn move fits much more pleasingly. Cecilia's postscript invitation to come in the summer becomes more apt, as does, 'We have a very nice garden with a great deal of wall fruit, *all of which had been eaten before we came'*. She also says that she is going to London 'soon' to visit Frederick. This visit took place at the end of November. Finally, arriving at five in the morning at the end of October would mean travelling in the dark and thus make losing their way between Waltham Cross and Beech Hill more plausible.

The retinue arrived on a Saturday morning. At five they had changed to a chaise at Waltham Cross, with Beech Hill only three more miles away. But the sun had not yet risen and they got lost, going five or six miles out of their way. They stopped at the wrong house and roused two spinsters from their beds. These ladies advised them to ask at the Inn, but they went instead to the local sergeant, owner of the house, and, as it turned out, their next-door-neighbour.

Mrs Tennyson, together with servants and one or two of the younger children, had already moved in. Cecilia does not mention who accompanied her on arrival, other than her dog Ariel, but it was almost certainly Alfred and Mary, since the three had been travelling together in the north. Spinks, one of the servants, was supposed to have met them at Waltham Cross, but he was an unreliable sort, given to obfuscating tales of self-justification.

They all liked the house, which was large, set on a hill, and had a creeper-festooned verandah. But the contrast with Lincolnshire made it difficult for any of them to feel at home.

Alfred was subdued. Before leaving Somersby he had heard rumours of Rosa Baring's engagement to one Robert Shafto, a cousin of Rosa's stepfather and member of a wealthy family from Durham. It was a pairing which bore all the hallmarks of having been 'arranged'. He went for walks with his sisters in Epping Forest but otherwise did not socialize.

He did not accompany his four sisters (Mary, Matilda, Emily and Cecilia) when they went, in December, to London to meet Frederick. The four girls squeezed into a three-seater fly to make the journey to Waltham Cross. Mrs Tennyson burst out laughing at the squash. Even the postboy was on hand with a grin. But Alfred was conspicuously absent.

The four girls could have done with his brotherly guidance. Instead of dropping them at the Four Swans in Bishopsgate, where Frederick was due to meet them, their coachman let them down beside a dingy-looking meat-stall. After due persuasion he let them back into the coach and carried them on to the Swans. However, Mary mistakenly entered a drapery shop. Realizing her mistake, she went out. A kindly customer pursued her and showed the girls on to a second shop, which they were too embarrassed to explain was not their correct destination. After a suitable delay they walked back to the Inn. But there was no sign of Frederick so the sisters boarded a second coach in order to travel to their lodgings. While waiting for it to set off the first coachman walked past and drunkenly asked if they were all comfortable. Cecilia does not record the gleeful giggles which inevitably ensued upon this enquiry, but the letter describing this muddled incident does explain that she used her visit to London to consult a physician about her repeated headaches. He prescribed some medicine which he said she must take 'for years'.

Ill-health was much on the family's mind at the end of the year, for Arthur, who had been left in Lincolnshire, developed smallpox. Aunt Bourne sent him a consignment of Ribston Pippins and Golden Russets to speed a recovery.

It had been a ragged year for Alfred. He had fallen out of love; he had left his home; not a single poem that could be counted amongst his finest work had been written. Right at the end of it he received an invitation from Tennant to visit him in Herstmonceux, where he was curate to Hare. 'Come then next Tuesday (January 2) by an Eastbourne coach, which leaves Golden Cross, Charing Cross, early in the morning and will bring you here to dinner; you must get off at Horsebridge; if it is a fine day I will meet you, and sending on your luggage by some man, we will walk; but if raining I will send a gig for you. Take care and bring lots of new poems.'

There was little to bring and though compiling a log of Tennyson's movements produces no alternative activity for early 1838, the poet's end-of-year mood and the homesick spirit in which he wrote to Mrs Rawnsley at the end of January, combine to suggest that Tennant's invitation was declined. A pity. The little place, lying inland midway between Eastbourne and Bexhill, and looking, in one direction, across the Pevensey Levels, and in the other towards the high Weald, became the home of no less than three Apostles – Tennant, Sterling and Garden – all curates to Hare, and Tennyson's work was often read aloud in the Rectory.

It was also proving to be one of the coldest winters on record – a fact which increased the contrast between the suburban formality of Essex and the warmly remembered sincerity of country life in Lincolnshire.

> You hope our change of residence is for the better. The only advantage in it is that one gets up to London oftener. The people are sufficiently hospitable but it is not in a good old fashioned way so as to do one's feelings any good. Large set dinners with store of venison and champagne are good things of their kind, but one wants something more; and Mrs. Arabin seems to me the only person about here who speaks and acts as an honest and true nature dictates: all else is artificial, frozen, cold and lifeless.[31]

During the next four years Tennyson was to be resident in London as much as he was at High Beech. The poem 'Black Bull of Aldgate' talks of 'thirty times at least beneath thy doorway stepping/I've waited for this lousy coach that runs to Epping'. His mother resented this incessant toing and froing and eventually the family took permanent rooms in Mornington Crescent so that they would all have somewhere to stay when in town –

although it remained Alfred who made more use of them than any other member of the family.

The hearty good cheer of his public coronation poem carried over into several poems of cosy bonhomie written during this winter. He wrote 'Will Waterproof's Lyrical Monologue' at the Cock Tavern 'To which I most resort'. Certain of the lines presage future dissatisfaction:

> For I had hope, by something rare,
>   To prove myself a poet:
> But, while I plan and plan, my hair
>   Is gray before I know it.

But the general impression is one of boozy celebration of earth's rich storehouse:

> This earth is rich in man and maid;
>   With fair horizons bound:
> This whole wide earth of light and shade
>   Comes out a perfect round.

The city which had once so bemused and anaesthetized him with its crowds and lights and traffic, now became something of a substitute for the network of friends he had known in Lincolnshire – the Rawnsleys, the Sellwoods, Rashdall, the Barings. Like many 'solitary' people he needed company in order to feel most keenly his own individuality. Of course he met FitzGerald often. But he saw Thackeray equally frequently. In 1838 the novelist moved into his house in Coram Street, right opposite another of Tennyson's Cambridge friends, John Allen. Alfred spent long hours in both homes, seeming to enjoy the domestic atmosphere of a marital household and no doubt contemplating afresh marriage to Emily.

Thackeray was impressed as much by Tennyson's appearance – 'great big yellow face and growling voice ... manliness and simplicity of manner go a long way with me'– as much as by his conversation, although this too was striking. 'He seems to me to have the cachet of a great man. His conversation is often delightful I think, full of breadth, manliness and humour: he reads all sorts of things, swallows them and digests them like a great boa-constrictor as he is.'

Nearly everyone remarked on his manliness. Still clean-shaven, he had a strong jawline and prominent mouth. An oil portrait done at this time by Samuel Laurence, now hanging in the National Portrait Gallery, had to be retouched by Burne-Jones (under later instruction from Hallam Tennyson) to reduce the 'blubber-lipt' impression.

Something else always remarked upon was Tennyson's utter lack of any sense of social decorum. More than rustic simplicity, it was a form of superior insouciance actively indulged in. But now that he was getting out and about with his friends in London some of his habits had to be curbed. Neither he nor the friends were any longer undergraduates. On a visit to the Reform Club with Brookfield, he was persuaded to take his feet down from the table.

In the spring of 1838, homesick for Lincolnshire, and anxious to see more of Emily Sellwood, Alfred went north. He may have visited Grasby, although questions which Cecilia had to ask Susan Haddelsey about Charles suggest that he did not. A note he wrote to Emily at this time seems to indicate that a distance had intruded itself between them since the move:

> I saw from the high road through Hagworthingham the tops of the elms on the lawn at Somersby, beginning to kindle into green. I remember you sitting with me there on the iron garden chair one day when I had first come from London (and when Miss Bourn of Alford called). It was earlier in the year than now. The morning three years back seems fresh and pleasant; and you were in a silk pelisse, and I think I read some book with you.[32]

This is wistful stuff, with none of the ardent immediacy one would expect of a note from one lover to another. Notwithstanding the caveat that it survives only in transcript, (in Hallam Tennyson's *Memoir* Vol. I), and was probably severely edited, it does suggest that the impending break with Emily was set in motion by the move to Essex, which simply seemed to parcel her up with the rest of Lincolnshire, and glaze her over with a nostalgic haze.

On his way south he spent a week in Cambridge. (Why not an extra seven days in the neighbourhood of Horncastle?) Blakesley found him 'complaining of nervousness. How should he do otherwise, seeing that he smokes the strongest and most stinking tobacco out of a small blackened clay pipe on an average nine hours a day?'

Of the atmosphere at High Beech, Cecilia Tennyson is the best source. She corresponded regularly with the Haddelseys of Caistor, in a graphic, if somewhat naïve, epistolary style. The Tennysons had bought themselves a black pony, costing £9, which Alfred thought a good price. A spirited, inexhaustible beast, its one fault was that it drew to the left when cantering. When the girls went riding Alfred would accompany them alongside on foot.

The Miss Sellwood whom Cecilia mentions as having visited High Beech was evidently Anne and not Emily. In early April both Anne Sellwood and Mary Tennyson left England for Guernsey – Anne for the benefit of her health, Mary to accompany her. They departed together at 7 am, from High Beech.

Recently arrived back from Cambridge, Alfred was there to see them off, and on the night of their farewell party kept them up till 1 am, entertaining them with mimicry. 'He made us laugh so much you should have heard him – would have amused you so.'

Alfred carried these good spirits on into London, where FitzGerald found him 'very droll and very wayward' with 'much sitting up of nights till two and three in the morning with pipes in our mouths'.

10 The Aphorist's Guide to Seduction

> Like men, like manners: like breeds like, they say:
> Kind nature is the best: those manners next
> That fit us like a nature second-hand;
> Which are indeed the manners of the great.
>
> ('WALKING TO THE MAIL')

By the summer of 1838 there were still no new poems of any note to celebrate. He was continuing to polish up his old ones and coming closer to the time when he would again agree to publish. But he had lost the centre of his existence (the Rectory at Somersby), and needed a new one.

In October he went to Torquay, apparently to be alone, and there wrote 'Audley Court', one in a series of English idylls begun with 'The Gardener's Daughter' and closely based on the pastoral poems of Theocritus. The poem is remarkable for its controlled objectivity and for the absence of any trace of Tennysonian morbidity. In the song sequence he seems to be trying on new attitudes for size.

> 'Oh! who would fight and march and countermarch,
> Be shot for sixpence in a battle-field,
> And shovelled up into some bloody trench
> Where no one knows? but let me live my life.
> 'Oh! who would cast and balance at a desk,
> Perched like a crow upon a three-legged stool,
> Till all his juice is dried, and all his joints
> Are full of chalk? but let me live my life.
> 'Who'd serve the state? for if I carved my name
> Upon the cliffs that guard my native land,
> I might as well have traced it in the sands;
> The sea wastes all: but let me live my life.
> 'Oh! who would love? I wooed a woman once,
> But she was sharper than an eastern wind,
> And all my heart turned from her, as a thorn
> Turns from the sea; but let me live my life.'

That is the song of Francis Hale, the friend and farmer's son with whom the narrator of the poem picnics. The hale and hearty mood of the poem may not be entirely convincing because of the detached way in which the idyll is conveyed, but there seems no doubt that Tennyson was entering a phase of his life in which he was determined to shake off the shadow and the shame of Arthur Hallam.

During this period the relationship with Emily Sellwood was conducted by post. The fragments of correspondence which survive are aphoristic and mannered:

'A known landskip is to me an old friend.'

'Sculpture is particularly good for the mind ...'

'Through darkness and storm and weariness of mind and of body is there built a passage for His created ones to the gates of light.'

We have no way of knowing what was the original balance of such observations. And we have forgotten, or cast aside, the sense of flirtation which people of the nineteenth century undoubtedly felt when exchanging such saws. The mind and soul of an adored one were as legitimate targets for seduction as the body, and the letter became the primary method of entreaty.

In circumstances that were rapidly, and hauntingly, to parallel the courtship between Hallam and Emily Tennyson, Alfred was forced, at first by lack of funds, and then by family edict, to court Emily Sellwood from afar. And she, in turn, became increasingly invalid and withdrawn, exhibiting symptoms almost precisely the same as Emily Tennyson's.

The name itself was no coincidence. It is questionable whether Tennyson would have been so attracted to an Anne (he didn't fall for *Anne* Sellwood) or a Jane. He had loved a Rosa and a Sophy, but his involvement with those two had been altogether more straightforward. There was no simple physical attraction between him and Miss Sellwood. His feelings for her were adumbrated with the shadow cast by brotherly-sisterly love, with the idealism that inevitably develops in a protracted exchange of letters, and with the recognition of a strong emotional response. Emily was no coquette, nor was she good at recognizing that men tend to like some resistance to their initial overtures. The barriers eventually put up to delay their marriage were of the wrong kind – they did not enhance her desirability, they merely held up an inevitable chain of events.

Tennyson spent some of the final weeks of the year in London, lodging at 23 Norfolk Street, and contributed a sovereign (per annum) to the Leigh Hunt appeal.

More letters passed between Horncastle and Beech Hill during the first part of 1839. Love letters of the famous nearly always have the power to take us aback, whether by their profanity, their babytalk, or their sheer mundaneness. But there is something more alarming than any of these in the following:

> I send thee all the sweetest and tenderest wishes for thy happiness here and hereafter, and if my wishes could make thee happy thou shouldst leap all day long like a lamb new to the field and the world ... may thy sisters and thy Father and thy Father which is in Heaven love thee more and more until thou rest satisfied in their love ...[33]

What is it that induced Tennyson to write as if Emily were nine years old, or less, and he was sending off a letter for an adult to read aloud to her? The answer is probably that he was trying to appeal to a side of her nature which by now he realized he had to win over before she would finally accept him; perhaps he had also led himself to believe that she could not be long for this world.

11   Rest and Motion

O me, my pleasant rambles by the lake,

('EDWIN MORRIS')

The family first used their Mornington Crescent residence in the spring of 1839. At the time, Mimosa Neville was once again staying with them, her marriage having finally broken up in America. Back in England she had befriended a twenty-five year-old named Louisa Lanesborough, an unconventional Methodist with a passion for poetry.

The Tennysons had invited Mrs Neville to Beech Hill so that she could go to London and consult Dr Currie, for she was reported to have been left in poor health after her trials across the Atlantic. Miss Lanesborough accompanied her, quite beside herself with the prospect of being amongst the Tennysons – 'they who are talked and dreamed of, but scarcely realised, whose notes are read, whose minds are unfolded, whose strange wild thoughts are followed out by my soul, in its lone wanderings. To see them, be in the same house and unknown, quite unknown.'

Louisa had decided to go disguised as Mrs Neville's nurse. The reason for this subterfuge seems much more bound up with the relationship between Mimosa and Louisa than it does with any real necessity to keep up a pretence at Beech Hill. It was as a servant called Marion Langlais that Louisa arrived in Essex, the two of them having made the crossing from Guernsey to Southampton.

Only Mary and Cecilia were at home, the rest of the family

being in London, 'moving in' to Mornington Crescent. After a day or two at High Beech Mary took them both, on 24 March, to the Crescent, leaving Cecilia alone in the Essex house. She was too ill with her headaches to accompany them. On her own she wrote to Susan Haddelsey, 'Mrs Neville is now with us. She went with Mary to London yesterday to consult her physician for she is in a very weak state of health indeed almost – nay I think quite – as weak as Emily Sellwood. She is thought by some to be in a consumption...' This is a most telling comparison, for it emphasizes yet further the contrast involved in Tennyson's switching of romantic allegiance from Rosa Baring to Emily Sellwood.

Miss Lanesborough, still disguised as a nurse, was introduced to the 'dirty, beastly kitchen' at Mornington Crescent and to the routine of the servants. It was a routine which gives considerable insight into the tenor of daily life for the Tennysons at this time.

After preparing the kitchen there were Frederick and Alfred's rooms to arrange, followed by the drawing-room and then Mrs Tennyson's bedroom. Mrs Tennyson, Horatio and the girls took breakfast together, while Fred and Septimus had theirs brought to them. During the rest of the morning there was shopping to be done and extra chores for the landlady Mrs Moore, who had a broken arm. Luncheon was taken in the drawing-room, as was dinner, which was at 4 pm. This always consisted of meat and an apple pudding for Alfred. Frederick and Septimus, ever the recluses, took their dinner upstairs, at 6 pm.

After this the servants had to sit up with the family, catering for their wishes until the early hours of the morning.

Late one morning 'Marion' passed Alfred's door as he lay in bed smoking and reading. He called her in and asked her to fetch a book from the drawing-room. It was a German book, and Alfred was impressed by the girl's ability to identity its strange title. That evening when another servant had trouble uncorking a bottle, Alfred called for Marion, saying that she could do it – she could do everything, from reading German to waiting at table.

On 3 April the party left Camden for Beech Hill – Alfred, Mary, Mimosa and Louisa crowded into one carriage. The doctor had advised a trip to Italy and the two visitors stayed in Essex for three more weeks while arrangements for this journey were made. Alfred, still somewhat infatuated with 'Marion', doodled pictures for her of the grim shapes he could see in the dying flames of a midnight fire. He read poetry to her and even gave her one or two copies of a sonnet when she left on 26 April, accompanied by Frederick and Mary, her disguise still not discovered. (It was apparently not until the party reached their hotel in Como that 'Marion' revealed her true identity, by deliberately stooping to kiss Mimosa.)

On the evening of 7 July the whole of southern England suffered a dramatic thunderstorm, with Beech Hill being visited by a freak fireball:

> What a thunderstorm we had the other night! I wonder whether it was so bad at Horncastle. It lasted the whole night and part of the previous afternoon. Lewis Fytche, who was with us then, was looking out of my window about half-past eleven o'clock, and saw a large fireball come up the valley from Waltham till it seemed to come quite over the pond: it then according to his account grew on a sudden amazingly large. How large? I asked him: he said, 'Like a great balloon, and burst with an explosion like fifty batteries of cannon.' I was so sorry not to have seen it, for it was a thing to remember; but I had just gone to my mother's room: she was grovelling on the floor in an extremity of fear when the clap came; upon which she cried out, 'Oh! I will leave this house: the storms are very bad here,' ... Such a scene, almost ludicrous in its extremes.[34]

Ludicrous; but also an indication of the taut nerves which held sway in the household. Alfred, for all the emphasis that has been placed upon his nervous instability, portrays himself here as a tower of strength, sorry not to have seen the fireball, but distracted by the need to comfort his distraught mother. This version of events is partially corroborated by Cecilia, writing a little later in the month, and after Alfred had left for Wales:

> Have you had many thunderstorms with you? We had a frightful one here not very long ago and a fire ball at no very great distance from us. Mama as you may suppose was shockingly frightened. We stood looking at it for hours by an open window which by the bye I do not think it right to do but some how or other I could not help it. There was a sort of fascination about it.

'I require quiet and myself to myself more than any man when I write', Tennyson was to confide in Emily Sellwood at this time. His journey to Wales, apparently alone, was almost certainly in response to the need to isolate himself from his family as much as from his annual attack of wanderlust.

The place itself was a disappointment – Aberystwyth a 'Cambrian Brighton' and only Barmouth, with its echoes of Mablethorpe, evoking a lively response. He wrote 'Edwin Morris' and 'The Golden Year' at Llanberis Lakes and continued his spate of aphoristic letters to Emily.

'Bitterness of any sort becomes not the sons of Adam.'

'How often it happens the things we count on least serve us best.'

'The Light of this world is too full of refractions for men ever to see one another in their true position.'

Nothing in Tennyson's earlier manner prepares us for this doggedness. But the need to woo Emily with such pithy canapés of philosophy and theology had a deepening effect.

In October, responding to a letter from Emily in which she quibbled with his latest injunction ('Annihilate in yourself these two dreams of Space and Time') Tennyson was moved to elaborate a personal, ontological viewpoint. It is a most revealing letter, for it delineates, at the age of thirty, the basic moral outlook which he would maintain till the end of his life, and it is a mark of the subtle, catalytic influence which a distant and imagined demeanour had the power to wield.

I chiefly meant by what I said to thee that where there is a mighty future before thee, thou should'st make it present by the hope that conquers all things. 'Why has God created souls knowing they would suffer' a question unanswerable. Man is greater than all animals because he is capable of moral good and evil – though perhaps dogs and elephants and some of the higher mammalia have a little of this capability. God perhaps might have made me a beast: but he thought good to give me power, to set good and evil before me that I might shape my own path. The happiness resulting from power well exercised must in the end far exceed the mere physical happiness of breathing, eating, and sleeping like an ox. Can we say that God prefers higher happiness in some to a lower happiness in all? It is a hard thing that if I sin and fail I should be sacrificed to the bliss of the Saints. Yet what reasonable creature, if he could have been askt beforehand would not have said 'Give me the metaphysical power' let me be the lord of my decisions: leave physical quietude and dull pleasure to lesser lives? All souls methinks would have answered thus and so had men suffered by their own choice, as now by the necessity of being born what they are, but there is no answer to the question except in a great hope of universal good. And even then one might ask why has God made one to suffer more than another, why is it not meted equally to all. Let us be silent for we know nothing of these things and we trust there is no one who knows all. God cannot be cruel. If he were, the heart could only find relief in the wildest blasphemies, which would cease to be blasphemies. God must be allpowerful else the soul would never deem him worthy of her highest worship. Let us leave it therefore to God, as to the wisest.[35]

Emily was also corresponding with the other Emily, Alfred's sister. She was jealous of their brother-sister relationship and suspected that Emily was to join Alfred in Wales. The subtext to all the correspondence to and from the Sellwoods at this time was the fact that Charles had once again become addicted to opium and that Emily's sister Louisa, following a nervous collapse, had had to separate from him, on doctor's orders. Emily Sellwood already feared that Alfred's move to the south, his apparent happiness within his own family, his holidays in Torquay and Wales (he could hardly have gone further away from Lincolnshire in each case, without actually leaving the country) were dragging him away from her.

The events in Grasby naturally coloured Mr Sellwood's attitudes towards any prospective marriage between Emily and Alfred. He had had one daughter harried and made miserable by a Tennyson, and was not keen for it to happen twice. Of course, there was gossip. And by implication Alfred became an opium addict too, with not even the solidity of a parish living to recommend him. Despite J.S. Mill's review and the high estimation in which Tennyson's poetry was held by a small coterie, to the public at large, and to the non-literary world, he was still something of a shiftless wastrel.

By the end of 1839 a wedding seemed further off than it had three years earlier. Publication, on the other hand, was once again a live issue. Dining with FitzGerald in November (sole, two boiled birds, apple tart, cheese) Alfred had pressure put on him to bring out a new volume. He came on as 'too lazy and wayward to put his hand to the business' but he did leave a large butcher's account book in FitzGerald's rooms. It was this notebook which contained, in addition to other poems of the period, numerous early drafts of *In Memoriam*.

Of the more recent poems 'Locksley Hall', 'Edwin Morris' and 'The Golden Year' were the best. The first of these had been begun eighteen months earlier, during the aftermath of the Rosa Baring affair, and is shot through with a wretched but temporary misogyny. It was the first time that Tennyson had used the 'voice' that would find best expression in the poem later most identified with the Tennysonian manner – *Maud*. Here were early tasters of that warped intensity: 'I myself must mix with action, lest I wither by despair.' Or 'Better fifty years of Europe than a cycle of Cathay.' As with several of his dramatic monologues Tennyson always insisted that the circumstances of the piece were entirely imaginary but it is impossible not to see biographical links in the poem – particularly Rosa Baring's 'arranged' marriage and the family feud between the Manor at Bayons and Somersby. The feelings expressed in the poem are complicated by continual self-questioning and denial. 'Comfort? comfort scorned of devils!' 'Can I relive in sadness?' 'Fool, again the dream, the fancy!' This last rap over the knuckles coming at the end of a reverie of purely material and animal fulfilment:

I will take some savage woman, she shall rear my dusky race.

Iron-joined, supple-sinewed, they shall dive, and they shall run,
Catch the wild goat by the hair, and hurl their lances in the sun;

Whistle back the parrot's call, and leap the rainbows of the brooks,
Not with blinded eyesight poring over miserable books—

Such might be fanciful folly, but at the heart of the poem there is a real sense of self-chastisement for the emotional energies he has wasted on a fruitless love affair. 'Weakness to be wroth with weakness! woman's pleasure, woman's pain –/nature made them blinder motions bounded in a shallower brain.' The confusion and contradictions in the poem, the presentation of confusion and contradiction in the voice of the speaker, made (and make) this an utterly 'modern' poem.

In 'The Golden Year'[36], another Theocritus-style idyll, Tennyson speaks with much greater equanimity.

> We sleep and wake and sleep, but all things move;
> The Sun flies forward to his brother Sun;
> The dark Earth follows wheeled in her ellipse;
> And human things returning on themselves
> Move onward, leading up the golden year.

And in a passage not included in the published version of the poem, but one which survives in manuscript, Tennyson gave expression to a deeply-felt belief in the continuing struggle. This is not a Belief in Progress, but in the moral imperative of not being content with one's current condition. The Romantic quest (for Beauty, Truth or Love) is gradually being transformed into a moral crusade.

> Motion: why motion? were it not as well
> To fix a point, to rest? again, it seems
> Most adverse to the nature of a man
> To rest if there be any more to gain.
> And there is all but what he is: no rest:
> Why then, to be resolved into the all.
> That will not do, being to lose myself.

Hence his preference for half a decade of European struggle over a cycle of Eastern resignation. 'Not in vain the distance beacons. Forward, forward let us range/Let the great world spin forever down the ringing grooves of change.' ('Locksley Hall')

'Edwin Morris' is a further variation on the theme of Rosa Baring. Much of the poem is built on early drafts of 'The Gardener's Daughter'. The climactic episode, when the speaker is beaten out of his embrace with Letty Hill by a host of Trustees, Aunts and Uncles, supported by a pack of pugs and poodles, went through several revisions before achieving a perfect pitch of humour and pathos. The ending of the poem suggests that the period of disintoxication was over.

> I have pardoned little Letty; not indeed,
> It may be, for her own dear sake but this,
> She seems a part of those fresh days to me;
> For in the dust and drouth of London life
> She moves among my visions of the lake,

While the prime swallow dips his wing, or then
While the gold-lily blows, and overhead
The light cloud smoulders on the summer crag.

Needless to say, this newly magnanimous position was contingent upon cycles in his hypochondria.

13   Knocking on Fortune's Door

And I must work through months of toil,
And years of cultivation
Upon my proper patch of soil
To grow my own plantation

('AMPHION')

Early in 1840 Alfred again turned up in FitzGerald's rooms. But this time he was in no state to contemplate publication, or have the thought pushed upon him. 'When I got back to my lodgings', FitzGerald reported in his correspondence, 'I found A. Tennyson installed in them: he has been here ever since in a very uneasy state: being really ill, in a nervous way: what with an hereditary tenderness of nerve, and having spoiled what strength he had by incessant smoking &c.'

Several factors combined to make him tetchy: his relationship with Emily Sellwood, about which he grew more and more equivocal; the condition of his brother Charles, who had stayed over Christmas at Beech Hill, before accompanying Mrs Tennyson to Cheltenham; the impending move out of Essex, to a small house in Tunbridge Wells, a town recommended by Mrs Tennyson's physician; and not least, the continuing lack of poetic inspiration.

The move to Tunbridge Wells compounded Tennyson's sense of misery. The new house was so small – 'a mere mouse-trap' –

he had to contemplate selling some of his books. The move was unpopular with other members of the household, particularly the servants, several of whom broke down in tears on the day of the move, a Monday.

Settling in to the new house and new place did not pacify Tennyson. Tunbridge Wells became his 'abomination', a place where his family was 'half killed by the tenuity of the atmosphere and the presence of steel more or less in earth, air and water'.

The mood was not universal, and other members of his family, like FitzGerald, were inclined to ascribe Alfred's disgruntlement to wilfulness and excessive smoking. 'The country is beautiful and it is a pity he should not see it', one of his sisters wrote. 'So infinitely better than smoking so much.'

Soon after the move he travelled into Lincolnshire and stayed at Mablethrope to see the spring tides. He must surely have visited Emily although there is no evidence that he spent any sustained period at Horncastle – on the contrary, there is every indication that he was not really welcome.

He found himself less able than in the past to 'commune *alone* with Nature', and spent much of his time indoors, at Mr Wildman's lodging house, reading anecdotes of Methodist ministers.

At thirty, Tennyson had, in the world's terms, made little progress since leaving Cambridge. His relationship with Emily had run into difficulty. The lack of improvement in his financial status brought the prospect of a wedding no nearer. Tennyson's failure to find work, his unkempt appearance, his melancholy and his lack of social inhibition must, to many people, in particular his prospective father-in-law, have hinted at the use of substances more potent than mere tobacco. The charge of opium addiction – dismissed as a scurrilous canard by Tennyson's previous biographers – cannot be so easily confined. Certainly the crones of Horncastle would not have been slow to draw conclusive parallels.

It would be extraordinary if Tennyson never used opium and there is good reason to suppose that, at certain periods of his life, he did resort to it. The sudden decline in his health which set in during 1840, just when he had seemed to be at his most hale and hearty, became another contributory factor in his difficulties with Emily. His illness followed close upon Charles Turner's stay at Beech Hill. There must have been conversations between the two brothers regarding opium's effects and it could very well be that the sudden deterioration and loss of vigour noticed by FitzGerald in February were attributable to some subsequent experimentation. It is, after all, just when we are feeling in perfect health that we become most vulnerable to those charms and temptations which, in sickly moments, are easy to resist or denounce.

His failure to keep up the creative momentum which had followed Hallam's death became connected in Tennyson's mind with his courtship of Emily. It might be time to think independently again.

On his way out of Lincolnshire he stopped a night in Leicester and then went on to Warwick, travelling at the front of the train in an open third-class carriage, and taking child-like delight in 'the curious lessons in perspective' derived from watching the two rails. FitzGerald happened to be in Warwick too. Alfred spotted his friend on the pavement as he drove past in a coach and immediately asked the driver to stop. Fitz got in and they spent an evening together at the George.

The two spent several days sight-seeing. Kenilworth was a disappointment because the ruins were smaller and less august than Tennyson had expected. At Warwick Castle he admired the atmosphere of feudalism and enjoyed the climb up Guy's tower, but best of all were two 'wonderful pictures', one by Rembrandt the other by Titian. (The castle in fact owned no such paintings – whether the mistake was Tennyson's, FitzGerald's, or a mischievous guide's, it is impossible to say.) Then they went to Stratford and found Shakespeare's monument, a bust by Gerald Johnson, whitewashed over. Alfred regretted this, saying that a physiognomist like himself would have been gratified to have been shown the probable colour of Shakespeare's hair and eyes. Going into the room of Shakespeare's birth Tennyson was seized, not for the first or last time, with the desire to add his name to those of other tourists on the walls. Though he was embarrassed afterwards he was not too ashamed to tell Emily, who received, in two instalments, quite detailed accounts of this mini-tour with Fitz.

In writing to her in such a lively way Tennyson was repeating the same tendency in the correspondence between Hallam and his own sister. But in Tennyson's case he seems to have been more ready to accept the implications. Close upon these reports came the letter which effectively suspended their engagement:

... I fly thee for my good, perhaps for thine, at any rate for thine if mine is thine. If thou knewest why I fly thee there is nothing thou wouldst more wish for than that I should fly thee. Sayest thou 'are we to meet no more?' I answer I know not the word nor will know it. I neither know it nor believe it. The immortality of man disdains and rejects it. The immortality of man to which the cycles and eons are as hours and as days . . .[37]

The vagueness of this letter – simply a masculine tactic of keeping all options open – cannot conceal its message. The love between himself and Emily was not for this world but for the next. The letter cost him much anguish, and was written in the company of madmen.

Septimus had stayed behind in High Beech after the family's move to Tunbridge Wells and had voluntarily put himself under the care of a Dr Allen in an asylum at Fair Mead. Allen was a friend of the Tennyson's High Beech neighbour and landlord, Mr Arabin, and had been present at several of the evening gatherings during the past year or so.

It was ostensibly to visit his younger brother that Alfred went to Fair Mead at the end of July 1840. He felt an immediate affinity with the resident patients, finding them 'the most agreeable and most reasonable persons' he had met with. He struck up a special relationship with the Doctor, and ended up staying a full fortnight. After he had left, Allen contacted him in London, saying, 'I have been very sad since we parted, and I can hardly tell you why, unless it were because you were so out of spirits'.

Tennyson reappeared in London, telling his friends he was going to leave the country. He 'is going today or tomorrow to Florence, or Killarney, or to Madeira, or to some place where some ship is going – he does not know where', wrote Spedding.

He was desperate for escape. In one sense he had intended his 'fleeing' letter to Emily to be taken simply literally – I must go away. She herself must have read it and re-read it to try and estimate its real meaning, and there was no clear break between them. Alfred's letters continued through the autumn, returning to their impersonal, aphoristic style, and claiming a continuing love for Emily – but a love that required no physical proximity. 'How hast thou come to me. Thou didst make thyself wings of love and faith and hast flown over the interval betwixt thee and me and hast settled in my bosom. But how thou should'st have found thyself there, without those wings, I know not.'

This was teasing cruelty for a young woman isolated in her father's house, and it is hardly surprising that Mr Sellwood quickly moved to put a stop to further correspondence. Equally unsurprising, for all his talk of flying off to the four corners of the globe, was the fact that Tennyson remained in England, spending more time in London than with his family at Tunbridge Wells. Allen regularly travelled into town to meet his new companion and by the late autumn Alfred was completely under the practical Doctor's spell.

A prime cause of the poet's anguish was his failure to make any practical impression on life – an anguish both specific (personal) and general (philosophical). Here was a man running his own business (the asylum) and doing good by helping his patients. There is no doubt that Tennyson, at this period, had fallen a little out of love with poetry, which neither did good, nor made good.

The Doctor's energy, and business creativity were immensely appealing and, in turn, Tennyson's rapt enthusiasm gave Allen the confidence to share an entrepreneurial dream – a dream which rapidly turned into monomania.

13   Stocks and Shares

Sit thee down, and have no shame,
Cheek by jowl, and knee by knee:
What care I for any name?
What for order or decree?

('THE VISION OF SIN')

Matthew Allen was in his late fifties in 1840. After working as an apothecary at the lunatic asylum in York, where he was appalled by the barbaric use of a machine known as the Tranquillizer (a quickly revolving chair which caused patients to vomit, empty their bladders and bowels, and then fall unconscious, all in the cause of re-establishing proper concentrations

181

of blood and other bodily fluids), Allen obtained a licence for his own establishment at High Beech in the Epping Forest. Here he followed a mild system of 'non-restrictive' methods, in which some categories of patient were free to discharge and re-admit themselves as they felt necessary. Coincidentally one of the patients residing at High Beech in 1840 was the poet John Clare. But Allen spread his patients amongst three separate buildings – in addition to Fair Mead (where Septimus and Alfred stayed) there were Springfield and Leopard's Hill – so it is by no means certain that the two men met.[38]

Tennyson's delight in the company of Allen's deranged residents is noteworthy. Both too much and too little can be made of it, however. Firstly, it is unlikely that he fraternized with any but the mildest of the patients. He always had a compulsive interest in the condition of madness, which is easy to portray as morbid, but which had its objective, clinical aspect. Allen was just the first in a series of psychologists or doctors with a special interest in that branch of medicine whom he befriended, though it must be admitted that Tennyson's interest in mental illness was never entirely detached. Belief in the inherited 'black blood' of the family, and in the extra-sensitive nerves which people of poetic temperament were, by common consent, expected to possess, determined a special degree of involvement. Tennyson naturally gravitated towards those of a despondent nature, and at Fair Mead he found despondency in large measure. The mood was catching. According to Allen, Alfred was very 'out of spirits' during his stay.

Three years previously, in an 'Essay on the Classification of the Insane', Allen had expounded a revealing attitude towards marriage. In his opinion it was likely to exacerbate instability in those of nervous disposition. He likened the complications of marriage to 'demons' plaguing 'man's health and peace' – with the potential to cause 'the most terrible forms of insanity'. If these were views which the Doctor elaborated on in discussions with Alfred and Septimus, Tennyson's letter to Emily Sellwood telling her that he must fly her for his own good, ('perhaps for thine, at any rate for thine if mine is thine'), takes on a rather more specific meaning.[39]

It was on an altogether unexpected basis that the friendship between Allen and Tennyson really evolved. The doctor had Micawber-like plans for a business venture and took Tennyson swiftly into his confidence. On 23 November Alfred passed over

£900, and was given a handwritten note of security in case of Allen's death.

The money was intended to fund a scheme of mass-produced wood-carvings for interior decoration. Allen dubbed it 'Pyroglyphs' or (more prosaically) The Patent Method of Carving in Solid Wood. It was, on the face of it, a fairly hard-nosed attempt to put the new power of the industrial age to artistic effect. The carvings were to be created by steam-driven machines.

Tennyson may have handed over his money too quickly and too eagerly, but he was not entirely unbusinesslike. Before November was out he had increased his initial payment to £1000, agreed to raise a further £2000 from his grandfather's bequest, and in return received five per cent interest, plus the mortgage on Fair Mead. He also expected to become rich. The fantastic dream of quickly becoming a wealthy businessman, and shaming the Barings into regretting their rejection of him, helped to muddy his judgement.

If Allen's scheme were to succeed, the mechanical process was all-important. Public interest was not a problem and churches, particularly, put in a flood of opening orders for high altar furniture and other ornamentation. So good were the prospects that Tennyson's sisters became desperate to buy into the scheme, but their uncle, Charles d'Eyncourt, was highly suspicious of the venture and prevaricated. The sisters grew vituperative:

> We have been very mild and patient with you hitherto although we have been told by those who understand the matter, that we are *shamefully treated* ... we are sadly afraid that the delay is on purpose, you do not deal openly with us and as you would that we should do to you under the same circumstances. Is the thing not simple enough! We merely want you to give up the deeds![40]

Allen was continually asking for more investment, whilst at the same time assuring all initial investors that success was guaranteed. Upbeat persuasion – the stock-in-trade of would-be speculators – came tripping off Allen's pen during the next few months:

> The business is progressing in progressive proportion. We shall have an immense business. All is hope, fear is gone and

I feel happy. We are all safe ... Orders are flowing in from all the great ones, Never was anything more promising. All things are a lie and all things are false if this fails. The World and human nature might be changed, but it is not so will not be so.[41]

An indication of the sort of profit that those handing over funds expected to receive can be gleaned from the figures given to Frederick Tennyson, when Allen attempted to squeeze yet further cash from the Tennyson family. An initial investment of £3000 would be worth £10,000 within the year and in five years would be worth that in annual premiums.

This being the general prognosis, and such the trust-making charisma of the man, it is easy to see how Alfred and his family were led to believe that their futures were made.

14   Alfred's Disturbing Hair

> ... the narrow brain, the stony heart
> The staring eye glazed o'er with sapless days,
> The long mechanic pacings to and fro,
> The set gray life, and apathetic end.
>
> ('LOVE AND DUTY')

Tennyson was initially buoyed up by his business involvement and took an extended holiday in Mablethorpe early in 1841. While there, he received a communication from the American editor and transcendentalist Charles Wheeler, informing him that Little and Brown intended publishing a Tennyson volume.[42] Alfred replied:

I am conscious of many things so exceedingly crude in those two volumes that it would certainly be productive of no slight annoyance to me, to see them republished as they stand at present, either here or in America. But I will tell you what I will do, for when I was wavering before, your letter has decided me. I have corrected copies of most that was worth correction in those two volumes and I will in the course of a few months republish these in England with several new poems and transmit copies to Little and Brown and also to yourself (if you will acept one) and you can then of course do as you choose with them.[43]

He was pestered from other directions regarding his new volume and wrote in irritation to FitzGerald: 'You bore me about my book: so does a letter just received from America, threatening, though in the civilest terms, that if I will not publish in England they will do it for me in that land of freemen – Damn! – I *may* curse knowing what they will bring forth, but I don't care.'

There was much frantic correspondence between Tennyson and Dr Allen during his stay, so that Alfred had to spend a considerable portion of his time in his room, waiting for the muffin-man. (The nearest postal town to Mablethorpe was Alford, and all mail was delivered and collected by the muffin-man.)

Confusion was caused by delayed or diverted letters and by the extreme illegibility of Allen's hand. In the end Alfred engaged a fisherman to drive him over to Alford so that he could see three important letters into the post in person. Then, receiving a fresh delivery, he had to write three more letters contradicting the first. After this, scared that the whole thing was turning into a muddle out of all proportion, he removed all six letters from the mailbox, much to the annoyance of the procedurally correct attendant, and then went and got drunk on gin with the fisherman, who waxed philosophical about God and the Devil before falling flat on the floor like a corpse.

From Mablethorpe Tennyson made another visit to Torquay – on the threshold of becoming a fashionable resort – and while there he wrote to Rawnsley, giving some details of his new business interest. The shares were selling for £20 a piece, but there had already been mechanical failure – 'They sent [a press] from Brummagen (wretched thing! split as soon as put into action ...)' – and not enough decisiveness – 'There has been too much talkee talkee as the niggers say and so little settled.'

By the end of March he was back in London – rather wild-haired and distracted. Brookfield bumped into him at the National Gallery at noon on 29 March – 'we coalesced and

185

evaporated' – and when Caroline Elton met him in April she found him 'very far from handsome and his hair quite disturbed me'. FitzGerald saw him at the same time 'with a little bit of dirty pipe in his mouth and a particularly dirty vellum book of Mss. on the sofa'. FitzGerald was highly sceptical of Dr Allen, as were most of Tennyson's friends, and warned Alfred and Frederick: 'There is a providence over fools and drunkards but not over poets I fear.'

If he was not staying with FitzGerald in Charlotte Street Tennyson was with Lushington and Venables at Mitre Court. It was one of his most restless years, and the place he resided at the least was the hated house in Tunbridge Wells.

Attending a breakfast given by Milnes at this time Tennyson had his first meeting with Browning, although there was no instant intimacy. Crabbe Robinson, also at the breakfast, described Alfred as a 'bandit of genius'.

He disappeared from London in May without telling his friends where he was going – he had actually taken himself off to Rotterdam and Amsterdam, returning by way of Paris – and did not return until the middle of August. These three private months abroad were probably much taken up with completing preparation for his 1842 volume, which was by now firmly planned with Moxon. Interludes such as this prompt speculation about his sexual life.

Those who accede to the view that Tennyson lacked sexual drive lay great store by the poet's own declaration that he had not so much as kissed a woman (in love)[44] before marrying Emily, and by his prudish attitude towards the pornographic interests of his friend Milnes. Even if the first assertion were true, neither one leads to the conclusion that Tennyson was a sexless being. Away from home, in continental cities such as Amsterdam and Paris, Tennyson may well have discovered more about his own physical appetites then he ever admitted to his friends. It is not a question worth fretting over. Whatever the extent or absence of the poet's amorous experience at this time it was certainly neither a preoccupation nor a vice.

Tennyson did make more American friends on the Continent, and wrote to thank Charles Wheeler for the gift of Emerson's essays. 'He has great thoughts and imaginations, but he sometimes misleads himself by his own faculty of talking brilliantly.'

In September Emily Tennyson announced her engagement to Richard Jesse. There was great consternation in the Hallam family, most of whom had come to expect that Emily would keep Arthur Hallam's memory sacrosanct. Jane Elton, cousin to the Hallams, wrote:

> Is it not extraordinary – painful – unbelievable, this intended marriage? Poor Julia felt it dreadfully at first – I remember her saying Emily would never *dream* of marrying – that she was a kind of *Nun* now, and that nothing was more *impossible* than her marrying – she had felt Arthur's death so much – it had even injured her health; and can you conceive anyone whom he had loved, putting up with another? I feel so distressed about this, really it quite *hurts* me, I had such a romantic admiration for her, looked at her with such pity, and now all my feeling about her is boulversed – and Alfred Tennyson falls headlong into the abyss with her ...[45]

There was speculation that Emily's £300 annual allowance from the Hallams would be cut off, but in the end Mr Hallam took the generous view and announced that it would continue.

It was not a long engagement. They were married on 24 January 1842, with Alfred acting as best man. But before this event there was a burst of domestic activity at the end of the old year. Much centred around the Allen speculation and Charles d'Eyncourt's continuing refusal to release funds. His angry letter to Mrs Tennyson is redolent of the Old Man's very worst huffs. He was replying to the supplications of Alfred's four sisters: 'I am sorry to say they have addressed letters to me so unpleasant and I fear I must add, offensive, that I cannot reply to them but must leave all future business to be settled without communication between them and me.' And later he repeats, 'I cannot permit anyone to write offensive letters to me.'

More interesting than the haughty petulance of this letter is the evidence it gives of a continuing contact between the Tennysons and the Sellwoods. Mr Sellwood had evidently offered to have the Tennyson deeds transferred to him – hardly the behaviour of a man supposed, according to some accounts, to have ostracized the family in exasperation over Alfred's treatment of Emily.

The uncle's letter was addressed to Boxley Hall, Maidstone, the Tennysons having moved out of their cramped Tunbridge Wells house at the end of the summer. The move brought them into close proximity to Park House, country home of the

Lushingtons. Edmund Lushington had gone to school at Charterhouse with Thackeray and Venables. He was at Trinity with Tennyson and became one of the Apostles. In 1838 he had been appointed Professor of Greek at Glasgow, a position he was to hold for the next forty years. He had two brothers who were also of importance in Tennyson's life. Henry, a year younger than Edmund, worked in the Temple from 1834 and was called to the Bar in 1840. A much younger brother, Franklin, a mere teenager in 1841, eventually became godfather to one of Tennyson's children.

Tennyson loved the sense of space at Park House and quickly fashioned himself a short-cut through from Boxley Hall. In later years he would recall a quintessential evening, still and starlit, sitting out on the lawn with the Lushington brothers and other friends, with candles burning on the tea-table, their steady flame disturbed only by the rush of a moth or cockchafer.[46]

What a mockery to that memory is the scene at Park House today. Not much besides the lawn has survived. Only the coach-house remains, converted into a modern family dwelling. Close by, a motorway roars throughout the day and the high-speed rail link from the Channel Tunnel seems set to be the next intruder. It is possible that Tennyson, looking down on this abuse, will not be too upset. The Lushingtons proved to be an ill-starred family, and Boxley became gradually associated with much sadness.

15   High Dudgeon

                              then my
        Eyes pursued him down the street, and far away,
           Among the honest shoulders of the crowd,
            Read rascal in the motions of his back,
           And scoundrel in the supple-sliding knee.

                                            ('SEA DREAMS')

Tennyson's separation from Emily Sellwood and the marriage of his sister, freed him to concentrate, poetically, on

the loss of Hallam, and the sections of *In Memoriam* grew apace during this autumn. It is difficult to imagine, had Tennyson married Emily in 1840, rather than ten years later, his long elegy ever having been written.

Edmund Lushington, on vacation from the north, came across from Park House to spend Christmas with the Tennysons at Boxley. 'The number of memorial poems had rapidly increased since I had seen the poet, his book containing many that were new to me.' One night he was sitting up late in the poet's bedroom when Alfred began to recite Section VI, making a profound impression with the deep melodious thunder of his voice.

> One writes, that 'Other friends remain,'
>   That 'Loss is common to the race' –
>   And common is the commonplace,
> And vacant chaff well meant from grain.
>
> That loss is common would not make
>   My own less bitter, rather more:
>   Too common! Never morning wore
> To evening, but some heart did break.

But as soon as Christmas was over Tennyson had to put the memorial poems aside and concentrate on settling the publication of a new volume with Moxon. By the middle of February he was still less than happy with the book and had not yet taken it to Moxon. 'However I intend to get it out shortly, but I cannot say I have been what you professors call "working" at it, that indeed is not my way. I take my pipe and the muse descends in a fume . . .'[47]

When he turned up in FitzGerald's rooms on 2 March he was immediately taken in hand, carried off 'with violence' to Moxon, and forced to arrange production of the proofs. This done, Tennyson moved out and went to stay with Spedding.

Ten days later he received the proofs and promptly suffered a crisis of confidence. The volume was not yet as perfect as he would like. He wished he had not been persuaded to publish. FitzGerald buoyed him up again, telling him that readers of poetry would not have seen the volume's like since the time of Keats. Tennyson obediently set to the correction of the proofs, and as he did so stripped the edges from pages of the long thin ledger-book filled with the original transcripts and used them as pipelights before throwing them in the fire.

Once the corrected proofs were with the printer FitzGerald tried his best to entertain his exhausted friend. On 26 March the two set off for Dulwich, but not in any great hope of excitement. 'When we get there of course the gallery will be shut because of Easter. Well, then we shall go in a bad humour to dine at a tavern: get heartily sick of each other: and so back to town', FitzGerald wrote to his friend Barton before setting off.

Looking back on this day a few months later Alfred would reflect, world-wearily, 'I don't know whether the Dulwich days were "good days": something good no doubt about them, but I don't look back with *much* satisfaction on them: I have not had a good day, a perfect white day, for years; I think I require delicious scenery to make a perfect day as well as friends – I don't know'.[48]

The two volume *Poems* of 1842 (Volume one consisting mainly of old poems from the previous two books significantly revised) was published on 14 May. FitzGerald regretted their joint publication. 'It is a pity he did not publish the new volume separately. The other will drag it down. And why reprint the Merman, the Mermaid, and those everlasting Eleanores, Isabels, – which always were, and are, and must be, a nuisance ... Every woman thinks herself one of that stupid Gallery of Beauties.'

Both volumes were immediately dispatched to America where they were published by W.D. Ticknor of Boston (publisher of Hawthorne's *Tales*). Tennyson received one of the earliest copyright payments ($150) given by an American publisher to an English author.

Eight hundred copies of the London edition were printed and sold at twelve shillings for the two volumes. This, even though there had been something of a slump in the book trade since 1836, compared with a run of only 450 for the 1832 *Poems*. The volumes were praised by Carlyle, Dickens and Rogers, but not everyone liked the revisions, which had been made to new as well as old poems. Browning was aghast: 'The alterations are insane. *Whatever* is touched is spoiled. There is some woeful mental infirmity in the man – he was months buried in correcting the press of the last volume, and in that time began spoiling the new poems (in proof) as hard as he could. *Locksley Hall* is shorn of two or three couplets ... I have been with Moxon this morning, who tells me that [Tennyson] is miserably thin-skinned, sensitive to criticism ... poor fellow!'

In revising the poems Tennyson's main aim had been to strip them of his youthful penchant for idiosyncratic word blends. Out went 'The yellowleaved waterlily/The greensheathed daffodilly' from 'The Lady of Shalott' and 'the goldensandalled morn/ Rosehued the scornful hills' from 'Œnone'. These revisions were sensible and cannot be regretted. It was where Tennyson recast whole segments or stanzas of a poem that his friends questioned his judgement. Lines 49–56 of 'The Miller's Daughter' had read, in 1832:

> I loved from off the bridge to hear
> 　The rushing sound the water made,
> And see the fish that everywhere
> 　In the backcurrent glanced and played;
> Low down the tall flagflower that sprung
> 　Beside the noisy steppingstones,
> And the massed chestnut boughs that hung
> 　Thickstudded over with white cones.

Ten years later it had been changed to:

> Or from the bridge I leaned to hear
> 　The mildam rushing down with noise,
> And see the minnows everywhere
> 　In crystal eddies glance and poise,
> The tall flag-flowers when they sprung
> 　Below the range of stepping stones,
> Or those three chestnuts near, that hung
> 　In masses thick with milky cones.

The awkward new version has exchanged the wonderfully exact 'backcurrent' for the vague and overly poetic 'crystal eddies', and throughout the revisions to this poem there are other examples of lost power. The evocative 'gummy chestnutbuds' became the ordinary 'chestnuts, when their buds/Were glistening ...' There can be no general assessment on the revisions, some of which, like these examples, are craven and indiscriminate, but others of which are unquestionable improvements – such as the altered ending to 'The Lady of Shalott'.[49]

As for Tennyson's contemporary critics, Leigh Hunt's review in the *Church of England Quarterly* was one of the first (appearing in the autumn issue) and one of the most negative. After that notices increased in warmth, up to the influential essay by R.H. Horne, which appeared in his book *New Spirit of the Age*, published in 1844.

Poems of 1842 was the start of a very satisfactory relationship between poet and publisher. Even Mrs Moxon was well-liked – she allowed Alfred to smoke in her drawing-room.

Hallam Tennyson's *Memoir* portrays Tennyson at this period basking in social admiration, dining out on his mimicry, and meeting past friends at the Sterling Club. This picture is not borne out by the evidence. FitzGerald, for one, hardly saw Tennyson during the first two months after publication. The fact is that Alfred was unable to concentrate on the reception of his poems. It was becoming increasingly apparent that the financial speculation with Allen had been a mistake. The family risked losing its entire investment. Not only would Alfred's own modest inheritance be lost, but that of his sisters too. The hurt went deeper than money. It is a hurt that a man or woman feels only once – and comes from the discovery that there are people in the world who, whilst appearing entirely genuine, are capable of gross deception.

In July he wrote to Allen a letter which burns with the indignation of freshly-lost naïvety:

My spirits have been dejected, my nerves shattered, my health affected by what I have heard. You must have seen how annoyed and worried I was the other morning at meeting you. I could not then say what was on my mind, nor can I now fully: for you seem to me for a long time to have made yourself as strange to me as possible; and I cannot help feeling and feeling deeply that it was not so before I lent you all I had in the world.

I think also that you must have seen that my last note to you was written in a state of great excitement and you might have answered it. My chief reason for writing that note was that I had been informed by two persons, whose veracity I had no need to question, that you had in their presence made use of expressions to this effect. 'That I had driven a hard bargain with you and that if this speculation succeeded, I could have no claims upon you.'

In the earlier days of our acquaintance if anything of this nature had been reported to me I should have rejected it at once as some monstrous perversion. At present I still hope that it is a misrepresentation and that you will be able to explain it away. The first part of the sentence is sheer absurdity: the last involves dishonour: and I am very unwilling to think any ill of a man whom I have regarded with affection and admiration for the valuable qualities of his head and his heart and what seemed to me his clear religious feeling. My faith in you has been strong – most strong. The stronger it has been the deeper and more poignant must be my distaste and loathing if I find you one of the herd, a mere commonplace man, ready, like all worldlings, after a thousand promises, at the first glimpse of prosperity, to kick down the ladder by which he mounted . . .'[50]

The manner in which people react in times of pressure and personal turmoil is always revealing, and particularly so are their carefully crafted epistolary expressions of high dudgeon. A fascinating anthology of such material could be concocted, and if it were, this letter of Tennyson's, neatly and carefully written and possibly never posted (like many such letters), might take pride of place. He closes it by wishing that he could return to his 'honourable poverty among gentlemen, after having drunk one of those most bitter draughts out of the cup of Life, which go near to make men hate the world they move in, and to look upon their brothers as a kind of vermine.'

Allen's response was to find a buyer for Alfred's sisters' shares. He also offered to buy out Charles, and even Alfred. But it was the 'women' Alfred was most concerned about; especially as Cecilia had become engaged to Edmund Lushington and was due to be married in October. Lawyers had advised the family that her new husband would become liable for any debts arising from the failure of the woodworks business.

Alfred's mother and sisters, either slower to come to their senses, or simply not privy to certain information, remained willing to believe in Allen for a little longer. They thought that Alfred was panicking and growing hysterical. And, like any people caught in the midst of a gamble, they were just as anxious not to miss out on any gains, as to avoid a loss. Eventually, though, they agreed, for their brother's sake, to request the sale of their shares. Mary wrote to Allen's wife: 'It would relieve Alfred's mind very much – he fidgets himself to death; I am afraid sometimes he will bring on again the complaint he has suffered from in London not long ago, and which he has been told is dangerous as it might at last reach the heart.' She continued by saying she had never been much alarmed by the possibility of the venture not succeeding. It was only Alfred who had the doubts and misgivings. When his fright is over, he will be himself again – that, she suggests, is the only motive for withdrawing.

To be fair to Mary (and to Alfred) it does need pointing out that she was looking for excuses so that the friendship with the Allens, which she valued, should not be utterly lost.

16 To Teach or to Delight

And oft, when sitting all alone, his face
Would darken, as he cursed his credulousness,
And that one unctuous mouth which lured him ...

('SEA DREAMS')

The family was thankful when Alfred agreed to accompany some of the younger Lushingtons to Eastbourne, where he stayed at 22 Seahouses. He relieved the tedium of the watering-place with much reading which included Henry Taylor's verse-drama *Edwin the Fair*. Tennyson was an avid reader of contemporary material – a fact which an over-emphasis on his classical and medieval allusions can obscure. But nothing he read at this time was able to shift his mind from the Allen business and he decided to take himself further afield by accepting an invitation from Aubrey de Vere to visit Ireland.

Before leaving England Tennyson called on Moxon to see how his book was selling. Moxon was not at home. Tennyson was jealous when he heard that his publisher had gone to the Pyrenees with William Wordsworth's two boys. The Pyrenees! Would that he were returning there himself. But the progress report on his book was encouraging. Moxon's brother told him that it had sold 500 copies, a number with which Alfred was very pleased. 'I have made a sensation. I wish the wood-works would make a sensation! ... What with ruin in the distance and hypochondriacs in the foreground I feel very crazy.'[51]

De Vere was five years younger than Tennyson and the son of an Irish baronet. He became involved in the network of

Trinity friendships through his cousin Stephen Spring-Rice. Some misunderstanding between himself and Tennyson (a rather good example of two poets failing to synchronize their practical arrangements) meant that Alfred spent a lonely fortnight in Ireland wandering from Limerick to Cork, from where he took a boat back to Bristol at the end of September, so that he could be home in time for his sister Cecilia's marriage to Edmund Lushington.

He went to Henry Lushington's place, at the top of the stairs in 2 Mitre Court. Somehow or other he had gone off to Ireland with Harry's key in his pocket, so he was able to let himself in. After the wedding reception (which was held at Park House) Tennyson stayed overnight, sleeping off a champagne hangover. But the wedding and the revelry could not blank out the woodwork worries and Tennyson was incensed to discover that Septimus had become the latest victim of Allen's hectoring. By this time he could not bring himself to confront Allen directly. Instead he wrote to Mrs Allen:

I have learned this morning that Septimus is about to lend Dr. Allen £1000 – and seeing that Dr. Allen has already at different times received from our family about £8000 – the result of which loan has been to my mother and sisters that they are at this time living upon my brother Charles – and to myself that I am a penniless beggar and deeply in debt besides ... it does strike me as most remarkable that Dr. Allen should have recourse for another 1000 to another member of the same family ...

It seems difficult to imagine anything altogether more indelicate and indecorous. What I have felt and suffered may rest unmentioned, but, I entreat you, if you have any regard for your husband's honour to do all in your power to prevent him making another victim of my family.[52]

To this letter Tennyson received a stalling reply. 'This tells me nothing', he stated bluntly. 'You will much oblige me by giving a specific answer to my petition.' It was straight talking, but tangentially directed. It might have been better to confront Allen himself, or even Septimus. By now, though, Tennyson seemed resigned to the Doctor's monomania, and as for Septimus, he 'seems latterly to have estranged himself from the family'.

Septimus was not the only younger brother to worry Alfred.

On 13 December Arthur Tennyson voluntarily entered the Crichton Institute in Dumfries. This was an insane asylum but one used by patients determined to cure themselves of any evil propensity. In Arthur's case the evil was drink. Entering the asylum short of funds, Arthur was forced to share a dormitory with seriously deranged patients. Efforts were made to get hold of some of his capital (through Charles d'Eyncourt) so that he could hire a private room. With one older brother addicted to opium and now two younger brothers in insane asylums, the prospect of losing the family's capital was terrifying.

Alfred became an uncle in January when his sister Emily gave birth to her first child. He was in Mablethorpe at the time, no doubt letting the winter wind blow some of his troubles away. On returning to town he kept up the pressure on Allen and by early March the Doctor was writing to Frederick, also an investor: 'I have done all that is possible for man to do to save your family, and I have *utterly ruined myself* in the attempt.' And in a postscript which seems to express disdainful exasperation with Frederick's brother's attitude, he adds, 'Every stick and stave is to be sold to pay A.T. *this day* – and yet people boast! I ail! and I suffer! and I die!'

In total the Tennyson family had invested £8000 in the scheme and for all Allen's protestations and promises to pay them back there was nothing left to return. Even the deeds and insurance policy issued as security on Tennyson's original loan proved worthless. The family had lost everything.

Edmund Lushington took out another insurance policy on Allen's life and gave it to Alfred. FitzGerald helped out. And there was still the £100 a year from his aunt, plus a similar sum in royalties. He was not destitute but the disappearance of generating capital was an unquestionable disaster.

Proof-reading for the second edition of the 1842 *Poems* took his mind away from troubles for a brief period and while in London Tennyson continued to be sociable. On 27 April he dined with Dickens, Thackeray and FitzGerald at Devonshire Terrace, playing cards and drinking mulled claret.

The new volume of *Poems* contained several that have come to be considered amongst Tennyson's finest work – 'Ulysses', 'Break, break, break', 'Morte d'Arthur', 'The Vision of Sin', 'The Two Voices', 'St Simeon Stylites', and 'Locksley Hall'. The idylls – 'Audley Court' and 'The Miller's Daughter', for instance – seemed to stand out from this first group with their attempt to represent contemporary life and Tennyson's readers had mixed feelings about them. However, the early reviews were mainly written by Tennyson's friends and fellow Apostles – Francis Garden, John Sterling, Monckton Milnes, and James Spedding.

Garden, writing in the *Christian Remembrancer*, while welcoming the disappearance of mannerisms, and the toning-down of youthful effervescence, noted that the poems were written from the standpoint of a poet who held himself aloof from the duties and cares of ordinary life. Tennyson was still failing to see that poetry, unlike painting and other 'fine art', is 'utterance; it is man speaking to man, man telling man his thoughts and feelings. Now, speech can never be long without having a direct moral character, without having aims in themselves foreign to art . . .'[53] This, as has been seen, was not such a pillar of Apostolic belief when the group in question were in their early twenties. Now, in a new decade of life, and approaching mature manhood, it was to be a message that Tennyson's friends would press home with increasing influence.

Sterling's review was significant for appearing in the *Quarterly*, the periodical which had carried the damaging piece by Croker ten years before. Although Sterling was privately a little disappointed that, at the end of a decade, Tennyson had not shown a more dramatic advance, his essay was generous. After a wide-ranging introduction in which he spoke of the social upheavals that had taken place in England since 1830, suggesting that it was a period rich in material for the contemporary poet, he singled out Tennyson's idylls for special praise. There were four other types of poem in the new volume – lyrical poems, including odes and songs; fanciful pieces; didactic poems; and mere 'facetiae', at which he did not think Tennyson very adept. Sterling linked his praise to his expansive opening remarks – 'The heartfelt tenderness, the glow, the gracefulness, the strong sense, the lively painting, in many of these compositions, drawn from the heart of our actual English life, set them far above the glittering marvels and musical phantasms of Mr Tennyson's metaphorical romances . . .'[54] Once again, it is necessary to remark that it *had* been just these glittering marvels of Tennyson which the Apostles had found so seductive in the first instance.

Monckton Milnes ended his review on the same earnest note as his friends. '[Tennyson's] command of diction is complete, his sense and execution of the harmonies of verse accurate and admirable; he has only to show that he has substance . . . worthy of these media; that he will not content himself with any ingenuity of conceit or fancifulness of illustration; that, in fine, he comprehends the function of the poet in this day of ours, to teach still more then he delights, and to suggest still more than he teaches.'[55] Spedding, whose review consisted in large part of fulsome appreciations of just four poems – 'The Palace of Art', 'St Simeon Stylites', 'The Vision of Sin', and 'The Two Voices' – ended with a slightly different injunction. 'If Mr. Tennyson can find a subject large enough to take the entire impress of his mind, and energy persevering enough to work it faithfully out as one whole, we are convinced that he may produce a work, which, though occupying no larger space than the contents of these volumes, shall as much exceed them in value, as a series of quantities multiplied into each other exceed in value the same series simply added together.'[56] This windy finale told Tennyson that his future poems should not only be didactic but on a much grander scale than up until then. Coming from friends and fellow-Apostles, it was compelling advice.

17   Crises

a full tide
Rose with ground-swell, which, on the foremost rocks
Touching, upjeted in spirits of wild sea-smoke.
And scaled in sheets of wasteful foam, and fell
In vast sea-cataracts ...

('SEA DREAMS')

At the beginning of November 1843 Alfred caught a 'villainous' cold and, lodging with FitzGerald, his mood became morose. He felt poisoned and panicked by the horrors of the past two years and, once his health had improved, took himself off to Cheltenham, where his mother, Charles, and one or two other members of the family were already.

Tennyson was to stay in Cheltenham for six months, lodging with a Mrs Morris of Prestbury, while undergoing a hydropathic cure, the new craze for health fanatics, neurotics and other hardy hypochondriacs. It is unsurprising that Tennyson should take to the water. He had long declared it his favourite element. And Cheltenham, famous as a spa town since pigeons had been seen pecking at salt grains on the site of the spring in 1716, had been a favourite place of refuge for the Tennyson family in his father's day.

Hydropathy – not introduced into England until 1840 – was the invention of Vincenz Priessnitz. A Hydropathic Society was formed in 1842, and in 1843 it was still very much a fresh fad. Priessnitz, an Austrian, was something of a quack. He was completely without medical qualification, but the use of pure water in his treatments made it difficult for the authorities to charge him with unlawful practice, as they had tried and failed to do in 1829. His centre at Grafenberg, once established, could boast the support of every kind of dignitary. In 1839 alone it was visited by a king, a duke, a duchess, twenty-two princes, 149 counts and countesses, eighty-eight barons and baronesses, fourteen generals, fifty-three staff officers, 116 captains, 104 civil servants, sixty-five divines, forty-six artists and eighty-seven physicians and apothecaries.[57]

The essential object of the treatment was purgative. To this end every variety of water application was put to use. In addition to hot and cold baths there were general packings (in which the patient's whole body was wrapped in layers of wet sheet and blankets), local packings (a wet stomach pack was known as 'Neptune's girdle'), hot air, steam and sitz-baths.

Priessnitz claimed that his technique was able to cure everything except epilepsy and consumption – both of which he refused to treat. He did not turn away syphilitics. Indeed, local soaking had long been used in the treatment of venereal disease. The sufferer might 'wrap up his whore-tackle in a linen cloth wet in strong vinegar and claret wine'.

A new patient would first of all be observed in a general bath and their skin scrutinized to ascertain the specific place of disease. An appropriate programme of treatment would then be instituted – the day probably beginning at 5 am with a series of general packings and immersions – and the onset of a 'crisis' eagerly awaited. A 'crisis' was the elimination of 'bad stuff' through the pus in a boil, or through dramatic openings of the bowels.

By February Tennyson was able to announce in a letter to FitzGerald, proudly, 'I have had four crises (one larger than had been seen for two or three years in Grafenberg – indeed I believe the largest but one that has been seen)'.

The establishment at Cheltenham, as yet the only one in England run according to Priessnitz's principles, was managed by the originator's nephew. The regime was strictly adhered to. Tennyson reported 'no reading by candlelight, no going near a fire, no tea, no coffee, perpetual wet sheet and cold bath and alternation from hot to cold: however I have much faith in it'. Such, one imagines, was a requirement of submitting oneself to such treatment.

The final paragraph of this letter makes it clear that Tennyson himself ascribed his nervous collapse entirely to what he had suffered at the hands of Dr Allen. But the fact that it occurred at the end of the year in which he had at last re-published is not without significance.

Much as he might echo the excitement of his publisher and herald the sale of 500 copies of his book a 'sensation', the reception was a disappointment. FitzGerald had promised that the public, knocked over by the poems, would rally to him as a new Keats. Suddenly, he was too ready with criticism. The piece by Leigh Hunt seemed likely to be the first in yet another series of negative reviews. He had worked so hard during the last ten years, and waited till he had what he considered to be as perfect a collection of poems as he was capable of producing, and the reception had turned out to be much more muted than he would have liked. Tennyson began to curse the Americans for pushing him before the public prematurely. His livelihood now depended entirely upon his reputation as a poet, and consequent sales. Moxon and his brother might be ready to convince their author, and themselves, that, in difficult times, the sale of 500 copies in three months was a 'sensation', but Tennyson would have looked for more graphic indications. Didn't the buyers of Byron queue up and hammer on John Murray's window when the next installments of *Don Juan* were due? Surely some such clamour ought to accompany a 'sensation'.

However exclusively Tennyson himself might blame his own ill-health on the financial tribulations of the woodworks business, it does seem clear that the anti-climax of his poetry's reception, after so long a fermentation, did disappoint him terribly. Pleasant reviews by one's friends are one thing, but a boost from a really neutral party is what the writer really craves.

He was still at Cheltenham in the early summer of 1844,

complaining to his Aunt Russell, of 'blood in the head'. 'This is the effect of Hydropathical treatment though a sitz bath always takes it away; I intended to leave off the water-cure soon after I left you but I find it is impossible, for I am not yet cured, as the recurrence of old symptoms sufficiently testifies: it is a terribly long process but then what price is too high for health, and health of mind is so involved with health of body.'

Tennyson was always curiously vague about his symptoms – 'blood in the head', and the recurring trouble with his eyes, is as specific as he became. Only occasionally did his anxiety produce a verifiable condition, such as the eczema on his legs which troubled him in mid-life. This has allowed speculation a fairly free rein. The waywardness of the epilepsy theory is reinforced by the Priessnitz system's refusal to treat epileptics. It is probably more accurate to take Tennyson's vagueness at face value, and to assume that his illness, where it was not purely hypochondriacal, was a form of neurasthenia, aggravated by his excessive drinking and smoking.

Tennyson's first break from the Hydropathic regime came at the end of June, when he took himself off to Aberystwyth and Barmouth. Failing to bump into his friend Venables as planned, he wrote to him in phrases which suggest he was growing tired of Cheltenham, although his intention was to return there for continued treatment. He talked of living 'a whole age away from the world in the abominable purlieux of a worse watering place' and ended significantly, 'it is only by the strictest temperance that I can keep myself tolerably comfortable'.

He returned to Cheltenham at the end of July but was unwilling to incarcerate himself for a further long spell. He had not lost faith in the system but the call of his friends and evenings in taverns was too strong. He wrote to Edmund Lushington before leaving for London: 'I shall have to go into the system again and carry it to the end. It is true I had ten crises but I am not yet cured.'

18   Macpherson's Farewell

Shy she was, and I thought her cold;
Thought her proud, and fled over the sea;
Filled I was with folly and spite,
When Ellen Adair was dying for me.

('EDWARD GRAY')

His arrival in London, late at night on 30 July, was inauspicious. The coach dropped him outside Hummuns, a
Turkish bath establishment in Covent Garden, and he went
immediately to the Temple to call, without success, on Spedding
and Benedict Chapman; (Chapman had been at Cambridge with
Tennyson, but not at Trinity and was neither an Apostle nor a
member of the Sterling Club, but became more closely
acquainted with Tennyson through being part of the Inner
Temple 'set' which included, apart from Spedding, Venables,
Harry Lushington and Kemble).

The next day he tried again at Mitre Court but without luck.
Spedding was out of town and the Lushingtons were in
Eastbourne, but Geraldine, one of the room-servants, let
Tennyson use the Lushington rooms. Feeling lonely, he wrote to
R.H. Horne, who was about to publish his essay collection *New
Spirit of the Age*, and had requested a portrait of the poet to use
inside it, 'I wish you could come and drink tea some night. I am
always at home at 8. Could you come Sunday? Why shouldn't
we know each other?'

This is a curious note. Horne is invited to drink 'tea', not to
share a glass of port or a pipe. And that 'why shouldn't we
know each other' is not the same voice as used by a healthier
more self-sufficient and remote Tennyson. Far from curing
Tennyson, hydropathy seems to have enfeebled him, making his
character temporarily dilute and insipid.

He was supposed to go and visit Carlyle in Chelsea (and did
at least say of the prospect 'with whom would I more willingly
smoke my pipe and fraternize on this side of the grave') but he
caught a fever which a doctor told him might become Scarlet

202

Fever without proper treatment. Accordingly, he dosed himself with six lemons a day, until strong enough to take himself into the country and join the Lushingtons.

He stayed at Park House for two months, writing no letters and very little poetry. FitzGerald complained, 'He never writes me a word. Hydropathy has done its worst; he writes the names of his friends in water.' His return to Prestbury was indefinitely delayed. Arriving back in London during early October, he made good his promise to visit Caryle. He arrived at Cheyne Walk at 2 pm and stayed until 11 pm, making an unforgettable impression upon Carlyle, who was left with an ugly headache which persisted for several days. Carlyle told Alfred the story of Macpherson's farewell: in brief, a highland robber played his own fiddle composition on the gallows, offered his instrument to the crowd, and when there were no takers, crushed it under his foot. Something in the story (perhaps his own fears of artistic failure) moved the inebriated Tennyson, and Carlyle was surprised to see the large man's lip quiver. In his dither, Alfred forgot to pick up his stick when he left. Typically, it was not his own but one he had 'borrowed' from Venables. It was found leaning against the wall in the small garden where he and Carlyle had had their first early afternoon smoke.

The general impression left on Carlyle was of 'a man solitary and sad . . . dwelling in an element of gloom'. Tennyson was full of his imminent return to Cheltenham and his determination to complete his cure. Just before his departure from London he received a letter from his new friend which ended in the valediction, 'Courage!'

Back in Cheltenham with other members of his family – Emily, Cecilia (briefly), Matilda, Charles, Mary, Horatio – Tennyson took a less rigid attitude towards the hydropathic regime. He ordered *Vestiges of the Natural History of Creation* from Moxon and borrowed Ruskin's *Modern Painters* from the London Library. The Tennysons moved out of their dingy lodgings at Bellevue Place into more comfortable rooms at 10 St James's Square. It was altogether a more relaxed sojourn, and although Tennyson talked of being no better, it was in his old bantering style. Writing to his Aunt Russell, he shared with her worries about the state of his eyes:

Those 'animals' you mention are very distressing and mine increase weekly: in fact I almost look forward with certainty to being blind some of these days. I have however no sort of inflammation to complain of – it is all failing nerve. As to health in other respects I cannot say on the whole I am much better – I am a 'creaking hinge' you know the proverb: but in my case I hardly credit its veracity ...[58]

While in Cheltenham a series of articles on Mesmerism, published in the *Athenaeum* on five consecutive weeks, fascinated Alfred. They were written by a Miss Martineau and when Cecilia left for Glasgow Alfred sent a copy to Edmund Lushington, who was impressed but sceptical. Alfred's sister Emily had been receiving treatment from a local practitioner in Cheltenham. 'The showwoman of Cheltenham is proved to be a great humbug', Lushington concluded, after reading the Martineau piece.

Cecilia, on arriving back in Scotland, wrote a long chatty letter to Frederick. As always, it is full of evocative family detail. 'Mrs. Russell is continually sending Mary and Till and Alfred money, which is very kind of her ... Old Allen still lives – it is a sad thing one is obliged to wish for the death of any man – I suppose thou knowest Alfred will get most of his money back when that desirable event takes place – to secure this Edmund pays some eight pounds a year for him ... Before we left Park House Emily had been staying with us for some time with her little boy – the meeting between them was very good, they stared at each other for some time, then came sounds of discontentment, presently little Arthur Henry showed signs of putting his fist into little Edmund Henry's face ...' Cecilia's husband did not have to pay out these premiums for very long. Allen died, of a heart attack, early in January 1845.

Alfred was still in Cheltenham when news reached him, but he immediately packed his bags and set out for Charlotte Street to meet up with FitzGerald. The new financial security did wonders for his health. Fitz found him looking twice as well as he had done a year before, and in better spirits.

Allen's death did, however, scupper a scheme, set up by some of the poet's friends, to secure for him a Civil List pension. The main movers were Rogers, Milnes, Gladstone and Henry Hallam. The petition was urged on the basis that the poet had lost his 'little property'. Peel did not offer a pension, but a single payment of £200. This Tennyson declined, as smacking too much of charity, but his friends continued the pressure on his behalf.

One evening at the end of January, Jane Carlyle was alone in the house at Cheyne Walk relishing the prospect of a long quiet time of 'looking into the fire', when a carriage drew up and deposited men's voices outside her window. It was Tennyson and Moxon, come to call on her husband who had gone to dine with the Chadwicks, much against his will. Although she welcomed both men into the house, it was the encounter with Tennyson which she found most worthy of comment.

Alfred is dreadfully embarrassed with women alone – for he entertains at one and the same moment a feeling of almost adoration for them and an ineffable contempt! adoration I suppose for what they *might be* – contempt for what they *are*! The only chance of my getting any right good of him was to make him forget my womanness – so I did just as Carlyle would have done, had he been there; got out *pipes* and *tobacco* – and *brandy* and *water* – with a deluge of *tea* over and above. – The effect of these accessories was miraculous – he *professed* to be *ashamed* of polluting my room, 'felt', he said, 'as if he were stealing cups and sacred vessels in the Temple' – but he smoked on all the same – for *three* mortal hours! talking like an angel – only exactly as if he were talking with a clever *man* – which – being a thing I am not used to – men always adapting their conversation to what they *take to be* a woman's taste – strained me to a terrible pitch of intellectuality.
When Carlyle came home at twelve and found me all *alone* in an atmosphere of tobacco so thick that you might have cut it with a knife his astonishment was considerable![59]

Tennyson had already begun writing *The Princess*, his long poem about the education of women. Jane Carlyle's self-assured and independent character was to be a strong influence.

19   Pensioner

In every land I thought that, more or less,
The stronger sterner nature overbore
The softer, uncontrolled by gentleness
And selfish evermore

('A DREAM OF FAIR WOMEN', 1832)

Tennyson spent the period between February and early April back in Cheltenham, staying with the family at St James's Square. If he did continue his hydropathic treatment it was half-heartedly, for there is no direct mention of it in his correspondence. He wrote some 200 lines of 'The University of Women' – sufficient to give a public reading in mid-April, when he returned to London and immediately indulged in a series of late nights with the likes of Brookfield, de Vere, FitzGerald, Spedding and Thackeray.

Wordsworth was also in London, for the official audience with the Queen following his appointment as Poet Laureate. This provided the opportunity for the first encounter between the older and the younger poet. The initial meeting occurred in Hampstead, where Wordsworth was staying with a Mr Hoare. According to de Vere it was Tennyson's idea to call on Wordsworth, but the meeting was a disappointment. Perhaps it was too early in the day. 'I could not inflame his imagination in the least!' Tennyson is reported to have said, although this is, to say the least, an uncharacteristic and scarcely believable remark. How would Tennyson himself have responded to a visitor on first introduction trying to inflame his own imagination?

A day or so later, Tennyson and Wordsworth met up again at a Moxon dinner. This was more of a success, and when it was time to sit at table, Wordsworth took the younger man's arm, saying, 'Come, brother bard, to dinner'. It was Tennyson's turn to feel withdrawn and when the meal was over he was too ashamed to pay Wordsworth compliments, so that when it was time to leave he felt uncomfortably conscious of a missed opportunity. At the last minute, outside the door, he impulsively said something about 'the pleasure he had taken from Mr Wordsworth's writings'. The old poet took his hand and returned the compliment.

It was a perfectly ordinary, and rather touching, encounter and the mutual embarrassment and reticence were equally understandable. It is overdramatic to try, as others have done, to turn the moment into something symbolical, as if Wordsworth's offering his hand was, in effect, a passing-over of the bardic secret, or, more sinisterly, an opportunity for Tennyson to suck the sap of a declining talent.

May was an exceedingly wet month, and the late-night dinner parties and drinking sessions continued without let-up. Tennyson and FitzGerald made plans for visiting Cornwall or Wales together, but Alfred finally took a short break in Eastbourne, where he continued to work on *The Princess*.

Something odd seems to have come over Tennyson on the Sussex coast, for when he returned to London he was secretive and reclusive. FitzGerald's exasperation with him bubbled over: 'Alfred Tennyson was to have gone with me to the coast, but I have not the least idea where he is now abiding; and, if I did, he would not write me a line to fix on anything; and if he wrote to fix, he would not do it. One can only rely on Chance for meeting him.'[60]

But the best impression of Tennyson at this time is given by de Vere:

1 JULY Driving in from Hampstead I met Alfred Tennyson, who was little pleased to see me, and seemed living in a mysterious sort of way on the Hampstead Road, bathing and learning Persian.

14 JULY Went out to Hampstead. . . . Called on Alfred Tennyson, who railed against the whole system of society, and said he was miserable.

16 JULY On my way in, paid a visit to Tennyson, who seemed much out of spirits, and said he could no longer bear to be knocked about the world, and that he must marry and find love and peace or die . . . He complained much about growing old, and said he cared nothing for fame, and that his life was all thrown away for want of a competence and retirement. Said that no one had been so much harassed by anxiety and trouble as himself. I told him he wanted occupation, a wife, and orthodox principles, which he took well.[61]

Tennyson returned to Eastbourne in mid-August, lodging once again in a group of cottages known as Mount Pleasant. A garden in front of the cottages and beyond that a cornfield was all that lay between the house and the edge of the cliff.

While there he was visited by Moxon (to discuss future publication) and by Edmund Lushington, who was shown new sections of *In Memoriam*, most notably the concluding wedding sequence which was based on his own marriage to Cecilia. 'Regret is dead, but love is more/Than in the summers that are flown/For I myself with these have grown/To something greater than before.'

He was in Cheltenham a month later, when he received a letter from Henry Hallam, informing him that the Prime Minister, Peel, had suddenly acceded to the continuing campaign of his friends and granted a Civil List pension of £200 per year. He immediately accepted the offer. This addition to his annual income, together with the prospect of increasing royalties, turned Tennyson into a relatively wealthy man. Certainly he could once again have contemplated marriage, should he so have wished.

Although the word 'pension' stuck in his gullet, he felt comfortable enough receiving it. 'I have done nothing slavish to get it', he said, honestly enough. He considered it as much a recognition of his artistic status, as a response to his financial circumstances. After all, Wordsworth received a pension, why shouldn't he? And when Bernard Barton was granted one also, Tennyson was gratified to hear that it was for just £100 per year, only half his amount. 'Certainly I am twice a Barton in verse', he said. It was his poetry which earned him the pension, which is perhaps the clue to his continuing to accept it even when he was a very wealthy man at the end of his life, making more than £10,000 a year from royalties.

Tennyson would be much criticized in later years for this, but there was an immediate reaction too, from all those who combined a natural dislike of his poetry with a feeling that more deserving claimants had been overlooked. The seventy-year-old actor and playwright James Sheridan Knowles had been strongly tipped to be included on the Civil List. The exclusion of this worthy and upright older man was just the excuse for someone like Edward Bulwer-Lytton to begin sniping. He immediately included in his long rhyming romance of London life, *The New Timon*, an attack on Tennyson:

Tho' praised by Critics, tho' adored by Blues,
Tho' Peel with pudding plump the puking Muse,
Tho' Theban taste the Saxon's purse controls
And pensions Tennyson while starves a Knowles.

This was tame enough. The fangs were bared at the bottom of the page, in the form of a footnote which reprinted part of the disastrous 'O Little Room' – and pointed out that Tennyson, in contrast to Knowles, was in the prime of life, without wife or children, and came from a wealthy family.

The criticism must have been echoed in private mutterings and mumblings by other aggrieved men and their supporters, but Lytton's attack did not lead to any further public onslaught. The tide seemed to be turning in Tennyson's favour.

20 A Wanderer Giving Wrong Messages

It is but bringing up; no more than that:
You men have done it: how I hate you all!

(THE PRINCESS)

On Saturday 20 September Alfred attended a private performance of *Every Man in his Humour* in Soho. It had been organized by Charles Dickens and amongst those present was Jane Carlyle – without her husband, who was in Scotland. It is an indication of how well Tennyson and Mrs Carlyle had hit it off at their previous encounter that Alfred arranged to visit her in Chelsea the following evening.

It was a wet night, and Tennyson caught a chill which he was still complaining of a month later. The cold was so thick it had made him deaf. Jane Carlyle was struck by the poet's anxiety to find a partner and establish a domestic rhythm to his life. After the meeting she heard from her friends that his anxiety had the proportions of desperation. Lady Harriet Baring, not without a cruel irony, told her that Tennyson 'must have a woman to live beside; *would prefer a lady*, but – could not afford one; and so must marry a maidservant'. Henry Taylor's wife, it was said, was seriously considering recommending her housemaid for such a *mésalliance*.

Although still staying in other people's rooms Tennyson did try and establish himself as an independent man about town. He issued invitations for dinner, entertaining, for instance, a thespian couple at Mitre Court in early October.

But by the middle of the month he was back in Cheltenham feeling frail and still recovering from his cold. In a letter to Rawnsley, he said, 'I begin to feel an old man myself. I have gone through a vast deal of suffering since I saw you last and would not have it over again for quadruple the pension Peel has given me, and on which you congratulate me.' The same letter contains the clearest expression of Tennyson's attitude towards the pension. Criticizing Miss Martineau for refusing to accept one, he goes on:

> ... if the people *did* make laws for themselves, if these things went by universal suffrage what literary man ever *would* get a lift, it being notorious that the mass of Englishmen have as much notion of poetry as I of foxhunting: meantime there is some meaning in having a gentleman and a classic at the head of affairs, who may now and then direct the stream of public bounty to us poor devils whom the [*hoi polloi*] would not only not remunerate but kick out of society as barely *respectable* ... [62]

The cold never really cleared itself and by the New Year (1846) Tennyson was still unwell and laid up in bed, where he continued working on *The Princess*. Rumour exaggerated his confinement and had it that he was seriously ill with 'an internal complaint'.

It was not only his physical condition which worried his associates. Many of them were concerned by his obsessive working on the University poem. When Elizabeth Barrett heard reports of it, from her brother who worked in the Temple, she expostulated, 'Now isn't the world too old and fond of steam, for blank verse poems, in ever so many books, to be written on the fairies? I hope they may cure him, for the best deed they do'. This was a common feeling, shared especially by FitzGerald, who was always critical when Tennyson chose to set his work in another period of time. What such criticism *does* bring out is the fact that a work which now seems to us quintessentially of the Victorian age – long, set in the Middle Ages, with trappings of folklore – at the time went very much against the grain. On the other hand Tennyson had been made to feel, by his friends' reviews of the 1842 volume, that he was in the process of creating just such a work as the age required.

He spent part of the spring of 1846 on the Isle of Wight. This was his first contact with the small island that was to be his home for the greater part of his life. It was a pleasant but not auspicious beginning. He found some good people there, a dramatist called Reverend White, and a minor poet, Edmund Peel – the cousin of the Prime Minister – who became an immediate admirer. White, in particular, was a significant figure on the island. Although only in his early forties he had given up his parish and retired to Bonchurch to live off money inherited from his father-in-law. He was a friend of John Forster and Dickens and a contributor to *Household Words*, as well as a dramatist.

When Tennyson returned to London at the end of April his friends found him haggard and listless. 'Surely no man has a right to be so lazy in this world', wrote the industrious Carlyle. Fitzgerald did his best to vivify Tennyson. 'Jowett, Tennyson and I are going to get a pint or two of fresh air at Richmond: and we are to wind up our day at Carlyle's by way of a refreshing evening's entertainment. I met Carlyle last night at Tennyson's; and they two discussed the merits of this world, and the next, till I wished myself out of *this*, at any rate.'

During the same week in May Tennyson again met Browning, who wrote: 'Moxon's care of him ... is the charmingest thing imaginable, and he seems to need it all – being in truth but a LONG, lazy kind of a man, at least just after dinner ... yet there is something "naif" about him, too ... the genius you see, too.'

June 1846 was the hottest summer month in living memory. The average temperature during the first twenty-two days was 84°F in the shade. On Friday 19 June the thermometer was within two or three degrees of 100°F. Alfred, already planning a continental trip with Moxon, escaped the city heat by making a second visit to the Isle of Wight. He seems to have given the three daughters of a Bradshaw family, taking their summer holiday on the island, excessive hope of a romantic involvement, and then offended them with too direct a reproach.

Sarah, the middle daughter, was the most confused and, retiring to the safety of the New Forest, Tennyson had to write an exculpatory letter to the mother:

> Out of the distance I stretch forth my hands to you for forgiveness. I shall always remember the days I past with you, always regret that any shadow came across them: nor can I ever forget that last sad morning. Sarah's mournful eyes pursued me during my whole journey to the extreme limit of the island. How kind you had all been to me, how unworthy I had seemed to your kindness! how ungentle must I have been to have caused, however unconsciously, a moment's uneasiness to such gentle creatures![63]

Enclosed with this letter was a poem written during a picnic which had been the scene of his sulky offence. It is worth quoting in full, not because it is one of Tennyson's best pieces, but because it is so straightforward an expression of the Romantic fly-by-night, and as such reveals much about the poet's self-image.

> Farewell, true hearts, with whom I felt
>   That mine might have one hour of rest!
> Farewell, dear maids, whose eyes have dwelt
>   With kindness on the passing guest!
>
> O happy he that finds a friend,
>   Or makes a friend wher'er he come,
> Who loves the world from end to end
>   And wanders on from home to home.
>
> But such sweet days are mine no more.
>   A sailor in a stormy sky,
> I see the peaceful light on shore,
>   And the wild tempest whirls me by.
>
> Not less, I count you kind and true,
>   I prize you more than I can tell.
> Give me a hand! and you – and you –
>   And once again – and so farewell.[64]

('THE WANDERER')

212

A part of Tennyson hankered after domestic rest. This was the part that spoke to Mrs Carlyle and some of his London friends. But another part was terrified of such stasis. The wild tempest whirling him past the homely niceties of a family with eligible daughters was only half-heartedly resisted. For the time being his relationship with Emily Sellwood was in abeyance and he was self-consciously trying out the role of isolated, wandering songsmith.

FitzGerald was still concerned by Tennyson's physical state. Before he had fled the city heat Fitz had found him in 'a rickety state of body; brought on wholly by neglect, etc'.

The hot summer continued into July, which Tennyson spent at Park House, joining Edmund and Cecilia there, and resting before the start of his tour to the Continent.

He set off with Moxon on 1 August, for Ramsgate, where they lodged at a fishmonger's, and the next day boarded the interestingly-named *Princess Maude*, bound for Ostende. Moxon was immediately sea-sick and Tennyson, alone, went below-decks for 'the very worst breakfast I ever had in my life'.

Almost a week into their tour there was a reticence between the two travellers which showed no signs of easing. A perfectly genial companion at London breakfasts and dinners, Tennyson's publisher was never as close to him as Brookfield or FitzGerald, and was not a natural traveller. The inevitable comparison between this tour, and the earlier tour of the Rhine, bore down on the poet, as it must also bear down on us. Then Tennyson had been a young man in the company of a close, beloved friend. Their relationship was complicated, as all intimate relationships tend to be, and that early trip up the Rhine had not been amongst their most delightful times together. Nevertheless, Tennyson was now a man of thirty-seven, his old friend was dead, travelling had lost much of the flirtatious excitement of the past, and his present companion was a professional associate first, and friend second. To make matters worse, Moxon was too frank with the poet. Walking behind Tennyson one day he told his companion that he discerned the unmistakable signs of encroaching baldness. The two travelled on to Grundelwald and Lantenbrumen, where Tennyson wrote 'Come down, O maid', one of the songs included in *The Princess*.

Come down O maid, from yonder mountain height:
What pleasure lives in height (the shepherd sang)

In height and cold, the splendour of the hills?
But cease to move so near the Heavens, and cease
To glide a sunbeam by the blasted Pine,
To sit a star upon the sparkling spire;
And come, for Love is of the valley, come,
For Love is of the Valley, come thou down
And find him; by the happy threshold, he,
Or hand in hand with Plenty in the maize,
Or red with spirted purple of the vats,
Or foxlike in the vine; nor cares to walk
With Death and Morning on the silver horns,
Nor wilt thou snare him in the white ravine,
Nor find him dropt upon the firths of ice,
That huddling slant in furrow-cloven falls
To roll the torrent out of dusky doors:
But follow; let the torrent dance thee down
To find him in the valley ...

Tennyson was teaching himself a lesson in this song and coming to realize that love and marriage must inevitably entail a settling down. However influential Matthew Allen had been in convincing Alfred that, for the soundness of his own mind, he must keep to the craggy, masculine independence of his bachelor life, he was beginning to see that femininity and the hearth were the keys to earthly happiness. Near the end of their trip Tennyson and Moxon called in on Dickens at Lausanne, a visit which was the most notable interlude in the whole tour.

The novelist was walking up and down in his colonnaded garden a little after 7 pm, having already eaten, and trying to think up a fresh plot development for *Dombey and Son*, when he was approached by two travel-stained men. He didn't recognize who they were until they were close. Moxon, his straw hat limp and weathered, kept ducking as he approached. As soon as the visitors were recognized Dickens entertained them with dry biscuits, Liebfraumilch and innumerable cigars. Dickens, who had earlier tried unsuccessfully to persuade Tennyson to join him and his family abroad, found Moxon snobbish and an odd companion for a man of genius. Tennyson enjoyed the encounter and immediately seemed at home, nonchalantly fingering a five-pound-note which had been worn down, during his travels, to some two thirds of its original size.

There must have been bad food and flea-ridden beds during Tennyson's tours with Hallam, but the emphasis and the state of mind were different then. This holiday with Moxon was an important interlude for Tennyson. It taught him much about the way he had altered and about what he could look for in the future. He might not be so keen or quite so fatalistic about being swept past the 'peaceful light on the shore' from now on.

21   Signs of Baldness

O Swallow, flying from the golden woods,
Fly to her, and pipe and woo her, and make her mine,
And tell her, tell her, that I follow thee.

(THE PRINCESS)

After a quiet month in London Tennyson joined his family for their autumn visit to Cheltenham. The lack of any developing intimacy between himself and Moxon was brought home to Tennyson when he received a parcel of books from the publisher – without any covering letter. 'You rogue you,' he wrote back, 'not to send me one line with that parcel, forgetful of our joint sweats up the Swiss hills and of our mutual mule.'

By way of compensation Tennyson put renewed emphasis on the depth of feeling he had for FitzGerald:

Don't you know that I esteem you one of those few friends who would still stick to me though the whole polite world with its great idiot mouth (wider than ever was a clown's at a fair, staring at a show) howled at me: if I write not, it is not because I do not love and remember, but from some small absurd cause of not having pen, or paper, or ink, or Queen's head within reach.[65]

He was growing increasingly fed up with Cheltenham – 'In this cursed watering-place I rust in ignorance of all things' – and moved back to London, staying at the home of Tom Taylor, another of the Inner Temple circle.

Moxon's remark about encroaching baldness had preyed upon the poet's mind, and he took himself to a Mrs Parker for

215

treatment costing ten shillings per session. The treatment consisted in scalp massages, the pulling out of dead hairs, and the application of tonics and creams. The woman had a very good reputation and was patronized by royalty. We don't know how long Tennyson used her services, but we do know that he remained supremely touchy about the state and colour of his hair.

He had a busy, mobile end to the year, moving from friend to friend and then going up to Cambridge for a commemoration dinner in January. Before that he spent a memorable day at the Clapton home of the Howitts, William and Mary, two Quakers prominent in the literary life of mid-nineteenth century London.

The retiring and meditative young poet, Alfred Tennyson, visited us, and charmed our seclusion by the recitation of his exquisite poetry. He spent a Sunday night at our house, when we sat talking until three in the morning. All the next day he remained with us in constant converse. We seemd to have known him for years. So, in fact, we had, for his poetry was himself. He hailed all attempts at heralding a grand, more liberal state of public opinion, and consequently sweeter, more noble modes of living. He wished that we Englanders could dress up our affections in a little more poetical costume; real warmth of heart would lose nothing, rather gain by it; as it was, our manners were as cold as the walls of our churches.[66]

This paragraph was written up in later life and included in Mary Howitt's *Autobiography*. The second half of it quotes verbatim from a letter she had received from Tennyson immediately after his visit. 'Mr Howitt's surprise at the hyacinths is a very pretty household picture. I wish that we Englanders dealt more in such symbols, that we drest our affections up in a little more poetical costume, real warmth of heart would lose nothing rather gain from it.'

In January of the New Year Alfred gave Emily Sellwood the Bible which was to become the family text, used for the recording of the births of all their children. It is the first tangible indication of a continuing affection for her, although the initial inscription was plain and unsentimental. 'Emily Sellwood/ January 1847/A. Tennyson'.[67]

He had returned to Cheltenham, 'tied by the apron-strings of home', and stayed there until the spring. Following the commemoration dinner Tennyson had been approached by Whewell, his old tutor and now the new Master, to write an Installation Ode (for the installation of Prince Albert as Chancellor of the University). He sweated over this for only a short time before giving up. 'You will understand that I decline from no unwillingness to oblige you but from sheer dread of breaking down.' It was his normal reaction to commissions.

Arriving in London at the end of March he was forced to take to one of the beds at Mitre Court, suffering from 'more than one ailment'. As soon as he was well he went to Park House in order to say goodbye to young Harry Lushington, who was going out to Malta as a government secretary.

The winter had been exceptionally severe and April remained bitter. Tennyson used the weather as an excuse for not responding to an invitation from Rev Rawnsley to visit Lincolnshire. Whatever the nature of his rekindled affection for Emily it was insufficient to tempt him away from the peaceful lawns of Park House. 'It was as much as I could do to get here', he told Rawnsley, and bid him give his kindest love to 'each and all of the "old familiar faces"'.

Despite much solicitous attention the stay at Park House did not leave Tennyson feeling fully recovered and he convinced himself that he had further need of a water-cure. Cheltenham had become too much associated with 'apron-strings' (the wrong kind) and he elected to visit the fashionable Umberslade Hall in Birmingham, travelling by express train, a journey which took just three hours. The establishment, run by a Dr Johnson, did not observe the principles of the Priessnitz system, but its regime still represented something of an ordeal.

He kept his move secret from his own family, and spent much of this retreat proof-reading *The Princess*. 'The printers are awful zanies, they print erasures and corrections and other sins they commit of the utmost inhumanity', he moaned to Moxon. Such was Tennyson's public prominence by this time, that his residence at Umberslade was eventually reported in the Press. So was the imminent appearance of a new book. Tennyson had to damp down speculation. He did not want to publish during a General Election; one took place at the end of July and resulted in the Liberals increasing their number of seats from 289 to 337.

Asked by the Burtons of Somersby to be a godfather to their latest child (a son, named Alfred) Tennyson immediately sent

217

his consent, and that of his brother Charles. After a brief visit to Cheltenham he went to London, intending at first to spend the late summer in Italy, but he was unable to find a companion for the trip and in the end he divided his time, during August, September and October, between Maidstone and London.

By mid-October, after much dining with friends, Tennyson had had his fill of society and needed to get away. He took the final proofs up to Mablethorpe and finished the job of correcting them there. In November he moved to Malvern and put himself under the management of Dr Gully, the English Priessnitz. Gully's hydropathy centre was aimed at a respectable middle class, although its regime was, if anything, stricter than its Austrian counterpart. All correspondence and reading was banned, whether by candlelight or daylight.

Every day the patients would climb one of the hills outside Malvern to St Anne's Well, to be accosted by young girls with baskets selling ginger beer and biscuits. The resistance of such temptation rapidly became the key element in the cure and Dr Gully the most popular means of receiving hydropathical treatment. Amongst his patients were both Mr and Mrs Dickens, Thomas Carlyle and Florence Nightingale. Carlyle was quick to identify the cure as being essentially an institutionalized opportunity to fast – he saw it becoming 'under better forms ... the Ramadhan of the overworked unbelieving English'.

One very big attraction to Tennyson of the Gully cure was that he could board with his old friend Rashdall, who was now vicar of the Priory church, Malvern. They quickly rediscovered their previous understanding and Tennyson was full of a long poem called *Festus*[68] by Philip Bailey, which he championed after having been introduced to it by the Howitts. Rashdall, never an automatic reflector for Tennyson's opinions agreed that the poem was 'grand' but found it 'bereft' in religion. The poem never did achieve the acclaim which Tennyson (temporarily) thought was its due, but it was not without its influence on Tennyson himself.

When he returned to London he took for himself new, independent quarters at 42 Ebury Street, a road in which the Brookfields also now lived, only fifty yards off. They helped Tennyson organize a house-warming, Mr Brookfield turning up early in the afternoon to find workmen dismantling Alfred's bedstead and the poet himself supervising. When asked what was going on, Tennyson explained that he was clearing his bedroom in order to provide a place of retirement for the ladies he had invited. Brookfield persuaded him that this was a piece of unnecessary chivalry, but both he and his wife were impressed by Tennyson's earnestness.

We are all full of good intentions for the future, trying to develop one particular trait, trying to dampen another. It is a mistake to consider that men and women of genius are any different and biography can often create the illusion that the gifted personality is blessed with a supreme confidence. The famous subjects of such books roll on through life simply being themselves, and all around them have to adapt to their points of view and attitudes. Self-criticism and self-disgust are not materials for the great and mighty.

It is true that there eventually comes a point in the career of an artist who attains fame in his or her own lifetime when self-belief becomes unshakeable. What makes Tennyson such an interesting subject is the force of his self-scrutiny and self-disgust, and the way this comes into play against his public persona.

With the publication of *The Princess* that persona was beginning to take form.

22   The University of Women

There at board by tome and paper sat,
With two tame leopards couched beside her throne,
All beauty compassed in a female form.
The Princess;

(*THE PRINCESS*)

*T*he Princess was published on Christmas Day, 1847. It was the first of Tennyson's volumes to be issued in green cloth boards, with gilt lettering on the spine – the standard binding from that time on, and the form to look out for on second-hand bookshop shelves.[69] The book, published on a sixty-six/thirty-three per cent profit share basis, became Tennyson's first financial success. The original print-run of 1500 sold quickly, making a second edition necessary early in the New Year. By February 1853, when the poem appeared in its final, extensively revised form, there had been five editions. The fifth edition was the first one to take more than a year to sell out. Tennyson's profits from each of the editions was in excess of £100. The book sold steadily for the next thirty years, Tennyson's royalties from it tailing off slightly, but holding at roughly £75 per annum.

The poem's composition had a long history. The original conception owed a lot to one of Tennyson's earliest reviews. 'Upon what love is, depends what woman is, and upon what woman is, depends what the world is, both in the present, and in the future. There is not a greater moral necessity in England than that of a reformation in female education.' This had been a powerful injunction. A poem called 'The New University' had been begun as early as 1839, but only 200 lines were completed. It was not until 1845 that friends had reported hearing or reading sections from a new poem called *The University of Women* (Tennyson's working title for first drafts of *The Princess*).

An early form of the Prologue – almost a self-contained English Idyll in the manner of 'Audley Court' and 'Edwin Morris' – may well have been written in July 1842, when Tennyson was at Park House for the Mechanics' Institute fête, which forms its setting. Seven young men were picnicking amongst the crowd of workers and country folk. The lawns of the house were filled with every kind of demonstration and activity. A ball was balanced on top of a fountain. Cannon were fired. A clockwork steamboat plied amongst the lilies of the lake, whilst a miniature railway ran around it. Boys played cricket. Toddlers tumbled in the grass. There was country dancing to a violin, playing 'Soldier Laddie', and

> overhead
> The broad ambrosial aisles of lofty lime
> Made noise with bees and breeze from end to end.

The scene is perfectly captured in what Tennyson himself considered to be some of the best blank verse he ever wrote. The realism of the Prologue prepares the way for the fantastic story that follows, told in seven episodes, ostensibly by each of the seven companions in turn. Tennyson subtitled the whole work 'A Medley'.

The public liked the poem better than either Tennyson's reviewers or his friends. (In broad measure this has remained the case. Although it has always been popular with the general reader, critics have found the poem evasive – Ricks – or lacking in artistic unity.) Albeit Tennyson's longest poem to date, many of those close to him considered it a lightweight affair. Fitzgerald thought it a 'grotesque abortion' and 'a wretched waste', but then he was little interested in women. Carlyle, writing five days after the book's publication, and having seen much of the poet during the previous three weeks, wrote to Emerson: 'He has bread and tobacco: but that is a poor outfit for such a soul. He wants a *task*; and, alas, that of spinning rhymes, and having it called "Art" and "high Art" in a time like ours, will never furnish him.'

These reactions – both public and (un)friendly – must have surprised Tennyson. While working on the poem he had been consciously responding to the critical reception of his *Poems* of 1842. In his book *Tennyson and the Reviewers*, Edgar Shannon Jr identifies five key points in the responses to the 1842 volume, and one of the most significant of these is that if Tennyson was to establish his claim to greatness, he must write a long poem – a sustained work on a single theme. It is easy now to point to subsequent long poems – Clough's *Bothie of Tober-na-Vuolich* (1848), Coventry Patmore's *The Angel in the House* (1854) and Elizabeth Barrett's *Aurora Leigh* (1857) – and to suggest that Tennyson was simply doing what other poets were doing. This is to ignore the fact that he went into print first, with *The Princess*, and subsequently *In Memoriam*, and that other poets, to a large extent, followed his lead. It also glosses over the important issue of form. Once a poem reaches more than a few hundred lines in length there is a tendency to assume that form ceases to be an issue. A long poem is a long poem, and simply needs to hang together, the suggestion goes. Despite the critics' adverse reaction to the structure of *The Princess* Tennyson was to keep the medley format for his two most accomplished long poems, *In Memoriam* and *Maud*. Neither *The Angel in the House* nor *Aurora Leigh* can be described as medleys (they are much more like verse novels), and it is therefore true to say that Tennyson's long poems are quite unlike most long poems of the Victorian period. They are, in fact, rather more in tune with modern taste, and modern styles, than anything by Browning or Arnold. The influence of Tennyson's long poems on T.S. Eliot's *The Waste Land* is well acknowledged.

The story, told 'from mouth to mouth' in the manner of an undergraduate game, concerns the arranged marriage between a Prince and Princess. They have never met, but the Prince has fallen in love with a painted portrait of Ida, and demands the marriage. But Ida's father informs him that she has gone beyond the borders of his kingdom to establish a college for women. No man is allowed to intrude, on pain of death. Too much in love to be daunted by such a decree, the Prince and several stalwart but knockabout friends dress up in drag and enrol themselves as students. Eventually, of course, their disguise is discovered and much mayhem ensues. At one point the Prince is set upon by eight 'mighty daughters of the plough' who 'so belabour'd him on rib and cheek/They made him wild'. When, yet later, the Prince is ignominiously unhorsed in a jousting contest, the Princess Ida's heart begins to melt and, in nursing her wounded suitor, love undermines the intransigence of her separatist position, and at the poem's close, she acquiesces to the Prince's view:

> For woman is not undevelopt man,
> But diverse: could we make her as the man,
> Sweet Love were slain: his dearest bond is this,
> Not like to like, but like in difference.
> Yet in the long years liker must they grow;
> The man be more of woman, she of man;
> He gain in sweetness and in moral height,
> Nor lose the wrestling thews that throw the world;
> She mental breadth, nor fail in childhood care,
> Nor lose the childlike in the larger mind;
> Till at the last she set herself to man,
> Like perfect music unto noble words;

Much of this (including, literally, the final injunction) became the code for Tennyson's actual marriage. But for the time being it was an ideal projection. One of Tennyson's most astute, and undervalued, critics – Valerie Pitt – recognized the symbolic message of *The Princess*, which was telling its readers that the author was ready to surrender his isolation and enter into a relationship with the world. What Tennyson wanted from marriage was the unification of his inner with the outer world. It was this poem of 1847, rather than the greater poem of three years later, which marked Tennyson's first conscious step towards becoming a public poet.

23   Turbulent Times

Casques were cracked and hauberks hacked,
Lances snapt in sunder,
Rang the stroke, and sprang the blood,
Knights were thwacked and riven ...

('THE TOURNEY')

In the New Year of 1848 Tennyson spent a fortnight at Cheltenham, followed by six weeks in Ireland with Aubrey de Vere, having agreed conditions for his stay which included being able to take breakfast alone, being allowed to smoke in his room, and being left alone for at least half the day. The Irishman's record of this visit contains a telling anecdote. 'One night we turned his poem of *The Day-Dream* into an acted charade; a beautiful girl whom he used to call "that stately maid" taking the part of the Sleeping Beauty; and the poet himself that of the Prince who broke the spell of her slumber.' Inexperienced he might be, and unworldly in terms of a Thackeray, but these glimpses of Tennyson suggest that he lived in a state of teetering erotic excitement.

Whilst he was out of the country, civil unrest in England reached alarming levels. There had been a riot in Glasgow, and on 13 March 20,000 Chartists attended a mass meeting on Kennington Common. A second demonstration was planned for 10 April, at which more than half a million marchers were expected to travel from Kennington to Westminster to hand in a Chartist petition. The Royal Family and many middle-class households were worried enough by the prospect of violent revolution to take refuge in the country. In the event the marchers (some 150,000) were outnumbered by special constables (numbering 170,000) and were prevented from crossing the Thames. It was an ignominious day for socialism which, according to Halevy, 'foundered not in blood but in ridicule'.

Emerson, who had been in England since the turn of the year, was cool about the unrest. 'People here expect a revolution. There will be no revolution, none that deserves to be called so. There may be a scramble for money. But as all the people we see want the things we now have, and not better things, it is very certain that they will, under whatever change of forms, keep the old system. When I see changed men, I shall look for a changed world. Whoever is skilful in heaping money now will be skilful in heaping money again.'[70]

The American Transcendentalist[71], mixing with Carlyle and Dickens, was party to some interesting table talk. Dining together with them at John Forster's – described by Emerson as having an 'obstreperous cordiality' – he was told that prostitution was so rife in the London streets that chastity in the male sex was as good as gone. Both Carlyle and Dickens claimed it was now so rare in England they could name all the exceptions. (They named neither themselves, nor anyone else.) Dickens added that incontinence was so much the rule that if his own son grew up chaste he should be alarmed and worried about his health. There may have been a good deal of bravado in this conversation; even a bit of leg-pulling of the American who sententiously informed them that such was not the state of affairs in America, where young men of good breeding went as virgins to the marriage bed.

Emerson eventually met up with Tennyson at Coventry Patmore's on Friday, 5 May. He wrote up their meeting at some length and his description is all the more interesting for being that of an outsider. The pure physical impression made on the American was much the same as he made on everyone: 'He is tall, scholastic-looking, no dandy; but a great deal of plain strength about him, & though cultivated, quite unaffected. – Quiet sluggish sense & strength ...' As for the moving, talking Tennyson, Emerson wrote, 'Take away Hawthorne's bashfulness, & let him talk easily and fast, & you would have a pretty good Tennyson'. To those familiar with the personality of Hawthorne, this is an evocative comparison[72]; for all the talk of Tennyson's shyness, when put beside a truly secretive or retiring nature he could seem positively sociable. Emerson was quick to recognize Tennyson's special relationship with his cronies. 'He lives very much with his college set, Spedding, Brookfield, Hallam, Rice, & the rest and has the air of one who is accustomed to be petted and indulged by those he lives with.'

Tennyson seems to have been on fine form that night, and to have recounted his adventures in Ireland with a braggadocio redolent of his father's bizarre stories of foreign travel. He told how he had been drinking in an Irish tavern when a youth pulled a sword and swore that he would drive it to the hilt into the body of an Englishman, if one were present. Tennyson, outraged, took out his penknife, went up to the drunken Irish youth, and said, 'I am an Englishman – there is my penknife and, you know, you will not so much as stick that into me'.

This scarcely credible story – was it, perhaps, Tennyson, and not the Irishman, who had been drunk? – says a lot about the fierce patriotism which lay beneath the surface of the poet's 'quiet sluggish sense', and which was about to burst forth in an outbreak of poetic expression. However, his *gasconnade* was undermined somewhat by an evident timidity in his reaction to Emerson's asking for his company in France.

The approach was made after they had left the Palmores' and taken an omnibus, with Brookfield, back to the Brookfield household. On the bus Brookfield had encouraged Emerson to take Tennyson with him. 'That is the way we do with him. We tell him, he must go, & he goes. But you will find him heavy to carry', went the warning. Tennyson, though, thought it madness to go to France at just that moment in time, in the middle of a revolution, and told Emerson he faced certain death. Wouldn't he prefer to go to Italy? Tennyson was prepared to leave at once if that could be the destination.

Poor Tennyson. He had been trying for years to persuade one of his friends to take him to Italy. That none of them did so says much about the 'heaviness' which Emerson was warned of, but also demonstrates the growing division between Tennyson and his associates – they, married and working, with domestic and professional commitments, he still single and footloose. It was a distinction he was becoming increasingly uneasy about and had talked incessantly in Ireland of how badly he now wanted to marry. He 'will not be right until he has someone to live with him exclusively', de Vere declared.

24 The Valetudinary Takes a Tumble

And he by wild and way, for half the night,
And over hard and soft, striking the sod ...

('PELLEAS AND ETARRE')

Having made his first, simple revisions to *The Princess*, Tennyson began to think of a follow-up book – another long poem – and he was drawn once again to the Arthurian myth.

At the end of May he set out, on his own, for Cornwall, arriving in Bude on the night of the 30 May. Eager for an immediate glimpse of the waves he asked a girl at his inn the way to the sea. She took him to a back door and pointed into the darkness. With several glasses already inside him he fell from a wall at the back of the inn and dropped more than six feet onto a 'pavement fang'd with cobbles', cutting his leg open badly. (The pavement was, in fact, the railway line, and the unusually sharp cobbles the stones between the sleepers. Given Tennyson's extreme short-sightedness – he boasted of being the second most short-sighted man in the country – and his prodigious intake of alcohol, it is a wonder he did not suffer more such accidents.)

Bleeding, but scarcely conscious of the seriousness of his wound, Tennyson picked himself up and walked over a 'dark hill' (probably the railway embankment) to the sea. The next day he was mobile enough to walk through the town in daylight and sit watching the 'angry waves rushing in'. But on 1 June he was too sore to move from the hotel room, and called in a Cornish doctor.

The Doctor was John Dinham, brother-in-law to R.H. Hawker, clergyman of Morwenstow, also a poet and writer of ghost stories (not to mention the originator of the Harvest Festival). Tennyson persuaded the Doctor to take him the next

226

day to Morwenstow. Hawker found him 'swarthy' and 'Spanish-looking'. They sat together on the brow of a cliff, Hawker talking about shipwrecks, and Tennyson explaining the purpose of his journey. 'He is about to conceive a Poem – the Hero King Arthur – the scenery in part the vanished Land of Lyonnesse, between the mainland and the Scilly Isles.'[73]

Tennyson spent the next week sight-seeing – going to Tintagel, Camelford and Bodmin – but his leg showed no sign of healing and on 9 June he had to call in a second doctor. He was laid up in Fowey till the 20th, nursed by the local doctor and by the geologist C.W. Peach, who showed Tennyson his fossils, let him look through his microscope, and revealed that he managed to maintain a wife and seven children on £100 a year.

From then on there was another month of pleasant hiking around the balmy Cornish coves. He 'supped on sas-ages', 'smoked with workmen' and did a lot of sea-bathing. In every village there seems to have been a poet or a naturalist to converse with, and in the main he was able to keep away from high society. The only exception came at the end of his tour when he was courted by Mr Rundle, MP for Tavistock. He was entertained by the Rundles at the MP's brother's house at Upland near Plymouth, and introduced to their twenty year-old daughter Elizabeth.

Elizabeth's own account of the meeting, printed in the *Memoir*, once again shows Tennyson in flirtatious mood, and thoroughly at ease in female company. Indeed he seems to have monopolized Elizabeth to the exclusion of other guests, who had collected in the house to meet him. When he was shown the crowded drawing-room he made it plain that he did not want to enter into the 'party' and Elizabeth was instructed to set a quiet tea in the dining-room. Over this tea Tennyson's conversation skated from tavelling to painting, from geology to revolution, of his dislike for pedantry in women, and his belief that Wordsworth was great but too one-sided to be dramatic. It was heady stuff for a twenty-year-old, and intended to be.

Tennyson returned the next morning and kept up the salvo. This time they sat on deck-chairs in the garden with Elizabeth's cousins and Tennyson talked of the ganglia of lower organisms, of his dislike for Miss Martineau, and of Carlyle and Goethe. He was engaged to dine with the architect George Whitewick but sent the fly away when it arrived to pick him up, saying, 'I would rather stay with you bright girls than dine with Mr.

Whitewick'. They went into the kitchen garden and Tennyson told weird stories about African women wanting to be cannibalized. He kept up till mid-afternoon, turning from stories to mimicry, and back finally to literature. It was – if the account is an accurate one – a bravura performance. In parting, Tennyson said, truthfully enough, 'I will be grave when next I meet you; I vary'.

After his Cornish tour Tennyson joined his mother and sisters in Cheltenham for August and then spent two further months with Dr Gully at Malvern. The stay this time does not seem to have been occasioned by any great ill-health and his letters during September and October are calm and good-humoured. He wrote to Moxon asking for *The Times* to be sent to him, but then withdrew the request, saying that a fellow patient had agreed to share his copy.

On 4 November FitzGerald reported that Alfred was back in town: 'He now drinks a bottle of wine a day, and smokes as before; a sure way to throw back in a week or two all the benefit (if benefit there were) which resulted from many weeks of privation and penance.'

Alfred's brother, Frederick, was also in London, preparing to return to Florence. Here was Tennyson's chance to visit Italy. The time of year was not good, nor was the company of his older brother, but FitzGerald was persuasive. On the 9 November Tennyson packed his bags and set off for the Continent with Fred.

Two days later he was back in London, banging on Fitz's door, having had cold feet at the port. FitzGerald could not hide his exasperation. 'A. Tennyson, having only two days ago set off with his brother to *Florence*, re-appeared in my rooms this day at noon, and has usurped my day till now it is five o'clock. I have packed him off with a friend to dine.'[74] And, in another letter, written during the same month, FitzGerald elaborated on his loss of faith in Tennyson:

Tennyson is emerged half-cured, half-destroyed, from a water establishment: has gone to a new Doctor who gives him iron pills; and altogether this really great man thinks more about his bowels and nerves than about the Laureate wreath he was born to inherit. Not but he meditates new poems; and now the Princess is done, he turns to King Arthur – a worthy subject indeed – and has consulted some histories of him, and spent some time in visiting his traditionary haunts in Cornwall. But I believe the trumpet can wake Tennyson no longer to do *great* deeds; I may mistake and prove myself an owl; which I hope may be the case. But how are we to expect heroic poems from a valetudinary? I have told him he should fly from England and go among savages.[75]

Tennyson was now entering upon his final year of 'genteel vagrancy'. The fact that it was not so genteel at times seems to have offended FitzGerald almost as much as any supposed shortcomings in the poetry. The poet's movements in and out of Town followed no pattern and his behaviour in company was becoming increasingly eccentric.

One night he had been sitting glumly amongst some of his London friends, puffing silently on his pipe, when he suddenly rose and departed, with the brief announcement, 'I am going to Cheltenham, I have had a glut of men'. Even when he was in London there was no certainty that his friends would see him. Carlyle wrote to de Vere in early 1849, 'Tennyson it seems has returned to Town: a glimpse of him was got the other day, walking with large strides into Regent Street, in a northerly direction; and then he went over the horizon again, and has not emerged since.'

When he was not simply hiding away in London he might be in Cheltenham, at Park House, in Mablethorpe, on the Isle of Wight, or visiting the parish of Shawell in Leicestershire, where Sophy Rawnsley was now married to the Reverend Elmhirst.

It is noteworthy that when Charles Tennyson wrote the biography of his grandfather in 1949 he was able to report that 'the tradition of these visits is still strong amongst the villagers' a hundred years later. They 'say that the Rector built him a wooden room in the garden where he could write and smoke undisturbed ... Most interesting of all is the still current belief that he had once proposed marriage to Sophie.'[76] This is interesting, for it means that the villagers were made fully aware that Tennyson visited Shawell principally to see Sophy. One wonders whether there were other traditions 'still current' which Charles Tennyson was too polite to repeat.[77]

The second edition of *The Princess* was selling well, and later reviews had been growing more favourable. It was in readiness for a third edition that Tennyson began writing the intercalated songs which he felt the need to include, both to emphasize the

229

importance of the theme of the child in the poem, and to strengthen the impression of its being a 'medley'.

Meanwhile, the elegiac, memorial poems had continued to accumulate and Tennyson had begun to mention to one or two close friends that he might have some half-dozen copies of the whole sequence printed, for private circulation. There was, however, a moment of panic in February 1849, when Tennyson discovered that the butcher's account book, in which the poems were written out, was missing. He was staying on the Isle of Wight at the time and immediately wrote to Coventry Patmore:

> I went up to my room yesterday to get my book of elegies – you know what I mean – a long butcher-ledger-like book. I was going to read one or two to an artist here. I could not find it! I have some obscure remembrance of having lent it to you. If so, all is well. If not will you go to my old chambers and institute a vigorous inquiry.[78]

Patmore found the book in Tennyson's rooms, despite the resistance of the landlady, and for his pains was rewarded with its safe-keeping – a charge which he made the most of. William Allingham, visiting the Patmores later in the year, was treated to the dramatic story: 'I have in this room,' Patmore began, 'perhaps the greatest literary treasure in England – the manuscript of Tennyson's *next poem*. It is written in a thing like a butcher's account book. He left it behind him in his lodging when he was up in London and wrote to me to go for it. He had no other copy, and he never remembers his verses. I found it by chance in a drawer; if I had been a little later it would probably have been sold to a butcher-shop.' The notebook was quickly flourished under Allingham's nose, but withdrawn before he had a chance to read any of its lines.

In fact there were several other manuscript copies of most of the poems, and Tennyson's memory of his verses was better than Patmore suggested. Nevertheless, the possible loss of the ledger-book put him in sufficient panic to return to London as soon as the weather permitted.

Once he was assured that the poems were safe, Tennyson paid a flying visit to Park House and there unexpectedly met up with Emily Sellwood who, according to a later entry in her Journal, was visiting Kent in the belief that Alfred was safely out of the country, in Italy. She immediately returned to her father's house, which was now near Farnham. (The Sellwoods had moved away from Lincolnshire in 1847.)

Returning to Town, Tennyson had his first meeting with a young man who was to become a lifetime companion. This was the twenty-six-year-old Francis Turner Palgrave. Like Arthur Hallam, Palgrave was the son of a historian. The meeting took place on 31 March, at the Brookfields'. Afterwards, walking in the night air towards Hampstead, the two of them 'conversed on Universities, *The Princess*, his plans etc.; he very open and friendly'. Three days later Palgrave visited Tennyson in his dingy lodging and the poet treated his new friend to readings of the new songs which he intended adding to *The Princess*, together with one or two sections from *In Memoriam*.

Tennyson returned to Park House for the early summer but left in early July, a few days before Edward Lear arrived in the company of Franklin Lushington, with whom he had been travelling in Greece. Lear, like Palgrave, was to be another important friend in the subsequent part of Tennyson's life.

For the time being Alfred was trying to recapture the independent, incognito ambience of his balmy Cornish summer, and there exists a charming anecdote told by a Mr Mitchell, about a coach ride to Pitlochrie, in which the narrator tells how he spent an entire day in Tennyson's company without knowing the true identity of the poet. (This sort of interlude must have been immense fun for Tennyson, since it corresponds to a common childhood fantasy.) The ending to the long account says it all:

> As I seated myself in the Gig, I said, I did not remember ever having spent a happier day, and that I could not bid him fare-well until I had learned his name. And that, he replied, I will not tell you, smiling, as he did so; but I insisted again, and again, when at last he said, Very well, I will give it you, but recollect you have wrung it from me. It is Alfred Tennyson.
>
> Is it possible! I voluntarily ejaculated, and felt a burning shame suffuse my face ... While these thoughts were coarsing through my mind, my friend looked silently on, when all at once he took hold of my hand, and said, you insisted on knowing my name, and now, I insist on learning yours.[79]

The episode tells us something interesting about Tennyson's

public standing at that time. Increasingly a literary lion, sought after in the salons of London[80], his name was beginning to spread wider afield, but his visual appearance was not yet commonly known, a state of affairs which was to change dramatically in a very short space of time.

The holiday, as a whole, was not a great success. There was not, in the North, the same profusion of interesting clergymen-poets and amateur geologists that there had been in the South-West. And the weather was terrible. At Auckeld he was 'drenched to the skin, till my very hat wept tears of ink'. The high-point of the trip was a visit to the birth-place of Robert Burns. 'I enjoyed no day more than the one I spent at Kirk Alloway by the monument of poor Burns and the orchards, banks and braes of bonny Doon. I made a pilgrimage thither out of love for the great peasant – they were gathering in the wheat and the spirit of man mingled with all I saw. I know you do not care much for him [Tennyson was writing to de Vere] but I do and hold that there never was immortal poet if he be not one.' For all his strangeness, one of the most endearing things about Tennyson are such glimpses of his ordinariness, and this visit of a great living poet to the birthplace of a dead writer cocks a snook at literary snobs who find such pilgrimages vulgar. Admirers of Tennyson may visit Somersby with an easy conscience.

Tennyson was in Lincolnshire himself during October and November, being fêted by his old friends, and spending much of his time with the Rawnsley clan. Those who had not seen the poet since his early youth were struck by the contrast between his coarse, scrubby-looking appearance, and his agreeable conversation. At one dinner he entertained the guests with a moral conundrum – one which has the flavour of being borrowed from another person's after-dinner repertoire: a Russian woman, travelling by sledge with three of her children, gets caught in a blizzard and is pursued by wolves. Three younger children are all alone in a log hut. The wolves gain on her and she throws them each of the three older children in turn, in order to preserve herself and reach home safely. Was she right? Or ought she to have died with her older children, leaving the younger ones orphaned in a wild terrain? Tennyson held that she should have died. He was opposed by most of the men present, supported by the women.

If Tennyson did borrow this story, and put on airs copied from his London cronies, what would it matter? He would have been inhuman not to have enjoyed the satisfaction of returning to the fold, a relatively successful and increasingly famous person. In one regard he had not changed. At a subsequent dinner Mrs Rawnsley had to gently warn him about putting his feet up on the sofa.

By the third week in November he was back in London, staying at the Sabonierre Hotel, Leicester Square, in room number four, and dining out constantly. During the day he was busy preparing the third edition of *The Princess* for the press, making his final choice of songs to fit between the separate sections. There is a tradition that Emily Sellwood was invited to choose between different versions of 'Sweet and low' and that a fair-hand copy, dated 24 November 1849, was sent to her for her opinion. But there is little evidence for this. Nor is there any evidence for the suggestion that Tennyson visited the Sellwoods in Farnham during December and 'resumed relations'[81] with Emily.

Certainly his recent visit to Lincolnshire had intensified his desire to marry, but he spent the last part of December, including Christmas, with Sophy Elmhirst at Shawell, and there met Charles Kingsley who was to play a key role in the events leading up to Tennyson's wedding. It was while staying with the Elmhirsts that he made the sudden announcement, in a letter to Mrs Rawnsley, dated Christmas Day, 'I have made up my mind to marry in about a month, I have much to do and settle in the meantime. Pray keep this thing secret. I do not mean even my own family to know.'

It is unlikely that he could have come to this sudden decision without having met Emily recently and without there having been some form of 'resumed relations' between them, but it is unnecessary to suggest that he had been to see her in Farnham. Emily herself recollected that in addition to their chance encounter at Park House they had also 'met at Shiplake where Drummond Rawnsley was vicar'. If this meeting also took place in 1849 it must have seemed to Tennyson that Providence was tugging at his sleeve and pulling him towards the inescapable.

He could have had little idea, at the turn of the year, quite how special the new one was to be.

PART FOUR
Hesperus I

1 Very *Kleinstadtisch*

Ring out the old, ring in the new,
Ring, happy bells, across the snow;

(*IN MEMORIAM* CVI)

E arly in the New Year Tennyson returned to Shawell and
spent a month with Sophy, chewing over his decision.
While he was there the third edition of *The Princess* was
published, but he was already thinking more of the publication
of his Elegies. A trial edition was set to be printed in March, for
circulation amongst his friends. The original proposal of half a
dozen copies had escalated to twenty-five. On the day of his
return to London from Shawell, Tennyson wrote to de Vere, one
of the planned recipients of a trial copy: 'With respect to the
Elegies I cannot say I have turned my attention to them lately – I
do not know whether I have done anything new in that quarter
since you saw them, but I believe I am going to print them ... I
shall print about 25 copies and let them out among friends
under ... condition of either return or cremation.'[1]

However, his final instruction to Moxon, in March, was to
print half a dozen copies. Known recipients were Edward
Lushington, Venables, de Vere, Spedding and Rawnsley. The
hand-written frontispiece read: 'Essentially inconceivably
private till its later tho longer brother appear then to die the
death by fire! Mind! A.T.'

The copy received by Drummond Rawnsley was passed, via
Catherine, to Emily Sellwood. Tennyson had expressly asked it
to be shown to her, and requested some form of written
response. Emily wrote the following note on 1 April, after
passing the volume back to the Rawnsleys:

Katie told me the poems might be kept until Saturday. I hope
I have not occasioned any inconvenience by keeping them to
the limit of time; and if I have, I must be forgiven, for I cannot
willingly part from what is so precious. The thanks I would
say for them and for the faith in me which has trusted them
to me must be thought for me. I cannot write them. 'I have
read the poems through and through and through and to me

they were and they are ever more and more a spirit monument grand and beautiful, in whose presence I feel admiration and delight, not unmixed with awe. The happiest possible end to this labour of love! But I think not its fruits shall so soon perish, for they are life in life, and they shall live, and as years go on be only the more fully known and loved and reverenced for what they are.'

So says a true seer. Can anyone guess the name of this seer? After such big words shall I put anything about my own little I? – that I am the happier for having seen these poems and that I hope I shall be the better too.

I cannot enter into things more particularly with him. I only hope he will not be vexed by this apology for a note.[2]

The 'true seer', whose encomium Emily chose to use, was Charles Kingsley, vicar of Eversley, which was only a dozen miles from Shiplake. Once Emily's reaction had been ascertained events moved quickly, Charles Tennyson doing his bit to smooth things over with his father-in-law, Mr Sellwood. When Alfred took out a marriage licence on 15 May, it was such that he and Emily could marry away from the Sellwood parish. No continuing rancour between the families need be read into this, however. The Sellwoods still felt relative newcomers in Farnham and it was natural for Alfred to want to be married by his friend Drummond. Mr Sellwood had been staying for some months in Eastbourne and although brief consideration was given to Grasby the vicarage there was considered to be too new and too far away.

As soon as their engagement was re-formalized Emily began bringing her influence to bear upon Alfred's work. She advised him to use the title of the Elegies' dedication as the title for the whole work, instead of the proposed *Fragments of an Elegy*. The book was duly published as *In Memoriam* on 1 June, a fortnight before they were married.

There had been a few last-minute waverings. Since taking out the licence[3] Tennyson had been reluctant to name the date – a frustration to Catherine Rawnsley, who had been given the task of preparing the cake and the dresses. His sudden announcement of the 13 June found her in a state of unreadiness. Neither the cake nor the dresses arrived in time and the white gloves were lost.

The marriage party was small, with his sister Cecilia being

the only direct member of his family present – a fact resented and seen as inauspicious by another sister. Mary, who had resented her brother's cruel silence about his engagement and was under the misapprehension that the ceremony had been conducted on Friday 13th (it was, in fact, Thursday), wrote: 'Well, all is over...*Friday and raining*, about which I feel very superstitious... I hope they will be happy but I feel very doubtful about it.'

The day after his wedding Alfred wrote two notes – one a brief thank you to Kate Rawnsley ('You managed it very well yesterday. Many thanks.'); the second a droll statement posted off to Sophy Elmhirst, whose daughter Jenny had acted as bridesmaid ('We seem to get on very well together. I have not beaten her yet.').

It is significant that Tennyson should think of Sophy a day after his marriage, and that the newly-wedded couple's first port-of-call on their honeymoon was the grave of Arthur Hallam at Clevedon. This was Tennyson's first visit to the burial place of his friend. Emily's remark – 'it seemed a kind of consecration to be there' – has suggested to some that the visit was her idea, and embarked upon in order to establish joint dominion over Hallam's memory. From Tennyson's point of view – and whoever suggested the visit it would not have been made had Alfred not wanted to go – the belated confrontation with his friend's resting-place tells us several things.

Firstly, it reveals something about composition. If Alfred had attended Hallam's funeral sixteen years beforehand it is questionable whether he would have written *In Memoriam*. Now that the poem was complete, and published, he could visit the grave without undermining the creative impulse. Implicit in the concurrence of the poem's publication and his marriage is an acknowledgement that Hallam had been an important element in prompting him to extend his bachelorhood beyond the normal measure. What happened beside Arthur Hallam's grave was much more an exorcism than a consecration.

The early honeymoon days included less highly-charged diversions. The couple went riding on the moors, Emily on a donkey and Alfred on a horse. The donkey proved obstreperous and Alfred had to change places with his wife, making them an amusing sight for locals. At Glastonbury Alfred renewed his interest in the Arthurian legend, and at Clifton there occurred the first in a series of calamities which, in the opening twelve months of their marriage, threatened to confirm his sister Mary's worst forebodings. Alfred developed an infection underneath one of his finger-nails and the doctor, deciding it would need cutting into, gave the poet chloroform. Emily, out of the room, heard him howl 'as if halloing the hounds' and when he came out of the room his chin was blistered. In addition to this discomfort he had been suffering, since just before the wedding, from severe hayfever.

The couple left Bristol for Cheltenham and stayed for a week during the first half of July, visiting Tennyson's mother and sisters. Then they travelled north, having accepted an invitation from a Mr and Mrs Marshall (sister of Stephen Spring-Rice) to stay at Tent Lodge, their house on the edge of Coniston Water, for an unlimited period.

On first arriving in the Lakes they booked into a hotel in Keswick and while there received an invitation from Spedding to visit Mirehouse. Spread out in the room provided for the couple was an assortment of holed socks, all rescued from one of Tennyson's bachelor lodgings and testifying to the poet's changed position and fortune. This rather earnest practical joke was typical of Spedding.

By late July they were settled in with the Marshalls at Tent Lodge, where they stayed till mid-October. For Alfred it was two and a half months of supreme relaxation. He rowed on the Lakes, ate well and drank well – and wrote no poetry. If the couple had experienced any difficulties earlier in their honeymoon in consummating their marriage after so long a delay, these were quickly overcome, for some time in August Emily conceived her first child.

During the long summer idyll several friends visited the Tennysons at Coniston and gave their early impressions of Emily. The most eloquent of these early visitors was Coventry Patmore. A day after his arrival he sent his wife the following portrait of Tennyson's bride:

Mrs. Tennyson seems to be a very charming person, and I have already seen enough of her to feel that any description of her from a short acquaintance is sure to be unjust. Her manners are perfectly simple and lady-like, and she has that high cultivation which is only found among the upper-classes in the country, and that very seldom. She has instruction and intellect enough to make the stock-in-trade of half-a-dozen literary ladies; but she is neither brilliant nor literary at all. Tennyson has made no hasty or ill-judged choice. She seems to understand him thoroughly, and, with the least ostentation or officiousness of affection, waits upon and attends to him as she ought to do. She is of very pleasing appearance, and looks about 32.[4]

Emily would have been pleased with that last sentence. She was in fact thirty-seven.

Two days later, after luxuriating in the easy-paced recreation of time spent with Alfred – Tennyson reading Allingham's poetry aloud among the water-lilies of the lake; dining at two then talking over wine for two or three hours; walking till dark; then tea and more talk till eleven – Patmore developed his portrait of Emily:

> I have just had a long talk with Mrs. Tennyson. She seems to be in all respects worthy of her husband. She is a thorough lady – according to my standard. She is highly cultivated, but her mind seems always deeper than her cultivation, and her heart always deeper than her mind, – or rather constituting the main element of her mind. She is familiar with the best modern books, Ruskin, Maurice, Hare etc. Her religion is at once deep and wide; so that upon this and most subjects I feel that I am most fortunate in having many opportunities forthcoming of talking with her.[5]

But Alfred remained the focus of Patmore's attention:

> I cannot value enough my advantage in seeing so much of Tennyson. It is a great good to me to find that I have my superior, which I have never found in the company of anyone else. In the society of the nearly tip-top men, like Thackeray, Carlyle and Allingham, I feel an inferiority only of the means of expressing myself ... but in Tennyson I perceive a *nature* higher and wider than my own; at the foot of which I can sit happily and with love.[6]

Carlyle's impression of Mrs Tennyson, on his first visit early in October was characteristically more graphic. 'The first glance of her is the least favourable. A freckly *round*-faced woman, rather tallish and without shape, a slight lisp too; something

241

very *kleinstadtisch* and unpromising at the first glance; but she lights up bright glittering blue eyes when you speak to her; has wit, has sense, and, were it not that she seems to be very delicate in health, "sick *without* a disorder", I should augur really well of Tennyson's adventure.' (See plate 7 for the portrait of the small-town, provincial Emily and also for the more favourable apppearance.)

By the time they left Tent Lodge they had been visited by Franklin and Edmund Lushington, Woolner and Lear. The Marshalls' offer to let them live on in the Lodge was turned down and they decided it was time to go house-hunting for a home of their own, the initial plan being that they should live near Alfred's mother, or even share a house with her. So they travelled to Cheltenham, going part of the way with Matthew Arnold who was then, according to Emily, 'in the hey-day of youth'. The encounter was unremarkable but part of their conversation at least must have focused on Tennyson's recent publishing success.

2　A Man Confessing Himself

I sometimes hold it half a sin
To put in words the grief I feel;
For words, like Nature, half reveal
And half conceal the Soul within.

(*IN MEMORIAM* V)

Tennyson received a £300 advance for *In Memoriam*, which was published in May, in an edition of 1500 copies bound in purple boards, and priced at six shillings. The immediate success of the poem is evident from the fact that Moxon had to print three further editions before the end of the year – a second edition (1500 copies) in July, a third edition (2000 copies) in August, and a fourth edition for the Christmas trade (3000 copies). A further edition (this time 5000 copies) was required the following year.

Tennyson's own projected title, before it was changed at Emily's suggestion, was *Fragments of an Elegy*, and this tells us that the work was essentially a compilation. Various clever, critical arguments have been put forward to show that the poem's looseness contains its own artistic integrity — a fragmented personality trying to pick up the pieces after a shattering loss. According to this view the poem is best read as it was written, a bit at a time. But once Tennyson decided to have the sequence printed he did give careful thought to the ordering and construction of the sequence, and there is a movement in the poem, culminating in the marriage verses, which can only be fully appreciated by a continuous reading, from beginning to end. The poem can be divided into nine parts:

Sections I–VIII The poet is grief-stricken at the loss of his friend

Sections IX–XX The ship carries Hallam's body back

Sections XXI–XXVII Recollections of walks and talks with Hallam 'Better to have loved and lost . . .'

Sections XXVIII–XLIX The first Christmas

Sections L–LVIII Doubt and uncertainty in the face of new evolutionary doctrines

Sections LIX–LXXI The spirit of Hallam

Sections LXXII–XCVIII First anniversary of death and second Christmas

Sections XLIX–CIII Departure from Somersby and third Christmas

Sections CIV–CXXXI Spring and hope culminate in the marriage of Edmund and Cecilia

Such a brief summary of the nine parts of the poem (the suggested groupings were Tennyson's own) can do no more than emphasize the chronological sequence. However, when most of the elegies had been first written, it had been without any thought of their being placed within such a structure. They had been written at different times, in response to the mood of the moment. In Tennyson's own words, 'The sections were written at many different places, and as the phases of our intercourse came to my memory and suggested them. I did not write them with any view of weaving them into a whole, or for publication, until I found that I had written so many.' In re-ordering them, so that they followed a strict chronological development, the poem was given its compulsive hold upon the reader. As Eliot said, *In Memoriam* is 'the concentrated diary of a man confessing himself', and he added, 'It is a diary of which we have to read every word.'

Eliot also drew attention to the extra dimension in the poem beyond its journalistic recording of the different moods and feelings of the bereaved, the dimension which gave it unique appeal for its mid-century audience – namely, a belief in the possibility of spiritual as well as scientific evolution. 'It is an attitude of vague hopefulness which I believe to be mistaken', Eliot wrote in an article for The *Listener*, fifty years after Tennyson's death. 'But that does not matter', he went on, 'what matters is that Tennyson felt it and gave it expression.'

After its publication Tennyson himself grew to think that the structural drift was too cheerful. 'It's too hopeful, this poem, more than I am myself.' This was the judgement of an older man, speaking to James Knowles many years after the poem's publication (Hallam Tennyson even denied that such a statement had ever been made by his father), but there were others – quite a few of them – who thought that the poem insufficiently reflected the strength of Tennyson's faith and optimism as it stood in 1850. It is easy to forget that we read the poem today in the context of all we know about the way in which the nineteenth century, and especially Darwinian theory, developed. Tennyson's poem actually preceded *The Theory of Evolution* (but not other similar works) by one or two years. This meant that it was read by its contemporary audience, on first publication, as predominantly a personal poem. And in an era when so many died in their twenties – from consumption or smallpox – it was an audience acutely tuned in to the extravagant expressions of grief. Nevertheless, not everyone thought the length of the poem justified. Charlotte Brontë, surprisingly perhaps, thought it 'beautiful, mournful', but 'monotonous'. She had to give up reading it when only half way through. And she was not the only one to find its stylized reaction to the all-too-common loss of a friend hard to take.

Undoubtedly, though, the poem struck a chord which reverberated throughout the second half of the century. One scientific book which had been published, and some time ago (in 1833), was Lyell's *Principles of Geology*. The importance of this book was its assertion that the process of creation was not over. There was no such thing as a finished order. And this, by inference, included mankind, as well as inanimate strata of rocks. Such an easy identification of geology with theology – one which Tennyson's poem appeared to support – led some to suspect the orthodoxy of his religious belief. Even an admirer like Coventry Patmore thought it worth remarking, when he visited the Tennysons in Tent Lodge, that he found Alfred to be much more of a conventional Christian than *In Memoriam* had led him to expect. There was nothing pantheistic about the poet's Christianity, he found, despite:

> My love has talked with rocks and trees;
> > He finds on ministry mountain-ground
> > His own vast shadow glory-crowned;
> He sees himself in all he sees.

(IN MEMORIAM XCVII)

And in one of the earliest and most substantial critical responses, published in *Fraser's Magazine* (September 1850) as an unsigned review, but known to be written by Charles Kingsley, the poem is applauded on the basis of its religious conviction. 'It enables us to claim one who has been hitherto regarded as belonging to a merely speculative and pieristic school as the willing and deliberate champion of vital Christianity, and of an orthodoxy the more sincere because it has worked upward through the abyss of doubt.' It was, quite simply, 'the noblest Christian poem which England has produced for two centuries'.

It was on those terms that the majority of general readers received it – the level of homely Christian elegy. The fact that the doubts of an entire generation and epoch were being vicariously confronted was not a matter that the several thousand people who purchased the book, and the thousands more who read it, would have consciously acknowledged. However, the speed with which the poem became a public document in the way that only works of literature which primarily address the preoccupations of their age can become, does justify those who see it now as the quintessential poem of the mid-Victorian period.

How consciously was Tennyson writing for this effect? The slowness of the poem's composition, and the later rationalization of its structure, might support the argument that he threw in some of the more general sections with just this purpose in mind. But it would be impossible to prove, and anyway, towards the end of its composition, Tennyson had a very much smaller audience in mind. Essentially the finished poem was addressed to Miss Emily Sellwood. It was his letter of seduction – his way of proving to her that he was both sufficiently Christian and sufficiently anxious to join his inner, imaginative world to the outer world of domestic, family life for her to take him as her husband.

Other readers would not have been drawn to the work in such large numbers if its theme had been entirely epistemological. It was the fact that questions of faith and doubt were expressed in a voice of 'warm humanity' and that the poem was full of the homely imagery of Christmas and wedding-bells that gave it such a broad appeal.

> Tonight ungathered let us leave
> This laurel, let this holly stand:
> We live within the stranger's land,
> And strangely falls our Christmas-eve.
> . . .
>
> But let no footstep beat the floor,
> Nor bowl of wassail mantle warm;
> For who would keep an ancient form
> Through which the spirit breathes no more?
>
> Be neither song, nor game nor feast;
> Nor harp be touched, nor flute be blown;
> No dance, no motion, save alone
> What lightens in the lucid east
>
> Or rising worlds by yonder wood.
> Long sleeps the summer in the seed;
> Run out your measured arcs, and lead
> The closing cycle rich in good.

> (*IN MEMORIAM* CV)

If Emily read the imagery one way, and Kingsley another, this was just as Alfred intended. He was making a romantic proposal *and* putting an important testimonial before the public.

3 Inexpressibles

I leave thy praises unexpressed
In verse that brings myself relief,
And by the measure of my grief
I leave thy greatness to be guessed;

(*IN MEMORIAM* LXXV)

T he Tennysons did not stay long in Cheltenham. By now it was clear that Emily was pregnant and the early prospect of a child had turned them against the idea of living with Alfred's mother.

Firstly they tried the neighbourhood near Henry Taylor at Mortlake, and met Mrs Cameron – 'a delightful picture in her dark green silk with wide open sleeves, the dress fastened by a silk cord round the waist....'[8] It was Emily's first meeting with her, but Alfred and the Camerons were already acquainted.

On 23 October they moved on to the Lushingtons' at Park House, with a view to finding a house in the south-east. There was another reason why they had decided against living near Cheltenham. The four months which had passed since their wedding had produced an immense change in the poet's fame. *In Memoriam* had been, and was continuing to be, a commercial and critical success. Since Wordsworth's death earlier in the year (on 23 April 1850) the Laureateship had been vacant. It had been offered to Samuel Rogers in May, but he had turned it down on the grounds of age – he was then eighty-seven. Before the publication of his Elegies, Tennyson was just one of several in contention. These included Leigh Hunt, Robert Browning, Elizabeth Barrett Browning (there were many who felt that it would be fitting for a Queen to have a female Laureate) and even Tennyson's old adversary Professor John Wilson (Christopher North). But after the summer there was only one favourite and the odds, had they been called, would have been very short.

Tennyson affected to be unconcerned. By the time he and Emily arrived at Park House the choice had already been made and the dispatching of a letter was all that remained to be done.

The Prime Minister, Lord Russell, had passed four names to the Queen in September – Taylor, Knowles, Wilson and Tennyson – a short-list which provided no contest, especially as the matter was referred to Prince Albert, a keen admirer of *In Memoriam*.

During the night of 9 November Alfred dreamed that the Queen and the Prince came to visit him in Cheltenham. In the dream the Prince – 'very kind but very German' – kissed him. The following morning a letter was received from Charles Phipps, keeper of the Privy Purse, offering him the office of Poet Laureate. Tennyson may have heard rumours that his name was being considered for the Laureateship and allowed these to prompt the dream, but all his life he was susceptible to premonitions and the real significance of this one is that the imagined episode took place under his mother's roof, suggesting that he was not yet thoroughly secure in his marriage.

Tennyson appeared to be genuinely torn between acceptance and refusal, valuing the honour involved in the appointment but worrying about the public prominence it would entail. He wrote two letters, one accepting, one declining, threw them on a table, and settled to deciding over a bottle of port. His friend Venables was also staying at Park House and helped persuade Tennyson in favour of acceptance by telling him that a Laureate would always be offered the liver-wing of a fowl when dining out.

Alfred posted his acceptance on the 13 November. (It is tempting to assume that he took pleasure in mocking others' suspicions of this date.) Meanwhile, house-hunting remained the married couple's priority, to the exclusion of any new poetry.

Monckton Milnes arrived at Boxley on the 14 November and stayed for four days, offering Alfred and Emily a wing of his house at Fryston. But Tennyson's relationship with Milnes was such that close proximity was not inviting. He wrote to Sophy Elmhirst asking if there was anything in her vicinity. 'We do not intend to give more than about £60 a year: Emily insists upon good airy rooms, particularly good bedrooms. Do you know of any such house in your parts?'[9] A letter to Sophy's father expresses his mixed feelings about the Laureateship:

I thank you for your congratulations touching the laureateship. I was advised by my friends not to decline it and I was even told that being already in receipt of a pension I could not gracefully refuse it: but I wish more and more that somebody else had it. I have no passion for courts but a great love of privacy: nor do I count having the office as any particular feather in my cap. It is I believe scarce £200 a year and my friend R.M. Milnes tells me that the price of the patent and court dress will swallow up all the first year's income.[10]

Sophy invited them both to Shawell at the end of the year, but by that time they were interested in a house in Sussex. Emily may also have resented Alfred's continuing attachment to the younger Sophy, and she seems to have been instrumental in declining this invitation. 'It is very kind of you to remember us but Emily does not think she will be able to travel: and as for myself I think that I have too much to do, I am told to say.' Thus begins a reply signed by both Alfred and Emily, and with the key excuse written in Emily's hand.[11]

He wrote again at the beginning of January, before moving to Sussex, a more personal note, the tone of which suggests that Sophy was quite desperate to see him. After explaining that he had been unwell for more than a fortnight, with excruciating face-ache and nervous headache he continued, 'But even were I quite well I could not come at present being just about to move into our new house near Cuckfield and having to be on the spot to superintend unpacking furniture etc. I am grieved that I cannot come but *really and truly* I cannot.'[12]

The house in Sussex was in the village of Warninglid, a few miles outside Horsham. How they picked upon this to be their first home is unclear, but it quickly dawned on them that they had made a disastrous choice. Moving in on the 20 January, they left 'the Hill'[13] for good on 2 February.

They stayed at the Talbot Hotel, Cuckfield, before moving into Buckingham Hall, taking Mr Sellwood's cook and housemaid with them. On their first morning Alfred took a long walk and returned claiming that he had not heard such birdsong since leaving Somersby. After a good breakfast he set to work writing out the 'seizure' insertions for the next edition of 'The Princess'; (these represented his only poetic output since the wedding, with the exception of the poem dedicated to Drummond Rawnsley).

Later in the day a storm blew up and Alfred was smoked out of his study. The dining room was too draughty to sit in in comfort and, to cap it all, part of their bedroom wall collapsed in the middle of the night, letting in a deluge. It seems they had been too enamoured with the age of the Hall to notice its state of disrepair. Alfred immediately resolved to return to Twickenham, where he had been house-hunting just after Christmas. Emily was left alone in Warninglid less than forty-eight hours after moving in.

In a note to Forster, scribbled on the day of his departure, Alfred said, 'I am in a peck of troubles' and, 'My own affairs are too urgent and harassing.' Indeed they were. He had just signed a contract for a year's lease on a house that was proving uninhabitable. His wife, thirty-eight years old, was six months pregnant. Travelling up to London on the train from Brighton he must have reflected that these were not the kind of cares he had anticipated from marriage.

In Twickenham he took a second look at Highshot House, originally rejected in favour of Warninglid. The rooms needed work done on them but £30–£40 would put them right and the landlord, Mr Cain, seemed willing to do it. But nearby Tennyson came upon another house, recently up for let:

> The most lovely house with a beautiful view in every room at top and all over the rooms are so high that you may put up your beds. A large staircase with great statues and carved and all rooms splendidly papered – with a kind *gentlemanly* old man as proprietor – and all for 50 guineas! A lady has taken it. I cursed my stars![14]

Tennyson's passion for this house and his desperation at finding Warninglid so inhospitable led him into hard bargaining with the old gentleman. No agreement with the woman had been signed and Tennyson begged the man to let him take the house. The response was sharp. 'My word's my bond!' What made the situation all the more infuriating was that, on his first visit to Twickenham, in the company of Weld, he had been on the point of looking at Chapel House when Weld said they ought to be getting home and he had yielded. 'I am half crazed at missing it,' he wrote.

Emily, meanwhile, had engaged workmen to come in during Alfred's absence to try and make the Hall more comfortable for his return. It was all to no avail. Alfred could not stop dreaming of Chapel House, the chimneys still smoked and the draughts were unbearable. To make matters worse the nearest doctor lived five miles away and there was no direct post. More disconcerting was the discovery that the Hall had once been the haunt of the devilish Cuckfield Gang and that an infant was buried somewhere on the premises. New home or not, they would have to leave.

On the day of their departure Alfred pushed Emily part of the way to the Talbot Hotel in a garden chair. From Cuckfield they travelled to Shiplake, to begin a new round of house-hunting there, still believing that Chapel House was a lost cause. They stayed with Drummond for a fortnight but the house-hunting around Shiplake was fruitless. However they did see a good deal of Charles Kingsley and both Alfred and Emily began to read his latest novel, *Alton Locke*. It was a wet two weeks – with particularly heavy rain at night – and one day while walking Alfred was fascinated to see two shadows of himself, one cast by the sun, the other reflected in a puddle. One shadow was dark, cast on a hard, unflinching surface; the other was coloured, shimmering and ready to dissolve. He felt they were like two sides of life, part of which was grey and sombre, while the other part was gay, flighty and shallow.

Admitting defeat in their search for a home they left the Rawnsleys on the 18 February and set off for Park House. Stopping overnight at the Clarendon Hotel Emily had a minor fall. She slipped on a step and suffered a bad sprain which kept her in bed the next day. Alfred administered a water-cure, and they were able to proceed to Maidstone on the 20th, where Emily was put under a doctor's care for some time, so that a careful eye might be kept on the last stages of her pregnancy.

While there, Alfred received a sulky letter from Sophy Elmhirst accusing him of being annoyed at her invitation. He sent her an indignant, but passionate reply.

Now I feel hurt at the letter you have written me. You ought to have known me better than to have accused me of expressing myself as annoyed at your invitation. I was really annoyed at your accusation and took some pains to enquire what you could mean. At last I find out that Emily said to Kate that I was annoyed that I could not come or annoyed that you wouldn't believe that I couldn't. Is being annoyed that I couldn't come or being annoyed that you wouldn't believe me the same thing as being annoyed that I was asked? is it not just the contrary? Sophy, Sophy, how could you?[15]

Emily added a comment in the flap of Alfred's letter: 'I told Kate that he was annoyed you did not take him at his word that he could not come but repeated the invitation immediately, as if not believing that he could not.' This, surely, is incriminating. It shows that Emily *did* in fact report that Alfred was made cross by the second invitation.

This petty fracas is suggestive of tensions in the Tennyson marriage – by no means unnatural or untoward, but easy to overlook in favour of a more straightforward treatment, much as it has always been tempting to underplay the tension in the friendship with Hallam.

Towards the end of the month Alfred had to leave for London to attend the Queen's levee, but could not find himself a set of court clothes. Venables offered him a waistcoat, but that was all he could lay his hands on. While in London he returned to Twickenham, looked over both houses again, and immediately requested an interview with the landlord, Mr Clifton. Exactly what bargaining passed between them is unknown, but the previous agreement with a 'lady' was now overturned and Alfred agreed to Clifton's terms. Pending the exchange of references, Chapel House was theirs, and Alfred moved back to Boxley to tell Emily the news. The servants, who had stayed on in Warninglid, were sent instructions to pack up the furniture there and Mr Clifton was asked to recommend a coal merchant and to send Emily a sketch showing her the 'disposition of the rooms at C.H. for I myself (who have what the Philosophers call a deficient locality) could not tell her very distinctly about this.'

Samuel Rogers let it be known that Tennyson could borrow his court dress, which had been used by Wordsworth, and so Alfred was able to return to London to attend the levee on 6 March. The costume was a little small, but 'the inexpressibles were not hopelessly tight'.

After one or two social engagements he went back to Park House in order to prepare for the move to Twickenham. There were more letters from Sophy awaiting him. He reassured her of his affection and then he and Emily left Bosley on the 10 March, after gathering daffodils from the Park House lawns, and moved into their new home the following day.

Apart from a legal argument which remained to be resolved with the Sussex landlord, regarding their breaking of the year's lease, all seemed at last, ten months after their wedding, to be

leading towards the settled home life which Tennyson had
supposedly been craving from marriage.

4   Awful Day

Little bosom not yet cold,
Noble forehead made for thought,

(POEM NO 300)

The first few weeks at Chapel House passed pleasantly
enough. The couple received little house-warming gifts,
such as a box of table ornaments from Alfred's friend and financial adviser Venables. Their early visitors included Spedding,
Patmore, Henry Taylor and the Marshalls. Of close family,
Charles and Louisa, and Mr Sellwood spent several days in the
house; but this last visitor fell down the stairs while trying to
look at one of the sculpted figures and badly bruised his eye and
legs.

Alfred took short, desultory, duty-walks besides the Thames,
conscious of suburban confinement and almost pining for the
open countryside around Warninglid. The landlord of the Hall
had refused to take the key off the servants, saying that boys
and tramps would break windows and do other damage if the
house were left unoccupied, and it looked as if Tennyson would
have a great bill to pay. He wanted Venables to settle the matter
by covering the year's lease in full.

Emily went into labour during Easter weekend and a sturdy-
looking boy was born on Easter Sunday – dead; strangled at
birth. The couple were led to believe, by their doctor, that
Emily's fall had contributed to the baby's end, but this was
unlikely to be the case, if death was purely by strangulation by
the cord, as appears.

Those of us who are attracted by mid-nineteenth century life,
and who find ourselves looking dyspeptically on our own time
as a consequence, are brought up short by events such as this.
Infant mortality was a horrible shadow cast over the whole
period, but the generality of its horror means that we have to

make an imaginative leap when considering parents' responses to the death of a baby. Emily's Journal records, simply, against 20 April, 'First child born', as if it were immaterial whether the child was alive or dead. But this entry was made some considerable time after the event, once she had composed herself.

Alfred's sudden rush of correspondence in the days following the 20 April is a better indication of the impact which the loss had upon them both. To Anne Weld, Emily's sister: 'The child got suffocated in being born. He was as grand-looking a little fellow as ever I saw, as large as if he had been three months old at least and the Doctor said he would have been very hefty.' To John Forster: 'My poor boy died in being born. My wife is safe as yet, but I rather dread the third day ... He was a grand, massive, manchild, noble brow, and hands, which he had clenched as in his determination to be born.' To Edmund Lushington: 'It was Easter Sunday and at his birth I heard the great roll of the organ of the uplifted psalm (in the Chapel adjoining the house)...Dead as he was I felt proud of him. Today when I write this down, the remembrance of it rather overcomes me.' And to Robert Monteith, most vividly and movingly of all:

I have suffered more than ever I thought I could have done for a child still born...I refused to see the little body at first, fearing to find some pallid abortion which could have haunted me all my life – but he looked (if it be not absurd to call a newborn babe so) even majestic in his mysterious silence after all the turmoil of the night before.

He was – not born, I cannot call it born for he never breathed – but he was released from the prison where he moved for nine months – on Easter Sunday. Awful day! We live close upon an English-church chapel. The organ rolled – the psalm sounded – and the wail of a woman in her travail – of a true and tender nature suffering, as it seemed intolerable wrong, rose ever and anon.[16]

The effort of this correspondence – he claimed to have written sixty letters in all – and the anxiety about Emily's health, took its toll on Alfred. By the beginning of May he was 'thoroughly unwell' and cancelled all of his engagements. In particular he had to put off attending the Queen's Ball.

There is no mention in any of the correspondence, or in

Emily's Journal, of how they spent their first anniversary but it cannot have been altogether festive. Alfred was unwell, and Emily still weak from her ordeal. As they looked back on their first year of marriage, apart from the late summer weeks spent in the Lakes, and the wonderful success of *In Memoriam*, there was not much to gainsay Mary Tennyson's sense of foreboding. And apart from the strange, but significant insertions put into the fourth edition of *The Princess* (published in April 1851), Alfred had written nothing of consequence during the whole twelve months. His latest piece, 'To the Queen', written as a dedication for the seventh edition of *Poems*, was pure Laureatese – exactly the kind of poem he had originally declared himself unwilling to write.

> Take, Madam, this poor book of song;
>   For though the faults were thick as dust
>   In vacant chambers, I could trust
> Your kindness. May you rule us long . . .

In June Tennyson met the young poet William Allingham, then twenty-seven years old. The Irishman had heard indirectly that Tennyson thought well of his first volume of work, and Coventry Patmore engineered an appointment for Saturday 28 June.

Allingham caught the train to Twickenham and then walked across quiet fields to the isolated line of terraced houses named Montpelier Row. Chapel House was the last on the south end of the terrace.

Tennyson was sleeping off a bad attack of hayfever when Allingham arrived and made a sickly impression on first introduction. 'Hollow cheeks and the dark pallor of his skin gave him an unhealthy appearance. He was a strange and almost spectral figure . . . He was then about forty-one, but looked much older, from his bulk, his short sight, stooping shoulders, and loose careless dress.'[17]

The two men went up to Alfred's study and Tennyson read aloud some of Allingham's own poems. Over lunch they discussed Wordsworth and a poet even younger than Allingham, whom they both admired – George Meredith. Tennyson liked Meredith's *Love in the Valley* best.

In the afternoon Patmore joined them, and the three discussed grave matters over port. Tennyson gave vent to his belief in Immortality, saying that if ever he lost it he should go immediately and throw himself off Richmond Bridge. Allingham found this image somewhat ludicrous, and laughed. Tennyson, short-tempered, asked him what he found funny, and, when told, said, 'I'd as soon make a comic end as a tragic.' Discomforted, Allingham went out into the garden and joined Mrs Tennyson and Mrs Patmore. Coming back into the house for tea he found Tennyson still in rebarbative mood. When he smiled at some offhand remark, Tennyson pounded, 'What are you laughing at? You don't know what I'm saying.'

After tea, over pipes, conversation again became more cordial and Tennyson eventually walked Allingham to the station.

5 Paris Nosegays

... where art thou, thou comet of an age,
Thou phoenix of a century?

('FRIENDSHIP')

During the summer of 1851 Tennyson made his long-anticipated visit to Italy – with his ready-made companion, Emily. They left the country with the intention of not returning until the following year. Stopping over in Paris they were recognized by Robert and Elizabeth Browning, who were travelling from Florence to London in reverse direction. The four of them took tea together at the Tennysons' hotel. Elizabeth and Emily had much in common – they had each married late, had each lost a child and were semi-invalid before their wedding – and they took to one another as sisters. The two men, who had only socialized across dinner tables and at large gatherings before this encounter, also hit it off, and Alfred gave the Brownings permission to use the house in Twickenham for their stay in England.

When the Brownings returned to say goodbye to the Tennysons they found their rooms empty but left Paris nosegays in mixed colours arranged in a Grecian pattern. (The dried remains of these were kept among the family treasures for many years.)

Of all Tennyson's contemporaries in the world of letters he had most respect for Browning. He did not think much of Browning's ear for language and often remarked on the irony that one so passionate and knowledgable about music should be capable of writing such leaden verse. But he was a true and dedicated poet, to be spoken of in a different breath from Matthew Arnold. Contemporary over-valuation of Arnold's intellectuality and the modern acceptance that the three of them together form a triumvirate of Victorian poetry was never at any time acknowledged by Browning and Tennyson themselves. They each knew who their true rival was, and their relationship was appropriately adversarious, but in the best possible spirit.

It was mid-August before the Tennysons arrived in Italy, making for Bagni Lucca, at the Brownings' suggestion. But they found the place flea-ridden and too overtly Catholic for their taste and so moved on to Florence, where they were able to stay with Frederick and his Italian wife, Maria.

They preferred Florence to Lucca but Alfred complained about the difficulty of finding decent English tobacco there, and when they were advised that their planned advance southwards, to Naples, would be dangerous after the unrest of 1849, Tennyson quickly abandoned the idea of spending the winter in Italy.

They began their homeward journey on 24 September, travelling through torrential rain. In Milan Alfred climbed to the cathedral roof but the journey as a whole passed without recorded incident. By late October they were once again settled inside Chapel House, ready for an English winter.

The trip had been shorter than planned and, as usual with Tennyson, less vivid and enjoyable than anticipated, but it was nevertheless restorative and he began the winter in better health than might have been the case had he stayed in London. Early in the New Year it became evident that Emily was again expecting a child, and the Tennysons grew anxious to find themselves another home. Alfred was beginning to find the proximity of Chapel House to London a mixed blessing. He rarely went into the middle of town himself, but it was all too easy for others to visit him. FitzGerald tried to renew their friendship, introducing Alfred to the Persian scholar, E.B. Cowell, and Patmore and Palgrave often came round. Callers were not confined to his close (although widening) circle of friends. He began to be pestered by aspiring poets wanting the Laureate to approve their efforts. The little terrace in Twickenham was all too accessible. What is more, Alfred never really took to living close to the river. It confined his walks and seemed to make the atmosphere of the locality dank. The trouble was that Chapel House was neither Mitre Court nor Somersby Rectory, and he began to hanker after a more rural home.

In the early part of January 1852 he went, alone, to Cheltenham, where the air seemed so much fresher. He had come to bid farewell to his sister Mary, who had married the previous summer and was about to accompany her husband to a posting in Antigua, in the West Indies.

6   Thrilled by the *Coup d'Etat*

O where is he, the simple fool,
Who says that wars are over?
What bloody portent flashes there
Across the straits of Dover?

('THE PENNY-WISE')

Louis Napoleon's *coup d'état* at the end of 1851 was the event which relit Tennyson's poetic imagination. The series of poems which resulted has confounded many of his admirers and is sometimes dismissed as an uncharacteristic outbreak of waywardness. The poems are patriotic popular songs or jingoistic outbursts of hysteria depending on one's point of view, but whatever their literary merits they have immense biographical importance, for they set in motion the next phase of Tennyson's development – a phase which was to conclude with the strange and equally confounding long poem *Maud*. They also stand as key testimonies to Tennyson's position on the issues of self-defence and armed struggle, and they illuminate his later reaction to the Crimean War.

Since outflanking Lamartine in the plebiscite of December 1848, Louis Bonaparte, (described as looking like an opium eater), had been biding his time to seize power. In the course of the *coup* of 2 December 1851, more than a thousand people were shot in the streets of Paris and many prominent soldiers and politicians imprisoned. Tennyson denounced the *coup* immediately. At least a part of his ill-feeling towards Louis was as a result of the curtailment of his Italian visit because of ferment caused by French aspirations in Italy.

The poems which burst forth were not Laureate verse. They were published either anonymously, or under the pseudonym 'Merlin' (always a favourite identification), and they voiced anti-establishment sentiments. The Queen, like her Lords, was anxious to mollify Napoleon and to go some way towards accommodating him in order to avoid hostilities. As for the pseudonym, it does hint that, thrown in on himself by marriage, and no doubt encouraged by the doting attentions of an admiring wife, Tennyson was beginning to cast himself in the role of a seer. Where the poems fail – and they do so only in part – it is not in their ardency or patriotism, but in the indignant voice-in-the-wilderness tone.

However, the best passages read well and ruggedly and it is easy to see why they were snatched up by the press. 'Rifle Clubs!!!', with its 'dead, the dead, the dead/Killed in the coup d'etat' refrain is short and punchy. 'Hands All Round', which Tennyson is said to have composed with tears streaming down his face, ends with a prophetic statement of that special relationship which has existed between the United States and Britain at times of international alarm. There is one poem addressed directly to the Press – 'Suggested by Reading an Article in a Newspaper' – which contains some of Tennyson's most barbed bolts:

I feel the thousand cankers of our state,
    I fain would shake their triple-folded ease,
The hogs, who can believe in nothing great,
    Sneering bed-ridden in the down of Peace,
Over their scrips and shares, their meats and wine,
With stony smirks at all things human and divine!

I honour much, I say, this man's appeal.
    We drag so deep in our commercial mire,

We move so far from greatness, that I feel
   Exceptions to be charactered in fire.
Who looks for Godlike Greatness here shall see
The British Goddess, sleek Respectability.

Alas for her and all her small delights!
   She feels not how the social frame is racked.
She loves a little scandal which excites;
   A little feeling is a want of tact.
For her there lie in wait millions of foes,
And yet the 'Not too much' is all the rule she knows.

Poor soul! behold her: what decorous calm! -
   She, with her weekday worldliness sufficed,
Stands in her pew and hums her decent psalm,
   With decent dippings at the name of Christ!
And she has moved on that smooth way so long,
She hardly can believe that she shall suffer wrong.

('SUGGESTED BY READING AN ARTICLE IN A NEWSPAPER')

This is strong enough, and hardly straightforward patriotism, but the strength is too outwardly directed. There is insufficient sense of self-disgust, although self-disgust *is* surely at the root of such a burst of protest verse. The poet, in attacking the littleness of others' lives, is implying that he too, by marrying, has in a sense chosen littleness himself. This tension, felt more by some writers than others, but usually afflicting those who opt for a traditional domestic life, has been dubbed by the writer Martin Seymour-Smith '*Kunstlerschuld*' ('artist-guilt') – a useful term which can be applied by way of short-hand to some later discussions of Tennyson's attitudes.

The poem quoted begins with a warning to the press to keep out of household privacies – only the large issues should be taken into the open arena. (It is diverting to consider what Tennyson's reaction would be to today's tabloid press.) Its closing verse encourages newspapers to join in the popular call of 'Prepare' (for War). But, as a commentary on Tennyson's sudden air of self-importance, it is interesting to note that he accompanied the contribution of this poem with a memo praising his own work. '*Sir*, – I have read with much interest the poems by *Merlin* [Tennyson's pseudonym for the already-published 'The Third of February 1852' and 'Hands All Round!']. The enclosed is longer than either of those, and certainly not so good; yet as I flatter myself that it has a smack of Merlin's style in it, and as I feel that it expresses forcibly enough some of the feelings of our time, perhaps you may be induced to admit it.' In part this simply plays out to the full the joke of anonymity, but the claim to be the voice 'of our time' is semi-serious, and it is a claim which it is difficult to conceive Tennyson making at an earlier date. At the same time he wrote to his brother-in-law Charles Weld explaining why he is not asking payment for the poems: 'I might have made £5 of it [*The Penny-Wise*] but I give it to the people.' In similar fashion this 'give it to the people' strikes a new note.

Whilst it is valid to point to Tennyson's married state in connection with this new tone of voice it would be wrong to ascribe any particular influence to Emily. Alfred was not at home in Twickenham when most of the Merlin poems were written. He was staying with his mother and family in Cheltenham. And we know that Emily disapproved of at least one of the pieces, and was anxious to prevent its publication. Of 'Rifle Clubs!!!' Alfred wrote to Patmore: 'My wife thinks it too insulting to the F[rench] and too inflaming to the English. Better not make a broadsheet of it say I.' (Patmore was at this time producing leaflets for distribution, advertising his Rifle Corps). In fact this poem – undeniably extreme in its fear-mongering – 'Bearded monkeys of lust and blood/Coming to violate woman and child' – never joined the Merlin sequence and was not printed in Tennyson's lifetime.

As for Patmore's Rifle Corps, Emily wrote to try and distance her husband from the organization. She and Alfred had agreed to pay a subscription and to help distribute leaflets but:

It seems to me he can be no more than an honorary member of your club (and an honorary member of such a club seems an absurdity), as you know we are trying to get a house in the country as soon as we can ... At all events do not speak of him as an 'agitator' for any cause whatsoever. Neither him nor yourself if I might be so bold as to say so. The word has come to have so evil a meaning, a sort of hysterical lady meaning if nothing worse.[18]

There is a hint here that, eighteen months into marriage, some of her husband's tendencies unsettled her. The popular respectability promised with the success of *In Memoriam* and the

261

presentation of the Laureate's crown might be endangered by the sort of wayward extravagance which her father would have warned her against. She had not liked being left alone in Twickenham and had fretted for Alfred's return, forcing him to send her a delaying reply:

> Canst thou not hold on till Monday evening without me. I shall barely have time to select what books I want by Monday. Yet I fear thou wilt be bothered by my not coming – particularly as thou callest thyself unwell. The Kers and Cissy are *not* coming back with me so do not plague thyself about them ... And on Sunday all trains are so slow that I should be hours on the road. So rest thee perturbed spirit till Monday afternoon and sleep sound upon the *certainty* that I shall come then ... Now bear up! be jolly – for to think of thee sad spoils me here for enjoyment of most things.[19]

Having returned to Twickenham Alfred stayed there for only two or three weeks before going on the hoof again. This time he decided to take Emily with him into the country, on a visit to his friend Rashdall, at the vicarage in Malvern. From there they could begin to look for a new home.

Sophy Elmhirst, hearing of this, and assiduous in her desire to have Tennyson living near her, obligingly and perseveringly suggested a place near Shawell, but it was too expensive for Alfred and Emily to consider.

The doctor who attended Emily at Malvern would not take a fee but asked Alfred, in exchange, to mesmerize a young woman who was very ill. Alfred did use hypnotism on Emily throughout their marriage but he was uneasy about using his skill on a stranger. The first attempt took an hour but subsequently he was successful within a few seconds. This was the only instance of Tennyson's using mesmerism outside his family.

After staying with Rashdall for more than a month Alfred took Emily to Cheltenham and then, on 16 June, they returned at last to Twickenham, taking Alfred's younger sister Matilda with them, possibly as a female companion for Emily, whose pregnancy was by now well-advanced. But Matilda seems to have spent much of her time sight-seeing and gallery-visiting with Alfred, who was much impressed when he saw Millais' painting *The Huguenot*. This picture, the full title of which was *A Huguenot refusing to shield himself from Danger by wearing the*

Roman Catholic Badge, was on display in the same Academy display as *Ophelia*, and art critics have detected in both works the first seeds of that vulgar sentiment which mar much Pre-Raphaelite art. Tennyson's enthusiasm, however, was thoroughly in unison with the popular taste of the time. The two pictures proved a great attraction.

At home the Tennysons saw a good deal of Franklin Lushington (always one of the more acerbic Tennyson-watchers), the Patmores, and Woolner. In the evenings Alfred read aloud from Herschel's *Outlines of Astronomy* and he and Emily had lengthy discussions together. But these cosy evenings did not last for long. By 7 July Alfred was off again, this time on his own. Mr Sellwood came to look after Emily in her husband's absence.

Tennyson travelled to Whitby, hoping that the north-east coast would clear his hayfever, which was particularly bad. The journey was colourful. After sleeping at Spedding's rooms in Lincoln's Inn he caught the 11am train and found that his hayfever was aggravated by the smoke and soot on the railway. It drove him 'nearly crazed' but his only companion in the carriage was a man who appeared in even worse discomfort, eyes and teeth clenched with the pain of gout and his shoe curiously split to ease the agony. This gentleman got out at Harrogate to drink the waters.

Tennyson could not smoke on the journey, having left his tobacco and gloves at Spedding's, so the first thing he did on arriving in York was to buy some 'weed'. The town was alight with electioneering and on his way from the tobacconist to the Black Swan Tennyson was caught up in a threatening mob. Similar shenanigans were afoot in Whitby.

There is the crackiness of an election going on and lots of pink and blue flags, and insane northland boatmen of Danish breed, who meet and hang each other for the love of liberty, foolish fellows. In the midst of the row yesterday came a funeral followed by weeping mourners, a great hearse, plumes nodding and mourning coach, and the gaunt old Abbey looked down with its hollow eyes on life and death, the drunkenness and the political fury, rather ironically as it seemed to me, only that it was too old to have much feeling left about anything.[20]

There is an obvious identification here between Tennyson and the old Abbey. It is as much the writer of the letter who stands at an ironical distance from the activity in the town as the Abbey – 'too old to have much feeling left' – but nevertheless he liked it in Whitby and stayed there a fortnight 'killed with hayfever', spending the days 'coasting' – Tennyson's word for beach-combing – and describing his finds in letters to Emily.

> I found a strange fish on the shore with rainbows about its wild staring eyes, enclosed in a sort of sack with long tentacula beautifully coloured, quite dead, but when I took it up by the tail it spotted all the sand underneath with great drops of ink, so I suppose a kind of cuttle fish...I found too a pink orchis on the sea bank and a pink vetch, a low sort of shrub with here and there a thorn. I am reading lots of novels. The worst is that they do not last longer than the day. I am such a fierce reader I think I have had pretty well my quantum suff...[21]

Tennyson had no inclination to find a house in the north despite being told that Whitby was remarkable for the longevity of its inhabitants. Moving on from the seaside town he spent a week with his brother Charles at Grasby and attended the local school's sports day.

He returned home to Twickenham in time for his forty-third birthday. Mr Sellwood moved out and left Alfred and Emily alone awaiting the birth of their child, expected in September or at the end of August at the earliest. Emily was still issuing dinner invitations for the middle of the month when she went into labour on the 11th.

This time Alfred was able to send off notes of celebration.

7   Brickfaced Monkey

Bless thy full cheeks my noble boy,
God bless thee, thou art all my joy.
Mayst thou grow to manly prime,
And wed a bride in the primrose time

('THE BABY BOY')

The child, a boy, was born at 9.30am on 11 August with just a nurse present. Julia Margaret Cameron, in the first of her mercy missions for Tennyson, dispatched herself to town to fetch a doctor, but in the event she was too late. It did not matter. The birth was an easy one and Emily, surprised and relieved, looked pleased with herself. Tennyson wrote in one of his letters that he had never seen anything more beautiful than this expression. As for the boy, he called him, in the early days when he had no name, his 'little brickfaced monkey'. Emily wanted to call the child Alfred and Mr Hallam received a request that they might use Hallam as the boy's middle name.

As for getting used to having a baby in the house, the Tennysons found it much as most parents do with their first child – absorbing and exhausting. Tennyson wrote the following to de Vere:

> sick as I am with last night's watchings and trying to soothe the mother to sleep while the young unconscientious monsterling kept wailing his hard fate which was yet not so hard as his mother's who suffers from an almost total want of sleep[22]

To Monckton Milnes, whose daughter Amicia had been born a week before the Tennysons' child, Alfred confided that he had been 'rather wishing for a little girl', but this was said at a time when the boy was roaring night and day – perhaps he thought a daughter would have been a quieter creature.

By the end of the month Alfred was claiming to have written close on a hundred letters. Emily, finding breastfeeding awkward and painful, remained weak and bedridden. She was now thirty-nine years old. A new nursemaid was employed at the beginning of September and Alfred left to spend a few days on the Isle of Wight. Not much is known about this brief visit, except that he stayed both with Rev James White at Bonchurch and at a hotel in Blackgang Chine. It has to be assumed that the birth of a child had made more imperative than ever the need to move away from Twickenham and that he had gone to the island to look for a house.

He was back with mother and baby on 8 September and set about organizing the christening, which was fixed for 5 October at 1.30pm, with the breakfast at 3pm. By the time of the ceremony it had been decided, by Alfred, to put Hallam's name first. F.D. Maurice and Henry Hallam were godfathers and Robert Browning held the baby. Charles and Louisa, and Matilda, represented Alfred's family, and other guests included Drummond Rawnsley, Edmund Lushington, Palgrave, Julia and Henry Cameron, Venables, Sir and Lady Duff Gordon, the Welds, and the Marshalls. Carlyle should have been there but his invitation had gone astray. Tom Taylor came the following day by mistake (and embarrassed himself by becoming ill on shag and port). The breakfast, organized by Milnes and supplemented with a haunch of venison donated by Rawnsley, was so perfect 'it was thought to have come from Gunters'. After the meal Alfred took Browning and Palgrave up to his study for a smoke and a whisky toddy. They talked until one in the morning and Alfred stuck to one subject – his *bête noire* – Louis Napoleon and the British lack of preparation for war.

He had been moved by the Duke of Wellington's death in the middle of September (with this last hero gone the country seemed well and truly defenceless) and was already working on the long elegiac 'Ode on the Death of the Duke of Wellington', which was to become his first signed publication as Poet Laureate.

An early draft was ready in time for the funeral and 10,000 copies were printed in pamphlet form, to be sold to the public at a shilling each. Moxon paid Tennyson £200 for this agreement. The poem sold well to the crowd outside St Paul's with people buying it as a memento of the occasion, but it was much criticized in the press. In his usual response to criticism Tennyson worked hard on the poem in readiness for a second edition (which appeared early in 1853).

Although not written at the Queen's request it must be considered Tennyson's first official Laureate poem, but it also has to be read as the culmination of his series of pseudonymous war poems of earlier in the year. It continues the complaint that the country is being left unprepared against her enemies. This secondary argument weakens its impact as an elegy. Compared with, for example, Whitman's 'When Lilacs Last in the Dooryard Bloomed' Tennyson's poem is too negative about death, and too simplisitic about war.

The contrast between the two poems is all the more noteworthy since Whitman was criticized at the time for allowing Tennysonian cadences to infiltrate into his earlier more rugged style. This was especially the case with his companion piece to 'Lilacs', 'O Captain My Captain', a poem that Whitman wished he had never written, so gratefully was its metrical regularity seized on by anthologists, to the exclusion of his more characteristic work. Whitman admired Tennyson and the structure of 'Song of Myself', at first apparently so un-English in its let-it-all-hang-out Yankee swagger, owed a lot to the medley format devised by Tennyson in *The Princess* and *In Memoriam*.

The 'Ode on the Death of the Duke of Wellington' is similarly loose in format – not unlike Whitman's Lincoln tribute in length and structure – but many have felt that its separate units do not gel, or that its sentiments are too stiff, and that it aims for too dignified and courtly a tone. Tennyson was so disturbed by its negative reception that he offered to let Moxon out of their agreement. 'If you lose by the Ode I will not consent to accept the whole sum of £200 which you offered me. I consider it as quite a sufficient bore to you if you do not gain by it.' Even his friends had thought little of the poem and he might have been prompted into making this offer to his publisher by something said by Thackeray: 'Perhaps the most remarkable thing about the few lines is that Moxon has given £200 for it,' although it is unlikely that this sort of comment was being made to his face.

Before the Duke's funeral the Thames flooded and Emily, worried that baby Hallam might suffer from the dampness and blocked drains of Twickenham, agreed to move away until drier conditions prevailed. In a letter sent to Spedding which makes it clear that it was only Alfred who was dissatisfied with Chapel House, she said, 'I have been so happy here I do not want to go and I hope we shall come back for the winter.'

At the end of October, then, they removed themselves to Seaford, renting Seaford House for £2 a week. In the middle of November Tennyson went up to London to get his 'Ode' through the press and to attend the funeral procession, after which he paid a brief visit to Shiplake for the baptism of Rawnsley's latest child.

Returning to Seaford House he seemed better able to work than in Twickenham, concentrating on making minor amendments to the proofs for the eighth edition of his *Poems*. Emily and the baby grew more healthy, the latter becoming 'very huge'. For company Emily had Alfred's sister Matilda, who had stayed on with them since the christening, and her own sister Louy, who came to stay with Charles. It is noticeable that Tennyson was most at ease when he was living in a full house.

Seaford was, in those days, a lonely place between Brighton and Beachy Head. Even today, in winter, it can be wild and bleak on the seafront, but the Tennysons' house apparently gave them good shelter. The garden had high ivy-clad arched walls to keep out the wind and its inner space was demarcated by a pretty fence made of two rows of saddleback tiles; at the beginning of December there were scarlet geraniums still in flower in various urns and vases. The sea, though, *was* wild, and Emily was content to stay in the garden, although Alfred did get out and about, enjoying walks near the sea and to Alfriston.

In the last days of the year he was joined by his old friend Edward FitzGerald, who had been spending Christmas with his mother in Brighton. Alfred and Fitz had two long talks and smokes, mainly about the 'Ode' and the disappointing general response, but the conversation kept turning to '*Invasion*' (FitzGerald's emphasis, in a letter to Mrs Cowell, wife of the Persian scholar) — the key tenor of Tennyson's year. However, FitzGerald noted in the same letter, something which was to become a more lasting tenor: 'I admired the Baby greatly and sincerely: and Alfred nurses him with humour and majesty.'

8 'I Must Have That View'

I found, though crushed to hard and dry,
This nurseling of another sky
Still in the little book you lent me,
And where you tenderly laid it by:

('THE DAISY')

The Tennysons stayed in Sussex into the New Year but moved, in January 1853, to a small house in Kemp Town, suggested to them by the Marshalls, who were also in Brighton. While there, Hallam was vaccinated, and Alfred went to London to have some teeth stopped. FitzGerald, still in Brighton with his mother, went up to town with Alfred and they both attended a performance of Flower's choral setting of the Wellington 'Ode'. Fitz found the music dull.

On their return to Twickenham in the middle of February they heard that a woman was going around telling the tale that Tennyson had married her in Cheltenham and then deserted her, on the basis of which story she was persuading various benevolent people to sponsor her efforts to join an emigrant ship in the capacity of matron. The woman was either making the story up or had been deceived by an impostor – although in the latter case she would surely have tried to trace the real Tennyson, which she had not done. (Impostors, however, were large in number before the days of photography made such trickery much more difficult.)

Alfred was concerned enough about the libel to write to a noted social benefactress: 'I do not recognise even the name of the woman...She is either a swindler or insane...' and, the crowning felony, 'I am told that she writes verses on pink paper.'

The episode never developed into a scandal but it destroyed some of the benefit that had accrued from his Sussex stay. Visitors to Twickenham noticed that he was drinking more than usual and that his teeth still gave him trouble. Although he hardly moved from Twickenham throughout February and March he could not settle to any fresh composition.

To a request from Monteith for some original verse Tennyson had to confess, 'I do not know that I have any such gear by me.' In the absence of anything absolutely fresh, he sent 'To E.L. on His Travels in Greece' which had been written eighteen months previously.

By the same letter Monteith had invited him up to Scotland and after initially thinking the journey 'too expensive and too extensive: self, wife, child and nurse' he changed his mind and persuaded Emily, although again pregnant, to join him on a northern holiday. Palgrave was invited to accompany the family, and when they reached York, Emily, feeling that she could not bear the fatigue of the journey into Scotland, left the train and went to stay with her sister Louy in Grasby.

It was an unhappy parting, with Emily perhaps feeling that Alfred should not abandon her so easily. One of the train guards commiserated with Tennyson on his wife's demeanour. For his part, Alfred probably felt that Emily should have been a little braver and persevered with the journey. Reaching Monteith's in Lanarkshire he wrote to her, 'I am grieved you did not come even if you had made three days of the journey. Such large lofty rooms for the babe and sweet outlooks through trees of the Clyde would have charmed you.'

Palgrave, insensitive to the marital sulk, had stopped behind in Edinburgh accusing Tennyson of a coldness and indifference towards friends. 'I told him that this would apply to him rather than me,' said Alfred. However, they rejoined one another and travelled to Iona and Staffa from a base in Oban, where they stayed at a cramped and crowded hotel. In a remarkable confession which demonstrates the extremity of Tennyson's self-consciousness in the presence of complete strangers, he wrote to Emily to apologise for missing out a 'Dearest' at the beginning of one of his letters to her. 'I crossed out the initial Dearest in my last night's note not liking to write it with people looking over one's shoulder and intending to add it afterwards. Perhaps it has hurt thee and if so I am vext at myself.'

Tennyson and Palgrave returned from Oban to Edinburgh in mid-August, from where they intended to set off on a month's tour of the Highlands. However, they were delayed; firstly by a plea from his brother-in-law, Alan Ker. Things were not working out in Antigua – Alan, Mary and their child had all had yellow fever and they desperately wanted to return to England. Alfred wrote on their behalf to Henry Hallam to see what could be arranged. Having done all he could in this regard he consulted a doctor about a petty disorder – probably a troublesome varicose vein. Although described simply as 'trifling' it required two surgical operations.

It was while recovering from the treatment that Alfred came upon the pressed flower inside one of his books and wrote the poem 'The Daisy', an epistolary poem to his wife commemorating their Italian tour in the summer of 1851 in terms that suggest such days are over. The 'throbs of pain' that he tries to lull in the final verse were real and not poetical. The memories are brought back by the discovery of a daisy pressed between the pages of a book he has with him.

It told of England then to me,
And now it tells of Italy.
    O love, we two shall go no longer
To lands of summer across the sea;

So dear a life your arms enfold
Whose crying is a cry for gold:
    Yet here tonight in this dark city,
When ill and weary, alone and cold,

I found, though crushed to hard and dry,
This nurseling of another sky
    Still in the little book you lent me,
And where you tenderly laid it by:

And I forgot the clouded Forth,
The gloom that saddens Heaven and Earth,
    The bitter east, the misty summer
And gray metropolis of the North.

Perchance, to lull the throbs of pain,
Perchance, to charm a vacant brain,
    Perchance, to dream you still beside me,
My fancy fled to the South again.

By the time he was well enough to get about, the opportunity for a Highland tour had been missed and he travelled to Grasby to rejoin Emily and Hallam. They did not stay long with Charles and Louisa and were back in Twickenham by the end of

September. Almost immediately Alfred went off house-hunting – again to the Isle of Wight. Staying with the Whites at Bonchurch, as on previous visits, he heard that a house called Farringford, near the village of Freshwater, was vacant. Going to view it he found it looked rather wretched and neglected, with wet leaves trampled into the surrounding grounds – but it was worth a second look with Emily.

And so, on a still November evening, with the sky a strange daffodil yellow, he and Emily were rowed across the Solent. They stayed the night in a Freshwater hotel (Plumbleys) and went the next day to look at the house. Emily was more enthusiastic than Alfred and, on observing the panorama from the dressing-room window, said to her husband, 'I must have that view.' Alfred was still cautious and thought that they might have to go and see a house in Lyme Regis which '*may* be preferable to this'. But the owner of Farringford, Mr Seymour, seemed willing to settle, and they took a lease for three years at a rent of £2 a week, with the option of buying before the three years were up.

Emily left Alfred to conclude the legalities while she rushed back to Hallam. With businesslike foresight Alfred asked Moxon for an advance of £1000 so that he could invest in some East Lincolnshire Line shares, with a view to accruing enough capital for the purchase of the house when the lease expired. Fortunately this proved a safer and sounder investment than the disastrous speculation with Matthew Allen, although the shares did give him cause for concern in the New Year, when the threatened outbreak of war in the Crimea depreciated the market.

They wasted no time in moving into their new home and left Chapel House on 24 November, having arranged for Tennyson's mother to take over the Twickenham lease. On reaching Lymington in the evening they booked into a hotel for the night, fearing to take Hallam across in a rowing boat. The next day their life at Farringford began.

9　Far From Noise and Smoke of Town

Come, Maurice, come: the lawn as yet
Is hoar with rime, or spongy-wet;

('TO THE REV. F.D. MAURICE')

Despite another inauspicious beginning (two of their servants burst into tears saying they could never live in such a lonely place) this was the real start of their married life, and the beginning of Tennyson's long period of creative maturity.

The estate the house was built on was an ancient one, the name of a certain Walter de Farringford occurring in fourteenth-century deeds. At one point in its history there had been a Priory attached and the names given by the monks to several landmarks were still current – Maiden's Croft and Abraham's Mead. The house which the Tennysons took over had been built in 1806 and was originally of modest size. But new rooms had been added – in particular the room to the south with its great twelve by sixteen-foot window commanding the view down to Freshwater Bay, about a mile away. The building and interior decoration were neo-Gothic – a style which Tennyson much preferred to any other.

The walls were covered in creeper and in the grounds several elms and pines added to the air of seclusion. However, in contrast to the dank confinement which he had always felt in Twickenham, here the open tops of the Downs were within a few minutes walk.

Soon after moving in Alfred built, with rushes and young willow shoots, a bower in the kitchen garden for his wife to sit in when the sun was shining. The kitchen garden, at the back of the house, a place of warmth and peace, was especially enjoyed by Emily. Eventually pink gooseberries, grown from a cutting taken from Somersby, and a plant sent from Mount Olympus by

Edward Lear were to grow there.

The move was clouded a little by a misunderstanding concerning the future domicile of Alfred's mother and by financial uncertainty regarding the shares. As regards Mrs Tennyson, the following letter sent by Emily to Alfred while he was away from the new house, tells us most that we need to know:

I fear Tilly has shown sad want of tact in what she has said to Mother. I said what I did to Tilly when Mother had hurt me by speaking as if we were striving with the Jesses to get her to live with us as matter of gain. Do not think however I said anything in the very least unkind even then. It sounds harshly put as Mother has put it but these were not my words.

I have written and said to her, '... it rather hurt me you should have spoken as if you thought we wanted you to live with us as a matter of help in a money point of view when your comfort and happiness alone made us think of the plan. ...'

I have told them as we should have to build and alter if they lived in the house with us I thought it best they should come first and try how they liked it ... I hope thou wilt approve of what I have done.[23]

Alfred thought that Emily had acted properly but gave slightly divergent reasons for so thinking. 'I believe I told her myself at Twickenham that I was afraid if she came to live with us the rest would flock there and that this was the sole objection to the plan of her living with us.'

The financial matter was less messy but of greater moment. 'The E.L. shares are down at 140 and the fees are £25 so ... if I were to sell out tomorrow I should lose £100,' he wrote to his financial guru, Venables. He wanted to know whether it would not be better to lose the £100 and sell, or risk waiting. But if the shares should fall further he might never be able to afford to buy the house. Everything hinged on the War. 'The shares will rise enormously if there is no war. But I cannot help thinking that war is all but certain.'[24]

Despite these headaches life at Farringford quickly settled into a distinctive rhythm – giving Tennyson the pattern and order he had craved but which he had never been able to realize during their days at Twickenham. He would normally breakfast alone and then spend half an hour in meditation over his first pipe of the day. Then he would work and break off for a long two-hour walk before lunch. In the afternoon there would be another long walk, with dinner taken between five and six. (The meal would invariably be a roast, followed by apple pie. In one regard at least, Tennyson was typically Victorian – his diet.) This was followed by another solitary pipe – the umpteenth of the day – and by port-drinking and further work. Then he would come down and read aloud and talk until late.

There were, then, three working periods in his study during the day. One in the morning soon after breakfast; one in the afternoon soon after lunch; and the last in the evening, immediately after supper. But much of his initial composition was done, as had long been his habit, while out walking, and the earliest draft of a poem would be a simple transcription of what had already been written inside his head. The first two sessions at his desk were devoted mainly to reading and thinking. It was in the evening that he spent most time working over his poetry.

The lawns at Farringord became something of an obsession. He spent hours rolling them, picking up leaves, and even digging them up. When he went away he left instructions about which activities were, and which were not, permitted on the grass. While his walking was thoroughly in tune with contemporary views on fitness, and had developed into an important mode of composition, he was driven by something much more manic in his labours with scythe and with rake.

Tennyson's worries about his investment need to be put in perspective. He still received £500 a year from his inheritance, the pension of £200, £100 from his Laureateship, and another £100 from his Aunt Russell – making a total of £900 assured income. By comparison, a skilled artisan, such as a printer, might expect to earn a little over £400 a year. But Tennyson had, in addition to his fixed income, the royalties from his poetry and these were by now effectively more than doubling his annual revenue, so that in the previous twelve months he is estimated to have brought in £2500 – a massive amount for a literary figure, in particular a poet. It was this relative wealth which permitted the Tennysons to take over Farringford in some style, employing a healthy retinue of domestics. They were helped by the fact that, to begin with, the house came ready-furnished.

That Tennyson consistently pleaded poverty, even at this date, stemmed from the insecurity he felt at his lack of backing capital – an insecurity which was bound up with his continuing resentment at the way his father had been disinherited by the Old Man of the Wolds. When he wrote to his Aunt Russell in March, acknowledging receipt of the latest £100, he was characteristically cautious about his current literary popularity:

> It was very kind of you to think of me and my expenses at this juncture. Your cheque was most welcome, however someone (I know not who, perhaps that cackling fellow, Jesse) may have been dilating to you about my 'elegant sufficiency'. If I were to die tomorrow I could only leave my wife and now two sons £150 per ann. in railway shares: that is surely no great matter: meantime my books make money but who can guarantee that they will continue to do so. A new name, and such must arise sooner or later, may throw me out of the market: even a Russian war (for books are nearly as sensitive as funds) may go far to knock my profits on the head.[25]

No doubt it was just such nervous realism which helped justify his continuing receipt of the Pension.

One of the first poems written at Farringford was the epistolary 'To the Rev. F.D. Maurice'. Maurice, godfather to Hallam, had left Trinity as a dissenter without a degree in 1827. He had published a novel, *Eustace Conway*, in 1834, and after serving as chaplain to Guy's Hospital, was now a professor of theology at King's College, London.

The poem is a perfect example of Tennyson at his most relaxed. The verse is rhymed, but colloquial. The invitation is warmly felt, and urbanely expressed. Written at a time when war was looming it expresses the quick sense of belonging which Tennyson developed towards Farringford:

> Should all our churchmen foam in spite
> At you, so careful of the right,
>   Yet one lay-hearth would give you welcome
> (Take it and come) to the Isle of Wight;
>
> Where, far from noise and smoke of town,
> I watch the twilight falling brown
>   All round a careless-ordered garden
> Close to the ridge of a noble down.

You'll have no scandal while you dine,
But honest talk and wholesome wine,
    And only hear the magpie gossip
Garrulous under a roof of pine:

For groves of pine on either hand,
To break the blast of winter, stand;
    And further on, the hoary Channel
Tumbles a billow on chalk and sand;

Where, if below the milky steep
Some ship of battle slowly creep,
    And on through zones of light and shadow
Glimmer away to the lonely deep,

We might discuss the northern sin
Which made a selfish war begin;
    Dispute the claims, arrange the chances;
Emperor, Ottoman, which shall win . . .

The ships of battle were indeed sailing out of the Solent and the
boom of cannon-practice echoed across from the naval docks
in Portsmouth. Just as war was developing and soldiers were
being sent to the front Tennyson was settling into his long-
sought seclusion. There was something delicious about sending
invitations and knowing that friends could not just 'call by'
without some such definite summons. But there were stronger,
more global forces that could not be controlled or kept at bay.
We have already seen how the war seemed set to scupper his
financial plans. It was a real concern, and not a matter for idle
after-dinner attitude-striking. Christopher Ricks has complained
that the Crimean reference in this poem weakens it, because the
nature of its form is too lightweight to take the burden of such
'politico-moral matter'. And a contemporary critic rather
pompously took offence at the picture of a poet 'chatting of the
war over his wine, while the men of war sailing outwards lend
another charm to the beautiful sea view.' The only reply to this
second criticism is that it interpolates too malignant a slant on
Tennyson's outlook on life, making him the unconcerned epicurean that he most clearly was not. Ricks's criticism is, as
usual, more searching, and is best countered by reaffirming the
biographical background. Tennyson *could* see such ships from
his window – they were not poetic window-dressing; and the

War which they represented was of direct concern, not at a moral or even political level at this stage, but at a personal one. Were Maurice to accept the invitation the two would almost certainly talk about the war. Remove the verses objected to and the poem becomes over-familiar, an articulation of measured urbanity, and indisputably light verse. Their inclusion gives it both a historical and a personal reference point – it does not particularly need a political or a moral one.

10   Specks in the Eye

Death and marriage, Death and marriage!
Funeral hearses rolling!
Black with bridal favours mixt!
Bridal bells with tolling!. . .

('FORLORN')

Alfred and Emily's second child was born on 16 March 1854. Towards the end it had been a difficult pregnancy and Emily remained bedridden for a considerable time after the event. Tennyson had been stargazing on the Farringford roof at the time of the birth (9pm) – he had complained to Moxon at the end of February that his telescope had been returned to him cleaned, but minus a night glass – and had just observed the culmination of Mars in the sign of the Lion. So the child was named Lionel and Alfred predicted a military career.

Once again he had to set about the task of writing letters. Lionel was described as 'a fine big boy', a 'fine lusty boy', 'a strong and stout fellow', but 'I don't think the younger one will turn out such a noble child as Hallam but who can tell.' Hallam's response to his baby brother was touching. 'He kissed him very reverently, then began to bleat in imitation of his cries; and once looking at him he began to weep, Heaven knows why: children are such mysterious things.' One of the last of such letters was written to Julia Cameron, in which he told her that he had been mesmerizing Emily, in an effort to ameliorate the pain she had suffered since the delivery.

During the late days of Emily's pregnancy, and the anxious ones immediately after the birth of Lionel, Tennyson immersed himself in the study of Persian and in correcting the proofs of his brother Frederick's collection *Days and Hours*. This close work, coupled with the general anxiety of the time brought a return of troublesome specks in his right eye and eventually a severe inflammation. Increasing his nervousness had been the behaviour of servants during Emily's confinement – they had been incessantly quarrelling among themselves and saying unkind things about their mistress. (Tennyson constantly fretted that his staff did not show him proper respect.)

In his letter to Aunt Russell, who also suffered from these 'musculantae', Tennyson wrote, 'I have got some 15 *new* specks in my right eye: these all occur together, like a group of dark Pleiads something in this position

not pleasant, rolling round as the eye rolls and damaging these splendid sea-views considerably. I cannot help thinking that these have resulted solely from house-bother and from having been put out, as they say, 3 or 4 times a day for at least 4 months. Muscae volitantes I believe do not lead to amaurosis, which if true is a comfort. The only advice I can give you or I believe that any Doctor could give is "Keep your mind easy".'[26]

Tennyson was still complaining of petty vexations in April. Writing to Patmore he said, 'When you call me such a happy man you lie. I have had vexations enough since I came here to break my back. These I will not transfer to paper though I can yet scarcely repeat with satisfaction the proverb of let bygones be bygones: for most of these troubles have not gone by ... Happy I certainly have not been. I entirely disagree with the saying you quote of happy men not writing poetry. Vexation (particularly long vexation of a petty kind) is much more destructive of the "gay science" as the Troubadours (I believe) called it.'[27]

Towards the end of April, with Edmund Lushington and Coventry Patmore visiting, (the early visitors to Farringford were all men) Emily finally got out of bed and Alfred and his two guests shared the task of pushing her up onto the Down in a little carriage acquired in the village soon after the move. The carriage – a form of basket chair on wheels – was to give good service and cover long mileage. It became Emily's main means of transportation when on the island.

On 15 May the guests left for London and Alfred joined them, staying in town for a week. It was his first trip away for some considerable time, and he wrote at the end of it, 'This little outing has done me good.'

It was an uneventful seven days – his most noteworthy excursion was to Sydenham to see the newly-moved Crystal Palace which was being prepared for the grand opening – but it was good to get away from servant-trouble and the trip also meant that his bad eye was rested.

While he was away Emily got together the small printed Persian grammar and the Persian book with minuscule type, and hid them. She felt secure in this subterfuge knowing that Alfred would blame absentmindedness on his failure to lay a hand on them.

Lionel's christening had to be postponed when the child caught thrush. It eventually took place on 6 June at a time when Edward FitzGerald was staying. Fitz stood proxy at the service for one of the godparents who could not be there – Drummond Rawnsley. This was FitzGerald's only visit to Farringford and although his stay seemed to pass pleasantly enough – with outdoor sketching, piano playing, and (from his own copy) translating aloud from the Persian for Alfred – there was something which made him sufficiently uncomfortable to decline future invitations. It is unlikely to have been disgust at the pretension of Farringford – in these early Freshwater days, before they owned the house and before the time of their greatest financial security, their manner of life was very simple. It is more likely that FitzGerald's discomfort was caused by the domestic and nursery atmosphere of family life, from which he felt himself temperamentally exiled. The fact that his visit coincided with a christening would not have helped.

11   Work of a Swell Man

I was walking a mile,
More than a mile from the shore,
. . .
And riding at set of day
Over the dark moor land,
Rapidly riding far away,
She waved to me with her hand.

(*MAUD* IX)

With the birth of his second child the life of father and family man, which had seemed so remote just a few years ago, had become reality. Tennyson was about to begin work on his next major poem and in the early part of June he received a letter which gives the clue to the poem's inception. It came from Sophy Elmhirst and contained an arresting piece of news. Tennyson's reply – 'I did not know that Rosa was at Ryde' – gives added significance to Emily's Journal entry for June: 'He took some very long walks in the great heat, to Bonchurch once and back, over the shingly shore, other walks almost as long to Newport & back & to Newtown. He knocked himself up but did not tell me.'

Tennyson usually walked on the Down, to the Needles, or, in the opposite direction, to Blackgang Chine. It was clearly the news in Sophy's letter which compelled him to walk across the island, in the direction of Ryde. Soon after receiving the news, and soon after these marathon and manic walks, he began work on *Maud*.

Six weeks later, after giving Hallam a birthday excursion on donkey-back to Alum Bay, Tennyson left the island and spent two weeks travelling in Somerset, alone. He visited Glaston-bury, Wells, and the Cheddar Gorge, seeming to be collecting impressions for a Merlin poem. He arrived back home 'in bad trim', suffering from a boil, but immediately settled down to working on his long poem.

Aubrey de Vere spent ten days at Farringford at this time and his account shows that the agitation of the Tennysons' first months in the house had been smoothed over. Of Alfred, he said, 'He is much happier and proportionately less morbid than he used to be; and in all respects improved. I never saw anyone richer in the humanities than he is, or more full of that cordiality and simplicity which are apt to accompany real genius, and which mere talents, or cleverness, seem to repel.' And of Emily: 'She is a woman full of soul as well as mind, and in all her affections it seems to me that it is in the soul, and for the soul, that she loves those dear to her.'

Other visitors who came to enjoy evenings in the candle-lit drawing-room included Sir John Simeon, Palgrave, and the Lushingtons, and it was during September and October that Alfred developed the routine of his nightly public readings to guests. Mostly these were of old poems – 'Edwin Morris', 'Audley Court' – but on 20 September, hearing news of the Battle of Alma, he did read to Simeon an early draft of one of the sections of *Maud*, the poem that was to become the stock-in-trade of his public readings.

It was a poem which many of Tennyson's contemporary readers were to find too hot to handle, but of all his major works, both in content and in tone of voice, it is the most readily accessible to the modern mind – an inspired and rabid monologue spoken by 'the heir of madness, an egoist with the makings of a cynic, raised to a pure and holy love which elevates his whole nature, passing from the height of triumph to the lowest depth of misery, driven into madness by the loss of her whom he has loved, and, when he has at length passed through the fiery furnace, and has recovered his reason, giving himself up to work for the good of mankind through the unselfishness born of a great passion.' So was the poem, in far too orderly a way, later paraphrased by Hallam.

What Tennyson succeeded in doing for the first time in *Maud* was to apply his splendid ability to write protest verse, hitherto confined to his minor political pieces, to a work of true stature. Emboldened by his new position as husband, father, and Laureate, he gave full rein to all the grievances that had bedevilled the first half of his life – the madness suffered by members of his family, the humiliating and ruinous deception wrought on them by Dr Allen, and, most pungently of all, the snobbery of wealth which had made futile and demeaning his advances on the rich girl, Rosa Baring.

The resulting torrent of injury falls in successive waves of varying intensity. Making use of a shifting, spasmodic pitch,

Tennyson accurately portrays a character on the edge, or in the midst of a crack-up. It would have been absurd to have delivered a controlled monologue in the conventional manner. And so he produced what he termed a 'monodrama', in which 'successive phases of passion in one person take the place of successive persons'.

When he was younger and unmarried, he had usually projected himself into the mind of an older character, such as Ulysses or St Simeon Stylites; now he did the reverse and wrote as a disaffected twenty-five-year-old, cast adrift by personal disappointments and the sense of cut-throat immorality in society. It was difficult to feel anything about anything:

> Our planet is one, the suns are many, the world is
>   wide.
> Shall I weep if a Poland fall? shall I shriek if a
>   Hungary fail?
> Or an infant civilisation be ruled with rod or with
>   knout?
> I have not made the world, and He that made it will
>   guide.

Such temptation to abdicate social responsibility speaks just as directly to us today. Initially Maud presents the character with the possibility of lifting himself out of such a hopeless state, through romance and marital bliss. When this hope is dashed, the prospect of a foreign campaign, and the chance for an act of nobility, seem to provide the only means of achieving dignity in a world grown loathsomely materialistic and acquisitive.

Alfred and Emily followed keenly every scrap of news from the Crimea. The landing had taken place on 17 September and the early success at Alma had given rise to an unrealistic sense of optimism characteristic of the start of most wars. A few days later when flags began to fly and they heard cannon fired Alfred and Emily believed that a swift victory was being celebrated. But the gun-salute turned out to be in honour of a coastguard wedding.

In the middle of November *The Times* carried reports of the disaster at Balaclava. While sweeping up leaves and burning them, Alfred began to compose 'The Charge of the Light Brigade' and, by the time he came to write it out, was ready to dash it off in the space of a few minutes. He worked on it a little for a day or two before asking Emily to post it on the 6 December to John Forster with a view to having it published in the *Examiner*.

First reports had mentioned a charge of just over 600 men but by the time Alfred had written out his fair copy this figure had been corrected to 700. He fretted over whether or not he should sacrifice metre for accuracy – the metre being a straight (but not frequently mentioned) crib of Michael Drayton's 'Agincourt'. Amongst the marginalia of Herman Melville, who was at this time turning to poetry, disillusioned with his failure as a novelist, there is a pencil drawing of a hand with its index finger pointing at the title of 'The Charge of the Light Brigade'. On the back of the hand is inscribed, 'Stuff by a Swell Man', and close beside it a verse from Drayton's poem.

> They now to fight are gone,
> Armour on armour shone,
> Drum now to drum did groan,
>   To hear was wonder;
> That with the cries they make
> The very earth did shake:
> Trumpet to trumpet spake,
>   Thunder to thunder.

('AGINCOURT' BY MICHAEL DRAYTON)

Tennyson followed the metrical pattern of the poem exactly, occasionally lengthening each verse with the addition of a line or two:

> Cannon to right of them,
> Cannon to left of them,
> Cannon in front of them,
>   Volleyed and thundered;
> Stormed at with shot and shell,
> Boldly they rode and well,
> Into the jaws of Death,
> Into the mouth of Hell,
>   Rode the six hundred.

('THE CHARGE OF THE LIGHT BRIGADE')

The poem was published instantly, in the edition of 9 December. Charles d'Eyncourt, increasingly irritated by the success and fame of his nephew, dubbed it 'horrid rubbish' and pontificated, 'What an age this must appear when such trash can be tolerated and not only tolerated but enthusiastically admired.' The enthusiasm was popular rather than critical, and buoyed up by the atmosphere of war.

In the meantime Alfred was continuing with the writing of *Maud*, working harder and more intensely ('morning and night' according to Emily) than at any time since his marriage. The working momentum was broken, in the middle of January, by the three-day visit of an American poet, Frederick Tuckerman. Tennyson, always deeply hostile towards long-distance visitors, particularly Americans, was cold and severe at their initial encounter, but as soon as Tuckerman began quoting from his favourite Tennyson poems, the ice was broken.

Tennyson read aloud as much of *Maud* as was completed, together with other poems, and drank brandy with the American, stretched out on the hearth-rug in his study. In his letter thanking the Tennysons for their hospitality, Tuckerman wrote: 'I may now say ... that portions of these poems have come back to me with a power and beauty unexampled and that I only wait until the curves come full circle to do justice to the perfection of the whole, in regard too, to your manner of reading or chanting, I feel that it must be the true one; at all events I cannot recite your lines – the exquisite ones for instance – "came glimmering through the laurels/in the quiet evenfall" – in any other way.'

This letter is of interest because it shows that even during its period of composition *Maud* was very much a performance poem, and that Tennyson's reading style – his chanting – was intimately matched to the poem itself, and not a late mannerism. (Nevertheless, it has to be admitted that, no matter how private or domestic the venue, readings of poems are performances and, like all performances which rely on a limited and often-repeated repertoire, have an inevitable tendency towards self-parody.)

Maud was completed in the throes of harsh winter weather, neuralgia, and desperate, seemingly hopeless news from the war front. In addition to receiving a handsome meerschaum and a bound Webster's Dictionary from Tuckerman, Tennyson also got from the American an edition of the works of Edgar Allan Poe and Emily's Journal records the fact that Tennyson was reading Poe's poems aloud during the evenings of February, at exactly the time he was adding the 'Mad Song' to the all-but-completed *Maud*. But the sense of despair in the poem remained authentically Tennysonian:

I keep but a man and a maid, ever ready to slander and steal;
I know it, and smile a hard-set smile, like a stoic, or like

A wiser epicurean, and let the world have its way:
For nature is one with rapine, a harm no preacher can
   heal;
The Mayfly is torn by the swallow, the sparrow
   spear'd by the shrike,
And the whole little wood where I sit is a world of plunder and prey.

We are puppets, Man in his pride, and Beauty fair in her flower;
Do we move ourselves, or are moved by an unseen hand at a game
That pushes us off from the board, and others ever succeed?
Ah yet, we cannot be kind to each other here for an hour;
We whisper, and hint, and chuckle, and grin at a brother's shame;
However we brave it out, we men are a little breed.

Maud is a poem still capable of unsettling the reader. It has generally been approached with caution by the critics, and held at arm's length; they have, by and large, shared the view of Tennyson's contemporary reviewers and concluded that it was an artistic misjudgement, uncontrolled and indulgent. It is a view which needs challenging, if only because *Maud* was always one of Tennyson's own most cherished poems. In its original form it was not divided into the three parts which stand today. Perhaps it is only their demarcation which makes Part III read as something cobbled on, but the concluding part adds little to our knowledge of the speaker, and what it does is intrusive, raising fresh issues. The closing lines of Part II – 'I will cry to the steps above my head/And somebody, surely, some kind heart will come/To bury me, buy me/Deeper, ever so little deeper.' – seem expressly written to end the whole work. It was an enormously courageous poem to bring before the public as his first book as Laureate, and perhaps the final verses and the character's conversion to the cause of war were in some part a means of mitigating his intrepidity. However, there are other ways of viewing this section and, in any event, they did not soften the critical onslaught. If anything, they exacerbated it.

During March and April Tennyson had completed the monodrama and the first fair copy was written out by Emily. In May they left Farringford for London, having to settle certain matters relating to the expiry of the Chapel House lease. Although they both left the island feeling hungry for change, Emily wrote to Edward Lear: 'It is too powerful a sea air to remain in it nearly a year and a half without going away for a day, but we admire the place quite as much as we did at first and if we were a little richer we should not hesitate about buying it.'

While in London they had a family outing to the Crystal Palace and then went to a party held at the Welds'. Other guests included Matilda and Horatio Tennyson, Edward Lear, Spedding and Venables. At the end of May they moved to Park House and left Hallam and Lionel there with their nurse, before going to Oxford, where Alfred was presented with an honorary degree, Doctor of Civil Law (DCL) – the same one held by his father. They stayed with the Master of Balliol, Robert Scott. Tennyson, excessively nervous in all public ceremonies, dressed carefully (he was often stung by remarks about his dirty clothing) but did nothing to control the lie of his hair. Emily, in the audience, thought he looked alarmingly pale. A heckler in the gallery was heard to call, 'Did your mother call you early, dear?' There were three other recipients of degrees – two commanding officers from the Crimean campaign and the Comte de Montalembert. Tennyson fancied he got the larger share of the undergraduates' applause, but recollecting this impression he prefaced it with the words, 'I'm afraid'. He could not help but be sensitive to a certain discomfort in receiving an award alongside men of action, who had risked their lives in the field of battle.

Returning to Twickenham he left Emily with his mother and went to fetch the two boys and their nurse from Park House, and then the entire family returned to Farringford.

Maud was published at the end of July, in a volume which included Tennyson's other significant compositions since his marriage: 'The Daisy', 'The Brook', the 'Wellington Ode', and 'The Charge of the Light Brigade'. The initial print run was large (10,000) and from the beginning sales lived up to Moxton's high expectations. A second edition had to be printed before the year was out.

The financial benefits of this success and the prospect of a popular triumph with a projected illustrated edition were somewhat offset by the force of criticism directed at *Maud*. Those who carped at Tennyson's later work – notably Meredith who said, for instance, of the 'Holy Grail', 'The lines are satin lengths, the figures Sevres china ... Why, this stuff is not the Muse, it's Musery. The man has got hold of the Muses' clothes-line and hung it with jewelry' – were being unfair for overlooking the critical reaction to *Maud*. He had written another type of poem and had it rejected. And Tennyson was never the type of artist to ignore critical opinion and go his own way.

One critic of *Maud* said that either one of the title's vowels could be omitted and all that needed to be said about the poem would be revealed. The Radical press, in particular, went to town on the poem, insisting that the character's views must be those of the poet. Verse parodies began to appear in various pamphlets attacking the Government's Crimean policy, defending the social progress of recent years, and generally reversing all the salient features of the character's state of mind. Tennyson was particularly upset to receive, from his favourite Aunt Russell, a letter taking umbrage at the passage in *Maud* describing a coal magnate, which she had read as a criticism of her husband's family. 'Sooner than would anyone in such a spiteful fashion [I] would consent never to write again; yea to have my hand cut off at the wrist.' In some measure, the critics did just that – cutting off, for many years, his nerve to write in such a fashion.

Before the main wave of this response broke, Tennyson heard from a chaplain in the Crimea that 'The Charge of the Light Brigade' was a great favourite among the soldiers, and that printed sheets of the poems would be greatly appreciated. He immediately arranged for 1000 copies to be run off. In doing so he reversed one or two amendments which he had made to it recently, and appended a note to all the soldiers at the front: 'Brave soldiers, whom I am proud to call my countrymen, I have heard that you have a liking for my ballad on the Charge of the Light Brigade at Balaclava. No writing of mine can add to the glory you have acquired in the Crimea; but I send you a thousand copies of my ballad because I am told that you like it and that you may know that those who sit at home love and honour you.' However, Emily felt that the tone of this note was too regal and John Forster advised likewise. The thousand poems, and later a second thousand, were sent without it.

At exactly the same point in the summer Alfred and Emily heard of Henry Lushington's illness and subsequent death in Paris. Alfred was reading the Memoirs of Margaret Fuller to Emily at the time – strange and incongruous material given the tenor of Fuller's life. They did not attend the funeral and Emily's letters to Lear, who had accompanied Franklin Lushington to be near the deathbed, established an intimacy between them that was to last the rest of Lear's life.

The letters reveal much about Emily's personality – much that is never conveyed by the consistent litany of Farringford visitors emphasizing her soul and her spirituality – and, by extension, they tell us a great deal about her relationship with Alfred.

On the 17 August she wrote: 'I feel one, or at least myself, often errs grievously through what in worldly parlance one calls shyness, what in higher and sterner language is want of faith in God and man ... For how much is lost that can never be recovered now? My heart is stupid. I cannot write only I have a dim sad feeling we must help each other, those who at all understand each other and love each other.' This dim sad feeling is suggestive of a gap in the understanding between herself and Alfred, a gap which Lear himself was to comment on at a later date. In another letter she told Lear that he must be a 'sofa to her shyness' – an oddly cosy and intimate metaphor, again suggestive that there was a want of warmth and emotional exchange in her marital life.

Emily wrote to Lear again a fortnight later, after Alfred had left for a hike in the New Forest and she had been left with Hallam and Lionel and had taught Hallam for the first time to say his prayers. 'I am sick at heart today, not having heard from Ally, though very likely I could not have heard ...' (It was only two days since his departure.) 'What right have I to feel sad who have so unspeakably much to make me cheerful; a love tried by all the changes and chances of a more than five years' marriage and tried only to prove it unimagined worth more and more.' Despite this unimagined worth, Emily was conscious of a continuing 'aloneness' which she had not expected to feel as a wife and mother. This same letter told Lear of her boys' boisterous games: 'Our tinies are well. Hallam's great delight is to ride on my back and then Lionel must ride too, so with her two romping boys Mother has a chance of being well tired.' Such romps jar against the conventional picture of Emily as sofa-ridden and invalid, just as her letters to Lear jar against the picture of a wife entirely fulfilled in the vicarious lives of her husband and children.

The song written by Alfred for insertion into the second part of *Maud* – 'Courage poor heart of stone' – had been completed just before Henry Lushington's death, and she found herself responding to its burthen of loneliness. 'Courage, poor heart of stone!/I will not ask thee why/Thou canst not understand/That thou art left for ever alone.' A letter did eventually arrive from the New Forest. Alfred was staying at the Crown Hotel,

Lyndhurst, and reported the loss of his umbrella and his tobacco-case, the latter being the colour of last year's leaves so that he did not see it when turning to leave the spot where he had stopped to smoke and read. He was grieved to lose the case. The whole letter, written at three different sittings is a dither of forgetfulness and incapability. Alfred says there is little to do at Lyndhurst but dine, and the incoherency of this letter suggests that the hotel cellars, as well as its kitchen, provided fair sustenance.

He decided to cut his trip short and asked Emily to meet him off Monday evening's 5pm packet. She did; but he was not on the steamer and so she took the fly back to Farringford. Alfred, who had come across on a rowing boat, was left to walk home alone.

Over dinner, in a curiously neutral way, reflected in Emily's rather flat Journal entry, he described some of the fine things he had seen in the forest. 'In a clear and rather rapid stream he had seen a cow standing with cataracts of light from the four legs,' etc. This presents a picture of a husband and wife who had both, in their different ways, been disarmed and unsettled by their brief parting, but were prevented by reticence and shyness from more passionate expression.

But the marriage was still young and Emily was at her healthiest at this time, able to get out walking on the Down with Alfred without the use of her wheelchair.

12   *Maud* Vindicated

Eyes, what care I for her eyes, those eyes that I did not behold.
Can they be more whether black or blue, fullrolling or small,
More than the beldam-tutored Demos commonplace eyes,
Lying a splendid whoredom to full-fed heirs at the Ball,
'Buy, me, O buy me and have me, for I am here to be sold.'

(*MAUD*, DRAFT)

On 25 September Tennyson went to London to visit his dentist and while in town was the guest at several evening gatherings. On the 27th he dined at the Brownings', with the Rossetti brothers both present. Tennyson drank two bottles of port and bored Dante Rossetti by repeating the same stories seven or eight times. His conversation, said Rossetti, was a 'perpetual groan'.

When invited by the Brownings to read from their volume of *Maud* he sat himself sideways on the sofa with one leg drawn up and, holding the book high in front of his eyes in his left hand, began at the beginning of the poem and continued to the end. Elizabeth Browning ascribed it to 'unexampled naïveté' that he should pause every now and then in the reading and remark 'There's a wonderful touch! That's very tender! How beautiful that is!' Perhaps; but it might also have had something to do with the two bottles of port.

The reading took two and a half hours. It had already been late when Tennyson began; nevertheless, there was still sufficient wakefulness (or competitiveness) at the end for Robert Browning to give a reading of *Fra Lippo Lippi*, allowing William Rossetti to compare the vocal delivery of the two poets. Where Browning was more dramatic, bringing out touches of character and conversational points and varying his tone, Tennyson was more rhythmical and much grander.

By the time Browning had finished it was 2.30 am and time to leave. Alfred and Dante Rossetti walked home together, and Tennyson repeated some of his stories and complaints for a ninth or tenth time.

As well as visiting his mother at Twickenham, he dined with the Camerons, describing Mrs Cameron as being 'more wonderful than ever ... in her world-bearing benevolence'. After this visit Julia Cameron immediately posted off a big ball for Hallam to play with at Christmas.

Soon after his return to the island there was a thunderstorm in which seven-inch hail-stones fell – but these, according to Emily, were as nothing compared to what the critics were continuing to pitch in Alfred's direction.

Their American friend, Tuckerman, sent a letter strongly defending Tennyson against the recent attacks and Emily thanked him with the argument that 'the freshness of nation breathed into your souls from your virgin forests and untrodden savannahs fit you better for hearing the voice of truth in *Maud*.'

'I do not wish to disparage England,' she went on, but her remarks show that she continued to consider the poem out of kilter with the national temperament. Of more solace to Alfred than Tuckerman's comradely, transatlantic reassurances was the first extensive critical acclaim published in the November edition of *Cambridge Essays* and written by George Brimley.

This essay, while not in any way a brilliant piece of criticism, *was* a welcome piece of support. It ridiculed the simplemindedness of critics who painted *Maud* as if it were nothing but 'a melodramatic story of suicide, murder, and madness, dished up for popular applause with vehement invective on the vices of the English nation, and claptrap appeals to the war-feeling of the day.'

In the previous month Tennyson had been equally heartened by a different kind of review, which appeared in the *Asylum Journal of Mental Science* and examimed *Maud* as case history, concluding that it was accurate in its portrayal of madness.

At the beginning of December he had occasion to write to Archer Gurney[28], whom he had wrongly and publicly suspected of being the author of an anonymous note which read, 'Sir, I used to worship you, but now I hate you. I loathe and detest you. You beast! So you've taken to imitating Longfellow. Yours in aversion, —.' After apologizing for this 'strange fancy', he went on to defend his new poem against some current misconstructions.

I have had Peace party papers sent to me claiming me as being on their side because I had put the cry for war into the mouth of a madman. Surely that is not half so wrong a criticism as some I have seen. Strictly speaking I do not see how from the poem I could be pronounced with certainty either peace man or war man. I wonder that you and others did not find out that all along the man was intended to have an hereditary vein of insanity, and that he falls foul on the swindling, on the times, because he feels that his father has been killed by the work of the lie, and that all through he fears the coming madness. How could you or anyone suppose that if I had had to speak in my own person my own opinion of this war or war generally I would have spoken with so little moderation. The whole was intended to be a new form of dramatic composition. I took a man constitutionally diseased and dipt him into the circumstances of the time and took him out on fire . . .

(P.S.) I do not mean that my madman does not speak truths too.[29]

The autumn and early winter after his return from London had been filled with leaf-sweeping and burning. Alfred had attended church regularly with Emily and on 12 December put into one of the bonfires of leaves a box filled with all his clay pipes. He had decided to give up smoking and burnt every last bit of tobacco on his study fire. However, by the first day of the New Year, Tennyson was regretting his 'little fumatory at Farringford'. Staying as a guest of Lady Ashburton at the Grange, he was surrounded by people smoking among the oranges, lemons and camellias.

His hostess was a famously professional entertainer and her Christmas and New Year gatherings attracted the luminaries of literary London. Tennyson had been invited in previous years, but declined. He feared it would be ungracious to decline again. Amongst the other guests was Carlyle, who had taken something of a shine to Lady Ashburton, and was becoming cold towards his wife Jane. Perhaps for this reason, or some other connected with Carlyle's disdain for poetry, he and Tennyson were not on the closest of terms during the visit, and in the middle of a reading of *Maud* Carlyle even had the audacity to go outside for a walk in the grounds.

In conversation with Lady Ashburton, Tennyson spoke of his desire that some rich man might buy up the Farringford estate and save it from being 'brick-box-dotted'. He said this in the quite serious hope that she would pass the word on to her husband so that he might take the requisite action. It is an example of how unsubtle and scheming the poet could be.

When he returned to the island he settled down to the writing of a new poem – the subject, Merlin, suggested by Emily. The first three months of the year were settled ones, full of star-gazing, garden-digging, readings from the *Odyssey* and the Bible, and work on his poem. But behind mundane activities like rolling the lawn and sweeping leaves, Tennyson's imagination kept up its feverish work. The writing of *Maud* proved just the prelude to a long period of creative gestation which resulted in *Idylls of the King*. Modern readers fight shy of epic verse set in the Age of Chivalry and the Idylls, although continuing to attract academic attention from literary critics, are most likely to be read today initially out of a sense of duty, or respect for Tennyson's more immediately compelling work. This is a pity, for the Idylls and, to a lesser extent, the later Dramas, give the lie to the notion propounded by some biographers, that following the critical débâcle of *Maud* Tennyson retreated into a shell of sedate and secluded respectability.

He learned to cast his social comment in a different mould but the Idylls, as any new reader will discover, are anything but sedate. They are a series of long narrative poems in which the themes of lust and infidelity predominate. It is of little matter that Emily prompted her husband to compose them, or that he based the essential characters and storyline on his extensive reading of Malory et al.; of much more interest is the fact that from the moment he returned from the Grange at the beginning of January 1856, for the next five years or more, his imagination was steeped in conflicts between intellect and sensuality. And this was the period covered by his increasingly close relationship with Julia Cameron.

Perhaps it was Carlyle's open flirtation with Lady Ashburton which proved the catalyst to beginning the composition with the enchantment of Merlin by Nimue, but a prolonged immersion in such dramatic and emotionally-charged subject-matter was bound, in due course, to impinge on Tennyson's own personality.

At the beginning of February Woolner, the sculptor, arrived on the island to work on a bust of Tennyson. The poet was not a good sitter and would only allow the sculptor a little time at night so that Woolner had to model with one hand, holding a candle in the other. It was slow work and he stayed in the house until 15 March.

A few days before Woolner had arrived Tennyson had gone to see his astronomer friend, R.J. Mann in Ventnor. They had done more than star-gaze while they were together; they had discussed *Maud* and the need for a public defence of the poem, a project first mooted by Mann in the autumn of 1855. When Tennyson went back to Farringford, taking a big top and trumpet for Hallam, Mann immediately set about composing his long and important essay 'Maud Vindicated', the proofs of which were received by Alfred on 13 March. Whilst the essay was less gratifying than Brimley's had been, it is of more intrinsic biographical interest because Mann had been privy to Tennyson's personal constructions on the poem.

The long essay concentrated on drawing out the moral 'so subtly enunciated' by the impulsive utterances of the mad speaker. 'The simple meaning which lurks within these passages, is obviously, that sad as open and declared war is, it has in it those touches of moral grandeur which make its horrors tolerable in comparison with the more dreadful social, and domestic hostilities, which seethe continuously in the dense populations of over-crowded lands, and set man against man, and brother against brother, causing base selfishness and cruelty to take the place of high principle and worthy aim.'[30]

Emily disapproved of the nature of the essay, believing, as she wrote to Spedding, 'that a thing must stand or fall of itself'. Tennyson must have been wondering how the first of his Idylls would stand or fall in her sight. Amidst the cosy atmosphere of Farringford, with continuous digging in his garden, readings aloud from the *Odyssey* and Shakespeare, Lionel's birthday (it was his second and Julia Cameron sent Hallam a present by mistake), overseeing arrangements for the transfer of his mother from Chapel House to a new residence in Hampstead, and frenetic financial arrangements preparatory to the purchase of Farringford, the Laureate was locked away in a private fantasy.

Just as his personal affairs became more solid and orderly, so did his imagination take flight. The mood of the Idylls, particularly of the first, (in the order of composition) has echoes of *The Devil and the Lady* and *The Lover's Tale*, those weirdly precocious and sexual compositions of the Somersby adolescent. At no period was the atmosphere of Farringford remotely like that of the Rectory at Somersby, but in many a secure family home either one of the parents may, at some stage, feel themselves, in a psychological and nostalgic sense, a child again. This is particularly so when the ambience of the household is dominated by one partner. Some such development was occurring in the Tennysons' relationship, with Emily taking care of correspondence, the invitations to guests, instructions to household staff, and so on.

Not all decisions were Emily's though. Left to herself she might well have suggested a move back to the mainland to be closer to her father, but at the end of a consultation with Venables and Sir John Simeon it was decided that they should press their case for outright purchase of the Farringford estate.

Tennyson had asked Seymour's agent, a Mr Eastcourt, to quote them a sum two months beforehand, when it became clear that a home needed to be found for the Chapel House furniture. They had heard nothing from the man, and the Twickenham belongings had had to be put in storage. Eventually it was settled that they could have the place for £6750 (plus an extra £150 payable for the orchard) with all moneys to be paid in full by 23 November.

After attending the Grand Review of the Fleet with Drummond Rawnsley and others, all became confusion for a month or so, while the process of moving into Farringford afresh, as new owners, began. They had taken the lease on the house as a furnished property, so first of all it had to be stripped of all Seymour's fittings. It was while this was in hand that Prince Albert decided to call upon the Tennysons, finding that 'every book was taken out of the room to be stowed away ready for the sale, how the chairs and tables were dancing, sofa and chairs stuffed with brown paper and all untidiness, the floor strewed with toys and cards and I know not what besides'. Someone in the Prince's group had gathered cowslips in the grounds and Albert said he would use them for making tea. One of the stems was dropped and Emily kept it for the children as a memento of their first meeting with royalty. The Prince seemed not fully to comprehend their predicament and gave them to understand that the Queen might call upon them any day so that they were forced to keep themselves in a state of preternatural readiness for the next week. But Queen Victoria did not come.

During the sale of Seymour's goods and the redecoration of some of the Farringford rooms, the Tennysons removed themselves to the Red House, in Freshwater. The greatest obstacle to making Farringford comfortable again was the 'ghastly appearance of the drawing room and dining room walls so woefully stained by pictures. Ally has a fancy for the drawing room paper,' Emily wrote to Woolner, 'and will not have it changed for he says whatever paper we had he should not be happy without red and flesh colours and bright frames.' She asked the sculptor to see what he could find in the pawnbrokers for a farthing a go. Some of these ugly marks at least were soon covered by a few of the paintings from Somersby, which had been hung for a time at Park House, and were now brought over by Edward Lushington.

At the beginning of June their Chapel House belongings arrived and had to be unpacked, a process which Alfred gave some assistance with, albeit in a self-consciously valorous style. 'Alfred has nobly stood out all the bustle and bother of the removal, helping to unpack and himself to place the things,' Emily wrote, again to Woolner, in the manner she had of unburdening herself in bursts of communication to various male correspondents in turn.

They tried to make the repossession of Farringford as special and as significant a break in their lives as possible. On the last day of May Alfred told Emily to ring the front doorbell when she returned from Communion so that he could let her into their new home. And on 4 June, after all the beds had been aired for a day on the grass and the whole family moved back permanently from the Red House, Alfred gave Emily a second welcome home. Her Journal entry for the close of this day is especially evocative:

A beautiful evening. We stop at the barn & look at Merwood's bits of carpet which he thought might do for us. I had sent to beg that he would not wait but there he sat in the barn his carpet spread out of doors. My A. gathered a rose and gave it to me as we walked thro' the kitchen garden. We went in at our back door. An evening to be remembered. A. gave me a welcome to our home which will be ever dear to memory. We had our tea in the drawing room. A. read me some of 'Enid'. It seemed as if we were the people of those old days. A Stag's horn beetle (I think it was) came into the room with a harp-like sound. We put it out & it sat on the window frame looking in at us & we admired its bright black eyes & its horns like the leaves of a Fan Palm, only they were brown yellow.[31]

A beautiful evening, beautifully described – with something emblematic signified by the entrance, and swift expulsion of the stag's horn beetle? Charles Tennyson rather detracts from the romance of Alfred's gallant picking of a rose for Emily when he imagines his grandfather 'recalling how his mother always used to gather a white rose on Sunday mornings at Somersby.'[32] As already implied, Alfred might well have been beginning to perceive Emily more strongly as mother than lover, but the identification would not have been that straightforward, and the wearing of a rose was always, for him, a talisman of femininity, (as shown, for instance, in *The Lover's Tale*). In picking the rose, and in making the homecoming special in other unelaborated ways, Alfred showed himself to be a sensitive husband, capable of managing events in a style which touched his wife deeply. Such private gestures went unobserved by the multifarious guests of the Laureate and it is important to weigh them against the accusations of some that Alfred was egotistically inconsiderate towards Emily.

The fresh homecoming was not the end of disruption. Carpenters were in the house from the 5–15 June, putting various things to rights, and it is little wonder that Alfred found 'Enid' harder going than 'Merlin'.

On the 22 June they saw the first naval ship returning from the Crimea, carrying its crew of bearded veterans, a sight which affected the two Tennysons in different ways. Emily, identifying with the wives and fiancées of the returning soldiers 'could not but think of the happy hearts that ship would make. How cold and blank the drawing room when I returned.' Even if we allow for the fact that Alfred was out of the house when she came into the drawing-room, that final sentence speaks of a strangely impassioned jealousy.

Alfred identified with the soldiers and, like many a man of the time, would soon grow a full beard.

13   A Process of Excretion

It is the little rift within the lute,
That by and by will make the music mute,

('MERLIN AND VIVIEN')

The first half of July was a happy fortnight. Alfred and Emily spent a good deal of time together. She was well and he was busily engaged with 'Enid'. His manner of working on the Idylls was described by Spedding: 'The Laureate cannot breakfast with anybody. The process of excretion (I speak spiritually) begins immediately after the last cup of tea; is accompanied with a desire of solitude and tobacco; followed (when no disturbing cause interferes) with the production of some five and twenty lines of Idyll.'[33]

Afterwards Alfred might lie in the sun by the strawberry bed or go for a walk with Emily. Her Journal is more full of 'we' at this time than usual. In the evenings they always played at least two games of backgammon together and, on Emily's birthday, Alfred gave her some verses beginning 'Why did you not tell me?', which she described as 'better than a hundred letters had he written them'.

Spedding's rather caustic description of Tennyson's working regime was coloured by objections he had formed towards 'Merlin'. In sending Alfred a new supportive-stocking for varicose veins, he wrote, 'I am still of opinion that Merlin would not have been talked over by that kind of woman; and that the effect of the poem is much injured by the predominance of harlotry.'[34] This discussion was to continue, but it was Emily who took the part of the Idylls. She replied before they left for a holiday in Wales, ending her letter, 'Pray do not defend the beard; of itself it will surely fall.' This was intended as a joke, echoing her objection to Dr Mann's essay, and her belief that a good poem should 'stand or fall of itself'. Nevertheless, she was genuinely irritated by Alfred's new beard and would later express the wish that the public might 'compel Alfred by act of Parliament to cut off his beard!'

As for Spedding's objections to 'Merlin', Emily dealt with these while alone in Builth in Wales in the middle of September.

Do you not think that the higher and more imaginative the man, the more likely he is to fall if he once yield ever so little to a base and evil influence. You think this, perhaps, but think also that in the case of Merlin, Nimue does not look, even at the beginning, enough the angel of light to have attracted him but it seems to me devotion or an appearance of it has more power over men than over women in itself. To a woman it is repulsive if she have no sympathy with him who pays it but I do not think it is so with men. Only I have looked at the world through such a very little chink all my life that I feel I have small right to give any opinion at all on the subject.[35]

Emily was far from naïve. The little chink through which she had looked at the world had been quite wide enough to show her that men could be dazzled by a purely frivolous or carnal charm. In saying this was she thinking, retrospectively, of

Alfred's own bewitchment by Rosa Baring? Of special interest is the fact that two days after writing this letter to Spedding she summarized these particular remarks for Alfred's benefit.

They had left for Wales on the 18 July and did not return to the Isle of Wight until the end of September. As they progressed through Wales, meeting local bards and schoolmasters, being entertained by harpists and singers, Alfred made steady progress with 'Enid'. For a while Emily attempted to chart his work in her Journal:

> *Aug 1st* He has finished the tournament in *Enid* and read it to me.
> *Aug 2nd* Today he made the stately queen's answer to Geraint ... He and I had long talks about the Infinity of the Universe and about God.

The two boys were with them and they journeyed as a family, with Alfred going off for long walks, until the leanness of their purse prompted him to leave wife and children in a hotel at Builth. He continued his research in and around Caerleon, concentrating on the main purpose of the trip, which was to collect details and impressions for his Arthurian epic, a theme which Emily was now ever more ardently espousing:

> The story of King Arthur gives me a feeling of awe reading it here alone. It is so grand and, in Welsh, so true. 'The Way of the Soul'. No story in the world is to be compared with it I think. It is made for thee I am sure. Thou must take care of thyself and husband thy energies to spend them on this.[36]

Soon after their return to Farringford Alfred began putting the finishing touches to 'Enid' and making arrangements for the sale of his East Lincolnshire shares, in order to raise the money in time for the November deadline, which was, in the event, extended to 2 December. The reason for the extension seems to have been Tennyson's nervousness about selling the shares at a loss; he wanted to give them every chance to rise again. However, his agent, Benjamin Baines, went ahead and sold them (indeed at a loss) at the beginning of November, much to Tennyson's annoyance.

They had not been back a fortnight before visitors and guests began to file through the Farringford doorway. Coventry

Patmore and his wife visited several times as did Arthur Clough and his wife Blanche, who were holidaying in a cottage just above Alum Bay. Clough, ten years younger than Tennyson, had published *The Bothie of Toperna-Fuosich* in 1848 and a collection of shorter poems in 1850.

To both Patmore and Clough Alfred read his first two Idylls and talked about the Welsh research. When they were back in London the two younger men assiduously began making enquiries on Tennyson's behalf. 'The best collection of Welsh books is, I am told, to be found in the Library of the Gynnedifion Society,' announced Clough. And Patmore, rather less encouragingly, declared, 'The Welsh publisher has vanished from Holywell Street.'

Sad news arrived at the end of October, when they heard that little Eddy, Edmund and Cecilia's boy, had died. Edmund had lost a sister (Louisa) in 1854, and a brother (Henry) the following year. Now his only son 'Just grown/To boyhood's prime' was gone. The three of them were placed beneath one memorial stone in the graveyard of Boxley church, the boy's inscription reading 'Edmund Henry/only son of Edmund Law Lushington/born December 31st 1843 at Glasgow/died October 20th 1856 at Eastbourne.'

The Tennysons set off for Kent on the 14 November, meeting Edmund at the railway station in London, having first taken the opportunity of visiting their dentist. The atmosphere at Park House was sombre and autumnal. Alfred read the completed 'Enid', but not 'Merlin'.

Passing back through London he went into a bookstore to buy an atlas and overheard a customer asking for copies of Tennyson's poems to be given as prizes. Not wishing to draw attention to himself he gave the name of Weld for his own purchase. This incident again shows that, in the 1850s, there was still no such thing as the instantly recognizable celebrity. Matters were changing quickly, however. During his Welsh holiday Tennyson had nervously concealed his identity knowing that once it was discovered he would be the object of vulgar curiosity. Within the next decade the spread of photography was to make such subterfuge impossible and to transform the public response to men and women of renown.

December contained the usual bustle of visitors, including Palgrave, Simeon and various plumbers, carpenters, glaziers and bricklayers. Christmas Day, however, was reserved for the family. They had a grand Yule log, and Lionel, who had been unwell, improved after treatment with some powders sent by Dr Mann. Alfred read aloud from George Sand's *La Petite Fadette*, when not digging and rolling in the garden. 'Diligently' is the adverb used by Emily to describe the manner of her husband's Christmas labours. But the word is too plain. The extent to which Tennyson continued to dig and roll the turf through the deep winter months is suggestive of a compulsive need to sweat off an inner tension.

14   Photography

I thought, but that your father came between,
In former days you saw me favourably,

('GERAINT AND ENID')

Tennyson had first met Julia Cameron at Little Holland House in West Kensington. Mrs Prinsep (the 'Principessa') who lived there with her husband Thoby, a former Indian civil servant, carried on an all-year-round sequence of Sunday at-homes to which most of London's literati and other notables were at some some time invited.

Sarah Prinsep had six sisters, nearly all of them celebrated for their beauty – Maria (grandmother to Vanessa Bell and Virginia Woolf) being, according to contemporary opinion, the most gorgeous of the lot. Even after their various marriages they were known as the Pattle girls; Julia Margaret was the second oldest, and the plainest-looking (see plate 10), a fact also borne out by the photographic record. Julia had, like her sister Sarah, chosen her husband from the Indian Civil Service. Charles Hay Cameron was ten years older than Julia and, long before it became fashionable to do so, sported a prodigious silver beard.

The Camerons lived in East Sheen and Julia, who had not taken up photography at this time, busied herself with charit-able acts for friends and acquaintances. She already considered

Right:
Charles Tennyson's
portrait of Alfred in the
margin of Horace

(Lincolnshire Library Service)

Below left:
Tennyson drawn by Weld

(Lincolnshire Library Service)

Below right:
Tennyson drawn
by Spedding

(National Portrait Gallery)

Above: On board ship, returning from their expedition (Tennyson, Hallam, Mr and Mrs Harden and their three daughters) (Lincolnshire Library Service)

Left: Rosa Baring (Lincolnshire Library Service)

Hallam and Lionel,
after their haircuts

(Lincolnshire Library Service)

Tennyson photographed
by Cameron

(Lincolnshire Library Service)

Tennyson and Carlyle smoking

(Lincolnshire Library Service)

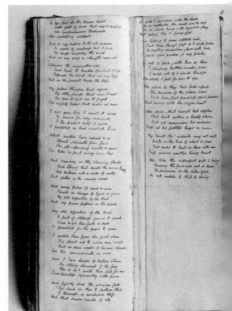

The 'butcher' notebook,
containing *In Memoriam*

(Lincolnshire Library Service)

The small-town, provincial Emily

(Lincolnshire Library Service)

The more favourable appearance:
a portrait by Watts

(Lincolnshire Library Service)

Tennyson, with Hallam on his knee, and the Marshalls

Tennyson family in the Farringford garden, 1863

(Lincolnshire Library Service)

Lord Tennyson in his skullcap

herself something of a special benefactress with regard to the Tennysons, sending birthday presents to the two boys (but typically mixing up the dates) and, most recently, helping with the acquisition of some special fittings for the Farringford fireplace.

Towards the end of February 1857 the Camerons went to stay on the Isle of Wight and saw a good deal of Tennyson. Alfred had not yet begun a third Idyll. He was still busy rolling and leaf-burning. One afternoon he had taken Emily with him into Maiden's Croft and covered her with his cloak while she lay on a long bench and watched the bonfire. Their handyman, Merwood, helped Alfred and when he put some brambles onto the fire they produced little feathery tongues of flame.

Beginning on 21 February, Emily's Journal shows that Alfred was most attentive and generous of his time with the Camerons. On the 22nd he showed them the Wilderness, Maiden's Croft, the garden and farmyard. On the 23rd they came to dinner.

In the midst of the Camerons' stay upon the island the Tennysons changed their dinner time, putting it back from 5 pm to 6.30 pm. When the Camerons arrived at the new hour, on the 26th, it was to find that cartloads of seaweed had been strewn across the Park. Tennyson's obsession with his grass began to take on monomaniacal proportions.

On the 28th the Camerons were back, for a reading of 'Enid'. Emily's Journal entries for March begin 'Daily meetings with the Camerons.' On the 6 March Alfred joined the Camerons for a two-day visit to Bonchurch. Emily remained at home, under orders from Alfred to turn the clay in Maiden's Croft. The daily intercourse with the Camerons continued throughout the whole of March and the greater part of April. Still Tennyson did not begin work on any new poem. There was a distraction in the middle of March when his younger brother, Horatio, married Charlotte Elwes at St Lawrence. After the ceremony Alfred and Emily threw a Lincolnshire cart-horseshoe and an old slipper after them for good luck.

While they were away Julia Cameron supervised her first Tennyson photograph session. The camera was not her own, and the subjects were Lionel and Hallam, rather than Alfred himself. Staying with the Camerons was a twenty-two-year-old medical student named Southey, who was also an enthusiastic amateur photographer. It was from this young man that Julia Cameron caught the photography bug.

After the wedding in St Lawrence the Camerons left the

island and Alfred became unwell. The effect of Julia Cameron upon Tennyson is worth consideration. Though no beauty, she was nevertheless vivacious and capable of controlling events in a manner which inspired admiration. Her escapades did not always work to plan, but deviations from the expected outcome were always entertaining. One day in March she had arrived at Farringford with a fire balloon and little lamps of Noah's Ark flags. The Cameron children ran races with Hallam and Lionel and the fire balloon burst into flames above them. It was all too much for Emily. She was so drained by the afternoon's excitement that Alfred had to ask all the guests to leave after 5 pm tea, and not stay until dinner.

Tennyson adored such fun and games and liked Mrs Cameron for initiating them. There was a childlike aspect to his temperament which could not bear stuffiness. One evening, when the dinner guests were rather sombrely and formally gathered, he insisted that everyone play a round of Blind Man's Buff. It is true that a hundred and fifty years ago an adult's sense of fun was different from our own, and that such party games were not the juvenile preserve that they have become. Nevertheless, the accumulative impression given by anecdotes concerning Tennyson's behaviour as father and husband does bear out this aspect of his temperament. Entertaining Hallam and Lionel was a source of delight for him, not an onerous paternal duty. Even the simple act of blowing bubbles could put him into a state of rapturous excitement.

Most often Emily was a supine observer of such merriment; although, when on form, she herself was capable of giving the boys piggy-back rides or acting out nursery rhymes with Alfred, in which each would take several parts – sometimes one of them would have to be a sausage, a role which must have taxed even Tennyson's powers of mimicry.

Emily's Journal makes it plain, especially for these early Farringford years, (undoubtedly the happiest of their marriage), just how generous Alfred was with his time, and when the social commitments arising out of the steady stream of visitors are added, it is hardly surprising that his rate of progress on the Idylls was excruciatingly slow.

For any creative person – where the essential act of creation requires sustained periods of prolonged endeavour – there is a conflict between artistic and social exigencies. The conflict is intensified by family life and a person can feel as if held in a double bind, incapable of guilt-free resolution. One of Tennyson's late poems, 'Romney's Remorse', shows how conscious he was that Art could come between a husband and a wife, but in these happy, domestic years no one could accuse the poet of allowing the Muse to act as marriage-breaker.

Farringford was a large house and the Isle of Wight could, in winter and in those days, be extremely desolate. It was Emily's judgement – for all invitations were sent through her – that Alfred thrived on company. In a sense she was right, but her Journal also shows that there was plenty to keep her husband busy: attending to her own needs, to the boys, and digging and rolling the turf. Once the Camerons burst upon the scene there was no hope of a reclusive life. Their holiday on the island determined Julia to find a house as close to the Tennysons as could be managed.

It is still possible to overhear, in some of the island's pubs, the dying murmurs of vulgar speculation concerning Tennyson and Mrs Cameron. As with the so-called 'canard' about opium, such gossip, because of its vulgarity, can be too easily swept aside. What Julia Cameron lacked in looks – and for the myopic Tennyson this was perhaps unimportant – she made up for in energy and dominance. The hurt caused by the failure of his affair with Rosa Baring endured partly because Tennyson liked to imagine himself in the arms of a vivacious lover. In the immediate aftermath of the affair, he had managed to convince himself that Rosa's ebullience was all froth and no bubble, but as the years passed, and as Emily's quietude became more and more established, he seemed less certain. Julia Cameron brought verve and industrious unpredictability to the island – qualities which were the much-needed complement to his own torpor.

Only a matter of days after she and her family left the island Alfred decided to go to London to attend his physician. The hectic and disorganized nature of his departure, on 27 April, indicated that he was ill-at-ease with the decision to go. The carriage which arrived to take him to the ferry was too small for Hallam and Lionel. They cried when told there was no room and in the end Alfred and Emily squeezed them onto their laps. But the delay made them late for the steamer. Tennyson had to leap into a rowing boat and board the ferry while it was heading for the Solent. The boys waved their handkerchiefs, but their father, not wearing an eye-glass, did not notice.

Woolner wrote to Emily the following day: 'I am glad that he

305

has come to this part of the Kingdom for I have no doubt the change will do him service.' Hardly a great change, for Tennyson stayed at Little Holland House, where he was bound to see a good deal of Julia Cameron.

On his first full day in town he called in at the London Library and bumped into FitzGerald. Although they had not met in a long time, it was not a great reunion. Later FitzGerald would remark on the apparent indifference shown by Alfred. This was not a good time for Fitz; he was in the midst of his disastrous marriage to Lucy Barton, and Alfred described him as looking 'thinnish and worn'.

The following day Tennyson's 'good hostess and nurse' – Sarah Prinsep – would not allow him out of the house. His foot was bad – not gout, but an ingrowing toenail – and he was awaiting the repair of his varicose vein stocking. On 30 April he wrote a strange letter home:

> Dearest
> I got the stocking which seems to have been repaired very swiftly and skillfully – this morning.
> Old Thoby Prinsep is a Prince of a man. You would delight in the gallant old fellow. Don't get ill, Madam, don't! So no more at present except
> A KISS FOR HALLAM AND A KISS FOR LIONEL
> and another for thee.
>
> > Thine
> > A.T.
>
> I ought to tell you there is a charming house to be had now for asking. Mrs C[ameron] will write to you about [it]. Don't leave this lying about.[37]

The final instruction – issued presumably to avoid alarming the servants – suggests that the postscript was written in earnest. Farringford had been their own property for less than six months, and here he was thinking of moving again. In a sense he was simply behaving true to form, as when he quickly became unhappy with living in Twickenham.

It is unlikely that he felt wealthy enough to contemplate owning two houses – Farringford and a second, town house – although just possibly he still held out high hopes for the success of the newly-published *Illustrated Edition*. The involvement of Mrs Cameron may simply reflect her busybody nature but it is also suggestive of a desire to have Tennyson nearby. And when nothing came of this she was more determined than ever to move to the Isle of Wight.

In the midst of his London stay Tennyson received a disturbing report concerning the conduct of the boy's nurse, Gandy. Discipline over the paid staff at Farringford was always rather lax, and appears to have deteriorated whenever Alfred was away. This, at least, is the impression given in the following letter:

> I am really grieved that Gandy's conduct has been so brutal. I wish I had been at home. I would not have allowed her to go on insulting you. This comes of treating a coarse nature *too* kindly.[38]

Gandy was dismissed, but not until Alfred had returned to the island. Emily seems to have resisted such a stern measure. 'I get up early to see dear Gandy off, obliged to send her away for fear of bad effects on our Hallam for favouritism to Lionel whom she had from the first. Dreary days of discomfort & sadness from parting.' Tennyson's anger at the nurse may well have reflected an opposite sense of favouritism on his part, for a number of remarks, and actions, throughout his life bear testimony to his special affection for Hallam.

The *Illustrated Edition* reprinted the 1842 *Poems* together with fifty-four wood-block drawings by eight different artists, chosen by Moxon. Once selected for the commission (a process not without its own disagreement — Emily's strong and surprising recommendation of Lizzie Siddall was rejected) the artists were free to choose their subjects. Production of the book was delayed because some of the artists, notably Rossetti, were late completing their work. As a result, the Christmas 1856 publication date had been missed. The Tennysons were cool about the venture and its prospects. Alfred disliked the notion of illustrating poems in general, and Emily disliked the particular interpretation put upon the poems. With few exceptions, she told Moxon, she would not even care to have the pictures as a gift. Moxon, a little disgruntled by this reaction, wrote to explain that no expense had been spared in the getting up of the book and he remained confident of its success.

Ten thousand copies were printed which was the same number as the first edition of *Maud*. But *Maud* had been sold at a standard price, whereas this new book went on sale at one and a half guineas. Many of Tennyson's readers already possessed the poems in earlier editions and the price proved too much – out of the gift season – to induce them to buy the poems in their new sumptuous format. The book sold just over a thousand copies in the first six weeks and then sales almost dried up. Six years later five thousand copies were remaindered to Routledge. Before the end of July Moxon was writing to Tennyson offering the poet a straight payment of £2000 'for your interest in the edition'. Tennyson immediately accepted.

The summer was tropical – one day in June was the hottest for twenty years – and Emily felt increasingly exhausted. But there was no abating the stream of Farringford guests: the Lushingtons, Horatio and his wife, Bayard Taylor, Edward Lear, and the Bradleys all stayed in the house during these sultry weeks.

On Emily's birthday the last of the guests departed. 'The first evening we have had alone for two months or more,' she noted in her Journal. Alfred set down cushions under the cedar tree and Emily lay down to admire the view across the bay. When she was comfortable he brought her the first lines of a new Idyll. At last he was working again. This early draft was the nucleus of the parting between Arthur and Guinevere – a strangely ominous birthday present to give to one's wife. While she read the lines to herself Alfred examined some snakes' eggs collected by Merwood. He took the baby snakes, in their jelly sheaths, out of the leathery eggs, and observed the beating of their hearts. The life-force pulsed away for two hours before coming to a pause. Tennyson's fascinated observation of these death-throes betrayed nothing of the naturalist's clinical interest; he was watching for the moment of death to see if any change, other than the cessation of pulse, passed over their frames as life ebbed away.

A week later they left Farringford for a tour of the north. They would be away for over three months, and after their return, in November, their life on the island would never be as fresh or as gallant again. Emily's sombre birthday present and the deaths of the baby snakes were talismans for an emotional separation and the demise of a certain phase in their life together.

15   A Most Romantic-Looking Person

But hither shall I never come again,
Never lie by thy side; see thee no more–
Farewell!

('GUINEVERE')

The Tennysons began their summer holiday by staying a fortnight with Charles and Louisa at Grasby. Charles had recently become re-addicted to opium, but he was in fine enough shape to act the considerate host as well as performing his parish duties. He took Emily and Alfred on long drives into the Lincolnshire countryside and one day they visited Bayons Manor. Only Mrs d'Eyncourt was at home but she took the trouble to show them all over the house, which was by now complete with its sham drawbridge and moat. The atmosphere, apparently cordial enough on the surface, must have seethed with the memories of twenty-year-old family rancours – indeed, it is difficult to avoid the suspicion that Alfred rather savoured the notion of turning up at Bayons Manor, the celebrated Laureate of the land.

On the last day of their stay in Grasby there was a school fête. Hallam and Lionel joined in the races and Emily helped Louisa with the cakes and toys. Mr Sellwood was also there and Emily was very happy, being with her father and sister again. It was with a sad heart that she said goodbye to them. Despite the very serious difficulties that existed in the Turners' marriage, Louisa's life as the wife of a country vicar had much to recommend it.

Charles took them to the station and set them on the train for Manchester, where they travelled in order to visit the immense Art Treasures Exhibition, which was on show in the specially erected 'palace' at Old Trafford.

They were in Manchester for six days and visited the

Exhibition at least five times. On 30 July the American writer, Nathaniel Hawthorne, nearing the end of his consulship at Liverpool, had Tennyson pointed out to him by Alexander Ireland. The description which Hawthorne put into his *English Notebooks* is well-known but bears repetition because it is such a full and evocative one. The fact that, according to Emerson, Tennyson reminded him of no American other than Hawthorne, gives it an added interest:

Tennyson is the most picturesque figure, without affectation, that I ever saw; of middle size, rather slouching, dressed entirely in black, and with nothing white about him except the collar of his shirt, which methought might have been clean the day before. He had on a black wide-awake hat, with round crown and wide irregular brim, beneath which came down his long black hair, looking terribly tangled; he had a long pointed beard, too, a little browner than the hair, and not so abundant as to incumber any of the expression of his face. His frock coat was buttoned across the breast, though the afternoon was warm. His face was very dark, and not exactly a smooth face, but worn, and expressing great sensitiveness, though not, at that moment, the pain and sorrow which is seen in his bust. His eyes were black, but I know little of them, as they did not rest on me, nor on anything but the pictures. He seemed as if he did not see the crowd nor think of them, but as if he defended himself from them by ignoring them altogether; nor did anybody but myself cast a glance at him.[39]

After 'gazing at him with all my eyes' Hawthorne scooted off to find his wife and took her back with him to the gallery of Old Masters. Tennyson was now talking to an elderly couple:

I heard his voice; a bass voice, but not of a resounding depth; a voice rather broken, as it were, and ragged about the edges, but pleasant to the ear. His manner, while conversing with these people, was not in the least that of an awkward man, unaccustomed to society; but he shook hands and parted with them, evidently as soon as he courteously could, and shuffled away quicker than before. He betrayed his shy and secluded habits more in this, than in anything else that I observed; though, indeed, in his whole presence, I was indescribably sensible of a morbid painfulness in him, a something not to be meddled with.[40]

The following day the Tennysons, having gone to hear Charles Dickens read *A Christmas Carol* in the Free Trade Hall the night before, were back at the Exhibition. This time they were spotted by Sophia Hawthorne, Nathaniel's wife. She was up in the gallery with her children, listening to the orchestra, when Una, the oldest child, suddenly exclaimed, 'There is Tennyson!' Mrs Hawthrone quickly confirmed the identification and also, she thought, spotted Emily and the boys:

> It was charming to watch the group ... The children were very pretty and picturesque, and Tennyson seemed to love them immensely. He devoted himself to them, and was absorbed in their interest. In him is a careless ease and noble air which show him of the gentle blood he is. He is the most romantic-looking person.[41]

The 'careless ease and noble air' of Tennyson's manner with his children is wonderfully captured in one of the photographs taken by Lewis Carroll a few weeks later (see plate 9).

The Tennysons left Manchester early in August to spend some time at Tent Lodge, the same house they had been lent by the Marshalls for their honeymoon. Although Tennyson suffered badly from hayfever this summer and from a heavy mood of melancholy – reports of his 'illness' reached Woolner in London – the two months which they eventually spent at Coniston were delightful ones. Both Alfred and Hallam celebrated their birthdays there, the boy being given a gun and a spinning whip by the Marshalls' daughter, Julia.

Relations with their hosts (whose own house was at Patterdale Hall in Ullswater) were very nearly ruined in the middle of August. Soon after arriving, Alfred, sulky with hayfever which was always made worse by travelling, had complained that the house was too much shut up by trees. The Marshalls decided to placate him by felling a small beech tree. However, their axeman, misunderstanding their instructions, or misdirected by Tennyson, took down a huge old beech in front of the dining-room window. Mrs Marshall was most upset, though she managed to maintain an air of geniality.

Alfred lost his watch during a picnic on the heath and a

servant had to return over the same ground in a vain search for it. Tennyson was miserable at the loss and asked for notes to be left at all the local farmhouses. Emily, conscious that her husband was being a nuisance, took the children back onto the heath herself to see if she could find it. Eventually it turned up – handed in by a farm labourer.

The children had been taken to church at Grasby for the first time. It was quite an amusement to see their Uncle Charlie dressed in robes and officiating at the altar. Emily took them again at Coniston, but 'I am sure it is not good for them. I could scarcely restrain Hallam from dancing during the sermon & he was continually asking me, "What does that mean?"'

A few days later she wrote to Elizabeth Browning:

Our boys are healthy and merry and quite simple children with small inclination for anything but play. I feel it should at present be indulged that they may have what chance we can give them of gaining strength to bear the weight of over – very, I will not say over, sensitive nerves that may have descended to them and that many signs make me believe have descended and I cannot wish it otherwise . . .[42]

It is unlikely that Emily would have been prompted to make such observations had not Alfred's own over- or very sensitive nerves been on edge. He was still very far from well and she began to think in terms of his having to see a London doctor.

Alfred's ill-health delayed the next stage of their holiday and Lewis Carroll arrived at the end of September just in time to take a set of photographs before the Tennysons finally packed up and moved further north. They went to Inverary and booked into the hotel there, hoping to stay with the Argylls the next day. But the timing of their visit was now out of kilter with the Duke and Duchess's own plans – they were both away on separate engagements. The Argylls' son, Lord Lorne, invited them to stay in the empty castle but they could not agree to this. Two or three days later the matter was sorted out when the Duchess, having chartered a special steamboat in order to get home quickly, arrived and welcomed her guests. The Tennysons stayed a week in the castle; Alfred, with a cold, was not at his best. There was the odd drive out, the odd reading of *Maud*, but nothing seemed to animate him.

Leaving the castle on 16 October they travelled south to Park

House, stopping off at Carstairs and Peterborough. They stayed a further week at Boxley and then another week after that at Ashburton Cottage, with the Camerons and Edmund and Cecilia Lushington. Finally they left for home on 4 November, reaching Farringford in the late afternoon, with rosy streaks in the sky, and the boys lavishing tender endearments on their favourite crannies and objects.

Emily was just as pleased to be back. She was quite worn out, in body and mind, and never fully recovered that little strength which, from time to time in the past, she had been able to muster.

Alfred, in between sweeping and lawn-rolling, managed at last to do some work. The poem which he produced was, and is, a surprise – not another Arthurian Idyll, but a modern fable about a ruined man and his wife on holiday by the sea. 'Sea Dreams' is a startling creation. During his brooding sickness in the north something must have induced him to think back to his own ruination at the hands of Dr Allen. Anything at all might have prompted this – a chance remark, the tour of Bayons Manor, one of the paintings at Manchester – but the visionary treatment in the poem (with everything hinging on dreams and their interpretation) and the contrasting attitudes of the husband and wife raises some intriguing biographical considerations.

Firstly, the poem prompts reconsideration about Tennyson's use of opium. In the early part of 1857 he had seen a good bit of his dentist and doctor, and might well have been prescribed a medicinal dosage of laudanum, particularly to dull the pain of his ingrowing nail. Meeting Charles, who was once again sorely addicted, would then have made him, and Emily, self-conscious about using it. There is in Emily's remark about the over-sensitive nerves of Alfred and the boys a considerable amount of underscored insinuation. And in Charles Kingsley's novel, *Two Years Ago*, published in the same year, one of the main characters, Elsley Vavasour, taken by many readers to be a caricature of Tennyson, dies of opium addiction. Of more interest than this fictional character is the carelessly-worded defence give at the time by F.D. Maurice: 'I believe Tennyson's life to be a perfectly simple & innocent one, & the charge about opium which I suppose Kingsley accepts to be utterly false. I know no reason to think there was any foundation for it in past years – he declares solemnly that there was not – I feel as convinced as I can be that he is entirely free from the sin now.'[43] Perhaps this was supposed to sound more categorical than it does, but Maurice's testimony is ultimately equivocal about the past and the present. Coming from Hallam's godfather, Tennyson might have expected a more robust rebuttal.

It is romantic nonsense to suggest that we should look for de Quincey-like visions in the work of a poet who made use of opium. As has already been observed, the sonnets of Charles Turner, a confirmed opium addict, could not be less visionary in their style and content. However, we know that opium is inclined to produce both waking dreams and lassitude. At the end of a year in which, apart from two new verses for *God Save the Queen*, written on request for the wedding of the Princess Royal, Tennyson's only composition was an uncharacteristic poem built upon a dream-sequence, it is quite legitimate to wonder whether there was a connection between his moody summer illness and his new poem.

Originally entitled 'An Idyll', 'Sea Dreams' was intended, according to one of Tennyson's own notes, for the 'glorification of honest labour, whether of head or hand, no hasting to be rich, no bowing down to any idol.' An office clerk, his wife and three-year-old daughter are taking a month's holiday by the sea to shake off the city dust and to take their mind off worries caused by the husband's foolish investment in a Peruvian mine. Tennyson uses the couple's dreams, and the interpretation each one puts on them, to contrast their different outlooks on life – the husband's jaundiced and pessimistic, the wife's believing and hopeful.

The poem is proof of the depth of hurt caused, or rather represented by the Allen episode. 'Is it so true that second thoughts are best?/Not first, and third, which are a riper first?/ Too ripe, too late! they come too late for use!' Furious with himself for being duped, the clerk dreams of being swept to the shore 'from out the boundless outer deep', entering a dark cave, and passing through to another exit. The natal imagery is explicit, so that the circumstantial background to the dream is generalized. This is the story of a much deeper deception:

> I thought the motion of the boundless deep
> Bore through the cave, and I was heaved upon it
> In darkness: then I saw one lovely star
> Larger and larger. 'What a world,' I thought,
> 'To live in!' but in moving on I found

Only the landward exit of the cave,
Bright with the sun upon the stream beyond:
And near the light a giant woman sat,
All over earthy, like a piece of earth,
A pickaxe in her hand: then out I slipt
Into a land all sun and blossom, trees
As high as heaven, and every bird that sings:

He dreams on and has a vision of

                a fleet of glass,
That seemed a fleet of jewels under me,
Sailing along before a gloomy cloud
That not one moment ceased to thunder, past
In sunshine: right across its track there lay,
Down in the water, a long reef of gold,
Or what seemed gold: and I was glad at first
To think that in our often-ransacked world
Still so much gold was left; and then I feared
Lest the gay navy there should splinter on it,
And fearing waved my arm to warn them off;
An idle signal, for the brittle fleet
(I thought I could have died to save it) neared,
Touched, clinked, and clashed, and vanished, and I woke,
I heard the clash so clearly. Now I see
My dream was Life; the woman honest Work;
And my poor venture but a fleet of glass
Wrecked on a reef of visionary gold.

The wife is sceptical. She tells him that as he woke he raised his
arm and knocked the young child's medicine bottle off the
bedside cabinet. 'Breaking that, you made and broke your
dream:/A trifle makes a dream, a trifle breaks.'

The poem is a little over-explicit where it should be suggestive but is never sentimental. The husband agrees, for his wife's
sake, to forgive the man who brought him to ruin, but does not
come round to her blithe view of the world. 'His deeds yet live,
the worst is yet to come,' he insists.

Later, when he began to write plays, Tennyson tried to
lighten them with intercalated songs in the Shakespearian
manner. None of them succeeds quite like the exquisitely placed
lullaby at the end of 'Sea Dreams'.

What does little birdie say
In her nest at peep of day?

Let me fly, says little birdie,
Mother let me fly away.
Birdie, rest a little longer
Till the little wings are stronger.
So she rests a little longer,
Then she flies away.

What does little baby say
In her bed at peep of day?
Baby says, like little birdie,
Let me rise and fly away.
Baby sleep a little longer,
Till the little limbs are stronger.
If she sleeps a little longer,
Baby too shall fly away.

16 The Centre Bits

And Sleep must lie down armed, for the villainous centre-bits
Grind on the wakeful ear in the hush of the moonless nights,

(*MAUD* I, xi)

In the early part of 1858 Tennyson regained a sense of artistic purpose. The winter was a mild one and in February, throwing off a dose of influenza, he began to construct with his own hands a summer-house for himself and Emily. At the same time he began to write the story of Arthur and Guinevere.

He was very much the master of the house during the days leading into spring and when, at the end of February, there was a sudden cold snap, he sealed up the window that Emily liked to sit beside so that she might keep warm and watch him sculpting a beautiful snow lady out on the lawn for her and the boys' amusement, dressing the icy beauty in a spare wide-awake hat.

By early March the basic summer-house construction was complete and once the milder weather returned he took Emily (who, it was assumed, was still suffering from a prolonged attack of 'flu) to Maiden's Croft, covered her in his cloak, and talked to her while he painted the walls of the suntrap.

The Guinevere Idyll was progressing quickly, large parts of it conceived during walks to the Needles. On 15 March there was an eclipse of the sun and Tennyson took all the servants onto the Down in order to observe the spectacle. Emily remained in the house. When Alfred returned he went to his study (still, at this time, a small bedroom situated at the top of the house) and finished copying out the completed 'Guinevere'. At tea-time he brought it downstairs and presented it to Emily.

Despite the good omen of his finishing 'Guinevere' so quickly Tennyson was still some way off being ready to publish a new edition. It was three years since the public had seen any new work from him and his friends were worried that the isolated negative response to the trial edition of *Edith and Nimue*[44] would throw him into a ten-year silence similar to the one which had preceded the *Poems* of 1842.

On this subject there was an interesting exchange of letters between himself and Jowett at the end of April. Benjamin Jowett had been a visitor to Farringford during the early part of the month and had had great fun with the two young boys, but when it came to literature Jowett was rather earnest:

May I say a word about 'mosquitoes'? Anyone who cares about you is deeply annoyed that you are deterred by them from writing or publishing. The feeling grows and brings in after years the still more painful and deeper feeling that they have prevented you from putting out half your powers. Nothing is so likely to lead to misrepresentation as the indulgence of it. Persons don't understand that sensitiveness is often combined with real manliness as well as great intellectual gifts and they regard it as a sign of fear and weakness.

A certain man on a particular day has his stomach out of order and the stomach 'getteth him up into the brain,' and he calls another man 'morbid'. He is morbid himself and wants soothing words and the whole world is morbid with dissecting and analysing itself and wants to be comforted and put together again. Might not this be the poet's office to utter the 'better voice' while Thackeray is uttering the worse one. I don't mean to blame Thackeray for I desire to take the world as it is in this present age crammed with self-consciousness, and no doubt Thackeray's views are of some value in the direction of anti-humbug.

But there is another note needed afterwards to show the

good side of human nature and to condone its frailties which Thackeray will never strike. That note would be most thankfully received by the better part of the world.[45]

Tennyson in a brief, almost terse, reply told Jowett he was not altogether right about the 'mosquitoes' but 'loving you and hating letterwriting' he would not elaborate.

Jowett was wrong about the mosquitoes and much else, but in his point about the 'better voice' he echoed a growing public perception of the Laureate as the Poet of Optimism or, if not optimism, of Condolence.[46] The notion that literature should be a balm to the contemporary proclivity for morbidity and self-scrutiny was not one which Tennyson naturally held, as should have been apparent to Jowett and other contemporaries from their reading of *Maud*, but the notion began to take sufficient hold on those people amongst whom the poet now moved, for it to affect the way in which he handled the material of the remaining Idylls. In large measure he would not break loose from this new role until writing 'Locksley Hall Sixty Years After', a poem of such pent-up morbidity that it fairly fizzes with fermenting bile.

After finishing 'Guinevere' Tennyson wrote a narrative poem on a subject directly recommended to him by Jowett. 'The Grandmother' is a sugary and lilting monologue spoken by an old woman who has outlived her husband and children. There is no emotion in it, just the sing-song resignation of a simpleton. 'The first that ever I bare was dead before he was born,/Shadow and shine is life, little Annie, flower and thorn.'

On a further visit to his dentist in London Tennyson was told that extensive treatment was required. He returned to Farringford briefly and while he was at home news arrived that Moxon, his publisher for more than fifteen years, had died. This was a professional disaster for, with the exception of the *Illustrated Edition*, Moxon had been an astute and very fair publisher. His death ushered in a period of distracting business worries.

For the moment though he was preoccupied with the prospect of dental treatment, for which he returned to London on 9 June. The night after having two teeth removed and two others filed down, he dreamed, probably under the influence of laudanum, that Hallam was calling out for help and, running out into the garden, Tennyson found the park full of soldiers. 'We had been talking about the invasion which made my dream,' he laconically commented. About the same time, and possibly on the same night, Emily's sleep was also disturbed, by a strange noise in her room. She thought she heard the 'Villainous centre-bits' (from line 41 in the first section of *Maud*) and sitting up in bed she tried to identify the sound, which was like the grinding of glass. With a lighted candle in one hand she moved across to the window and saw a snail on the outer sill scraping at the pane with its shell. The fact that Emily should immediately associate the unfamiliar noise with lines from her husband's poetry shows both her intimate knowledge of it and the degree to which her range of references were determined by his work.

After the extractions Tennyson was forced to remain in London for several more days while Barrett, the dentist, waited to make a mould for the setting of false teeth. Tennyson passed his time in the usual way for this period, moving between Argyll Lodge, Burlington House, and Little Holland House. He had in large measure drifted apart from the Trinity set – Brookfield, Venables, FitzGerald, and especially Milnes. His college companions had all contributed in their chummy and supportive way to the kind of poetry Tennyson had written before being made Laureate. The trial audiences which he chose for the readings of the early Idylls were of a different cast. Between the intimate encouragement of his wife, Emily, and the rather mannered and polite encomia of his society friends like the Argylls, there was insufficient editorial influence. People like Jowett, as we have observed, did their bit, but it was a far cry from the days when fair copies of poems were passed between Cambridge, London, Somersby and Herstmonceux, and friends would fulminate over crass revisions or salivate over a new masterpiece.

Tennyson has had a finger or two wagged at him for this, as if he were somehow blameworthy for the state of affairs. But marriage, family life, ownership of property, celebrity – these all carry inevitable penalties. They need not be penalties of course, and viewed in a straightforward and positive light Tennyson's marriage was good both for his work and for his temperament. But in darker perspectives the 'villainous centre-bits' were busy grinding away.

17   Look to Your Butts

Ready, be ready to meet the storm!
Riflemen, Riflemen, Riflemen form!

('RIFLEMEN FORM!')

During September and October there was the usual constant stream of visitors to the island, notably F.D. Maurice, who lost his hat while chasing the boys on the Down and had to have his head covered with a handkerchief, and Edmund and Franklin Lushington. Franklin had resigned from his post in Corfu and returned to England in August in the company of Lear, with whom he had been travelling. Lear had long nurtured a homosexual longing for Franklin and had been given some surprisingly knowing advice from Emily on how to advance the friendship. As it was, Lear was busy at this time painting in St Leonard's and hawking his portfolio of Near East sketches.

The autumn was dominated by a serious deterioration in Alfred's relations with his publisher. Tennyson's agreements with Moxon for each book issued had been purely verbal, a matter of honour between friends. The new firm now handling the business, Bradbury and Evans (owners of *Punch*), with Moxon's younger brother William acting as front-man, insisted that a written contact should be drawn up. Tennyson, too far away to deal with the matter in person, appointed Emily's brother-in-law Charles Weld to act as his agent. Weld sent Alfred his first report on 27 October 1858. It contained staggering information:

[Moxon] informed me that...the estate of the late Mr. Moxon had claims on you to the amount of £8886. 8. 4 – on my demanding how this could possibly be he proceeded to tell me that in consequence of *your* earnest solicitations his late brother had embarked in the unfortunate speculation of publishing an illustrated edition of your Poems of which he printed 10,000 copies and that 7790 copies remain unsold...[47]

The offence which this caused Tennyson is expressed in his irritable reply:

> After very weary waiting for months and rejecting splendid offers from first rate publishers because I chose to stick by the house of Moxon, I am treated at last discourteously and untruthfully by William Moxon. I decline entering into any business till all this is explained and apologized for.[48]

In fact there was double cause for outrage. The Tennysons heard directly from Bradbury and Evans that they were proceeding with an illustrated edition of *The Princess*, (a venture for which there had never been a verbal agreement), and that Maclise had been in Italy preparing the sketches for it.

Weld's assignment was complicated by the fact that all agreements between Tennyson and Moxon had been casual and assumed. Emily did what she could to dig out letters and find references, but in the end all she could furnish her brother-in-law with were vague recollections such as 'In conversation Alfred stated that it was impossible for him to furnish funds to pay the artists and I think, as far as I remember, Moxon said, "Oh we can manage all that."' This hardly clinched the matter.

These were tiring days for Emily, and her Journal entries for the first part of November are made all the more gloomy by the reporting of damage to the great ilex outside the dining room. The tree split down the middle and had to be supported with strong iron chains. She is a reticent diarist, but sometimes the juxtapositon of remarks and events achieves a poetic and metaphorical suggestiveness. Here we see Emily afraid that the constant secretarial demands on her time will break her, like the ilex: '*Nov 1st* ... We have another weary day of letter hunting and letter writing. The great Ilex opposite the dining room planted in the year of the battle of Waterloo has split. This split is filled with clay & it is girded by strong iron chains & soon moves itself by its branches.'

As well as poring over old correspondence, and writing to Weld, she had to copy out a long 'statement of facts', carefully going over the contested points. Written as if it had come from Alfred's own pen it was in all probability composed by Emily herself. 'The Illustration of the Poems was entirely the late Mr Moxon's own proposal on the occasion of the encouragement given him to mrk. a publication by different book sellers ...That

I accepted the 2000 in lieu of the much larger sum I had reason to expect proves that I was not greedy of gain ...'

In the middle of November Tennyson could bear the tension no longer, and went to London in person to help draw the matter to a conclusion. He would not permit Emily to accompany him on the trip because of the cold east wind. The 'great stink' which hung about the city during the whole of this winter, and emanated from a pollution of the Thames, would have helped convince him that he was right to insist she stay at home.

The publishing firm had already invested a great deal in the new edition of *The Princess* and despite the recent disappointment of the *Illustrated Edition*, Tennyson was still the mainstay of their list. He was in a strong position; in the end Moxon & Co. relinquished their claim for £8886 8s 4d and gave Tennyson a new written contract in which he was allowed to take ninety per cent on books sold, a royalty margin which beggars belief.[49] Unsurprisingly, he agreed to stay with the firm under its new management but remained determined not to let Maclise's designs 'be published this Christmas if possible: they are too wide of the text.'

Alfred returned from London with Mrs Gatty, a woman of exactly his own age, herself an author of short stories, children's books and the editor of a magazine for young people. During her stay in his house Alfred took her to the beach to collect sea anemones and read *Maud* and 'Locksley Hall' to her. Following this and other visits Mrs Gatty showered Alfred, Emily and the children with gifts of her books, homeopathic medicines and other special items, like a lesser Mrs Cameron. One of the first presents to arrive was a new scythe and, despite it being December, Tennyson went straight outside to mow the grass with it.

As an indication that Emily could still, from time to time, make an effort to recover some intermittent vitality, she played a little shuttlecock with Alfred on 7 December, at a time when they were both suffering from colds and their chests were smeared with thick flour and honey poultices, a favourite remedy. The game must have been a messy affair.

Some of the tension over the Moxon business was relieved when Woolner arrived on Boxing Day. The boys went wild with excitement. Woolner turned the dining room into his studio while he worked on a medallion of Emily, but found time to blow bubbles with Alfred for the entertainment of Lionel and Hallam (who, it appears, were not allowed to blow their own bubbles).

Tennyson was now engaged in writing 'The Maid of Astolat', later known as 'Elaine', a subject first proposed by Woolner the previous summer. He seems to have been able to concentrate well on the poem, despite the sculptor's presence, and later that of Jowett. Both men helped Alfred push Emily up onto the Down – covered in Alfred's great cloak with only a peep-hole to see through.

By 8 March Tennyson was able to tell the Duchess of Argyll that four Idylls were complete – these being 'Enid', 'Vivien', 'Elaine' and 'Guinevere' – but as for plans to publish them, he could not say. He had not been well for some weeks and the end of January had been made sombre with the news of Henry Hallam's death, and with the death of a sick dove which Alfred had found in the grounds, under a fallen tree. Tennyson was asked by Mr Hallam's daughter, Julia, to compose the epitaph for her father's tombstone. The simpler the better, he said, and suggested: 'HERE WITH HIS WIFE AND CHILDREN/RESTS/HENRY HALLAM/THE HISTORIAN/ONLY SON OF THE LATE JOHN HALLAM, D.D., DEAN OF BRISTOL/BORN 9TH JULY 1777: DIED 21 JANUARY 1859'.[50]

At the end of March Tennyson went to Town to collect the proofs of *Idylls of the King* and to have another portrait painted by Watts. He spent a whole morning declaiming 'Merlin' to Walter White, standing by the mantelpiece in White's office and reading in a deep sonorous voice all 140 pages of the manuscript.

The next day he was 'carried off' to Little Holland House and on Saturday 26 March read 'Elaine' to Woolner, the Argylls and other company. Emily, getting his letter of the 25th, wrote back, rather self-pityingly, 'So thou art in the Enchanted Palace once more. I do not doubt that thou art happy and I hope it will do thee good.'

Returning to Farringford with proofs of the *Idylls*, Alfred set about checking them and nursing Emily who was at this point bed-ridden and in extreme pain. 'It is almost worthwhile to have the pain to be tenderly nursed as I am by A.', she recorded in her Journal, in what was perhaps an unguarded moment, but which became an increasingly frequent refrain.

Lewis Carroll was on the Isle of Wight during the latter part of April and visited the Tennysons two or three times.

Significantly, he did not make much of an impression on Hallam or Lionel, in contrast to the fun-loving Woolner, or the visually eccentric Lear. Tennyson was out in the grounds when Carroll first turned up, with Mrs Gatty's scythe glinting in a strong Easter sun. Indoors Carroll saw proof-sheets of the *Idylls* lying about, but Tennyson would not let him read them. He had already written to Sarah Prinsep begging her to burn a copy of 'Guinevere' which he had left at Little Holland House, fearing it would be broadcast before publication. 'O Principessa' he had addressed her, 'I petition the Goddess to burn – burn – burn.' After Carroll's satire on 'The Two Voices' he did not trust the young man.

Emily Tennyson, still on her sofa, was too weak to look at the book of photographs, containing the family shots of the Tennysons at Coniston, and so Carroll left them overnight.

Soon after this visit, and as a result of scything in the deceptively cold spring weather, Tennyson became ill with face-ache and headache. Whilst his head was in pain, news of the Franco-Austrian War and of the treaty between France and Russia was published in *The Times*. In response to what he perceived as the renewed threat of war with France, Tennyson wrote two more patriotic pieces, 'Riflemen Form!' and 'Jack Tar'. The first of these was a reworking of one of the patriotic songs from 1852. He sent it to the Gattys and to Weld, who was told to try it with *The Times*. The newspaper published it on 9 May and the poem had a decisive influence on the formation of a volunteer movement. The second poem was not published. Both told the nation to stop all factional politics for a time and address the international crisis.

> Let your reforms for a moment go!
> Look to your butts, and take good aims;
> Better a rotten borough or so
> Than a rotten fleet and a city in flames!

Such patriotic outbursts were not blips in the Tennysonian manner. Facial neuralgia might have deepened his sense of foreboding but it did not produce an inconsistency of thought. Christopher Ricks, through detailed analysis of the various manuscripts, including those at Trinity, has brilliantly identified the 'deep biographical roots of [Tennyson's] self-borrowing'. His first political poem as a peer – 'Freedom', dated 1884 – is in fact a reworking of poems written when Tennyson was in his early twenties. This self-borrowing was a characteristic cast of Tennyson's mind and poetic method. In the many descriptions of him that can be found in the memoirs of his contemporaries there are frequent references to the way in which he would talk about words and prosody as a painter might talk about colour and brush-technique. His manuscript books and early drafts became like half-finished old canvasses stacked in a studio, ready to be taken up at a later date.

The decision to base 'The Charge of the Light Brigade' on Drayton's 'Agincourt' was no coincidence. He had been brought up on the patriotic ballads of the Elizabethans and knew many of them by heart. Turning to nationalistic political verse was no surprise to himself – it was a conscious attempt to work in the best of English traditions.

18   A Tennysonian Fix

I wither slowly in thine arms,
Here at the quiet limit of the world,

('TITHONUS')

During May and June some major renovation was carried out at Farringford, to provide Alfred with a larger study and to improve the light in certain parts of the house. It meant the gutting of Alfred's attic haunt. 'Poor little room, it is sad for A. and me when we see its barnlike rafters & we grow quite sentimental over it when A. talks of all the pleasant evenings spent under its low ceiling, all the thoughts & all the feelings thought and felt then.'[51]

As best they could they ignored the building work, the whole family involving itself in the planting out of greenhouse flowers. Emily chose the positions, Hallam and Lionel carried out the plants, and Alfred dug the holes. Deprived of his study, Tennyson did the last stages of his proof-reading in the summer-house. Working outdoors brought on an early attack of hayfever and he put off a trip to London until 10 June. Ostensibly to deliver the proofs, the purpose of the visit was also to visit Barrett, who had a new set of teeth (supposedly indestructible) ready for the poet. Most of his time was spent, as usual, at Little Holland House, reading to the assembled company, which included, on 17 June, Gladstone and his wife. Two or three days later Tennyson received an invitation to breakfast with Gladstone, but sent a gracious refusal, saying that although he used to breakfast occasionally with Mr Rogers and Mr Hallam, they were men of so great an age it would have been irreverent to refuse them.

Watts still had a little to do to his new painting of Tennyson – later to be dubbed the 'moonlight' portrait – but on 27 June, accompanied by Mrs Cameron and Frederick, Alfred returned to Farringford. Although the carpenters had worked hard to finish the improvements in his absence, Alfred and the visitors arrived to find that there was much left undone. On the first day of July a fearful thunderstorm, producing hailstones the size of bullets, flooded the kitchen and let water into the newly furnished bedrooms. Merwood was called in to drill holes in the bathroom ceiling to let off a vast amount of water that threatened to collapse the plaster.

In the midst of this dramatic weather Mrs Cameron, who had left the house for another part of the island, sent Ellen, her maid, to collect the manuscript of 'Guinevere'. Alfred had apparently promised it to her but she was scared he would give it to the first set of dinner guests who asked for it. 'A. does not care about his manuscripts,' Emily wrote in her Journal. 'He gives them to anyone who asks. To me they are more precious than words can say. Every page almost a memory. He is so good as to say that if I do not like to part from it and he has promised it he will copy it out rather than that I should have to part from it.' These sugary words do not quite succeed in suppressing the sense of jealousy which lurks behind them.

On 10 July they received the first copies of *Idylls of the King*: 40,000 copies had been printed, in the familiar green boards, priced at seven shillings. A quarter of this print-run was sold in the first six weeks and a second edition was required within six months. There would be six more editions before the next series of Idylls was completed in 1869.

These early Idylls were not allegorical, but exemplary. Sub-titled 'The True and the False', Enid and Elaine represented true love, and Guinevere and Vivien false. It was only later, with the addition of successive Idylls, that Tennyson began to work out the elaborate pattern of symbolism that can be read into, for instance, 'Gareth and Lynette'. For the moment his concern was wholly centred on adultery.

It is impossible, in the broad sweep of a biography, to give these poems the prominence which their length and influence might seem to demand. Perhaps it is better this way, for they have become overburdened both with what the Victorians themselves made of them, and with more recent attempts to defend them as a large-scale achievement. They are best read, and most likely to be enjoyed, as poems entirely in keeping with the rest of Tennyson's work. What they form when put together is still a fragmentary poem, like *In Memoriam* and *The Princess*; it is just that each fragment this time is more of a piece.

Certainly, as each new Idyll is read, the allegory which the Victorians themselves loved to see in the poems – with Arthur as the monarchy, and the Knights of the Round Table as missionary exponents of British imperial wisdom – recedes, and the rough, critical voice that was used in *Maud* begins to be heard again. For no one can read these poems as anything but a sombre, regretful prophecy of the dissolution of the Empire.

The surprising weakness of the language in the Idylls – they indisputably contain some of Tennyson's worst writing – has been well documented. He wrote them first as prose drafts, and it has to be admitted the translation from prose to poetry sometimes does not go much beyond a counting of syllables and the introduction of frequent inversions. But the very clumsiness of the verse (in comparison with his usual metrical precision) lends it a dramatic weight which is especially effective in the set speeches. Here, Merlin speaks to Vivien:

'O did ye never lie upon the shore,
And watch the curled white of the coming wave
Glassed in the slippery sand before it breaks?
Even such a wave, but not so pleasurable,
Dark in the glass of some presageful mood,
Had I for three days seen, ready to fall.
And then I rose and fled from Arthur's court
To break the mood. You followed me unasked;
And when I looked, and saw you following still,
My mind involved yourself the nearest thing
In that mind-mist: for shall I tell you truth?
You seemed that wave about to break upon me

And sweep me from my hold upon the world,
My use and name and fame ...'

If the unaccustomed use of prose drafts was Tennyson's way of protecting himself from an inappropriately lilting dexterity, such passages prove the wisdom of the technique.

The summer 'holiday' came a little later this year. The Tennysons were still at Farringford in the middle of July, suffering in the tropical heat and entertaining another American visitor, the publisher James T. Fields who wrote to Longfellow:

> I had already met Alfred the Great in London where he had gone to read the proofs of his new volume. We sat down together over the sheets one day in the Temple and talked over certain passages about which he seemed doubtful. The title then was *The True and the False* which he afterwards altered as it now stands. As you have never seen him I will try to make him out on paper for your inspection. A tall stooping figure clad in sober grey, beard full and flowing, moustache, long stringy hair, and spectacles. His voice is shaggy-rough, and his gait moves with his voice. His near sight does not improve his general appearance, as you may imagine. In his own house and grounds ... he stumbles about in a kind of Tennysonian fix which he does not seem to be trying to move away from ... I shall have much to say to you of him when we meet which I cannot write, but I will note down here that he strikes me constantly as the greatest man I have ever met in England. His Knowledge is most wonderful, and when he talks he says things that are apt to send a thrill with the words. His usual tone is a low unmelodious thundergrowl, but when he chooses he can melt as well as rasp with his Lincolnshire tongue. When he appears at the table in the morning with his old slouched sombrero hat, reading his letters while he takes his breakfast, he is apt to stick dagger-words up and down the present Emperor of France whom he variously designates as a beggar and a scoundrel. But I will not *write* of him any more.[52]

This reiterated suggestion that there is more to be said about Tennyson when Fields and Longfellow meet face to face is an obvious invitation to speculate. What was it about the great man's habits, conversation, health, or treatment of his wife that could not be written down? And whilst this description of

Tennyson echoes previous ones – the rasping voice, the near sight – it introduces a new dimension. The stumbling about in 'a kind of Tennysonian fix' suggests more than the air of languid self-absorption which had been his characteristic since early youth. It gives us the picture of an artist who has reached a certain threshold in his career and is temporarily on automatic pilot.

Towards the end of the month he and Emily finally got away, travelling firstly to Park House, and then to the Camerons' at Ashburton Cottage. From here Tennyson made speedy preparations with Palgrave for a trip to Portugal. They left on the 16 August, sailing from Southampton, where they were joined by Grove, and waved off by Brookfield.

After a journey of five days, aboard the P.&O. steamer *Vectis*, they booked into the Braganza Hotel, Lisbon. Toothache, the heat, the flies and the fleas eventually put paid to plans of travelling on to Tangier or Malaga, and on the 2 September they decided to board a boat home. Meanwhile, Emily, who was unwell, had taken the boys to Park House, where they were initiated into the game of cricket. Alfred did not join them there but went into the New Forest with Palgrave, who continued to be 'as kind to me as a brother, and far more useful than a valet or courier, doing everything.'

A sudden desire to be in Cambridge came over Tennyson on their return to England and after a few days in the Forest he travelled there with Palgrave. Such is the impression given by texts of letters published in the *Memoir*. However, a rather different slant is put upon this sudden jaunt in a letter from Woolner to Lady Trevelyan. According to Woolner: 'He enjoyed tolerably his trip to Lisbon, but was exceedingly ill for some days, brought on by the wine and vile food of the country: Palgrave, who was with him, was in a fright about him for some while: his and Tennyson's fear was lest the fact should get into the papers and frighten Mrs Tennyson at home.'[53] The trip to Cambridge was not, then, so much a nostalgic impulse, as an act of self-preserving panic; but the return was not without its sentimental moments. Tennyson met and talked to his old tobacconist from Trinity days, but a more important meeting was with Alexander Macmillan, after which Macmillan straightaway wrote a long letter to Emily explaining the very personal valuation which he put upon her husband's writing, particularly *In Memoriam*. This poem had helped him in two family bereavements – both his younger brother Daniel, and his brother-in-law, George Brimley, had died within a month of one another in 1857.

It is difficult to take the letter's sincerity at face value. At their meeting in Cambridge Tennyson would undoubtedly have mentioned his recent difficulties with the Moxon firm and the businessman in Macmillan would immediately have sensed interesting potentialities. Tennyson might also have remarked that a large proportion of his affairs were in the hands of his wife. And so the letter to Emily – a letter which produced a more rapid, if a more trifling, response than he had sought.

When Macmillan visited Farringford between 7 and 10 October he was given 'Sea Dreams' to publish in the first edition of his new monthly magazine. In letting Macmillan have the poem (for £300) Tennyson let down his friend Thackeray who asked for something to go into the first number of the *Cornhill Magazine*, due out in January. Tennyson explained, somewhat embarrasedly, that he had just parted with his only new poem. 'I don't think he would have got it, except that he had come to visit me in my island, and was sitting and blowing his weed vis a vis.' His claim that Thackeray's request for a poem had arrived after he had given one to Macmillan was perfectly true. The first part of Thackeray's letter, written in a marvellous 'ardour of claret and gratitude' – Thackeray had been tippling in the cellar of a Southampton hotel with the landlord – although dated September, was not sent until after 16 October, when a post-script request for a contribution to Smith & Elder's periodical was added.

Tennyson rummaged around in old albums and scrap books but could find nothing satisfactory. The matter played upon his conscience though, and before the end of the year he had written, and sent off, 'Tithonus', the painful sense of obligation producing a tone poem of the highest order. It was based on an early 'pendant' piece to 'Ulysses' entitled 'Tithon' and which he had never used. In this instance the revisions cannot be faulted:

> The woods decay, the woods decay and fall,
> The vapours weep their burthen to the ground,
> Man comes and tills the field and lies beneath,
> And after many a summer dies the swan.
> Me only cruel immortality
> Consumes: . . .

The early version had 'substance' in place of 'burthen' in line 2, and 'rose' instead of 'swan' in line 4; and in line 5 immortality was 'fatal' rather than 'cruel' – small but priceless changes. Its classical allusion is to the character beloved by the goddess Aurora and given eternal life but not eternal youth. As a poem about one of Tennyson's lifelong obsessions – immortality – it is of special interest, and there are clear invitations to read the poem as one more expression of abandonment by his dead friend Arthur Hallam. Benjamin Jowett, who had visited Hallam's grave earlier in the year and been deeply moved, had written to Alfred, saying, 'It is a strange feeling about those who are taken young that while we are getting old and dusty they are as they were.' Nevertheless, the poem's classical frame does need to be acknowledged for a sensible understanding of its metaphorical passages.

> Thy cheek begins to redden through the gloom,
> Thy sweet eyes brighten slowly close to mine,
> Ere yet they blind the stars, and the wild team
> Which love thee, yearning for thy yoke, arise,
> And shake the darkness from their loosened manes,
> And beat the twilight into flakes of fire.

This is perhaps too obviously an epical conceit to be misunderstood, but the temptation to anthropomorphize the image is stronger later in the poem when Tithonus remembers with what mortal joy he once surveyed the dawn:

> I used to watch – if I be he that watched –
> The lucid outline forming round thee; saw
> The dim curls kindle into sunny rings;
> Changed with thy music change, and felt my blood
> Glow with the glow that slowly crimsoned all
> Thy presence and thy portals, while I lay,
> Mouth, forehead, eyelids, growing dewy-warm
> With kisses balmier than half-opening buds
> Of April, and could hear the lips that kissed
> Whispering I knew not what of wild and sweet ...

Of more importance to the Hallam theme than the eroticism of the imagery is the note of caution – 'If I be he that watched.' Still there was the fear that as the living changed while the dead remained as they were their meeting again in Paradise would be a paradoxical affair.

19   Piano Posse

Thine the liberty, thine the glory, thine the deeds to be celebrated,
Thine the myriad-rolling ocean, light and shadow illimitable,
Thine the lands of lasting summer, many-blossoming Paradises.
Thine the North and thine the South and thine the battle-thunder of
God.

('BOADICEA')

The drawing-room drama whimsicalities of Virginia Woolf's play *Freshwater* pale into insignificance beside the reality of life at Farringford. One of the early domestic incidents of the New Year (1860) typifies the laughable bathos of some of the events recorded in Emily's Journal. 'The poor little Squirrel given to the boys by Afton escapes while Henri is clearing the cage. He throws a stick up at it to bring it down from a tree which kills [it] and makes us all sad. It had such pretty ways. We were all fond of it.'[54]

Mrs Cameron at last realized her dream of living near the Tennysons, as neighbours. Having waved her husband off to Ceylon, she acquired Dimbola, a house just a few hundred yards below Farringford, and moved in with her children in early 1860. One of her first acts was to deliver, in person, two legs of Welsh mutton, and a few weeks later she arrived bearing a quantity of vivid blue wall-paper. 'The vivid blue neither she nor we like,' Emily noted, rather crisply. But added, already with an air of neighbourly resignation, 'We as usual protest against her prodigal kindness.'

Affectionate though Alfred and Emily remained towards one another, there is a growing sense of isolation in Tennyson's personality in the first year of the new decade. He had already begun to spend the annual 'move' – what Emily called his 'wanderingfit' – away from his wife and children. Emily began to spend more and more time on the sofa or confined to her bed, and Alfred felt increasingly alone. His trips to London, ostensibly to visit the dentist, or to deliver proofs, were extended beyond the few days strictly necessary. His dependence on valet-like male companions became ever more marked. Mrs

Cameron, and even young girls like the Thackeray daughters, provided a greater proportion of his female company.

As his image became public property – through paintings, cartoons, sculpture, photography and, eventually, postcards – his reaction was defensive, petulant, irrational and paranoid: he stubbornly refused to come to terms with his fame. He began to imagine 'cockney' autograph hunters in innocent passers-by, and any talk of building on the island within range of his estate put him into paroxysms of rage. How dare they invade his private domain?

Having passed the age of fifty, Tennyson evidently now viewed himself as a senior man of letters, in a position to curry favour in support of his friends. In January 1860 he recommended Woolner to Tuckerman for the Washington Monument, and in February he wrote to Milnes and Gladstone to try and obtain a junior clerkship in the House of Commons for his nephew Arthur Jesse. These were considerate acts, but they gave to his contacts with old friends an increasing air of expediency.

More and more frequently the poetic impulse needed a kick-start. Living a life apart from friends and varied sensations, Tennyson was glad to listen to suggestions for new poems. He looked for material in stories and anecdotes printed in periodicals or passed on to him by his friends, and increasingly the staple content of his poetry became narrative and dramatic in character.

Despite the instant success of *Idylls of the King* Tennyson did not immediately return to the Arthurian material. Early in March he completed the strangely experimental 'Boadicea', a poem full of his patriotic impulses and hatred of European viciousness. In its long lines and repetitive naming of names it has an uncharacteristically loose and Whitmanesque feel, giving us a tantalizing taste of what Tennyson might have produced, and the direction in which English poetry might have gone had he chosen to explore further this style of poetic utterance, rather than turning to verse-drama. Perhaps Emily's opinion was influential '["Boadicea"] is very fine, I think, though I would not have him do many such things. I think all metres that properly belong to a language are born in the minds of the poets of the land and not adopted children.'[55]

The poem was written at a time when Emily and the boys were very unwell. Alfred sent to Newport for a doctor and whooping cough was diagnosed. The sufferers were shut away in three separate rooms and several visitors had to be put off, or sent to the hotel in Freshwater Bay. The wallpaper in one of the newly-decorated rooms was found to contain a 'great quantity of Arsenic', thought to be the source of the cough – so it had to be stripped off.

Over the next few weeks Alfred entertained such visitors as were not put off by the cough – these included Woolner, Venables and the Argylls – and brought Emily little bunches of primroses to brighten her room. Mrs Cameron, of course, was a constant presence, helping to amuse the boys and keep their spirits up. By mid-April they were all well enough to get out of bed. Alfred carried Emily down to the drawing-room and then brought Hallam and Lionel to her – 'so here we all are once more, thank God.'

However, 'Tomorrow A. has to go to his dentist', prompts the suggestion that Alfred was less thankful than Emily for the return to normality. He was in town for a week, the most notable event of these seven days being a long night spent at Macmillan's during which he wrote his name in capitals on the rim of the big round table.

On his return Tennyson was delighted to find how neat Heard, their new gardener, had made the kitchen garden. Merwood, who now managed the farm, had always protected his special expertise and would not let the Tennysons advise or assist. Heard, although less interesting in himself, was much more congenial and even let Alfred help out with the digging.

Julia Cameron's new proximity to Tennyson affected her view of the man and by the early summer she had begun to reach some fairly acerbic conclusions. His general dissatisfaction with life infuriated her. 'He sees the beauty but he *feels* it not – his spirits are low – and his countenance serious and solemn. Every trifle of life disturbs him – the buildings *getting* up are a nightmare to him – the workmen *not* getting on are a daily vexation to him – his furniture has not come – the sculptures for his hall have miscarried or been delayed – the tradesmen cheat him – the visitors look at him – Tourists seek him – Ladies pester and pursue him – Enthusiasts dun him for a bit of stone off his gate – These things make life a burden and his great soul suffers from these insect stings....'[56]

If Julia Cameron showed a want of imagination in these observations and a failure of that modern sentiment called 'empathy', it was largely because she took a heroic view of life and art. A 'Poet' was not supposed to be subject to the everyday bother of dealing with tradesmen and hangers-on. Artists – whether they be writers, painters or musicians – continue to live in substantially the same world as their audience and it is often more revealing to observe the ways in which they respond to the petty trifles of life than it is to pretend that such trivialities pass them by.

The month of June was the happiest of the year, filled with good weather and a rush of guests. Alfred's brother, Arthur, brought his young bride, Harriet West; the Kers came, the Prinseps, and Edward Lear, with Franklin Lushington. The adults went kite-flying with the children and eclipse-watching on the Downs. Dr Wolff came to give a lecture in the church, an occasion held up for the arrival of Tennyson and Julia Cameron, who had chosen to walk together rather than go by horse and cart.

During Lear's stay Julia Cameron surpassed herself. Emily was resting after dinner when she heard tramping on the drive. Her first thought was that it was a posse of American sight-seers and she steeled herself for the ridding of them. But on going to the window she saw eight men struggling towards the house with a grand piano. Mrs Cameron had sent it so that Lear could accompany his settings of Tennyson songs on his last night in the house. When Lear wrote to Woolner to report the incident he used seven exclamation marks. It was, even by Julia Cameron's standards, an extraordinary gesture.

Tennyson seems to have played a purely passive part in all of this – the whole year is a self-effacing one, as if he were gathering his resources for the later rounds of life. Like a boxer in round six of a ten-round fight he kept to the perimeter of the ring, on guard, and breathing deeply.

The summer move was again delayed, this time by petty troubles. They did not get away until after Alfred's birthday, which Emily celebrated by decking him in flowers and a briary wreath. 'A peaceful day. A. in good spirits,' she recorded. This picture of Tennyson allowing himself to be decked in flowers and foliage is in keeping with the rather muted, passive bearing which he adopted in these days.

They finally got away from the island in early August and went to Burlington House, staying in the Welds' rooms. Entertaining Palgrave, Woolner and Walter White at the house the following day, Tennyson was full of plans to go to the Levant, or even the West Indies, for a few weeks. But over the course of the next week – a week otherwise filled with family excursions to Westminster Abbey, to Alfred's mother in Hampstead, and to the National Gallery to see the recently acquired *Madonna and Child* by Titian – the travel programme became attenuated to a short tour of Cornwall. Emily, meanwhile, took the boys to Grasby.

Although a trip to Cornwall in the company of Palgrave and Holman Hunt had been intended to re-awaken Tennyson's Arthurian inspiration, he began no new poem this autumn. Instead, much of his care and attention went into entertaining and diverting his friend John Simeon, whose wife had recently died, and supervising work on a new sunken road beside the park at Farringford. Trees had to be felled and a small bridge built over it so that it would be possible to pass through the green gate and straight across the road into the Wilderness.

As little as a day or two after his arrival home from Cornwall the visitors began to appear – the Lushingtons, the Welds, Coventry Patmore, and Frederick with his son Giulio (otherwise known as Julius). In November he and Emily heard of the government's plans to fortify the end of the island by the Needles – news which put them in an awkward position. Forever wary of new development in the region of Farringford, and of a growth in population, they could hardly complain about a decision which Tennyson's own poetry had probably encouraged.

By early December the trees had been felled and both the road and the bridge were nearly finished. They were officially opened on the 19th, the day Palgrave arrived for his Christmas visit.

During Palgrave's stay Tennyson helped him to finalize the selection for *The Golden Treasury*, a project which had developed out of the Cornish trip. The editorial process had been continuing (by post) throughout the autumn, with Palgrave using Woolner and Tennyson as arbiters, but giving the latter the power of veto and casting vote. Poems were marked 'P' for 'Print', 'O' for 'Out' and 'OW' for 'On the Whole', with Tennyson showing his approval with a cross, or special approval with a double cross.[57] One of the poems that was included on Tennyson's insistence – Richard Lovelace's 'To Lucasta' – demonstrates the degree to which his belief in the after-life rested on literary as much as religious principles. Heaven was not so much a spiritual as an imaginative resting place. In Lovelace's poem two separated lovers meet one another in their imagination,

> So then do we anticipate
> > Our after-fate,
> > And are alive i' the skies,
> > If thus our lips and eyes
> Can speak like spirits unconfined
> In Heaven, their earthy bodies left behind.

('TO LUCASTA' BY RICHARD LOVELACE)

20   All Along the Valley

> All along the valley, while I walked today,
> The two and thirty years were a mist that rolls away,

'IN THE VALLEY OF CAUTERITZ'

I n writing of Tennyson during the 1860s we are confronted by a poet whose creative impulse is severely disrupted by illness, domestic upheavals, and a growing restlessness, compounded by the increasing numbers of tourists streaming onto the island in summer. It was not until well into the second half of the decade that he felt empowered to continue the sequence of Idylls.

It is always tempting for biographers to blur the focus of their book once they are past the mid-point in a life. For those writing about Tennyson the temptation has been particularly strong – Christopher Ricks, in his critical biography, presents only half a life, ending his chronological account in the year 1850, with the extraordinary assertion that by that time Tennyson 'had undergone all that truly formed him'. But the real challenge for a biographer whose subject lived on, actively, into old age is to examine later experiences as tellingly as those of youth.

The year of the Prince Consort's death, 1861, has been chosen by historians who dislike the conventional three-way analysis of the Victorian period, as the transition from the early to the late phase of the Queen's reign. There are alluring reasons for allotting it a special place in Tennyson's own development. Jowett, arriving for his annual visit on 15 January, gave a description of Tennyson which lacks the usual misty, adulatory tone.

He has been ill, and greatly suffering and depressed I fear. The more I see of him the more I respect his character, notwithstanding a superficial irritability and uneasiness about all things. I have a pleasure in repeating this about him, because I find he is so greatly mistaken by those who don't know him or only know him a little. No one is more honest, truthful, manly, or a warmer friend; but he is as open as the day, and, like a child, tells any chance comer what is passing in his mind ... The subject on which he is most ready to converse – sometimes over a pipe – is (what do you think?) a future state, of which he always talks with a passionate conviction. He is the shyest person I ever knew, feeling sympathy and needing it to a degree quite painful. Please not to repeat this to the vulgar, who can never be made to understand that great mental troubles necessarily accompany such powers as he possesses.[58]

This is a convincing portrait. The poet's passionate obsession with the nature of a 'future state' – not, of course, a political obsession, but a spiritual one – would gradually alienate him from the domestic felicities of family life. The first change in affairs came in February 1861, with the arrival of Henry Graham Dakyns, who had been employed as tutor for Hallam and Lionel. Dakyns, a twenty-two year-old scholar from Rugby School and Trinity College was procured for the Tennysons by Bradley. The position appealed to the young man, who had just been awarded a second-class degree, because it would offer him the opportunity to go on 'self-educating'.

The boys, who were nearly nine and seven, were rather young to be much interested in the kind of study that would have contributed to Dakyns's self-education, but they responded warmly to his playful personality and he spent as much time with them in pure fun as he did in instruction. After he had left, and a series of new tutors had been employed, Emily would frequently wish that the new tutors might extend their labours beyond the classroom, as Dakyns had done.

Above all, Dakyns was a success with Tennyson; which is just as well, because the poet continued, after Jowett's visit, in a gruff and irritable state. When Dakyns arrived, Tennyson had just been to London to visit his dentist (accompanied by one of the Cameron daughters) and had returned with a version of the 'Northern Farmer' in manuscript. That poem marvellously captured the cantankerous idiom of an old and dying tenant farmer refusing to obey the doctor and keep off the ale. There was sufficient grouchy obstinacy in Tennyson's own nature to make the dialect mimicry entirely convincing.

Lionel had prepared a welcoming ditty for Dakyns, which he planned to sing while waving a flag, but on the day of the tutor's arrival, 19 February, courage failed him, and instead he put a pot of snowdrops in the newcomer's room. Emily, while delighted to find Dakyns so intelligent and amenable, was percipient enough to realize immediately that his arrival marked a watershed in her marriage. 'I cannot but miss the life we have hitherto had, however good I hope the change is in some way.'

Dakyns was quickly introduced to the potential for tension at Farringford. A month after his arrival, Edward Lear, distraught at the death of his sister Ann, arrived at Farringford hoping to find comfort and solace. He had been promised as much by Emily in a letter sent just days before he arrived. 'You must come to us when you are equal to it . . .' she had said, which he took as an immediate invitation. But he arrived to find the Tennysons in a bustle of preparation for the arrival of Horatio and his family and, feeling awkward about imposing himself, he booked into the Royal Albion Hotel. He did dine at Farringford but the conversation hardly touched upon his own sense of sadness – instead, it was all about Alfred's recent publishing disagreements and the disgrace of the Tennysons' brother-in-law, Charles Weld, who had been dismissed from office on the discovery of some undisclosed misdemeanour, and who, as a result, was suicidal. Weld had long acted as Alfred's London representative in financial matters, but there has never been any suggestion that the Laureate's affairs were in any way implicated in the man's fall from grace.

The lack of interest in and sympathy for himself so distressed Lear that he left Freshwater without bothering to go to Farringford to say goodbye. The discovery that Lear had left suddenly put Emily into a mood of desolate remorse, and she took to her bed for a week. Dakyns did his best to rise above the ponderous atmosphere, by concentrating on his work and games with the boys, and by making himself something of a companion for Tennyson. While Emily was confined to bed the two of them crossed the Solent in a ferry and bought up a collection of bedding plants and shrubs from a nursery in Lymington. The whole family helped to position the plants, including Emily, now up and well. Alfred, hearing a nightingale call, took Dakyns aside to go in pursuit. Emily, left behind with the boys and the head gardener must have felt that this incident merely compounded the prescience of her earlier Journal entry.

The arrival of the youthful Dakyns unsettled Tennyson in ways beyond the outward rhythm and routine of his life. In April Emily recorded that 'Alfred has not been after his best form lately,' and the next month, en route to Cambridge with Emily, he suffered an attack of palpitations which put him in a serious enough panic to cause the journey to be curtailed. The attack prompted his second attempt to give up tobacco. In the garden of the Oatlands Park Hotel he smoked his pipe one last time, broke it and scattered the tobacco to the winds.

He stopped in the New Forest on the way back to the Isle of Wight, sending Emily and the boys on ahead of him, and tried to regain some fitness by hiking. Back at Farringford at the end of May the palpitations returned and Emily persuaded him to go back to Lyndhurst for more walking. It was a short excursion. He spent only two nights away from home, in the company of Edmund Lushington.

Alone in his room, fighting (unsuccessfully) the need for tobacco, he resorted to making an alphabetical list of his library – the action of an insecure man temporarily abandoned by the Muse. At the same time, a plan – 'overventuresome' Emily described it – for the whole family to visit the Pyrenees took shape. The decision to 'move' the whole family together for the summer was at their doctor's suggestion. The boys were still affected by whooping-cough (eighteen months after the onset of the illness) and medical advice was that a journey to a warm climate would be the best possible thing for them.

And so they set off – accompanied by the boys' nurse and by Dakyns, who acted as general courier throughout the trip. The journey was no holiday for Emily. The difficulty of finding rooms and carriage, and the impossibility of obtaining food that the children would eat, took away most of the pleasure of being on the move. Alfred, through the offices of Dakyns, was able to isolate himself from these petty frustrations of family travel, and the trip became for him a journey filled with the poignant echoes of lost youth.

On 21 July they happened (as English travellers on the Continent frequently did in those days) to 'bump into' someone they knew – Arthur Clough, who was making his way to Florence. Emily Tennyson was full of complaints about the inconvenience of inns and, sensing that Tennyson needed time away from his family, Clough set Dakyns and the poet on the road up to Pic de Sancy. They returned at 7.30 pm, having enjoyed a long day alone in the hills.

Clough kept in touch with the Tennysons off and on for the next six or seven weeks, turning up in Luz, Luchon and Cauteritz, doing his best to ensure that Tennyson and the young tutor could remain independent of Emily and the boys. By the beginning of September Emily was still in an ill-humour and the boys sickly. Clough decided it would help Tennyson and Dakyns if he accompanied Emily, Hallam, Lionel and the nurse to Cauteretz, but as it happened they all remained in Luc for five more days, and it was Tennyson and Dakyns who set off for Cauteretz, on foot, ahead of the others. They took the same route Tennyson had followed with Arthur Hallam in the summer of 1830, then the inspiration of 'Œnone', and now for 'In the Valley of Cauteretz'. Clough accompanied the rest of Tennyson's family in a caleche. He was anxious to get on to Florence; he had left England just after the birth of his third child, the intention being that his wife would join him in Italy as soon as she was strong enough. But now it seemed that Dakyns was talking of returning to England. Clough quickly changed his schedule. 'It would among other things be ... a charity to these Tennysons; for Dakyns is to go away for a month most likely, perhaps this next week, and A.T. is but helpless by himself and thinks himself even more so than he is.'

Later, as housemaster at Clifton College, and as a friend and confidant of J.A. Symonds, Dakyns became infatuated with several young boys. Although he and Alfred spent much time alone together on this trip there was no strength of feeling between them. Tennyson was too self-absorbed and affected by powerful recollections to share much with his young companion. It was not the voice of his son's tutor which he heard, but the voice of his dead friend Arthur Hallam. To his credit, Dakyns did the sensitive thing and kept himself to himself, letting Tennyson walk on ahead at some distance, alone with his thoughts, rolling back the mist of 'two and thirty years'.

When the two of them rejoined Emily and the boys, Alfred observed that Dakyns was 'no fool'. 'In the Valley of Cauteretz', the single poetic offering of this re-identification with the past, consists of just ten lines, half of them beginning 'All along the valley'. Good as it is, the poem represents only a modest re-emergence of Tennyson's musical manner – a 'lyrical flash' he termed it himself, when sending it eighteen months later to the Duchess of Argyll.

It was possibly the meagreness of this flash, and the emotional disturbance of being reminded of his comradeship with Hallam – of a time when he was free of care and responsibility (barring the call of Poetry) – which unsettled Tennyson on his return to Farringford. Emily ascribed Alfred's illness to a chill caught at Cauteretz, made worse by the pouring rain on their return journey. The London doctor whom he consulted a week or so after the return pronounced him 'below par' – but the treatment, a rigorous four-week course of chlorine baths, suggests that he was in rather a worse state than merely 'under the weather'. The doctor was John Jackson, Julia Cameron's brother-in-law, and there was more to the treatment than chlorine baths. 'He says that I am in an amoenitous, ie. blood-less and bileless, condition and must take nitric acid or some-thing of that kind,' he wrote to Emily '. . . and a mustard plaster for three nights, ten minutes at a time – he gave me a long consultation.'

The month in London was not all medical and dental treat-ment. He saw Lear, who showed him paintings of the Dead Sea and an Egyptian sunset. He found his mother wonderfully well and hearty. Frederick and Giulio were staying with her and Frederick was full of stories of automatic, devil-powered writing.

The musician, Sterndale Bennett, arriving at Mitre Court to collect Tennyson's 'Exhibition Ode', which he was to set to music, found the poet absorbed in drying tobacco on the hobs of the grate. Tennyson's reading of the poem was 'curiously monotonous'. His heart was not in the venture, and the following day he confessed to the Duke of Argyll that, 'I should never have volunteered, for I hate a subject given me, and still more if that subject be a public one.' Reading a second-rate novel, *Zohrab the Hostage* by James Morier, and reflecting on the pomp and vanity of the Lord Mayor's Show, his 'torpid liver' deprived him of finding pleasure in anything.

His mood was not made any better by the knowledge of changes that had taken place in Freshwater during their absence. The military road had been begun; bricks and mortar were going up everywhere; and there was 'talk of laying out streets and crescents'. Then came news from Emily that several pines had fallen in the autumn gales, thus exposing more views of the wretched new brick.

By mid-November Emily still had no idea when Alfred would be allowed to return. She was told, presumably by Alfred himself, that even when he did 'the doctor says he will for some time require great care'. A recovery was not helped by the news of Arthur Clough's death, in Florence, on the 13 November. It was a sad loss, and the similarity in circumstances and timing to the death of Arthur Hallam cannot have escaped Tennyson. He must have felt, in his sickly despondency, that friendship with him carried some kind of curse or luckless influence. In his own life he had thrown off the ill-fortune of his father's line, but there was sufficient of it abroad, affecting some of his brothers and sisters, and families he was closely associated with (notably the Lushingtons) for him to feel that the 'black blood' of the Tennysons was still a potent force.

During this stay in London he also met Browning, looking very pale, with a silver beard since losing his wife – she had also died in Florence, on 29 June – and the recognition that his friends and acquaintances were ageing, some of them dying, coupled with his recent attack of palpitations, produced an obsession with survival, both in this world and the next, which was to dominate and drive him during the next thirty years of his life.

21   A Beast in its Burrow

He woke, he rose, he spread his arms abroad
Crying with a loud voice 'A sail! A sail!
I am saved,' and so fell back and spoke no more.

('ENOCH ARDEN')

Tennyson returned to Farringford on 3 December. It was to be a freezing month and another death, that of the Prince Consort, was only days away. He brought with him the prose draft of a fisherman's story which Woolner had been pressing on him for many a month, and during the bitter cold of December, still far from recovered from the anaemic biliousness, began work on the poem that was to become 'Enoch Arden'.

Dakyns had to leave shortly after Tennyson's return, to tend a sick father, and, to all intents and purposes, his period as tutor was over. But he continued to visit the island during 1862 and it is from the affectionate letters that Hallam and Lionel wrote to him that we can gain much of our knowledge of Tennyson's family life at this time. Hallam, we learn, cut himself on Christmas Day with a penknife given to him by Lewis Carroll. Both boys received a sovereign from Grandpa Sellwood, and a rake and a box. On 3 January Hallam wrote to Dakyns, 'Papa's better. Mama does not drink more coffee. She eats meat at luncheon.'

Tennyson did indeed seem to begin the New Year with a determined vigour. On the first day of January Emily recorded that he was skipping about like a young man. But this physical and mental agility did not last long. By the 6th Emily was writing to tell Dakyns that, 'Alfred has been very unwell again yesterday and today,' and Bradley, who was spending his annual New Year holiday on the Isle of Wight, also told Dakyns, 'He [A.T.] is more worried by his small enemies – the fleas of Farringford – than I like to see him.'

However, he started work on the fisherman story, writing through a spell of snow at the end of January, and on into February. It had been some considerable time, since finishing the first cycle of Idylls in fact, since he had been able to absorb himself in any long composition.

In the second half of February, while Dakyns was visiting, Tennyson was ready to read sections of his new poem aloud, and to begin writing out a fair copy manuscript. He played backgammon with the young tutor, now engaged to begin his career as master at Clifton College, and joined him for long walks at night.

He and Emily were supposed to visit Shiplake together, where they had been married, and from where the Rawnsleys were about to move away, but the weather was too bad for Emily to travel and Alfred went there alone. Kate Rawnsley found him in good health and when he returned to Farringford on the 1 March Emily thought he looked young and fit. 'The most absolute regularity and quiet home ways seem necessary to A. now.' Apart from Bradley, Jowett, Dakyns and Simeon, the first two months of the year had been comparatively free of visitors, and perhaps Emily was at last conceding that the hectic entertaining of past years was no longer, if it ever had been, conducive to Alfred's health.

Tennyson himself recognized that the reclusive element in his nature was gaining ascendancy. 'I ... am grown an old fellow, crystallised in my ways, and sticking all the year round to my own hearthstone,' and 'I am a shy beast and like to keep in my burrow,' he wrote in letters of this time (turning down invitations to visit) with an essential rather than literal accuracy.

These are views of himself which help the reading of the poem he was now working on. 'Enoch Arden', knocked up from the story given to him by Woolner, describes the 'heroic' decision of a fisherman, long thought lost at sea, who returns hale and hearty only to find his old home up for sale, his wife bigamously remarried and domiciled with another man. The local barmaid fills him in on the unexpected developments; he trundles off to view his wife's new place and peeps through the window at the happy family scene; instantly he vows 'not to tell her, never to let her know'; he returns to the barmaid and unburdens all, in tearjerking detail; three days later, from some mysterious weakness born of years of solitude and sudden grief, he dies; and is given as grand a funeral as the little fishing-port has ever seen.

On this occasion, it is hard to defend the poem from the likes of Meredith. 'I'm a little sick of Tennysonian green tea. I don't think Byron wholesome – exactly, but a drop or so – Eh? And he doesn't give limp, lackadaisical fishermen, and pander to the depraved sentimentalism of our drawing rooms. I tell you that

'Enoch Arden' is ill done, and that in twenty years' time it will be denounced as villainous weak, in spite of the fine (but too conscious) verse, and the rich insertions of tropical scenery.'

The poem (two-thirds of it) is too much preamble. The one vivid and evocative scene – Enoch peering in at the new household's window – is underplayed, but the terms in which it is conceived and the sailor's act of renunciation speak of a growing ambivalence on Tennyson's part towards domesticity. Though 'cups and silver on the burnished board/Sparkled and shone; so genial was the hearth,' the way of heroism lay outside the house. This was Tennyson's *kunstlerschuld* speaking again, but in a voice too gentle and too 'literatesque' (the term comes from Bagehot's review of the poem) to be much use as self-reprimand.

At the end of March Tennyson received an invitation he could not refuse. Through Argyll, he was sent the Queen's command to go to Osborne House, her official residence on the Isle of Wight. Still in mourning, and with the highest regard for *In Memoriam*, she wanted an audience with the Laureate. It took place on 14 April. At first sight the Queen was taken aback by Tennyson's peculiar appearance, but was glad to find that 'there is no affectation about him'. For his part, Tennyson was extremely nervous, feeling that much was being asked of him and that he should be powerless to give the consolation the Queen craved. He had already asked Argyll's advice on the best way of speaking and behaving in the Royal presence. 'Come out of your burrow,' had been the Duke's response. 'Talk to her as you would to a poor woman in affliction, that is what she likes best.'

More trifling aspects of the interview also worried Tennyson. How should he bow? How should he leave the room when the audience was over? Walk backwards? But as soon as the encounter began, with Tennyson standing with his back to the fire and the Queen walking up to within five paces of him, saying, dolefully, 'I am like your Mariana now,' all sense of reserve vanished. Tennyson conversed freely and afterwards had a very imperfect recollection of what it was he had said, except that he had spoken with considerable emotion. He remembered little of what the Queen said either, other than that she spoke with a stately innocence.

When he emerged to be driven back to Farringford by Jowett, there were tears in his eyes. The watery swoon in which this meeting was conducted tells us much about the priorities of that time. We are inclined to call the Victorians 'mannered'. Their readiness to break into tears offends the modern sense of decorum, and smacks of effusive, exhibitionist posturing. Certainly there was more theatrical behaviour around. The middle and upper classes, for a start, had more energy to spare for it than they do today. They were less likely to be exhausted by professional and business concerns and much of the drudgery of domestic life was performed by servants. The absence of cinema or television (the media which above all have promoted the controlled intensity of the modern manner) meant that the only models for behaviour came from the stage and from novels. On the stage there was comedy or tragedy, both acted with emotive histrionics. In novels there were descriptions of highly-wrought emotion. And so, whether it is Dickens weeping over a reading of *A Christmas Carol*, or Tennyson crying in the presence of the Queen, we are no more justified in calling this insincere posturing than in assuming our own less volatile behaviour to be more 'natural'.

22   Dear Old Ways

Below were men and horses pierced with worms,
And slowly quickening into lower forms,
By shards and scurf of salt, and scum of dross,
Old plash of rains, and refuse patched with moss.

('THE VISION OF SIN')

A fter a flying visit to Yarmouth with Emily, followed by some days in London (where he found his mother bent double with rheumatism) and some more in Clevedon (where he was accompanied by Argyll and Gladstone), the next month – April 1862 – was haunted by a legal wrangle with a man called Woodford. This was not the only difficulty. There was a problem with a Mr Squire, and more trouble with the servants, one of whom had to be dismissed. The new tutor, Atkinson, was in

347

marked contrast to the popular Dakyns. He spent the minimum amount of his time with the boys and formed no relationship with Alfred.

It was a withdrawn and harrowing month which, combined with the onset of hayfever, prevented Alfred from working. But the coming of summer had its compensations. The boys were thrown less on the capacities of their tutor, and spent much time with the Cameron children, playing soldiers and cricket. At the end of June the entire Tennyson and Cameron households played an organized game of cricket which the Tennysons won, and Julia Cameron awarded them as prize some translucent window stickers.

Tennyson was beginning to spend more and more time with Julia Cameron. In the middle of the month he read, at her request, 'The Vision of Sin' (that grimly macabre poem which was a personal favourite) and two days later invited her, Henry Taylor, and Mr and Mrs Jackson to Farringford for a reading of 'Enoch Arden'. The poem had a dramatic effect on Mrs Jackson. Near the story's climax she went into hysterics, a reaction which prompted Taylor to criticize (privately) the poem's artistry. 'The poem is too purely painful, the pain not being the rich and pleasing pain which poetry ought to produce. It is not so coloured and glorified by imaginative power as to exalt the reader above his terrestrial distress.' This comment is of interest because it is one example, of many, of the way in which Tennyson was often regarded by his contemporaries to be writing verse which was too near the knuckle, poetry which presented the truth with too little flesh on the bone – a view of his work which has been almost totally obscured in recent times by the emphasis on his early, ornate and Keatsian poems. The underestimating of this aspect to his work has also contributed to the near-outright neglect of his Dramas, works which, whatever their merit, occupied him for a considerable period of time from the 1870s onwards, and were taken seriously by nearly all of his contemporaries. The Dramas can be properly appreciated only by those readers willing to acknowledge that in 'Enoch Arden' and in 'Aylmer's Field', the second new poem begun in 1862, Tennyson was moving towards a new artistic standpoint, closely allied with his private musings and reading on the matter of Immortality. Even Alfred's brother Charles noted, and did not refrain from commenting on, the rather bookish seriousness of this period, and wrote to him in the middle of the 1860s warning about the 'tyranny of books'. 'This reading about a subject if not the subject itself which damages the intellect so much.'[59]

But that brotherly jibe was three years away, and was not to have much impact upon Alfred anyway. He worked on 'Aylmer's Field' throughout December, and in mid-month Emily remarked on the return to 'dear old ways' – by which she meant that Alfred was safely involved in composition, the house troubles were over for the time being, and the boys were gainfully employed in their studies.

The summer and autumn had been unexceptional. In July they had been lent Ashburton Cottage by the Camerons, and from there Alfred, leaving Emily and the boys at Grasby, had gone on a tour of northern England with Palgrave, who was under strict instructions to try and preserve the poet's anonymity – a tall order, given Tennyson's striking and increasingly well-known appearance. The tour was notable only for a revealing titbit of conversation recalled by Palgrave in an account of the trip later given to Hallam Tennyson. Seeing a deserted farmstead, Palgrave said he might well choose to live in such an isolated place, 'with its own sky', where it should be possible to live in peace and forget the world. Given Tennyson's obsession with privacy, Palgrave was probably expecting polite assent. But the poet demurred, saying that if he had to choose between *all* London or *no* London, *all* London it would have to be.

Returning to Farringford in September and coming back to the 'tinkle of the horrible trowels' Tennyson continued to spend much time with Julia Cameron. They, and both sets of boys, worked together on the farm and even Emily had to admit that Julia looked 'gorgeous in her velvet dress and red cloak walking over the newly-mown grass'. The tutor, Atkinson, who had had to write an amusingly desperate letter to Dakyns asking to 'whom one has to apply for one's quarter's salary!', was now teaching the Cameron and Tennyson boys together, when they were not busy on the farm. But he continued to have trouble with discipline, particularly as regards Hallam and Lionel.

Both of them show a largish amount of distaste for work in general. Did you ever find it so? Perhaps it is that I am rather *too* particular about their being *quiet* and *sitting* still during lesson time – and yet it is what they *must* learn sooner or later at school or suffer for not doing so ... They are *dear* boys, and the peculiar interest they cannot fail to arouse in anyone's mind renders one painfully aware of any defects of character . . .[60]

There is more of that 'peculiar interest' to come.

On the eve of Guy Fawkes night, wishing that Dakyns was still their tutor in place of this well-meaning but priggish moralist, Hallam wrote one of his evocative letters:

> My dear Mr Dakyns
> When will you come here again? . . . I wish you were here to make Guy Fawkes. Fanny is fat. I had two very pretty rabbits on my birthday . . . I've got a little house and a padlock and I keep the key myself . . . The Monday before last we went to Alum Bay. The sea was too rough and so we could not get down except Charlie Cameron and me. I cannot write to you very often but I thought as I could not get out I would take the chance. The post is going, So Love from all[61]

For some time Tennyson had given up his habit of reading aloud to Emily, but on the 18 December he began reciting from Carlyle's *Frederick* (Volume III) – 'a return to our dear old ways most welcome to me'. An attempt was made to establish other old habits. On the 19th the whole family was outside, transplanting rhododendrons. And on the 24th there were reassuring preparations for Christmas Day, with Alfred and Emily putting 'the gifts from Uncle and Auntie Charley and Grandpapa and ourselves by the side of the boys' beds.'

An early version of 'Aylmer's Field' was ready to read to Emily on Christmas Day.

If, in this end-of-year domestic activity, there was an attempt to return to the measured, epicurean days of the boys' younger years, it did not succeed. In several ways, 1863 was to prove a bad year.

23   Tea With the Queen

Dust are our frames, and, gilded dust, our pride
Looks only for a moment whole and sound

('AYLMER'S FIELD')

I t was during May that the year's troubles really began to pile up. 'Things seem upset, and things make me sad,' Emily wrote to Dakyns. Once again there was a sense of mutiny amongst the domestic staff. A couple of the servants actually walked out, although the Tennysons preferred it to be known that the men concerned had been dismissed.

A man called Cooper, and one other, had found some Roman coins while digging at The Terrace, a property on the Farringford estate. They were chiefly copper coins from the time of Gallienus. The two men had divided their treasure-trove between themselves and were sorely offended when Tennyson admonished them and demanded they hand the coins over to him. A third servant walked out in sympathy with these two, and in protest at Tennyson's imperious behaviour. Whatever the rights and wrongs of the matter, the episode shows that Tennyson was a poor manager of men, too self-centred to be able to foresee the reactions of other people and to predict the outcome of his own dealings with them.

This mini-mutiny was closely followed by the resignation of the hapless Atkinson. According to the tutor himself his departure from Farringford was due to a straightforward exasperation with Hallam and Lionel. 'The boys are getting quite beyond my management,' he told Dakyns. But there was more to it than that. As the boys grew older there was a mounting tension between the Tennysons' remarkably laissez-faire approach to discipline and Atkinson's own rather more martial ideas.

My own opinion is that they ought to go to school as soon as possible where they would be subject to discipline – a thing they do not as yet understand.... I have not accomplished my darling project of eradicating their really serious faults – chiefly, I *must* say, because I have not been 'backed up' in my endeavour.[62]

Emily, also writing to Dakyns, put it more succinctly. 'He is to leave.' She immediately tried to tempt Dakyns back to Farringford, offering him a salary of £250, double the sum he had received previously – an increase made possible by the fact that the Cameron boys would also receive his tuition.

It is clear that this offer was made without consulting Julia Cameron, for a few days later Emily had to cover her tracks. 'Lest by any chance I should have unsettled you at all, I write immediately to say that Mr Cameron says the coffee accounts are so bad he can have nothing to do with our arrangements.'

In fact, the Camerons wanted their boys to attend a local school, if one could be established, and Dakyns was, by this time, perfectly content to stay at Clifton. Much as he got on well with Hallam and Lionel, and enjoyed Tennyson's company, there was no future for a young man of his age and circumstances returning to the position of a personal tutor.

In the midst of these domestic changes, just over a year after Alfred's first interview with the Queen, the whole Tennyson family was invited over to Osborne House. This was a very different encounter from the intense and emotional meeting of a year before. It was very much a family and social visit, with introductions to the large number of princes and princesses.

The visit began, after dinner, with a drive around the estate and then the six year-old Beatrice showed them her model shop, with miniature tea caddies which she used for serving pretend cups of tea to the Queen. The twelve year-old Prince Arthur displayed a home-made fort, called Victoria Fort & Albert Barracks. The ten year-old Leopold showed Hallam how he made paper boats and set them alight before launching them on the water.

And then, finally, the Queen came in to talk with them. Emily went down on one knee and kissed Victoria's hand. Although the atmosphere was as relaxed as it could be, with the Queen laughing at one or two of Alfred's anecdotes, it was still very much a formal encounter, with none of the charged emotionalism of the previous year. Young Hallam concluded his boyish account of the visit with the observation, 'You must stand until the Queen asks you to sit down. Her Majesty does not *often* tell you to sit down!'

Visits from old friends – Spring Rice and Venables – helped cheer Alfred briefly towards the end of May, but in June he fell ill with a gouty infection of the leg (an exacerbation of the eczema he was always prone to), which he attributed to a tainted vaccination received on 19 May. He had been talked into succumbing to the needle, along with the rest of the family (plus his visitors, Spring Rice and daughter Ailene) by, inevitably, Julia Cameron.

There are two slightly variant versions of this story, but in both of them Julia Cameron is the active force, pursuing Tennyson with the local doctor behind her, needle at the ready. In the most colourful version Alfred locks himself in his smoking room; Julia hammers at the door and calls out, 'Alfred, you are a coward'; Tennyson replies, 'Go away, I will be vaccinated tomorrow.' Whatever the truth, it appears that no one else was affected by the injections, and the connection with his bad leg was probably fanciful.

The inflammation might have had more to do with a late-night tumble into a mud-hole in the company of a visiting American preacher, Moncure Conway. It is worth giving the American's account of this amusing incident:

> It had been a stormy evening, and the night was of pitchy darkness when I started out, against invitations to remain, to go to the *Albion*. Tennyson insisted on showing me a nearer way, but in the darkness got off his bearings. Bidding me walk close behind him, we went forward through the mud, when suddenly I found myself precipitated six or seven feet downward. Sitting in the mud, I called on the poet to pause, but it was too late; he was speedily seated beside me. This was seeing the Laureate of England in a new light, or rather, hearing him under a novel darkness. Covered with mud, groping about, he improved the odd occasion with such an amusing run of witticisms that I had to conclude that he had reached a situation which had discovered in himself unexpected resources. His deep bass voice came through the congenial darkness like mirthful thunder, while he groped until he found a path. 'That this should have happened after dinner!' he exclaimed; 'do not mention this to the temperance folk.'[63]

Conway was fascinated by the unexpected roughness and bluntness of his English host. 'His fondness for strong Saxon words, such as would make a Tennysonian faint if met in one of his lines, his almost Quaker-like plainness of manner, albeit

353

softened by the gentle eye and the healthy humanity of his thought, did not support my preconception that he was the drawing-room idealist.'[64]

By the end of the month Alfred's leg was bad enough to require medical treatment and he travelled to London with Julia Cameron, hoping once again to consult her brother-in-law, Dr Jackson; but he was also unwell, with bronchitis, and Tennyson decided to seek a consultation with the Queen's Surgeon-General, James Paget. Paget became a close friend of the Laureate and never charged him a fee. However, he was unable to see Tennyson until 10 July and meanwhile Alfred was attended by the French medic, Henri de Mussy, who told him that although the condition was annoying, it signified little. He was to stop wearing his elasticated varicose-vein stocking and give the leg rest and air.

So he stayed at Little Holland House, bed- and sofa-ridden, his bad leg propped up on pillows. When he finally saw Paget the prognosis was the same. 'There is no danger of any kind, only need of patience.' After this consultation he moved, keeping his leg up, to the Palgraves', from whose house he wrote Emily a series of rather tetchy notes:

'I hope no one will pluck my wild irises which I planted – if they want flowers there is the kitchen garden.' 'I don't quite like children croquetting on that lawn. I have a personal interest in every leaf about it.'

His doctors (the combined consultation consisted of three opinions – Jackson's, de Mussy's and Paget's) recommended that he go to Harrogate for spa treatment and that he stop drinking so much port and switch to claret, which he hated, or Amontillado sherry, which he liked little better.

As for going to Harrogate, he wrote to Emily:

I don't know whether, all things considered, it would be better for you to go along with me or not. I purpose starting on Monday but I could wait later here if you could join me and Mrs. Prinsep offers her house to you: then whether it would be better in case you came to leave the children with the tutor at Farringford or to bring children and tutor to be left at Grasby or to go all to Harrogate I don't know ... Then, there is no absolute necessity for your coming. Think about these things and arrange as you think best. Of course it would be more comfortable to have you with me but I don't know what money I have in the Bank, and am half afraid to draw.[65]

Emily did accompany Alfred to Harrogate, but the trip was not a success. The cold and damp weather there proved so harmful to her own health that as soon as the doctor would let him go Alfred took himself back to London, while Emily and the boys went for a lightning visit to Grasby. On the 11 September Tennyson met his wife and sons at the mainline station in London. The cabman, despite their objections, put all their luggage in one cab and then took a wrong direction. Turning sharply to right himself the whole contraption overturned and it was a miracle that several members of the family were not seriously hurt, the calm docility of the horse saving them from all but cuts and bruises.

When they were eventually home again, the weather was no better – it was stormy and rainy – but Alfred's leg, at last, began to improve. Beginning to feel better he was able to continue work on 'Aylmer's Field'. Some time during October he completed the important sermon section and read it aloud to Emily. In her Journal she described it as 'magnificent', but she did not much care for this poem and wrote to Woolner, 'He will not give *The Sermon* up, though I advise him, wicked creature that I am, you will say. I long for him to be at the *San Graal*, feeling sure that is his work, and the days are going for him and for me.'[66]

William Allingham, always a highly descriptive visitor, was amongst the guests at Farringford this autumn. His characteristically long diary entry for this visit gives us an insight into the blunt no-nonsense tone of the poet's light conversation:

ALLINGHAM: That large tangled fig tree looks like a breaking wave.

TENNYSON: Not in the least.

Or

ALLINGHAM: Rather crude, that green you have chosen for the woodwork round the windows.

TENNYSON: I don't know why you shouldn't like it.

Quite possibly Tennyson reserved this degree of querulousness for Allingham – a continuation of the tone established at Twickenham all those years ago, when Allingham was still in

355

his early twenties (he was now approaching forty). But, although others were often too polite to record such details of the Laureate's tone of voice, the mention of bluntness and prickliness is too frequent to suggest that Tennyson behaved with Allingham in anything but a slightly exaggerated version of his usual manner.

He took the younger man up to his rooftop look-out and confessed that he had once tumbled headlong through the hatchway, a drop of ten feet. And there was the usual tirade against curious impostors. One day he had been 'pursued full cry along the road by two fat women and sixteen children!' Another day he saw the face of a man who had climbed up onto the outside fence and was looking over into the garden. Tennyson had said: 'It isn't at all pretty of you to be peeping there! You'd better come down.'

This was Tennyson reporting himself, and probably editing out some of the Saxon saltiness which the American, Conway, had been surprised by. His hatred of Peeping Toms makes it unlikely that he would have confined his chastisement to the word 'pretty', even in its negative form.

A new tutor, Thomas Wilson, (taking over from a Mr Butterworth, who had lasted a mere couple of months) was employed at this time, and stayed with the Tennysons for a year. Hallam, with Christmas in mind, wrote to Dakyns in mid-December asking for a football 'about the same size as you gave us from Rugby'. Dakyns sent the ball, but it arrived one day late, on Boxing Day. Allingham was again visiting and was dragooned into a game with the boys. Such a diversion was welcome, for on Christmas Day news had arrived at Farringford of William Thackeray's sudden death. Alfred had last seen him during his recent bout of treatment in London, but only briefly. Emily had been unable to read any of the novelist's books, finding the cynicism not to her taste. But Alfred remembered the man from younger days – 'a man of most kindly nature, with a heart of true flesh and blood. It was only his outer husk that was cynical and that only in his books – as far as I knew him.'[67] Thackeray was the first of Tennyson's contemporaries to die of natural causes (if we discount those who died prematurely) and we can fully believe that 'His loss has much saddened my Christmas to me.'

But he too joined in the games of football, and the treks on the Down. He was rather full of classic metres at this time (and had recently composed a series of 'Attempts at Classic Metres' – published in the *Cornhill* that December), an aspect of Tennyson's work which few modern readers can get excited about, and many of his impromptu recitations were illustrations of various measures. Some, however, were given purely for effect.

Higgledy-piggledy, silver and gold,
There's a louse on my back
Seven years old.
He inches, he pinches,
In every part,
And if I could catch him
I'd *tear* out his *hearrt*![68]

Tennyson spoke the last line in mock-tragic fury.

Immediately after their father's death and funeral (which Tennyson did not attend) Thackeray's two daughters came over to the Isle of Wight to stay in one of the Dimbola cottages, lent to them by the ever-helpful Julia Cameron (their mother had, for some time, been shut away in an asylum).

Anne Thackeray gave a weirdly suggestive account of their arrival. It was bitterly cold. Snow lay thickly on the ground. The two sisters walked up and down the ground floor of the house, warming themselves by a freshly-lit fire – unable to settle. Suddenly, they became aware of a figure, silhouetted against the snow, standing outside the window in a heavy cloak and wide-awake hat. It was Tennyson.

Charles Tennyson and Robert B. Martin record this incident in their biographies without remark, both adding, simply, that Tennyson had come to give the girls his silent sympathy. There is, however, something in the haunting atmosphere of the depicted scene which cannot pass without comment. Two young and pretty girls, lit in a half-light by flickering coals, being stared at by a shrouded and bearded man. It is as if the three protagonists have been carefully positioned by a painter keen to capture one of those pregnant moments so beloved by Victorian art.

And what might have passed through Tennyson's mind, as he stood outside in the cold? Something more than silent sympathy, one fancies. His horror of Peeping Toms makes it highly unlikely that he left Farringford with the clear intention

357

of stopping outside the girls' window, as the two earlier biographers imply. Much more probably he walked down to the Dimbola cottage, fully intending to knock on the door; or perhaps he was simply on his way to see Julia Cameron.

The vision of the two sisters, pacing up and down in their speechless grief beside the domestic hearth, presented Tennyson with a cameo of a world from which he felt increasingly excluded. Like Enoch Arden looking through the casement at the family scene he dare not disturb, Tennyson could only observe and pass on.

24   Sell-Out

> He therefore turning softly like a thief,
> Lest the harsh shingle should grate underfoot,
> And feeling all along the garden-wall,
> Lest he should swoon and tumble and be found,
> Crept to the gate ...
>
> ('ENOCH ARDEN')

The year 1864 was a crowded, though rather insignificant, one. Its flavour can best be given by means of a swift description of the main events in Tennyson's life.

In the middle of January Dakyns visits, plays football with the boys, and gives the whole family a cold. On 3 February the Queen rejects the first four lines that Alfred has sent for the Duchess of Kent's tombstone, and he is forced to revise them. That done, he leaves for London, on the 8 February, to supervise the printing of 'Enoch Arden'.

Having dinner with Palgrave on the 11th, he meets Gladstone who, when told the boy's age is 'very decided about the necessity of sending [Hallam] to school instantly.' Tennyson changes the subject to smoking. 'I would not have my children smoke,' he says. 'It's all very well for a studious man, but it ruins an active man.' He is sorry to hear the Prince of Wales smokes. An English King should be an active man. Then he argues with Browning (who was there to have his will signed and witnessed) about an imagined insult delivered by Forster:

FORSTER: How about dining with me one night?

TENNYSON: It is against my principles to dine out.

FORSTER: All your principles are eccentric.

This has stuck in Tennyson's gizzard. Browning tells him not to be so sensitive.

On 13 February Alfred dines with his friend, Walter White, who offers him Hungarian wine in place of the usual port, which is still under doctors' edict, and the following morning White and Tennyson breakfast in Spedding's rooms. They take an early morning walk together, Tennyson trying, unsuccessfully, to outstrip White. On the way back Tennyson pulls up at some spilt milk, bends down, and fingers its congealed surface, to see whether it is milk or chalk. Looking up at White – 'We should be mobbed,' he says, 'if this were a week day.' As if to prove this point, the very next day a portrait of Tennyson appears in the *Illustrated News*.

The Workingmen's Shakespeare Committee take advantage of his presence in the capital to request from him, by 23 April, (the bard's tricentary) some memorial verses. 'They all look upon me as a bootmaker,' he complains, 'and think that I can make a poem as a bootmaker does a pair of boots – to order.'

At the end of February, before returning to Farringford, Alfred writes to Forster, calling a truce to their tiff. Back at home he spends much of each day laying turf and playing football. In the evening he plays backgammon with Emily and the new tutor. On Lionel's birthday, 15 March, while riding on the Down, the boy's cap blows off and frightens Fanny, the white pony. He is thrown and dragged in the stirrup, but not badly hurt. In the afternoon there is a grand football match, with a large crowd, and in the evening a game of charades, with Julia Cameron and the servants as the audience.

Alfred's new friend, White, comes to stay on 25 March, arriving on the 9am steamer from Yarmouth. Allingham, Jowett, and the artist, Lawrence, are also staying at Farringford. There is much tiresome conversation about the pronunciation of words like 'photography'. On the 28th there are fourteen to luncheon.

April is dominated by a grand official visit from Garibaldi, said at that time to be the most famous man in Europe. Alfred and the boys position flags outside the front door and opposite the drawing-room window; and they set up a screen, made from old editions of *Punch*, at the spot where a Wellingtonia is to be ceremonially planted. A crowd, on foot and horseback, waits for two hours at the gates.

Tennyson takes his guest to the study and the two men talk politics, Alfred finding that the retired guerilla general has the 'divine stupidity of a hero'. Julia Cameron arrives to photograph the visitors. She drops down on her knees and holds up her blackened hands, stained with developing chemicals. Garibaldi thinks her a crazed beggar.

After the planting of the Wellingtonia ('the waving pine which here/The warrior of Caprera set') scavenging strangers break into the grounds and take branches from the young tree to carry away as souvenirs.

Tennyson spends most of June in London, putting his latest collection of poems in order. He is intending to call the new book *Idylls of the Hearth* but Emily writes to him indicating her disapproval and suggesting two alternatives – either *Idylls Chiefly of Seventy Years Ago* or *Enoch Arden and Other Poems*. A few days earlier she has posted Alfred a transcript of a recently composed air, 'The Son of the Alma River', for Tennyson to hawk about.

How good in thee, dearest, to take so much trouble! Thy praise is all I can desire. I should think it due to Chappell and to Santley to give my name. If they approve, that is sufficient I should think . . . *Idylls of the People* let it be. I am anxious and urgent about it. That thou shouldst be true to thyself even in such a thing is much to me. Never mind if some of them are printed *Hearth*, let the rest be *Idylls of the People* . . .[69]

In the same letters she suggests attaching the monogram Æ, a combination of AT and ET, to the air; rather than modesty, this speaks of a woman who thinks very highly of herself.

On the day of receiving Emily's title suggestions Alfred replies that *Home Idylls* seems to him the best, but two days later he announces, 'I now think of *Enoch Arden etc.* as a title.' Emily has had her say, and her way.

On Thursday 30 June he takes the final proof sheets to Woolner's and settles down to begin proof-reading. A barrel organ begins grinding away outside and Allingham, who is also present, rushes out to shoo the man out of the street. In such ways is the concentration of the Laureate assisted.

The final days of this London visit are spent at the House of

Commons – not in the Public Gallery but, at Gladstone's invitation, on the opposition's side. 'Gladstone spoke with real passion. Dizzy never seemed to me to lose himself although he doubled up his fist in a sort of pseudo-rage,' he writes to Emily.

He returns to Farringford two or three days before Emily's birthday, which he nevertheless ignores, and which Emily celebrates privately. 'Letters from my dearest Father and Louy with good wishes. A. does not like keeping birthdays so I do not tell him or the boys that it is mine.'

The new volume is published in August, under the title *Enoch Arden & Other Poems*, while the Tennysons are on holiday (this year as a family) in France. They follow an arduous itinerary. Crossing to Boulogne, where they temporarily lose their baggage, they go on to Amiens. Then to Paris; to Versailles and Trianon; and back to Paris. From there they go to Augers, where they are allowed a private view of the castle. Then to Nantes, by train; by boat to Gavr'inis and Carnac. Then Quimper, Morlaix and Guinguamp; Mont St Michel, Caen and Bayeux.

From Honfleur they take a boat to Rouen, a journey once taken by Tennyson and the other Hallam. It is a stormy passage and everybody aboard is sick, except the Tennysons. From Rouen they go to Dieppe, and then home.

Once home the Tennysons begin at last to think seriously about sending the boys to school. It is a matter upon which there will be much disagreement. They consider sending Hallam and Lionel to a private tutor near Wimborne, but they are told there will not be any spare places until Easter. And so they employ one more tutor at Farringford, a Mr Lipscombe, who arrives in November. This, at any rate, is how Emily portrays it to friends like Mrs Gatty. The real reason for the postponement is in truth nothing to do with the school, but owing to Emily's reluctance to cut the boys' long hair at the beginning of winter.

Edward Lear, visiting the Tennysons this autumn, comments on the altered atmosphere in and around Freshwater.

I found all that quiet part of the Island fast spoiling, and how they can stay there I can't imagine. Not only is there an enormous monster Hotel growing up in sight – but a tracing of the foundations of 300 houses – a vast new road – and finally a proposed railway – cutting thro John Simeon and A.T.'s grounds from end to end. Add to this, Pattledom has taken entire possession of the place – Camerons and Prinseps building everywhere: Watts in a cottage, and Guests, Schreibers, Pollocks, and myriads more buzzing everywhere.[70]

In November Alfred returns to London, staying in an apartment at the top of the Woolners' house. He basks in the success of 'Enoch Arden'. Meeting Walter White, they share a bottle of Oedenberg and, while drinking it, White presses the case of buying land in Haslemere.

Gladstone, on being met up with again, repeats his view that Tennyson's boys should be at school. In preparing a selected edition of his own poems Tennyson agrees to have a new photographic portrait of himself taken. The lithograph, it is said, will add 2000 to the sales.

He arrives home on 3 December with a bad headache and raw throat. He and Emily immediately walk out together to see what can be done to block out the hideous new houses. Already they are having an artificial mound constructed to hide some new stables on neighbouring land, and they consider doing something similar to hide the view of the red-brick houses. But it is beginning to seem like a losing battle, and they are pleased to receive a letter from Mrs Gilchrist, the widow of Blake's biographer, inviting them to stay with her, should they wish to examine the land on offer in Haslemere.

At the end of the year Jowett arrives for his annual visit. The boys bring out the chessboard at once, and then a new football, yet another 'splendiverous' gift from Dakyns.

By 31 December the first edition (60,000 copies) of 'Enoch Arden' has sold out.

25　To School

. . . now it seems some unseen monster lays
His vast and filthy hands upon my will

('LUCRETIUS')

Two sombre developments in the early part of 1865 affected Tennyson deeply. In February he received a letter from Hampstead informing him that his mother was dangerously ill.

He left at once. Charles was already there. 'We were summoned by a note announcing my dear mother's serious illness *zeitz* to Hampstead, where we only arrived in time to see her alive, but not soon enough, I fear, for recognition by her. We cannot expect in this severe weather that there shall be any gathering of relatives except ourselves.' Alfred arrived too late. 'Mother had gone before I came. She went at 10pm, age 84.' It was an easy, natural death. In Charles' words, she died 'worn out with old age and an attack of bronchitis'.

Tennyson was relieved to be told that his mother had not asked for him especially, and his general attitude to her death was in marked contrast to the bullish and adolescent bravura with which he had met the demise of his father. In recent years he had not let a visit to London go by without dropping in on his mother to see how she was. It was a severe loss, because she represented (as mothers often do – rather more than brothers and sisters) a link with the past and, in his particular case with the highly-charged years spent in the Somersby Rectory. While she was alive there was still some connection with his origins, some regular reminder of his birth and beginning, some echo of the child in the adult heart. With her gone, the echo's final reverberations were slowly to fade away.

'I dare not see her,' he wrote back to Emily, fearing that sorrow and separation would undo him. How different from the night spent in his father's bed, and his attempt to lure forth a ghost.

Emily and the boys did not go to London for the funeral but Hallam and Lionel were measured up for mourning suits so that they could enter the spirit of the day – Monday 27. Tennyson described his mother to the clergyman conducting the service as 'the beautifullest thing God Almighty ever did make.' He was sorry that she could not be buried in a country churchyard, rather than being laid to rest in Highgate Cemetery.

Seeing her so infrequently during adult life, he was able to preserve this idealization of her. As the portrait of Mrs Tennyson in the early part of this book has shown, she was a much more spirited and gritty woman then the saintly character so often depicted. Alfred took that into full account when he described her in such glowing terms. Because Emily was (or, again, is so often depicted as being) sickly, reticent, lacking in energy, Tennyson has often been accused of admiring just these qualities in a woman above all others – in other words, subscribing to the Victorian suppression of the female sex. His mother was not that kind of woman and he respected her for her eventual resistance to his father. There are some languid and submissive beauties amongst his early 'girly' verses, but against these we have the resilient figures in *The Princess* and *Maud*. Those Idylls which he had already written reveal a surprisingly modern understanding of woman's sexuality (surprising only because insufficiently credited), and he was soon to begin writing the most sexual of all his poems, 'Lucretius', before going on to explore the character of woman more deeply in the Dramas.

He did not stay at Rosemount during the days leading up to the funeral but went into town to lodge with his younger brother Arthur. Nevertheless, there were opportunities for conversation with Charles, who had, only a fortnight ago, sent Alfred a letter eulogizing the study of Theology.

> I have never in my old desultory heady days found such a charming interest as in the study of the Queen's Science as Trench calls 'Theology', and those who assume that they will find in it no food for the mature reason will be surprised at the large provision for the intellect & rich satisfaction for the highest imagination.[71]

It was in this same letter that he advocated the 'study of the Prophets' to save one from 'the tyranny of books'. Tennyson seems to have taken some note of this brotherly advice, whatever expansion it was given in London, for on his return to Farringford he began to teach himself Hebrew, so that he might read his favourite Old Testament books in the original.

When Frederick, his other older brother, came to stay for a few days at the beginning of March, it was Emily who had to bear the brunt of his interminable talk about Swedenborg.

Less than a month after the death of his mother his Aunt Mary died, and later there was news of the death of Stephen Spring Rice, who had been sick for some time, but neither of these affected Tennyson much, except insofar as he was remembered in his Aunt's will.

Far more momentous was the final departure of the boys to school, in May. The tutor, Lipscombe, left on the 2nd, to become a schoolmaster at Winchester. Emily had a half-hearted attempt to cut Hallam and Lionel's hair on the 9th but could not bring herself to complete the task, and the job had to be finished by a barber a few days later.

Parting from the boys on the station at Baillie, Emily recorded in her Journal, 'A sorrowful sight to us both, our two boys on the Baillie platform, alone, for the first time in their lives as our train left.' The grand welcome home which the servants prepared for Alfred and Emily – a wagon 'gay with flags and banners' was sent to pick them up from the late-night ferry – could not disguise the newly-desolate mood of the household. Gone were the games of football and cricket; gone the boys' help with digging and with pushing Emily in her chair; gone too, the need to employ a tutor and the consequent presence in the house of a succession of young men. The boys had helped create a continuous rhythm to an otherwise haphazard family life, so that behind the breathless comings and goings of house-guests there was an undercurrent of permanency. This too was gone; and the occasional re-establishment of it at holiday-times only served to emphasize the jaggedness of their life.

Alfred immersed himself in the reading of Job, Isaiah and Solomon, and thought for a time of creating modern renderings of the Hebrew. Emily had no such means of escape, though the management of the household continued to occupy a good deal of her time, and in particular she had to prepare for a special visit by Queen Emma of the Sandwich Islands.

26   Lust

These prodigies of myriad nakednesses
And twisted shapes of lust, unspeakable,
Abominable, strangers at my hearth
Not welcome, harpies miring every dish.

('LUCRETIUS')

After a summer tour of Belgium and Germany the Tennysons arrived home in the middle of September 1865, in time for Hallam and Lionel's return to Baillie for the new term. A week after getting back to school the boys were given special leave of absence to return to the island to meet Queen Emma. She was a young black Queen who had come to England to raise money for an Episcopal Mission in Honolulu. The Tennysons were invited to receive her by Lady Franklin (Emily's aunt) who was the Queen's London hostess, and was eager for a few days' respite.

Emily's preparations were lavish. A great arch was put over the entrance by the road, decorated with a flowery wreath and the Union Jack. Across the front porch was woven a combination of dahlias and ivy, arranged so that the flowers spelt out the greeting, 'Aloha'. A throne chair was made for her out of some ilex wood that had fallen in a storm.[72]

The young Queen, a widow of only twenty-nine years old, was attractive and described by Emily as having an affectionate nature. She spent four days at Farringford and was alone with Alfred on several occasions. Driving out to the Needles they ran on the Down together, and when she wanted to hide from the other guests for a while he took her to the summerhouse and talked with her there. When she left he gave her two magnolia blossoms.

After she, and the boys, had gone he began working on a new poem – his first for some considerable time. It was a poem which reflected his recent reading of Lucretius and the Prophets, and was based on a legend of Lucretius' death, but its eroticism is not in the least bookish.

The news that Tennyson was working on this subject did not please Matthew Arnold. He wrote to his mother:

I am rather troubled to find that Tennyson is at work on a subject, the story of the Latin poet Lucretius, which I have been occupied with for some twenty years ... every one, except the few friends who have known that I had it in hand, will think I borrowed the subject from him. So far from this, I suspect the subject was put into his head by Palgrave, who knew I was busy with it. I shall probably go on, however, but it is annoying.[73]

Arnold's suspicions are credible (rather discreditable too) because Palgrave and Woolner were forever passing suggestions on to Tennyson. 'Enoch Arden' had evolved from a prose-sketch sent in by Woolner, as had 'Aylmer's Field'. But Tennyson did have a personal interest in the Latin writer and had read passages aloud to Emily as long ago as 1857.[74] More recently he had been reading the new edition published by Hugh Munro in 1864.

Of all Tennyson's poems 'Lucretius' is the most likely to surprise readers only familiar with four or five of his best-known titles. It is based on the legend of Lucretius' death by suicide in a deranged state, after being administered a powerful aphrodisiac by his wife. There are passages in it which did shock his contemporary readers but not, apparently, Emily, whose job it was to copy out the poem. '*She* says she does not think it will shock people.' One passage, in particular, caused a flurry of debate and was slightly cut for its first publication in *Macmillan's Magazine* (1868). It is the erotic description of an Oread, or mountain-nymph ('how the sun delights/To glance and shift about her slippery sides/And rosy knees and supple rounded-ness/And budded bosom-peaks') but there are also passages which seem suffused with a strong sense of personal identification. Speaking directly to the Gods, Lucretius says:

I thought I lived securely as yourselves –
No lewdness, narrowing envy, monkey-spite,
No madness of ambition, avarice, none:
No larger feast than under plane or pine
With neighbours laid along the grass, to take
Only such cups as left us friendly-warm,
Affirming each his own philosophy –
Nothing to mar the sober majesties
Of settled, sweet, Epicurean life.
But now it seems some unseen monster lays
His vast and filthy hands upon my will,
Wrenching it backward into his; and spoils
My bliss in being . . .

Could the comely Queen Emma have made possible such an identification? She was as likely a catalyst for the poem as Matthew Arnold's implication that Tennyson was trying to steal a march on him.

The autumn brought wild weather and more fallen trees. Progress on 'Lucretius' was interrupted in December by a long and busy visit to London. His departure, on the 1st of the month, was typically chaotic. The steamer lost its way over from Lymington in the fog and never arrived at Yarmouth so

Tennyson had to board a rowing boat. On the other side he missed the train by ten minutes. He went to Allingham's place and together they walked to the station at Brockenhurst, where he was able to catch the 5.35 for London. The journey took four and a half hours.

He was in London to be introduced to the Royal Society but took the opportunity of seeing Queen Emma again, at Lady Franklin's. In fact, he saw her twice, the second time on the pretext of having forgotten to thank her for the gift of a Book of Common Prayer – in Hawaiian translation. He carried with him a note, in case she was out. The letter was, 'colder than I felt – for I was a little hampered with court European forms'. (Without such forms it might still have been difficult to find words to express one's gratitude for such a gift.)

Moving between the Woolners' and the Palgraves' he found fault with the tea he was given and recommended Mrs Palgrave change to Ridgways, his favourite. He was inducted into the Royal Society on 7 December. It was, he told Emily, 'a merry dinner with lots of anecdotes'; but a more significant gathering occurred the following night when the party at Woolner's included Gladstone, Holman Hunt, and a Bristol physician, Dr Symonds, together with his son, John Adington Symonds (who did not arrive until the gentlemen were just finishing their dessert).

The young man Symonds settled confidently into an armchair and began to eavesdrop on the after-dinner conversation. The subject was the recent massacre of a mob in Jamaica by the Governor, Edward Eyre. Gladstone carried the argument against Eyre. He had just been reading official papers which included evidence wrung from a black boy held with a revolver to his head. Tennyson was all for excusing the cruelty, not really entering the debate, but muttering *sotto voce* various prejudices and convictions: 'Niggers are tigers; niggers are tigers.' 'We are too tender to savages; too tender to savages.' And, apropos of nothing specific, but spoken with a much louder voice, in a tone of rasping hatred: 'I could not kill a cat. Not the tomcat who scratches and miawls over his disgusting amours, and keeps me awake.'

Gladstone developed the argument more logically, citing Eyre's hanging of a woman because some women – though not necessarily the one condemned – had mutilated a corpse. Tennyson twisted the subject round to a matter of personal courage. 'As far as I know my own temperament, I could stand any sudden thing, but give me an hour to reflect, and I should go here and go there, and all would be confused ... I have not got the English courage. I could not wait six hours in a square expecting a battery's fire.'

Palgrave arrived at this point and Symonds was able to stop listening and reflect on the contrast between Tennyson and Gladstone. The dual portrait he draws is a convincing one:

> Gladstone with his rich flexible voice, Tennyson with his deep drawl rising into an impatient falsetto when put out: Gladstone arguing, Tennyson putting in a prejudice; Gladstone asserting rashly, Tennyson denying with a bald negative; Gladstone full of facts, Tennyson relying on impressions; both of them humorous, but the one polished and delicate in repartee, the other broad and coarse and grotesque. Gladstone's hands are white and not remarkable. Tennyson's are huge, unwieldy, fit for moulding clay or dough. Gladstone is in some sort a man of the world; Tennyson a child, and treated by him like a child.[75]

Woolner was the perfect host. Palgrave, the new arrival, was rasping and assertive. Hunt silent. It was, thought Symonds, like being present at the performance of a concerto, scored as follows:

> Gladstone – 1st violin
> Dr Symonds – 2nd violin
> Tennyson – cello
> Woolner – bass-viol
> Palgrave – viola
> Hunt – 2nd, very subordinate, viola

After Palgrave had been accommodated the conversation turned to metaphysics and the young Symonds was able to record some of the most extensive transcripts of Tennyson's moral thinking that survive. What struck the observer and listener was the childlike simplicity of the poet (a familiar reaction). There was nothing original or startling about his philosophical thought. Indeed, what was startling was his ability to treat as real, agitating questions, matters which most mature men were happy to treat as insoluble – and to treat them with an engaging moral earnestness.

'I do not know whether to think the universe great or little. When I think about it, it seems now one and now the other. What makes its greatness? Not one sun or one set of suns, or is the whole together?

I cannot form the least notion of a brick. I don't know what it is. It's no use talking about atoms, extension, colour, weight. I cannot penetrate the brick. But I have far more distinct ideas about God, of love and such emotions. I can sympathise with God in my poor way. The human soul seems to me always in some way, how we do not know, identical with God. That's the value of prayer. Prayer is like opening a sluice between the great ocean and our little channels.

Huxley says we have come from monkeys. That makes no difference to me. If it is God's way of creation, He sees the whole, past, present and future, as one.

I cannot but think moral good is the crown of man. But what is it without immortality? Let us eat and drink, for tomorrow we die. If I knew the world were coming to an end in six hours, would I give my money to a starving beggar: No, if I did not believe myself immortal. I have sometimes thought men of sin might destroy their immortality. The eternity of punishment is quite incredible. Christ's words were parables to suit the sense of the times.

There are some young men who try to do away with morality. They say, "We won't be moral." Comte, I believe, and perhaps Mr Grote too, deny that immortality has anything to do with being moral.

Why do mosquitoes exist? I believe that after God had made His world the devil began and added something.'

Eventually Tennyson was persuaded to read his 'Achilles Over the Trench' and the remainder of the night (until 1 am) was filled with a discussion about translating from the Greek.

The meeting with Dr Symonds proved useful to the Tennysons because when Lionel returned from school for the Christmas vacation he was in a stammering and high-strung state of weakness. Alfred and Emily took the condition seriously, although the younger boy had never been quite such a favourite of his father's as Hallam. While in London he sent Emily such notes as, 'I don't much like Lionel's sporting propensities but then you know man is naturally a beast of prey.' Stammering – with its beast-like symptom of inarticulacy – was superstitiously considered a sign of sinfulness. Neither Emily nor Alfred would have openly admitted giving such a belief serious credence, but with Lionel on the threshold of adolescence the spectre of masturbation hovered half-spoken behind each of the boy's inarticulate utterances.

The ever-popular Dakyns came to visit early in the New Year of 1866. He was just recovering from measles and his visit had at one time appeared in jeopardy. Dakyns was friendly with John Addington Symonds, and therefore knew Dr Symonds Sr. Emily proposed that Lionel should go to Dakyns, firstly to be tutored for Clifton College, and secondly to be treated by Dr Symonds. The doctor responded to this proposal by sending his written agreement in the following effusive terms:

> I cannot let a post go by without sending my assurance that I shall be really glad and proud to do my best for your son, and if I fail to remove or lessen his infirmity, it will not be want of effort on my part. The case would for its own sake interest me. But it would be an intense satisfaction to me to render any service however slight to Mr Tennyson to whom I live under a great weight of obligation. To no contemporary have I owed through many many years so much support and solace and delight as to the father of your Lionel. He could not have a better home away from his own than with Mr Dakyns, whose kind and judicious care has been given to a young friend of mine . . .[76]

By 17 January everything seemed settled:

> My dear Mr. Dakyns
> Our best thanks. If you will have him, he shall come as your little private pupil, to be transferred to the College if you see fit. Till Easter would probably not be too long if Clifton suits him . . .
> Will you kindly manage as is right about fees for Dr. Symonds? . . . You need only write 'ready' . . . .[77]

However, the message 'ready' never arrived. Within a week of dispatching this letter Emily's plan was withdrawn, and it is worth speculating as to the fate from which Lionel was saved.

On 11 October Dakyns had written to Alfred and Emily, saying that he envied Mr Paul (their new tutor) very much:

I envy Mr. Paul very much. There is one little boy here who reminds me of them (H & L). I call him a little boy because he is only 13 and he is certainly not big in his limbs. But in his mind and spirit he is anything but little. The soul, moreover, of Beethoven is in him ... This child's name is Arthur Carre. And it is he who in the last few months has brought back in tenfold vividness all the pleasant happy days I spent with you. You know that this is the oasis of my life on which I am ever looking back, and, by comparison with which, all other beautiful scenes are a tantalising mirage. But I ought not to talk foolishly to you; I mean I ought to check myself: so I suppose.[78]

The fact that Dakyns did not feel the need to check himself is testimony to the special allowance that was made for the adoration of young boys. As is well known by now, the word 'homosexual' was not in use at that time and men could be quite open about ardently platonic attachments for one another (and for boys) without feeling ashamed. Emily Tennyson had, after all, played her part quite comfortably as an *agent provocateur* in the relationship between Edward Lear and Franklin Lushington.

Quite who was fooling whom is difficult to determine because it is clear, from our perspective, that there was often a sexual element to these 'crushes' and the 'bad habits' rife in boys' boarding schools were common knowledge. It is difficult, then, to avoid concluding that there was some form of unspoken collusion in operation which allowed liaisons of this kind to go on, providing things could be managed in a decorous and restrained way.

As the century approached its *fin de siècle*, relationships between men and young boys became less and less restrained and, indeed, in many cases amounted to nothing less than pederasty, as the interesting, but rather fey book *Love In Earnest* by Timothy d'Arch Smith (1970), shows.

In the case of Dakyns, we know that his friend John Addington Symonds was one of those who more and more openly confessed his 'homosexuality'. (Whitman was greatly embarrassed by the explicit interpretations put upon 'Calamus' by Symonds.) The boy referred to in Dakyns' letter, Arthur Augustus Carre, was, according to Robert Peters, editor of the Dakyns correspondence, the subject of sexual attentions from both Symonds and Dakyns. 'By the late 1860s ... there was sufficient gossip to cause Dakyns to think of leaving Clifton.'[79]

Suddenly, Lionel's stammer takes on a new and disturbing significance. Somehow or other the risk of sending him to Bristol was made known to the Tennysons – although quite how it was explained is impossible to ascertain. In the immediate correspondence of January 1866 Emily simply suggests that it would be taking too great advantage of other people's kindness, but a subsequent letter from Dakyns, written over twenty years later, in November 1886, makes it clear that Dr Symonds Sr stepped in personally, at the last minute, to prevent the move:

> ... the decision of Dr Symonds', which though I acquiesced in its wisdom, was a great blow to me, and robbed me of the charge of Lionel in January 1866. I have often thought what a difference to me it would have made probably had I had him on my own ...[80]

The change of mind by Dr Symonds does tend to suggest that he was suddenly made aware of the undercurrent to the proposed arrangements.

27   Naïveties and Niaiseries

The frost is here,
And fuel is dear

('THE WINDOW')

Alfred began the New Year unwell with flu and bursitis, conditions which lasted into the spring. He was also having rancorous dealings with Mr Payne, the new proprietor of Moxon & Co. Once it was clear that alternative arrangements had to be made for Lionel, he went with Emily and the boy to London, where they consulted Dr Paget.

The visit turned into a mini-season of sociability. They did not return to the Isle of Wight until 23 March, by which time they had been away for seven weeks. They went to Westminster Abbey (which Alfred was always fond of strolling about in, preferably by himself), and met and dined with the usual people – Watts, Gladstone, Forster, Palgrave, Woolner, Browning, and the Carlyles. It was the last time they were to see Mrs Carlyle and her 'fatal little dog'. Lionel stroked its fine black coat. The boy didn't have much else to do, his parents seeming to believe that a round of dull social life amongst adults might calm his nerves and strengthen his constitution.

A month after their return to the island they heard of Jane Carlyle's death. The black dog had been hit by a carriage in the street and she had overtaxed herself in its rescue. Since his marriage Tennyson had had less and less to do with Carlyle, and his meetings with Jane had become very infrequent. The interesting relationship that had begun to develop between them during their early encounters never amounted to anything, and her death did not move him particularly.

He was still far from fully fit, and writing nothing. 'Lucretius', for all its power, had not been the beginning of a new poetic vein.

There were too many domestic and personal cares. Lionel's stammer was no better. Emily was suffering from severe toothache and had to go to London for dental treatment. Hallam had to be taken to Marlborough, where he had enrolled at the beginning of the year. They were still no nearer finding the longed-for second home. And there were the minor petulances provoked by journalistic inaccuracies about Tennyson's circumstances. In June he grew positively apoplectic about an article by an unidentified American:

'A porch completely festooned with woodbines,' there is not a woodbine anywhere about it. 'Ancient oaks threw their spreading branches *completely over the broad approach to the house*': a complete fiction. 'Wide level lawns extended on either side': there is not a bit of level ground anywhere near the house. 'A Butler': I don't keep a Butler ... I am *'perhaps* 5 feet 9 if I hold myself up.' I am 6 feet. 'His gait is feeble.' I dare say I had corns ... 'Plentifully mixed with grey' he says my hair is. I haven't a grey hair in my head.[81]

The slander about the hair was the most loathsome of all.

There was a family trip to the New Forest for a fortnight in July. Alfred, Emily and both the boys were accompanied by Grandpapa Sellwood. Lionel had caught sunstroke just before leaving and Emily had had to spend three nights in his room. As they moved about the Forest, Alfred and Hallam, father and eldest son, commonly went on foot, while the weakened Lionel rode with Emily and Grandpapa. If part of the problem of Lionel's stammer had its roots in a sense of being the less favoured of Tennyson's sons, as seems likely, this was hardly the way to go about seeking an improvement in his condition. Tennyson's insensitivity in his treatment of the two boys can be explained – and partially exonerated – by remembering that the cause of all his own childhood tribulation was a father's favouritism for the second-born son. In growing so close to Hallam and seeming to leave Lionel to Emily, Tennyson was perhaps simply overcompensating for what he still felt to be that earlier act of ancestral injustice.

None of this seems to have spoilt the relationship between the two boys themselves. They still played well together and on their return to the Isle of Wight were both called out by the Freshwater Cricket Club. As far as life at home was concerned, though, it was a brief vacation. Hallam went back to Marlborough on 7 August and Lionel was taken to a special school in Hastings ten days later.

The school was run by a Dr James Hunt, a specialist in the treatment of speech disorders. Charles Kingsley and Lewis Carroll had attended his clinic at Ore House, with some success, although Carroll at least did not think much of the character of the man. 'It might be disagreeable for a lady to be in the house,' he said.

Hunt believed that a stammer was merely a symptom of constitutional weakness and treatment consisted simply of a masculine and strengthening regime based on red meat (three times a day), beer and cross-country exercise. Alfred and Emily did not find out about the beer drinking until after they had abandoned Lionel to the Doctor's care. It was not an easy parting. The boy sobbed and begged not to be left. Alfred had to 'walk twice back along the road with him to comfort him.'

From Hastings, the Tennysons drove through Battle and Tunbridge Wells, to visit Edmund Lushington at Park House. Alfred revisited his mother's old Boxley home, showing Emily the room which had been his, and spent several evenings talking metaphysics with Edmund.

While at Park House they received their first letter from Lionel. Emily responded to the worrying news that he was being provided with beer. 'Speaking of the half-glass of beer not being enough for anyone in this hot weather, you say you "buy some". Does this mean beer, or what do you buy? I scarcely know what to recommend but I should think seltzer or soda water would be best. Certainly not beer . . .'

There was greater anxiety for Emily and Alfred when, having moved on to Haslemere to continue their search for a second home, they heard of an outbreak of cholera in the Hastings area. Emily wrote at once to Lionel, warning him not to eat 'uncooked fruit or anything unwholesome'.

They were in Haslemere to see The Jumps, a house which had been recommended to them some time ago by Mrs Gilchrist. She found Tennyson looking older than expected, but still very grand and eccentric in manner. A girl of seven came into the room. The poet called her over, kissed her and began to stroke her sturdy legs. He asked Emily to feel them too. Then he put the girl on his knee. Afterwards, he explained himself to Mrs Gilchrist:

TENNYSON: I admire that little girl of yours. It isn't everyone that admires that very solid kind of development of flesh and blood. But I do. Old Tom Campbell used to say that children should be like bulbs – plenty of substance in them for the flower to grow out of by-and-by. How many children do you have?

MRS GILCHRIST: Four.

TENNYSON: Quite enough! Quite enough!

Alfred did not like what he saw of The Jumps – it was too barren and desolate – so they looked at some alternative sites in the same region before returning to Farringford on 21 September.

Anxiety about Lionel continued. Dr Hunt sent the family few progress reports, a fact which Lionel explained in a letter to his brother. 'The reason why Dr Hunt never says anything about me is that his system is carried on in very simple terms so that if it were once known then everybody would be setting up establishments for curing stammers.' This amusing prospect was followed by a worrying suggestion that Lionel was being treated with less than the special attention which the Tennysons expected. 'There was a procession all round the field of Battle because it was the 800th anniversary, but I did not go to see it because Dr Hunt did not want me, he had not enough tickets for all of us & so I gave up mine.'[82] When this effrontery was compounded with news that he had been in bed for a week with a bad headache, Alfred wrote to Hunt, 'This never occurred to him before,' and asked for further information. What was forthcoming was no comfort at all. They were told merely that the weakness contributing to Lionel's stammer was continuing.

They did their best to allow the distractions of Farringford to put poor Lionel out of their minds. Julia Cameron presented Emily's father with a bright violet poncho, which he was told to wear as a nightshirt, but in fact used as a cape on his frequent ferry crossings. In October Grove and Sullivan (then a twenty-four-year-old aspiring musician) came for a ten-day visit and prompted Alfred into writing his first new poem of the year – a sequence of lyrics known variously as 'The Window' or 'The Song of the Wrens'. The idea was essentially Grove's, who thought Tennyson might care to try writing something in the vein of Heine's 'Lieder'.

During Grove and Sullivan's visit Tennyson completed three of the proposed series of seven song lyrics, and Sullivan began to work out medleys on Farringford's 'very tinkling' out-of-tune piano.[83] At night the three men retired to the top of the house and talked till two or three in the morning about 'death and the next world, and God and man.'

At the beginning of November both Alfred and Emily had to go to their dentist, Barrett, in London. After treatment they returned to Haslemere to continue looking for land, but it was another wasted and rather fractious effort. Emily suffered from an inflamed eye and Alfred grew cross with her for failing to remind him to look out for the great fall of meteors on the night of 13 November.

On his return to Farringford Tennyson was in an excitable mood. One morning he complained about the retinue of servants and ubiquitousness of guests. 'I should like to sneak about and get a cup of tea by myself.' Emily smiled at this, as if to suggest that her husband might find such exertion taxing. 'I breakfasted alone for quarter of a century,' he pointed out. It was a telling little exchange.

Later the same day Tennyson outraged a parson's wife with some rather agnostic-sounding remarks on the death of children. 'Mere chop-logic,' the bravely enraged woman declared. Tennyson left the table and went to his room, to be joined by Allingham. To begin with Tennyson tried to ignore the interlude and created diversionary literary talk. But Allingham brought him round to it:

ALLINGHAM: You shocked Mrs F.

TENNYSON: Can't help it.

The next day he was in high spirits, reciting his 'Song of the Wrens' while jumping around most comically, like a cock-pigeon. 'He is the only person I ever saw who can do the most ludicrous things without any loss of dignity,' wrote Allingham.

'Very like Shakespeare,' Tennyson thought some of his new verses. 'Naïveties and niaiseries,' said Allingham, more accurately.

28   Such an Age

Ring out the old, ring in the new,
Ring, happy bells, across the snow:
The year is going, let him go;
Ring out the false, ring in the true.

(*IN MEMORIAM* CVI)

Much to Alfred and Emily's delight Lionel came home for Christmas 'looking rosy and happy, thank God, and his stammering nearly cured'. This was in large part wishful, and seasonal, thinking, but the parents were happy enough at least to send him back to Dr Hunt for another term in the New Year.

Hallam was getting on well at Marlborough, the Bradleys sending constant eulogies about the boy's character. At the end of the Christmas vacation Hallam wrote to Dakyns complaining that none of his letters from Marlborough had been answered – an indication of a continuing cloud following the collapse of plans to send Lionel to Clifton.

The last day of an extended Christmas vacation fell on 7 February. Alfred, in a change to normal domestic routine asked the boys to stay and sing to him after supper. He made a bowl of punch and gave them a little. They both left home the following day, and this time it was to be Hallam who would give his parents the most anxiety, growing seriously ill with pneumonia in March. As soon as news of the lad's illness reached Freshwater, the Tennysons sent a telegraph to Dr Symonds asking him to attend their son. At the same time they immediately left home, bearing gifts from Julia Cameron – a set of Indian pyjamas coloured purple and gold, an embroidered poncho and two Japanese trays. 'Doesn't he look nice,' the nurse said, when Hallam was arrayed in his new costume.

But this was two weeks later. When Alfred and Emily first arrived at the school Hallam seemed to be at death's door – 'the pulse stopt and he was seized with a coup des neufs.'[84] Alfred reacted morbidly and fatalistically. Emily said, in her Journal, of 'this terrible time':

> A. was very calm but deeply moved. At the crisis he said, 'I have made up my mind to lose him. God will take him pure and good, straight from his mother's lessons, he is very simple & religious. Surely it would be better for him than to grow up such a one as I am.'[85]

For Emily the ordeal was doubly worrying. Her father had suffered a stroke at the end of January and she had been concerned for his recovery ever since. Standing to lose a father and a son, she bore up bravely, with an emotional resourcefulness which belied her physical frailty.

Allingham, in visits to Farringford early in the year, had found Tennyson obsessed with human destiny and, it seems, more than usually concerned for his own survival. While walking along a cliff-edge path, Tennyson began speaking of people who had fallen over the edge. Allingham, walking behind him, said, 'Suppose I were to slip and catch hold of you, and we both rolled down together.' Tennyson stopped, considered, and said, 'You'd better go on first.' A good story, and one that amusingly testifies to the poet's sense of self-preservation.

There had been another visit to Queen Victoria. Alfred went alone this time, it being (in his view) too cold and wet for Emily. The conversation was rather droll. The Queen found Tennyson's anti-cockney obsession comical. 'We are not much troubled by them here,' she said.

'Perhaps I should not be either, Your Majesty – if I could stick a sentry at my gates.'

The Queen asked about the latest developments in poetry. Tennyson mentioned Browning and Swinburne, and added, 'Everyone writes verse nowadays. I dare say Your Majesty does.' Victoria denied it. In fact, she had no time for books.

'Why don't you do some great work?' she asked.

'Oh, it is *such* an age,' Tennyson answered, and went on to air his views about universal suffrage and vote by the ballot. Possibly to take him off this tack, the Queen asked about the boys. Marlborough was the best of schools, she had heard.

In all the worry about Hallam, Lionel was not forgotten. Indeed, while at Marlborough, and in response to hearing that paper chases had been the ruin of several members of the Bradley family, Alfred wrote to Dr Hunt demanding that Lionel be excluded from such activity forthwith. He took the precaution of also sending a note to Lionel:

I have been just writing to Dr Hunt to prevent your running such long paper-chases. Everyone here (all the Masters) exclaim against it as ruining and breaking up the constitution. Arthur Bradley is knocked up at this moment from having run only 5 miles and you say you have run 16. You must not do it.[86]

Dr Hunt took umbrage at this and kept Lionel in Hastings over Easter. Hallam, safely recovered and home at Farringford recuperating, complained to Dakyns about 'that savage monster Dr Hunt.'

29   To the Cobb

Over the thorns and briers,
Over the meadows and stiles,
Over the world to the end of it
Flash for a million miles.

('THE WINDOW')

During their last visit to Haslemere Tennyson had taken out a two-year lease on Grayshott Farm so that, until they had found a permanent site for their second home, they would at least have somewhere to escape to. They left Farringford for Grayshott on 29 April, by which time Hunt had relented and allowed Lionel home. Tennyson wrote to the Doctor politely thanking him for his treatment but deciding that it would be better for Lionel not to return to Ore House in the summer.

Being shut up for six weeks in an undrained farmhouse in the middle of nowhere was no holiday for Emily, and she longed to get back to Farringford – so much so that she rather impishly and uncharacteristically celebrated Alfred's onset of hayfever in a letter to Mrs Gatty: 'Now that we have no longer the induce-ment to remain here that we had so long as he was well I *trust* that we may soon be going home.'[87] She also worried that the place was too primitive and lacking in cultured pursuit for the boys. 'One feels that even this little time may have a large influ-ence & one is anxious notwithstanding continual rides & drives & walks.'

In addition to excursions there was the unchanging conveyor belt of visitors: Drummond Rawnsley, Palgrave, Allingham, Jowett, and even Lear, who fell in love with the neighbourhood to such a degree that he rather optimistically asked the Tennysons to look out for an extra plot for him.

At last they were successful in their search and signed an agree-ment for a wooded area of land called Greenhill. As celebration they arranged a picnic on their newly-acquired property. Emily rode part of the way on a donkey. Alfred and Hallam carried her across terrain that was too difficult for the beast of burden and at one point all three of them tumbled to the ground in a fit of laughter. Later the same day Alfred arranged to meet Knowles, the man who was to design and build their second home. They had bumped into one another by chance a week beforehand at Haslemere station and Knowles, knowing how short-sighted Tennyson was, went up to the poet and spoke to him. Learning why the Tennysons were in the area Knowles said, 'I am an architect,' and Tennyson replied, 'You had better build me a house.' So the commission was given.

There was already a common bond between the two men. In 1862 Knowles had published, with a dedication to Tennyson, a book of Arthurian stories. It was to be the basis of a long and influential friendship. Although young, Knowles was a forceful, practical and dynamic character, quite capable of bringing his own views to bear on those of the older man.

The land which the Tennysons had bought, consisting of some thirty-six acres, was high up on Blackdown. The steepest point was ringed with pine trees and known as the Temple of the Winds. At once the biggest drawback and also the greatest attraction was the fact that there was no road to the property, only deeply-rutted cart-tracks. The price of this inaccessible refuge was £1400.

The final resolution of his need for a second home brought a sense of purpose back to Tennyson's life. On a practical level he felt the need to earn back the money that he was paying out for the land – even though he could well afford it on past and continuing earnings. Recent disagreements with Mr Payne had convinced him that it was time to move publishing house, and in September he appointed a deputy to look into Payne's financial position.

This was after a summer in which his only tour away from the island was a fortnight's ramble in Dorset and Devon, initially with Allingham. Tennyson had decided to go to Lyme Regis, having wanted to see the Cobb ever since reading *Persuasion*. He met Allingham by chance in Lymington and talked him into coming along.

They took the train to Dorchester, then walked through fields and stubble to Maiden Castle. After booking rooms at the Antelope, they walked through the town, visiting its museum, then decided to visit William Barnes. Allingham led the way to Came vicarage, a small cottage just a mile outside Dorchester. It was a late decision and they did not get to Barnes' door until 10 pm. Nevertheless, Barnes was delighted to see them.

The following day they were transported to Bridport and then set off on foot for Lyme Regis, taking a beer and cheese lunch at Charmouth, where Tennyson surprised Allingham by flirting with the waitress. In Lyme they took rooms in The Cups and after dinner sat smoking on a bench and talking very openly about marriage.

Tennyson was up early the following morning and walked down to the Cobb before breakfast. He returned with Allingham later, the two of them taking a copy of *Persuasion* with them, and reading aloud the passage describing Louisa Musgrove's injury.

Palgrave, who was staying in the town with his wife, met up with them later in the day and rather spoiled the free-and-easy atmosphere. On the way back to The Cups Tennyson seized Allingham's arm and begged him not to go back to Lymington, as he said he should. 'Is it the money?' Tennyson asked. 'I'll pay.' But duty called for Allingham. Tennyson, however, remained hopeful, and a day or two later a dry note arrived in Lymington, signed by Palgrave, saying, 'Tennyson asks me to say he hopes you will join us at Moreton Hampstead – Dartmoor – au revoir.' However, Allingham was expecting the imminent arrival of Dante Gabriel Rossetti, and could not get away.

Tennyson returned from his week-long incursion into Devon to family sadness. Henry Sellwood, Emily's father, died on 15 September, never having properly recovered from the stroke.

To his first tentative enquiry about the financial soundness of Moxon & Co. Tennyson received an unsatisfactory response from Payne. He wrote back frankly explaining that he was regularly in receipt of anonymous letters claiming that the publishing house was close to bankruptcy and giving a formal warning that a representative (formal authors' agents were a later breed) would be making further, more searching enquiries.

> Seeing that I have stuck to the house of Moxon from the beginning through evil report and good report, and really have been and am the main pillar of it, it seems to me (and I say it with all kindness) that you cannot but feel that it is not only due to me but also your duty to yourself that I should be fully informed of the state of affairs: and with this view, and in accordance with your offer that you can afford me reasonable proof of your financial soundness, I propose deputing a friend in whom I have confidence to confer with you respecting our mutual business relations.[88]

There had been a small error in Tennyson's recent account – £74 had been omitted – and this, coupled with his reminder to Payne that 'some few years ago there was an absolute error to a much greater amount,' had drained his confidence in the firm.

30   Foundation Stone

The purchase of land at Haslemere had lifted a great weight off Tennyson's mind. In the past four or five years he had written only one major poem ('Lucretius'). Now he began composing again in comparative profusion. At the close of the year he wrote 'The Higher Pantheism', 'Wages', and 'The Spiteful Letter'.

The first of these, written in December (and later read aloud by Knowles at the inaugural meeting of the Metaphysical Society in June 1869) is a meditation on man's failure to make proper connection between the material and the spiritual:

> Dark is the world to thee: thyself art the reason why;
> For is He not all but that which has power to feel 'I am I?'

> Glory about thee, without thee; and thou fulfillest thy doom,
> Making Him broken gleams, and a stifled splendour and gloom.

Also written in December was 'The Spiteful Letter', a protest at some annual hate-mail which he had been receiving at the close of each year from an anonymous source. Like many of Tennyson's complaining poems it is rather weak, his anger couched in convolutions: 'Greater than I – is that your cry?/And men will live to see it./Well – if it be so – so it is, you know;/And if it be so, so be it.'

'The Victim', also published at this time, but written before May 1866 is not a good poem. In fact, it is so bad it reads like a third-rate schoolmaster's attempt to turn a legend into a verse narrative suitable for young students to declaim. The whole point of the original story – as it appeared in Charlotte Yonge's *Book of Golden Deeds* – is thrown away. Priests have ordered a heathen king to give up that which is dearest to him in sacrificial offering to avert a famine. They do not know whether to seize his baby son, or his wife. They take the child. At the moment of sacrifice, the wife rushes forward to save her baby. On an impulse the king tries to save her from the knife. In the original, the high priest, having had a demonstration of the king's true balance of feeling, plunges his knife into the woman. The effect of this dramatic moment is sentimentalized in Tennyson's version, with the queen committing suicide on the offered blade.

As evidence of continuing dissatisfaction with Moxon & Co. Tennyson decided to publish three of these four poems in periodicals.

The health of both Tennyson sons continued to give concern. Lionel's stammer was no better and Hallam's lungs remained weak enough to warrant his staying at home during the early part of 1868. The presence of both boys made for some high-spirited entertainment – the acting out of the Burnand and Sullivan sketch *Cox and Box*, or games of football in 'Little Dakyns Hollow' – but if Emily was holding on to the boys in an effort to regain earlier family happiness, by exaggerating the risk to their health, she was making a futile stand and more or less admitted it. Accompanying a spate of letters from Hallam and Lionel to Dakyns, she added a page herself:

I scarcely ever have our pleasant evening readings now, for we are scarcely ever alone – Ally and I. Hallam still reads; but the want of vigour in his reading grieves me. He does not know it himself but he has by no means regained his own strength. Lionel stammers very much in damp or from over-fatigue; but in dry weather and when not over-fatigued the least little only. We are very much puzzled what to do with him. At present we are well off with Mr Digby, tho' I know that the training and emulation of school is wanted for both boys.

The old home ways have been in a measure broken in upon and something is wanted to supply that which is gone.[89]

Tennyson had plenty to occupy him. At the end of January he went to Haslemere and fixed the precise site for the new house with Knowles. Then, at Knowles' home in Clapham Common, the two men discussed the design for the house, Emily and Alfred's originally modest conception, as shown in their sketch (see plate 14), becoming more and more elaborate.

On 23 April, Shakespeare's birthday, the foundation stone was laid and building commenced. In the meantime Tennyson had begun writing 'The Holy Grail'.

PART FIVE
Hesperus II

1   The Second House

O brother, had you known our mighty hall,
Which Merlin built for Arthur long ago!
For all the sacred mount of Camelot,
And all the dim rich city, roof by roof,
Tower after tower, spire beyond spire,
By grove, and garden-lawn, and rushing brook,
Climbe to the mighty hall that Merlin Built.

('THE HOLY GRAIL')

While Alfred Tennyson was having a grand second home built for himself, his brother Charles was busy overseeing the construction of a new church in his parish of Grasby. Nothing more dramatically displays the difference – both in temperament and in circumstances – between the two brothers.

The building of Aldworth has often been compared with the building of Bayons, by Tennyson's uncle, Charles d'Eyncourt, who had died in 1861. According to this view, we behold Tennyson the hypocrite, reneging on all his old, healthy adolescent expressions of disgust at his uncle's self-importance and pretence. There were indeed superficial similarities between the two buildings, especially their Gothic ugliness, and the attempt to attribute the scale of the building wholly to the influence of Knowles has always seemed suspect, but Bayons had been built self-consciously for display, whereas Aldworth was genuinely conceived as a family retreat.

It is essential, in this period of Tennyson's life, to determine the seriousness of the poet's aspirations for social position; but there is no more reason to look for consistency in a poet than in anyone else. After a few glasses of port with Knowles he might well have started thinking grandly of himself as a d'Eyncourt, at last vindicating the humiliation of his poor, abused father. Why not, then, throw a few coats of arms on the stonework? Sober, he worried more about the plumbing and whether or not to have the luxury of a bath in the new house.

The bathroom was eventually positioned on the first floor, overlooking the porch, and was, together with the study, a major feature of Knowles's design. Tennyson was so taken with the novelty of having a bath that when he moved in he immediately began having three or more baths a day. The study was grander and more open than the one at Farringford and decorated with marble figures of various Roman emperors.*

A broad hall-corridor ran the whole length of Aldworth's ground-floor, this feature having been included in the design so that Tennyson might take his constitutional walk even in inclement weather, pacing up and down beside his Edward Lear oils and watercolours. Coming off the corridor were no less than three sitting-rooms. Emily's own drawing-room, and an anteroom in which Tennyson took his dessert and pint of port after dinner. The kitchen, domestics' hall and housekeeper's room were all on the opposite side of the corridor, and the warren-like second floor contained sufficient rooms for staff, guests and additional family.

The interior of the house was large and expansive, but hardly extravagant. The design did not include, for instance, that prerequisite of country house life – the billiard room. It was in its exterior touches that the house was most pretentious – a motto and heraldic beasts cut into the stone of the cornice, shields on the windows, and the arms of the Tennyson

---

*Some time after the house was eventually sold out of the Tennyson family, at the end of the First World War, these figures turned up in a second-hand shop in the Brompton Road – or so Tennyson's grandson, Charles, believed. However, the figurines were mass-produced and it seems unlikely that Tennyson's could have been recognized with such certainty.

While writing this biography I have been shown many items – inkwells, candle-snuffers, paper-weights, brass dogs – purportedly once used by Tennyson in his study, and now carefully cherished in ordinary households. Some of these may be genuine. On the Isle of Wight in particular many objects were unofficially 'saved' from Farringford when the house was eventually sold by Tennyson's heirs. However, the profusion of these objects leads one to be sceptical. There also seem to be rather too many capes, wide-awakes, pipes and tobacco jars in the various museum display-cases at the Tennyson Research Centre, the Usher Art Gallery, Carisbrooke Castle, and Farringford Hotel.

As a general principle it might be better if a writer's literary executors, rather than burn letters and diaries, were to make a large bonfire of all their personal effects, in order to avoid tawdry and morbid displays such as the collection of sickbed paraphernalia offered for our delight at one of these venues.

d'Eyncourts marked on the chimney-pieces.

In many respects the building of the house – as so much construction work is inclined to be – was a messy and shambolic affair. For months after the Tennysons moved in, the workmen continued to labour on the drains and the laying of the lawn, amidst a mess of sand and apparatus. Annoying as this was to Emily, Alfred evidently enjoyed the atmosphere of activity. He had always admired busy people. That was what impressed him most about acquaintances like Bradley and Knowles. The building of the house was much more a straightforward display of his own belief in the virtue of wilful betterment than any attempt at an empty gesture of grandeur. It was a way of proving – to himself, primarily – that his station in life was steadily advancing. The house was built as a retreat, but it was to be a retreat in which the work could go on.

One night, in December 1867, he had composed the short poem 'Wages', in which the reward for all virtuous endeavour is seen as no easy retirement in this world, but a passport into the next:

> She desires no isles of the blest, no quiet seats of the just,
>   To rest in a golden grove, or to bask in a summer sky:
> Give her the wages of going on, and not to die.[1]

The emphasis on 'going on' stemmed, in part, from Tennyson's recent Hebrew studies and reading about the Talmud. For a time, in 1868, he toyed with the idea of creating a modern verse translation of either the Book of Job or the Song of Solomon, before turning finally, and to Emily's satisfaction and relief, to 'The Holy Grail'.

Meanwhile, Tennyson's dissatisfaction with the new management of Moxon & Co. eventually led to a change of publisher. Added to his worries about the firm's financial position was his anger at the way Payne had gone about recovering copyright fees from a religious association which had innocently printed a Tennyson poem in one of its tracts. And in the background were worries about competition from younger poets and a concern that the taste of the reading public might suddenly turn away from him.

The final straw, as far as Tennyson's dealings with Payne were concerned, was an advertisement in the *Publishers' Circular* of 2 March 1868 of a new standard edition of the poems, in a cheaper format than the existing seven volumes. The advertisement appeared without the poet's permission and its commercialism infuriated Emily:

What I do really care for is that my Ally should stand before the world in his own childlike simplicity and by this he would be made to appear a mere low, cunning tradesman and it shall not be if I can prevent it. I say I, but he hates it all, of course, as much as I do, only he does not see the consequences as clearly as I do, perhaps not having turned his mind to the subject.[2]

On the same day that she sent this to Woolner Emily wrote in her Journal: 'Very much annoyed by Mr Payne who cannot understand our love of absolute simplicity in advertisement business arrangements so that we may be free to take thankfully what comes in this way. Be it much or little. What grieves me is that his love of excitement may mislead the public as to A., who has nothing to do with these matters.'

Tennyson himself was more businesslike in his response, but equally annoyed. He saw that the advertisement put him in a difficult position. He did not want to go ahead with the new edition, but realized that its announcement was likely to deflate sales of the old one. Throughout the second half of 1868 he managed to concentrate on the composition of his new poem, 'The Holy Grail', whilst keeping in touch with the progress of building at Greenhill.

There was a significant visitor during July – Henry Wadsworth Longfellow. It was an interesting encounter, for, superficially, the American poet was something of a Tennysonian clone – bearded, wide-awake-behatted, becloaked. Longfellow was accompanied by two sisters, three daughters, a son, a brother and a brother-in-law, so there was no prospect of the party being accommodated at Farringford. They had to stay at the hotel, but were twice entertained at the house. Each occasion was rather crowded and formal, with other eager guests being introduced to the American. Longfellow's manner was straightforward and his character appeared all on the surface. There was a marked contrast between his smooth, unfurrowed countenance, and the hard, lined face of Tennyson.

Although Tennyson quite liked *Hiawatha*, he did not hold

Longfellow's poetry in high regard and went so far as to criticize the man's hexameters to his face; then seemed surprised when the American defended himself. There was a long talk between them on the subject of spiritualism but, possibly because Longfellow always had to leave before Tennyson had finished his bottle of port, the discussion was muted. He took the American to be photographed by Mrs Cameron and left him to face the camera alone. His parting remark – 'I will come back soon and see what is left of you' – reflects as much on his view of Longfellow as a rather ineffectual figure as it does on the well-documented bossiness of the photographer.

There were other visitors through the summer and autumn, of course; indeed it was at just this period that the guests became more numerous, and from a variety of backgrounds. Tennyson found himself drawn less and less to a few individuals, and more and more to the crowd.

One exception was still Allingham, who was always privy to late-night discussions whenever he called. On the night of 11 August they were locked out of the house. A number of dinner guests, including members of the Darwin family, departed at midnight, and Tennyson and Allingham went out beneath the sky, to talk about Immortality. Tennyson seemed desperate for an assurance of eternity; Allingham could do no more than restate his own belief in God. Emily, not realizing that Alfred had left the house, had ordered it to be locked, and the two stop-outs had to rouse a servant to let them back in.

Not until November did Tennyson really turn his mind to the matter of finding a new publisher. By this time 'The Holy Grail' was finished and had been given its first trial readings. He went to London, for talks with his solicitor Arnold White, and stayed with Knowles. Payne, realizing by now that he was about to lose Tennyson, was going around portraying the poet as selfish, mean and unfriendly. Other publishers soon realized that a prime commodity was up for grabs, and on this visit Tennyson was offered £4000 a year to sign with Alexander Strahan, the proprietor of *Good Words* and *Argosy*. Apparently Tennyson and White warned the prospective publisher that it might be difficult to make back such money, but Strahan shrugged their caution aside, saying that *Good Words* alone made him £7000 a year and that Tennyson would bring 'no end of grist to his mill'. Tennyson might have been expected to find all this rather unedifying, and did in fact appear over-anxious to settle. He even sent Strahan a copy of the 'Grail' to be printed, as well as *The Lover's Tale*, which he wanted made into a trial edition, before any agreement had been signed.

The tension had its effect on his health, bringing on an attack of lumbago which confined him to his bed in Clapham. But he did get out one night, to a table-rapping session after which Browning heard him read the 'Grail' and pronounced it the 'best and highest' thing he had done. In return Tennyson listened to Book One of Browning's *The Ring and the Book*. He found it a strange and vigorous work but doubted whether it could ever be popular.

From his sick-bed Tennyson kept in constant touch with Emily, and she became anxious that without her active counselling Alfred might be too rash and generous in what he offered to Strahan.

> Pray do not let the poems go into *Good Words*. As to people having no reason to complain if they were, there I differ, for part of the object of those who have thy other poems would of course be to have these as a volume in the series. And when it is taken into consideration that *Enoch Arden* in one year brought in about £6,000 it is perfectly absurd to think of £700 ... Make a stand at once; it may save future trouble. Put it on me, if thou wilt, for I do entirely object ...[3]

Any attempt to convert that £700 into its current worth highlights Tennyson's enormous earning power – and Emily Tennyson, supine and spiritual saint that she is supposed to have been, wanted more.

Before returning to Farringford, Tennyson travelled to Paris with his friend Locker. They stayed for about ten days and Tennyson returned to Farringford to find the house in some chaos. A maid had contracted scarlet fever and it was decided to evacuate the house while it was scoured. Emily and the boys, who were home for Christmas, went to Headon Hall in Alum Bay. Alfred joined them from time to time but returned to the house to work alone in his study. On Christmas Eve, with the rest of the family still at Headon, he wrote angrily to Palgrave, telling him to stop passing the trial edition of 'The Holy Grail' around.

> You distress me when you tell me that, without leave given by me, you showed my poem to Max Muller: not that I care

about Max Muller's seeing it, but I do care for your not considering it a sacred deposit. Pray do so in future; otherwise I shall see some boy in some Magazine making a lame imitation of it, which a clever boy could do in twenty minutes – and, though his work would be worth nothing, it would take away the bloom and freshness from mine.[4]

This was fair comment and perfectly consistent with his attitude towards the manuscripts which he had passed amongst his Trinity friends. They were sacrosanct, for a select circle only, until the time of publication.

He also told Palgrave that he did not intend publishing the 'Grail' 'for a year or two', and would write three or four more Idylls first. Nevertheless, he was keen to make the move from Moxon official and on the 31 December he signed an agreement with Strahan which gave him £4300 a year. The extra £300 was to go towards an allowance which he had decided to have paid to Moxon's widow, up until her death. In the letter which accompanied the signed contract Tennyson made it clear that in the event of Mrs Moxon's death the amount payable to him by Strahan & Co. should be reduced to £4000.

When Payne heard of the agreement he fixed a pair of ass's ears to the painting of Tennyson which hung in the Moxon offices.

2
The Reality of the Unseen

Let visions of the night or of the day
Come, as they will; and many a time they come,
Until this earth he walks on seems not earth,
This light that strikes his eyeball is not light,
The air that smites his forehead is not air
But vision ...

('THE HOLY GRAIL')

D uring the Bradleys' New Year visit to Farringford – this year they brought with them a Perigord pie (which, had it not been eaten, might well now be in a glass case alongside other exhibits) – Tennyson gave another trial reading of 'The Holy Grail', 'explaining the realism and the symbolism, and how the natural, if people cared, could always be made to account for the supernatural.' Just as the order and structure of *In Memoriam* had only gradually formed itself in Tennyson's mind, so did the unifying structure of the Idylls only take shape after each successive one had been written.

It was the metaphysical and moral constructions that could be put upon the poems which was the inspiration to the formation of the Metaphysical Society, the original idea of which was hatched by Knowles and Tennyson during the poet's November visit to Clapham Common. His reading of 'The Holy Grail' led naturally into a chat about the 'mystical meaning of the Poem' and 'led to almost endless talks on speculative metaphysical subjects.' Tennyson remarked that it would be good if such themes could be argued in the form of a learned society, and the energetic Knowles immediately offered to 'endeavour to get it up.'

Originally, the group was to be known as the Theological Society, but then it was decided, in order for real discussion to take place, to enrol members of all shades of opinion. It was Dean Stanley's wife who suggested the final name. Knowles stated the purpose of the society as follows: 'that those who were ranged on the side of faith should meet those who were ranged on the side of unfaith, and freely interchange their views.' Adopted as its motto was a remark of Tennyson's tossed off in the middle of some vociferous debate – 'Modern science ought at all events to have taught men to separate light from heat' – and the discussions generally condensed down into the fundamental clash between scientific materialism, and religious mysticism. Not only did the Society form itself in the wake of Darwin's theory of evolution, but also in the midst of popular interest in spiritualism and the occult. Tennyson listened with interest to papers like 'The Verification of Beliefs' (Henry Sidgwick) and 'On the Emotion of Conviction' (Walter Bagehot) but he did not attend every meeting and, as with the Apostles, he never read a paper himself. William Carpenter, a provocative member, presented his paper 'Principles of Mental Physiology' in which he argued that all dreams and visions were tricks of the mind.

Tennyson was likely to turn this argument on its head and

argue the same thing for ordinary perception. His own mind at any rate, during the early part of the New Year, was kept firmly on his business affairs. He was especially niggled by reports in the *Publishers' Circular* suggesting his move to Strahan had been motivated by avarice. He was convinced – to a paranoid degree – that the offending articles had been 'planted' by Payne, and even spoke to his lawyer about it, but was wisely counselled to keep silent. Strahan did, however, complain, in a letter published in one of his own periodicals. It was good, open, spiteful sparring, and not at all the type of gentlemanly decorum that many persist in imagining the world of Victorian letters to have been.

When, a month or two later, an anonymous article appeared under the title 'The Poetry of the Period', in which his poetry was subjected to its fiercest criticism for over thirty years, Tennyson immediately jumped to the conclusion that it was another vindictive 'plant' by Payne, and quickly (in a letter to Locker) dashed off one of his occasional darts of vitriol.

Ancient Pistol, peacock Payne
Brute in manner, rogue in grain,
How you squeezed me, peacock Payne!
Scared was I and out I ran
And found by Paul's an honest man.
Peace be with you, peacock Payne,
I have left you, you remain
Ancient Peacock, sealskin Payne.[5]

As with his earlier attacks on Bulwer Lytton this squib never really explodes. It splutters and fizzles and gets a certain amount off Tennyson's chest, but that is all. He never considered it worth publishing, having learnt no doubt from his previous misjudgements.

Tennyson's relationship with his new publisher hit early rough water when he heard, from Edmund Lushington, that Strahan had been sending out copies of the trial edition of 'The Holy Grail', as if they were the proofs for a bona fide forthcoming publication.

This annoyance, together with certain domestic worries, provoked a return of what Emily called Alfred's 'nervous affliction'. She later elaborated, 'A. still suffering from the solar plexus' – a remark which suggests that its physical manifestation was digestive.

Domestically the main concern during the first months of 1869 followed on from the death of Charles Weld, who had not been in good health since his dismissal from office. After his death Emily commented that in his final days he had been 'quite changed – never lost his temper', implying that Anne Weld, her sister, was well rid of him.

For a while there was talk of having Emily's sister and niece move in with them at Farringford. Eventually they found a house of their own in a neighbouring part of the island but as a letter from Emily to Hallam written later in the year makes clear this was only after a period of emotionally-charged deliberation.

> I think Auntie is now quite convinced that I intended the best in opposing their living with us and did the best, which is of course a comfort great in proportion to the trial of her first misunderstanding and difference of opinion ... I do feel it a great relief not to have the daily pressure of three separate families however glad I hope I am to do what I can for Uncle Horatio and Aunt Nanny.[6]

Such trials might have been bad for Tennyson's solar plexus, but they were good for his Muse. During the first half of the year he completed three new Idylls – 'The Coming of Arthur', 'The Passing of Arthur', and 'Pelleas and Etarre' – and would soon be ready to begin a fourth – 'Gareth and Lynette'. But first came the move to Aldworth.

3   More Turf

And all talk died, as in a grove all song
Beneath the shadow of some bird of prey;
Then a long silence came upon the hall,
And Modred thought, 'The time is hard at hand'

('PELLEAS AND ETARRE')

Tennyson had enjoyed a short tour of Switzerland with Locker during June and the first part of July, leaving the second end of the month free for packing. They were in the new house in time for Alfred's birthday – his sixtieth – a 'day which I always feel inclined to pass like a Trappist without speaking – or to keep it sitting in sackcloth and ashes.' As usual Emily did nothing to disturb this mood, except for making sure that new curtains were hung in his study.

The isolation of Aldworth was profound. There was no road, and no post. During the building of the house their application for an access road had been blocked by their neighbour, Lord Egmont, and because the stables were not yet finished they could not even get about on horseback. Walking was their only means of escape. Lionel and Emily grew so weary of the loneliness that they walked to the gate each evening to watch the local workmen and villagers go home, and for the chance of a chat.

Typically, Tennyson did not feel constrained to take false delight in his new home. After so long at Farringford it was to be expected that a brand new house would take a bit of getting used to, and so it did. 'Papa does not get reconciled to his room at all; though we keep it quiet for him, the windows and the ceiling are as displeasing to him as at first.'

The new dwelling was no more pleasing to Emily, but she probably affected more satisfaction with it than she confessed in writing to her confidant, Edward Lear:

Thou ask me how I like Blackdown. For my own private opinion I much prefer Farringford as to its beauty. The absolute solitude of this place at present is not displeasing to me or would not be if there were not so many workmen about . . . and if the terrace were green instead of a waste of sand . . . and I don't care so much for want of the road which Lord Egmont denies as most people would, I suppose, even though I have more reason to care having not the power to walk.'

During September, to counteract their isolation, there was a stream of visitors including Alfred's new publisher, Strahan, the Welds, the Turners, and Edward Lear. Lear's visit ended in dispute and rancour.

Emily and Alfred began to discuss which of the paintings Lear had brought with him they should buy. Alfred was cagey. The money might be better spent on the house. He was not so keen on the paintings as Emily. Lear became irritable. Alfred pointed it out and Lear responded by telling the poet he was a worrier, and that 'everyone knew it'. There was a brief explosion of rage and then Lear went to his room to pack his things. When he came down he tried to apologize. Tennyson was unmoved. It was the assertion that 'everyone' said he was a worrier that cut to the core. Writing to Hallam the day after Lear's departure Emily made no reference to this stormy scene and in mentioning Lear said only that 'it distresses one to find him in for another cold. I am afraid he must be imprudent.'

The Tennysons stayed at Aldworth until the early part of December, having loaned Farringford to the Knowles for the autumn. Their long stay gave Alfred the chance to oversee further work on the house, as well as to begin writing another Idyll – 'Gareth and Lynette'.

The major work outside the house consisted in shaping and levelling the terrace, followed by the laying of turf. Given Tennyson's obsession with the lawns at Farringford, it is hardly surprising to find that he made extravagant plans to have turf cut from the Farringford Down and several wagon-loads of it conveyed to Yarmouth to be ferried over to Southampton. Emily told him he was mad and that the locals of Haslemere would call him 'the mad poet on the hill'.

This observation carried more earnestness than usual. She had been annoyed by his brusque treatment of Lear, and now Alfred was refusing to allow Lionel a visit home, just when 'he has set his dear little heart on doing so'. There had been a spate of train accidents, the latest one (10 October, Nottingham) having killed seven people and Tennyson, worrier that he was, felt nervous about the risks of mechanical travel. Nevertheless – a fact not lost upon Emily – he had gone to London to sort out the facts behind an unexpected publication by his old firm. Payne had sanctioned the release of a Tennyson Concordance which included, scurrilously, a complete text of 'The Window'.

Emily found Aldworth more dreary than ever without Alfred but she recognized his need for companionship. 'I am very anxious to enlarge the borders of his circle', she told Hallam 'which from death and other causes is growing painfully narrow, and surely great talk is a great help.'[8]

While in London he attended a Metaphysical dinner and checked the final set of proofs for *The Holy Grail and Other Poems*, which was published early in December. Soon after Tennyson's return to Aldworth he, Emily and the servants moved back to Farringford. Both boys returned from school – Hallam from Marlborough and Lionel, suffering from measles, from Eton.

4 'Mr Tennyson'

Flower in the crannied wall,
I pluck you out of the crannies,
I hold you here, root and all, in my hand,
Little flower, – but if I could understand
What you are, root and all, and all in all,
I should know what God and man is.

('FLOWER IN THE CRANNIED WALL')

In addition to *The Holy Grail* volume – which included three other Idylls ('The Coming of Arthur', 'Pelleas and Etarre' and 'The Passing of Arthur') and a number of shorter poems (including 'The Victim', 'Wages', 'Lucretius' and 'Flower in the Crannied Wall') Strahan brought out an updated book of Idylls containing all eight that Tennyson had so far written and entitled *Idylls of the King*. Both books came out in time for the Christmas gift-trade.

It was some considerable period (more than five years) since Tennyson had put to his readers so many new poems, and he was even more nervous than usual of their reception. He suspected that Payne, especially after their recent disagreement over the Concordance, would do all in his power to snipe at the new work. The anonymous article which had appeared in the May issue of the *Temple Bar* had in fact been written by Alfred Austin, who was at that moment in the process of revising it for inclusion in his book of essays *The Poetry of the Period* (1870).

The essay, 'Mr Tennyson', is testimony to two things – firstly to the general veneration in which Tennyson was held at the end of the 1860s, and perceived to be unquestionably a great poet; secondly to a rapidly developing reaction amongst the younger generation. Tennyson was now sixty years old. He had been writing and publishing at the peak of his powers for over twenty years. The time was obviously right for some bright spark to come along and take a few pot-shots.

For dramatic effect Austin speaks in his essay as if his is a lone voice but the courage to publish must be accompanied by the belief that the ideas expressed will find at least some sympathetic ears. Austin's was simply the first really critical voice to come into the open. Five years beforehand, in a private letter, Gerard Manley Hopkins had made his famous 'Parnassian' attack on Tennyson. Reading 'Enoch Arden' he had been struck by the automatic quality of much of the writing. It was, he analysed, in the nature of many great writers, that at a certain stage in their career 'they can see things in this Parnassian way and describe them in this Parnassian tongue, without further effort of inspiration'. The criticism is convincing because it is made with such a sense of personal sadness. 'I think one had got into the way of thinking, or had not got out of the way of thinking, that Tennyson was always new, *touching*, beyond other poets, not pressed with human ailments, never using Parnassian. So at least I used to think. Now one sees he uses Parnassian; he is, one must see it, what we used to call Tennysonian.'[9]

Austin's attack is more brittle and opinionated. He is out to quash the notion that Tennyson is a 'great' poet. Quite the contrary, he is 'not even at the head of poets of the third rank, among whom he must ultimately take his place.' Where is his great subject? he asks – his *Faery Queen*, his *Paradise Lost*? If King Arthur is his subject then he has 'funked it', and all he has managed to produce are 'exquisite cabinet pictures'. The uniform 'exquisiteness' of Tennyson's poetry is a mark of its mediocrity. Great poets always produce a good proportion of disastrous nonsense, but 'Mr Tennyson' has too few faults. In fact, he has only one, 'the fault of not being great enough to commit any.'

One of the most withering passages in the essay imagines Shakespeare, Byron and Wordsworth meeting in the Elysian fields and recognizing greatness in one another. Tennyson comes along but is immediately given the cold shoulder. He has too much of the 'pouncet-box' about him, and is left to languish in 'the garden that he loves' beside the 'slow broad stream'. Tennyson has been popular in this life for writing poetry that the age could warm to and, 'It is natural enough that the age, having got in Mr Tennyson a poet that it vastly likes, should want to persuade itself that he is a great poet.' But – and disingenuously Austin pretends that this is the main point of his essay – in doing so the age is risking the ridicule of its grandchildren. The 'Age of Tennyson' indeed. What could be more preposterous?

As Austin's essay was even more critical of the taste of the age than it was of Tennyson's actual poetry, it was inevitable that the critics should seize the two new books as opportunities for defending their position. Consequently, their enthusiastic reception rather masked the poet's loss of favour amongst a younger generation.

Both books were a commercial as well as critical success. Tennyson received more than £10,000 for sales of *The Holy Grail and Other Poems* during its first year – by far his largest annual royalty to date. The voice of Austin was largely ineffectual.

5   Two More Deaths

All in a death-dumb autumn-dripping gloom

('THE LAST TOURNAMENT')

One evening in August 1870 Alfred and Emily, again at Aldworth, were sitting on iron chairs on the lower terrace, watching the turfers at work. Alfred was more unsettled than on their last stay. The physical manifestation of his discomforture had moved from his solar plexus to his skin. Eczema had broken out on his back and his legs. Emily was rather despondent to discover that the acquisition of a second home had done nothing to bring him peace of mind. 'Papa does not settle here one bit,' she had written to Hallam in July, 'so things are rather embarrassing.'[10]

Two recent deaths had contributed to Tennyson's state of mind. The most affecting of these was the death of his dear friend Sir John Simeon, who had become unwell while on holiday in Switzerland. The body was returned to Swainston for the funeral and Alfred, having been at Aldworth for just one week, went back to the island to attend the burial, which was conducted with Roman Catholic extravagance. The body lay in an open coffin surrounded by candles, and Lady Simeon, shrieking and sobbing, threw herself upon it for a final embrace. Tennyson escaped into the garden, borrowing a pipe, a cloak and a hat of Sir John's. The garden at Swainston had long been famous for its nightingales and from the trees came their warbling song. Tennyson lay full length beneath the shade of one of the trees, smoked the pipe, took off the hat, and, with tears in his eyes, composed the first draft of the short elegy 'In the Garden at Swainston'.

> Nightingales warbled without,
>   Within was wailing for thee;
> Shadows of three dead men
>   Walked in the Woods with me,
>   Shadows of three dead men and thou wast one
>   of the three.
>
> Nightingales sang in his woods:
>   The Master was far away:
> Nightingales warbled and sang
>   Of a passion that lasts but a day;
>   Still in the house in his coffin the Prince of
>   courtesy lay.
>
> Two dead men have I known
>   In courtesy like to thee;
> Two dead men have I loved
>   With a love that ever will be;
>   Three dead men have I loved and thou art last
>   of the three.

The three men have been widely taken to be Arthur Hallam, Henry Lushington, and Simeon himself. The importance of the closing verse is the finality it expresses – Tennyson is left bereft, not just of old friends, but of the possibility of making new ones. Just these three he will have known and loved, it seems. Simeon was the last. There will be no more.

Significantly, from this moment on, Tennyson was more inclined to put his trust in female company, especially young female company, than in the company of men, and it was probably the realization that deep, fellow understanding (of a kind that men in the nineteenth century sought much more assiduously than they do today) would be known to him no more, that made him such gloomy company on a shopping trip into Guildford a few days after the funeral. 'His loss haunts him,' Emily recorded bleakly in her Journal, on their return to Haslemere.

Just two days later another shock came – the death of Dickens. Tennyson attended the funeral in Westminster Abbey, an occasion which more graphically than any other illustrates the degree to which he had become a celebrity. At the end of the service the congregation, instead of turning to leave, surged forward to get a proper sighting of the Laureate. Decorum was thrown to the wind; women climbed onto the pews; children were held high by parents. Tennyson had to be led into a side chapel and out of a private door before the crowd could be persuaded to disperse. (It was not only such public occasions which brought outward displays of homage. 'People in Town take to bowing to him now as he walks in the streets,' Emily told Hallam that summer.)

Dickens had been, in so many ways, the opposite of Tennyson – industrious, flamboyant, a moral campaigner – but there were similarities too. Both men shared the same political perspective, the same belief in the moral obligation of walking, and a similar sense of patriotism and religion. Although in physical stature the simian figure of Dickens was so unlike the lanky, loping Tennyson, their facial features had, in recent years, become strikingly alike. When Tennyson saw Millais' death-bed pencil sketch of Dickens he exclaimed, 'This is the most extraordinary drawing. It is exactly like myself.'

The death of Dickens was not the personal blow that the death of Simeon had been, but it had far greater implications for his career. For so long Dickens had commanded huge swathes of public sentiment, which was kept loyal by his energetic dramatic readings and his consistent output. Now that he was gone a large proportion of this popular sentiment was transferred to Tennyson, or so it seemed. Just at the time when critical murmurings were beginning to rumble, and a younger generation of poets was starting to challenge some of the Laureate's cherished artistic tenets, so did he find himself the darling of a mass audience. Much of this audience was not his natural audience, and his imminent switch to poetic drama can be traced to this day in Westminster Abbey, when a multitude pressed their allegiance upon him.

6 Eczema and Moths

What I've come to, you know well,
What I've gone through none can tell.

(EPIGRAM)

During January Tennyson had taken a lease on an apartment on the top floor of the new Albert Mansions in Victoria Street – 'top of the house, 2nd door to the left at the top of the stairs' – so that he would once again have a London base. He used it for the first time during March and April. Emily, worried how he might fare on his own, posted him a box of butter and biscuits, and Houghton sent some port from Fryston.

An extraordinary insight into the degree of forgetfulness and paranoia that Tennyson's heavy drinking made him subject to is given by a letter of 15 April. Written to Knowles, it begins with a description of his muddled departure from the London terminus. In the confusion he became separated from his luggage.

> The worst of all is that I had, or believe I had, in the breast pocket of my coat an open letter to my wife which I had written that morning, when I was intending not to go home till Saturday: it was not signed by me but directed to her ...
> Now when I got into the train this letter was gone; and my fear is that in pulling out my purse which was in the same pocket as the letter it dropped to the ground among the feet of the crowd and will appear in *The Queen's M[essenger]* or some other place a few days hence.

This was a reasonable fear, so far cogently described. But the letter goes on:

> It is just possible that I lost it in the Victoria Station restaurant where I took a plate of soup. I forget the names of the restaurateurs something like Spiers and Ford I think – two monosyllables. Would you mind asking there whether a letter was found? Another faint hope I have that I *may* have burnt it before starting. Another faint hope that I may have

thrown it into one of the top drawers of that chest of ditto in my bedroom.[11]

Losing one's luggage, and mislaying an important personal document can put the sharpest of minds into confusion. But it seems a little odd that Tennyson could not remember whether he had burnt the letter or not, and did not think twice about confessing his uncertainty.

At the time of the two funerals his eczema was at its worst. He was receiving treatment from Paget, which made a prolonged stay in London necessary. As so often in the past it is difficult to know how far his symptoms were exaggerated in order to make such stays possible. Certainly Aldworth was a mess, with men working night and day on the drains and the terrace, and we have it on Emily's own authority that he was unable to settle there. However, she did not sympathize with this need for treatment in London. 'For myself thou knowest I have more faith in lying up on the lawn with the down breezes all around thee. I hope thou are not to be in bed.' And in this same letter to her husband she makes a telling observation on her own diffident temperament:

Louy [Simeon] says she must go to her Uncle Cornwall's tomorrow. I have felt as I used to do in old days talking with her for I can only talk when I may say just what I like, and to her I can, and I know that she likes it. I have grown too diffident of myself to think that anyone else does, having a strong feeling that one must have rosy cheeks, etc., to make one's talk generally acceptable. Thou wilt say that this is cynical. Perhaps it is . . .[12]

What this says to Alfred, in coded but easily decipherable language, is that they do not talk together as they used to, and that, because of her own paleness and sickliness, he does not give her the credit he used to for uplifting companionship.

Still laid up in Victoria Street, Alfred wrote to his young nephew, Percy, one of Horatio's five children: 'Uncle's leg is better than it was a week or two ago but not so well as it was on Saturday. Uncle is afraid he has walked too much but he has been lying down a long time and now is rather tired of it.'

He returned to Aldworth in time for a visit from Dakyns, who reported, two months later, that the poet's leg was no better and that he was seeking homeopathic treatment.[13] But by this time Tennyson had at last begun to settle down in the new house. He was not working there yet, but on 23 September Emily recorded in her Journal, 'A divinely happy talk alone with my A. One to be remembered as long as I live.'

There is no reason to doubt the reciprocity of this feeling. One of the dangers of a detailed, domestic biography is that it can demythologize relationships and make people appear petty and feckless. It is important, therefore, to bring out the highlights and contrasts, and to acknowledge that there could still be occasions of 'divine' communion between them. However, it is difficult to disguise the fact that, with the possession of Aldworth, a sense of emotional marasmus enters into the Tennysons' life. The family returned to Farringford for Christmas, Emily and Lionel travelling on ahead to ensure Alfred's study and books were in order. They found his sofa and chair ruined by moths and his clothes covered in damp-spots. Emily's wardrobe was affected too, including her wedding dress. In writing to Hallam about the discovery, she tried to mask the despair of this homecoming with a muted optimism: 'If luck comes only when the wedding dress is worn out mine must come now – but what better can I have than I have had with my Husband and my boys. I ask nothing but the old days ever anew, in Him who makes all things new.'

This backward-looking and, in contemporary terms, feminine point of view goes some way towards accounting for the increasing disparity between Alfred and Emily during the last twenty years of their marriage. Once again, Emerson's recognition of a similarity between Tennyson and Hawthorne is instructive; for if they were similar in their individual personality, they were also similar in their choice of partner. The Hawthorne marriage is one of the most idyllic in literary family histories, but it foundered with the move to Europe. Hawthorne the novelist and Tennyson the poet shared a love of the 'old days' but neither was content with a mere repeat of feelings already enjoyed.

Now over sixty, Tennyson might have been tempted to recline in sedate seclusion, and to end his career as a mere Longfellow, or to live the life of the country squire he had always, in fancy, hankered after. But there were still massive reserves of energy hidden in his languid frame, and remaining idle was a torture for him.

On Christmas Day the photographer, Mayall, took a portrait

of Tennyson standing on the Farringford porch. In all the photographic portraits of these last years the eyes, although hooded and myopic, look out into the distance.

7
We Are not Angels Here

What I most am shamed about,
That I most am blamed about;
What I least am loud about,
That I most am praised about.

(EPIGRAM)

E arly in 1871, inspired by alterations that Julia Cameron had had made at Dimbola, the Tennysons decided to have two new rooms built at Farringford. The first, on the ground floor, was a large room designed for parties and dances, and above it, a new study for Alfred, more on a scale with the one he was slowly growing used to at Aldworth. The contract for the new extension was signed on 14 March. Ominously, a few days beforehand a great poplar had fallen, smashing many of the Tennysons' favourite plants.

The building work, which included demolition of part of the greenhouse, and the stripping back of the vines, unsettled Tennyson. Suffering once again from palpitations and a 'fluttering of the nerves', he resolved to go away to Aldworth by himself. He was gone for just three days. On his return, Emily observed, 'A day never to be forgotten. Surely love as one grows older has the tenderness of the eve of parting – the long parting. A. never seemed to me so beautiful & touching & I never had moments of the same sort of happiness. Thank God forever for this time alone with him & our boys.'

One of the last poems written in the old study was a new Idyll, 'The Last Tournament'. This powerful work was composed on a diet of cold milk and bread, and in the wake of a shocked reaction to Swinburne's latest collection, *Songs Before Sunrise*, which Tennyson found blasphemous. Both facts are crucial to an interpretation of the poem.

He had been speaking to Emily about 'the deadly curse of these days' – the loss of belief in a personal God and in the existence of the human soul. 'He feels that we are on the edge of a mortal strife for the life of all that is great in Man and that this will be the cause.' Swinburne's poems were passed to the Tennysons by Julia Cameron, who asked if they were suitable to send to her husband in Ceylon. Not at all, thought Tennyson.

The red/white colour symbolism which suffuses his new poem falls into place in the context of this revulsion and in view of the fact that it was written by a man who had given up red meat and red wine for white bread and milk. As with so many of the Idylls it continues Tennyson's obsession with the theme of sexuality and illustrates a certain equivocality in his revulsion. King Arthur's little fool, Dagonet (a revealing name), is given self-incriminating rein:

> Swine? I have wallowed, I have washed – the world
> Is flesh and shadow – I have had my day.
> The dirty nurse, Experience, in her kind
> Hath fouled me – an I wallowed, then I washed –
> I have had my day and my philosophies –
> And thank the Lord I am King Arthur's fool.

Late in the poem Tristram gives voice to the central loss of faith:

> Vows! did you keep the vow you made to Mark
> More than I mine? Lied, say ye? Nay, but learnt,
> The vow that binds too strictly snaps itself –
> My knighthood taught me this – ay, being snapt –
> We run more counter to the soul thereof
> Than had we never sworn. I swear no more.
>
>   ...The vows!
> O ay – the wholesome madness of an hour –
> They served their use, their time; for every knight
> Believed himself a greater than himself,
> And every follower eyed him as a God;
> Till he, being lifted up beyond himself,
> Did mightier deeds than elsewise he had done,
> And so the realm was made; but then their vows –

410

First mainly through that sullying of our Queen –
Began to gall the knighthood, asking whence
Had Arthur right to bind them to himself?
Dropt down from heaven? washed up from the deep?
They failed to trace him through the flesh and blood
Of our old kings: whence then? a doubtful lord
To bind them by inviolable vows,
Which flesh and blood perforce would violate:
For fell this arm of mine – the tide within
Red with free chase and heather-scented air,
Pulsing full man; can Arthur make me pure
As any maiden child? lock up my tongue
From uttering freely what I freely hear?
Bind me to one? The wide world laughs at it.
And worldling of the world am I, and know
The ptarmigan that whitens ere his hour
Woos his own end; we are not angels here
Nor shall be: vows – I am woodman of the woods
And hear the garnet-headed yaffingale
Mock them: my soul, we love but while we may;

It is impossible and unrewarding to fix a single network of meaning to such a long multi-layered poem as the Idylls. It is the
kind of work which inevitably contains as much subconscious
implication as it does a designed message. Reading the final
Idylls within the context of Tennyson's biography provokes
the feeling that Tennyson was making, probably unawares,
something of a protest against the high-mindedness to which
Emily bound him. This is not the same as saying, as the biographers of the 1920s said *ad nauseam*, that marriage to Emily
destroyed his romantic and lyrical ability. It comes nearer to
identifying with the kind of observation that was increasingly
made about the Tennyson marriage by contemporary visitors of
the 1870s. Most notably, Mrs Gilchrist found Emily's industrious
devotion misdirected. After visiting the Tennysons she wrote to
William Rossetti, 'No one can see Tennyson's profoundly *ennuye*
air and utter lack of the power of enjoyment without realising
what a mistake it all is. Mrs. Tennyson, watching him with
anxious, affectionate solicitude, endeavours to find a remedy in
the very things that cause it — surrounds him ever closer and
closer with the sultry, perfumed atmosphere of luxury and
homage in which his great soul – and indeed any soul would –
droops and sickens.' Anne Gilchrist, a fanatical believer in a life

of solitude and simplicity, was a biased observer, but there grew up a general feeling, much more than in the early days of their marriage, that Emily's efforts and aspirations were not entirely in accord with her husband's nature. At times it seems as if Tennyson, speaking through one or other of the Knights of the Round Table, is apologizing to Emily for failing to live according to her expectations.

8 To Vow or not to Vow

The vow that binds too strictly snaps itself –
My knighthood taught me this – ay, being snapt –
We run more counter to the soul thereof
Than had we never sworn

('THE LAST TOURNAMENT')

Tennyson was in much better health after completing 'The Last Tournament', which he read to Emily at the end of May 1871. She pronounced it 'very grand and terrible'.

Now that much of the work on the house and grounds was completed he felt more settled at Aldworth. They moved there in June and, barring short breaks in London and a ten-day tour of North Wales with Hallam, Tennyson stayed in Sussex for a full six months. His first visitor of the season was the novelist, Turgenev, who entertained them with graphic stories of Russian life and legend, and played backgammon with Alfred.

Early in July he went to London in order to attend the Prime Minister's garden party. Thinking Hallam was likely to join him he bought a new bed to put in the dressing-room of his tiny flat. 'It is touching to hear that A. sees himself to the airing of the bed,' Emily remarked, with the patronizing air of a wife who considers her husband incapable in the practical sphere. But, partly put off by puzzling communications from his father –

'I think it hardly worthwhile for Hallam to come ...'

'Let him do as he wishes ...'

'Decide between yourselves ...'

'He had better not ...'

412

'I dare say Hallam is in the right to his own nature, not to come ...'

'He need not have been afraid of a garden party ...'

Hallam did not make use of the bed. He informed his father of the fact in a telegram which the Post Office incorrectly addressed to Alexander T., 6 (instead of 16) Albert Mansions.

While in London he saw a lot of the Thackeray girls and took Louy Simeon to the British Museum. Before returning to Aldworth on 14 July he wrote a letter to Walt Whitman, thanking him for the gift of his poems, which he had found waiting for him in his London Chambers. The letter was the first in a short but important burst of correspondence between the two writers. From the start Tennyson was both polite and positive in his response to Whitman's work: 'I had previously met with several of your works and read them with interest and had made up my mind that you had a large and lovable nature. I discovered great "go" in your writings and am not surprised at the hold they have taken on your fellow countrymen.'[14]

On the train back to Haslemere Tennyson met up with George Lewes, who was staying at Shottermill with his companion 'Mrs Lewes' (George Eliot). Lewes took Tennyson home with him. It was the first time the poet and George Eliot had confronted one another, but Tennyson, avid novel-reader that he was, had read all of her books and was able to tell her that his favourites were *Adam Bede* and *Silas Marner*. Ever frank, he matched this by saying that he thought *Romola* a little out of her depth.

Despite this criticism, Tennyson was welcomed back to Shottermill a week later. He and Hallam had gone to Haslemere station to meet the Gladstones off the train, but a telegram informed them that their guests would be on a later train. With time to kill, Tennyson decided to take his son to meet the noted author. They were both struck by an unexpected softness in George Eliot's voice, which her strong masculine face did not lead one to expect.

Gladstone joined Alfred and Hallam for long walks on the downs during his visit. At dinner, somewhat intimidated by the Tennysons' reputation for reactionary opinion, Gladstone assured them that he was 'conservative & that he has been driven into measures which he deprecates for fear of more extreme measures from the opposition'.[15]

A few days after the Gladstones had left, Lord Houghton

turned up accompanied by Fanny Kemble and one Mrs Sabine Greville, an eccentric in the Julia Cameron mould. Houghton and his female companions had considerable trouble getting away from Aldworth. Their two horses were unable to manage one of the steep hills surrounding the Tennyson house, despite Houghton's dismounting from the box to ease the load. 'As I should have had to carry Mrs. Greville, you can imagine what we escaped,' Houghton wrote to his wife, after the three of them had been rescued by a London cab returning from Goodwood.

Mrs Greville lived at Milford, near Godalming, so – transport permitting – she was a close neighbour of the Tennysons. But on this occasion she had been overshadowed by Fanny Kemble, who recited passages from Shakespeare in a magnificent voice, with tears streaming down her face.

The day after his birthday – 'A. has a happy birthday tho' we do not mention it to him' – Alfred set off with Hallam for North Wales. Emily was sorry to see them go, but just as vexed, it appears from her Journal, to lose the peacocks which had been adorning the terrace. These birds had been doing too much damage to Tennyson's beloved lawns and were being banished to a neighbouring farm.

After Alfred and Hallam were back at Aldworth, both he and Emily called upon the Leweses at Shottermill, a fact suppressed by early biographies as George Eliot's unmarried state contravened contemporary proprieties. Whilst it was appropriate for Tennyson to call on her as a fellow-professional, it was considered bad form for a woman to condone the arrangement with a purely social visit. On the last day of the month – the day before the Leweses moved away from Haslemere – Alfred went on his own again and read, apparently at Lewes' request, 'Guinevere'. Given the circumstances surrounding the couple's relationship it was a strange choice. George Eliot wept profusely and for once the Victorian waterworks do not seem out of proportion to the stimulus.

9 Parabolic Drift

'Know ye not the Riddling of the Bards?
Confusion, and illusion, and relation,
Elusion, and occasion, and evasion?'

('GARETH AND LYNETTE')

On her return to Farringford at the end of the year Emily suffered a minor collapse. She lost her voice and quite lacked the energy to write letters, a task which Hallam, in addition to acting the perfect nurse, took over. Lionel also helped at the bed and couch-side and Alfred is quoted in her Journal, which she managed to continue for the time being, as saying, 'I leave you to your sons.'

One of the last letters Emily wrote herself, before the onset of her illness, was her half-annual report to Edward FitzGerald, in which she revealed, extraordinarily, that 'Alfred is sorely tempted to go to – Ceylon! – with some friend who is going out there ... to fulfil the dream he has so long had of the Tropics.'[16] There is no mention of this intention elsewhere amongst the Tennyson papers, but if it was seriously held – and there would seem to have been no point in Emily's talking of it to Fitz if it were not – it puts Emily's collapse into a curious perspective. All through their marriage she had been vexed by Tennyson's restlessness and had only gradually come to terms with his forays into London and his summer jaunts. The prospect of a prolonged parting – as a trip to Ceylon must inevitably entail – would not have been faced with fortitude. Emily's illness, which previous commentators have unanimously and too quickly ascribed to overwork, seems more likely to have been initiated by a personal sense of panic. Writing letters and managing two households can certainly be arduous but hardly prostrating. How consciously Emily deployed her ill-health to personal advantage can never be determined; but genuine symptoms of exhaustion were no doubt played for maximum effect.

It is tempting to imagine Tennyson considering a trip to Ceylon with Julia Cameron, but it is much more likely that he anticipated going with one of the Cameron sons. And it was, anyway, like some of his earlier yearnings for the South, a luxurious fantasy rather than a realistic option.

Julia Cameron was still very much a figure in the Tennysons' lives. At the end of their journey from Aldworth, at the beginning of December, she had been at Lymington station to meet them 'with open arms'. But she was not in the best of health herself, being made anxious by the problems of adolescent sons who, in their father's absence, were leading wayward and reprobate lives. Henry gave her greatest worry. He had gone to London to make his name on the stage, inspired no doubt by his mother's own amateur theatricals.

Despite Emily's illness and Julia Cameron's sense of distraction, good use was made of the new ballroom at Farringford during the early part of 1872. Tennyson had returned to 'Gareth and Lynette', which he had abandoned nearly two years beforehand. The poem was still giving difficulty but it was a purely technical problem, unconnected with the diversions of Farringford social life, or the worry about Emily. His explanation of the problem, written to Knowles, indicates how direct exigencies of his art, as well as more amorphous influences, were prompting him towards the writing of plays. 'If I were at liberty, which I think I am not, to put the name of the speaker "Gareth", "Lynette", over the sharp snip-snap of their talk, and so avoid the perpetual "said" and its varieties, the work should be much easier.'[17]

The poem was eventually sent to the press in July but not published until December, a delay caused in the main by Tennyson's own carelessness with the fair copy and the number of necessary revisions entailed. While revising and proofreading the new Idyll, he was also busy making hundreds of minor alterations to the other Idylls, in preparation for a new 'Library' edition. It was a process which allowed him to give renewed thought to the overall structure of the work, and he came to the conclusion that the new Idyll completed the cycle.[18]

It must be frankly stated that some of Tennyson's claims about his early intentions to write an Arthurian epic, in twelve books, do not ring true, and Hallam Tennyson's datings of one or two of his father's early drafts need treating sceptically. The uncertain progress of the Idylls when he did finally begin them seems to give the lie to these early drafts. Why did he not continue with the Idylls after the initial publication of the first four, if his plan was so well laid-out? His excuses were various – he doubted whether he could keep up the same high level – and even while working on these first sections he did not behave like a man writing to a preconceived scheme. 'He troubles himself that the *Idylls* do not form themselves into a whole in his mind and moreover that the subject has not reality enough,' Emily told Alfred's friend Venables.[19] As to clever readings of his intentions by the critics, Tennyson had this to say: 'They have taken my hobby, and ridden it too hard, and have explained some things too allegorically, although there is an allegorical or perhaps rather a parabolic drift in the poem ... Of course Camelot, for instance, a city of shadowy places, is everywhere symbolic of the gradual growth of human beliefs and institutions, and of the spiritual development of man ... The whole is the dream of man coming into practical life and ruined by one sin. Birth is a mystery and death is a mystery, and in the midst lies the tableland of life, and its struggles and performances. It is not the history of one man or of one generation but of a whole cycle of generations.'

It was this aspect of the cycle which he sought to draw out in the new Idyll. Lynette has taken Gareth into a cave, to show him some figures carved into the rock:

'Sir Knave, my knight, a hermit once was here,
Whose holy hand hath fashioned on the rock
The war of Time against the soul of man.
And yon four fools have sucked their allegory
From these dark walls, and taken but the form.
Know ye not these?' and Gareth lookt and read –
In letters like to those the vexillary
Hath left crag-carven o'er the streaming Gelt –
'PHOSPHORUS,' then 'MERIDIES' – 'HESPERUS' –
'NOX' – 'MORS,' beneath five figures, armed men,
Slab after slab, their faces forward all,
And running down the Soul, a Shape that fled
With broken wings, torn raiment and loose hair,
For help and shelter to the hermit's cave.

It suited him for Emily to think that he was writing a pretty, heroic pageant in which the soul was set against the passions and where, however tragical the outcome, the overriding mood was optimistic – the soul might one day vanquish all its foes. But the real theme of his poem was something much more awful and deeply pessimistic, the inexorable and soul-destroying march of Time which, 'slab after slab', routs every good intention and noble scheme.

10 Knocking on Walls

so thou pass
Beneath this archway, then wilt thou become
A thrall to his enchantments, for the King
Will bind thee by such vows, as is a shame
A man should not be bound by, yet the which
No man can keep; but, so thou dread to swear,
Pass not beneath this gateway, but abide
Without, among the cattle of the field.

('GARETH AND LYNETTE')

Tennyson was now wealthy and famous enough to become prey to requests for money. Some of these were easier to ignore than others. As has been shown, where he could be of influence to help younger men he rather enjoyed doing what he could in the way of letters of recommendation. In his own early life he had been highly dependent on gifts from his aunt and from Edward FitzGerald, and during 1871 he had shown a commendable readiness to support a younger poet in a time of need. The thirty-year-old Scottish poet, Robert Buchanan, had written to Tennyson in June importuning him for money. Tennyson sent him £200. Later in the year, after publication of his book *The Drama of the Kings*, Buchanan asked for another £100. The request was wrapped up in a ten-page letter which might have been cause enough for Tennyson to reconsider his earlier generosity. In Buchanan's favour, however, was the fact that he had recently published an article in the *Contemporary Review* entitled 'The Fleshly School of Poetry', attacking Rossetti, and airing many sentiments with which Tennyson was in agreement. Whether Buchanan got his extra £100 or not, by the middle of the following year Tennyson had learnt to be much more wary of being touched for money. In replying to a begging letter from an unknown correspondent, he explained: 'I have within the last two months parted with more than £1000 to one of my own family who was in difficulties. I have given a friend £200 more ...'

Despite the new ballroom, and the extra entertaining that it made possible, those who met Tennyson for the first time in these years, found him self-absorbed. One such was a Yankee Abolitionist and Unitarian minister, the editor of Emily Dickinson, Thomas Higginson. He came to Farringford in June 1872 and, like others before him, was surprised to find not a 'decorous and well-groomed Englishman' but something more resembling a 'reformed Corsican bandit' or 'imperfectly secularized Carmelite monk.'

> He talked freely about his own books, and it seemed to me he must be like Wordsworth ... a little too isolated in his daily life, and too much absorbed in the creations of his own fancy ... I noticed that when he was speaking of other men he mentioned as an important trait in their character whether they liked his poems or not – Lowell, he evidently thought, did not. Perhaps this is a habit of all authors, and it was only that Tennyson spoke out, like a child, what others might have concealed.[20]

This is an important observation. Much criticism of Tennyson's character is hypocritical and lacking in elementary psychology. As for being 'too much absorbed' in his own work, we have to ask – too much for whose or what's sake? Ultimately such statements bring us to absurd hypotheses, whereby we can claim that Tennyson would have been happier had he only aimed at being a minor poet and given only half a mind to his work, and that he might have been more content among the 'cattle of the field'.

Tennyson was fairly brusque with Higginson. He complained of Bayard Taylor's publication of a magazine article about a visit to Farringford, more or less warning the present American guest not to go blathering away about his own visit. (Higginson's autobiography, including the above account, was published several years later.) But this was in healthy defence of his privacy, not anti-American spite, as can be seen from his continuing, friendly correspondence with Walt Whitman.

On 23 May Tennyson wrote again to Whitman, having already sent him the promised picture of himself, one of John Mayall's photographic portraits, which Whitman pronounced 'superb', and kept near him whenever he replied to the Englishman. Tennyson had chosen this photograph because he had been told by several of his friends that it was the best one taken of him. In September, acknowledging receipt of *Democratic*

Vistas, Tennyson felt bold enough to mention a remark he had once made in a conversation about America, to the effect that 'There is a chance that your country may turn out the most immoral the world has ever seen.'

The *Democratic Vistas* had been waiting for Tennyson on his return from a short European tour. Emily was either well enough, or ill enough, as the case may be, to want to accompany Tennyson and the boys. From either point of view, her presence made the trip one of the less notable of Laureate holidays. It is an uncomfortable truth for those of us who are loyal to our families to be forced to acknowledge that sensitivities and perception are at their most acute only when we are on our own or living, temporarily, the single life. This was the essence of Tennyson's visits to London, and his domestic routine was designed to preserve a set proportion of the day as, in effect, a bachelor's domain.

They were away for a month and Emily's letters to Hallam, who was left in Fontainebleau with his French tutor, give the impression that she was again very much the family's impresario. The itinerary took in mainly churches and holy tombs, but Alfred and Lionel also enjoyed a good deal of hiking and mountain climbing. Waiting for a carriage to take them to the top of the Chartreuse they were left in the queue for two hours. Tennyson became overheated and exclaimed to the carrier 'Je croy ais que tu all assiez a la grand Chartreuse: ah je suis troupe.' They left the queue and went to cool off by a mountain stream, returning to the carrier's post just as a carriage pulled up. The vehicle was licensed to carry five passengers but, seeing that his father's 'steam was beginning to rise' again, Lionel persuaded the carrier to take six – '4 fat-French-women and us two.' The miserable horse couldn't take the strain and Lionel jumped out to walk beside it on the narrow track, the French coachman giving dire warnings that he would fall and break his neck.

There were other comical episodes. One evening at the hotel Tennyson knocked on the adjoining wall between his room and Lionel's. However, his sense of layout (notoriously and self-confessedly bad) let him down. He was thumping on the wrong wall and Lionel did not hear. Leaving his room, Lionel 'tried Papa's door, couldn't open it & so locked him in.' Going on to midnight Mass it slowly dawned on him what had happened and he raced back to the hotel to let his father out. They returned to the church for the long Mass, sitting in the gallery and able to see little of what was going on.[21]

They managed one success, climbing on foot to the top of the 6148 ft Dent du Chat, and their guide proclaimed them both good *montagnards*, but Lionel, he added, was like *un oiseau*. Whilst it was good for Tennyson to spend time with his other son, this little remark of the guide's is an indication that Lionel's company was rather too combative to be entirely relaxing.

However, the sporty competition was good for Tennyson's physical health and when Allingham met him later that autumn he described the poet as looking 'well and *big*'. Tennyson and Knowles had called on Allingham in his London lodging. Allingham was invited to join them both for dinner in Clapham and the three walked together over Chelsea Bridge. Tennyson recited Lincolnshire nursery rhymes, but the conversation was sprinkled with heavier matter.

TENNYSON: If I ceased to believe in any chance of another life, and of a great personality somewhere in the Universe, I should not care a pin for anything. People must have some religion.

KNOWLES: I said to Manning – we're all coming back to you by and by.

TENNYSON: I've often thought the day of Rome would come again.

Tennyson was in London to correct the final sheets of 'Gareth and Lynette'. They were delayed, and while he waited for them he composed a warsong for the knights in the first Idyll.

> Blow trumpet, for the world is white with May;
> Blow trumpet, the long night hath rolled away!
> Blow through the living world – 'Let the King reign.'
>
> Shall Rome or Heathen rule in Arthur's realm?
> Flash brand and lance, fall battleaxe upon helm,
> Fall battleaxe, and flash brand! Let the King reign.

The song was written quickly and immediately dispatched to Aldworth. Tennyson was pleased with it – 'I must say that to me the song rings like a grand music' – and justified its rousing tone to Emily, who must have carped a little. He had to send her this defence: 'It seems to me all right for the knights going forth to break the heathen. It is early times yet, and many years are to elapse before the more settled time of "Gareth".'

The point of the song, as Hallam was to observe, was also to emphasize that the aspirations and ambitions of Arthur and his knights were doomed to downfall. As Tennyson stood back from the whole work, tinkered with it, and added the final Idylls, he saw more clearly than he had at first that its religious theme had a contemporary interpretation. The 'Rome' of the opening Idyll was, historically, the Rome of an occupying army, but thematically it was the Rome of the Holy See, the Catholic church. Arthur, again historically, was a native hero imposing law and order on a land left to rot by an absentee imperialist power; thematically he was sometimes Christ himself, the King to whom the holy vows were made, and at other times he and his order represent the Protestant opposition to Catholicism. As Tennyson's part in the snippet of conversation recorded by Allingham makes clear, he was not unmoved by the notion, encouraged by Manning, Newman and the whole 'Oxford' movement, that Protestantism had had its day. Manning, a Roman Catholic since 1851, was then Archbishop of Westminster, and also a member of the Metaphysical Society. Tennyson met him at the meeting on 12 November and gave him a copy of 'Gareth', for which he was warmly thanked.

An important defence of Tennyson was published in the December issue of *Macmillan's Magazine*. It was written by R.H. Hutton, editor of the *Spectator*, eminent reviewer and religious commentator. The tone of the piece is more important than its content, for it was written in the context of an increasing backlash against Tennyson's work. The criticism, which had begun in the late 1860s with Alfred Austin, was continued into the early 1870s, with essays by Swinburne and his sympathizers. The scale of the onslaught was every bit as savage as the early onslaught of the 1840s but has always appeared of less significance because of his current fame and commercial success. However, fame is of no protection in these matters; Tennyson continued to take every review of his work, every essay and book about him, very much to heart. He even found things to complain about in Hutton's supportive piece.

The thrust of Swinburne's case against the Idylls was that Tennyson had stripped the ancient story of all its tragic authority, by making Arthur a rather incredible wittol, unblemished by the history of incest which, in original versions of the story, sets in motion the tragic train of events. 'Treated as he has treated it, the story is rather a case for the divorce-court

422

than for poetry.' Swinburne had a fair point to make about the figure of Arthur, but spoilt his case with too high-minded an attack on the figure of Vivien. In criticizing Tennyson for creating a character more abominable than anything in French literature, he was more interested in scoring self-righteous points and, by implication, defending the morality of his own poetry, than in making useful observations. In fact, what he said about Vivien was accurate – 'it is the utterly ignoble quality of Vivien which makes her so unspeakably repulsive' – but his conclusion that she is therefore 'unfit for artistic treatment' and 'simply a subject for the police-court' proves that Tennyson had the more modern outlook.

Hutton's essay was long and covered the whole of Tennyson's career (it was updated for inclusion in his *Literary Essays* of 1888) but it dealt specifically with Swinburne's criticism of the Idylls. Tennyson welcomed the defence but carped at some of the reservations which Hutton, with typical honesty, mixed into his piece. These were all linked to a general notion that the 'gorgeous inward-picture gallery' character of his very early verse continuously threatened to subvert the governing notion of a poem. 'Whenever Tennyson's pictorial fancy has had in it any degree in its power to run away with the guiding and controlling mind, the richness of the workmanship has to some extent overgrown the spiritual principle of his poems.' The essay also resurrected Coleridge's early criticism of Tennyson's juvenilia, and this rankled the poet. He wrote to Grove: 'It is true that in the folly of youth I played some tricks with orthography and metre – but Coleridge ought – only odd men get shut up in themselves – to have seen that it was from wantonness not from ignorance.' Odd men shut up in themselves take exception to the staunchest of defences, but in one regard Tennyson was justified in reacting coolly to Hutton's piece. 'His calling the Idylls an Epic which they are not is to me a misnomer and may set my foes blaming ...' Hutton had vigorously dismissed Swinburne's jibes about Arthur and Vivien, but all in terms of Tennyson's supposedly epic conception. In the case of Arthur he had had to choose between two inconsistent elements in the Arthurian legends – on the one hand the element of primordial shame and on the other the element of Christian mysticism and spiritual glory. And so Arthur is there as Christian hero, priggish in his perfection perhaps, but necessarily so. Swinburne, Hutton said, had quite simply missed the point about Vivien's lack of dignity. She was in the poem to show 'the power which sensual creatures, partly *because* they are without dignity, may attain over the highest and most experienced intellects unprotected by something higher yet.' However, Hutton had to agree that her place in the poem was premature, in terms of the thematic movement of the epic. Although Tennyson's conception of the poem had been changing, with each successive addition of a new Idyll, he was quite right to cavil at this insistence that a long poem must necessarily be in the epic tradition. Swinburne's attack on the Idylls is pompous and wrong-headed simply because he insisted on reading the poem as a traditional epic, instead of a modern medley of vignettes on a medieval theme.

11   High-kitsch

their fears
Are morning shadows huger than the shapes
That cast them, not those gloomier which forego
The darkness of that battle in the West,
Where all of high and holy dies away.

('TO THE QUEEN')

W. G. Ward, the Roman Catholic theologian, had had property on the Isle of Wight since 1858, but he did not begin to get to know Tennyson well until he built a house at Weston, a mile or so from Farringford, in 1871. The friendship between Tennyson and Ward was far more important than any surviving papers hint. The fact that they were such close neighbours meant that they had no need to correspond, and their friendship was built upon philosophical and theological conversation of the kind that men indulged in late into the evening over wine and tobacco. This tendency of the 'Victorians' for high-minded conversation is easily ridiculed, but our own age is probably unique in the paucity of attention it pays to problems of being and belief. Certainly, Tennyson's need for such companionship was profound and Ward – 'subtle at tierce and quart of mind with mind' – was the ideal companion, sufficiently different in opinion to be provocative. By the winter of the early part of 1873 the association was well-established, and Emily reported to Hallam on 3 February: 'Poor Papa has not a soul to speak to now for Mr. Ward is gone away for some weeks.'

'I must do my best,' she added, acknowledging in that brief sentence her own inadequacy to satisfy Alfred's need for a certain kind of spiritual companionship which, almost by definition, had to be masculine. And as if in response to this pessimistic testimony, Tennyson set off for London a week later. Soon after arriving he was giving hints that he was about to change publisher again. Amidst worldwide financial collapse it was known that Strahan was in difficulties and Tennyson wrote home to Emily that Arnold White, their lawyer, would 'decide whether I am to remain with my publishers or not'.

There were negotiations of a more domestic kind as well. Lady Franklin had proposed sharing the lease of 4, Seamore Place with Alfred and Emily, who were to decide which part of the year they would like it for. The arrangements, as in the case of most of Tennyson's money matters, were a mixture of precision and imprecision. He agreed to lend Lady Franklin £3500 (at an interest of four and a half per cent) so that she could complete purchase of the lease, and the first possibility was that 'We should hire it for the season from February to July, live there for the first half of the season, and let it for the second half, paying Lady Franklin £500 but almost recouping ourselves by subletting it.' However, 'Nothing is fixt,' he told Emily in a letter of 20 February.

In return for receiving a copy of the 'very fine new edition' of the Idylls – the Imperial Library Edition, containing the new Epilogue 'To The Queen' – Queen Victoria invited Tennyson to Windsor so that he might be shown Prince Albert's mausoleum. The invitation was not immediately welcome. He had already been in London a fortnight and was keen to return home. He wrote to Emily, 'I said deuce take all kings and Empresses and deuce take the Bruce, but I suppose I shall have to go and stop here till I go.' What is worthy of remark here, rather than the irreverence, is the relaxed nature of his letters and notes to Emily at this time – in marked contrast to the self-consciousness of earlier years.

The visit took place on 6 March. The Queen, in the presence of the Dean of Westminster and Lady Augusta Stanley, showed him some of the detailed decoration on the building and Tennyson admired the light brightness of the design, remarking that he wished funerals could be in white. 'Why should death, which was already so dreadful in itself, be clothed with everything to make it worse, as if it were the end of all things?' the Queen paraphrased her Laureate in her diary. Tennyson's own report of the visit, sent to Emily, was somewhat abbreviated. He and the Dean 'pottered about till the Queen and Princess Beatrice arrived – the Queen took me into the building and explained everything.'

A fortnight after this meeting with the Queen, when Tennyson had returned to Farringford, he received a letter from Gladstone offering him a baronetcy. The offer was not immediately agreeable. Following the visit to Frogmore, the Dean of Westminster had made representations on Tennyson's behalf, fully primed 'with all the history, as far as I know it, of the d'Eyncourt title' by Knowles, with a view to his getting a peerage. The offer of a lesser, non-hereditary title put him in a quandary, and his wily way of trying to play the situation for maximum advantage was testimony to the bargaining abilities developed in his dealings with publishers. Prompted by Knowles – 'I do not see why you should not say to G. that you accept it, but that if possible it should be given to your son' – Tennyson sent Gladstone two letters in reply. One was a short and gracious acceptance of the offer. The other:

I do not like to trouble you about my own personal matters in the midst of your absorbing public work; but not only on account of my feeling for yourself, but also for the sake of that memory which we share, I speak frankly to you, when I say, that I had rather we should remain plain Mr. and Mrs., and that, if it were possible, the title should first be assumed by our son at any age it may be thought right to fix upon: but like enough this is against all precedent and could not be managed; and on no account would I have suggested it were there the least chance of the Queen's construing it into a slight of the proffered honour. I hope that I have too much of the old-world loyalty left in me not to wear my Lady's favour against all comers, should you think that it would be more agreeable to H.M. that I should do so.

In that case please to accept the accompanying letter as the expression of my acceptance . . .[22]

Gladstone responded promptly. Attempting an innovation such as was suggested by Tennyson would not be 'advisable' and he could only suggest that, 'if the idea of the posthumous honour meets your view, it would be easy for me to place the Queen's wish upon record, in some document which could be handed on till the arrival of the (I trust) distant period when it would come to be acted upon'.

Tennyson, somewhat miffed that his bargaining position had met with such a nimble but emphatic response, told Gladstone that as far as his personally receiving a baronetcy was concerned he, 'was not likely to change his mind on the subject. For the rest I leave myself to your hands'. And there the matter was left, the ball once more in Gladstone's, or his successor's, court.

It was perhaps to make up for this disappointment that Julia Cameron contrived one of her final grand gestures on the island. Making a wreath of red and white blooms, and gathering together a sizeable body of people, she processed to Farringford, announcing that the Doge of Freshwater was to wed the sea. There was the usual battle of wills – and the usual outcome. Alfred, taken down to the bay, was made to throw the wreath upon the waves and, conducting himself with proper solemnity, recite some appropriate lines. If ever a television documentary is made about Tennyson's life on the island, this scene will surely be in it. One imagines that whoever plays the part of Tennyson will be made to declaim some verses from the main body of his work (an extract from 'The Sea-Fairies' perhaps.) My own hunch is that, however solemn the manner of delivery, the lines spoken are more likely to have been of the impromptu character of some of his Epigrams – shot through with pugnacious wit. It was not in Tennyson's character to allow himself to be made the puppet of such high-kitsch.

Current with his machinations for the baronetcy there was ongoing uncertainty about his publisher. With Strahan's financial failure now apparent, Tennyson found himself the subject of overtures from two of the publisher's ex-partners, James Virtue and Henry King. Virtue's method of wooing an author was a peculiar one. He blamed Strahan's failure on the generosity of his terms with the poet. 'The result of the last four years arrangement has shown that the principle of giving a certain fixed sum per annum ... is not a sound one,' he wrote to Knowles, who was once again acting as informal agent. Virtue's proposal was that, to help the new house 'recoup ourselves' the

'Pocket' and 'Library' editions should be published for the next five years 'without royalty'.

By comparison, King's competing proposal, offering £5000 a year for the next five years, and just five per cent commission on new titles, was obviously the more favourable and Tennyson instructed White to see to the formalities. It is not insignificant, though not often remarked upon, that this latest change of publisher and the rather depressed financial climate coincided with the start of a new phase in Tennyson's career. Although he was busy adding 'Balin & Balan' to the Idylls (he now thought 'Merlin and Vivien' came too early in the sequence) – he knew well-enough that his Muse was drying up. 'Your Muse is prolific as Hecuba and mine by the side of her an old barren cow,' he wrote to Browning, on receipt of *Red Cotton Night-Cap Country*. It may well have been that receipt of a fixed sum per annum was giving his Muse the wrong signals.

12   Two Voices

Hast thou no voice, O peak,
That standest high above all?
'I am the voice of the Peak,
I roar and I rave for I fall.'

('THE VOICE AND THE PEAK')

On Hallam's twenty-first birthday, 11 August 1873, he and his father set off on a month-long tour to the Italian lakes. 'A.T.' – as Hallam referred to his father in his Journal – was in fine form, obsessed with the sound of rushing torrents and the cascades of water 'flowing in great gusts'. On 18 August, standing beside one such cataract, Tennyson recited, in a voice which sounded 'very awful', the following sonnet by Wordsworth:

Two Voices are there; one is of the sea,
One of the mountains; each a mighty Voice:
In both from age to age thou didst rejoice,

They were thy chosen music, Liberty!
There came a Tyrant, and with holy glee
Thou fought'st against him; but hast vainly striven:
Thou from thy Alpine holds at length art driven,
Where not a torrent murmurs heard by thee.
Of one deep bliss thine ear hath been bereft:
Then cleave, O cleave to that which still is left;
For, high-souled Maid, what sorrow would it be
That Mountain floods should thunder as before,
And Ocean bellow from his rocky shore,
And neither awful Voice be heard by thee![23]

How stirring it must have been to hear the 'very awful' voice of Tennyson, using the words of a previous Laureate as vehicle for expression. The moment is full of meaning. The sonnet, written 'On the Subjugation of Switzerland' would seem, in the awesomeness of its delivery to have taken on a special personal significance, which eventually found expression in the muddled but pregnant 'The Voice and the Peak' begun later in this holiday. Remembering the ceremony on the shore of Freshwater Bay it might have come to seem to Tennyson that from now onwards his Muse would be confined to one Voice – the mature voice of the Ocean. No longer was it fleet enough to skitter down ravines – the voice of Fancy, of the torrent, was mute. But 'Cleave, O cleave to that which still is left' – there is the line which brought out the full 'very awful' tone in Tennyson's delivery, giving voice to an artistic commitment to carry on with whatever powers remained.

In contrast, much of the month was filled with merry-making and father and son returned to Farringford on 11 September. A month later Hallam and Lionel both left for Trinity. By now it might be expected that Tennyson had grown used to these autumnal partings but this one made him as morose as some of the earliest. 'A. wanders forlorn,' Emily recorded.

For a diversion, and as he had no work to settle to, Alfred took Emily to London at the end of October. During this stay Tennyson went to Woolner's studio daily, to sit for a new bust. In the evenings there were meetings with old friends such as Venables, Spedding and Forster. When Carlyle met Tennyson at a dinner on 11 November he found the poet, 'distinctly rather wearisome; nothing coming from him that did not smack of utter indolence'. But Carlyle never had any sympathy for poetical insouciance, and it is easy to imagine that Tennyson's torpor was exaggerated on this occasion by the effects of port and for Carlyle's benefit. He had a roguish sense of playing various parts of his personality for best effect, and this element of his character grew more pronounced as the years went by.

In the middle of November Alfred left Emily in London and went to Cambridge to visit Hallam and Lionel. Although Hallam remembered that his father was 'as happy as a boy' on this visit, the memories which it brought back eventually put him into a sombre mood and by 27 November, when he had been back in London for ten days, Emily described her husband as 'out of spirits'. As usual, especially in her correspondence with Edward Lear, she gave vent to an air of frustration in connection with Alfred's insisting on staying in a place which brought him no peace of mind:

> ... nothing short of the Premiership and the modest confidence of genius befitting could make me happy in London, I think, unless it were the fact that our boys found work suited to them here and that their home was with us, or that I saw my Ally really the better and happier for being here. On the contrary he has been poorly here and out of spirits and at Aldworth he was well and cheerful. However notwithstanding he is convinced that it is good for him to be here. I suppose it is and so here I am content to be ...[24]

It was almost certainly memories of the past, stirred by his recent visit to Cambridge, and feeding into the resigned but stalwart facing up to failing powers (within a certain range) that put Tennyson so out of sorts.

The Tennysons stayed in London until 23 December, making full use of the facilities at Seamore Place for entertaining. Hallam and Lionel joined them from Cambridge, together with one of their new friends, R.C. Jebb, who saw in Emily 'something of the sweet queenliness of a French mistress of the manor of the old regime.' The queen was glad to have returned to her court in time for Christmas. 'No doubt it is good for one to be a little in London but how glad & thankful I am to be in our peaceful home.'

13 Neuromimesis

I would I were a milkmaid,
To sing, love, marry, churn, brew, bake, and die,
Then have my simple headstone by the church,
And all things lived and ended honestly.

(ELIZABETH IN QUEEN MARY III, v)

Soon into the New Year of 1874 Tennyson, working in Hallam's room for extra warmth, began the first of his dramas, *Queen Mary*. Much of his reading aloud at night, while in London, had been from Shakespeare, and he continued the practice at Farringford. In January he began reading the Tragedies; by the end of the month he was on *Othello*, but did not get past its opening act. 'We agree that Othello is too tragic to be read aloud,' Emily wrote, and it was put aside in favour of *Henry IV*.

That Tennyson should have considered writing historical dramas at this time was not, as Edmund Gosse observed, a 'curious trait'. There was an inevitability about it, almost an obligation. If there was no longer any strong financial incentive to publish a new collection of poems, the rewards he stood to make from a successful staging of a script were real enough, as evidenced the previous year by the outstanding success of *Charles the First* by W.G. Wills.

Whilst making a start on his first play (studying the historical sources – J.A. Froude's *Mary*, the ecclesiastical histories of Collier, Fuller and Burnett, and of course Holinshed), Tennyson was given a Laureate's duty to perform.

'A Welcome to Alexandrovna', composed for the home-coming of the Duke of Edinburgh and his bride, a Russian Duchess, caused him some anguish, but he delivered it to the Queen a few days before the newly-weds landed in England. It was published in *The Times* on 7 March and Tennyson went to London for the procession through the capital on the 12th. Knowles had taken seats in Regent Street so that Tennyson had a good view. The Princess was large, imperial-looking and neither pretty nor plain. She and the Queen were both wagging their heads as if they were made of India rubber. The day was spoilt by the weather – cold and snowy, with *The Times* reporting that 'the Russian princess had surely brought down upon us true Russian weather' – and by the information that in the chorus to his poem Tennyson had put the accent on the penultimate rather than the antepenultimate (as Emily put it) syllable of Alexandrovna.

Tennyson stayed in London at Seamore Place, with Emily's Aunt Franklin. There was continual entertaining. 'There is another party today here and I wish there was not, and another tomorrow at Knowles' and I wish there was not,' he wrote to Emily, rather disingenuously – for by all accounts he unfroze at these gatherings in the time-honoured way, taking an entire bottle of port to himself at each meal.

Back on the island, and while working on the first Act of *Queen Mary*, Tennyson received the gift of an essay by Benjamin Blood, American mystic and philosopher. Replying to Blood, Tennyson gave a long description of his trance-like experiences:

> ... all at once as it were out of the intensity of the conscious-ness of individuality the individuality itself seemed to dissolve and fade away into boundless being – and this not a confused state but the clearest of the clearest, the surest of the surest, utterly beyond words – where Death was an almost laughable impossibility – the loss of personality (if so it were) seeming no extinction but the only true life.[25]

Blood's own speciality was for explicating the revelations associ-ated with anaesthetics. Tennyson was making the point that although he had once had a dreamlike experience under the influence of chloroform, the state which he was really interested in was that which came upon him when he was wide awake. His ability to talk of death as a laughable impossibility helps to explain the new wave of energy he was able to muster for the writing of his plays. Apart from the odd twinge of gout and rheumatic ache, his hypochondria was at a low ebb during the next ten years.

In July he was saddened by news of his friend Brookfield's death. They had seen a good deal of one another during the winter and this sudden loss affected Tennyson – but not deeply.

> You man of humorous-melancholy mark,
> Dead of some inward agony – is it so?

Our kindlier, trustier Jacques, past away!
I cannot laud this life, it looks so dark:
Σκιας ὄναρ – dream of a shadow, go –
God bless you. I shall join you in a day.

('TO THE REV. W.H. BROOKFIELD')

Of all Tennyson's Trinity friends, Brooks, as he was affectionately known, seems the most benign – a nice chap who could
put others at their ease. The sonnet, from which the lines above
are taken, is a smooth piece of work, lacking the emotional force
of most of Tennyson's memorial verse. Was he becoming
inured to the deaths of his contemporaries? There is an inevitable and perfectly human sense in which this was true; but
despite the poem's final line (which is not, of course, intended
literally) it is clear from Tennyson's reactions to bereavement
from this time on that he had girded himself for the long haul.
There was work to be done, and working in a new medium must
have been a little like starting over again.

He put *Queen Mary* aside for a month in the summer and the
whole family travelled to France, first of all staying in Paris,
where they went to see several plays at the Théâtre Français.
Moving on to Tours, Lionel was left to attend on Emily, while
Alfred took Hallam on to the Pyrenees. There was much walking
and mountain-climbing, and a final trip through the Valley of
Cauteretz. But although Tennyson was in a region charged with
memories, his mind was on other things – and perhaps this was
one return too many. He and Hallam headed back to Tours and,
with the family complete, started for home.

Soon after arriving Emily made the final entry in her Journal,
which had been left blank since February of this year: 'I had to
answer many letters from unknown correspondents, asking
advice from A. as to religious questions, and desiring criticism
of poems, etc. and I became very ill and could do but little, so
my Journal ends here.'

Once again it is unclear why letter-writing should suddenly
have caused her to collapse, especially so soon after a month-
long holiday. There were emotional as well as physical strains
involved in being the wife of the Laureate and it might be to
these that we should look to explain her illness. There had been
a trial-run, so to speak, of her debility more than two years
beforehand. On that occasion her sickness was, in part, trig-
gered by her husband's threatened trip to Ceylon. He did not

go. She made a partial recovery. And whilst he was not working, but taking her to London and joining her in evening entertainments, although she might complain and wish she was in her own home, she seemed in reasonable shape. But now he was hard at work on an intensive venture, and had less time for her. Even on holiday, she had been deposited in Tours so that he could go off to the mountains with Hallam.

When Tennyson wrote to Palgrave in the middle of October informing him of Emily's illness, and describing his month away, there is a marked coldness in the references to his wife: 'We had not much of a tour. We stayed a week in Paris and then went on to St. Germain which she found too cold for her. Then on to Tours where we stopped some weeks at Hotel de l'Univers but where it was still very blustering and by no means warm.' And at the end of the letter he adds again, 'Not much of a tour.'[26]

Emily was, throughout her life, physically frail, and it would be wrong to suggest that there was *no* physical cause for her collapse. But physical energies can be depleted in psychological ways. She was an emotional woman with a deep love of her husband and a reverence for the ways of the home. But she also had a high regard for her own person and intellect, and did not like to be ignored. She did not take to her couch in a petulant attempt to be nursed and petted but, on the other hand, just as it is wrong to suggest this as her sole motivation for sickening, it is just as wrong to suggest that there was no element of self-interest in her newly-exaggerated invalid state – that she was a saint, incapable of selfish feelings.

Tennyson was too aware of the symptoms of nervous hysteria, not to have some inkling that much of Emily's disability was psychosomatic. One of his own doctors, Sir James Paget, had published a series of lectures in the *Lancet* during the 1870s detailing the different conditions in which 'nervous mimicries' manifest themselves. One of the most notable disorders of those suffering a nervous complaint was 'spinal neuromimesis'. To read Paget's descriptions of this disorder, you would think that he had used Emily Tennyson as a case-study. The patient will complain of 'a sense of weakness in the lower limbs, so that they are scarcely capable of supporting the weight of the body; and even actual paralysis.'[27] The editor of Emily's letters, James O. Hoge, believes that her weakness was indeed physical, although he acknowledges that 'her specific ailments are rarely particularized.' His suggestion that her infirmity was to some extent the product of wish-fulfilment on Alfred's part – who, it seems, was a 'husband predisposed to regard the highest type of woman as a rather unphysical being' – is both undermining to his own position and wrong-headed. It is particularly wrong-headed in relation to the attitude towards and understanding of women contained in Tennyson's dramas.

During the final part of the year he managed to work on with *Queen Mary* getting Hallam and Lionel to send him books from Trinity when they were not available from the London Library. Emily, under the treatment of a young doctor named Dabbs, from Newport, was receiving phosphorous, a homeopathic treatment associated with hypersensitivity, but there was no significant improvement and Alfred had to inform Lady Franklin that they would not be taking up their share of the winter lease of Seamore Place that year.

14   Not Much of a Send-off

There's no glory
Like his who saves his country

(KNYVETT IN *QUEEN MARY* II, i)

At the end of the year the baronetcy question was again raised. Disraeli, the new Prime Minister, prompted by the Queen's Private Secretary, who seemed not to have been informed of the outcome of the previous communication between Gladstone and Tennyson, repeated the offer of a baronetcy. Tennyson replied saying he had already been made such an offer, had refused it for himself, but accepted on behalf of his oldest son who, it was understood, would be offered it on his, Alfred Tennyson's, death.

This was all news to Disraeli and in his reply he was quick to quash any illusions the Laureate might be under regarding the informal understanding he had reached with Gladstone:

It would be presumptuous in me to comment on any understanding beween Mr. Gladstone and yourself, that after your
death, provided he is Prime Minister, a baronetcy should be
conferred on your oldest son; but to prevent misconception, I
think it my duty to apprise you, that no person, except Mr
Gladstone, can be bound by such an agreement, and that to
attempt to extend it to the Crown, would be a course not only
anomalous but unconstitutional.[28]

Tennyson sent a copy of this letter to Gladstone, without
comment.

On her sofa, Emily's mind was not idle. She invented some
form of device for cutting the emission of smoke from chimneys.
'It is so simple that it has no doubt been tried before,' Alfred
told Knowles. 'She requests you to have it put – by Act of
Parliament – in every house in London before we come thither
again, that we mayn't die of fog.'

Alfred stayed at Farringford with Emily until the middle of
March, by which time he had completed *Queen Mary* and was
ready for some days away. He visited Knowles at The Hollies
and, very impressed with some cheap Co-operative port, wrote
to Emily to tell her that he had reserved a bulk order for himself.
On 20 March he went to the Boat Race (there were five Trinity
men in the crew) and afterwards had tea with the children's
writer and fabulist George Macdonald. He found much of
interest in Macdonald's modest but diverse library and
borrowed a copy of the Gaelic *Ossian*.

He did not stay away long and on his return found Emily
continued 'exceedingly unwell'. By the beginning of June he had
a trial edition of his play ready. Knowles had read it and given
his reaction. It appears that Emily was too unwell to give hers.
She only had energy to read for two minutes at a time.

Everything seemed propitiously set for *Queen Mary*'s success.
The theatre in London was enjoying a renaissance. There were
over forty houses open and the introduction of gas had
improved the lighting of stage and auditorium. A newly-
educated middle-class was looking for more intelligent fare than
the popular melodramas and in their place developed a genre of
domestic comedies known as 'tea cup and saucer' plays. In 1871
an American had taken over a derelict theatre called the
Lyceum, had engaged an actor called Henry Irving, and was
soon glorying in the successes of plays like *The Bells* and W.G.

Wills's *Charles The First*. In 1874 Irving performed at the Lyceum as *Hamlet*. It was, at that time, an unorthodox interpretation of the part, and Tennyson often claimed that Irving's originality in the role depended heavily on advice he had given the actor the previous year.

First reactions to *Queen Mary* were good. Froude, who received one of the proof copies, wrote to say that its anti-Papist message struck 'a more fatal blow than a thousand pamphleteers and controversialists.' Browning thought it 'astonishingly fine' and was immediately going to read it again.

The modern reader approaches the play with much more trepidation, so undermined has been the standing of the Dramas. Indeed, there is no good, authoritative edition of them. Part of the trepidation involves a fear that the plays will use language similar to that found in *Idylls of the King*, which will make the reading difficult, and render all the dialogue false. In fact, most of the plays are very easy to read and *Queen Mary* is one of the best. It is easy to follow and, if anything surprises or disappoints the reader in a play conceived on a Shakespearian scale, it is the very absence of exalted moments and high poetry. Everything is on too even a keel. Taken a scene at a time, Tennyson's reconstruction of the key historical moments is very effective, but there is insufficient variety of tone. Henry James's well-known criticism only glances at the problem. 'It is simply a dramatised chronicle, without an internal structure, taking its material in pieces as history hands them over, and working each one into an independent scene – usually with rich ability. It has no shape; it is cast in no mould; it has neither beginning, middle, nor end, save the chronological ones.'[29] For historical (and biographical) purposes the chronological events are given, and a work has to derive its shape from the method by which it makes its selection. It is not true that there is no development between Tennyson's scenes – the historical theme, and its contemporary implications, are skilfully handled. The trouble is purely that Tennyson has gone to his task too seriously and the result is too unrelentingly earnest. There is insufficient acknowledgement that a play needs to enthrall its audience, not on the page, but in its action on the stage.

By the time the play was in print Tennyson already had a commitment from the Lyceum to stage it, and had asked Charles Stanford – then only twenty-two and introduced to his father by Hallam who had met the young musician as an organist at

Trinity – to compose the incidental music. The petty jealousies and brazen subterfuge which this commission set in train was just one of the means by which Tennyson was quickly initiated into the ways of the theatre. He was also told, very quickly, by Irving that the play would need shortening before it was ready for performance.

Although Hallam was still officially registered at Trinity he had been at home looking after his mother for most of the year, and for all of the summer term. Tennyson's summer was disturbed by news of a pirated edition of *The Lover's Tale*, the poem about which he was always so preternaturally sensitive. 'I am in a great rage at this scandalous business!!!' he wrote to the parties concerned, insisting that every copy of the book should be handed over to him.

His rage was somewhat alleviated by the continuing arrival of reactions to his play – nearly all of them good. Gladstone praised his friend on 'the grace and ease with which you move in new habiliments' and FitzGerald wrote to say he had already bought the play before his 'gift-copy' arrived. 'Still your old Fitzcrotchet', he carped a little at the loss of 'thee' and 'thou' from the characters' speech – a reservation not likely to be shared by many a modern reader – but it was a chummy letter, quite unlike the coldness he had exhibited to some of Alfred's new work in the past.

After receiving Browning's appreciation, Emily, from her sofa, directed Alfred to reply, which he did, giving an exact transcription of their conversation.

EMILY: Why don't you write and thank Mr. Browning for his letter?

ALFRED: Why should I? I sent him my book and he acknowledged it.

EMILY: But such a great and generous acknowledgement.

ALFRED: That's true.

EMILY: Then you should write: he has given you your crown of violets.

ALFRED: He is the greatest-brained poet in England. Violets fade: he has given me a crown of gold.

EMILY: Well I meant the Troubadour crown of golden violets: pray write: you know I would if I could; but I am lying here helpless and horizontal and can neither write nor read.

ALFRED: Then I'll go up and smoke my pipe and write to him.

EMILY: You'll go up and concoct an imaginary letter over your pipe, which you'll never send.

ALFRED: Yes I will. I'll report our talk.[30]

Tennyson revealed his cavalier attitude towards revising his play for the stage in a reply to another correspondent. 'Although I meant my play to be acted, I would not let that bias me from writing a full Historical Drama. I knew that half of it would have to be excised, but I leave all that business to Mr. Irving and the Batemans.'

And leave it he did – by going off on another family tour of the Continent. Although Emily was still very unwell it was thought the southern sun would do her good. Eleanor Locker, the daughter of Tennyson's friend, accompanied the family to serve as Emily's informal lady-in-waiting. The holiday fell into the same pattern as the previous year's. Emily, Eleanor and Lionel were deposited at Pau, while Hallam and his father again set off for the Pyrenees, Tennyson taking several Balzac novels with him for holiday reading.

Holed up at Pau, Lionel and Eleanor, with Emily's blessing and encouragement, became engaged. Tennyson, in theory, was a great supporter of young love being offered no impediment. He too blessed the engagement but made it known that with Lionel aged only twenty-one and still at university it would be some time before they could marry. However, he was soon doing all he could to help Lionel find a position.

The Tennysons were back at Farringford by the end of September and Alfred, refreshed from his month away, was quick to take up the cause of his play. Mrs Bateman, who had taken over management of the Lyceum from her deceased husband, was apparently back-tracking on her commitment to stage *Queen Mary*. 'I cannot but think Mrs. B. has used me badly in keeping the agreement so many months unsigned and then stating an objection,' Tennyson told Knowles, ending in exasperation, 'Altogether I have ceased to care whether the Batemans have it or not.'

This autumn was not a good time for Tennyson. The southern sun had done nothing for Emily; antagonisms in connection with *Queen Mary* escalated, interrupting the start he was trying to make on a new play; and Julia Cameron left the island for good, moving permanently to Ceylon.

Published at the same time as *Queen Mary*, a new edition of the *Idylls* was illustrated with a series of twelve woodcuts taken from photographic settings on which Mrs Cameron had expended a vast amount of time and energy. Two hundred and forty-five photographs had been taken to arrive at the final dozen. Julia had given the photographs for Alfred's volume 'out of friendship', but his failure to consider offering her anything for her efforts hurt.

As a photographer, 1875 marked the high point of Julia Cameron's success. In addition to the publication of the *Illustrated Idylls* she had exhibitions in London and Bournemouth; there was a growing market for her prints; and a special folio edition of some of her best pictures. Her biographers have not been able to ascertain with certainty her reason for leaving England. Some believe it was at her husband's insistence. He was now over eighty and wanted to live out his days in Ceylon. Some think it was for the sake of her older sons, who had taken over the estates. And some suggest it was merely a ruse to take the rakish Henry away from the temptations of the English capital. The truth probably involves a combination of reasons, including the lack of tangible gratitude shown by Tennyson for all her support.

Her relationship with Farringford was not what it had been. The Tennysons were now on the island for only a small part of the year; their sons were a good deal away; Emily was unwell; Alfred was working earnestly. Very simply, the period of 'high-kitsch' was over.

There is no record that Tennyson ever said goodbye to her, although he was on the island at the time. No doubt he did, if not in any extravagant way. He was too absorbed in vexations arising over the revisions to his play for a grand send-off, and in dealing with the mounds of packets and letters accumulated while they had been away. He was working slowly through them but with Emily unwell and incapable he could hardly keep up with each new day's post, let alone the backlog. Much of his correspondence these days consisted in requests for donations to charities and memorial funds, or even straightforward begging letters. He sent £5 here and £2 there and did his best to discriminate between genuine and unworthy causes.

But it was the bother with his play that concerned him most. He wrote to Irving repeating that 'if Mrs Bateman does not care to have the play acted, neither do I.' No sooner had he posted the letter than he regretted it, seeing the fun the press might have after a public announcement of the play's withdrawal.

MRS BATEMAN CANNOT MEET MR TENNYSON'S TERMS.

MR TENNYSON STANDS OUT AGAINST AGREEMENT.

Suddenly he was in the mood for going on 'let it be damned or not.' Furious that his lawyer, White, was away – 'White had no right to go and leave me foundered' – he wrote to Knowles seeking advice and assistance.

Knowles quickly arranged for a fresh contract to be drawn up and posted it to Alfred for approval and signature. Emily wanted him 'to throw the thing over' and he had nearly returned to the same conclusion himself. However, he signed the paper and sent it back to Knowles who, it seems, had added in a 5 December deadline for the signature of other parties.

The deadline came and went and Tennyson heard nothing. He wrote to Knowles on the 10th: 'Altogether I feel I have not been treated well. I suppose that Irving may be something of a coward in the presence of his patroness but that should not make him uncivil to me.'

The next day he received the long-awaited news from the Lyceum. It was from Mrs Bateman herself, and explained the delay in signing the contract as follows:

> I have thought it best to write and ask if you will undertake the requisite curtailment yourself. It is always an onerous task to propose the alteration of beautiful language but the exigencies of the stage demand that the play be reduced in length and that it may not be longer than Hamlet – and it ought to be half an hour shorter and not fuller of characters ... I should like to receive this acting copy as soon as possible as I propose doing the play at Easter ... There is no immediate haste about the contract and I have thought it best to have a clear explanation with you as to the acting play without the formula of law in the matter.[31]

Tennyson replied in a pet, cross that he was still not being told exactly what revisions to make. However, during the three or four weeks either side of Christmas he worked assiduously at reducing his play and Mrs Bateman was able to acknowledge receipt on 14 January 1876. 'I am delighted to find your father took the mutilation of his words so patiently,' she wrote to Hallam, a certain masochistic glee in her tone.

No sooner had the problem with the text been settled than

Mrs Bateman began having objections to Stanford's score for incidental music. It required too large an orchestra, she said, and there would not be room enough in the pit. Tennyson suggested that if this were so he would gladly defray the costs of, and lost revenue from, removing the front two rows of the stalls. Ultimately it was always clear who would have their way. As Hallam put it to Stanford, 'Fight for the right as you like but in the end of course you must yield the right to sing the songs to Mrs Bateman – whatever music there is – whether to your music or some other – because otherwise the play cannot be acted.'

Queen Mary opened on 18 April – with a different score (requiring the same number of musicians as Stanford's arrangement). Tennyson did not attend the first night but received reports from Browning, among others – 'I want to be among the earliest who assure you of the complete success of your Queen Mary last night.'

When he remarked to a friend that he would never go and see the play unless he could smuggle himself in under a disguise he was told he would be recognized and the audience would yell for him to go onto the stage. 'They might yell and be damned,' he said.

The first-night audience was stuffed with Tennyson admirers; none so extravagantly ardent as Sabine Greville. After the curtain she sent Alfred both a telegram and a letter. The letter is a peach:

Dear Heart – Dear Master
Through all her chronicles hereafter England acknowledges you as a Playwright, – and that is the crown of crowns for a Poet ...
Hallam behaved like an angelic gentleman.
I behaved very nicely till the curtain dropped and then was inflamed by familiar Devils ...
The Poetry rolled like the waves of the sea. I am trying to explain to myself the Power of a Tragic Poet. Beyond all other human Power assuredly. I cannot express myself. I wanted to write a nice critique and I feel I am preying on the garbage of used out words ...
Good night – God bless you.
The dawn of Wednesday.[32]

Tennyson received £10 for each performance, but after the

opening week audience figures fell back and the production was closed after the twenty-third final curtain. This was not sufficient enough a failure to dissuade Tennyson from continuing his work in the theatre and there was no shortage of excuses that could be, and were, found for the general public's lack of enthusiasm. Much of the play's richness had been shorn in the course of revisions – after that Yankee manageress had slashed at it with her bowie knife, as one of Tennyson's friends put it – and Kate Crowe, Mrs Bateman's daughter, was not a powerful enough actress for the main part.

Tennyson returned to the writing of *Harold*, confident that he could build on the lessons learned.

15   Late for the Wedding

O Garden blossoming out of English blood!
O strange hate-healer Time! We stroll and stare
Where might made right eight hundred years ago;

('SHOW-DAY AT BATTLE ABBEY, 1876')

*H*arold was much shorter and he had it mostly finished by the end of August, when he took Hallam on a tour of East Anglia. Earlier in the summer, as part of his research for the play, he had taken Hallam to the battlefield at Senlac, and had there written, on 9 May, his poem 'Show-Day At Battle Abbey, 1876'.

This longer holiday included a notable reunion. Passing through the village of Woodbridge on 14 September Tennyson looked out FitzGerald's address and left his calling-card. Little Grange was being decorated and so FitzGerald put his two guests up at the nearby Bull Inn, where they stayed for two nights.

The impromptu visit was a complete success in spite of FitzGerald characteristically speaking his mind and telling the poet it was time to 'ship his Oars'. During the full day of their visit, Friday 15, they took a steamer to Harwich and told each other some of the 'Old Stories'. The only blot on the day was a report in *The Times* which (wrongly) accused Tennyson of refusing Longfellow permission to publish anything of his in a new collection called *Poems and Places*. Despite being on holiday Tennyson immediately dispatched a note to the American giving him 'full leave' to insert anything he liked in the collection.

FitzGerald admired Tennyson's relationship with his son and remarked that it was good to hear Hallam refer to his father as 'Papa' instead of the fashionable 'Governor'. Sitting next to his old friend on an iron bench in the garden of Little Grange, with doves fluttering in the trees overhead, Tennyson began complaining of some recent criticism in the *Quarterly*. Courageously FitzGerald told him that had he, in the manner of Scott or Shakespeare, led a more active life, or even, as Byron, played the Devil a bit more, he might have done more and talked about it less.

This was near-the-knuckle and Tennyson tolerated it probably because he was as aware as FitzGerald that this was likely to be their last meeting. 'I suppose I may never see him again,' FitzGerald wrote, after getting home from the sending-off at the station. Somehow or other, in those remote parts of East Anglia, no disguise was necessary to make it possible for Tennyson to travel incognito. When the landlord of the Bull Inn next spoke to FitzGerald, he said, 'And what pray, was the name of that gentleman?'

Harold was published in November. Tennyson was staying with Gladstone at Hawarden at the time and while there he treated his host family to a complete reading of the play. Begun at eleven in the morning it lasted for two and a half hours, forcing the Gladstone's domestic staff to postpone luncheon. Mary Gladstone, whose diaries give several vivid insights into Tennyson at this time, observed that the poet read 'with great vigour and power and enjoyment to himself.' As was usually the case with a Tennyson reading, and as so delicately put by Miss Gladstone, the enjoyment was not universal. Mary's father 'seemed sleepy and not forthcoming', her brother 'giggling' and one of her sisters 'fierce'.

At breakfast the next day Gladstone tried to exact repayment by regaling Tennyson with the divine teachings of James Mozley and attempting to draw him into discussions about theology. Mary's description of the breakfast-table conversation is revealing: 'Conv. at breakfast got on to eternal punishment (in which T. firmly disbelieves), the immortality of the soul, and prayer, in which he has great faith. Papa great in deploring the levity of the age. T. does not appear to be much of a Christian, and I suspect is no theologian, but is very religious.'

The Lyceum did not offer to produce *Harold* – perhaps in part because it did not contain a suitable role for Irving – and nor did anyone else. But Tennyson immediately began preparing to write a third play, this time about Thomas à Becket. It was a substantial subject, requiring several months of plying through the historical sources and other background reading.

Early in the New Year (1877) Alfred, Emily and Hallam rented a small house in Upper Wimpole Street for the winter season. During his stay in London Tennyson saw a good deal of Browning and on 28 February the two of them went together to Elliott and Fry's photographic studios at 55 Baker Street in order to have their pictures taken for a new periodical called *The Portrait*. Each had agreed to appear in the monthly, if the other would do the same. On their way a drunk stopped them in the street and accosted Tennyson.

DRUNK: You are Mr Tennyson; I know you from the photos.

TENNYSON: Well, if I am, there is no reason why I should be stopped in the street in this way.

DRUNK: Mr Tennyson, I've been dead drunk half a dozen times this week; if you'll only shake hands with me I'll never get drunk again.

The source for this anecdote, Alfred Domett, reported that Tennyson complied, but 'without any faith in the efficacy of his touch as a cure for this kind of King's evil'. One should think not. His own heavy drinking was being more and more remarked upon. A month later Henry James, dining with Lord Houghton, and sitting next but one to the 'Bard', noticed that all his talk was about port and tobacco. 'He seems to know much about them, and can drink a whole bottle of port at a sitting with no incommodity.'

As well as old friends, and memorable new acquaintances such as Mr James, Tennyson was naturally introduced to many minor socialites. His increasing forgetfulness, which cannot have been helped by his drinking, could prove highly embarrassing. 'Haven't an idea who you are,' he would bellow at someone he had sat beside and talked to just a day or two before.

Whilst on this social round Tennyson composed a sonnet entitled 'Montenegro', his tribute to a small band of rebels who had been 'beating back the swarm of Turkish Islam.' He had been told about Montenegro by Gladstone, and sent the poem for his approval before its publication in the May edition of the *Nineteenth Century*.

Tennyson had enjoyed his London season 'among all the Poets, Wits and Philosophers' and, with Hallam in attendance, seemed to be living a fulfilled existence. There were those who remarked, sometimes with ribald innuendo, that Hallam seemed able to perform all the wifely devotions that had once been Emily's province. Tennyson's new, positive and gregarious spirit – Hallam's part in which was so crucial – in fact shows how different the masculine companionship of his son was, and gives an insight into the type of artist Tennyson might have become had his friend, the other Hallam, survived for longer. The retiring, domestic Tennyson had always concealed a temperament that fed on large companies. This is why it is silly of those who berate Emily for having issued too many invitations during the early Farringford years. She understood her husband, in this respect, better than her critics.

A family disappointment – Lionel's failing his Foreign Office Entrance Examination – did nothing to dampen the mood of confidence and Tennyson proceeded apace with his studies for the new play. In August he took Hallam to Canterbury in order to see each of the scenes of Becket's martyrdom.

By the beginning of 1878 he was ready to begin the writing of his new play, a task he concentrated on admirably well despite the distraction of Lionel's wedding, which took place in Westminster Abbey. The last time Tennyson had been there, for Dickens's funeral, his presence had been turned into a crude public spectacle. To avoid a repeat of this – although the assembled congregation was made up of the most worthy and well-behaved notables – he arranged with the Dean that a side door in the north transept should be left open so that he could take his seat at the last moment. But on the day of the wedding the Dean (Stanley) was unwell, and his place was taken by F.W. Farrar. The little north transept door was left locked and Farrar had already begun the service while Alfred and Hallam struggled to find their way around the Abbey precincts with the frail body of Emily in Hallam's arms. Eventually they gained admittance through the Abbot's private entrance. Hallam put his mother down, for dignity's sake, and merely supported her on his arm. Entering through the choir stalls and hurriedly being ushered to their places, they were just in time to hear Farrar pronounce Lionel and Eleanor man and wife.

Although Tennyson was apparently not to blame for their late arrival, this undignified and shambolic entrance will have been regarded by some (not least by Lionel and his new wife) as typically disorganized and insensitive.

The register was signed by Gladstone, Browning and the Duke of Argyll, as well as by the parents. With Farrar steering him through the murky Jerusalem Chamber, Tennyson was gripped by a woman's hand and told, 'I am glad you got in just in time.'

Scared that this might be the arm of some cockney autograph-hunter, and the start of another public onrush, he quickly barked out what was coming to be a reflex defence, 'I have not the least idea who you are.'

It was, in fact, George Eliot, but he had not recognized her.

16   A Fistful of Tension

'I have fought for Queen and Faith like a valiant man and true;
I have only done my duty as a man is bound to do:
With a joyful spirit I Sir Richard Grenville die!'
And he fell upon their decks, and he died.

('THE REVENGE')

I n 1878 and for subsequent winters in London the Tennysons resided at 14 Eaton Square, an address which became the focus for much dark-season entertainment. Joseph Joachim, the Hungarian violinist, frequently provided the musical diversion for guests as various as the Duke of Argyll, Locker, Browning, Arnold, Henry Bradshaw, the Listers, the Ritchies and Professor Huxley's two funny tightly-dressed crop-headed daughters – all there, according to Mary Gladstone, on Saturday 30 March.

But Miss Gladstone's list was not exhaustive. Also present were the Allinghams, Dr Paget, Lewis Morris, F. Pollock and Spedding. Much of the early, sober conversation concerned the topical talking-point – the 'Eastern Question'.

The revolt against Turkish misrule which Tennyson had

celebrated in his recent Montenegro sonnet had been ruthlessly crushed by Turkish troops. The brutality with which the Slavonic cause had been routed prompted Russia to declare war on Turkey, and on 3 March 1878 the Turks were forced to sign a humiliating peace treaty making Turkey, in effect, a satellite of Russia. Despite the sentiments of his poem, Tennyson held on too strongly to the vestiges of old Crimean spirit not to share the Tory alarm at this Russian victory. A war-like mood swept through London and gung-ho songs became the order of the day on the music-hall stage.

> We don't want to fight, but by jingo if we do,
> We've got the ships, we've got the men, we've got the money too!

Although Tennyson regaled Allingham, 'I can't agree with you about Russia, you damned Irishman! I've hated Russia ever since I was born, and I'll hate her till I die!'; and after a burst of the Hungarian's violin went on, 'I hate Dizzy and I love Gladstone; still I want Russia subdued' – for all this, in comparison with previous periods of bellicosity, Tennyson's warlike mood was subdued, and confined to his private drawing-room. It is not unlikely that the age of his sons had something to do with such judiciousness.

After midnight, when only a handful of guests remained, Tennyson, by way of apologizing to Joachim for his apparent neglect of the music, invited the violinist up to his private sanctum for a smoke and a short recitation. They were joined by three others, and all reacted to a reading of a brand-new poem, 'The Revenge'.

The poem was read in thunderous voice, interrupted, in the poet's normal manner, to throw in remarks like, 'How would you do that on your violin?', and at the end of it he said, more quietly, 'I am afraid I shall be waking up the cook who is sleeping next door and I had better not read any more tonight.'

'The Revenge' received a second airing a few days later, on an evening described by Mary Gladstone in her usual frothy manner as 'great fun'. (Although she writes as a perpetual teenager Mary was in fact over thirty years old at this time.) The reading consisted of 'Boadicea', and *Maud*, as well as the new poem, which he read in an increasing rush, shouting out the climax.

There had been another shriek earlier on in the poem. Whenever Tennyson read aloud it was his custom to grip something in one hand – often the corner of a cushion – and release some of the tension in his reading through the intensity of his grip. On this occasion he took hold of Emily Ritchie's hand and at a dramatic point in the reading squeezed it so hard that she cried out.

He stopped and apologized. 'Didn't know I was pinching you.'

'Never mind,' said the noble Miss Ritchie.

'Must hold onto something, but a table-leg will do just as well,' Tennyson explained, less than chivalrously.

By this time, the middle of April, he was tiring of London and wanting to go to Farringford to make better progress with *Becket*. His displeasure with London was fuelled by an increasingly acrimonious relationship with his publisher, and in particular with the manager Kegan Paul.

As the publisher of Tennyson during these years, Paul's problem was how to keep marketing Tennyson's poems through a period when he was not writing sufficient new verse for a fresh collection. The answer was to keep bringing out new and novel editions. One novelty involved using illustrations of some of Tennyson's personal haunts – an engraving of Aldworth, of the Farringford porch etc. – an innovation which Tennyson vigorously but abortively resisted, although Emily clandestinely encouraged it.

Two years earlier there had been a protracted dispute regarding Paul's plans for an Annotated Edition. The publisher had begun preparing material for the edition without there being any firm agreement for it. The notes which he submitted to Tennyson for consideration were disappointing – far inferior to those in the annotated Byron. Paul replied that that was because 'Byron was reviewed with better criticism' and because local colour and biographical details, which lent great interest to the Byron book, were neither so necessary in Tennyson's case, nor so welcome to the poet.

In the end Alfred and Hallam had to get White to pin Paul down to the terms of Tennyson's agreement with King & Co. which gave the poet a veto on any insertions in new editions. Paul had to drop his plans. He was not pleased, and from that time on he took every opportunity of disparaging his leading author.

At the end of 1877, due to ill-health, Henry King retired from publishing, leaving Kegan Paul in sole charge of the firm. The early part of 1878 was therefore spent jockeying for position, in advance of signing new contracts. On 14 April, White, at Tennyson's instruction, gave notice to Paul that the existing agreement (as signed with King) would be terminated at the end of the year. This was intended as a signal to Paul that he could not take for granted Tennyson's automatic transfer to the new list. And to show that this was not bluff, when Paul's first offer (of 7 June) was unsatisfactory, White began approaching other publishers – particularly Macmillan, who had long wanted to act on Tennyson's behalf.

By mid-July Paul made a second, much more flexible offer. Hearing nothing from Macmillan, but believing that Routledge was preparing to make a handsome offer, White was all for rejecting Paul again. But caution was counselled by Knowles, who did not think Routledge would 'deliver'. In the end, Tennyson had no choice but to try and get the best deal possible with Paul. The timidity of other publishers was all bound up with the difficulties of taking over an author late in his career with so many collections and editions already extant.

Kegan Paul was, in terms of literary and business acumen, Tennyson's most astute publisher since Moxon. An earlier family connection – this was the same Kegan Paul who, as vicar of Sturminster Marshall, had run a school in his home in Baillie attended by Hallam and Lionel – might have been a good omen. But Paul had changed since his days in the church, which he was forced to leave because of his liberal quasi-Unitarian views, and in his dealings with Tennyson he was always hard-headed, totally impersonal, and intellectually hubristic. He had once said, of his early liking for Tennyson's verse, 'I did not then recognise how little thought is contained in that pomp and melody of verse, still less of how very little of what thought there is, is the poet's own.'

By August Tennyson had a rough draft of his new play ready and wrote to Lewes inviting him and Miss Greville to come and read it. 'You should come early as it takes some time to read it or better if you would stop all night.'

Leaving George Eliot at home with a sick headache, Lewes brought Sabine Greville to Aldworth in time for lunch. After the meal he settled down to read the play. 'Greatly interested by many scenes of it, though I had some serious doubts which I did not express, and some which I did.' While Lewes was forming his mixed reservations Alfred was entertained by Mrs Greville. Some of Lewes' reservations were later written down and posted to Tennyson, who was unable to act on them until after a holiday in Ireland with Hallam.

17   De Sade Charade

Election, Election and Reprobation – it's all very well,
But I go tonight for my boy, and I shall not find him in Hell.

('RIZPAH')

When he returned from this trip, one of constant travel and sight-seeing, Tennyson found the letter he had written to Whitman returned to him for redirection. He had omitted 'Camden' from the address. He added a note on the flap of the letter, apologizing, and put it back in the post.

Emily wrote to her sister, Louisa, in October to explain how settled they were at Aldworth that year:

I don't think we shall go to Farringford very early this year unless we are frozen out here. Ally's study is so light here and so much less drafty than at Farringford that this is a great temptation to stay and besides to say the truth I hear of so many fresh people at Freshwater where already there were far too many to our taste that I am in no hurry to encounter them ...[33]

In his light and draught-free study Alfred was putting together a new poem, worked up from an article in the *Leisure Hour*, which had been shown to him earlier in the year by Mary Brotherton. The article opened with the tombstone epitaph of one Phoebe Hessel, who had died in Brighton at the age of 108 in 1821. The venerable old lady's claim to fame had been that, in her younger years, she had served as a foot-soldier under the Duke of Cumberland at the Battle of Fontenay. But the part of the article which stamped itself on Tennyson concerned a train

451

of events occurring in her middle years. As a travelling fish-monger, serving the villages around Brighton on the back of a donkey, she obtained information which led to the arrest and conviction of two mail-robbers. They were gibbeted on the scene of their crime and, it was claimed, after their clothes had become well weathered and their flesh decayed, one of the crook's mothers would steal out to the Downs in the middle of the night and collect up as many of her son's bones as had been blown from the gibbet-cage, wrap them in her apron, and carry them home.

> Wailing, wailing, wailing, the wind over land and sea –
> And Willy's voice in the wind, 'O mother come out to me.'
> Why should he call me tonight, when he knows that I cannot go?
> For the downs are as bright as day, and the full moon stares
>   at the snow.
>
> We should be seen, my dear; they would spy us out of the town.
> The loud black nights for us, and the storm rushing over the
>   down,
> When I cannot see my own hand, but am led by the creak of the
>   chain,
> And grovel and grope for my son till I find myself drenched
>   with the rain.
>
> Anything fallen again? nay – what was there left to fall?
> I have taken them home, I have numbered the bones, I have
>   hidden them all.
> What am I saying? and what are *you*? do you come as a spy?
> Falls? what falls? who knows? As the tree falls so it must
>   lie.

This poem (only three of its seventeen verses are quoted), in its early form called 'Bones', but later re-titled 'Rizpah', is one of the strongest pieces of Tennyson's later period. The anguish and despair of the woman, raking the Downs and ducking the carrion birds, is given a perfect vehicle of expression. The Biblical title helps to universalize the emotion so that the rather eccentric and desperate figure of the woman becomes a tragic emblem of life's endemic doom, which has the power to make grovellers of us all.

During a visit to Mrs Greville's Surrey home, Henry James made his first visit to Aldworth. 'She is not young, and she is ugly,' James wrote about his hostess, and described her as an 'intimate' friend of Tennyson – 'to the point of kissing him somewhere – quite *en famille* – every quarter of an hour.'

It is clear from James's various accounts of this visit that the American was not of much interest to Tennyson. Probably he wasn't keen enough on his port, or sufficiently eager to share a pipe. There was a reading of 'Locksley Hall', but a rather solemn, lacklustre performance. 'It was a large and simple and almost empty occasion,' James summarized, adding 'yet empty without embarrassment.'

The conversation at the luncheon table was a case in point. Mrs Greville happened to mention, quite innocently, that one of her relatives was named Mademoiselle Laure de Sade. Tennyson immediately proceeded at great length to describe the infamy of the author bearing that name:

He proceeded admirably – admirably for the triumph of simplification – to the very greatest length imaginable, as was signally promoted by the fact that clearly no one present, with a single exception, recognised the name or the nature of the scandalous, the long ignored, the at last all but unnameable author; least of all the gentle relative of Mademoiselle Laure, who listened with the blankest grace to her friend's enumeration of his titles to infamy, among which that of his most notorious work was pronounced. It was the homeliest, frankest, most domestic passage ... and most remarkable for leaving none of us save myself ... in the least embarrassed or bewildered; largely ... because of the failure ... of all measure on the part of the auditors and speaker alike of what might be intended or understood, of what in fine, the latter was talking about.[34]

What, indeed, is *James* talking about? His implication that Tennyson himself, whilst knowing the facts of de Sade's life and work, had no comprehension of its real import is an absurd attempt to appear superior. With friends like Lord Houghton, Tennyson was perfectly well-informed about the darker predilections of the human temperament.

He became a grandfather on 20 November, with the birth of Alfred Browning Stanley Tennyson, a combination of names which did not meet with Emily's approval. 'Our little bairnie has his fine name of Alfred spoilt in one way by the addition of

Browning and Stanley, the names of his godfathers which it is now considered etiquette to impose.'[35] Pleasure at this new birth was marred a little a few days later with news of George Lewes's death. Alfred sent his 'affectionate' sympathies to George Eliot.

Emily was improving slightly and writing very regularly to her sister Louisa, who was suffering from severe depression. The letters are full of good Christian advice, the key tone of Emily's last years, in which she seems wrapped up in God, and partially estranged from Alfred and even Hallam. She was disappointed when neither of them would agree to supporting her niece Agnes Weld's charitable work on the island. 'I cannot conceive of anyone more entirely absorbed in the welfare of others than she is. A most truly Christian love she has I do believe.'

In order to keep her sister busy and her mind off her personal troubles she asked Louisa to knit Hallam a new scarf in white wool, 'two yards and a quarter long please.'

Becket was completed early in 1879 and sent to Irving, who was now the manager of the Lyceum. But Irving was frightened off by the play's length (and its other faults) and suggested that Tennyson write a much shorter play, on a different theme. Without entirely giving up hope that *Becket* would be produced Tennyson did turn his mind to finding a new subject.

At the end of January he was unsettled by news of Julia Cameron's death in Ceylon. Having seen little of her on her recent return to England, this unexpected death, and the knowledge that he would see no more of her in this life, put him in a ponderous state.

The Tennysons went to Eaton Square for the winter season but it was neither as full nor as jolly as the previous year. Mary Gladstone found Alfred 'very tired and faint'. She asked if he needed medicine. The only tonic he needed, he replied, was the sight of her wholesome face. It was a rather weary riposte. At the end of one evening together the 'old fellow' became very affectionate. 'Goodbye, dear, be happy – till I die, and afterwards.'

It was an odd thing to say. But death hung in the air and three weeks later he received news that his brother Charles was dead. The end had come in Cheltenham, where Charles had been staying with Mary Ker and her husband, a doctor.

Emily sent a box of primroses and forget-me-nots from Farringford. There is no indication that Alfred travelled to the funeral but his brother's death, closely followed less than a month later by his unhappy wife, Louisa, affected him morbidly. He became prey to perpetual ghostly voices. Fortunately there were business distractions. A pirated edition of *The Lover's Tale* was being sold, and this persuaded Tennyson, at long last, to allow the poem, with the addition of 'The Golden Supper', to become a bona fide publication.

News that a review of *Becket* had appeared infuriated him, 'If Irving has let my cat out of the bag, it is very dishonourable. Pray see him if possible,' he instructed Hallam, 'I am in a great rage.'

18   Nose-stroking

'What can it matter, my lass, what I did wi' my single life?
I ha' been as true to you as ever a man to his wife;

('THE FIRST QUARREL')

Tennyson's mind was taken off his ghosts and irritations at the beginning of June by a visit from the vivacious Miss Gladstone. Arriving on the 4th, Mary's first impressions of Farringford were that it was 'very bleak inside, with large empty table and sofa ungracefully placed.' At dinner, Mary and her companion, Margaret Warren, were made to feel a little 'hot' by the poet's tendency to say 'near-the-wind' things, and by the household habit of changing tables at each course. There were four moves in all, and a game of backgammon at the last. Alfred played with Maggie, leaving Mary to cool off. But when it was time for the two guests to retire her cheeks reddened again when Tennyson came right up to her and asked earnestly, 'What colour *are* your eyes? I cannot make out.' And following them upstairs he stopped beside a queer Chinese print and said, 'We shall all turn into pigs if we lose Christianity and God.'

Next day, after a late breakfast, Tennyson and Hallam accompanied the two young women onto the Down and then to the beach. Mary longed to take a dip but Alfred said it was bad to bathe if one was perspiring, and put his hand to her cheek. The girls just laughed and jumped into the 'p.b.' sea – 'p.b.' being an abbreviation of Passionate Brampton which was slang for Pre-Raphaelite. After luncheon, still tingling and glowing from her swim, Mary rested with Henry James's new book, *Daisy Miller*.

Later in the afternoon she and Margaret were taken for a drive across the golden gorse to Alum Bay. It was a marvellously still summer's afternoon. The sea was calm and quiet, and sparkled a silvery grey. As they watched from the shore, beside the famously coloured cliffs, a steamer sailed past. 'Very pathetic, that ship sailing away into the grey,' said Alfred.

Driving back to the house he again began harping on about the colour of Mary's eyes, making out that there was something remarkable about them. She went very red in the face and Hallam, to make a joke of it, held up a rug to shield her. 'Hallam has a great respect for that young woman – she has a remarkable face,' Alfred told Margaret, who gave the impression of being gravely unamused by his attentions.

After tea Tennyson read them both two new poems. One was 'Rizpah', the other 'The First Quarrel', a domestic narrative about a story which had been told to the poet by Dr Dabbs. The story – like a compressed Hardy novel – tells of the broken marriage between two childhood sweethearts. Before they are able to wed, the young man has to leave the Isle of Wight to work on a relative's farm in Dorset.

> I was a child, an' he was a child, an' he came to harm;
> There was a girl, a hussy, that workt with him up at the farm,
> One had deceived her an' left her alone with her sin an'
>   her shame,
> And so she was wicked with Harry; the girl was the most to
>   blame.

After several years he returns to the island and weds the girl who has remained faithful to him. The marriage begins well, but then while he is away, once again finding work away from the island, she discovers a letter from the milkmaid he has abandoned.

> 'What can it matter, my lass, what I did wi' my single life?
> I ha' been as true to you as ever a man to his wife;
> ... Come, come, little wife, let it rest!

The man isn't like the woman, no need to make such a stir.'

But she sends him away from the house, unforgiven, and the boat which he takes for Jersey goes down under the waves.

The poem is remarkable for the way it combines the obsessions of the age with Tennyson's personal mania about marital fidelity. It is also an admirable example of Tennyson's ability to write colloquial narrative verse, an ability unequalled by any other English poet of the first rank. In a revealing comment on the poem Carlyle was to say, after he had heard it read for the first time, 'Poor fellow, he was just an honest plain man, and she was a curious production of the century ...' *A curious production of the century*. This phrase says much about the Victorians' ability to distance themselves from their own time.

Mary's comment was less incisive. She found both the poems 'awfully sad'. After the reading Tennyson began stroking her nose. He told her it was a 'petit nez retroussé' which meant, he said, all sorts of naughty things – these, apparently, he left to her imagination. When it was time for bed Mary sat up late with Maggie who had had a 'terrific scene' with the poet. They both privately complained about the excessive personal attention they were expected to withstand.

There was no respite. Immediately after breakfast the next day Tennyson stood beside Mary, staring at her face. 'Those wonderful eyes of yours. I do believe they are grey,' he said.

The four of them – Alfred, Hallam, Mary and Margaret – went for another drive, visiting Watts, Ward and an old shepherd who gave them a large cabbage. Walking in a copse Tennyson quizzed Mary about the names of all the wild flowers and then stood her back to back with Margaret to find which was the taller. It was Mary, by an inch.

That night he read another new poem, 'The Northern Cobbler', his temperance ballad in Lincolnshire dialect. He then made Mary cross by chafing her unmercifully in a theological vein, saying things that jarred, and treating her like a baby.

On the fourth day Mary began to feel that she and Margaret were being played off against one another. Alfred suddenly announced that he had solved the mystery concerning her eyes. They were like Carlyle's! And then he was heard to say that he liked Maggie 'better and better'. It was a rainy day and the two young women clung to one another 'The moment one rises the other does ditto' – but by the evening their sense of self-protection had relaxed. Mary went to Alfred's sanctum 'and had some alarm. *He kissed me.*'

Hot sunny weather returned the next day and that night there was more theological discussion. Tennyson said that if ever he lost his belief in an after-life he would commit suicide. He planned to write a satire entitled *A Suicide Supper*. Mary wrote in her diary, 'I am disappointed in his religion. It is purely founded on the chaos and failure of a godless world, and there is a want of reverence wh. is a shock . . .'

The visit was beginning to pall. On Monday there was a dull trip to Yarmouth, where Maggie decided to stay the night with her sister. Back at Freshwater, on her own, Mary had a 'dreadful evening . . . I did my best and talked and talked to cover the . . . silence. And played and played [the piano] with my heart in my mouth. Father and son had a game of backgammon, in the midst of which I vanished drearily to bed.'

But she could not sleep and by the time a new day dawned she was in no mood for bright sunshine. She described the sunny morning as 'a satire on the inside of the house'. She felt wretched at breakfast, partly through lack of sleep, and partly through the absence of Margaret, and during the morning she sat silently in the garden with Alfred and Hallam, who read aloud from a book of Plato, breaking into sobs when he reached the passage describing the death of Socrates. Mary sat stonily unmoved. Alfred called her a 'hard little thing.'

At last Margaret came back from Yarmouth. They could not get off the island quickly enough and left that afternoon.

Hallam belonged to a self-effacing generation. He was not the only child who would dedicate so much of his life first to his father's old age and then to his memory. The end of the century was to witness a profusion of memoirs and biographies compiled by loyal offspring, Hallam's own *Memoir* merely being the archetype. Too often Hallam has been spoken about as if his obsequiousness to his father was somehow freakish, instead of its being in large measure the manner of the times. If only we had on record more of his own feelings during interludes such as the one just described. How did *he* feel about Mary Gladstone's eyes? What were his actual emotions when he had to hold up the rug to hide her embarrassment at one of his father's near-the-wind remarks? In short, what was his attitude to his father's flirtatious behaviour with young women?

Clearly, eye-gazing, cheek-pinching, palm-stroking and even kissing were more prominent vehicles for intercourse between men and women than they are in our own hard-hearted times. But just as clearly, Tennyson was extravagantly attentive towards Mary and other young women. Nearing seventy he might perhaps have considered that he was permitted to take liberties on the grounds of his age. It is also highly probable that he was wooing Mary on behalf of Hallam. Invitations to young women in households with elegible bachelors are rarely made without some vague view to match-making. Again, how good it would be to know Hallam's point of view. It is significant, however, that nowhere in Mary's diaries or letters (and she wrote many to Hallam) does she show much romantic interest in Hallam.[36] (She was five years older than him, a fact which, from either perspective, might have made the match unenticing.)

19   Busy Times

> my son will speak for me
> Abler than I can in these spasms that grind
> Bone against bone.
>
> ('COLUMBUS')

L ate at night, at the end of June, Tennyson wrote a prefatory poem to be used for the collection of his brother's sonnets being compiled by Spedding. It is a beautiful poem, written by and not for the occasion. In seven short verses Tennyson conveys the deep sense of desolation which his brother's death induced. The contrast between their brotherly partnership during childhood and youth – when they had strode the Somersby lanes shouting couplets at one another across the hedgerows – and their separate ways during manhood, underscores the poem but does not swamp it.

> And, now to these unsummered skies
> The summer bird is still,

Far off a phantom cuckoo cries
From out a phantom hill;

And through this midnight breaks the sun
Of sixty years away,
The light of days when life begun,
The days that seem today,

When all my griefs were shared with thee,
As all my hopes were thine –
As all thou wert was one with me,
May all thou art be mine!

Miserable as his brother's death made him, the poem also shows why the loss coincided with a late burst of poetic energy. True, this outflow had begun with 'Rizpah', but the momentum was maintained by the re-identification with his ten-year-old self, and with all the old hopes that had been shared with Charles.

In addition to working on a one-act dramatization of a Boccaccio story – *The Falcon* – Tennyson was hard at work during the last half of the year composing some longer poems. 'In The Children's Hospital' is a very pathetic tale, taken from a true story he had been told by Mary Gladstone, about a young girl in a children's ward scared that she will die on the operating table. In its authentic rendering of the nurse's sentimental and credulous Christianity – a form of belief treated affectionately by, but not necessarily shared by, the poet – this poem captures the morbidity of the Victorian period more closely than any other example of Tennyson's work. As such it is hardly typical and indeed might be difficult to identify as his work if stumbled upon out of context and un-credited.

In his poem about Columbus – a dramatic monologue by an old, abused explorer – he at times seems to be talking through the voice of the Spaniard:

> And more than once in days
> Of doubt and cloud and storm, when drowning hope
> Sank all but out of sight, I heard (God's) voice,
> 'Be not cast down. I lead thee by the hand,
> Fear not.' And I shall hear his voice again –
> I know that he has led me all my life,
> I am not yet too old to work his will –
> His voice again.

In the failure of his plays to capture the public imagination he must have felt more slighted than he let on. The facts of the poem were taken from just one source (Washington Irving's *Life of Columbus*) but the emotion has its source in Tennyson's own life. 'I am old and slighted,' the poem ends, but:

> you will tell the King, that I,
> Racked as I am with gout, and wrenched with pains
> Gained in the service of His Highness, yet
> Am ready to sail forth on one last voyage,
> And readier, if the King would hear, to lead
> One last crusade against the Saracen,
> And save the Holy Sepulchre from thrall.

This was no fanciful self-identification. There were clear indications during Tennyson's final years, even in something as superficial and relatively straightforward as his relationship with Gladstone, that he felt himself burdened with the duty of prophetic and warning utterance.

'The Voyage of Maeldune' is a reworking of a Celtic legend about a chieftain who searches the world for his father's murderer. After a long and fruitless voyage, in which he and his crew visit differently paired islands – the Silent Isle/the Isle of Shouting, the Isle of Flowers/the Isle of Fruits – each one capable of symbolical reading, they sail forlornly home.

> And we came to the Isle we were blown from, and
>   there on the shore was he,
> The man that had slain my father. I saw him and let
>   him be.
> O weary was I of the travel, the trouble the strife
>   and the sin,
> When I landed again, with a tithe of men, on the
>   Isle of Finn.

This final verse illustrates both the punchy energy of the poem and a recurrent motif in much of Tennyson's later verse – the attainment of moral wisdom at the end of a journey through life. There are distractions on the way. In the Silent Isle, a peace that charms all strength away; in the Isle of Shouting, the hubbub of aggression; in the Isle of Flowers, a fruitless wallowing in sensuality; in the Isle of Fruits, the temptation of gluttony; in the Isle of Fire, the fierce light of aggression; in the Bounteous Isle, the

461

life of ease and ennui; in the Isle of Witches, the seductive prancings of sexuality; and in the Isle of Double Towers, the distractions of religious argument and schism. These readings, although fairly obvious, are not obtrusive, and the poem can be enjoyed as much for its humour and swift rhythms as for its allegory.

By the time the Tennysons were ready to begin their winter season in London during February 1880, Alfred had finished a second one-act drama (*The Cup*) and had produced nearly a dozen new poems during the previous twelve months. The outflow of creative energy continued and in due course he was to have sufficient new poems for his first collection in eight years.

In the meantime he, Emily and Hallam, unable to make immediate use of Eaton Place, took a new town house in Upper Belgrave Street. It was here, in March, that Tennyson had his first and only meeting with the novelist Thomas Hardy.

Hardy was no juvenile worshipper. He was forty years old with half a dozen volumes of fiction to his credit, but, considering himself primarily a poet, he approached Tennyson with awesome preconceptions. When he arrived – the visit was arranged and chaperoned by Mrs Anne Procter – Emily was 'lying as if in a coffin,' but she got up to welcome him. For lunch (the other guests included Locker and Lady Russell) Emily reclined at the head of the table and Tennyson, surprising Hardy with his sociability and humour, asked Mrs Procter absurd riddles – (Q: *Who is the first man mentioned in the Bible? A: Chap first*) – and told Hardy about the funniest misprints that had appeared in his work. Hardy, who never took up an invitation to visit the Tennysons at Farringford, is just one more of those reliable sources on record as saying that the flesh-and-blood Tennyson belied the somewhat grave and patrician public image of the man.

Another visitor later in the month, by which time the Tennysons were settled in their usual London dwelling at Eaton Place, was James Russell Lowell, the American poet, who found Tennyson looking old and seedy. However, his impression of the Englishman was soured by a characteristically mischievous charade of dotage, amusingly captured by Lowell's compatriot, Henry James, who was also at the luncheon.

Both of them arrived early and took their places at a table set for 'possible when not assured guests.' James sat at one end, near Emily, and Lowell was told to sit at the other 'near the window, where the Bard would presently join him.' Hallam breezed in, and breezed out.

Several minutes passed without any other guests arriving. Finally, Tennyson came in and sat himself down opposite Lowell, saying not a word. The silence between the two poets rapidly (to James) 'took on monstrous proportions.'

> I converse with my gentle neighbour during what seemed an eternity – really but hearing, as the minutes sped, all that Tennyson didn't say to Lowell and all that Lowell wouldn't on any such compulsion as that say to Tennyson. I like however to hang again upon the hush – for the sweetness of the relief of its break by the fine Tennysonian growl. I had never dreamed, no, of a growling Tennyson – I had too utterly otherwise; but no line of Locksley Hall rolled out as I was to happen soon after to hear it, could have been sweeter than the interrogative sound of 'Do you know anything about *Lowell*?' launched on the chance across the table and crowned at once by Mrs. Tennyson's anxious quaver: 'Why, my dear, this *is* Mr. Lowell!'[37]

An amusing story, consistent with others; but James is perhaps too much the craftsman to be entirely reliable. In all his comments about Tennyson he also showed that he was amongst the minority who completely missed, or stubbornly refused to acknowledge, the playfulness of the man. This was linked to his inability to fully understand the English temperament.

In May Tennyson became embroiled in some petty politicking connected with the Rectorship of Glasgow University. Following a deputation to Farringford, the two parties of which were acting on advice given by Edmund Lushington, Tennyson had agreed to his being nominated – but in ignorance of the fact that the deputation consisted of the president and secretary of the university's Conservative Club, that he would therefore stand as a Conservative candidate, and would have a Liberal opponent.

As soon as he became aware that he was being asked to stand as a 'party candidate' he withdrew. The Conservatives of Glasgow did not let him off the hook so lightly. They used every means of influence, including Lushington, and managed to persuade Tennyson to withdraw his withdrawal. He did so, on the understanding that some of his original conditions would be complied with, notably that he would not be required to be present at the installation. There was more pressure on him from the Liberal wing to withdraw, including a letter to *The Times*, and eventually he did drop out. But only to take up an offer to become the nominee of the non-political Independent Club. These shenanigans, and Hallam's role in them, disturbed Lionel. He thought his father was receiving unsound advice. 'The mistake was in the first instance consenting to stand at all. Papa's policy throughout life has been to keep clear of politics & questions may possibly arise during his rectorship which would oblige him to declare himself for one party or another.'[38] The whole saga proved to be a futile distraction when John Bright, the Liberal candidate, easily won the election.

20   Ave Atque Vale

Infinite Ideality!
Immeasurable Reality!
Infinite Personality!
Hallowed be thy name

('THE HUMAN CRY')

On doctor's orders – Tennyson was tired and unwell, as much from overwork as from the emotional trauma of his brother's death – he and Hallam took an early summer holiday. In June, trying first of all without success to book places on a liner to Canada, they went overland to Venice, (another decision criticized by Lionel). In Munich they visited art galleries and went to see Lord Acton in Tegernsee. Acton, crisply intellectual, was not predisposed to Tennyson's 'want of reality, the habit of his walking on the clouds, the airiness of his metaphysics.' However, the two of them finally warmed to one another, 'chiefly at night, when everyone was in bed.'

After several days travelling beside beautiful mountain meadows, gay with gentians and forget-me-nots, they arrived in Venice in the middle of a thunderstorm. Tennyson was disappointed with the canals, which did not match the picture of them he had dreamed about all his life, and his sight was too weak to pick out the poorly preserved artwork in the dimly-lit churches. His favourite part of the city was the Jewish burial-ground. Overgrown with poppies and thistles it was a pathetic place but spoke more to Tennyson's temperament and mood than did the images of Bellini and Tintoretto.

On the journey home they passed through Sirmio, the little promontory on the shore of Lago di Garda, where Catullus had had a villa. Catullus was one of Tennyson's favourite Latin poets, and in recent months he had read several times the famous lament for a lost brother, 'Ave atque vale'. Tennyson now wrote his own 'Frater Ave atque Vale'. Written in trochaic tetrameter it blends both a tribute to a revered forerunner (brother-poet) with a softened sadness for his own dead brother, Charles.

> Row us out from Desenzano, to your Sirmione row!
> So they rowed, and there we landed – 'O venusta
>   Sirmio!'
> There to me through all the groves of olive in the
>   summer glow.
> There beneath the Roman ruin where the purple
>   flowers grow.
> Came that 'Ave atque Vale' of the Poet's hopeless
>   woe,
> Tenderest of Roman poets nineteen hundred years
>   ago,
> 'Frater Ave atque Vale' – as we wander'd to and fro
> Gazing at the Lydian laughter of the Garda Lake
>   below
> Sweet Catullus' all-but-island, olive-silvery
>   Sirmio!

After he had written the poem, conscious that his own preface to Charles's sonnets, and this rather sunny tribute, hardly matched the sadness of the old Roman poem, Tennyson wrote to Gladstone to explain that, in his view, no modern elegy could ever hope to surpass the pathos of desolation found in the old classical authors, 'so long as men retain the last hope in the afterlife of those whom they loved.' This was an extremely interesting comment, for it revealed an underlying ambivalence in his attitude towards religious faith. From a personal point of view the possibility of losing faith in the after-life was an abomination, but from a literary or artistic perspective the prospect that death was a finality had a certain astringent allure. It was an ambivalence which illuminates another aspect of Tennyson's *kunstlerschuld.*

Returning to England and settling at Aldworth for the rest of the summer, Tennyson set to the task of completing his new play *The Cup* and of collecting together the new poems which he hoped to publish at the end of the year.

One of the poems contained in the new collection – the book was eventually titled *Ballads and Poems* and published in December at five shillings, the same price that Tennyson's first individual collection had sold at over fifty years ago – was *De Profundis* ('Out of the Deep'). Supposedly begun at the time of Hallam's birth in 1852, the completed poem draws also on the birth of his grandson, and is about the 'main-miracle, that thou art thou', the mystery of Individuality.

> O dear Spirit half-lost
> In thine own shadow and this fleshly sign
> That thou art thou – who wailest being born
> And banished into mystery, and the pain
> Of this divisible-indivisible world
> Among the numerable-innumerable
> Sun, sun, and sun, through finite-infinite space
> In finite-infinite Time – our mortal veil
> And shattered phantom of that infinite One,
> Who made thee unconceivably Thyself
> Out of His whole World-self and all in all –
> Live thou!

It has to be said that Tennyson is not at his most mellifluous when philosophizing in this way, and the result here is of the kind which sends readers running a mile when the poet is a known sophist of one school or another. But Tennyson's lifelong obsession with the conundrum of personality – the extent to which it permeates his collected work and the degree to which it burned at the very core of his lived experience – lifts the poem onto another realm, and is another demonstration of the way in which his art cannot be fully appreciated without reference to context.

Apart from the poems already discussed the collection contained 'The Revenge', 'The Sisters', 'The Defence of Lucknow', 'Sir John Oldcastle', and, as dedication, 'To Alfred

Tennyson, My Grandson', originally titled in manuscript 'To Alfred Tennyson, babe, from Alfred Tennyson, septuagenarian.' (The volume omitted 'Frater Ave atque Vale' which was not published for another three years, when it first appeared in the *Nineteenth Century*.)

21   Overmastered

a power to make
This ever-changing world of circumstance,
In changing, chime with never-changing Law.

('TO THE DUKE OF ARGYLL')

T ennyson's one-act drama *The Falcon* had been produced at the end of 1880. It had a run of sixty-seven performances but was less enthusiastically received than this statistic might suggest. Part of the production's attraction came from the use it made of a live falcon – up until the time the bird entangled itself in its own chain and expired on stage. This followed its earlier, theatrical deaths, demanded by the script, when it was cooked off-stage and offered as food to the guest who had come to ask it as a gift for her son. The play, a curious piece, was produced at St James's by the Kendals, not by Irving at the Lyceum. After the live bird's replacement with a stuffed specimen, audiences dwindled.

The Cup opened at the Lyceum, on 3 January 1881. Another short piece – produced in tandem with a revival of *The Corsican Brothers* – it nevertheless demanded a large cast, elaborate costumes, and a set carefully authenticated with advice from the British Museum. The two leading roles – Synorix and Camma – were taken by Irving and Ellen Terry. When he finally saw the play, well into its run, Tennyson thought Irving's interpretation of Synorix rather crude, missing 'the subtle blend of Roman refinement and intellectuality, and barbarian, satisfied sensuality.' But it proved to be Tennyson's biggest stage success to date, running for 127 nights.

At a commission of just £5 a performance, play-writing was

still a financially insignificant part of Tennyson's work. But the success of *The Cup* encouraged him to go on and write another script. Indeed, the pitch at which he worked during the next two years, both at dramas and poems, is reflected in the thinness of detail which survives about his social life at this time.

The Tennysons did spend the end of the winter in London but apart from sitting for a portrait by Millais and continuing to disconcert Mary Gladstone with remarks about her wild eyes there were few notable encounters. While they were still in London, however, Alfred's old friend James Spedding was run over by a cab and seriously injured. Tennyson tried to visit him in St George's hospital but was turned away. Spedding survived for just over a week before dying of his injuries. He and Alfred had seen one another only infrequently in recent years, their friendship declining after Spedding's marriage and his becoming, 'no longer the comeatable, runuptoable, smokeable J.S. of old but as a family man, far in the West, sitting cigarless among many nieces, clean and forlorn'.

There is nothing by which we can measure Tennyson's reaction to this death – no memorial poem, no mention of it in his letters, and no response to FitzGerald's suggestion, sent to Emily, that Hallam should undertake the task of editing Spedding's papers. The increasing rapidity with which friends and relations were dying was, however, testing and torturing Tennyson's belief in the existence of an after-life and the survival of the soul.

Amongst Tennyson's society friends in the vicinity of Haslemere were Lord Selborne[39] and his daughter Sophia Palmer. They lived across the border, in Hampshire, but at a distance of only ten miles from Aldworth. Sophia, in her late twenties, was another of those young women with whom the older Tennyson liked to philosophize. Some time after Spedding's death he had the following conversation with her.

TENNYSON: Tell me, if you saw your father's and mother's bones, skeletons, lying in the grave, saw their bodies overmastered by corruption, would it over-master you? Would you feel they were there? That was all? Think! Just their bones – corruption! Would you?

SOPHIA: No; I would not be overmastered. The bones would not be those I had loved. *They* would be still alive, only more so than before.

TENNYSON: You are sure?

SOPHIA: Why, yes.

TENNYSON: Ah well; yes, I too hold it so. I have tried to say it –
to show it – that the body is the husk – the shell. But at times
these new lights, this science wearies and perplexes me; yet I
know they cannot reach, cannot explain . . .[40]

As he began having to face the inevitability of his own end, it
was hardly surprising that doubts about the after-life were to
obsess him. His personal struggle with pessimism and despair
was played out in the context of a more general crisis in
religious and philosophical debate concerning individuality and
personality. The Society for Psychical Research, founded in
1882, and its inquiries into material manifestations of the spirit
world, testified to the general hunger for confirmation of the
after-life.

In June Tennyson began a poem which, when it was
published later in the year in the *Nineteenth Century*, produced
something of a furore. The subject of the poem had once again
been suggested to him by Mary Gladstone, who had posted
Alfred a newspaper cutting reporting the case of a husband and
wife's attempt at joint suicide by throwing themselves in a river.
The man was rescued; the woman drowned.

Tennyson substituted the sea for the river and, in the form of
a dramatic monologue, put himself into the mind of the saved,
would-be suicide. 'Despair' is one of the triumphs of Tennyson's
later life. It is easy to see why the poem provoked so much bitter
criticism, for the voice of the speaker, unremittingly sustained
through twenty-one verses, damns both the religious and materialistic pieties of the age. It was a poem bound to upset
believer and non-believer alike.

In the face of attacks on the poem and various vicious
parodies (including Swinburne's 'Disgust'), Tennyson's instinct
was to distance himself from the despairing attitudes expressed
by reiterating that it was a dramatic monologue, not a con-
fessional ode. There can be no doubt, however, that he shared,
to the point of having personally felt, many of the would-be
suicide's thoughts.

In a short poem composed two months beforehand on the
occasion of the Duke of Argyll's resignation from office, he had
(in an early draft) urged the Duke to 'maintain/The spirit of the
age against the time.' This short poem ('To The Duke of Argyll')
was dredged from a much earlier poem about the Duke of
Wellington, and many of the sentiments in 'Despair' are best

explained, not by reference to the supposed, morbid disillusion of Tennyson's old age, but by comparison with much of his youthful verse in which can be found a similar tone of protest.

'Hail Briton!', never published in Tennyson's lifetime, had been written some fifty years before 'Despair'. It contains some of Tennyson's most powerful political and social comment:

> For babbling voices vex the days
>   We live in, teaching hate of laws,
>   And teaching lose their own applause
> To win a shallow journal's praise—
>
> Men loud against all forms of power,
>   Unfurnisht foreheads, iron lungs,
>   And voluble with windy tongues
> To compass all things in an hour.
>
> Still changing, whom no change can please,
>   Despotic hearts reviling kings,
>   They deal with names and know not things
> And handle types of emptiness.
>
> . . .
>
>   We faint unless the wanton ear
>   Be tickled with the loud 'hear hear'
> To which the slight-built hustings shake.
>
> One pants for place: one seeks relief
>   From life's monotony: one runs
>   For any goal: another shuns
> The pressure of a private grief.
>
> Uncertain of ourselves we chase
>   The clap of hands: we jar like boys:
>   And in the hurry and the noise
> Great spirits grow akin to base.
>
> . . .
>
> He seeing far an end sublime,
>   Contends, despising party-rage,
>   To hold the spirit of the Age
> Against the spirit of the Time—

> O civic Muse, for such a name,
>   Deep-minded Muse, for ages long
>   Preserve a broad approach of song
> And ringing avenues of fame.

The last verse quoted was later reworked as part of Tennyson's 'Ode on the Death of the Duke of Wellington' and he continued to plunder this unpublished text of his youth, using a verse from it as late as 1889 in 'To The Marquis of Dufferin'. Christopher Ricks's notes to the three-volume edition of Tennyson's poems abound with such references back to earlier work. This is not evidence of a failing power having to plunder past inspiration, but of a consistency of vision which had the confidence to see itself as a fixed eye amid a sea of shifty glances. The prophetic voice was one of many that Tennyson had at his disposal – alongside the elegiac, the colloquial, the lyric, the martial – and if it now took his readers aback, this was partly because, ever since the 1850s, he had chosen to make little use of that particular tone. However, a good deal of the reaction was that of a people genuinely affronted to have had their fixed and cherished positions soundly mocked – and by the Laureate of the day. A poem like 'Despair' is not written to pass without comment.

As the speaker recalls stepping out on the sands and preparing to wade into the deep, he describes the night-sky, stripped of mystery and promise:

> And the suns of the limitless Universe sparkled and shone in the
>   sky,
> Flashing with fires as of God, but we knew that their light was a
>   lie—
> Bright as the deathless hope – but, however they sparkled and shone,
> The dark little worlds running round them were worlds of woe like
>   our own—
> No soul in the heaven above, no soul on the earth below,
> A fiery scroll written over with lamentation and woe.

And, as part of the explanation of their disillusionment:

> Why should we bear with an hour of torture, a moment of pain,
> If every man die for ever, if all his griefs are in vain,
> And the homeless planet at length will be wheeled through the
>   silence of space,
> Motherless evermore of an ever-vanishing race,

When the worm shall have writhed its last, and its last brother-
worm will have fled
From the dead fossil skull that is left in the rocks of an earth
that is dead?

Have I crazed myself over their horrible infidel writings? O yes,
For these are the new dark ages, you see, of the popular press,
When the bat comes out of his cave, and the owls are whooping at
noon,
And Doubt is the lord of this dunghill and crows to the sun and the
moon,
Till the Sun and the Moon of our science are both of them turned
into blood,
And Hope will have broken her heart, running after a shadow of
good;
For their knowing and know-nothing books are scattered from hand
to hand—
We have knelt in your know-all chapel too looming over the sand.

It is not so much Tennyson's contemporary public who read the
poem wrongly, but those modern critics who find the poem too
shrill or strident to be counted one of his best. Tennyson uses
the ranting of the failed suicide to show how important are
meaning, hope and belief, to a calm and settled existence. If the
ranting is convincing it is because he allowed his own belief to
be more uncertain and unsettled than the average person of his
period.

22   Disturbance in the House

a red fire woke in the heart of the town,
And a fox from the glen ran away with the hen,
And a cat to the cream, and a rat to the cheese,
And the stock-dove coo'd, till a kite dropt down,
And a salt wind burnt the blossoming trees.

('SONG – 'THE PROMISE OF MAY')

In the autumn Tennyson had gone with Hallam to Sherwood
Forest, to make notes for the play he was still writing, *The*

Foresters. After his return the script was quickly finished but, like *Becket*, failed to convince Irving and others that it was worth producing. It was, he was told, not sensational enough for a modern audience. And so he immediately turned to very different material. Urged on by Sabine Greville and her set, he began to write a modern village tragi-comedy entitled *The Promise of May*.

But 1882 proved to be a nightmare year. It began with his managing to offend his old friend and honorary agent Knowles. At the request of Alexander Kinglake, historian of the Crimean War, Tennyson had written a new poem about it entitled 'The Charge of the Heavy Brigade'. Somehow or other Knowles was under the impression that he had been promised the new piece for the *Nineteenth Century*. Tennyson was adamant that he was mistaken:

> I cannot understand how you can say that the Charge of the Heavy Brigade was not offered to you – more than once – first, when you were here talking on the terrace with me. You distinctly refused it ... If you had even said I cannot have it now but will insert it in some future number, I should never have dreamed of offering it to Macmillan. You may in the multiplicities of business have forgotten all this but not I.[41]

This was rather an inconciliatory way to write to such an old friend and suggests that Tennyson was growing irritable from over-work and suppressed disappointment at the failure of his plays. The social life at Eaton Place was in something of a time warp. 'Joe', the Hungarian violinist, was always there; Alfred would invariably read *Maud*; and Mary Gladstone would introduce a new friend or cousin to the Laureate. She was growing irritated by Tennyson's habit of repeating himself. 'He glared at me and explained everything as if I had never heard of it,' she said, following a reception on the 16 March.

Four days later it was the Queen's birthday, in celebration of which Tennyson had been persuaded to recast 'Hands All Round!', written in 1852, into a patriotic song set to music by Emily who, for many years, had been nursing aspirations as a popular composer.[42] Emily's part in this debacle is significant because she was normally very astute in realizing when Tennyson was laying himself open to ridicule, and advising accordingly – as when she had told him not to send a personal letter to the Crimea. Her judgement evaded her on this occasion – perhaps because her own creativity was involved.

Tennyson's poem was sung all over England and the Colonies on 15 March. Every British subject was invited to raise a glass and drink

> To all our statesmen so they be
>   True leaders of the land's desire!
> To both our Houses, may they see
>   Beyond the borough and the shire!
> We sailed wherever ship could sail,
>   We founded many a mighty state;
> Pray God our greatness may not fail
>   Through craven fears of being great.
>   Hands all round!
>   God the traitor's hope confound!
> To this great cause of Freedom drink, my friends,
>   And the great name of England, round and round.

The modern frame of mind is quick to find such stirring patriotism laughable, but there were a good number of people in Tennyson's time who also found it unpalatable. The song brought trouble from two different camps. Temperance societies objected to its repeated invocation to 'drink', and wanted the word replaced with 'cheer'. Instead of ignoring such crassness Tennyson answered it by arguing somewhat sententiously that 'the common cup has in all ages been the sacred symbol of unity.' One wonders if he thought of his glass of port in such terms. More difficult to reply to was the stream of satires printed in the daily press during the days following the 15th. The *Daily News* rattled:

> A health to Jingo first and then
>   A health to shell, a health to shot!
> The man who hates not other men
>   I deem no perfect patriot.

Tennyson's imperialism, however, did not annoy everyone. Indeed, it might be rather cruelly said to have pleased the people who mattered. From the modern viewpoint there is something moving about Tennyson's naïve, romantic faith in England as an imperial power. It is a mood utterly alien to us now but, in contrast to Kipling's later less-forgivable patriotic ballads,

Tennyson's grand statements strike home as sincere and essentially good-natured. They were not built on any serious social or political perspective (he was hopelessly out of touch) but on a historical and sentimental identification with the nationalistic songs of Michael Drayton and James Sherry. The only modern English poet to have attempted to write in similar vein is Charles Sisson.[43]

In July came another blow. Tennyson's friend W.G. Ward died. In addition to the loss of his brother and of Spedding, the recent months had also brought the deaths of Carlyle, Dean Stanley, Drummond Rawnsley, and Longfellow. Ward's death left him particularly saddened, for it robbed him of a neighbour in Freshwater who had given support and encouragement to his religious musings. At the graveside (on the day after the funeral – Tennyson loathed the idea of attending an actual burial, probably because of his horror of contemplating the possibility that the lowering of a body beneath the ground might mark the end of everything) he recited the whole of 'Death the Leveller' by James Sherry. Repeatedly forced to face his own mortality – Sherry's poem concludes, 'Only the ashes of the just/Smell sweet and blossom in the dust' – he accepted an invitation to write a poem to mark the nineteenth centenary of Virgil's death. 'Thou majestic in they sadness/At the doubtful doom of human mind.' It was the element of doubt concerning the existence of the after-life which so haunted him. The composition of 'To Virgil' and a summer trip to Dovedale were positive interludes in an otherwise ill-starred year.

When Irving saw the finished prose play, *The Promise of May*, he was unimpressed; Kendal thought that it needed further development; but Mrs Beere, one of the leading actresses of the time, decided to produce it (and star in it) after hearing Tennyson read it aloud in October.

The play began its run at the Globe after a very brief rehearsal time, on 11 November. Despite the rush it was a well-prepared production, with effective village scenery, and well-designed programme. However, the first night was a fiasco. Opening on a Saturday was always foolhardy in those days, because a weekend audience was acknowledged to be unruly. A delay in the start of the production (scheduled for 8 pm, the curtain did not rise until 8.45 pm) caused the audience to become even more restive than usual. 'The Poet Laureate, poor innocent man! was led into a deep pitfall,' reported a columnist in *Theatre*.

Mary Gladstone, at the first night with Hallam, Lionel and Eleanor, summarized both the play and the evening as 'miserable work!'

Its reception on this first night has made it the most notorious of Tennyson's Dramas and, sadly, set the tone by which the rest are judged. This is a pity because it is by a long way the worst of his plays. The central character, Edgar, was too plainly a conduit for Tennyson's propaganda against materialism and Free-thought. The part had been devised and created against the background of a public controversy concerning the attempt of an MP, Charles Bradlaugh, to take his seat in the Commons without making the oath on the Bible. The viewing audience saw in Edgar a thinly-veiled attack on the likes of Bradlaugh, and the fact that the actor portraying him spoke great chunks of his lines as if he were making debating-points did not help dispel this assumption. The *Memoir* prints a lengthy attempt by Lionel to justify Edgar entirely in terms of the play's plot, and the relationship between its characters, but the play never had the pleasure of an audience willing to take it on its own dramatic terms. On the fourth night the Marquess of Queensbury[44], a leading supporter of Bradlaugh and Free-thought, stood up in his seat at the end of the first act, and shouted out, 'I am an agnostic, and I protest at Mr. Tennyson's gross caricature of our creed.' It was this public protest which prompted Lionel to write his piece, which appeared in the *Daily News* on 16 November.

Many suspected that the unrest on the first night had been the work of saboteurs. Sophia Palmer, who was at the performance with her father, noticed that the 'noise always began from one man ... Mr Labouchere & a large party of clearly intimate friends were present and father thought some of the same way of thinking were the noise-makers in the pit.'[45]

Tennyson himself tried to remain above the affray, and adopted a rather lofty, self-satisfied attitude towards the commotion he had set off. He wrote to one of his supporters:

I had a feeling that I would at least strive to bring the true Drama of character and life back again. I gave them one leaf out of the great book of truth and nature ... That old sonnet of Milton came into my head when I heard of the ruffians in the gallery ...

'I did but prompt the age to quit their clogs' (their melodramas, their sensationalisms, their burlesque – burlesque, the

476

true enemy of humour, the thin bastard sister of poetical caricature who I verily believe from her utter want of human
feeling would in a revolution be the first to dabble her hands
in blood)

'When straight a barbarous noise environs me
Of owls and asses, cuckoos, apes and dogs –
But this is not by casting pearl to hogs.'

On the whole I think I am rather glad of the row for it shows
that I have not drawn a bow at a venture.[46]

Despite this point of view Tennyson instructed Kegan Paul to
withdraw the play from publication. The type had already been
set and the book's cancellation meant that Tennyson had not
published any of his Dramas since *Harold* in 1876.

23   The Earliest Pipe of Half-awakened Bards

Old Fitz, who from your suburb grange,
Where once I tarried for a while,
Glance at the wheeling Orb of change,
And greet it with a kindly smile;

('TO E. FITZGERALD')

T he experience of having his play rejected – the run came to
an end early in December – hung over the early part of the
following year (1883). In his depression he took up and began to
rework an early poem, 'Tiresias', about an old, abused, blind
prophet.

I would that I were gathered to my rest,
And mingled with the famous kings of old,
On whom about their ocean-islets flash
The faces of the Gods – the wise man's word,

> Here trampled by the populace underfoot,
> There crowned with worship – and these eyes will find
> The men I knew, and watch the chariot whirl
> About the goal again . . .

Lines written so long ago; but just for this moment. There had been a time when his friends had blessed his every word. Now those friends were gone, and a frivolous public trod him into the ground.

One of the faces he did not yet reckon on being among the famous kings of old was that of FitzGerald, a rare surviving friend from more gracious times. Fancying to send the reworked poem as a birthday present, Tennyson began composing an epistolary prologue. But even as he wrote he received news of Fitz's death, at the age of seventy-five:

> The tolling of his funeral bell
>   Broke on my Pagan Paradise,
> And mixt the dreams of classic times,
>   And all the phantoms of the dreams
> With present grief.

Much diverted by thoughts about prophecy and sooth-saying, Tennyson easily identified with the figure of Tiresias, who, in classical mythology, had been punished with blindness for seeing too much (the naked Pallas Athene) but recompensed with the power of divination. More and more, in his last years, Tennyson's own poetry would carry a message, or tackle questions of faith and despair.

The Queen, who early in the year had lost her tried and trusted servant, John Brown, sent Tennyson a special invitation to visit her at Osborne House in August. He was at Aldworth at the time, but on the 7th made a special trip over to the island. It seems that ever since March, the month of Brown's death, there had been an exchange of letters between the Laureate and the Queen. She had been reading *In Memoriam* again, and sought comfort in a private meeting which, Tennyson had been told, would be 'in Her own room without any form.'

The meeting lasted for an hour and Alfred – 'He is grown very old – his eyesight much impaired – and he is very shaky on his legs' – talked of all the friends he had lost and spoke with horror of all the unbelievers and philosophers who would make you believe that there was no other world and no Immortality.

As he left her, he said, 'You are so alone, on that terrible height, it is terrible. I've only a year or two to live, but I'll be happy to do anything for you I can. Send for me whenever you like.'

There is something both sentimentally touching and archly pompous about his putting himself at Her Majesty's Service in this way, and there can be little doubt that the new intimacy in his relationship with the Queen intensified his view of himself as a modern prophet. When Victoria wrote to thank him for taking the trouble to visit her the letter was the first she had written in the first person – 'as the other form is so stiff.' She was soon taking the poet at his word. 'You say that you are glad to be of service to me ... Could you help me in choosing one or two lines to be put on the pedestal of the bronze statue of my faithful servant.'

Tennyson sent her three appropriate quotations from Shakespeare, Byron, Pope, and a fourth, marked 'Anonymous'. The Queen chose the anonymous couplet – 'Friend more than servant, loyal, truthful, brave!/Self less than duty, even to the grave!' – suspecting, correctly, that the lines were by Tennyson himself.

During September Hallam and his father joined the Gladstones as guests on a trial cruise around western Scotland aboard the *Pembroke Castle*, a 4000-ton vessel belonging to the shipping magnate and philanthropist, Donald Currie. The itinerary for the journey was extremely loose and unpremeditated. Indeed, when *The Times* initially reported the prospect of the Prime Minister's cruise, on 5 September, it was under the misapprehension that the boat would be sailing in the Channel – where, in recent days, there had been severe storms, denuding the beaches at Brighton and Hove of most of their shingle.

Alfred and Hallam met the Gladstones aboard a train at Chester. Crowds shouted out for Gladstone at every station they passed, a fact which nettled the poet. When they were safely aboard the *Pembroke* he complained of the fact that poets were less known by face to the public than actors and orators. Gladstone thought it only natural – the public, realizing that they were unlikely to meet a writer in the street, did not take the trouble to learn their faces from photographs. This hardly mollified Tennyson, who was further put out by the long and corrected report in *The Times* on 10 September, headed 'Mr Gladstone' (as all such reports of the cruise were to be) and giving a colourful description of the station-platform adulation which greeted the Prime Minister the full length of the train's route. The presence of the Poet Laureate in the party was given the briefest of mentions.

Tennyson was uncomfortable amongst the other dignitaries on board and discomforted by the bantering holiday mood. He failed to see the joke of a remark made by the Home Secretary in response to his saying that the tobacco in his first pipe of the day always tasted the best. 'The earliest pipe of half-awakened bards,' Sir William Harcourt quickly chipped in, burlesquing a line from 'Tears, idle tears'.

Mary Gladstone thought Alfred was ill-at-ease because the company and environment of the boat had put him out of 'all his old-maidenish habits'. But he and her father were as jolly together as two boys out for a holiday. Except for a brief and dangerous conversation about Bradlaugh, they took care to keep their conversation away from politics.

Politics of a more intimate and personal nature than national or international affairs did, though, raise its head in the course of the cruise. One morning Tennyson made it known to Sir Arthur Hamilton Gordon, Gladstone's Private Secretary, that if the offer of a baronetcy were to be made again his response might be different from in the past.

When Gordon told Gladstone about this the latter said, that being so, he would of course renew the offer. He then wondered aloud if he ought not to go one step further and make it a peerage, but hesitated. 'Could I be accessory to introducing *that hat* into the House of Lords.' It was typical of Gladstone that he should make this a serious reservation. He told Gordon, after thinking it over for a day, that he would offer a peerage, 'subject to certain information he required'.

Sidling up to Hallam when Tennyson was not around, Gladstone told him of the decision. 'The only difficulty in Gladstone's mind,' remembered Hallam, 'was that my father might insist on wearing his wide-awake in the House of Lords.' There were other questions too. Would Tennyson vote, if an urgent question of state policy required it? Was the poet's annual income sufficient to bear the dignity of a title?[47] And was Lionel settled in life? This was a surprising question, given that Lionel was married and a father, but it reflected the continuing high spirits of Tennyson's youngest son and the fact that his marriage was not strictly in accord with Tennysonian principles.

When told by Hallam of Gladstone's intention to offer him a

peerage Tennyson, contrary to the impression he had gone out of his way to give Gordon, told his son he did not want it. There followed several days of game-playing, with Gladstone even bringing in his ex-Private Secretary to help in the persuasion.

What was the point of such studied coyness on Tennyson's part? As so often with his behaviour in situations of this kind it is too easy to take the most ungracious view. Tennyson was vain, and liked to have people begging him to change his mind. His emotions in the matter were quite simple. He wanted the peerage, had wheeled and dealed over several years to get it, and was now going to savour his triumph.

But such a view takes insufficient account both of Tennyson's own naturally wavering character and of the psychology of public figures. If the rich are different from you and me, so are the famous. When Tennyson told Hallam that the title would 'do no good to literature' and make many literary men jealous, he was only saying aloud what he suspected to be true, and wanted to be convinced otherwise. In the end it was at Gladstone's urging that because a peerage had never before been offered purely and simply for service to literature, 'he owed it to the literary guild to accept this recognition on the part of the Queen and her ministers of the dignity and worth of letters. When put to him like that he felt it his duty to the craft to accept.'[48]

Severe minds may find this typical of Victorian pretension – people could not say they wanted something for itself but had to dream up a civic and honourable defence of their desire. It was quite common for people to weigh in the balance perfectly mundane decisions about their personal life for much longer than we do today. Even if there was an air of posturing about such deliberation and the concoction of sometimes fanciful rationalizations around an inevitable outcome, it is dangerous to treat such high-mindedness as if it were pure charade.

Emily was not aboard the *Pembroke Castle* so her immediate influence on Tennyson's acceptance of the peerage was minimal. He knew that it would please her, especially for Hallam's sake, but it is unlikely that she would have been able to persuade him otherwise had he been against accepting. Frederick, writing from Jersey (to his son Julius), and therefore out of touch with the mood at Farringford and Freshwater, read Emily's strength of character much more accurately than others, who were fooled by her physical infirmity, but the view of his brother as a mere plaything following in her wake is wildly off the mark:

As to the Peerage, which is the crowning honour – at least so considered – of a literary life, I do not believe that the desire to obtain it originated in your uncle's mind. Mrs. – now Baroness T. of Aldworth and Freshwater – has not been laid upon her back most of her life without nursing ambitious dreams, now realised. She, of course, will plead the advantages accruing to her children, & theirs. Many years ago the Queen – whose heart he had gained by the poetical incense offered to the late Prince Consort – would have done the same – but he did not then seem to regard it in any other light than as an empty adjunct to an already honoured & illustrious name. But doubtless he has been drawn into the wake of his wife's worldliness.[49]

As ever with Frederick the minor inaccuracies speak of a much broader misreading of events. Years ago, even when living in the same house as Alfred, he had told others that his brother was ready to publish a new volume of poems when this was quite untrue. His caustic view of Emily was influential on those who wrote upon Tennyson in the 1920s, encouraging their view of the poet as a split personality, the one half his natural self as represented by the poems written before 1850, the other half manipulated into high-thinking verse by a moralistic wife.[50]

Tennyson was used to others following in his wake, and that included his wife. It also included the other passengers on board the *Pembroke* for, on 13 September, at his suggestion, the boat suddenly left Scottish waters and set sail across the North Sea for Norway. In Copenhagen the party was given a state reception and at the Castle of Fredensborg there was a large dinner, the guests for which included the Kings and Queens of Denmark and Greece.

Queen Victoria, when she heard about this, was furious with her Prime Minister for setting foot 'on a foreign shore' without her permission. Gladstone was quick to tell her that the direction the cruise ended up taking was entirely the Poet Laureate's idea, which emolliated her.

One day Tennyson set fire to his coat by putting a lighted pipe in his pocket. He chided Mary Gladstone, saying that she had looked at it and burned a big hole over his heart. By now she was finding the old man's flirting more tiresome than intimidating, and mended the hole for him. *The Promise of May* had become part of Tennyson's repertoire for nightly readings.

'And the papers called that a failure,' he would say, as he reached the last words. 'Why, it's a perfect gem.'

'This he said,' wrote Miss Gladstone, 'in the most naïve way, and took our silence for consent.'

For the homecoming Tennyson was less inclined to be content with silence. On arriving in Gravesend on Friday 21 September Gladstone spoke to the crowd and prompted three cheers for Tennyson, remembering perhaps his disgruntlement on being ignored on the train-ride north. Of Tennyson and the peerage, of course, he said nothing, and there was no immediate public announcement. Although the Queen quickly gave her approval, all concerned were anxious that it should not be associated too closely with the cruise, and it was decided to delay the formal notification until early the following year.

In the meantime Tennyson had his title to consider. He explored the possibility of taking the d'Eyncourt name. As he told Gladstone, if the younger branch of the family could claim a descent from the time of Charles II, so could he. The exchange of letters between Tennyson and Gladstone during the autumn and early winter contained much about this and other matters:

Gladstone says that the Queen would leave the announcement till February but that he has advised Christmas. What would Tennyson prefer?

Tennyson replies that the date is for the Queen to fix.

Over a month later Gladstone 'presumes' that Tennyson will soon consider which date he prefers – Christmas or February.

Tennyson writes back, 'H.M. must decide when I am to be Peered.'

Gladstone, who has some Arthur Hallam letters of his own which he would like to print, tells Tennyson of a book by Charles Milnes Gaskell which includes other Hallam correspondence. Gladstone has given Knowles his own letters with a view to printing some of them.

Tennyson, who has not seen the Gaskell book – (it has been hidden from him by Emily and Hallam who fear its consequences on his 'very sensitive nature') – writes back in haste, 'Don't let Knowles print A.H.H.'s letters.' In a post script he tells the story of an old woman who, after reading Froude's biography of Carlyle burnt all the letters she had received from the great and famous. 'They were written to *me*, not the public,' she said. And Tennyson adds, in case Gladstone has not got the point, 'I should like to raise an altar to that old lady and burn incense on it.'

To Tennyson's suggestion of the d'Eyncourt title Gladstone replies that he does not think it likely to be possible. 'However reprehensible the act of disinheriting may have been,' the name has already been appropriated by the younger branch.

The College of Arms ruled against Tennyson anyway, so he had to be happy to become Lord Tennyson of Aldworth and Freshwater. The announcement was made in December and there was an immediate flurry of cartoons and lampoons, but little evidence of the literary jealousy which had been his main fear.

PART SIX
Nox

1 · The Bard is Crowned

O Statesmen, guard us, guard the eye, the soul
Of Europe, keep our noble England whole,
And save the one true seed of freedom sown
('ODE ON THE DEATH OF THE DUKE OF WELLINGTON')

Tennyson took his seat in the Lords on 11 March 1884, introduced by the Duke of Argyll and the Earl of Kenmore, the latter in place of Lord Houghton, who was away in Greece. The clerk read the Royal letters patent, Tennyson took the oath, entered his name on the roll, and was then led with the usual ceremony to his seat on the cross benches. (He had decided not to pledge himself to any one party, so that he could be free to vote without obligation.)

When he arrived home at Farringford he re-enacted the ceremony for Emily and a guest, Mary Brotherton, using a tea-cosy in place of a cocked hat.

1884 brought another significant change in Tennyson's circumstances. A further distrust had developed between himself and his publishers, Kegan Paul, by the time their five-year agreement expired at the end of 1883. In September an offer had been received from Macmillan which included a one third royalty and an annual advance of £1500, in return for a ten-year contract. At this stage of his life the length of the newly proposed contract had much to commend it, for it meant that in all probability Tennyson would feel settled with his new publisher for the remainder of his career.

Macmillan had tried on three previous occasions to secure Tennyson for his list. In 1858 he had attempted to poach the poet on Moxon's death; in 1868 he had been outbid by Strahan; and in 1878 he was outmanoeuvred by Kegan Paul. His delight in at last capturing the prize was infectious:

It is just forty-two years since I first read 'poems by Alfred Tennyson', and got bitten by a *healthy mania* from which I have not recovered and dont want to recover. I then tried to bite others, with some success. I have now *other*, I cannot say *deeper* motives for continuing the process. How much I owe to

Alfred Tennyson for the increase of ennobling thought & feeling, no one can tell. Now our closer connection will not lessen my desire to repay the debt.[1]

The relationship with Macmillan was much more friendly than it had ever been with Kegan Paul. For several years the Tennysons had been buying their books from the Macmillan shop, a habit begun when Lionel was at Eton, for Macmillan had a son there too. As far as the state of the Macmillan business in 1884 was concerned, the acquisition of Tennyson was a major addition to an already thriving concern – perhaps the major reason why business relations were so cordial. In addition to textbooks Macmillan published Meredith, Hardy, James, Pater and, subsequently, Kipling – as well as better-selling authors such as Charlotte Yonge and Mrs Oliphant. Then there were the popular editions and reference works such as the *Globe Library* and *Grove's Dictionary of Music and Musicians*.

The first new volume of Tennyson's work came out in February, with the publication of his two short dramas *The Cup* and *The Falcon*. The Macmillan accounts for 1884 are missing but however well the plays sold in the first year, public interest in them waned sharply. Only thirty-three copies were sold during 1885.

In March Tennyson was asked to write two epitaphs, one on Lord Stratford Canning, an Ambassador at Constantinople, and the other for Prince Leopold, youngest son of the Queen. H.D. Rawnsley was staying at Farringford while he worked on the first of these and noted how diligently, despite trouble with his eyesight and a natural antipathy to this kind of assignment, he tried out various drafts before settling on the best. 'I hate doing this kind of thing ... but they bother one out of one's life if one refuses.'

They also kept him from two longer poems he had on hand, for the flush of narratives which had begun six years before with 'The Revenge' and 'Rizpah' was continuing. One of the new pieces, 'Tomorrow', was in Irish brogue. Originally titled 'Molly Magee', the poem was based on a story de Vere had once told Tennyson about an old woman discovering the body of her first love, buried many years ago but preserved by the peat bog just as she remembered him. Allingham spent some time a month or two later helping Tennyson to make the brogue as effective as possible. He told Alfred that the Irish would not like it, 'but he didn't see why not.' The fascination of the story for Tennyson clearly lay in the reburial of the young man beside the body of the old woman who had fallen dead at the sight of him. The different states of the two bodies, one still fresh and youthful, the other aged and wrinkled, represented a difference in life experience which it was hard to envisage being bridged in Heaven. The two bodies might lie next to one another in the same grave, but could the uneven portions of Time they took with them to Eternity ever be balanced? It was a problem he had confronted in other, rather more seriously poetical verse – in 'Tithonus' and in *In Memoriam*:

> Yet oft when sundown skirts the moor
>   An inner trouble I behold,
>   A spectral doubt which makes me cold,
> That I shall be thy mate no more.
>
> Though following with an upward mind
>   The wonders that have come to thee,
>   Through all the secular to-be,
> But evermore a life behind.

(IN MEMORIAM XLI)

The personal fear that Arthur Hallam, and other loved ones already dead, might be unapproachable when the time came for his own entry into Paradise was a haunting one. If anything, the presentation of the peerage had sharpened Tennyson's preoccupation with death, for he seemed to see it as the 'crowning' of his career and a sign that his number was about to be called. Writing to the French translator of *Idylls of the King* he said, 'I thank you for your kind congratulations about the peerage; but being now in my seventy-fifth year, and having lost all my youthful contemporaries, I see myself, as it were, in an extra page of Holbein's "Dance of Death", and standing before the mouth of an open sepulchre while the Queen hands me a coronet, and the skeleton takes it away, and points me downward into the darkness.'[2]

But there was a pleasant domestic distraction in June when Hallam married Audrey Boyle in a side chapel of Westminster Abbey. (Audrey was the sister of Cecil Boyle, the special doted-upon charge of Henry Dakyns and John Addington Symonds at Clifton.) This was a smaller, less public occasion than the wedding of Lionel had been. The gathering, select and distinguished, included Browning, Lord Houghton, Arnold and the

Allinghams. Tennyson disappointed public onlookers by turning up dressed in a conventional suit, rather than his cloak and wide-awake hat. The stripping-away of his eccentric outer layer left him looking like an ordinary old gentleman.

During the ceremony Allingham sat with his wife behind two of Tennyson's sisters, Matilda ('always most simple, friendly, and a pleasure to talk to') and Cecilia. Browning winked an acknowledgement across the aisle. Tennyson himself was 'cool and self-possessed'. Emily, already frail, was rather overcome and could not enter the Jerusalem Chamber for the signing of the register. Nor was she able to go on to the reception at Lord and Lady Spencer's; instead, she and the servants were looked after at the Deanery until Alfred returned later in the day to take her back to Aldworth.

Hallam and Audrey honeymooned at Great Berkhampsted in Hertfordshire, taking over the Spencers' country house for a few weeks. Although Hallam's place at Aldworth was taken by Lionel, Eleanor and the children, his services were sorely missed. Emily was far too ill to begin all over again with the job of looking after Alfred's correspondence and Lionel had his own affairs (both general and particular) to attend.

There was no question of Hallam's abandoning his parents for good. It was agreed that, following the honeymoon, he and Audrey would return to Aldworth to begin their married life with Hallam's parents – Hallam continuing to consider his secretarial work for his father as a full-time occupation.

2   Taking a Stand

Men loud against all forms of power –
Unfurnished brows, tempestuous tongues –
Expecting all things in an hour –
Brass mouths and iron lungs!

('FREEDOM')

While they were away Tennyson had to confront his first political issue as a peer. The Franchise Bill, passed by a large majority in the Commons, was brought before the Lords, where the Tories were determined to vote it down. Gladstone, keen to muster every vote in its support, naturally considered this an early occasion for Tennyson to be called upon to return a favour. He wrote to Lionel (still temporarily in charge of his father's affairs) trusting that, 'We may count upon his being in his place on Thursday for the division.'

The Tory opposition to extension of the franchise was based on a fear that it would give Liberals an unfair advantage in future elections and they wanted a parallel bill brought in to redistribute and re-align the allotment of seats. After he had been apprised of the issues by Lionel, Tennyson took stock and informed Gladstone on 4 July, in a terse note of a single sentence, 'I cannot vote with you and I will not vote *against* you.'

Gladstone, 'considerably exercised' by this response, immediately wrote back to Tennyson from his London residence at Dollis Hill, Kilburn, in the midst of 'bustle and baddish lumbago'. He told Tennyson that he was the only peer with Liberal leanings who was hesitating to vote against Lord Salisbury, that a number of Conservative bishops would be voting with the Government, that the battle between the two Houses was likely to lead to a great humiliation of the Lords and pressure for a change in its composition.

Believing that Emily's influence on Alfred was all-important in matters of public concern, Gladstone wrote a companion-letter to 'Lady Tennyson' emphasizing the irresponsibility of the Lords in trying to overrule the Commons. The whole drift and purpose of this letter was to suggest to Emily that Alfred would be made to look like an accomplice in an irresponsible prank if he withheld his vote. 'I rely on your coming to the conservative view on the subject,' he ended, choosing his words carefully, and meaning, 'I hope you will resist joining the Tory extremists.'

Tennyson, in a letter written out by his daughter-in-law, Eleanor, replied by setting down his position on the issue. The time had come to extend the franchise, he accepted. But it could not be considered in isolation. Will town votes dominate country votes? (The Tory fear.) Will the loyal North of Ireland be over-ridden by the disloyal South? These were important questions for the House of Lords to consider. 'If you solemnly pledge yourselves that the Extension will not become Law before Redistribution has been satisfactorily settled, I am quite willing to vote with you and in proof I come up to town notwithstanding gout.'[3]

Although Tennyson's view, thus stated, was not far off Lord Salisbury's, it was good enough for Gladstone who gave a positive pledge that redistribution would follow at the earliest opportunity. So, on the night of 8 July Tennyson recorded his vote. It was not enough to save the Government from defeat but its scale (fifty-nine) was less than had been feared. Tennyson remained in London until the 17th to vote in favour of a proposal, put by Lord Wemyss, suggesting passage of the Franchise Bill, with a commitment to consideration of Redistribution to follow. The motion was rejected again, this time by fifty votes, and so the matter rumbled on for several more months.

In the meantime Tennyson was able to move to Aldworth for the summer. Hallam came home with his bride towards the end of July – a Welcome Home banner having been hung across the avenue. It was still there a few days later when the Allinghams visited and had to get used to calling Emily 'Lady Tennyson'.

They were frequent visitors during the summer season. Allingham, admirably unintimidated by his new Lordship presented Tennyson with some copies of the *Justice*, a socialist paper. They were quickly returned, with the comment that they had made him 'vomit mentally', fast becoming a favourite expression. In contrast he told Allingham he had read Baudelaire's *Les Fleurs du Mal* and, although he allowed that the subjects were shocking, found the French poet to be a 'kind of moralist'.

One day, sitting in the drawing-room with the Tennysons, the Allinghams were treated to an exhibition of domestic playfulness which showed that his title had not dampened any of Alfred's sense of fun. When the two five- and six-year-old grandchildren (both boys) raced into the room Tennyson left his chair and came back with a soap-dish and a lump of soap, which he rubbed into a lather for the blowing of bubbles. The boys jumped about to try and catch them or watched them burst in the high corners of the room after Allingham had fanned them up to the ceiling. Next, Tennyson turned his pipe upside-down and blew directly into the soapdish, bringing up a domed cluster of bubbles which grew and grew until it spilled over onto his trousers. The Allinghams, showing Lordly reverence at last, sprang forward with some newspaper to preserve the peer's hose.

The scene recalled previous bubble-blowing episodes and, remembering a trick he had been shown by a French hornplayer[4], Tennyson took his tobacco pipe, lit it, drew in some smoke and then blew marvellous opaque bubbles which burst like miniature explosive shells, much to the boys' (and their grandfather's) delight.

His conversation was full of talk about England going downhill and entering a 'sort of decadence', an attitude which it would be easy to dismiss as an old man's fancy, were it not for the fact that 'decadence' has since become the key-word in social historians' treatment of the *fin de siècle*.

Gladstone re-introduced the Franchise Bill into the Commons on the 24 October and it was again passed to the Lords on 13 November. In the interim Tennyson had composed 'Compromise', an eight-lined volley of advice for the beleaguered Prime Minister:

Steersman, be not precipitate in thine act
   Of steering, for the river here, my friend,
   Parts in two channels, moving to one end—
This goes straight forward to the cataract:
   That streams about the bend;
But though the cataract seem the nearer way,
Whate'er the crowd on either bank may say,
Take thou the 'bend', 'twill save thee many a day.

Gladstone's reply, beginning with a certain lack of straightforward honesty, 'I think it a great honour to receive from you a suggestion in verse,' was to the effect that he *had* taken the circuitous route of compromise urged upon him and found himself no better off than when he had started.

In his next letter Tennyson told him categorically to go before the House and give his personal pledge that as soon as the Franchise Bill was passed a Redistribution Act would be tabled. The Prime Minister made just such a declaration on the afternoon of 17 November, and on the 18th the Bill was passed in the Lords, Salisbury having been satisfied by Gladstone's statement. *The Times*, on the 19th, praised Gladstone for having 'steered' a moderate course, an obvious reference to Tennyson's poem, which had appeared in *St. James's Gazette* at the end of October. (Although the opening word of that version had been 'Statesman', the *Gazette*, in its introductory paragraph, had wondered which 'steersman' – Gladstone or Salisbury – was being addressed. Tennyson preferred this word, and made the revision.)

Gladstone's malleability and apparent lack of sensible intuition over this issue had been a shock to Tennyson. During a conversation between Emily Ritchie and himself, recorded by Allingham, he made his view plain.

RITCHIE: What a pity Mr Gladstone sees so many sides of a subject.

TENNYSON: No, that he does not do – he cannot see all round a thing.

RITCHIE: I suppose there's no country where the people care so much for politics as in England.

TENNYSON: I hate politics! The Queen said to me, 'I hate politics,' and no wonder she does. As to this Bill, I don't believe the people care anything about it.

Tennyson's relationship with Gladstone and the Liberal Party deteriorated as the months went on, partly because he did not confine such critical views to private conversations. In the spring of 1885 he attacked the Gladstone administration's reduction of the Fleet in a poem published in *The Times*. 'The Fleet' is not a good poem and it deserved the short shrift it got from the *Spectator*, which called it a 'bit of doggerel'. Hallam, incensed on his father's behalf at the attack, threatened to write to Hutton and cancel the family's subscription.

Tennyson thought Gladstone's foreign policy partly to blame for the death of General Gordon in the Sudan and he put himself at the head of a committee whose aim was to establish a Gordon Boys' Home in the General's memory. The Tennyson household was especially sensitive towards the issue in the Sudan because Audrey Tennyson's brother, a Major with the King's Rifles, had fallen ill with enteric fever while serving there, an illness which eventually caused his death.

The Queen, writing to Tennyson to invite him to Princess Beatrice's wedding, complained about the 'fatal mistakes' made in Egypt and the Sudan, when 'they were always too late, thereby being the cause of the death of that noble hero Gordon, whose abandonment is an eternal blot on our Crown.'

Their likemindedness on this subject encouraged Victoria to try and persuade Tennyson to bring his influence to bear on Gladstone in the form of encouraging retirement. His administration had been defeated in June but the Queen worried that he would return to the fray in the autumn elections, repeating the turmoil of his Midlothian Campaign in 1880. 'Radicals wish to push him on at 75½ to do what will ruin his reputation more than this last Government has already done.'

Tennyson told the Queen that he would 'try' but he was uncomfortable about his mission. He braced himself, however, and instructed Hallam to include the following sentence in a letter congratulating the Gladstone family on the birth of a grandson: 'I am also to say to you from him that he hopes for *every* reason that you will *not tax your strength* in going for an autumn campaign but that you will retire from the distractions of political conflict.'

The Queen pressed him for news in August, but Gladstone's reply had been equivocal and Tennyson could only tell her that he 'goes no further than to say he will not if he can help it.'

3   The Better Land

I would that I were gathered to my rest,
And mingled with the famous kings of old

('TIRESIAS')

During the autumn Tennyson had frequent visits from the Allinghams, who had been living at Sandhills, six miles away, for the past four years. The conversations recorded by the dutiful Allingham tell us much about Tennyson's views at this time: that he found Trollope prosaic and dull; that he remembered William Barnes with affection; that he contemplated attaching a phonetic code to his poems to help readers sound them properly. In between these autumn walks and visits Tennyson was mulling over the proof copy of *Tiresias and Other Poems*, which was finally published in December. The book was a mixture of poems that had already appeared in periodicals (including 'Despair', 'Frater Ave atque Vale', and 'Hands All Round') and entirely new poems ('The Wreck', 'The Ancient Sage' and 'Balin and Balan'). It was some five years since Tennyson had published a similar collection and both the public and the critics responded enthusiastically. But perhaps not quite as rapturously as Macmillan had expected. Of his optimistic print-run of 20,000 copies the book sold 15,000 in its first year. Despite the guaranteed income from the Macmillan contract and from continuing sales of old stock, Emily had recently given notice that family funds were falling low. 'This year I have been reduced to the purchase of 2 black woollen dresses,' she wrote to her niece Agnes, 'so you will divine that we are not very flourishing. Indeed I do not know who is, except it be Mr Chamberlain.'[5]

In October Lionel and Eleanor had left England for India, at the invitation of Lord Dufferin. Their two boys remained behind with an aunt in Scotland. Early in the New Year (1886), during a hunting trip in Assam, Lionel caught jungle-fever and returned to his base in Calcutta. There his condition hung in the balance for many weeks. The Tennysons first heard that Lionel was ill in mid-February but they were informed by Dufferin in terms of classic British understatement. Lionel was 'laid up' and had 'caught a chill ... we regard attacks of the kind pretty much in the same light as we do colds in England.'

Eleanor's telegrams at first carried hope, but Lionel's lungs were affected and he had to be operated on. Suffering from post-operative abscesses he was put on a ship and sent home. Sailing through the Red Sea his condition became desperate.

Under a silvery moon the coffin was lowered into the phosphorescent sea.

> And now the Was, the Might-have-been,
>   And those lone rites I have not seen,
> And one drear sound I have not heard,
>
> Are dreams that scarce will let me be,
>   Nor there to bid my boy farewell,
>   When that within the coffin fell,
> Fell – and flashed into the Red Sea
>
> Beneath a hard Arabian moon
>   And alien stars. To question, why
>   The sons before the fathers die,
> Not mine! and I may meet him soon;
>
> But while my life's late eve endures,
>   Nor settles into hueless gray,
>   My memories of his briefer day
> Will mix with love for you and yours.
>
> ('TO THE MARQUIS OF DUFFERIN AND AVA')

This lovely, measured poem was written some two years after the event. At the time Tennyson was torn to pieces, and working on a poem of a radically different mood. Some suggest that Lionel's death once more demonstrated the emotional strength of Emily, and that it was she who helped bring Alfred through the crisis with her rock-firm faith. However, the description given by Mrs Brotherton to illustrate Emily's 'serene courage'[6] could equally well describe the facile tranquillity of a fanatic. 'I never saw so radiant a look in any happiest human face as in hers. I really think she spends half the time already in the Better Land with her son. Nothing else could give so wonderful an expression of joy. It is not resignation. It is bliss.'

It is hard to see how Tennyson might have found such a fundamentalist spirituality supportive. There are some slightly spurious stories of his having attended seances after his son's death, in an attempt to make contact with Lionel's spirit. Such stories need not be true for their existence to demonstrate that he did not share his wife's inward sense of transportation to the Better Land.

The poem which he completed in the days following Lionel's death – 'Locksley Hall Sixty Years After' – is a work of splenetic isolation and disillusion.

4   Poor Old Voice

Poor old Heraldry, poor old History, poor old Poetry, passing hence,
In the common deluge drowning old political common-sense!

Poor old voice of eighty crying after voices that have fled!
All I loved are vanished voices, all my steps are on the dead.

All the world is ghost to me, and as the phantom disappears,
Forward far and far from here is all the hope of eighty years.

('LOCKSLEY HALL SIXTY YEARS AFTER')

Late in July Hallam and Audrey went with their father to London where Tennyson was examined by Doctor Andrew

Clarke, physician to Gladstone and other notable figures. Hallam's report to his mother that the patient was pronounced 'absolutely sound' suggests that more than just his physical condition had given cause for concern. The prescription, however, was down-to-earth and typically Victorian. He needed a liver-pill. (A few days later Lord Tennyson's picture appeared unauthorized in an Eno's advertisement alongside a promotional recommendation reputedly signed by him.)

Tennyson was cheered on this visit to London by seeing the first production of his *Becket* – not, however, the whole play, and not performed by a professional company. Scenes were acted out by an amateur group (led by Lady Archibald Campbell) in a Wimbledon wood.

Leaving London, Hallam took his father to Cromer to visit the Locker Lampsons and while they were there a report appeared in *The Times* giving notice of the existence of Tennyson's new poem. 'The hero of [Locksley Hall] re-appears as a broken-down man of 80, whose modified views of life and liberty may be taken to reflect the Laureate's own.' Such an autobiographical interpretation of his work always infuriated Tennyson but in this case his rebuttals were somewhat unconvincing. The character in the new poem could not possibly be himself, he said, because the poetical figure was grey-haired, whereas he, no matter how close to eighty he may be, did not have a grey hair in his head.

The poem was eventually published in December 1886 in a book entitled *Locksley Hall Sixty Years After Etc.* – the 'Etc' referring to just three other poems and his play, *The Promise of May*, now some four years old, and an inclusion which has puzzled most of his critics. Why did he bother to take up so much space by putting into print a drama which carried with it so many bad associations, and which had been withdrawn from publication when it was first completed? The answer can only be that he continued to believe that it contained a message to which he wanted people to listen. Commercially, the volume enjoyed a success almost identical to the previous year's collection, selling just over 14,000 copies in the first year. But there was extensive criticism of the new, long poem, not least from Gladstone.

For many readers a new book by Tennyson was an echo of older, more positive times, and therefore welcomed, not uncritically, but with an expansive frame of reference. Mrs Ritchie

(Anne Thackeray), although she was of another generation, greeted the book in exactly this spirit:

> In the evening it came, and I began – no not began – I went on reading out of the book that I have read and loved all my life, and who knows, perhaps, when we are all peacefully together again (and I always think of old days on the Freshwater Downs as the nearest thing to heaven I ever could imagine) you will still walk ahead and point to the sea and to the sky, and touch things and make them shine for us and flash into our hearts, as you have ever done.[7]

The inclusion of *The Promise of May* in the Locksley Hall volume did more than demonstrate Tennyson's continuing faith in the play. He was, in fact, negotiating with Bram Stoker for a second production. But in his higher hopes for the play Tennyson misjudged the mood of the time. The Queen's Jubilee was to be celebrated in February 1887 and a large section of Tennyson's readership resented the sour note struck by the title poem. None more so than William Gladstone, who read it as a straightforward criticism of the social and economic progress he had fought so hard for half a century to achieve. In reply he wrote an article which appeared in the *Nineteenth Century* listing the reforms achieved since 1842. 'Justice does not require,' he ended, 'nay rather she forbids, that the Jubilee of the Queen be marred by tragic notes.' The essay, which also carried an implicit suggestion that Tennyson was not intellectually equipped for social comment, was a controlled outburst of all the irritation Tennyson had caused Gladstone since accepting the peerage.

There were other critical voices, particularly from younger poets who felt Tennyson had become a whingeing old man who had demonstrably survived longer than was good for himself and his country. Contemporaries of Tennyson, however – friends like Jowett – were impressed by his continuing vigour.

5   The Corpse of Pleasure

Love for the maiden, crowned with marriage,
no regrets for aught that has been,
Household happiness, gracious children,
debtless competence, golden mean;

('VASTNESS')

There were two upsetting events in Tennyson's personal life early in the New Year. His favourite sister Emily (Jesse) died. And Eleanor, Lionel's widow, became engaged to a young barrister called Birrell. 'Why do you want to force your way into my family?' is alleged to have been Tennyson's unprepossessing response to the young man's initial entreaties.

In June he accompanied Hallam and Audrey on a cruise around the south-west coast. They set sail from Portland Bay on the 11th and were pleased to find on board the same cook that had travelled with them on the *Pembroke Castle*. With no Mary Gladstone aboard to tease, Tennyson took to spending much of his time with his daughter-in-law. The two of them would get up early, while Hallam dozed on, and walk along the quayside together.

Sailing past Torquay, Brixham and Berry Head, they weighed anchor in Dartmouth. Then they sailed on to Tintagel and Lundy, where they landed and stayed for four days and nights, travelling around the island on a two-wheel jig without springs which nearly broke Alfred's back in two. On one occasion the horses took fright and they all thought their last hour had arrived. 'His father and I sat perfectly still, perfectly silent, awaiting our doom,' Audrey wrote in her travel journal.[8]

Leaving the island, Audrey was given the job of steering the small tender back to the yacht. Constantly reprimanded by Hallam she took herself to bed with a racking headache and stayed in her cabin all the next day. The next time she was offered the tiller she made Hallam steer 'as it is a task most thankless I find & not pleasant.'

There was a serious storm on the night of the 18 June. They were passing back round Land's End and the yacht rolled and tossed terrifyingly. A crash and a strong smell of sal volatile told

Audrey that the bottle she had put out for her father-in-law's pipes had smashed.

As he lay in his bunk, at the mercy of the seas, Tennyson might have reflected on the poem he had written two or three years earlier, exploring the theme of 'What is the point of it all?'

Pain, that has crawled from the corpse of Pleasure,
  a worm which writhes all day, and at night
Stirs up again in the heart of the sleeper, and stings him
  back to the curse of the light;

('VASTNESS')

In these late years he remained genial in company and although everyone noticed that death was continuously on his mind, it was not morbidly so. Allingham and his wife visited Aldworth in November and were taken to Tennyson in his room where they found him sitting by the window reading, uncharacteristically dressed in a red fisherman's smock. After going outside to walk on the lawn with them both, and discussing Darwin and French philosophy, he said suddenly, 'The only tolerable view of this life is as the vestibule to a better.' Then, taking Helen's hand, he added, 'I am very glad to have seen you. Perhaps you'll never see me again till I'm dead.'

The roll-call of visitors fell off slightly. He saw rather more of those brothers and sisters who lived close by (Arthur, Horatio and Matilda) and as his grandchildren grew older so did he spend time with them. Taking them for walks he would amuse them with his eccentric behaviour towards other children. Flapping his cloak like some huge, sombre bird, he would make barking noises at them and express surprise when they ran off in terror.

At the end of one of his solitary walks he returned home carrying his hat upturned and filled with dangerous-looking fungi. Despite Emily's and Hallam's protests he ordered them to be cooked for lunch and ate them all himself. The cook was ordered by Emily to make sure the episode was never repeated. She was happy to obey.

Relationships between the Tennysons and their staff were now very good. The large retinue of servants – extending to grooms and gardeners – had mostly been with the family for many years and a blind eye was turned on their occasional 'lapses from sobriety'. One of the longest-serving was their coachman William Knight. He remained in the family's service until he was eighty years old, having begun working for Alfred when he was only fifteen. Knight, who had an uncouth dignity, later published his own recollections of Tennyson.

Early in 1888 Edward Lear died at his Villa Tennyson in San Remo. Emily's Christmas letter to him at the end of 1887 had been sober in the extreme. She wrote as an old woman with only the view from her window as comfort.

> All is changed here since you were here. You would be startled every now and then by a railway whistle were you with us now. The cars only carry gravel at present but in March the whole way is to be open to Carisbrook, we are told ...
> Fortunately one's eyes look out only on the old prospect from the windows. The old prospect but a little narrowed to the north by the growth of trees ... My Ally has been working but he is changed since you saw him though he can walk well and write wonderfully still.[9]

It cannot have been a very heartening letter for the sickening Lear who himself, by that time, having lost his cat Foss, took little pleasure in life beside looking out of the window onto the terrace of the Villa Tennyson.

Lear's last years had been devoted to the production of several hundred illustrations for Tennyson's poems, a project in which Tennyson himself never showed great interest. Although some effort was made to publish all of the drawings, only a few were made available in Tennyson's lifetime, in a limited edition containing illustrations to just three poems, 'The Daisy', *The Princess* and 'The House of Art'.

Despite these two events and the continuing furore over the new Locksley Hall, Tennyson began 1888 in good form. An American actress, Mary Anderson, showed an interest in producing *The Cup*. Tennyson also pressed the case of *The Foresters*, implying that it was a new play still being worked on. To help fire her enthusiasm he and Hallam took Miss Anderson and her mother on a two-day tour of the New Forest. They were driven round by Willingham Rawnsley, son of Drummond, and headmaster of the school near Lyndhurst to which Lionel's boys had been sent. The touring group visited Alfred's grandchildren and took them on a picnic in the forest. Tennyson was introduced to Gordon Wordsworth, a teacher at the boys' school and a grandson of the poet. He asked Wordsworth how old his grandfather had been when he died. When he was told eighty, he announced, rather grimly, 'One more year.'

However, most of the time he was in puckish form, attempting to hide his identity at the Inn by posing as a Mr Hood.

In July he was visited by the Earl of Carnarvon who found him as fresh and capable in his mind as ever before. 'In conversation one is struck by the power and force of what he says, though it is the speech of a man who has lived in books; or in a very small world of his own and who sees things through a narrow vista – the constant contrast of broad and fine ideas with very narrow ideas is unusual – and from the same cause I suppose he brings everything back to himself. His own writings are the central point of all his thoughts.' This last thought echoed criticisms made about the old age of Wordsworth but whereas Wordsworth's self-centredness could be priggish Tennyson's, according to Carnarvon, 'is almost like a child'.

As with others Tennyson tried to persuade the Earl that the new Locksley Hall was purely 'dramatic' but his visitor was unconvinced. 'The poem does mean a change and a very great one; and Tennyson's conversation bears witness to it. He hates the modern Radicals, he has lost any admiration he may have had for Gladstone, and if he expresses an occasional belief in human or social progress it is a very frigid and doubtful profession of faith. But the old impulsive character of the man is there ... In him one sees the two natures in conflict – the impulsive, hopeful, sanguine believer in progress of former days, and the timid Conservative of the present who fears the tendency of modern times and is inclined to look at everything from a very narrow point of view.'[10]

August passed pleasantly enough with no hint of ill health, but during the first part of September Tennyson noticed that there was swelling around both his knees. It was the beginning of a serious illness.

6 The Snows of Age

What hast thou done for me, grim Old Age, save breaking my bones
on the rack?

('BY AN EVOLUTIONIST')

Dr Andrew Clarke, Gladstone's physician, attended him, as
did Dr Dabbs from the Isle of Wight. It was Dabbs who,
two months later, accompanied Tennyson in a specially commissioned ambulance carriage, when the family returned to
Farringford for the winter. Hallam was told that his father was
suffering from rheumatic gout brought on by his habit of
walking in all weathers. Whether the illness was rheumatic fever,
gout, or a combination of both, is difficult to determine.
Certainly Tennyson himself considered it to be gout, and was
supported in this by various remarks made by his doctors.
Clarke once declared his patient to be 'saturated with gout'.

Toward the end of September he seemed to be getting better.
Emily wrote to Venables, who had made his last visit to Alfred a
few days earlier (and who became seriously unwell himself
during the stay with what proved to be the onset of a fatal
illness) that Alfred no longer needed to be 'lifted from bed to
sofa in a sheet and fed like a baby.' He had even gone out for a
drive.

But there came a serious relapse early in October, severe
enough for Emily and Hallam to keep secret the news that
Venables had died on the 6th and to put off all visitors.

Allingham, who had to delay a trip to Aldworth until the
beginning of November found Tennyson in his study, leaning
back across two chairs and wearing a black skull-cap. He was
reading a book by the extra light of two candles, the illumination
from which lit up just one side of his face, creating a striking
and noble profile. Allingham thought him thin and pale but
otherwise not looking his age.

During November the effect of the medication Tennyson
received produced a series of vividly colourful dreams. He
dreamed that Priam appeared before him, and he probably
identified with the King of Troy, portrayed in the *Iliad* lamenting

the death of his sons and bewailing the sufferings of his people; he dreamed that the face of a clock expanded and filled up the whole end of the room, its hands pointing to 6.15 – 'Superstitious people would say that I die then,' he told Hallam; he dreamed that he opened a letter to himself after his death – what it said, he wasn't telling; he dreamed he was the Pope, bearing all the sins and miseries of the world on his shoulders; he dreamed of building a tower of brightly coloured pagodas reaching up to Heaven. And accompanying these dreams was a rush of thoughts about God, the Universe, and the after-life.

That Tennyson was dangerously ill, and near death, is attested by his mood and the detailed notes on his condition kept by Hallam, who was told by the doctors to record 'not only the state of his physical health, but also something of what was occupying his mind.'[11] After a small recovery at the end of November (it was this which allowed him to be transported back to Farringford) there was an immediate relapse. His doctors tried various regimes – milk, broth, quinine – and drugs to ease the severe rheumatic pain.

Although a nurse (Miss Durham) was employed to attend to Alfred, Hallam spent many hours by his father's bedside, sometimes sitting up through the night when Tennyson was very feverish and restless. Just after Christmas there was a gradual improvement – the patient began to chaff both Nurse Durham and Hallam over their assiduous treatment. 'You are like a brooding mother,' he told Hallam one day, as his son helped the nurse to dress him. Once his temperature began to return to normal he started to complain that they were wrapping him up too warmly: 'it feels like the geese tied by the fire to make their livers big.' And he was able to share in the humorous enjoyment of the various prescriptions sent through the post by multitudes of well-wishers. One – perhaps not a well-wisher, this – suggested that burning cork should be placed under his bed.

During respites in his illness he had been writing down epigrams and he now assembled these into one poem, 'By an Evolutionist'.

I have climbed to the snows of Age, and I gaze at a
    field in the Past,
        Where I sank with the body at times in the sloughs of a
        low desire,

> But I hear no yelp of the beast, and the Man is quiet at
>   last
>   As he stands on the heights of his life with a glimpse
>   of a height that is higher.

When he was beginning to recover he wrote out a rare personal invitation to one of the few surviving friends from the past – Merivale – who had just sent him an edition of his rhymed translation of the *Iliad*. But although his doctors were soon to pronounce him fully recovered there were still setbacks. At the beginning of March Emily wrote to her sisters, '[Ally] is very weak and poorly now. The cold is too much for him we suppose. He has not been well enough to be carried down for some days. Thank God we may hope for Spring in another month.'[12]

In the middle of May he walked outside with Hallam in the kitchen garden and a little way into the 'wilderness'. But although the ground was a colourful mass of primroses and cowslips, and the first turtle-dove of the year called in the trees, Tennyson quoted aloud from Milton's *Paradise Lost*: 'O foul descent! that I who erst contended/With Gods to sit the highest, am now constrain'd/Into a Beast, and mixt with bestial slime/This essence to incarnate and imbrute,/That to the highth of Deity aspir'd . . .' He was pronounced physically fit enough to be taken by Hallam on a summer cruise aboard Lord Brassey's yacht, the *Sunbeam*, but the aftermath of his illness left his mental outlook very darkened.

The *Sunbeam* was famous for having toured the world ten years earlier with Brassey, then Liberal MP for Hastings, at the helm. It was a 170ft, three-masted craft, whose steampower was temporarily out of action. When Tennyson boarded the boat, with his son and his nurse, fellow passengers were struck by how diminished in body he had become. (He had been weighed, in his clothes, at the end of the winter, and registered only nine and a half stone on the scales. Despite his hypochondria, his body-weight had never been an overriding obsession and nothing is known of how great a weight loss this signified. But for a tall man, with a large frame, nine stone was a seriously underweight condition.)

Despite physical weakness and frailty Tennyson seemed in fairly good spirits, telling 'endless stories'. However, he was loath to go ashore and risk contact with crowds and always insisted the boat was anchored well beyond the sight of curious stare-mongerers. After an abortive push for Iceland, the boat turned and contented itself with hugging the now-familiar south-west coast.

Tennyson's jocularity at the start of the cruise quickly ebbed away. On the morning of 26 May he wrote out part of a new poem, 'Parnassus', expressing a fear that haunted him at the end of his life – that, for all his achievement, the influence of Poetry was being overshadowed by two terrible modern Muses, Astronomy and Geology.

What be those two shapes high over the sacred fountain,
Taller than all the Muses, and huger than all the mountain?
On those two known peaks they stand ever spreading and
    heightening;
Poet, that evergreen laurel is blasted by more than lightning!
Look, in their deep double shadow the crowned ones all
    disappearing!
Sing like a bird and be happy, nor hope for a deathless hearing!
'Sounding for ever and ever?' pass on! the sight confuses
These are Astronomy and Geology, terrible Muses!

After finishing the draft he was tired and in low spirits. The weather was very cold and blustery, and the boat took refuge at Dartmouth. Tennyson's readings on this cruise departed from his normal repertoire. He recited 'Despair' and, on the 30 May, 'Guinevere', choking on the words and with tears streaming down his cheeks.

It was not until the end of the voyage, with the boat passing round the Needles on its way back into port, that his spirits rose again. But even after he was home at Farringford the depression continued. As his eightieth birthday approached he gathered his powers and, with thoughts of death still hanging over him, composed a poem capable of standing as a final statement. 'Merlin and the Gleam' is both potted autobiography and a clarion call to younger poets:

Not of the sunlight,
Not of the moonlight,
Not of the starlight!
O young Mariner,
Down to the haven,
Call your companions,
Launch your vessel,

And crowd your canvas,
And, ere it vanishes
Over the margin,
After it, follow it,
Follow the Gleam.

The short lines and chant-like rhythm (– u u – u) give the poem
remarkable freshness. Not only is it one of the best poems of
Tennyson's old age, it is a marvellous poem by any standard.
His long illness seemed to have burnt out the cantankerous and
vituperative pessimism that powered 'Locksley Hall Sixty Years
After'. No matter how depressed and out of spirits he might
appear to others – Emily frequently said that he was never the
same again after his illness – and no matter how he might feel
that his own power to follow the gleam was gone – 'And so to
the land's/last limit I came –/And can no longer/But die
rejoicing' – he did in fact go on, not simply rejoicing, but
working. Working to the last.

7   Eighty Years Old

Eighty winters leave the dog too lame to follow with the cry,
Lame and old, and past his time, and passing now into the night.

('LOCKSLEY HALL SIXTY YEARS AFTER')

On the afternoon of his eightieth birthday he was visited by
Emily Ritchie. Having seen him so thin and ill earlier in
the year she was braced to find him void of the poetic temper.
But he took her into his study and read her his new poem. 'It
was a happiness, an unexpected one, to hear it; the freshness,
the inspiration and the novelty of the metre in which he set
forth the course of his poetic life seemed wonderful. Anyone
who knows the poem will understand how moving it was to
hear Tennyson read it – Merlin himself speaking.'[13]
There was no keeping his birthday quiet this year, of course,
and even Emily did not attempt to do so. She arranged with
Craik, the manager of Macmillan, for a new desk to be sent – 'a

good solid old-fashioned desk to *stand* on his writing table & we should much like to place it there on the 6th. I ask you to choose one for us.'[14]

As the telegrams arrived Alfred told Emily, 'I am sick of all this publicity, all this fulsome adulation,' and she was perhaps too ready to take the negative surface of such statements at face value. Tennyson's birthday did in fact bring him considerable pleasure. There was a big box beside him containing the hundreds of telegrams and congratulatory letters, mostly from people who mattered nothing to him. But, puffing on his pipe, he would occasionally put in his hand and pull one out. There was the odd plum – a beautiful letter from Edmund Lushington and a similar one from Robert Browning. Such heartfelt admiration from close and respected friends made him wonder what he had done to make people feel as they did towards him.

Emily's readiness to believe that Ally was too morose to enjoy his birthday is partly explained by her concern for Hallam who had had to undergo an operation on his mouth at the end of July and was still recuperating. This appears to have been connected with trouble that Hallam had had two years beforehand. It was not, judging from Emily's comments, a dental problem. As he recovered from that earlier illness, she wrote to her sister, 'He can even yawn without much pain now & the lip goes on ... Dr. Hollis never having had a similar case makes one rather more anxious than would otherwise be.' The recent operation, for which Hallam had to be given chloroform, was successful. 'The doctors think the evil is eradicated'; however, 'he will, I fear, be in bed at least another week.'[15]

Tennyson himself seems not to have been much diverted by his son's illness. Soon after his birthday he began writing 'Romney's Remorse', a powerful monologue, loosely based on the life of the artist, George Romney (1734–1802), who married at nineteen but then abandoned his bride because he was told that marriage would spoil his art (only to return to her to be faithfully nursed through his last sickness). Tennyson freely acknowledged that the central point of the poem (the 'remorse') was a pure fabrication. In order to justify his invention he put his speaker under the influence of an opiate: 'Words only born of fever, or the fumes/Of that dark opiate dose you gave me – words/Wild babble.'

A biographical reading of the poem cannot fail to conclude that the 'remorse' was not invented at all but sharply and painfully felt by Tennyson himself, with respect to Emily. If Romney's remorse can be seen as the objective correlative of Tennyson's own remorse, in what manner might Tennyson have considered that he had abandoned his family for his art? *Kunstlerschuld* works irrationally, and especially so upon those artists who have no occupation other than their art. In this sense, Tennyson, the poet par excellence, was a prime victim. Leaving aside his theatrical excursions, and his early financial speculation, he never wavered from his Muse – never, and this is extraordinary in terms of his Victorian 'pre-eminence', gave a lecture or wrote an essay. The whole of his working life was dedicated to poetry and he was bound to feel at times that such fidelity was, in its way, an *in*fidelity to those around him, particularly to Emily, Hallam and Lionel. A large part of his obsessive preoccupation with immortality was not religious in nature at all, but a direct symptom of his artist-guilt. If he could be convinced that there was no after-life, he would say, he would throw all to the wind; 'eat drink and be merry, for tomorrow we die'. At the back of such statements lay a horrifying suspicion that all would be lost in the grave and he might just as well have lived a life of sentient ease. What fame he has at eighty will burst like a bubble once he is dead and gone: 'Mine that grew/ Blown into glittering by the popular breath,/May float awhile beneath the sun, may roll/The rainbow hues of heaven around it – There!/The coloured bubble bursts above the abyss/Of Darkness, utter Lethe.'

How, in actuality, could it be said that he had abandoned Emily? In one sense the abandonment was mutual, with Emily's hysterical spinal condition representing her attempt to claim some individual space in response to her husband's all-encroaching one. 'Here, on this sofa, I am Queen.' Tennyson's own studies of madness and psychology make it likely that he was fully aware of what lay at the root of Emily's state, and the element of his own responsibility for her condition. In many ways he was a considerate husband – pushing her in her bath chair, reading to her, but these actions were not enough. Increasingly, as the boys grew older, husband and wife had become estranged – Tennyson entangled in his work and Emily first of all in her secretarial duties and then in her illness. By the time Hallam usurped her role this estrangement was quite pronounced. Some contemporary visitors and observers of the Tennysons at home thought Alfred supremely insensitive to his wife's ministrations – in these accounts we see Emily enshrined as the ministering angel serving the selfish genius. But Emily was neither so saintly nor Tennyson so singleminded as this sentimental viewpoint implies.

The dramatic setting of the poem – the mental meanderings of a doped and dying man – suggest that the full impact of his guilt may have dawned on Tennyson in the course of his recent illness. He might better have been an outright sinner than bury himself for so many hours in books and manuscripts. Art is going to seem a feeble excuse to proffer to the Almighty:

'Nay, Lord, for *Art*,' why, that would sound so mean
That all the dead, who wait the doom of Hell
For bolder sins than mine, adulteries,
Wife-murders, – nay, the ruthless Mussulman
Who flings his bowstrung Harem in the sea,
Would turn, and glare at me, and point and jeer,
And gibber at the worm, who, living, made
The wife of wives a widow-bride, and lost
Salvation for a sketch.

The poem has other, minor biographical reference-points. The white heather mentioned in line 105 had its basis in an actual sprig which Tennyson discovered on one of his walks during the period of composition and immediately presented to his guest at the time, William Gordon McCabe.[16]

Through the rest of the summer and early autumn he worked hard at putting together a new collection and on 1 November 1889 Emily told Craik, 'He is writing away at his poems. I hope you will have them with you in two or three days.' And exactly three days later, on the 4th, she wrote again to say, 'I have just been packing off the poems to Hallam. He wished to give them to you himself. I have told him that his Father does not wish a post to be lost.' Indeed, there seems to have been some disagreement over the dispatch of the new poems. Enclosed with the new manuscript was a note to Hallam, 'I have told Papa that I thought you would be disappointed if the Poems were not sent to you but sent direct to Mr Craik, so he lets me send them to you by this post and bids me say that he has not forgotten those points you discussed together but he has decided on leaving them as they are and does not wish any word to be altered.'[17]

Tennyson's eagerness to bypass Hallam and have the poems

sent straight to the publisher suggests an attempt to avoid the question of revisions. Apart from 'Romney's Remorse', which Hallam might have been concerned about on his mother's behalf, the collection also contained 'The Roses on the Terrace', his father's tribute to the memory of Rosa Baring:

Rose, on this terrace fifty years ago,
    When I was in my June, you in your May,
Two words, '*My* Rose' set all your face aglow,
    And now that I am white, and you are gray,
That blush of fifty years ago, my dear,
    Blooms in the Past, but close to me today
As this red rose, which on our terrace here
    Glows in the blue of fifty miles away.

8   Firing the Dirigible

Cannon to right of them,
Cannon to left of them,
Cannon in front of them
(THE CHARGE OF THE LIGHT BRIGADE')

The keen reception of his new collection, published as *Demeter and Other Poems*, was all but ruined for Tennyson by the deaths of his two most enduring friends. William Allingam had died on 17 November, following complications arising from an operation he had undergone in the summer, and Robert Browning died on 12 December, (the same day that *Demeter* was published) while visiting his son, Pen, in Venice.

Tennyson and Hallam immediately set about persuading the Dean of Westminster to allow Browning to be buried in Poet's Corner. Amongst those who joined as signatories on the letter were Palgrave, Swinburne, Leslie Stephen, Jowett and Froude. There were several separate testimonials, notably one from Gladstone, and the case was made. The funeral took place on the last day of the year. Tennyson pleaded feebleness and Hallam took his place as pall-bearer – but it would have been surprising if he had broken his long-term hatred of funerals, even for a fellow poet and friend of Browning's standing.

Still feeling low and despondent about the two deaths, Tennyson fell ill with bronchial pneumonia. He was bedridden for most of February and part of March. Once again it was feared that this was the end. 'My father is very ill indeed,' Hallam wrote to the American raconteur and essayist, Dr Oliver Wendell Holmes. 'He has had a sharp attack of bronchitis and sleeps day and night and it is often difficult to persuade him to take nourishment. He hates the idea of doing nothing, he says – it is pathetic, intensely pathetic.'[18]

In the feverish bouts of the illness he was beset by memories of the past, particularly the deaths of his first-born child, and of Lionel (whose thirty-sixth birthday it would have been on 16 March). When the weather turned warm in the middle of March Tennyson was able to convalesce in the summer-house, covering the bald crown of his head in a red cap which Emily thought unbecoming and effeminate.

Although the bronchitis had cleared he still felt depressed and idle. Encouraged by Watts, who gave him a small water-colour set, Tennyson took to painting and also made a wood carving of ivy leaves which was then cast in clay and used to decorate the porches in some local cottages.[19]

These practical labours did indeed prove therapeutic and throughout April and May he was in good spirits, entertaining large tea-parties held in the ballroom, even taking to the dance-floor once or twice himself. During May the Tennysons received one of Thomas Edison's American representatives who brought with him a phonograph. Tennyson was encouraged to recite part of the 'Charge of the Light Brigade' through the amplifying tubes. His nurse, Miss Durham, gave a great jump at the noise and Hallam and Audrey's young baby, Lionel, shouted with delight. Tennyson enjoyed using the contraption and Edison's man was permitted to arrange a formal recording session, part of which survives. Although the quality of sound obtained from the original wax cylinders is very poor (partly, no doubt, because they were apparently stored next to a radiator), the modern disc or cassette gives a reasonable impression of Tennyson's reciting style and of the enduring Lincolnshire vowel sounds in his voice.

Such distractions only temporarily alleviated a growing mood of gloom and despondency. An experimental firing of the dirigible torpedo[20] impressed him with the conviction that nineteenth-century science had set loose a malignant evil spirit upon the world. He felt his own body to be rapidly declining. He walked before luncheon, but not after, and was convinced that he was going blind. At the beginning of July Hallam took him to London to be thoroughly examined by Sir Andrew Clarke.

They stayed with Knowles who, although somewhat disgruntled at having been dislodged by Hallam as Tennyson's special assistant and confidant, remained outwardly hospitable. He accompanied them on their medical visits. After they had been to see the oculist (not Clarke), who told Lord Tennyson categorically that his eyes were free of disease, the poet was heard to mumble miserably, 'No man shall persuade me that I'm not going blind.'

While the Tennysons stayed with him Knowles entertained a large number of distinguished guests. When Tennyson heard one night that Gladstone had been invited he refused, in protest at the Home Rule bill, to sit at the dinner table. He took his meal in his room, inventing an indisposition. After the meal was over Knowles persuaded Gladstone to go and knock on Tennyson's door. He did, and was invited inside. Ten minutes later the two old men descended the stairs arm in arm and sat down to talk. Most of the discussion was about Browning and Homer but Gladstone could not resist delivering some propaganda for Home Rule. Tennyson was too tired to resist. At the end of the evening he told Knowles, 'He has quite converted me,' but at the breakfast-table the following morning, cross at his own soft malleability, he crashed his knife and fork down on the plate and said, 'He spellbound me for the time and I could not help agreeing with him ... His logic is immense, but I have come back to my own views. It is all wrong, this Home Rule and I am going to write and tell him so.'

Back home at Aldworth one of Tennyson's visitors, Dean Farrar, reminded him of a story he already knew from Charlotte Yonge's *Book of Golden Deeds*. It seemed, Farrar thought, a perfect subject for a poem, and after the Dean's visit Tennyson began to write 'St Telemachus' which he considered as a pendant for 'St Simeon Stylites'.

During the summer and autumn the Tennysons entertained other guests but most of their domestic life now centred around their own family – with visits from their two grandchildren Ally and Charlie and the fun of observing the growing antics of the youngest resident, little Lionel.

Two new dialect poems were started – 'The Church-Warden' and 'Charity'. The second of these shows the influence of his avaricious reading of sensational novels. In twenty-two succinct couplets it tells the story of a woman betrayed by her lover and abandoned while with child; he marries an heiress for her fortune, but is crushed to death in a train crash; the child is still-born and on her sickbed the abandoned woman is charitably looked after by the widowed heiress, who leaves her a fortune, and then dies of a fever caught while visiting a hospital ward. An eighty-year-old poet who can turn from the tale of Telemachus to such material is wide-ranging indeed.

There were renewed attempts to have his Dramas staged. Mary Anderson's plans to produce *The Foresters* had foundered on her decision to retire from the stage, but there was talk in the autumn of Irving taking over the project, and in December Tennyson was encouraged by news that an American actor, Lawrence Barrett, had signed a contract to perform *Becket*.

Christmas at Farringford was loud and busy. W.G. Ward's son, Wilfred, his wife and five children were guests, and they joined in fully in the family festivities. Servants and estate dwellers were welcomed into the ballroom to gather round the Christmas tree for present-opening. Alfred took special pleasure in his fourteen-month-old grandson and although his health had been precarious enough in October (he had once again required a specially-commissioned train from Haslemere to Lymington for the move to the Isle of Wight), young Ward found the old man perky enough, able to climb a five bar gate and run down the slope of the Down.

There was early disappointment in the New Year when Irving finally decided to forget the idea of producing *The Foresters*. 'Public taste I fear is in a very *sensational* condition,' and he did not feel the play was startling enough. Six weeks later, in March, the American actor Barrett died, and with him went the hope that *Becket* might at last be granted an audience.

Tennyson's manner became more eccentrically withdrawn. One day, when he received a young admirer, he hid his face behind a copy of the *Spectator*, like a child wanting to be coaxed into the open. Those who knew him well were able to cajole him out of such moods by playing the fool with him, but Emily, in her serious way, found such behaviour symptomatic of an inner disturbance.

In June he was well enough to be taken on yet another cruise, this time aboard a boat lent by his neighbour Colonel Crozier. It was called the *Assegai* and it sailed once again along the south-west coastline. Tennyson took with him a small library of books about Akbar the Great, to research a new poem on a subject suggested by Jowett.

The poem had been begun before this holiday but he continued it on the voyage, writing the final Hymn to the Sun while the boat was passing Dulverton. 'Akbar's Dream' is one of Tennyson's great final works. Imbued with his spirit of tolerance and his hatred of rigid, formalistic creeds, it needs to be read by anyone who persists in hearing in Tennyson's voice only the tone of a nationalistic imperialist.

At the end of the year agreement was at last reached on the staging of one of the plays – but it was one which he did not care passionately about (*The Foresters*) and the contract signed with Augustus Daly and Ada Rehan was for an American production. Before signing away the rights Tennyson made some enquiries about the actress, Miss Rehan. Irving sent R.D. Blumenfeld to convey his opinion in person to the poet. When he arrived at Aldworth the butler told the visitor that Lord Tennyson was out walking and directed him down the path the poet had taken. Blumenfeld pursued and caught up with the unmistakable figure in the cloak and wide-awake hat. But when he began to introduce himself Tennyson wheeled round, raised his sturdy stick and barked out, 'I have not the least idea who you are. Go away!' Blumenfeld did just that and returned to London, mission unaccomplished.

The American production went ahead in the spring of 1892 and toured various American cities, including Baltimore, Philadelphia, Chicago and Boston. It proved to be Tennyson's longest-running and greatest stage-success – but it all happened too far away for him to take much pleasure in.

9   The Chalice of Life

Will my tiny spark of being wholly vanish in your deeps and heights?

('GOD AND THE UNIVERSE')

During the spring there were renewed signs that Tennyson's strength was failing. For the first time his voice began to break down in the middle of readings, and all recitations were likely to bring on severe bouts of facial neuralgia.

Taken with a desire to see his brother Frederick, he and Hallam again borrowed the *Assegai*, stopping once more in Dartmouth, and then sailing on to Jersey. It was five years since the two brothers had seen one another. Frederick was now leading a reclusive widower's life upon the island, still interested in Swedenborg, spiritualism and, more recently, a masonic form of astrology. (He had helped to edit Henry Melville's arcane work *Veritas: the Meridian and Persian Laws*, published in 1874 and purporting to be the key to a lost secret of the universe.) He was still writing poetry and had recently had printed two collections, *The Isle of Greece* in 1890, *Daphne and Other Poems* in 1891. 'What can be more mournful than a retrospect of childhood?' he once wrote, but when the two brothers were together they talked as much about the long lost past as about the uncertain future.

Some aspect of the encounter with his brother prompted Tennyson, immediately on his return to Farringford, to request a private communion in his study. On the 29 June the vicar of Freshwater was summoned and duly administered the Holy Sacrament. It was received in the spirit of a life-giving feast, rather than a mass – Tennyson insisted on this, calling up a line from one of Cranmer's speeches in *Queen Mary*. In receiving communion at this time he was perhaps making a conscious effort to put into practice the mood of one of his last poems, 'The Silent Voices':

When the dumb Hour, clothed in black,
Brings the Dreams about my bed,
Call me not so often back,

517

Silent Voices of the dead,
Toward the lowland ways behind me,
And the sunlight that is gone!
Call me rather, silent voices,
Forward to the starry track
Glimmering up the heights beyond me
On, and always on!

Although increasingly troubled by the gout in his jaw, he was still hard at work. Three poems are worth particular mention – 'The Making of Man', 'God and the Universe', and 'The Dawn'. All three reflect Tennyson's interest in astronomy and the revelation of earth's position in a vast system of other suns. While visiting London in July he was told that 500 million stars had now been counted, and when Hallam took him to the Natural History Museum they both looked with wonder at the statue of Darwin which stood at the head of the hall. It was a graphic symbol of the ascendancy of the new sciences, geology and astronomy; they were responsible for discoveries so wonderful that inevitably much of the glory of poetry, as celebrated in classical times, seemed diminished.

Returning from London to celebrate his eighty-third birthday, a stream of visitors descended upon Aldworth, notably Norman Lockyer, who helped answer Tennyson's questions about the ages of the sun, earth and stars. He was no longer fit enough to go for walks. Hallam sometimes took him for a drive but most of the time he sat in the sun, protected from the wind by a hedge, a velvet skullcap on his head. By now, according to his own account, he was completely blind in one eye, and the other was not much good for reading. There were moments in the day when he would sit doing nothing, his features relaxing into the morose vacancy of senility.

Emily had retired further and further into her shell. For more than a year she had been confined to two upstairs rooms at Aldworth.[21] Attending to Alfred was left to Hallam, Audrey, the nurse and various visitors. One frequent caller during the last months of Tennyson's life was Henry Dakyns, who had recently moved to Haslemere with his family. (After the poet's death he was to give significant assistance to Hallam with correspondence accompanying the compilation of the *Memoir*.)

At the beginning of August the sale of the Rectory at Somersby was announced. Tennyson's lawyers apparently encouraged him to consider purchasing it[22] but the asking price was excessive. Even contemplating the matter was too much for the old man and his depressive state worsened. Hallam agreed to travel to Lincolnshire to look over his father's childhood home. In his absence further visitors to Aldworth were discouraged. The separation from Hallam, and the ban on visitors, were not good for Tennyson's seriously depressed state, and when Hallam returned in the middle of September he was shocked at his father's decline and immediately telegraphed Dr Dabbs.

There was sufficient improvement for a few visitors to be allowed to resume their calls. Amongst old friends who came to see him were Helen Allingham and Jowett. The latter found Tennyson clear-headed, but with insufficient vigour for philosophical debate. On 25 September Bram Stoker came to discuss new plans of Irving's for a production of *Becket*. Tennyson knew he would not live long enough to see such an event come to pass and was more inclined to talk to Stoker's companion, a young classical scholar. Their discussion about the authorship of the *Iliad* and of Shakespeare's plays animated him briefly, but he would sometimes yelp in mid-sentence, saying the gout was flashing through his jaw.

Craik came two days later to discuss the proofs for a new volume. After a final ride into the town of Haslemere on 28 September, the persistence of his father's weakened condition at last persuaded Hallam to call Sir Andrew Clarke. He arrived the same evening and was somewhat annoyed to find that the patient, supposedly on the verge of death, had that same morning been taken out in the carriage. He examined Lord Tennyson and pronounced his heart and lungs perfectly healthy. Dabbs, the local doctor, was called on to persuade Clarke of the seriousness of Tennyson's condition and Sir Andrew agreed to conduct a re-examination. This time a rapid pulse, high temperature and sickness convinced him that all was not well. But he still did not think it serious enough to warrant his staying at Aldworth and left by the 9am train the next morning.

Tennyson was fed on pulped mutton, which he managed to keep down with a calomel pill. Audrey would visit him after he had eaten and read him articles from *The Times*. By 30 September he was in agony with his throat and could not keep awake to listen to Audrey's new reports. He was given drugs to take away the pain and linseed poultices every two hours. A glass of port offered to him that evening made him sick.

The next day the grandchildren were sent away. Lionel asked if he might see his 'Baba' in bed beforehand, and had to be taken to his grandfather's bedside twice before he was happy to leave.

PART SEVEN

Mors

The Passing of Alfred

Moon on the field and the foam,
Moon on the waste and the wold,
Moon bring him home, bring him home
Safe from the dark and the cold,
Home, sweet moon, bring him home,
Home with the flock to the fold –
Safe from the wolf to the fold.

(THE CUP)

On the afternoon of Sunday 2 October 1892, although he had seemed better in the morning, Tennyson's pulse and temperature began to rise. His breathing became rattly and irregular. Hallam clung to the hope that this was a similar attack to the one two years before when his father had slept for sixty hours, and told Audrey and Dabbs to expect a recovery soon. He sat up through the night and was pleased when, after coughing up a quantity of phlegm, Tennyson seemed much improved.

The next morning he asked for Shakespeare's plays, resting the book open on the bedcovers rather than reading. He was convinced he would not recover and when Audrey asked him if he was a little better replied, 'The doctor says I am.' Three times in the afternoon he was given champagne, which he took and enjoyed. But tea made with milk and brandy made him vomit.

By now his condition was becoming public knowledge and telegrams began to pour in. Tennyson's mind was wandering, except when he heard the clock strike the hour. He counted it correctly each time, perhaps out of a morbid fear that his earlier dream of the giant clockface had been a premonition of his time of death. There were other moments of clarity. Turning to Hallam some time after midnight he said, 'I make a slave of you.'

In the early hours of the morning he was given sulphonal to quieten his delirium and was alert enough the following morning to be able to object to the indignity of being given an enema and having to be massaged with castor oil. By this time the doctors were openly preparing the family for the worst and a bulletin placed outside the gate at 10.30 that morning read 'Lord

Tennyson is worse ... Debility increases.'

At midday he cried out again for his Shakespeare and for the blinds to be put up. It had been a sunny morning and Hallam agreed to raise the blinds and open the windows, but early in the afternoon it clouded over and they were shut again. Most of that Tuesday afternoon he slept, occasionally waking and talking about a journey which he did not feel up to. In the evening his fever suddenly fell and for an hour or two he was calm and collected, but by nightfall he was wandering again and Hallam heard him say something about Mr and Mrs Tennyson and poison, and about walking with Gladstone in the garden that morning, showing him the trees.

Between these bouts of irrationality there was a vacant far-away look in the sick man's face and Hallam felt really hopeless for the first time. Everyone stayed up through the night, thinking it might be the last, and Emily was brought to the room and lay on the sofa.

Sir Andrew Clarke, finally responding to Hallam's frantic tele-grams, arrived at 10.30 that night and immediately prescribed a strong sedative. Audrey wiped some eau de cologne on her father-in-law's forehead as it was administered and he said, 'That's nice.'

On Wednesday 5th it was impossible to tell what he was saying, so heavily drugged was he, but upon a private message from Emily being conveyed to him he called again for his Shake-speare, managing to make himself understood. Hallam told him he was not well enough to read, but his father was insistent. When given the book, which was not his familiar volume but the most handy edition, he opened it at a certain page and laid it on his chest.

It was his final deliberate act. He drifted in and out of consciousness throughout the remainder of the day and night. A full moon rose at 6 pm and flooded the bedroom with a silvery light that, for a time, fell directly on his face. The servants were allowed into the room to say their goodbyes and when the moonlight moved to another part of the room Audrey lay on the bed stroking his hand.

At 11 pm, with the moonlight having shifted still further, a fire was lit, and just after midnight the final spasms began. The end came at 1.35 am on 6 October.

When Hallam took the volume of Shakespeare from the bed where it had been lying jacket uppermost the following morning, he was amazed to see it opened at a particular passage in the fifth act of *Cymbeline*. This had been one of three favourite passages, but what surprised Hallam was the fact that his father had been handed the book at a time when all those observing him had thought him incapable of seeing, let alone reading. And yet the book seemed to have been opened as the result of a deliberate action. It was Hallam's view, conveyed to Dakyns[1], that the passage it had been turned to comprised a coded response to his mother's private message. If so, it clearly demonstrates that both Alfred and Emily were fully conscious of the gulf that had opened between them in the last years of their marriage. Emily's sofa-ridden condition does not fully account for her very minor role during the course of his illness. She is hardly mentioned in the relevant sections of the *Memoir*, nor in Audrey's otherwise morbidly detailed death-bed Diary.

Emily did not attend the funeral in Westminster Abbey, which was inevitably a grand occasion, (too grand according to one of the congregation, Thomas Hardy, who characteristically thought a country churchyard would have been a more appropriate venue) and her letters to her sisters following the death reveal an air of languid resignation. She speaks as one who had lost the spirit of her husband long ago, the body's recent departure being purely incidental. Several times she states explicitly that her Ally had never been the same since his first serious illness. 'We who love him best know that he has never been the same since his bad illness four years ago and that from last February there was, we fear, no enjoyment of life.'[2]

Her own health did not deteriorate. If anything, it improved; she became fully involved in Hallam's efforts to compile the *Memoir*, a task which he embarked upon with the help of Dakyns, Sidgwick and Palgrave almost immediately.

Emily's comment – 'it is very difficult to piece things neatly together' – accurately conveys the unscrupulous, cut-and-paste method of the *Memoir*'s composition, and Hallam had no qualms about excising passages from letters and diaries, or even re-writing them.

'Crossing the Bar' has been traditionally placed at the end of all subsequent Tennyson collections, but at the time of the first complete volume of poetical works published after his death, by Macmillan in 1895, Hallam urged that this place should be reserved for 'The Death of Œnone', which Tennyson had once described as his last will and testament.[3] Written during the onset of his earlier sickness, biographical knowledge gives a terrifying insight into the possibilities behind its composition.

> 'Œnone, *my* Œnone, while we dwelt
> Together in this valley – happy then –
> Too happy had I died within thine arms,
> Before the feud of Gods had marred our peace,
> And sundered each from each. I am dying now
> Pierced by a poisoned dart . . .'

> The morning light of happy marriage broke
> Through all the crowded years of widowhood,
> And muffling up her comely head, and crying
> 'Husband!' she leapt upon the funeral pile,
> And mixt herself with *him* and past in fire.

Emily did not seem over-anxious for such immersion. She survived for another four years, dying on 10 August 1896. She was buried in the churchyard at Freshwater, the distance between her grave on the Isle of Wight and Alfred's in London, representative of the emotional and physical space which had come between them in the final years. Her last words to Hallam were, 'I have tried to be a good wife.'

And what of that coded message contained within the pages of *Cymbeline*? Imogen is speaking to Posthumus:

> Why did you throw your wedded lady from you?
> Think that you are upon a rock; and now
>   Throw me again.

> *Posthumus*:
>   Hang there like fruit, my soul,
>   Till the tree die!

This says much about Emily's relationship with Alfred. He treated her in life as his guiding spirit, from which his sensual and imaginative interests were wholly separate, centred in himself. Long ago, when he had tried to tempt from the dizzy Somersby night a vision of his father's ghost, it was to seek assurance that Heaven preserved intact the central features of personality. If Tennyson, one hundred years after his own death, has found Paradise to be much as he hoped for, he will be little changed from the man he was in this life: self-absorbed, humorous, hypochondriacal, a bottle-of-ambrosial-champagne-a-day-man.

Should this be the case, will Emily be enjoying a fuller relationship with her heavenly husband? It is doubtful. One day in May 1863, Rejlander took some extraordinarily evocative photographs of the Tennyson family walking in the garden at Farringford (see plate 11). We see Emily's arm linked loosely in the crook of Alfred's elbow, she looks admiringly up at him, Hallam contemplates his marvellous parents, Lionel stares sullenly at the camera, while Alfred's eyes glance grandly and independently off-frame.

> I found Him in the shining of the stars,
> I marked Him in the flowering of His fields,
> But in his ways with men I find Him not.
> I waged His wars and now I pass and die.
> O me! for why is all around us here
> As if some lesser God had made the world,
> But had not force to shape it as he would,
> Till the High God behold it from beyond,
> And enter it and make it beautiful?
> Or else as if the world were wholly fair,
> But that these eyes of men are dense and dim,
> And have not power to see it as it is:
> Perchance because we see not to the close; –
> For I, being simple, thought to work His will,
> And have but stricken with the sword in vain;
> And all whereon I leaned in wife and friend
> Is traitor to my peace, and all my realm
> Reels back into the beast, and is no more.
> My God, thou hast forgotten me in my death:
> Nay – God, my Christ – I pass but shall not die.

('THE PASSING OF ARTHUR')

NOTES

As this book is intended for the general reader and library user, all references are made to the most accessible *printed* collections in preference to manuscript locations. In the account of Tennyson's early years much use has been made of materials held in the Tennyson Research Centre (*TRC*) and Archives Office, Lincoln. Abbreviations are noted below:

Lang & Shannon (ed.), *The Letters of Alfred Lord Tennyson*, Clarendon 1982, 1987, 1990 (*Letters* I/II/III).

Hallam Tennyson, *Alfred Lord Tennyson: A Memoir*, Macmillan 1897 (*Memoir*).

James O. Hoge (ed.), *Lady Tennyson's Journal*, University Press of Virginia 1981 (*Hoge*).

James O. Hoge (ed.), *The Letters of Emily Lady Tennyson*, Pennsylvania University Press 1974 (*ETJ*).

June Steffensen Hagen, *Tennyson and his Publishers*, Macmillan 1979 (*Hagen*).

John Jump (ed.), *Tennyson, the Critical Heritage*, Routledge 1967 (*Jump*).

Robert Peters (ed.), *Letters to a Tutor*, Scarecrow 1988 (*DAK*).

Alfred McKinley Terhune and Annabelle Berdick Terhune (ed.), *The Letters of Edward Fitzgerald*, Princeton University Press 1980 (*Fitz*).

Jack Kolb (ed.), *The Letters of Arthur Henry Hallam*, Ohio State University Press 1981 (*AHH*).

Charles Tennyson, *Alfred Tennyson*, Macmillan 1949 (*CT*).

Robert Bernard Martin, *The Unquiet Heart*, Clarendon 1980 (*RBM*).

Christopher Ricks, *The Poems of Tennyson*, 3 vols, Longman 1987.

Tennyson Research Bulletin, Tennyson Society, (*TRB*).

1   Phosphorus

1. Hallam Tennyson, *Alfred Lord Tennyson: A Memoir*, I, 72: 'My father told me that within a week after his father's death he slept in the dead man's bed, earnestly desiring to see his ghost, but no ghost came.'
2. Thackeray, *Pendennis*, ch. 7. By the time Tennyson reached middle-age the railway had superseded the horse as the means of long-distance transport but the whole of his restless youth spanned the heyday of the stagecoach, 1820–1850.
3. The village of Somersby is little changed today. Although it is possible to buy Tennyson book-marks and car-stickers at Stockwith Mill two or three miles down the road, and in summer months coach parties tour the villages of 'Tennyson Country', the Rectory building (now a private household), the neighbouring Manor House, and the squat, rather ugly church on the opposite side of the lane stand in surroundings which can aptly be described as unspoilt.
4. A.T. to B.P. Blood 7 May 1874, *Letters* III, 78.
5. *Petit mal* seizures usually occur in childhood and rarely continue into adult life. Chronic alcohol abuse, according to the *Oxford Textbook of Medicine*, is now recognized as the potential trigger for epileptic-type fits. The same book's definition of partial seizures is so all-embracing (ranging from drop attacks, through *déjà vu*, to vertigo) as to warrant a special certificate marking it unsuitable for all hypochondriacs.
6. These were first brought to general notice by Christopher Sturman in *TRB*, November 1987.
7. Paul Turner, *Tennyson* (Routledge & Kegan Paul 1976), 35.
8. *Memoir*, I, 5.
9. David Urquhart, proprietor of Jermyn Street baths, quoted in *The Healthy Body and Victorian Culture* by Bruce Haley (Harvard 1978), 17.
10. *Letters*, I, 6.
11. The volume actually contained poems by *three* brothers. Although the majority of the poems were by Charles and Alfred, three or four were by Frederick.
12. The sun goes down in the dark blue main,
    To rise the brighter tomorrow;
    But oh, what charm can restore again
    Those days now consigned to sorrow?
    ('The sun goes down in the dark blue main')

2 Meridies I

1. George Moore, *The Use of the Body in Relation to the Mind* (1846).
2. The feminist reading of Tennyson's life and work by Marion Shaw, despite its obsessively confrontational view of the sexes, does have the merit of emphasizing the importance of erotic attraction to Tennyson. She is also one of the few critics to identify the significance of the brother–sister relationship in *The Lover's Tale* and other poems.
3. *Letters*, I, 23.
4. I had the good fortune one afternoon to meet Mr and Mrs Bamber, direct descendants of the Baumbers, in the churchyard at Somersby. Their own assiduous researches into the Baumber/Bamber family tree have helped me to see this episode in its correct light.
5. 'Bones of great lovers lie in this oasis:
   Browning and Tennyson, who showed what the English meant
   By marriage: rose-flush in a hushed garden,
   Sheath of oak-shade, massive and wholesome,
   Folding the plain vein, a pledge
   Of ancient power and knowledge,
   Northern and Christian.'
   (Jack Clemo)
6. As an example of the close inter-relationships amongst the intellectual and literary coterie of the mid-nineteenth century, Gaskell was also, in due course, father-in-law to Francis Turner Palgrave.
7. *Letters*, I, 41.
8. Hallam Tennyson, *Tennyson and his Friends*, 451.
9. *AHH*, 326.
10. *AHH*, 319.
11. The renowned oculist was Henry Alexander.
12. Douglas Heath, his brother John, and sisters Julia and Emma were good friends with all the Tennysons. John was to become engaged to Alfred's sister, Mary.
13. Count Platen, homosexual poet and playright, died aged thirty-nine.
14. *AHH*, 322.
15. Francis (later Sir) Doyle (1810–1888) became professor of poetry at Oxford between 1867 and 1877.
16. Charles Tennyson Turner, *Sonnet* VII '*Love of Home*'.
17. *AHH*, 354.
18. The prim empathy with which this scene is imbued in *RBM* is entirely fanciful. Ojeda's bravado remark about cutting the throats of the priests was doubtless taken in better humour than suggested in that account.

19. *AHH*, 374.
20. Susan Baur, *Hypochondria* (1988).
21. Steven Marcus, *The Other Victorians* (1966).
22. John Allen became a close friend of both FitzGerald and Thackeray.
23. *Jump*, 30.
24. The bracketed part of the title was dropped when the poem was reprinted.
25. Tennyson's talk of the 'black' blood of the Tennysons was in part another manifestation of his hypochondria – a belief that he had inherited various infirmities. But he did also use the term descriptively, in association with his moods rather than his health. Later, Emerson was to say that Tennyson reminded him very much of Hawthorne and it was perhaps in their 'mossy blackness' that they were alike.
26. *AHH*, 416.
27. As a letter written by William Burton to the Bishop in July 1835 (LAD 28.7.35) makes clear, it was eventually the eldest and not the youngest son who took over from Robinson.
28. *AHH*, 431.
29. *Memoir*, I, 117. It has to be said that this is a secondary quotation, taken by Hallam from Canon Ainger in his *Tennyson for the Young*. It is therefore of doubtful authority.
30. *AHH*, 446.
31. *AHH*, 553n.
32. *AHH*, 597.
33. *AHH*, 553.
34. *AHH*, 604.
35. *AHH*, 618.
36. *AHH*, 622.
37. *AHH*, 643.
38. *AHH*, 687.
39. Halllam's nick-name for Emily. His nick-name for Alfred – 'Nal' – was later used by Emily Sellwood.
40. *AHH*, 694.
41. Edward Bulwer-Lytton (1803–1873) was a prolific poet and novelist, Member of Parliament for Lincoln, and a noted dandy.
42. *AHH*, 761.
43. *CT*, 143.
44. *Ricks*, I, 583 ref. Trinity.
45. *AHH*, 768n.
46. *AHH*, 767.
47. *RBM* acknowledges his sleight-of-hand, but only in his notes on p. 599. 'My dating is conjectural, since it would have been difficult for AT in Scotland to receive a letter from Somersby or London on Wednesday, 31 July, and to return to London before AHH's depar-

ture, as the *Memoir* indicates.' He adds that 'Either the dating of [Hallam's] letter or the account of the visit to London must be in error.'

48. *AHH*, 789.
49. *AHH*, 793n.
50. *AHH*, 792.

3 Meridies II

1. Sinfield, *Alfred Tennyson* (Blackwell, 1986), 57.
2. Thompson to Blakesley, 11.11.33.
3. *Letters*, III.
4. *Fitz*, I, 140.
5. *Letters*, I, 104.
6. *Letters*, I, 94.
7. *AHH*, 102.
8. *AHH*, 105.
9. *TRC*, I, 230.
10. *Letters*, I, 106.
11. Rashdall diary, 14.1.34 (Bodleian).
12. *Memoir*, I, 106.
13. *Letters*, I, 112.
14. *Letters*, I, 113.
15. *Letters*, I, 115.
16. *Letters*, I, 110.
17. *Letters*, I, 130.
18. Edwin to CT, 29.3.35.
19. FitzGerald wrote many letters to Frederick Tennyson, who had been his exact contemporary at Cambridge. Unfortunately, most of the letters written by FitzGerald to Spedding were destroyed by Spedding's sisters, for being too full of things 'intended solely for masculine eyes'. Another sad hole in the correspondence is the loss of nearly all the letters exchanged between FitzGerald and Thackeray during the 'immortal summer of foolscap' in 1831.
20. *Memoir*, I, 155.
21. RBM's view that AT wanted to keep the visit secret from Fitzgerald gives too cringing an impression of the poet, and commonsense suggests that neither Spedding nor Wordsworth would fall in with such petty subterfuge.
22. *Fitz*, I, 164.
23. *Letters*, I, 134.
24. *Letters*, I, 138.

25. The biographer is RBM.
26. The large Massingberd family is described as 'tangential' by Lang & Shannon. However, it included Francis ('Frank') Massingberd, Vicar of Ormsby, and eventually husband of Fanny Baring, sister of Rosa.
27. *Jump*, 84.
28. *Letters*, I, 146.
29. 22 and 23 May, according to C. Sturman in *TRB*, November 1988. These dates are not, however, on their own, evidence for an early move.
30. Charles Turner to Susan Haddelsey, 12.2.37.
31. *Letters*, I, 157.
32. *Letters*, I, 159.
33. *Letters*, I, 168.
34. *Letters*, I, 170.
35. *Letters*, I, 174.
36. The final line of this poem
    'I heard them blast
    The steep slate-quarry, and the great echo flap
    And buffet round the hills, from bluff to bluff.'
    is a fine example of Tennyson's occasional use of onomatopoeia.
37. *Letters*, I, 182.
38. *Tennyson and Madness* by Ann C. Colley (University of Georgia Press 1983) contains an interesting comparison of Tennyson's (objective) and Clare's (subjective) approaches to their own moods and emotions. The book as a whole borrows too heavily from the 'unquiet heart' theme of the *RBM* biography and as a result portrays an over-melodramatic picture of Tennyson tottering on the edge of sanity, but it is thought-provoking and contains helpful details about some of the lesser figures in Tennyson's life.
39. The letter in question is undated. Lang & Shannon estimate that it was written in July or August 1840. If August, this interpretation holds.
40. *Letters*, I, 198.
41. *Letters*, I, 197.
42. In fact Ticknor was Tennyson's first US publisher.
43. *Letters*, I, 187.
44. The crucial parenthesis (rather an important rider) is Tennyson's own.
45. *Letters*, I, 194.
46. *Memoir*, I, 205.
47. *Letters*, I, 200.
48. *Letters*, I, 204.
49. For those who want to make their own judgement there is no alternative to reading the poems in the splendid (though prohibi-

tively expensive) three-volume Longman edition, edited by Ricks, which shows all variants, including those contained in the Trinity manuscripts.

50. *Letters*, ɪ, 205.
51. *Letters*, ɪ, 209.
52. *Letters*, ɪ, 213.
53. *Jump*, 102.
54. *Jump*, 122.
55. *Jump*, 138.
56. *Jump*, 152.
57. These and other details about hydropathy are taken from the wittily informative book *Taking the Cure* by E.S. Turner.
58. *Letters*, ɪ, 230.
59. *Letters*, ɪ, 233.
60. *Fitz*, ɪ, 500.
61. *Letters*, ɪ, 239.
62. *Letters*, ɪ, 246.
63. *Letters*, ɪ, 255.
64. The poem is quoted in the variant enclosed in a letter to Catherine Bradshaw, *Letters*, ɪ, 255. Another version, Poem #285b is in Ricks, ɪɪ, 184.
65. *Letters*, ɪ, 264.
66. *Autobiography* by Mary Howitt, ɪɪ, 27–28.
67. *TRC*, Cat No 525.
68. This poem is worth tracking down, if only to be read for its influence on *Maud*.
69. At the time of writing, a first edition copy of *The Princess*, signed by Tennyson and containing a handwritten poem, was being offered at an American auction with a guide price of $1000 – a very moderate price considering the antique special editions book market. My local second-hand book dealer advises me that an ordinary first edition might fetch as little as £20. Subsequent editions in the Moxon binding can still be found for under £5.
70. Emerson's *Journals*, 1848, ed. Merton Sealts (Harvard University Press 1974).
71. Although influenced by Kant, the American Transcendentalists, principally Emerson and Thoreau, are not to be confused with the pure philosophical school.
72. If Hawthorne had been more Tennysonian, how much more satisfactory the friendship with Melville would have been!
73. *Letters*, ɪ, 289n.
74. *Fitz*, ɪ, 622.
75. *Fitz*, ɪ, 623. For connotations on the word 'valetudinary' see p. 70.
76. *CT*, 233.
77. There is still a good deal of mischief spread about in connection

with a future female companion of Tennyson, Julia Cameron.
78. *Letters*, I, 297.
79. *Letters*, I, 303.
80. His dinner engagements for May 1848 left hardly a single night free. See *Letters*, I, 286.
81. Charles Tennyson, *Aldworth*, p. 5: 'In 1849, when relations were resumed, he had stayed at an old inn at Farnham – now 21 West Street – and walked daily across the market-place and past the castle to visit her.' This circumstantially exact statement suggests it was based on written or oral evidence no longer available.

4   Hesperus I

1. *Letters*, I, 320.
2. *Letters*, I, 322.
3. The dating of the original licence (15 May) is given by Willingham Rawnsley in *Tennyson 1809–1909*.
4. *Letters*, I, 335.
5. *Letters*, I, 336.
6. *Letters*, I, 336.
7. *Letters*, I, 339.
8. *ETJ*, 21.
9. *Letters*, I, 343.
10. *Letters*, I, 343.
11. *Letters*, I, 346.
12. *Letters*, II, 2.
13. The house in Warninglid was referred to variously as 'The Hill' and 'The Hall'.
14. *Letters*, II, 3.
15. *Letters*, II, 4.
16. *Letters*, II, 15.
17. Allingham, *Diary*, 60–61.
18. *Hoge*, 57.
19. *Letters*, II, 23.
20. *Letters*, II, 32.
21. *Letters*, II, 33.
22. *Letters*, II, 40.
23. *Letters*, II, 66–67.
24. *Letters*, II, 77.
25. *Letters*, II, 83.
26. *Letters*, II, 84.
27. *Letters*, II, 86.

28. Archer Thompson Gurney (1820–1887), one of the multitude of fascinating 'lesser lights' of the literary scene, was a friend of Charles Kingsley, who confided in him on the failure of his own monodrama *Santa Maura*, 'I have deserted poetry as rats do a sinking ship. I have refused to publish my poems, actually ashamed of being called a poet, of being caught out in such a bad company (not yours of course) and have taken to monosyllabic prose, as the highest achievement of man ... I can tell more truth in prose than I can in verse, and earn ten times as much money.'

29. *Letters*, II, 138.

30. *Jump*, 211.

31. *ETJ*, 72.

32. *CT*, 300.

33. *RBM*, 406.

34. *Letters*, II, 154.

35. *Hoge*, 102.

36. *Hoge*, 103.

37. *Letters*, II, 173.

38. *Letters*, II, 174.

39. Nathaniel Hawthorne, *The English Notebooks* (ed. Randall Stewart, OUP 1941), 553–4.

40. Ibid.

41. Sophia Hawthorne to E. Peabody, 1.8.57, *Memories of Hawthorne* (Rose Hawthorne Lathrop 1897), 332–3.

42. ET to E. Browning, *Hoge*, 113.

43. *RBM*, 421.

44. By common consent the critic and old friend was Monckton Milnes.

45. *Letters*, II, 197.

46. The persistence of this perception in the modern mind was amusingly exemplified in an episode of *Neighbours* broadcast by the BBC on 27 December 1990, in which Hilary, in mourning for a dead relative, was sent a bouquet of flowers by her schoolteacher admirer – the accompanying verse was by Tennyson.

47. *Hagen*, 107.

48. *Letters*, II, 209.

49. Taken from *Hagen*.

50. *Letters*, II, 223.

51. *ETJ*, 134.

52. *Letters*, II, 234.

53. *Letters*, II, 241n.

54. *ETJ*, 143.

55. *Hoge*, 148.

56. *Letters*, II, 257.

57. *TRB*, November 1988.

58. *Letters,* II, 271.
59. *TRC,* CT to AT 6.2.65.
60. *DAK,* 48.
61. *DAK,* 52.
62. *DAK,* 62.
63. Conway, *Autobiography, Letters,* II, 331.
64. Ibid.
65. *Letters,* II, 339.
66. *Hoge,* 176.
67. *Letters,* II, 346.
68. *Letters,* II, 347.
69. *Hoge,* 182.
70. *Letters,* II, 383n.
71. *TRC,* CT to AT, 6.2.65.
72. The chair, a little rickety and somewhat holed with woodworm, but still quite grand, can be seen in the Usher Gallery, Lincoln.
73. Matthew Arnold, *Letters,* I, ed. G.W.E. Russell (Haskell House 1982).
74. *ETJ,* 104, 105.
75. This, and other details about the dinner are taken from *Letters and Papers of John Addington Symonds* (1923), extracted in *Letters,* II, 415.
76. *DAK,* 95.
77. *DAK,* 96.
78. *DAK,* 88–89.
79. *DAK,* 90n.
80. *DAK,* 118.
81. *Letters,* II, 437 (the recipient is unidentified).
82. *TRC,* LT to HT, October 1866.
83. The songs were eventually published, with Sullivan's musical notation, in December 1870.
84. *Letters,* II, 455.
85. *ETJ,* 260.
86. *Letters,* II, 455.
87. *TRC,* ET to Mrs Gatty.
88. *Letters,* II, 467.
89. *DAK,* 108.

5   Hesperus II

1. George Grove, editor of *Macmillan's Magazine,* offered £50 for the poem on 3 January 1868.
2. *Hoge,* 218.
3. *Hoge,* 227.
4. *Letters,* II, 510.
5. *Letters,* II, 523.
6. *Hoge,* 240.
7. *Hoge,* 239.
8. *Hoge,* 248.
9. *Jump,* 280.
10. *Hoge,* 261.
11. *Letters,* II, 547.
12. *Hoge,* 262.
13. *DAK,* 110.
14. *Letters,* III, 9.
15. *ETJ,* 328.
16. As reported in *Fitz* to Frederick Pollock, in *Letters,* III, 21.
17. *Letters,* III, 28.
18. For an admirable summary of the textual and conceptual development of the Idylls, see Ricks, III, 255–262.
19. *Letters,* II, 148.
20. Higginson, *Cheerful Yesterdays,* in *Letters,* III, 32.
21. *TRC,* LT to HT 20 August 1892.
22. *Letters,* III, 57.
23. Wordsworth, *Thoughts of a Briton on the Subjugation of Switzerland.*
24. *Hoge,* 303.
25. *Letters,* III, 78.
26. *Letters,* III, 87.
27. Colley, *Tennyson & Madness,* 42–3.
28. *Letters,* III, 94n.
29. Quoted in *TRB,* November 1973.
30. *Letters,* III, 106.
31. *Letters,* III, 116.
32. *CT,* 430.
33. *Hoge,* 310.
34. Henry James, *The Middle Years,* 590–591.
35. An interesting study could be made of the fashions in middle names (and no doubt has been). It was common, and not considered vulgar, to name children after men of letters at this period. The 'etiquette' was most evident amongst men of letters themselves. One of Charles Dickens's sons was christened Alfred d'Orsay Tennyson.

36. There is at least one instance, though rather muted. During the later cruise she noted in her diary that another passenger's eyes were growing bluer every day, and followed this observation with, 'Hallam grows too ... not blue, but nice.'

37. Henry James, *The Middle Years*, 589.

38. *TRC*, LT to HT 1 June 1880.

39. Lord Selborne, recently returned to office, was at this time the subject of a vitriolic campaign in the press, according to which he was 'broken in health' and 'losing his memory'. Tennyson was touched by the way Sophie stuck by her father.

40. *CT*, 460.

41. *Letters*, III, 220.

42. Those interested in forming their own estimate of Emily's talent can refer to *With Tennyson at the Keyboard* by Joan Hoiness Bouchelle (1985).

43. See particularly Sisson's 'Vigil and Ode for St. George's Day' (in *God Bless Karl Marx!*, Carcanet 1987).

44. The Marquis of Queensberry is also notorious as the father of Alfred Douglas and the instigator of Oscar Wilde's conviction.

45. *TRC*, Sophia Palmer to HT, 13 November 1882.

46. *Letters*, III, 237 (correspondent unknown).

47. Tennyson did in due course worry that the peerage would mean having to drink more expensive port. A Lord would not be able to fill his cellars with cheap bottles from the Co-operative.

48. As reported in the *Century Magazine* and quoted in *Letters*, III, 258n.

49. *RBM*, 545.

50. Some of the short biographies of that period are worth reading despite their polemical and warped viewpoint. The books by Harold Nicolson and Hugh Fausset are representative of a type and scale of biography which is very refreshing when compared with the present re-emergence of the double- and even triple-decker Life.

6   Nox

1. *Hagen*, 160.

2. *Memoir*, II, 304.

3. *Letters*, III, 297. (This letter, it must be said, was not an entirely accurate expression of Tennyson's views on the franchise. Neither he nor Emily was a true democrat and both feared the people's vote.)

4. *Letters*, II, 176.

5. *Hagen*, 177.
6. Both RBM and CT take this view. 'Serene courage' is the grandson's description of his grandmother.
7. *CT*, 495.
8. *TRC*, Audrey Tennyson, *Ms Yachting*.
9. *Hoge*, 339.
10. *Letters*, III, 370.
11. *Memoir*, II, 347.
12. *TRC*, ET to Anne & Agnes Weld 2 March 1889.
13. *Letters*, III, 400.
14. *TRC*, ET to Craik, Summer 1889.
15. *TRC*, ET to Anne Weld 3 May & 12 May 1887; ET to Gordon Wordsworth, 25 July 1889; ET to Craik, 11 August 1889.
16. *Letters*, III, 400, 409.
17. *TRC*, ET to Craik, 4 November 1889; *TRC* and *Hoge*, ET to HT, 4 November 1889.
18. HT to Holmes, *Letters*, III, 413.
19. The carving can be seen in the Usher Gallery.
20. The experimental torpedo was fired on 5 July 1890 from the clifftop fort at the western end of the Isle of Wight. Tennyson was just one of a crowd of notables, including other Peers and MPs, who watched its launch.
21. *DAK*, 124.
22. *Hoge*, 356.

7. Mors

1. *DAK*, 126.
2. *Hoge*, 359.
3. *DAK*, 150.

Index

551

349–50; sons' departure for school and, 361, 365–6, 385; search for second home ends with building of Aldworth, 381–2 *et seq*; death of father, 383; AT's peerage and, 481–2, 487; death of son Lionel, 497; plays minor role in AT's illnesses, 404, 506, 508, 525; AT's death, 524; does not attend funeral, 525; assists son Hallam with *Memoir*, 525; her death, 526

Tennyson, Emily (later Jesse) (sister), 43, 45, 46, 59, 133–4, 139, 163, 203, 204, 274; love for Arthur Hallam, 5, 63, 68, 73, 77–8, 81, 86–9, 91, 94–100, 101–2, 105 6, 109, 112, 114–15, 131, 179; poor health, 83–4, 85–8, 91, 101, 105, 109, 133; Hallam's death and, 118, 127, 138, Mr Hallam makes allowance, 127, 187; Husks society and, 152–3; marries Richard Jesse, 135, 186–7, 188; first child, 196; death, 500

Tennyson, Frances (Fanny) (wife Charles d'Eyncourt), 19, 21, 111, 131, 159, 309

Tennyson, Frederick (brother), 5, 9, 10, 12, 14, 24, 30, 67, 81, 82, 84, 87, 92, 95, 99–100, 113, 126, 130, 133, 144, 148–9, 156, 159, 162, 171–2; to Eton, 15–16, 18–19, 37, 42; at Cambridge, 23, 24–5, 28, 37, 40, 41, 80, 89, 90; rusticated, 41–2; father and, 41–5, 51; as tutor in Paris, 51, 122; inheritance, 144, 149; Julia d'Eyncourt Tennyson and, 151; settles in Italy, 151, 154, 222, 257, 326, 336, 364, 481–2, Dr Allen's scheme, 184, 186, 196; married, 257

The Isle of Greece (1890)

Daphne and Other Poems (1891) 517

last meeting with AT, 517

Tennyson, Dr George (father), 3, 19, 20, 38–9, 41–2, 49, 73, 83, 97, 111, 124, 144, 199, 225, 287, 343, 389; at Cambridge, 7; ordained, 7; Benniworth living, 7, 8; Rector Somersby & Bag Enderby, 8; final illness and death of, 3–5, 18, 78–81, 128, 144, 363; temperament, violence, 4, 8–9, 11, 18, 21, 31, 39, 40, 42–4; educates sons, 4, 10, 14, 15, 22, 23, 25; disinherited, brother Charles favoured, 6–7, 8, 9, 15, 17–18, 42, 276; relations with Charles, 9, 11, 14, 15; marriage problems, wife Elizabeth, 26–8, 29, 31, 39, 43–5, 70; son Frederick and, 41–5; year's exile, 45–6, 51–2, 59, 114; return, 64–51; health, 15–17; epilepsy and, 12–13, 23; breakdowns, instability, 13, 15, 16, 23–4, 26–8, 29, 32

Tennyson, George Clayton (the Old Man) (grandfather), 4, 6, 8, 9, 18, 23–4, 28, 39, 49, 51, 79, 81–2, 85, 89, 90, 99–100, 111, 114, 128, 130, 135, 187; favours younger son Charles, 6–9, 15, 17–18, 42, 276; allowances to both sons, 11; grandson Frederick and, 24–5, 100; son George's illnesses, marriage difficulties and death, 27–9, 43–4, 51–2, 64, 65, 80, 114; custodian of George's children, 29ff, 40–41, 52; death and will, 143–4, 145

Tennyson, George (cousin), 40–41, 46, 80, 100, 126, 131, 133, 159

Tennyson, Giulio (Julius) (nephew), 336, 342, 481